Praise for *A Companion to the Eighteenth-C*
English Novel and Culture

"A team of two dozen prominent scholars . . . here report on the state of the art in 18th century novel studies. Nearly all the work is cutting edge, and almost every page challenges conventional wisdom . . . specialists in the early novel will find this wide-ranging and theoretically sophisticated work provocative. Highly recommended." *CHOICE*

"Editors Paula R. Backscheider and Catherine Ingrassia have assembled an impressive collection of authors . . . visiting or revisiting a complex cultural topography." *ECF*

"The variety of texts treated in this volume is rich, unapologetic, and one of its real pleasures." *The Journal for Early Modern Cultural Studies*

Blackwell Companions to Literature and Culture

This series offers comprehensive, newly written surveys of key periods and movements and certain major authors, in English literary culture and history. Extensive volumes provide new perspectives and positions on contexts and on canonical and post-canonical texts, orientating the beginning student in new fields of study and providing the experienced undergraduate and new graduate with current and new directions, as pioneered and developed by leading scholars in the field.

Published

A COMPANION TO THE

EIGHTEENTH-CENTURY ENGLISH NOVEL AND CULTURE

EDITED BY PAULA R. BACKSCHEIDER
AND CATHERINE INGRASSIA

WILEY-BLACKWELL

A John Wiley & Sons, Ltd., Publication

Registered Office
John Wiley & Sons Ltd, The Atrium, Southern Gate, Chichester, West Sussex, PO19 8SQ, United Kingdom

Editorial Offices
350 Main Street, Malden, MA 02148-5020, USA
9600 Garsington Road, Oxford, OX4 2DQ, UK
The Atrium, Southern Gate, Chichester, West Sussex, PO19 8SQ, UK

For details of our global editorial offices, for customer services, and for information about how to apply for permission to reuse the copyright material in this book please see our website at www.wiley.com/wiley-blackwell.

Library of Congress Cataloging-in-Publication Data

A companion to the eighteenth-century English novel and culture/
edited by Paula R. Backscheider and Catherine Ingrassia.
p. cm.—(Blackwell companions to literature and culture ; 30)
Includes bibliographical references and index.
ISBN 978-1-4051-92453 (pbk)
ISBN 978-1-4051-0157-8 (hbk: alk. paper)
1. English fiction—18th century—History and criticism—Handbooks, manuals, etc.
I. Backscheider, Paula R. II. Ingrassia, Catherine. III. Series.

A catalogue record for this book is available from the British Library.

Set in 11/13pt Garamond 3 by SPi Publisher Services, Pondicherry, India
Printed in Singapore

1   2009

Contents

Illustrations

Notes on Contributors

Srinivas Aravamudan joined the English Department at Duke University in 2000. He is the author of essays in *Diacritics*, *ELH*, *Social Text*, *Novel*, and other periodicals. His study, *Tropicopolitans: Colonialism and Agency, 1688–1804* (1999) won the first book prize of the Modern Language Association in 2000. He has also edited *Slavery, Abolition, and Emancipation: Writings of the British Romantic Period*, volume VI, "Fiction" (1999). His book, *Guru English: South Asian Religion in Cosmopolitan Contexts* was published by Princeton University Press in 2004. He is working on a book-length study of the eighteenth-century French and British oriental tale and is also editing William Earle's antislavery romance, entitled *Obi: or, The History of Three-Fingered Jack*.

Paula R. Backscheider is Philpott-Stevens Eminent Scholar at Auburn University and a past president of the American Society for Eighteenth-Century Studies. She is author of the biography, *Daniel Defoe: His Life* (1990), which won the British Council Prize in 1990, and four critical books, including *Spectacular Politics: Theatrical Power and Mass Culture in Early Modern England* (1993), and *Reflections on Biography* (1999). She has published articles in *Biography*, *Theatre Journal*, *ELH*, *PMLA*, *Eighteenth-Century Fiction*, and many other journals.

Ros Ballaster is Fellow in English Literature at Mansfield College, Oxford University. She is author of *Seductive Forms: Women's Amatory Fiction from 1684 to 1740* (1992). Her latest book, *Fabulous Orients: Fictions of the East in England 1662–1785*, and an accompanying anthology, *Fables of the East*, will be published by Oxford University Press in 2005.

Elizabeth A. Bohls of the University of Oregon is the author of *Women Travel Writers and the Language of Aesthetics, 1716–1818* (1995). She is finishing *Caribbean Crossings: Identity and Place in the British West Indies, 1770–1833*, an anthology of travel writing and a study of identity and place in the colonial British Caribbean.

Toni Bowers teaches English and Women's Studies at the University of Pennsylvania. She is the author of *The Politics of Motherhood: British Writing and Culture, 1680–1760* (1996), and of numerous articles and reviews. She is writing a book about eighteenth-century seduction stories and, with John Richetti, editing a teaching abridgement of Richardson's *Clarissa*.

Elizabeth Maddock Dillon is Associate Professor of English and American Studies at Yale University. She is the author of *The Gender of Freedom: Fictions of Liberalism and the Literary Public Sphere* (2004) and has published articles on gender in early America, transatlantic literature and culture, aesthetics, and sentimentalism.

Robert A. Erickson is Professor of English at the University of California, Santa Barbara. He is co-editor of John Arbuthnot's *The History of John Bull* (1976), author of *Mother Midnight: Birth, Sex, and Fate in Eighteenth-Century Fiction* (1986), and *The Language of the Heart, 1600–1750* (1997). He is presently at work on a book on Milton and the poetics of ecstasy. He was Fulbright Professor in Comparative Religion and Literature at the University of Helsinki, 1999–2000.

Christopher Flint is Associate Professor of English at Case Western Reserve University and is author of *Family Fictions: Narrative and Domestic Relations in Britain, 1688–1798* (1998) and various essays on the eighteenth-century novel. He has recently published several articles on fiction and print culture and is currently working on a book on the subject, tentatively titled "The Fate of the Page: Fiction and Print in the Eighteenth Century."

Carol Houlihan Flynn is Professor of English at Tufts University. She has written *Samuel Richardson: A Man of Letters* (1982), *The Body in Swift and Defoe* (1990), *Washed in the Blood* (1982), a novel, and articles on Austen, Cleland, Sterne, Smollett, Fielding, Boswell, and Burney. She is writing "The Animals," a fictional memoir, and "Becoming Urban: Learning London in the Eighteenth Century."

George E. Haggerty is Professor and Chair of English at the University of California, Riverside. His books include *Gothic Fiction/Gothic Form* (1989), *Unnatural Affections: Women and Fiction in the Later Eighteenth Century* (1998), and *Men In Love: Masculinity and Sexuality in the Eighteenth Century* (1999). He has also edited *Professions of Desire: Lesbian and Gay Studies in Literature* (1995) and *Gay Histories and Cultures: An Encyclopedia* (2000).

Catherine Ingrassia is Professor of English at Virginia Commonwealth University. She is author of *Authorship, Commerce, and Gender in Early Eighteenth-Century England: A Culture of Paper Credit* (1998), co-editor (with Claudia Thomas) of *"More Solid Learning": New Perspectives on Pope's Dunciad* (2000), and editor of Eliza Haywood's *Anti-Pamela* and Henry Fielding's *Shamela* (2004). She is also editor of volumes 33 and 34 of *Studies in Eighteenth-Century Culture*.

Kathryn R. King is Professor of English at the University of Montevallo. She is author of *Jane Barker, Exile: A Literary Career 1675–1725* (2000) and co-editor (with

Alexander Pettit) of Eliza Haywood's *The Female Spectator* (2001). She is the author of essays in *The Eighteenth Century: Theory and Interpretation*, *Studies in the Novel*, and *ELH*.

Susan S. Lanser is Professor of English and Comparative Literature and Chair of Women's Studies at Brandeis University. Her publications include *The Narrative Act: Point of View in Prose Fiction* (1987), *Fictions of Authority: Women Writers and Narrative Voice* (1992), two co-edited books, and numerous essays. Her current book focuses on sapphism and the engendering of modernity.

Devoney Looser teaches at the University of Missouri, Columbia and is the author of *British Women Writers and the Writing of History, 1670–1820* (2000), the editor of *Jane Austen and Discourses of Feminism* (1995), and the co-editor of *Generations: Feminist Academics in Dialogue* (1997). She is working on a book on women writers and old age in Great Britain, 1750–1850, and is co-editing (with George Justice) *Correspondence Primarily on Pamela and Clarissa*, which will be volume 10 in the Cambridge Edition of the *Correspondence of Samuel Richardson*.

Robert Markley is Professor of English at the University of Illinois, and editor of *The Eighteenth Century: Theory and Interpretation*. His books include *Two-Edg'd Weapons: Style and Ideology in the Comedies of Etherege, Wycherley, and Congreve* (1988), *Fallen Languages: Crises of Representation in Newtonian England, 1660–1740* (1993), and *Dying Planet: Mars and the Anxieties of Ecology from the Canals to Terraformation* (2004). *Fictions of Eurocentrism: The Far East and the European Imagination* was published by Cambridge University Press in 2005.

Paula McDowell is Associate Professor of English at Rutgers University. She is the author of *The Women of Grub Street: Press, Politics, and Gender in the London Literary Marketplace, 1678–1730* (1998) and *The Early Modern Englishwoman: Essential Works: Elinor James* (2004). She has published articles on subjects ranging from the history of the book to Henry Fielding, and is currently completing a book titled "Fugitive Voices: Literature and Oral Culture in Eighteenth-Century England."

Ruth Perry is Professor of Literature at MIT, and has written widely on eighteenth-century English literature and society. Her publications include *Women, Letters, and the Novel* (1980) and *The Celebrated Mary Astell: An Early English Feminist* (1986). Her most recent *Novel Relations: The Transformation of Kinship in England 1748–1818* examines the effects of capitalism on family structure and was published by Cambridge University Press in 2004. She is a landlady.

Adam Potkay is Professor of English at the College of William and Mary. He is author of *The Fate of Eloquence in the Age of Hume* (1994) and *The Passion for Happiness* (2000), and co-editor of *Black Atlantic Writers of the Eighteenth Century* (1995). He has published numerous articles in journals including *PMLA*, *Raritan*, *Eighteenth-Century Studies*, *William & Mary Quarterly*, *Nineteenth-Century Literature*, and *Studies in Early Modern Philosophy*.

John Richetti is A. M. Rosenthal Professor of English at the University of Pennsylvania. He is author of *Popular Fiction Before Richardson: Narrative Patterns, 1700–1739* (1969; 1992), *Defoe's Narratives: Situations and Structures* (1975), and *Philosophical Writing: Locke, Berkeley, Hume* (1983). His most recent book is *The English Novel in History 1700–1780* (1999). He is currently editing the *Restoration and Eighteenth Century* volume of the *New Cambridge History of English Literature* and completing a critical biography of Daniel Defoe.

Laura L. Runge is Associate Professor of English at the University of South Florida, and is the author of *Gender and Language in British Literary Criticism, 1660–1790* (1997) and the editor of Clara Reeve's *The Old English Baron* with Horace Walpole's *The Castle of Otranto* (2002). Currently she is working on a facsimile edition of essential texts from the *querelle des femmes*, 1641–1700, for the Early Modern English Woman's series from Ashgate Press.

Charlotte Sussman is Associate Professor of English at the University of Colorado. Her publications include *Consuming Anxieties: Consumer Protest, Gender and British Slavery, 1713–1833* (2000), as well as articles on Aphra Behn, Walter Scott, Charlotte Smith, and Mary Shelley. This essay is drawn from her current research project, "Imagining the Population: Literature and Demographic Theory in Eighteenth-Century Britain," which has been supported by an ACLS Burkhardt Fellowship.

Kathryn Sutherland is Professor of Bibliography and Textual Criticism at Oxford University and a Fellow of St. Anne's College. She has published widely on fictional and non-fictional writings of the Scottish Enlightenment and Romantic periods, including her edited work, *Electronic Text: Investigations in Method and Theory* (1997).

James Grantham Turner teaches at the University of California, Berkeley, and has authored four books: *The Politics of Landscape: Rural Scenery and Society in English Poetry, 1630–1660* (1979), *One Flesh: Paradisal Marriage and Sexual Relations in the Age of Milton* (1987, 1993), *Libertines and Radicals in Early Modern London: Sexuality, Politics and Literary Culture, 1630–1685* (2001), and *Schooling Sex: Libertine Literature and Erotic Education in Italy, France, and England, 1534–1685* (2003). He also wrote the chapter on "Literature" in the Blackwell *Companion to the Worlds of the Renaissance* (2002).

Roxann Wheeler is Associate Professor of English at Ohio State University. She is the author of *The Complexion of Race: Categories of Difference in Eighteenth-Century British Culture* (2000). Her most recent essay, "Colonial Exchanges: Visualizing Racial Ideology and Labour in Britain and the West Indies," appears in *An Economy of Colour: Colonialism, Visual Culture, and Identity in the Atlantic World, 1700–1840*, edited by Kay Dian Kriz and Geoff Quilley (2003).

Introduction

Catherine Ingrassia

The questions scholars ask about texts determine the knowledge they create. In fact, the originating questions are often more important than the answers, for they initiate broader interrogations and ultimately help construct a discipline. The essays in this collection consistently ask provocative and interesting questions that challenge, revise, or resist previous inquiries into the eighteenth-century novel. In doing so, the essays – both singly and collectively – contribute to and potentially revise our understanding of that genre as it has been constructed in the late twentieth century. The publisher's charge for this volume was for essays that were theoretically informed, academically rigorous, and anticipating (or establishing) new directions in the field. These essays strive to do just that, creating a dialogue that potentially advances the way we think about the novel and, perhaps, eighteenth-century studies generally.

The essays upend some of the traditionally held "truths" about the novel that students and scholars have all too often used as a kind of critical shorthand, and they foreground information that qualifies previous interpretations of "novel culture." The novel was not the most popular genre of the period – "the novel" was not even a recognized or codified genre until well after mid-century (and, arguably, later). It is a generic marker that is, at best, provisional. Homer Brown is correct to observe "we must always guard ourselves against the supposition that the meaning of any genre or institution, or even any text or utterance, is fully manifest, let alone contained, in any single historical moment or context."[1] The idea of "the novel" was not located in British culture, but was consistently European and often global in its scope and influences. Early in the century, extensive seepage existed between and among contemporaneous strains of discourse such as the "oriental" tale, the spy tale, or the "it" narrative, and novelistic fiction. The genre was inchoate, unstable, and contingent – what one critic describes as "a perfect Creole."[2] Our understanding of the period's dominant writers is also profoundly unstable, framed by constructions of scholars' own making, not always the literary culture of the author's own day. These essays question the received knowledge inherited from other literary histories and the models with which we've consistently read the novel. While the exigencies of the classroom, the monograph, and the scholarly article demand the use of a recognizable rubric or paradigm with which to frame analyses, these essays demonstrate the inventive and liberating possibilities that emerge when we eschew such ultimately limiting habits of mind.

Thus, this volume does not seek to be a traditional collection of essays on the novel; it is not concerned with providing a tidy history, but rather with exploring the diverse and often unsettling contexts that inform the genre. Consequently, this book is not a coverage-based model. The volume is organized into three sections: "Formative Influences," "The World of the Eighteenth-Century Novel," and "The Novel's Modern Legacy." The essays in the first section explore the discursive threads that inform the emergent novel. Those in the second focus on the social, economic, ideological, and cultural fields in which the novel is situated. And essays in the third section consider the way the novel has changed our thinking and, in turn, the way our thinking has changed about the novel. As the description of the essays makes clear, shared themes and concerns run through all three sections of the book. While many authors are discussed – some of whom have been previously little mentioned – the book does not offer essays that are focused only on one author, nor does it attempt to cover canonical authors exhaustively. It instead situates the fictional text in a field with other discourses and explores the ways in which that "genre" as it is being formulated interacts, reflects, informs, and qualifies other reading experiences. It brings to the fore concerns, interpretative strategies, and modes of engagement that have not always been addressed. In addition, the essays are slightly longer than those often found in such collections, enabling the authors to engage the material deeply and suggestively, highlighting the crosscurrents between and among their texts, and the ongoing dialogue within our field.

Watt and the "Rise" of Novel Studies

A vast body of scholarship offers narratives that attempt to explain the "history" of the novel, typically constructing it as the evolutionary triumph of a stable, monolithic, and British genre. Indeed the history of the history of the novel is itself a rich subject for examination. While a comprehensive discussion of what one scholar terms the "canonical criticism"[3] of the novel is not appropriate here, a sense of the dominant voices – the "formative influences" as it were – is useful as a point of entry into the volume, for these essays allude to, depart from, and interact with the history of the novel as it has previously been written.

Charges of irrelevance and ephemerality assailed early popular fiction in the eighteenth century. As Jane Austen famously observed in *Northanger Abbey* (1818):

> Although our productions have afforded more extensive and unaffected pleasure than
> those of any other literary corporation in the world, no species of composition has been

so much decried ... there seems almost a general wish of decrying the capacity and undervaluing the labour of the novelist, and of slighting the performances which have only genius, wit, and taste to recommend them.[4]

An academic version of "undervaluing the labour of the novelist" similarly limited serious consideration of the novel until the mid-twentieth century and the publication of Ian Watt's *The Rise of the Novel* (1957).[5] That book recuperated the novel from its status as a disreputable form and "opened up eighteenth-century fiction as an area of serious scholarly engagement."[6] Earlier histories of the novel certainly existed and, indeed, they anticipated the preoccupation with realism that would mark Watt's study. Wilbur Cross's *Development of the English Novel* (1899) explored the "imaginative success" of Defoe and Richardson, among others, who made the fictitious "seem real."[7] Ernest A. Baker produced a ten-volume *History of the English Novel* (1924) that variously focused on "circumstantial" and "intellectual" realism.[8] Just a year before Watt's book, Alan McKillop's *The Early Masters of English Fiction* (1956) shared a concern with the same authors and qualities of fiction (class, realistic narrative detail), albeit in different terms.[9] But Watt's book institutionalized the study of the novel, introduced the concept of "formal realism" as an essential characteristic of the genre, and provided a useful critical vocabulary. Watt didn't just chart the development of the novel; he was the first scholar to attempt to explain it with an approach that combined literary criticism, history, philosophy, and sociology. As he recounted in 1978, the intellectual influences on his text were multiple and profound, including the "empirical, historical, and moral elements" of his Cambridge training, and the theoretical elements of the European tradition (Marx, Weber, the Frankfurt School).[10]

Watt's argument, greatly simplified, suggests that the novel "rose" concomitantly with the "middle class," an emergent, diverse social group that possessed discretionary income and leisure time (especially among women) – two key components to reading for pleasure. Simultaneously, the changing social, political, and ideological context contributed to what Watt termed an "individualist" culture in which the subjects had increased control over their lives. "Individualism"[11] was also tied closely to "formal realism," a term that encompasses both the presentation of the details of daily life and the production of texts that purport to be an "authentic account of the actual experiences of individuals" (27). Thus, according to Watt, the narrative of Crusoe not only illustrated the life of a man who realized individual ambitions apart from traditional social structures, but also did so with narrative detail (time, space, material items) and psychological and philosophical "realism." Heralded at the time as the first comprehensive history of the novel, *The Rise of the Novel* took a genre regarded as merely "popular" and gave it a solid academic grounding. Though its teleological, formalist, undeniably masculinist, and at times monolithic perspective became the object of subsequent critique,[12] the text remained a touchstone for subsequent studies of the novel, whether challenging or affirming Watt's approach.

Watt's text initiated a more sociological and cultural focus in the scholarship on early fiction and changed the nature of inquiry into the genre. For example, with

Popular Fiction Before Richardson: Narrative Patterns, 1700–1739 (1969), John Richetti, influenced by Watt, was the first scholar to take seriously purely popular fiction – the largely ephemeral texts that had been previously ignored – to demonstrate what he termed "the relevance of the unreadable."[13] He discussed the "entertainment machines" and "fantasy inducers" (263) of early women writers like Aphra Behn, Delarivier Manley, and Eliza Haywood, and the cultural function they served for a nascent reading public. His tremendous contribution by engaging undiscussed, unregarded texts was often overshadowed as he became too easy a target for feminists revising the history of the novel. While the popular fiction Richetti addressed has, in many cases, edged closer to the "canon" and been interpreted from different theoretical perspectives, Richetti's early work (to which he suggestively alludes in his own essay here) remains important.

McKeon, Armstrong, and "The New Eighteenth Century"

Certainly the kind of popular fiction Richetti examined has increasingly become the object of focus in the last two decades, as feminist, Marxist, New Historicist, and cultural studies approaches expanded the field and literary studies as a whole. The 1980s was an incredibly rich and generative period for scholarship on eighteenth-century fiction, producing significant histories of the novel as well as theoretically informed, narrowly focused books that connected the development of the novel to very specific cultural phenomena. During this decade, arguably the two most influential studies of the novel were Michael McKeon's *The Origins of the English Novel, 1600–1740* (1987) and Nancy Armstrong's *Desire and Domestic Fiction: A Political History of the Novel* (1987).[14] These two books, the first an amplification of Watt, the second a reconsideration of the novel as a political and gendered genre, remain current. Serious students of the novel need to engage them both. McKeon's massive and exhaustively detailed study explores the "origins" of the English novel (and they are many in his rendering) in a way that directly resists Watt's attempts to distill the essence of the form. McKeon, instead, seeks to account for the novel's "emergence as a simple abstraction"[15] which, for him, occurs around the time of Samuel Richardson's *Pamela* (1740). Two sets of questions, born of the period's generic and social instability, guide McKeon's text: "Questions of Truth" and "Questions of Virtue." The first involves how to tell (and discern) the truth in a narrative; the second, how to recognize the relationship (if any) between social position and inner worth or "virtue." Both these questions pose "problems of signification" (20) that are worked out, in part, through fictional narratives. Constructing two overarching dialectics that structure his argument, McKeon suggests that, generically, there is a movement from romance to history to the novel in a way that corresponds with an epistemological shift from romance idealism to naïve empiricism, resolving into extreme skepticism. Similarly, social instability results in a movement from aristocratic ideology to progressive ideology to conservative ideology. As with all dialectics, the emergent factor not only critiques the dominant one but also absorbs elements of the originating, ultimately residual, component. Thus the aristocratic ideology's investment in ideals of virtue and honor, which is critiqued by the financially oriented, self-actualizing impulse of the progressive ideology, reappears, albeit nostalgically, in conservative ideology's counter-critique of progressivism. So elements of the romance, which is overmined by the newly found importance of "truth" claims in history, reappear in the novel. McKeon's effect on subsequent discussions of the novel is difficult to over-estimate. While not all critics agree completely with the generic, epistemological, and ideological shifts his study details, few would dispute the rigor, significance, or persuasiveness of his argument. While his text may not supplant Watt's, it is a powerful supplement.

Nancy Armstrong is similarly ambitious in her Foucauldian discussion of the invention of the "domestic woman" through fiction and conduct books of the eighteenth century. For Armstrong, the eighteenth-century domestic novel played a – indeed *the* – central role in forming not just women, but the modern political subject, for it provided the "written representations of the self" that allowed the modern individual to become "an economic and psychological reality" (8). The modern subject was "first and foremost a woman" through whom an assertion of middle-class power is ultimately realized in private and domestic terms. The novel negotiates and contains this reorganization of political power; thus, *Pamela* "repackages political resistance as the subjectivity of a woman" (132) and it is on this point that Armstrong's book is seen as profoundly revisionary. Armstrong also made discursive constructions of desire, as it is historically and culturally determined, central to the novel and linked the history of the novel inextricably to the history of sexuality. In examining the cultural constructions of gender, sexuality, and desire, their connection to class, and their effect on the history of the novel in the eighteenth and nineteenth centuries, Armstrong advanced a provocative, complex, if not always completely accepted, thesis.

The same year McKeon's and Armstrong's texts were published, Laura Brown and Felicity Nussbaum edited a collection of essays entitled *The New Eighteenth Century: Theory, Politics, English Literature* (1987) that changed the way many scholars of eighteenth-century studies regarded their work.[16] While the term "the new eighteenth century" itself has become a cliché, the volume left an indelible and still vital imprint on subsequent scholarship. It urged a revision of the field's critical practices with theoretical approaches that embrace new feminist, Marxist, historicist, and cultural studies. The collection attempted to revise and problematize traditional constructions of period, genre, and the canon. In the introduction, the editors articulated some of the then new, now acknowledged theoretical underpinnings of a new critical practice: the historically constructed nature of subjectivity; gender's position as both a cultural construct and an important category for interpretation; the instability of dominant ideologies of the past and scholars' attempts to write about them. The effect of the collection (quite evident in this volume) was the discipline's move from formalism to historicisms, and a resistance of the top-down, rarefied voice of Augustan literary history. Completely new issues and subjects – domesticity (including servants, work, family), nationalism and imperialism, and cultural identity (in terms of race, class, gender, and nation) – become fertile avenues for investigation. While subsequent studies of the novel do not necessarily note this text directly (it actually included only a few essays on the novel), its effect was palpable in terms of the texts and cultural forms examined and the critical practices used.

Indeed, some of the other important studies of the novel from this period share a theoretical orientation with this broader move in the field. Instead of regarding the novel as a stable, recognizable genre, these studies focused on the narrative response to the generic and social instability of the early eighteenth century. In *Factual Fictions: The Origins of the English Novel* (1983), Lennard Davis examines the "ensemble" of written texts surrounding and leading to the formation of the novel, including literature, newspapers, advertisements, laws. Rather than attempting to chart a "series of genres displacing each other," he suggests scholars should look at a "discourse that is forced to subdivide."[17] Ultimately the division of fact and fiction, or the news and novels, within this wider discursive field contributed to the development of the novel. A study also informed by Foucault is John Bender's *Imagining the Penitentiary: Fiction and the Architecture of Mind in Eighteenth-Century England* (1987). Bender continues Watt's connection between social change and literature, but with the assertion that novels are "the vehicles, not the reflections, of social change."[18] Bender suggestively argues that the novel and the development of the modern penitentiary were homologous cultural systems: both are mechanisms for social control and both create realistic "narratives" about solitary fictional subjects and the relatively solitary process through which they are reformed or improved. In *Masquerade and Civilization: The Carnivalesque in Eighteenth-Century English Culture and Fiction* (1986), Terry Castle explores the historical phenomenon of the English masquerade and what she terms the "phenomenology" of the masquerade, its profound effect both on self-representation and literary representation.[19] By discussing the powerful dimension of disguise and masquerade, and their potentially subversive and liberating powers, Castle introduced a new vocabulary for exploring previously unaccounted dimensions in the novel. These studies of the novel and the cultural systems in which it emerged were original, provocative, and revisionary, and continue to inform the way the novel is taught and discussed.

Changes in the discipline also resulted in theoretically sophisticated, archivally based, and culturally oriented work focused on women writers. For example, Ros Ballaster's *Seductive Forms: Women's Amatory Fiction from 1684–1740* (1992), in a sense continues an exploration of the texts Richetti engages, though with a distinctly feminist approach. *Seductive Forms* focuses on the "novelistic writing" or "amatory fiction" of Behn, Manley, and Haywood, to understand "the importance of ideologies of gender in the construction of genre."[20] By focusing on amatory or seduction fiction, Ballaster demonstrates how profoundly a consideration of gender, class, and sociopolitical and ideological issues informs a genre previously discounted as pure entertainment. *Seductive Forms* unpacks the cultural work done by early women's novelistic fiction. Ballaster's book is complemented by a study like Cheryl Turner's *Living by the Pen: Women Writers in the Eighteenth Century* (1992), which offered a very quantitative, cogent analysis of the actual financial conditions for early women writers. In the same vein, Janet Todd's *The Sign of Angellica: Women, Writing, and Fiction, 1660–1800* (1989), provided a structured (and pedagogically friendly) discussion of four generations of women writers.[21] In addition to exciting, theoretically sophisticated new work on women writers, they were also increasingly treated with the same academic consideration as their male counterparts, as evidenced by the new availability of modern editions of their work as well as serious literary biographies of their lives. Certainly a study like Catherine Gallagher's *Nobody's Story: The Vanishing Acts of Women Writers in the Marketplace, 1670–1820* (1994) owes much to these tremendously important (and continuing) developments.[22] A book that Terry Castle described as "the true successor and necessary supplement to Watt,"[23] *Nobody's Story* explores the reciprocal shaping of the terms "woman," "author," and "marketplace." Discarding the notion that women resisted remunerative authorship, Gallagher instead suggests "they relentlessly embraced and feminized it," constructing an authorial persona that accentuated "numerous ingenious similarities between their gender and their occupation" (xiii). Gallagher's history of the novel not only depends on the centrality of women as writers and readers of texts, but also the new focus on the professionalization of authorship and print culture generally, a subject that has received increasing attention in the last decade.

For example, in *Before Novels: The Cultural Contexts of Eighteenth-Century English Fiction* (1990), J. Paul Hunter asks, simply, "What was new about the novel?"[24] His answer attempts to explain both what constitutes a "literary species" and why that species emerged. To do so, he creates a rich context or "prehistory" for the emergence of the genre. By focusing on the characteristics of first-generation novel readers, the structures of their literacies, and the diverse textual world in which they lived, he profiles not only the early reader but the cultural context of their engagement with the text. His analysis of "texts," "contexts," and "pretexts" subtly demonstrates the complexities of the form and its historical moment, and attempts to explain both fully. William Warner shares a concern for the culture in which the novel emerges, though in distinctly different terms in his equally important *Licensing Entertainment: The Elevation of Novel Reading in Britain, 1684–1750* (1998). Warner performs a "genealogy of the literary history of the rise of the British novel" as he revises Watt's fundamental premises about generic stability and, instead, locates the earliest novels in the marketplace as a form of "early modern print entertainment."[25] By making the novel "entertainment" and authors "print-media workers" within a larger, commercialized print culture, he dramatically changes the terms in which the novel is engaged. For Warner, the "cultural location and meaning of novel reading took a decisive turn" with the publication of *Pamela*. Not only did that novel generate a "media event" that demonstrated the genre's commercial and cultural possibilities, it also successfully began fiction's move from popular diversion to elevated (and thus authorized) literary text. As the genre developed, suggests Warner, early "scandalous" fiction (typically by writers like Haywood and Behn) were "overwritten" by their male successors, who retained the titillating discourse but recontextualized it in a didactic vehicle that responded to anti-novel rhetoric.

As Hunter's and Warner's work suggests, scholarship on the novel, with an emphasis on historicist approaches, increasingly focuses on the complicated contexts for reading and embraces the instabilities and complexities of the genre and its time. For example, John Richetti's *The English Novel in History, 1700–1780* (1999) examines how social change and social representation shift with England's economic, political, and cultural transformation.[26] Similarly, an interest in the print trade, reading practices, and other aspects of material culture has generated a number of important studies focused variously on the production, sale, and form of the novel.[27] Scholars are focusing on the importance of the book as a material object.[28] The "new economic criticism" facilitated scholarship that examined the ways in which the new instruments of exchange and speculative investment manifest themselves both within the narrative and in the relationship between reader and text.[29] The continued interest in sexuality and gender has produced alternate histories of the novel that attempt to theorize it beyond the heteronormative constructions of gender relations.[30] This suggestive rather than exhaustive survey demonstrates the various directions of scholarship on the novel, which share a resistance toward monolithic, linear, or codified characterizations. By destabilizing the history of the novel, recent scholarship identifies new areas for challenging questions about the genre and its cultural context.

Influences, Contexts, and Legacies

The essays in this volume examine discourses that inform the novel in often unexpected ways. They share a concern with locating the often un- or under-discussed aspects of the novel and the culture in which it emerged (thus words in their titles, like "secret," "hidden," and "unwritten"). They attempt to cast into relief aspects of the text that have seemingly defied analysis. They write about what cannot be represented and try to explain why it can't. Exploring elements as diverse as the relative value of literacy, the importance of "old age" as a new category for analysis, and representations of poverty and homelessness, these essays share a consistent focus on previously ignored dimensions of the novel. They remind us how the private is the political, and how those two intersect narratively, structurally, and culturally. Though diverse in their approaches and subject, the essays all contextualize the novel in new and expanding ways. They all resist the teleological, progressive story of the rise of the novel, as well as the claimed superiority of realist fiction.

A number of essays focus on the generic and stylistic effects of previously unconsidered genres – tales of spying, surveillance, or the "orient." In "Fiction/Translation/ Transnation: The Secret History of the Eighteenth-Century Novel," Srinivas Aravamudan suggests the novel has been incorrectly characterized in ways that exclude influential transnational (and translational) discourses. Using the surveillance narrative as his example, he points out the "nation-centered gate-keeping function" of literary history. To recognize and eradicate it would ultimately revise the origins of the early English novel as "a multi-sited translational utopianism, a clearinghouse for multiple languages, polities, religions, and ethnicities." Rather than investing so fully in the word "novel," he suggests that scholars, like most other European language literary critics, embrace cognates of words, or concepts, that link the novel back to the many strands of "history" and "romance." Aravamudan's inclusionary revision shifts the groundwork for understanding early fiction by asking what happens when the novel is defined "transnationally" rather than in relation to a particular country.[31]

Like Aravamudan, Elizabeth Maddock Dillon in "The Original American Novel; or, The American Origin of the Novel" problematizes the easy nation-novel conjunction that has guided much criticism of the novel, particularly in America. She suggests, instead, that discussions of the novel should be framed by the eighteenth-century nascent global market shaped by the forces of colonialism, mercantile capitalism, and imperialism. The insistently domestic and familial content of the early novel stems not from the particularity of national identity but rather the social, economic, and cultural effects of colonialism. Within this changed context for reading, the incest and miscegenation that emerge in eighteenth-century texts such as William Hill Brown's *The Power of Sympathy* (1789) and Sally Sayward Wood's *Julia and the Illuminated Baron* (1800) act as indices of concern with the circulation of persons and relationships in the shifting terrain of a transnational, globalizing economy.

A concern with the same kinds of transnational threads can also be found in Robert Markley's essay, "'I have now done with my island, and all manner of discourse about it': Crusoe's *Farther Adventures* and the Unwritten History of the Novel," which examines the assumptions and values central to the "the homology of 'bourgeois' identity, the rise of the novel, and early-modern capitalism" that has informed both the premises and conclusions of much scholarship on *Robinson Crusoe* (1719). By ignoring the two sequels to *Crusoe*, critics have focused on the narrative of capitalist triumph (which conforms to Watt's premise) and disregarded Defoe's subsequent dismantling of that ideology. The two sequels' focus on global travel (to China and Siberia) not only closely connects the texts to the tradition of travel literature, but also undermines the construction of British identity – and the significance of the same – so central to Defoe's first novel. Markley explodes many of the generic assumptions about Defoe and, by extension, about the development of the novel. Ros Ballaster similarly complicates the emergence of the novel in Britain by focusing on the profound influence of the oriental tale, previously read as separate or unrelated to the novel. In "Narrative Transmigrations: The Oriental Tale and the Novel in Eighteenth-Century Britain," she demonstrates how some of the central characteristics associated with the British novel – its "use of narrative as a survival strategy, the notion of the 'otherness' to be found within the self… and the casting of epistolarity as an unstable and volatile alienation of the self" – actually originate in the oriental tale. In these essays, the novel is one of many discourses in a dialogic, polyglot world.

Like Ballaster, Markley, and Aravamudan, James Grantham Turner in "The Erotics of the Novel" resists the "monoglot" interpretation of the novel that reads its sources as primarily British. He notes how widely read and highly desirable French texts of all genres were to the early reading public. The demonstrable influence of French texts – particularly spy narratives, "magical elements," and surveillance discourse – serves as a powerful corrective to the privileging of "realism" as a dominant characteristic for the genre. Seemingly opposite impulses – romantic myth and novelistic practice, discursive constructions of desire, and the detailing of ordinary life – are not only deeply intertwined but also mutually influential on the development of the novel. By reinserting desire, sexuality, and the hidden nature of the self into our consideration of the novel, Turner complicates the genre and the motivations of its readers. The mobility of the population and the cultural preoccupation with travel and travel narratives, as discussed by Elizabeth Bohls, provides a material context for the global influences common to these essays. "The Age of Peregrination: Travel Writing and the Eighteenth-Century Novel" not only demonstrates how fully travel – as narrative and action – consumes the eighteenth-century novel but also implicitly suggests how travel is driven by desires that, in turn, fuel the novel. The essay's focus on intercultural encounters and the negotiation of national identity that ensues provide useful information for reading these other essays.

A focus on national identity, desire, and self-definition also informs Toni Bowers's "Representing Resistance: British Seduction Stories, 1660–1800." Seduction stories, which seem far removed from politics, became a narrative vehicle for the most controversial debates of the age – debates about the relative humanity of persons from different class positions, about the meaning and value of consent in relationships where power is unevenly distributed, about what it meant to be "British" during this time. By unpacking the tension between collusive and non-collusive resistance to seduction or rape (the fine line between the two frequently obscured during that period), Bowers illustrates how the seduction narrative addresses issues of identity and subaltern resistance. As such, she lays the groundwork for consideration of the changing ideological functions of seduction writing across the eighteenth century. Seduction is also the subject of Robert Erickson's essay, though in distinctly different terms. "Milton and the Poetics of Ecstasy in Restoration and Eighteenth-Century Fiction" examines the often unexpected influence of *Paradise Lost* (1667) on the early novel. The original reception of *Paradise Lost* as an "oral narrative" rather than as "poetry" illustrates the generic fluidity of the late seventeenth century and anticipates its discursive influence on fiction. Milton's representation of human sexual relations and eroticism in terms of ecstasy, imagination, and confession, in Erickson's argument, became a kind of "ur-text" or model for plotting heterosexual eroticism. His discussions of Aphra Behn's *The Fair Jilt* (1688), John Cleland's *Fanny Hill* (1747), and Daniel Defoe's *Roxana* (1724) provocatively illustrate how the concept of "ecstasy" as an interpretive tool might help shape our reading of novel.

Paula McDowell re-examines the period's attitude toward literacy, asserting that education could be a liability rather than necessarily an asset, depending on one's subject position. "Why Fanny Can't Read: *Joseph Andrews* and the (Ir)relevance of Literacy" subtly unpacks how the meaning and consequences of literacy were vitally dependent on sociohistorical context. While literacy is potentially liberating, it can also reinscribe restrictive and hegemonic values that solidify rather than challenge the existing social hierarchies. Though a contemporary reader might embrace literacy as socially progressive, this carefully argued essay that focuses on *Joseph Andrews* (1742) demonstrates that attitudes toward literacy and education were much more equivocal than we think. Adam Potkay also uses *Joseph Andrews*, among many other texts, to situate the terms "joy" and "happiness," the title of his essay, in their broader discursive contexts to illustrate their importance to eighteenth-century novelists of and after the 1740s. "Joy and Happiness" emphasizes that those terms are not interchangeable or synonymous, but finely distinguished and fundamental to the novel's "mimetic and moral aims." Part of the novel's didactic agenda, suggests Potkay, is teaching people to feel appropriate emotions. Joy is a more transient state, an emotional response to a stimulus, while happiness is an ethical evaluation or state of rational contentment. Reinvesting these terms with discriminating meanings affords an opportunity to reconsider what they meant in an eighteenth-century context and, perhaps, our own time as well.

In contrast, Ruth Perry and Charlotte Sussman's essays share a concern with poverty and population and their literary representation. In a strongly suggestive essay, Perry observes that depictions of poverty had a very direct relation to actual historical conditions, particularly regarding shelter. "Home Economics: Representations of Poverty in Eighteenth-Century Fiction" demonstrates how spatial allowances – the size and condition of one's living space – played a central role in denoting impoverishment, particularly during a period when property was increasingly designated for exclusive private use. Scenes of eviction and restitution become commonplace in the novel, and Perry convincingly demonstrates how a kind of dystopic home economics appears in fiction: an observation that provides tremendous insight into the way market forces were radically changing how people lived. In a different way, Sussman is also concerned with the (dis)placement of the population when she connects the novel and another emergent concept of the period: the population. Demographic theory changed the way people were regarded and thus how they could be valued, moved, or deployed. The potential transience of individuals, indeed whole communities, created the problem of capturing "communal memory in the face of large-scale human mobility." "Memory and Mobility: Fictions of Population in Defoe, Goldsmith, and Scott" explores different narrative strategies for addressing the question of memory's relationship to space as well as time, the question of memory's capacity to travel, and to link disparate locations as well as eras. It suggests the ways the novel becomes a supplement, or perhaps a substitute, for memory when it tells collective stories, the title's "fictions of population." Carol Flynn's piece "Whatever Happened to the Gordon Riots?" complements these two essays in its similar concern with the unrecognized, willfully ignored, or ultimately unrepresentable. By suggesting the problems with representing revolution, Flynn asks the general question of what's missing from novels and why. Her subtle delineation of narrative representations of the violence in the Gordon Riots, and the way those negotiate an axis of class and national identity, considers the limits and possibilities of fictional discourse. In a related way, Susan Lanser's wide-ranging essay, "The Novel Body Politic," urges a recognition of how profoundly political the novel is as it "engages the pressing eighteenth-century question of who shall participate in civil society... of who shall have public power and whose interests shall be recognized and served." Her nuanced reading of Mary Shelley's *Frankenstein* (1818) demonstrates how, through the representation of the monster, it articulates the terms of participation in a human community and in the body politic, and the implications of that participation – or exclusion – for women. Similarly, that novel, like Mary Wollstonecraft's *The Wrongs of Woman; or, Maria* (1798), illustrates the divide between narratively representing the claims for greater political rights and effecting any real change. The essay has implications for other essays in this volume, such as Bowers's, as well as the political claims for the novel Armstrong makes in *Desire and Domestic Fiction*.

Lanser's concern with non-normative behavior intersects with the focus of George Haggerty's "Queer Gothic." The essay demonstrates the deep imbrication between the history of the novel and the history of sexuality. When Haggerty asks, "What does it mean to call gothic fiction 'queer'?" he launches an essay that problematizes the genre's transgressive sexual-social relations and demonstrates how the gothic novel challenges or undermines heteronormative configurations of human interaction. While he is careful not to make too broad a claim, since gothic fictions never significantly challenge the "dominant fiction" of the age, this stimulating essay adds new insights into both the novel and sexuality in the latter part of the eighteenth century.

Kathryn King, Devoney Looser, and Laura Runge all address issues relevant to the assessment and understanding of women writers during the period; each asserts the need for a new category of cultural consideration. King explores misunderstandings of Eliza Haywood's life and author function as she dismantles the construction of her as primarily a commercial, scandalous author to take "a fuller measure of the meaning of her early novels in her own culture." Situating Haywood firmly in Aaron Hill's literary and social circle, she argues for understanding the heightened language of Haywood's early prose fiction not as bad writing or erotic shorthand but as part of an effort to express the sublime and the shared sensibilities of her "reading community." "New Contexts for Early Novels By Women: The Case of Eliza Haywood, Aaron Hill, and the Hillarians, 1719–1725" offers original insight into Haywood's career and promises to make a significant contribution to the continued attempts to grasp Haywood's fiction, as well as new contexts for reading other women writers.

Such re-envisaging also informs Runge's essay, as she uses published reviews of the latter part of the eighteenth century to demonstrate how female novelists at this period enjoyed fame and professional respect equal to their male peers; her essay clarifies their acknowledged importance as writers within the genre. Though the reviews were inflected by gender, it did not yet limit their opportunities for publication or evaluation. The enormous and largely untapped resource of literary reviews offers a completely new way to understand not only the specific novelists she discusses – such as Frances Burney, Charlotte Lennox, and Elizabeth Inchbald – but the authority and innovation granted to women as writers of fiction at the end of the eighteenth century. Looser uses similar resources but to different ends as she, in a sense, creates a new category for interpretation – the aging woman writer. Authors who successfully negotiated sexism in their early careers were confronted with ageism in their latter years. "Women, Old Age, and the Eighteenth-Century Novel" asks why older women writers, previously prominent, were forgotten when they aged. Using Frances Burney and Maria Edgeworth as examples, Looser explores both their complex and varied representation of older women in their fiction, and their often ill treatment by critics and audiences in their own old age. Her preliminary answer to the question "why did we forget women writers in their old age?" indicates how promising this area of research may be. What can be learned about women, aging, and the novel potentially opens an entirely new field of inquiry.

The complex gendering of sociability, conversation, and education, and their effects on the eighteenth- and nineteenth-century novel are the subject of Kathryn Sutherland's "Conversable Fictions." Sutherland suggests that large-scale narratives of authority such as Samuel Johnson's *Dictionary of the English Language* (1755) or Adam Smith's *Wealth of Nations* (1776) represent personal and intellectual development as a monologic state of self-communion. By contrast, more modest narratives by women represent growth as a dialogic process, the development, correction, and adjustment of a literate self within community – e.g. as forms of conversation. This divergence contributed to gendered methods for constructing social identity and mapping the production of knowledge. Prose fiction and the novel from the late eighteenth century developed by exploiting the opportunities within this division. The essay's skillful reading of Maria Edgeworth, Hannah More, and Sarah Scott demonstrates the rich implications for recognizing the conversational model for education within the development of women's fiction and the novel as a genre. Similarly Roxann Wheeler's essay, "Racial Legacies: The Speaking Countenance and the Character Sketch in the Novel," expands contexts for reading with the observation that the eighteenth-century novel functions as a technology of racialization that is located in a concern with national identity. The consistency in appearance among novels' protagonists implicitly privileges (and disseminates the image of) European features in a way that could be subsequently deployed to specific politic and economic ends. The discourse of the novel intersects with the discourses of physiognomy and natural history as they all converge in their attention to the body's surface in ways previously unrecognized.

Rather than expansively positing a new approach to the novel, in "The Eighteenth-Century Novel and Print Culture: A Proposed Modesty," Christopher Flint urges critics to offer "a more modest account of the novel" that is aligned more closely with the realities of eighteenth-century print culture. This thought-provoking essay returns to Roger Chartier's principal categories – the Reader, the Author, the Book – to effectively question much of the "information" or "facts" about the eighteen-century novel.[32] As he examines each category for analysis, he essentially dismantles received assumptions about them, strongly pressing for the need to locate the novel firmly in the history of the literary marketplace and the material conditions of production. Only when we recognize the complex ways individuals (writers, publishers, readers) interact materially and discursively can we gain a better, albeit more modest, sense of the novel in eighteenth-century culture.

In a similar way, John Richetti proposes the reconsideration of literary value as a category for assessment of the novel. With his essay, "An Emerging New Canon of the British Eighteenth-Century Novel," Richetti offers not only a wonderful condensed intellectual history, but also a stimulating engagement with the nature of value. The emphasis on texts' far-reaching historical and ideological resonances engendered by the feminist, New Historicist, and cultural studies work has provided important insight into sociocultural contexts for the novel. Yet such work, to Richetti's mind, has often abandoned the question of value or constructed it as serving the purposes of a dominant culture. Richetti suggests the question of literary value should be reintegrated into our consideration of eighteenth-century texts. Perhaps canonical texts actually possess a superior sociocultural fullness and density value, the very qualities privileged by a new generation of scholars. Reading Haywood and Defoe together, Richetti elegantly suggests that the nature of value in eighteenth-century fiction be redefined and attended to.

Paula Backscheider's essay bears the mark of her editorial role in this volume; it continues interpretative threads and revisionary lines of thinking touched on in a number of the other essays. As such, its position as the last essay appropriately synthesizes, and benefits from, nuanced approaches other authors engage. Backscheider explores the non-commercial side of writers' consciousnesses and suggests that genre was a major part of the schema that was a fundamental constitutive element in their composing and compositions. The essay discusses texts that self-consciously integrate multiple genres, create innovative forms, and capitalize on permeable genre boundaries. Using Nathaniel Lee's *The Princess of Cleves* (1678), Eliza Haywood's *The History of Miss Betsy Thoughtless* (1751), Oliver Goldsmith's *The Vicar of Wakefield* (1766), and Helen Maria Williams's *Julia* (1790) as its basis, "Literary Culture as Immediate Reality" illustrates how, for writers and fictional subjects, literary consciousness functioned as a dominant schema; genre exists within and outside the text, impinging on both the text and lived experience. The extremely detailed and textured treatment of these works illustrates the possibilities for this new category of interpretation to deepen profoundly our understanding of writers, their narrative and generic choices, and potentially readers' understanding as well.

Finally, if we consider why eighteenth-century authors write the kinds of texts they do, we should also consider why we write the kind of criticism we do. Are scholars preoccupied with writing about print culture because it seems threatened in our own time? Does a new interest in attitudes toward the aged and elderly writers emerge in a time of aging baby boomers? Does the increased focus on the global nature of the novel stem from the present varied globalization? Does a focus on the body politic allude to questions about access to political systems in the world today? Does the desire to resist the monoglot emphasis acknowledge our culture's increasingly polyglot dimensions? The list of intertextual crosscurrents could continue. Perhaps the questions we ask about the literature we engage reflect, in some way, the intellectual problems that vex us in our own cultures. We hope these essays will generate questions in their readers and in turn contribute to the ongoing interrogation of the eighteenth-century novel.

NOTES

1. Homer Brown, "Prologue: Why the Story of the Origin of the (English) Novel Is an American Romance (If Not the Great American Novel)," in *Cultural Institutions of the Novel*, ed. Deidre Lynch and William B. Warner (Durham, NC, and London: Duke University Press, 1996), 15.

2. Nancy Armstrong and Leonard Tennenhouse, *The Imaginary Puritan: Literature, Intellectual Labor, and the Origins of Personal Life* (Berkeley and Los Angeles: University of California Press, 1992), 198. The quotation continues: "Novels characteristically claim to have begun as another kind of writing, as a diary, a journalistic account, a handbook for letter writing, a travel narrative, a criminal confession, a romance, or just plain history."

3. Leila Silvana May, "The Strong-Arming of Desire: A Reconsideration of Nancy Armstrong's *Desire and Domestic Fiction*," *ELH* 68 (2001): 268.

4. Jane Austen, *Northanger Abbey*, ed. R. W. Chapman. Vol. 5 of *The Novels of Jane Austen* (Oxford: Oxford University Press, 1923; rpt. 1988), 37.

5. Ian Watt, *The Rise of the Novel: Studies in Defoe, Richardson, and Fielding* (Berkeley and Los Angeles: University of California Press, 1957).

6. David Blewett, "Introduction," *Reconsidering the Rise of the Novel*. Special issue of *Eighteenth-Century Fiction* 12:2–3 (2000): 141.

7. Wilbur L. Cross, *The Development of the English Novel* (New York: Macmillan, 1899), 33.

8. Ernest A. Baker, *The History of the English Novel*. Vol. 3, *The Later Romances and the Establishment of Realism* (New York: Barnes and Noble, 1924; rpt. 1950), 137. For a fascinating discussion of the persistence and prevalence of Watt's text, despite the presence of other more extensive histories of the novel, see Margaret Reeves, "Telling the Tale of *The Rise of the Novel*," *CLIO* 30 (2000): 25–49.

9. Alan Dugald McKillop, *The Early Masters of English Fiction* (Lawrence: University of Kansas Press, 1956).

10. Ian Watt, "Flat-Footed and Fly-Blown: The Realities of Realism," *Eighteenth-Century Fiction* 12:2–3 (2000): 153. This talk, originally presented in 1978, provides a wonderful intellectual history – in the truest sense of the term – of Watt and the development of his landmark study.

11. *The Rise of the Novel*, especially chapter III, "Robinson Crusoe: Individualism and the Novel," 60–92.

12. Watt's text is central to all subsequent histories of the novel both for critics who embrace his text as a model and those who work strenuously to revise it. In addition to the special issue of *Eighteenth-Century Fiction* noted above, two other pieces that suggest the significance of Watt's contribution are: John Richetti, "The Legacy of Ian Watt's *The Rise of the Novel*," in *The Profession of Eighteenth-Century Literature: Reflections on an Institution*, ed. Leo Damrosch (Madison: University of Wisconsin Press, 1992), 95–112; and Daniel R. Schwartz, "The Importance of Ian Watt's *The Rise of the Novel*," *Journal of Narrative Technique* 13 (1983): 59–73.

13. John Richetti, *Popular Fiction Before Richardson, Narrative Patterns: 1700–1739* (Oxford: Clarendon Press, 1969; rpt. 1992), 262. The phrase comes from the title of Richetti's epilogue.

14. Michael McKeon, *The Origins of the English Novel, 1600–1740* (Baltimore, MD: Johns Hopkins University Press, 1987) and Nancy Armstrong, *Desire and Domestic Fiction: A Political History of the Novel* (New York: Oxford University Press, 1987).

15. Quoting Louis Althusser, McKeon notes "there is no longer any original essence, only an ever pre-givenness, however far knowledge delves into its past" (19).

16. Felicity Nussbaum and Laura Brown, eds., *The New Eighteenth Century: Theory, Politics, English Literature* (New York: Methuen, 1987).

17. Lennard Davis, *Factual Fictions: The Origins of the English Novel* (New York: Columbia University Press, 1983), 44.

18. John Bender, *Imagining the Penitentiary: Fiction and the Architecture of the Mind in Eighteenth-Century England* (Chicago: University of Chicago Press, 1987), 1.

19. Terry Castle, *Masquerade and Civilization: The Carnivalesque in Eighteenth-Century English Culture and Fiction* (Stanford, CA: Stanford University Press, 1986), vii.

20. Ros Ballaster, *Seductive Forms: Women's Amatory Fiction from 1684–1740* (Oxford: Clarendon Press, 1992), 2.

21. Cheryl Turner, *Living by the Pen: Women Writers in the Eighteenth Century* (London: Routledge, 1992); Janet Todd's *The Sign of Angellica: Women, Writing, and Fiction, 1660–1800* (New York: Columbia University Press, 1989).

22. Catherine Gallagher, *Nobody's Story: The Vanishing Acts of Women Writers in the Marketplace, 1670–1820* (Berkeley and Los Angeles: University of California Press, 1994).

23. Quoted in Lennard J. Davis, "Reconsidering Origins: How Novel are Theories of the Novel?" *Eighteenth-Century Fiction* 12:2–3 (2000): 480.

24. J. Paul Hunter, *Before Novels: The Cultural Contexts of Eighteenth-Century English Fiction* (New York: W. W. Norton, 1990). The question is the title of chapter 1, 3–28.

25. William B. Warner, *Licensing Entertainment: The Elevation of Novel Reading in Britain, 1684–1750* (Berkeley and Los Angeles: University of California Press, 1998), 2, xiii.

26. John Richetti. *The English Novel in History, 1700–1780* (London: Routledge, 1999). This extremely useful study, designed for students, provides a very accessible account of the context for the novel.

27. For example, Paula McDowell, *The Women of Grub Street* (Oxford: Clarendon Press, 1998); Brean S. Hammond, *Professional Imaginative Writing in England, 1670–1740: Hackney for Bread* (Oxford: Clarendon Press, 1997); and George Justice, *The Manufacturers of Literature: Writing and the Literary Marketplace in Eighteenth-Century England* (Newark: University of Delaware Press, 2002), among others. The interest in early readers of the novel has resulted in work such as James Raven, Helen Small, and Naomi Tadmore, eds., *The Practice and Representation of Reading in England* (Cambridge: Cambridge University Press, 1996).

28. For example, Janine Barchas, *Graphic Design, Print Culture, and the Eighteenth-Century Novel* (Cambridge: Cambridge University Press, 2003) and Leah Price, *The Anthology and the Rise of the Novel* (Cambridge: Cambridge University Press, 2000).

29. Sandra Sherman, *Finance and Fictionality in the Early Eighteenth Century* (Cambridge: Cambridge University Press, 1996) and James Thompson, *Models of Value: Eighteenth-Century Political Economy and the Novel* (Durham, NC: Duke University Press, 1996) are good examples.

30. For example, Lisa Moore, *Dangerous Intimacies: Toward a Sapphic History of the British Novel* (Durham, NC: Duke University Press, 1997) or George Haggerty, *Unnatural Affections: Women and Fiction in the Later Eighteenth Century* (Bloomington: Indiana University Press, 1998). Interesting suggestions for theorizing such a history of the novel appear in Sally O'Driscoll, "Outlaw Readings: Beyond Queer Theory," *Signs* 22 (1996): 30–51.

31. Though written from a distinctly different theoretical perspective, Margaret Doody's similarly inclusive *The True Story of the Novel* (New Brunswick, NJ: Rutgers University Press, 1996) argues for recognition

of the influences of the "ancient novel" and also resists the "chauvinism" that "leads English-speaking critics to treat the Novel as if it were somehow essentially English" (1).

32. Roger Chartier, *The Order of Books: Readers, Authors, and Libraries in Europe Between the Fourteenth and Eighteenth Centuries*, trans. Lydia G. Cochrane (Stanford, CA: Stanford University Press, 1994).

Shared Bibliography

Adams, Percy G. *Travel Writing and the Evolution of the Novel*. Lexington: University Press of Kentucky, 1983.

Anderson, Benedict. *Imagined Communities: Reflections on the Origin and Spread of Nationalism*. London: Verso, 1983.

Aravamudan, Srinivas. *Tropicopolitans: Colonialism and Agency, 1688–1804*. Durham, NC: Duke University Press, 1999.

Armstrong, Nancy. *Desire and Domestic Fiction: A Political History of the Novel*. Oxford: Oxford University Press, 1987.

Backscheider, Paula R., ed. *Revising Women: Eighteenth-Century "Women's Fiction" and Social Engagement*. Baltimore, MD: Johns Hopkins University Press, 2000.

Bakhtin, Mikhail. *The Dialogic Imagination: Four Essays*. ed. Michael Holquist and trans. Caryl Emerson and Michael Holquist. Austin: University of Texas Press, 1981.

Ballaster, Ros. *Seductive Forms: Women's Amatory Fiction from 1684–1740*. Oxford: Clarendon Press, 1992.

Barchas, Janine. *Graphic Design, Print Culture, and the Eighteenth-Century Novel*. Cambridge: Cambridge University Press, 2003.

Bartolomeo, Joseph F. *A New Species of Criticism: Eighteenth-Century Discourse on the Novel*. Newark: University of Delaware Press, 1994.

Bender, John. *Imagining the Penitentiary: Fiction and the Architecture of Mind in Eighteenth-Century England*. Chicago: University of Chicago Press, 1987.

Bohls, Elizabeth A. *Women Travel Writers and the Language of Aesthetics, 1716–1818*. Cambridge: Cambridge University Press, 1995.

Bowers, Toni. "Sex, Lies, and Invisibility." In *The Columbia History of the British Novel*, ed. John Richetti. New York: Columbia University Press, 1994, pp. 50–72.

Brown, Laura. *Ends of Empire: Women and Ideology in Early Eighteenth-Century English Literature*. Ithaca, NY: Cornell University Press, 1993.

Burgess, Miranda. *British Fiction and the Production of Social Order, 1740–1830*. Cambridge: Cambridge University Press, 2000.

Castle, Terry. *Masquerade and Civilization: The Carnivalesque in Eighteenth-Century English Culture and Fiction*. Stanford, CA: Stanford University Press, 1986.

Cheek, Pamela. *Sexual Antipodes: Enlightenment Globalization and the Placing of Sex*. Stanford, CA: Stanford University Press, 2003.

Colley, Linda. *Britons: Forging the Nation 1707–1837*. New Haven, CT: Yale University Press, 1992.

Corman, Brian. "Early Women Novelists, the Canon, and the History of the British Novel." In *Eighteenth-Century Contexts: Historical Inquiries in Honor of Philip Harth*, ed. Howard Weinbrot, Peter Schakel, and Stephen Karian. Madison: University of Wisconsin Press, 2001, pp. 232–46.

Damrosch, Leo. *God's Plot and Man's Stories: Studies in the Fictional Imagination from Milton to Fielding*. Chicago: University of Chicago Press, 1985.

Davis, Lennard. *Resisting Novels: Ideology and Fiction*. London: Methuen, 1987.

Davis, Lennard. *Factual Fictions: The Origins of the English Novel*. Philadelphia: University of Pennsylvania Press, 1997. [First published in 1983.]

DeJean, Joan. *Tender Geographies: Women and the Origins of the Novel in France*. New York: Columbia University Press, 1991.

Donoghue, Frank. *The Fame Machine: Book Reviewing and Eighteenth-Century Literary Careers*. Stanford, CA: Stanford University Press, 1996.

Donovan, Josephine. *Women and the Rise of the Novel, 1405–1726*. New York: St. Martin's Press, 1999.

Ezell, Margaret J. M. *Writing Women's Literary History*. Baltimore, MD: Johns Hopkins University Press, 1992.

Flint, Christopher. *Family Fictions: Narrative and Domestic Relations in Britain, 1688–1798*. Stanford, CA: Stanford University Press, 1998.

Foucault, Michel. *The History of Sexuality*, trans. Robert Hurley. 3 vols. New York: Pantheon, 1978.

Foxon, David. *Libertine Literature in England 1660–1745*. New Hyde Park, NY: University Books, 1965.

Gallagher, Catherine. *Nobody's Story: The Vanishing Acts of Women in the Marketplace 1670–1820*. Oxford: Clarendon Press, 1994.

George, Dorothy M. *London Life in the Eighteenth Century*. Harmondsworth, UK: Penguin, 1966. [First published in 1925.]

Goldmann, Lucien. *Toward a Sociology of the Novel* [*Pour une sociologie du roman*], trans. Alan Sheridan. London: Tavistock, 1975.

Gonda, Caroline. *Reading Daughters' Fictions, 1709–1834: Novels and Society from Manley to Edgeworth*. Cambridge: Cambridge University Press, 1996.

Haggerty, George E. *Unnatural Affections: Women and Fiction in the Later Eighteenth Century*. Bloomington: Indiana University Press, 1998.

Halberstam, Judith. *Skin Shows: Gothic Fiction and the Technology of Monsters*. Durham, NC: Duke University Press, 1995.

Hammond, Brean S. *Professional Imaginative Writing in England, 1670–1740: "Hackney for Bread."* Oxford: Clarendon Press, 1997.

Hulme, Peter, and Tim Youngs, eds. *The Cambridge Companion to Travel Writing*. Cambridge: Cambridge University Press, 2002.

Hunt, Lynn. *The Invention of Pornography: Obscenity and the Origins of Modernity*. New York: Zone Books, 1993.

Hunter, J. Paul. *Before Novels: The Cultural Contexts of Eighteenth-Century English Fiction*. New York: W. W. Norton, 1990.

Ingrassia, Catherine. *Authorship, Commerce, and Gender in Early Eighteenth-Century England: A Culture of Paper Credit*. Cambridge: Cambridge University Press, 1998.

Jameson, Fredric. *The Political Unconscious: Narrative as a Socially Symbolic Act*. Ithaca, NY: Cornell University Press, 1981.

Johnson, Claudia L. *Equivocal Beings: Politics, Gender, and Sentimentality in the 1790s: Wollstonecraft, Radcliffe, Burney, Austen*. Chicago: Chicago University Press, 1995.

Justice, George. *The Manufacturers of Literature: Writing and the Literary Marketplace in Eighteenth-Century England*. Newark: University of Delaware Press, 2002.

Kahn, Madeleine. *Narrative Transvestism: Rhetoric and Gender in the Eighteenth-Century English Novel*. Ithaca, NY: Cornell University Press, 1991.

Keymer, Tom. *Richardson's Clarissa and the Eighteenth-Century Reader*. Cambridge: Cambridge University Press, 1992.

Kidd, Colin. *British Identities Before Nationalism: Ethnicity and Nationhood in the Atlantic World, 1600–1800*. Cambridge: Cambridge University Press, 1999.

Lukács, György. *Theory of the Novel: A Historico-Philosophical Essay on the Forms of Great Epic Literature*, trans. Anna Bostock. Cambridge, MA: MIT Press, 1971.

Lukács, György. *The Historical Novel*, trans. Hannah and Stanley Mitchell. Lincoln: University of Nebraska Press, 1983.

Lynch, Deidre. *The Economy of Character: Novels, Market Culture, and the Business of Inner Meaning*. Chicago: University of Chicago Press, 1998.

Lynch, Deidre, and William Warner, eds. *Cultural Institutions of the Novel*. Durham, NC: Duke University Press, 1996.

Mayer, Robert. *History and the Early English Novel: Matters of Fact from Bacon to Defoe*. Cambridge: Cambridge University Press, 1997.

McDowell, Paula. *The Women of Grub Street: Press, Politics, and Gender in the London Literary Marketplace 1678–1730*. Oxford: Clarendon Press, 1998.

McKeon, Michael. *The Origins of the English Novel 1600–1740*. Baltimore, MD: Johns Hopkins University Press, 2002. [First published in 1987.]

Michaelson, Patricia Howell. *Speaking Volumes: Women, Reading, and Speech in the Age of Austen*. Stanford, CA: Stanford University Press, 2002.

Mullan, John. *Sentiment and Sociability: The Language of Feeling in the Eighteenth Century*. Oxford: Oxford University Press, 1988.

Pateman, Carole. *The Sexual Contract*. Stanford, CA: Stanford University Press, 1988.

Pocock, J. G. A. *Virtue, Commerce, and History: Essays on Political Thought and History, chiefly in the Eighteenth Century*. Cambridge: Cambridge University Press, 1985.

Pollak, Ellen. *Incest and the English Novel, 1684–1814*. Baltimore, MD: Johns Hopkins University Press, 2003.

Pratt, Mary Louise. *Imperial Eyes: Travel Writing and Transculturation*. New York: Routledge, 1992.

Price, Leah. *The Anthology and the Rise of the Novel: From Richardson to George Eliot*. Cambridge and New York: Cambridge University Press, 2000.

Raven, James. *Judging New Wealth: Popular Publishing and Responses to Commerce in England, 1750–1800*. Oxford: Clarendon Press, 1992.

Raven, James, Helen Small, and Naomi Tadmor, eds. *The Practice and Representation of Reading in England*. Cambridge: Cambridge University Press, 1996.

Ribeiro, Alvaro, and James G. Basker, eds. *Tradition in Transition: Women Writers, Marginal Texts, and the Eighteenth-Century Canon*. Oxford: Clarendon Press, 1996.

Richetti, John J. *Popular Fiction Before Richardson: Narrative Patterns 1700–1739*. Oxford: Clarendon Press, 1992. [First published in 1969.]

Richetti, John J. *The English Novel in History, 1700–1780*. London: Routledge, 1999.

Robert, Marthe. *Origins of the Novel* [*Roman des origines et du roman*], trans. Sacha Rabinovitch. Bloomington: Indiana University Press, 1980.

Runge, Laura L. *Gender and Language in British Literary Criticism, 1660–1790*. Cambridge: Cambridge University Press, 1997.

Schellenberg, Betty A. *The Conversational Circle: Re-reading the English Novel, 1740–1775*. Lexington: University Press of Kentucky, 1996.

Sedgwick, Eve Kosofsky. *Between Men: English Literature and Male Homosocial Desire*. New York: Columbia University Press, 1985.

Sill, Geoffrey. *The Cure of the Passions and the Origins of the English Novel*. Cambridge: Cambridge University Press, 2001.

Siskin, Clifford. *The Work of Writing: Literature and Social Change in Britain, 1700–1830*. Baltimore, MD: Johns Hopkins University Press, 1998.

Sorensen, Janet. *The Grammar of Empire in Eighteenth-Century British Writing*. Cambridge: Cambridge University Press, 2000.

Spencer, Jane. *Rise of the Woman Novelist: From Aphra Behn to Jane Austen*. Oxford: Blackwell, 1986.

Stanton, Judith Phillips. "Statistical Profile of Women Writing in English from 1660 to 1800." In *Eighteenth-Century Women and the Arts*, ed. Frederick M. Keener and Susan E. Lorsch. New York: Greenwood Press, 1998, pp. 247–54.

Sussman, Charlotte. *Consuming Anxieties: Consumer Protest, Gender and British Slavery, 1713–1833*. Stanford, CA: Stanford University Press, 2000.

Thompson, James. *Models of Value: Eighteenth-Century Political Economy and the Novel*. Durham, NC: Duke University Press, 1996.

Todd, Dennis, and Cynthia Wall, eds. *Eighteenth-Century Genre and Culture: Serious Reflections on Occasional Forms: Essays in Honor of J. Paul Hunter*. Newark: University of Delaware Press; London: Associated University Presses, 2001.

Todd, Janet. *Sign of Angellica: Women, Writing and Fiction, 1660–1800*. New York: Columbia University Press, 1989.

Tompkins, J. M. S. *The Popular Novel in England, 1770–1800*. Lincoln: University of Nebraska Press, 1961. [First published in 1932.]

Trumbach, Randolph. *Sex and the Gender Revolution*. Volume 1. *Heterosexuality and the Third Gender in Enlightenment London*. Chicago and London: University of Chicago Press, 1998.

Trumpener, Katie. *Bardic Nationalism: The Romantic Novel and the British Empire*. Princeton, NJ: Princeton University Press, 1997.

Turner, Cheryl. *Living by the Pen: Women Writers in the Eighteenth Century*. London: Routledge, 1992.

Turner, James Grantham. "Pornography and the Fall of the Novel." *Studies in the Novel* 33 (2001): 358–64.

Varey, Simon. *Space and the Eighteenth-Century English Novel*. Cambridge: Cambridge University Press, 1990.

Wahl, Elizabeth Susan. *Invisible Relations: Representations of Female Intimacy in the Age of Enlightenment*. Stanford, CA: Stanford University Press, 1999.

Warner, William B. *Licensing Entertainment: The Elevation of Novel Reading in Britain, 1684–1750*. Berkeley and Los Angeles: University of California Press, 1998.

Watt, Ian. *The Rise of the Novel: Studies in Defoe, Richardson and Fielding*. London: Chatto and Windus, 1957; Berkeley and Los Angeles: University of California Press, 1957; second edition, 2001.

Zionkowski, Linda. *Men's Work: Gender, Class, and the Professionalization of Poetry, 1660–1784*. New York: Palgrave, 2001.

Part One
Formative Influences

"I have now done with my island, and all manner of discourse about it": Crusoe's *Farther Adventures* and the Unwritten History of the Novel

Robert Markley

The Crusoe Trilogy and the Critics

During the last two decades, feminist, Marxist, and New Historicist critics have transformed our understanding of the eighteenth-century novel, but none of them has questioned the iconic status of *Robinson Crusoe* (1719). Even those critics skeptical of the hero's justifications for colonizing "his" island accept the commonplace that Defoe's first novel transmutes the raw material of Puritanical injunction and moral self-scrutiny into the psychological realism that helps define the novel form. In turn, Crusoe's individualistic psychology, most critics agree, marks the transition from a residual aristocratic to an emergent bourgeois, capitalist, and (since the 1980s) broadly Foucauldian ideology of selfhood. The titles of many of these critics' works – centering on "rises" and "origins" – reveal a tendency to write the history of modern identity, the rise of the novel, and the rise of financial capitalism in mutually constitutive and mutually reinforcing terms.[1] Paradoxically, *Robinson Crusoe* retains its crucial role in revisionist histories of the novel precisely because Defoe can be credited with (or blamed for) developing a colonialist model of subjectivity: conquering the wilderness and exploiting the labor of native peoples allow the colonizer the luxury of becoming a bourgeois subject.[2] Seen in this light, Crusoe's economic moralizing and religious proselytizing may not quite open a window to the soul, but they do offer a compelling novelistic strategy for representing the psychological complexities of Defoe's reluctant pilgrim.

This consensus view of *Robinson Crusoe*, however, holds up only if critics ignore or explain away the two sequels that Defoe published shortly after his successful first novel. In this essay, I call into question some of the assumptions and values that underlie the homology of "bourgeois" identity, the rise of the novel, and early modern capitalism that inform much *Crusoe* criticism. Volumes two and three of the trilogy, the *Farther Adventures of Robinson Crusoe* (1719) and the *Serious Reflections* (1720), I suggest, represent Defoe's self-conscious *rejection* of the interlocking discourses of "psychological realism," economic self-sufficiency, and one-size-fits-all models of European colonialism. In both works, Defoe abandons the narrative strategies that he employs in his first Crusoe novel. Rather than seeing the *Farther Adventures* as an unsuccessful sequel, I want to take seriously Defoe's contention that "the second part . . . is (contrary to the usage of second parts) every way as entertaining as the first, contains as strange and surprising incidents, and as great variety of them; nor is the application less serious or suitable; and doubtless will, to the sober as well as ingenious reader, be every way as profitable and diverting."[3] His contemporary readers apparently agreed with Defoe's assessment: published four months after *Robinson Crusoe*, the *Farther Adventures* went through seven editions by 1747 (only two fewer than the original) and was republished regularly with its predecessor well into the nineteenth century.[4] In their eagerness to identify *Crusoe* and its hero as standard-bearers of an emergent modernity, however, many critics have taken at face value the notion that his fictional island is a template for a European colonialism that dominated the eighteenth-century world. In crediting the "realism" of this fantasy of emergent Eurocentrism, they give short shrift to the hero's subsequent Asian adventures in the second volume of the trilogy, particularly his hyperbolic attacks on every aspect imaginable of Chinese culture. In its obsession with China, *Farther Adventures* marks a significant turn in Defoe's career. Instead of elaborating a colonialist parable, this novel depicts and seeks to counter nightmare visions of an embattled English identity in a hostile world. In this regard, Defoe's explicit rejection of many of the values and assumptions associated with Crusoe's twenty-eight years on the island has significant implications for any history of the eighteenth-century novel. Rather than considering his first novel a triumphant innovation, Defoe seems to have regarded it as an experiment that did not bear repeating.

In the most compelling analysis of Crusoian identity to date, Hans Turley has reread the three novels as efforts to describe a piratical, homosocial self as an alternative to the domestic ideology of a feminized, psychologized identity.[5] According to Turley, Defoe yokes capitalist expansion and Protestant evangelism to privilege Crusoe the Christian apologist over Crusoe the poster-boy for the bourgeois self. In extending Turley's argument, I argue that the Crusoe novels are marked by a crucial fantasy – one always in danger of collapse and therefore always in need of shoring up – that centers less on "identity" than on the dream of economic self-reliance. In analyzing the liberties that Defoe takes in *Crusoe* with the history of ceramic manufacturing, Lydia Liu has called attention to the strangeness at the heart of "an otherwise thoroughly known text and context"; his shipwrecked hero produces a usable facsimile of Chinese porcelain, a feat beyond the ability of European manufacturers in 1719.[6] If Crusoe's earthenware pot is emblematic of a fantasy of economic self-sufficiency, it also suggests how little attention has been paid to *Crusoe*'s

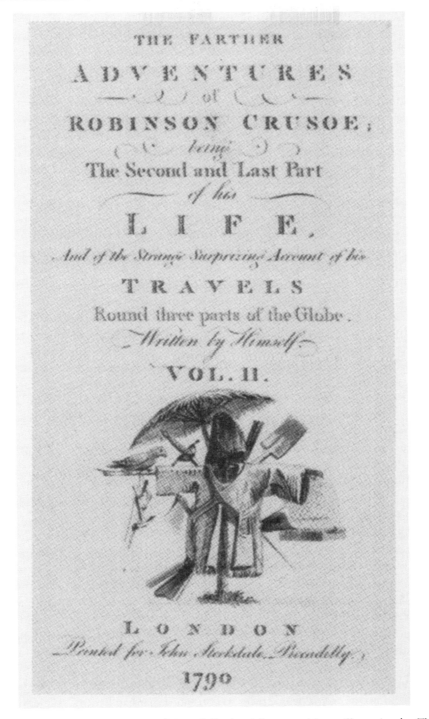

Plate 1. Title page from the 1790 edition of *Farther Adventures* with an illustration by Thomas Stothard, the first important illustrator of *Robinson Crusoe.*

"context," especially a sequel that becomes increasingly obsessed with the problems posed by the Far East for western conceptions of "capitalism" and national identity.

In the context of the trilogy as a whole, Crusoe's island and its attendant assumptions and values — the hero's puritanical self-scrutiny; the colonialist exploitation of the natural world and non-European peoples; the willing submission of "pagans" to Christianity; and economic self-reliance — constitute only one half of a dialectic. Once Crusoe leaves his colony midway through the *Farther Adventures*, Defoe develops the narrative strategies and anatomizes the ideological concerns that shape the rest of his literary career. First, economic self-sufficiency is jettisoned in favor of a discourse about the networks of communication and credit — the merchants, bankers, and middlemen — essential to Asian trade; Crusoe's implication in these networks provokes a desire to re-establish a religious and national identity that can insulate the hero from cosmopolitanism and contamination. Second, the colonialist parable of *Robinson Crusoe* is abandoned for a different kind of fantasy: the *Farther Adventures* is the first of Defoe's fictional narratives that promote visions of an infinitely profitable trade to the Far East and the South Seas. Third, the figure of the cannibal as convert, a testament to the powers of European technology and religion, is replaced by the hero's — and the novelist's — obsession with far more dangerous "others," the Dutch and the Chinese. And lastly, puritanical self-scrutiny becomes far less insistent in the sequel; Crusoe's formulaic protestations of his "follies" give way to fervid, nearly hysterical assertions of European — specifically British and Protestant — superiority to Asian cultures. By the end of the trilogy, in *Serious Reflections*, the transition from psychological self to fanatic crusader is marked by the bone-chilling prescription that Crusoe offers for national prosperity in a world in which "Infidels possess such Vast Regions, and Religion in its Purity shines in a small Quarter of the Globe": convert or exterminate the brutes.[7] But as the hero's adventures in the Far East demonstrate, his call for a *jihad* against the Eastern world can take place, at least in 1720, only in armchair fantasies thousands of miles from the Great Wall.

The bizarre prospect of Crusoe trading diamonds in Bengal; opium, cloves, and nutmeg in the Indonesian archipelago; and silks and bullion in China marks Defoe's fascination with the travel narratives of the seventeenth century and their pursuit of profit, national glory, and the spreading of the gospel.[8] Written at the height of the speculation in South Sea Company stock, *Farther Adventures* seeks to jump-start British ventures in the Pacific by reinvigorating the fantasies of "infinite" wealth to be made in the region. Defoe's fictional forays into the Far East in *Farther Adventures*, *Captain Singleton* (1720), and *A New Voyage Round the World* (1724) are marked by both fascination and fear. Defoe recognizes — as his contemporaries did and as Europeans had done for two centuries — that trade with China and Japan could return enormous profits; at the same time, he reacts viscerally against the difficulties that Europeans faced as supplicants for trade during a period when China and, to a lesser extent, India and Japan, dominated world trade, bullion and financial markets, and the traffic in luxury items (from spices to porcelain) that had become staples of upperclass consumption, and of elite social identity, in Europe. Although the English had significant trading ventures in Mughal India, the Ottoman Empire, and Persia, China presented both practical and conceptual difficulties as a trading partner. As the richest and most populous nation on earth, it could dictate the terms of trade to Europeans, levy customs, restrict trading privileges, and force merchants and missionaries to accommodate themselves to Chinese practices.[9] Yet, despite these widely reported barriers to trade, Defoe remains obsessed by the travel literature on which he drew: in dozens of seventeenth- and early eighteenth-century accounts, China, Japan, and the Spice Islands fulfill two crucial, and imaginary, roles: they are both insatiable markets for European goods and a vast, inexhaustible storehouse of porcelain, spices, silk, tea, and other goods that can command premium prices in Europe. In the Jesuit sources that Defoe cites throughout *Serious Reflections*, China represents the apex of civilization – the order and government necessary to carry on an ever-expanding trade; Southeast Asia and the Pacific are characterized frequently as regions where Europeans can either gather commodities with little effort or strike one good deal after another with cooperative natives. The promise that the Far East holds, and the myth it embodies for Europeans, then, is that it can sustain an unending, and infinitely profitable, trade. The reality that Defoe must deal with is that the Chinese cannot be transformed into the subjects or dupes of European imperialism. In his farther adventures, Crusoe confronts a nightmare that lurks everywhere in early modern accounts of the Middle Kingdom: the irrelevance of western conceptions of identity and theology in a sinocentric world.

Crusoe's Nameless Island

Crusoe's *Farther Adventures* and *Serious Reflections* have troubled critics who come to the novels with expectations that these works should continue the project of defining an emergent selfhood. While the first half of the former novel has Crusoe return to his island and deal with the problems of the colony he left behind, the second half follows the hero through an episodic series of adventures in Southeast Asia, China, and Siberia. By recasting mercantile visions of the endless generation of wealth as the very stuff of Crusoe's "farther" adventures, Defoe presents a compensatory narrative for the problems of colonization – the social, theological, and administrative headaches that occupy Crusoe when he returns to "his" island.

Reading the *Farther Adventures*, one is struck by how little Crusoe has learned from his experiences. Repeatedly in this novel, Defoe uses the same language of folly and sin to describe his hero's obsessions, wanderlust, and rejection of middle-class comfort that he had employed in his first novel. Yet the abrupt transition midway through the novel from the island to the exotic lands of merchant adventuring necessitates new narrative strategies to describe both individual and national identity. The difference between the two halves of *Farther Adventures* is defined by two dreams that Crusoe relates at length: the first, at the beginning of the novel, describes his longing to return to the island; the second, years later, recounts his "anxieties and perplexities"

(415) as a merchant in Southeast Asia. Although, seven years after returning to England, the hero is living comfortably, he is obsessed with returning to the island. This "chronical distemper" troubles his dreams and dominates his life:

> The desire of seeing my new plantation in the island, and the colony I left there, run in my head continually. I dream'd of it all night, and my imagination run upon it all day; it was uppermost in all my thoughts, and my fancy work'd so steadily and strongly upon it, that I talk'd of it in my sleep; in short, nothing could remove it out of my mind; it even broke so violently into all my discourses, that it made my conversation tiresome; for I could talk of nothing else, all my discourse run into it, even to impertinence, and I saw it my self. (251–52)

Crusoe succumbs to "such extasies of vapours" that he imagines himself back on the island, conversing with the marooned Spaniard and Friday's father, and concludes that, while he cannot account for the etiology of his dreams or "what secret converse of spirits injected it, yet there was very much of it true" (252). His dreams, however, reveal little about what Crusoe wants to do when he returns to the island or what the moral significance of his obsession might be. While his dream may foreshadow the action of the first half of *Farther Adventures*, the collapse of distinctions between dreaming and waking underscores the cautionary remarks offered in *Serious Reflections*: "Dreams are dangerous things to talk of ... the least encouragement to lay any weight upon them is presently carried away by a sort of people that dream waking, and that run into such wild extremes about them, that indeed we ought to be very cautious what we say of them."[10] The nature of Crusoe's obsession, his tendency to "dream waking," is not made explicit; but if "very much" of his dreaming about the island is "true," then his "desire" takes the form of exercising an authority that the hero describes as "patriarchal." His dreams become both externalized, half-attributed to supernatural powers, and introjected so that the fantasies of commanding subjects and administering justice express his desire to repossess the island and reassert the socio-political integrity of a self committed to colonial administration and religious instruction. Yet midway through the novel, Crusoe's daydreams about the island give way to nightmares in the Far East. These violent dreams give shape to fears that are greater than those of being eaten by cannibals – fears of bodily and psychic dissolution that are emblematic of the threats to the Christian, mercantile self in a hostile world.

The first half of *Farther Adventures* set on Crusoe's island "colony" is didactic, even theologically coercive, in its insistence that administrative and juridical control depend on reclaiming sinners, notably the hell-raising Will Atkins, and reintegrating them into a social order of penitence and probity. Battles with natives are interspersed with long colloquies about the necessity for religious toleration and the virtues of Christian marriage – native women must be converted and married to their pirate and Spanish lovers. But if the enabling fiction of *Robinson Crusoe* is that self-interest and colonization are compatible, that enterprising individuals can transform the wilderness without draining England's wealth or exhausting indigenous resources, then in *Farther Adventures* Crusoe confronts the dilemmas that had been finessed in the first volume: competing economic interests within the colony, contested political authority, and religious differences between Catholics and Protestants.

His concern with colonial politics and Christian conversion may explain why, in fictionalizing the account of Alexander Selkirk, Defoe changes the location of the island in *Robinson Crusoe*. Juan Fernandez, off the coast of Chile, was a resort for buccaneers, a stopover for European expeditions to the Pacific, and a potential naval base. Much to Defoe's chagrin, England had no "plantations" in the Pacific, and the East India Company's voyages to the Far East were, by and large, not efforts to establish colonies but to insinuate its way into regional trading networks.[11] By shipwrecking Crusoe in the Caribbean, Defoe locates his narrative within a New World economy of slave trading and colonial development. This setting renders plausible the "colonization" of the island in a region where England could point to some success, and where Crusoe's dreams, as the hero tells the reader in *Serious Reflections*, reconfirm the prospect of eventual rescue: "in my greatest and most hopeless banishment I had such frequent dreams of my deliverance, that I always entertained a firm and satisfying belief that my last days would be better than my first" (*SR* 261–62). These frequent dreams of "deliverance" – not depicted in *Robinson Crusoe* – serve as after-the-fact confirmation of the moral and theological values that Defoe promotes. They are, in a sense, geographically specific to a Caribbean world that by 1719 was well-known and well-prospected by the English in their efforts to contain Spanish influence in the Americas. Displaced into East Asia, Crusoe confronts the nightmares of English irrelevance that he can ignore on his island.

The problems that Crusoe adjudicates, however, cannot mask the fact that his island is an unprofitable backwater. He has no dreams that foreshadow the colony's profitability. Rather than rehash the adventures of the first Crusoe novel or continue the moralizing of the first half of its sequel, Defoe abruptly abandons the projects of colonization and conversion. Having cajoled, proselytized, and shamed the European men on the island into marrying their native wives and having brokered agreements among bickering colonists, Crusoe denies any long-term plans or nationalist intention: "I never so much as pretended to plant in the name of any government or nation, or to acknowledge any prince, or to call my people subjects to any one nation more than another; nay, I never so much as gave the place a name" (374). His earlier obsession is gone, and he leaves the nameless island unceremoniously, never to return. He entrusts colonial administration to a nameless partner and the new governor, Will Atkins, declaring, "I have now done with my island, and all manner of discourse about it; and whoever reads the rest of my memorandums would do well to turn his thoughts entirely from it" (374). The vehemence of this admonition is startling, and Defoe is explicit: as an experiment in or as a model of colonialism, Crusoe's island is a failure. Neither ideals of toleration nor the internalized discourses of self-control can prevent the island from succumbing to the well-known problems of early eighteenth-century colonies – diminishing resources, political conflicts, and external threats:

> the last letters I had from any of them was by my partner's means; who afterwards sent another sloop to the place, and who sent me word, tho' I had not the letter till five years after it was written, that they went on but poorly, were malecontent with their long stay there; that Will. Atkins was dead; that five of the Spaniards were come away, and that tho' they had not been much molested by the savages, yet they had had some skirmishes with them; and that they begg'd of him to write me, to think of the promise I had made to fetch them away, that they might see their own country again before they dy'd. (374–75)

This outright rejection of the discourses and practices of colonialism suggests that the hero already has succumbed to the lure of trade and that his creator has recognized the incompatibility of the languages of administrative self-policing and infinite profits. In retrospect, then, the hero's rejection of the dictates of colonialism reveals that the "realism" of *Robinson Crusoe* has been predicated all along on the fantasy that one man is an island – economically and psychologically.

To introduce his subsequent adventures, Crusoe berates himself in much the same language that he uses to describe his first leaving England forty years earlier: "expect to read of the follies of an old man, not warn'd by his own harms, much less those of other men, to beware of the like; not cool'd by almost forty years' misery and disappointments, not satisfy'd with prosperity beyond expectation, not made cautious by affliction and distress beyond imitation" (374). But this moralistic rhetoric hardly describes Crusoe's adventures in the Far East. When Crusoe leaves the island, he leaves behind the moral-juridical structures that he has sought to establish as well as the internalized "reflections" of a man well aware of his own "follies." Although Friday is killed in a battle at sea and Crusoe is forced off his nephew's ship after remonstrating with the crew for massacring 150 villagers on Madagascar, he realizes a fortune from his years in Asia as a trader. His "new variety of follies, hardships, and wild ventures; wherein . . . we may see how easily Heaven can gorge us with our own desires" is long on gorging and short on both physical and psychological consequences of this septuagenarian's "wild-goose chase" (374). Crusoe's characteristic self-doubts and upbraidings quickly give way to denunciations of Asian civilizations and ultimately, in Siberia, to violence. The self, it seems, is no longer held together by moral injunctions and Foucauldian self-scrutiny but rendered coherent only as an instrument of providential fury against threats to Christianity.

"Inhuman tortures and barbarities": Crusoe's Nightmares in the Far East

Crusoe's second set of dreams occurs when he and his partner discover they have bought, inadvertently, a pirate ship and fear that they will be captured and hanged by the Dutch authorities in the Indonesian archipelago. In recounting these nightmares, the hero mentions no Christian patience, no martyrdom, no sense of placing himself in divine hands:

> both my partner and I too scarce slept a night without dreaming of halters and yard-arms, that is to say, gibbets; of fighting and being taken; of killing and being kill'd; and one night I was in such a fury in my dream, fancying the Dutch men had boarded us, and I was knocking one of their seamen down, that I struck my double fist against the side of the cabin I lay in, with such force as wounded my hand most grievously, broke my knuckles, and cut and bruised the flesh; so that it not only wak'd me out of my sleep, but I was once afraid that I should have lost two of my fingers. (414)

This dream extends beyond individual "imagination"; it is shared by Crusoe's partner and forces the hero to lash out in his sleep and break his knuckles. Crusoe does not use the rhetoric of guilt, sin, and unworthiness to describe his psychological turmoil; if this language has a precedent in his adventures, it is in his fantasies of massacring the cannibals after he has discovered human remains on his island. But the "fury" of this dream, "of killing and being kill'd," seems to threaten the hero's own person as much as it does the Dutch. The self-inflicted wound to his hand signifies a threat more troubling than his fear of cannibals in *Crusoe*. The nightmares that Crusoe and his partner experience, in the Dutch-dominated waters of Southeast Asia, mark the irruption of a national bogeyman into their consciousness: the trial and execution of twelve British merchants on the island of Amboyna a century earlier by the Dutch East India Company (VOC).

This 1623 incident was the epilogue to two decades of contention in the region that culminated in the British East India Company being forced out of the spice trade by the more numerous, better financed, and better equipped agents of the VOC. The execution of British merchants on Amboyna is a crucial – indeed defining – national trauma for the British until the 1760s: it marks England's exclusion from the lucrative spice trade for over a century and a half; it underscores the limitations of British naval power; and it exposes the tenuousness and contingency of a British national identity that takes commercial success as a providential sign that England, and not the Netherlands, is the true defender of the Protestant faith.[12] In *Atlas Maritimus and Commercialis* (1728), Defoe denounces at length "the horrid Massacre" of English merchants by the Dutch, "a Scene so full of Barbarity, and not only unchristian but also inhuman Cruelty," that its specifics of torture, forced confession, and execution are "not to be express'd."[13] By invoking Amboyna in *Farther Adventures*, the novelist conjures up a threat to the fundamentals of a national identity founded on the interlocking value systems of enlightened self-interest, civility, and religious faith: the martyred Englishmen, he declares in 1728, "were used in the most violent and inhuman manner, without respect to their Quality or Nation, being Merchants of good repute, and Men of untainted Character."[14] Social status, nationality, professional honesty, and moral probity all are undone by the nightmare on Amboyna.

Plate 2.　Map of Scythia and Asiatic Tartar, ancient tribal regions of Europe and Asia.

Although Crusoe visits the usual stations of the cross by acknowledging that "Providence might justly inflict this punishment, as a retribution" (415), his own dream is not that of a penitent grappling with the consequences of his sin but of violence and vengeance.

The hero's analysis of his nightmares describes a pattern that is repeated later in *Farther Adventures*: the threats he encounters in Asia are compared to and found more terrifying than the prospect of being eaten by "savages." His response to the cultural memory of Amboyna oscillates between "talking my self up to vigorous resolutions, that I would not be taken" and fears that he will be "barbarously used by a parcel of mercyless wretches in cold blood." The Dutch are far more terrifying than New World cannibals:

> it were much better to have fallen into the hands of savages, who were man-eaters . . . than [into] those who would perhaps glut their rage upon me, by inhuman tortures and barbarities . . . it was much more dreadful, to me at least, to think of falling into these men's hands, than ever it was to think of being eaten by men, for the savages, give them their due, would not eat a man till he was dead, and kill'd them first, as we do a bullock; but that these men had many arts beyond the cruelty of death. (415)

Dutch "cruelty" both subsumes and goes beyond the fear of disincorporation. "Inhuman tortures" threaten the integrity of the body politic – the metonymic identification of the merchant's body with the coherence and self-reliance of the nation. If "his" island represents a failure of colonialism, Crusoe's obsession with Amboyna reveals "the anxieties and perplexities" that attend making himself an instrument of his overriding desire for profit. Torture lays bare the greed, "barbarism," and amorality that providentialist and patriotic justifications for international trade mystify. Consequently, the hero's response to his dream is radically different from the soul-searching and moral accounting that he undertakes in *Robinson Crusoe*; he externalizes the divisiveness of sin, projecting a false "national" identity as a means to safeguard body, nation, and profits. Crusoe is the first, but not the last, of Defoe's heroes to fly a false flag at sea, to counterfeit a "national" identity in order to escape the consequences of a "free commerce." In this respect, his fears of being victimized by pirates and mistaken for a pirate represent the ambiguities of the independent trader seeking cargoes and profits in the entrepots of Southeast Asia: the "patriarch" of the island has become enmeshed in the ongoing negotiations of commercial identities in the East.

His nightmare of being tortured by the Dutch, however, may be the most serious threat that Crusoe faces in the second half of the novel. The colonial authorities in Batavia remain offstage; there is no heroic confrontation with the Dutch, no grappling with internal demons, no vindication of Crusoe's honor and honesty against an evil commercial rival. In short, no consequences follow from his dreams: Crusoe sells the ship and follows a trading opportunity to China. Idolatry, Catholicism, and despair – the principal threats against which Crusoe struggles to define his moral identity in the first part – pose far fewer difficulties for the hero (or his creator) in the sequel. Although the Dutch may haunt Crusoe's nightmares, his true antagonists in *Farther Adventures* are the Chinese because they embody a fundamental contradiction that Defoe cannot resolve – a virtuous and prosperous "heathen" civilization that threatens the mutually constitutive fantasies of infinite profits, religious zeal, and a secure national identity.

A long-time critic of the India trade, Defoe consistently, even obsessively, advocated British expansion into the South Seas; trading posts on the the west coast of South America, he maintained, could establish a profitable trade with both New Spain and the Far East. As it reworks material from Defoe's *Review of the State of the English Nation* (1704–1713), *A New Voyage Round the World* reveals his and his culture's fascination with trade across the Pacific as a means for England to realize its dreams of a coherent national identity and international economic power. The Crusoe trilogy appeared at a significant time in British efforts to open new markets and amid ongoing debates about the value of the East India trade. Throughout the seventeenth and much of the eighteenth century, Britain imported far more from the East than it exported, and almost all of its exports were in bullion. In 1718 and 1719, when Defoe was writing his Crusoe novels, four East India Company ships called at Canton, and all four carried more than 90 percent of their cargo as silver. As late as 1754, 80 percent of England's exports to Asia were in bullion.[15]

In *A New Voyage*, Defoe voices his long-standing critique of the East India trade: "we carry nothing or very little but money [to the orient], the innumerable nations of the Indies, China, &c., despising our manufactures and filling us with their own." He characterizes these imports as either "trifling and unnecessary" – "china ware, coffee, tea, japan works, pictures, fans, screens, &c." – or as "returns that are injurious to [Britain's] manufactures": "printed calicoes, chintz, wrought silks, stuffs of herbs and barks, block tin, cotton, arrack, copper, indigo."[16] Defoe's criticism of the India trade – sending out bullion and receiving either luxury items or cotton cloth which competed directly with British woolen mills – is extended in *Farther Adventures* to the burgeoning tea trade.[17] Although East India Company merchants "some times come home with 60 to 70 and 100 thousand pounds at a time" (393), the trade imbalance threatens England's economic security. "The innumerable nations of the Indies, China, &c." become, for Defoe, *both* an imaginative space of infinite profits *and* a nightmarish realm where personal and national identity become uncertain. To counter the prospect of the economic domination of the Dutch in Southeast Asia and of China to the north, *Farther Adventures* develops compensatory narratives that deny or repress the limitations of European power in the Far East.

Crusoe in China

Crusoe has no dreams in China or Siberia, but his characterizations of both lands assume an almost hallucinogenic quality; Eurocentric fantasies of Protestant commercialism replace the moral realism of *Robinson Crusoe*. His obsessive vilification is without precedent in the vast European literature on the Middle Kingdom. As Jonathan Spence notes in his discussion of *Farther Adventures*, "every previously described positive aspect of China [by the Jesuits and others] is negated, and every negative aspect of China is emphasized."[18] By rejecting accounts that celebrated China's wealth, socioeconomic stability, good government, and presumed monotheistic religion, Defoe dismisses the arguments that made China a difficult target for Europeans to attack. For sinophiles, the Middle Kingdom was an ancient empire that had escaped the fate of the pagan regimes of the Mediterranean and Near East and continued to prosper; it boasted a written history that, in its antiquity and moral probity, apparently rivaled the Old Testament; it seemed, to many commentators, to provide a model of sociopolitical order; and in its immense potential for trade, it reinforced centuries-old perceptions of "China's world economic preeminence in production and export."[19] Eyewitness accounts almost uniformly agreed that "Of all the Kingdoms of the Earth *China* is the most celebrated for Politeness and Civility, for grandeur and magnificence, for Arts and Inventions."[20] Although Defoe shares his contemporaries' views of the potential for trade to China and the East Indies, he resists the sociopolitical lessons that Jesuits, sinophiles (notably Leibniz), and English royalists draw in idealizing the Middle Kingdom as a model for Europe to emulate.[21] The prospect of an empire resistant to his critiques of tyranny, sin, and idolatry forces

Defoe into fervent efforts to counter the challenges that China poses to his vision of an infinitely profitable trade.

In both *Farther Adventures* and *Serious Reflections*, Crusoe castigates the Chinese at far greater length than he does any other people or culture. In fact, his long digression on China's civilization is the only time in his travels that he singles out a nation for explicit comment. "As this is the only excursion of this kind which I have made in all the account I have given of my travels," he maintains, "so I shall make no more descriptions of countrys and people; 'tis none of my business, or any part of my design" (423). In *Serious Reflections*, he dismisses the Mughal empire in two sentences and the entire Islamic world in a couple of pages but devotes twenty-three hefty paragraphs to castigating the Chinese for their pride, immorality, technological backwardness, corrupt government, hideous art, and political tyranny. Lashing out at the Chinese enacts rhetorically a compensatory fantasy of European pride and supposed superiority; what Crusoe can only dream about – fighting back against the Dutch – becomes a structuring fantasy for a Eurocentric identity. In identifying the Chinese, not the "cannibals" of the Americas as the "other" against whom he defines his theocentric identity, Crusoe finds the structure of fantasy more certain than the uncertainty of his dreams.

In his satiric fantasy, *The Consolidator* (1705), Defoe targets China as the antithesis of his political and religious values. His satire takes the form of a mock-ironic encomium that travesties Chinese learning, technological accomplishments, absolutist politics, and claims to a pre-Mosaic antiquity. Satirizing John Webb's theory that China was founded by Noah and that the Chinese therefore preserve the ancient language spoken by Adam and Eve, Defoe has his credulous narrator promise his readers "A Description of a Fleet of Ships of 100000 Sail, built at the Expense of the Emperor *Tangro* the 15th; who having Notice of the General Deluge, prepar'd these Vessels," escaped the Flood, and consequently preserved the antediluvian "Perfections" of their culture and a "most exact History of 2000 Emperors."[22] For Defoe, China's widespread renown for its antiquity, virtue, and social stability is merely a cover for noxious political and religious doctrines – notably monarchical absolutism and passive obedience. His narrator avows that there is no "Tyranny of Princes, or Rebellion of Subjects" in any of China's histories, and concludes that these annals offer proof "that Kings and Emperors came down from Heaven with Crowns on their Heads, and all their Subjects were born with Saddles on their Backs."[23] If such absolutism has been decreed by heaven, then Chinese history can be invoked by apologists for tyranny to "explain, as well as defend, all Coercion in Cases invasive of Natural Right."[24] In *The Consolidator*, China symbolizes the political repression and false religion that Defoe spent a lifetime attacking.

Fifteen years later, Crusoe's obsession with the Chinese occasions his vehement attacks on Jesuit accommodationism – the efforts by missionaries, part-belief and part-strategy, to identify Chinese moral philosophy with western monotheism.[25] Although Defoe accepts the Jesuits' wishful characterization of "Confucius's maxims" as an analogue of European "theology," he denounces these texts (widely translated into European vernaculars by 1720) as "a rhapsody of words, without consistency, and, indeed, with very little reasoning." He goes on to declare that there are "much more regular doings among some of the Indians that are pagans in America, than there are in China" (*SR* 123). As he does in vilifying the Dutch, Crusoe compares the Chinese unfavorably to the "pagans" of the Americas. But in China "idolatry" goes beyond ignorance or devil-worship to violate the principles that anchor western conceptions of reality. In a garden outside of Nanking, Crusoe finds a horrific Chinese "idol":

> It had a thing instead of a head, but no head; it had a mouth distorted out of all manner of shape, and not to be described for a mouth, being only an unshapen chasm, neither representing the mouth of a man, beast, fowl, or fish; the thing was neither any of the four, but an incongruous monster; it had feet, hands, fingers, claws, legs, arms, wings, ears, horns, everything mixed one among another, neither in the shape or place that Nature appointed, but blended together and fixed to a bulk, not a body, formed of no just parts, but a shapeless trunk or log, whether of wood or stone, I know not. (*SR* 126)

This "celestial hedgehog" is too grotesque "to have represented even the devil"; yet, if the reader wishes to form a picture in her mind's eye of Chinese deities, Crusoe asserts, "let imagination supply anything that can make a misshapen image horrid, frightful, and surprising" and the Chinese will worship "such a mangled, promiscuous-gendered creature" (*SR* 126). Crusoe overreacts: Chinese art by 1719 was well known in the west: porcelain was a prized import, silks, furniture, screens, fans, and illustrations in travel books made Chinese artistic conventions familiar and popular. Defoe's insistence on the "hedgehog's" confusions of physiology, gender, and religion, in this respect, is prompted by his recognition that this "idol" challenges a European ideology of representation and therefore an entire worldview. It is not simply that this "incongruous monster" represents the "other" against which an English Protestant self must be defined, but that Chinese theology and representational practices threaten to rewrite the very principles of theology, gender, and self-identity. Cannibals, like Friday, can be converted; they are amenable to reason and candidates for revelation. Catholics, like the helpful French priest on Crusoe's island, can become allies against idolatry. Even the Dutch, with their "inhuman tortures and barbarities," are Protestants who can be understood within a dialectic of national interest and international rivalry for trade. But it is the Chinese *lack* of interest in Europe, its culture, and its merchants that poses a greater threat than disincorporation by cannibalism or psychic disintegration at the hands of torturers. China threatens to *incorporate* Europeans within its standards of civilization, its conceptions of reality. Even as he tolerates "subtle *Jesuites*" in his country, the Kangxi Emperor and his subjects remain largely unmoved by their designs, forcing the missionaries to adapt "their Model [of religion] to the philosophy of *Confucius*, seldom or never Teaching the Crucifixion and Godhead of Christ, and frequently allowing the worship of *Pagods*."[26] Going native in early Qing China does not mean reverting to "savagery" but conforming to the assumptions, values, and standards of an alien civilization.

Yet even Defoe's insults reveal his familiarity with the vast literature on China published in Europe by the early eighteenth century. Crusoe's route from Beijing to Archangel follows, in large measure, the itinerary described by the Czar's emissary to Kangxi, Evret Ysbrants Ides, in *Three Years Travels from Moscow Over-Land to China* (1706).[27] Defoe reads Ides selectively. After lavishly praising China's wealth, civility, architecture, magnificence, and women, Ides spends the final two pages of his narrative criticizing the "rude and barbarous" judiciary system of the Chinese and the "perfect Pagan idolatry" of their religion; he concludes that the "great share of Wisdom, Arts and Sciences, for which they are so highly extolled by many Writers, comes far short of the *Europeans*."[28] Such belated denunciations and qualifications often are used by European writers to mitigate or contain the threat China poses to western notions of religious, political, and cultural supremacy. However eager Europeans may have been to flatter the Emperor and the Mandarin officials in the interests of securing trade, they are quite conscious of their patrons, who invested huge sums of money in both trading ventures and religious missions. Employed by Peter the Great and seeking to establish himself in the caravan trade between Beijing and Moscow, Ides seems eager to placate a monarch who has his own imperial ambitions, especially since he returned with a mixed message from Beijing: the Czar's official letters to the Kangxi Emperor were rejected by the Board of Rites because they violated the proper protocols for a barbarian tributary mission – they failed to address the Emperor as a supreme monarch and Ides did not kowtow. Similarly, Le Comte flatters Louis XIV, bogged down in a costly war in Europe, by reflecting "on the facility with which *Lewis* the Great would subdue those Provinces [bordering the Great Wall], if Nature had made us a little nearer Neighbours to *China*."[29] Given the praise that the French Jesuit elsewhere lavishes on Chinese civilization, this is less a military assessment than an enticement for the King to continue supporting missions to the Far East.

Defoe amplifies Ides's perfunctory criticism and Le Comte's formulaic compliment into an all-out assault on Chinese civilization. He is shrewd enough to know that he cannot mimic the density of detail that characterizes first-hand accounts of China so generic diatribes substitute for the descriptive strategies of literary cartographic "realism." China's vaunted prowess, Crusoe asserts, is the effect of the low expectations that Europeans hold for "a barbarous nation of pagans": "the greatness of their wealth, their trade, the power of their government, and the strength of their armies, is surprising to us, because ... we did not expect such things among them; and this indeed is the advantage with which all their greatness and power is represented to us; otherwise in it self it is nothing at all" (421). It is difficult to convey how jarring an assertion this is in the early eighteenth century: the idealized Empire of Jesuit-inspired literature is replaced by a country caricatured as at once backward and decadent. In confronting the threat that China poses to his vision of national identity and economic prosperity, Defoe describes a land he has never seen only in debased relation to European standards of religious truth, military power, and technological sophistication. Crusoe elaborates authoritative-sounding comparisons that structure his (and his creator's) fantasy of European superiority. "A million of their foot [soldiers]," he claims, "could not stand before one embattled body of our infantry . . . 30,000 German or English foot, and 10,000 French horse, would fairly beat all the forces of China" (422). This vision of well-trained and well-equipped European forces united against the Chinese army, "a contemptible herd or crowd of ignorant sordid slaves" (422), becomes an imaginary compensation for the wealth and "greatness" of the Chinese empire, not to mention the 900,000 soldiers garrisoned along its northern frontier. This battle of East and West takes place only in a virtual realm where fictional pronouncements about military capabilities take precedence over material reality: European garrisons in the Far East well into the eighteenth century, at most, could muster only a few hundred men, and no British, French, or German soldiers were stationed within 2,000 miles of Beijing. Crusoe's claim is not a serious challenge or a reflection of the relative strengths of the two nations but an impotent gesture in the face of superior power.

Crusoe's tirades cannot disguise the fact that Chinese luxuries remain objects of intense desire, such as the £3500 of raw silk, cloth, and tea which the hero brings back to sell in Europe. Much of his stay in China is devoted to negotiating with shady, often dishonest traders who are presented as characteristic of their nation. These scenes, too, present fantasies of wealth and empowerment as a discourse of hard-headed realism. All the eyewitness accounts which Defoe could have read testify to the wealth, business acumen, and ingenuity of the Chinese. Englishmen such as Alexander Hamilton, who in 1703 in Canton had to sell his ship's cargo at half its market value, were all too aware that they were dealing with clever merchants who drove hard bargains.[30] Some sense of how shrill, even hysterical, Defoe's attack on China must have seemed to his contemporaries can be gleaned from two important eyewitness accounts published at the same time as *The Consolidator*, Fernandez Navarette's *An Account of the Empire of China, Historical, Political, Moral, and Religious* and Giovanni Francesco Gemelli Careri's *A Voyage Round the World*, which devotes its longest section to China.[31] Careri, an Italian jurist who traveled to China in 1695–6 with no governmental or religious authorization, echoes earlier travel narratives. Noting the "extraordinary industry" of the "very sharp Witted" Chinese, he admits that they "exceed the *Europeans* in Ingenuity."[32]

This view is shared by Navarette, a Dominican friar who drew on his two decades in China to produce an engaging and detailed account of social and economic life during the early Qing period. The "Nature, Method, and disposition of the *Chinese* Government is admirable," Navarette asserts, "and may be a Pattern or Model to many in the World."[33] This sociopolitical stability is reflected in the economic life of the empire. Canton is a city of superb workmen, who produce both exotic items and knockoffs of European imports "counterfeited . . . so exactly, that they sell them in the Inland for Goods brought from *Europe*." Even as they undercut the market for imports, though, the Chinese more than hold their own against the Europeans as manufacturers of luxury merchandise:

> The Curiosities they make and sell in the Shops amaze all *Europeans*. If four large Galeons were sent to the City *Nan King*, to that of *Cu Cheu*, to *Hang Cheu*,

or any other like them, they might be loaden with a thousand varieties of Curiosities and Toys, such as all the World would admire, and a great Profit be made of them, tho sold at reasonable Rates. All things necessary to furnish a Princely House, may be had ready made in several parts of any of the aforesaid Citys, without any further trouble than the buying, and all at poor Rates in comparison of what is sold among us.[34]

Navarette is explicit: the Chinese are better businessmen than the Europeans, equaling or bettering the quality of European goods at much cheaper prices. Throughout his narrative, he quotes the prices he has paid for various staples, marveling at how inexpensively he can purchase food, paper, clothes, and servants. His view of commercial life in China, in short, differs starkly from the fictional descriptions that Defoe offers. Navarette describes Chinese "Traders and Merchants" as "all very obliging and civil; if they can get any thing, tho never so little, they don't slip the opportunity."[35] This willingness to negotiate prices marks the Chinese as members of a civilized, transnational class of merchants whose business practices indicate that they share the same moral, social, and financial values as the Europeans. In turn, these values become the external manifestations of a fundamental similarity of worldviews. Careri finds that in dealing with merchants "their Oath is Inviolable, and they will hazard their Head to keep their Word."[36] This "civil and obliging" behavior guarantees, in effect, that the Chinese share a psychological interiority that can be understood in terms of *universal* desires for profit, civility, and ultimately, Navarette implies, Christian enlightenment. In this regard, like Careri, Navarette accepts his status as a foreign guest in a empire that – except for religion – out-civilizes as well as out-produces the nations of western Europe.

Le Comte, in many respects, confirms Navarette's account of the Chinese, but his comments suggest a darker perception of the psychological costs of commercial acumen. The desire for profit turns inward upon China's merchants so that they become the victims as well as the perpetrators of mercantile obsession:

> There is no Nation under the Sun, that is more fit for Commerce and Traffick, and understand them better: One can hardly believe how far their Tricks and Craftiness proceeds when they are to insinuate into Mens affections, manage a fair Opportunity, or improve the Overtures that are offered: The desire of getting torments them continually, and makes them discover a thousand ways of gaining. . . . Every thing serves their turn, every thing is precious to the *Chinese*, because there is nothing but they know how to improve. . . . The infinite Trade and Commerce that is carried on every where, is the Soul of the People, and the *primum mobile* of all their Actions.[37]

With a few rhetorical changes, this passage might have been lifted from Defoe's *Complete English Tradesman*. Chinese merchants embody the very strategies that Defoe's heroes and heroines adopt over the course of their careers. Like Moll and Roxana, these profit-seekers thrive on their ability to outmaneuver European men. As Le Comte warns his European readers, "a Stranger will always be cheated, if he be alone." Most threateningly, for Defoe, China's "infinite Trade" marks the sinicization of capitalist self-interest, a pre-emptive appropriation of the strategies of bourgeois self-definition, including the psychological "torments" of Crusoian obsession. If a European, says Le Comte, employs a "trusty *Chinese*, who is acquainted with the Country, who knows all the Tricks . . . you will be very happy, if he that buys [for you] and he that sells [to you], do not collogue together to your Cost, and go snips in the profit."[38] In contrast to the fictions of economic self-sufficiency, labor, and the devotion of a virtuous servant, China presents Crusoe with confusing networks of "infinite Trade and Commerce," double-dealing and dependency, and untrustworthy locals. In China, Defoe's hero threatens to falls from "patriarch" to dupe. The prosperity and acumen of the Chinese, in this regard, undermine the links between sin and scarcity, virtue and abundance that are crucial to Protestant visions of self-identity and national greatness. Consequently, Defoe must gloss over how an empire "imperfect and impotent" in "navigation, commerce, and husbandry" (428) can produce the riches that dominate European markets for luxury goods and for re-export to the Americas. His invective can prompt no action; his assertion that the English could "batter . . . down in ten days . . . this mighty nothing call'd a wall" (431) can have no consequences, provoke no vindication such as his victory over the cannibals. His taunts can be acted on only after he has left the Qing Empire and the crises of self-representation that it provokes, only when the opportunity arises for Crusoe to assert the superiority of Christian culture against a far weaker antagonist.

Crusoe The Avenger

To get his hero back from Beijing to Europe, Defoe creates a fictional Russian caravan. The nine caravans that followed Ides's route between 1696 and 1719 were the monopoly of the Czar, an effort to control the trading of furs to China in exchange for gold, damask, and silk.[39] Although Ides had returned a forty-eight percent profit on the state's investment, by 1710 Chinese imports had saturated the tiny Russian market for luxury items and had to be resold in the Baltic for considerably less than they had previously commanded.[40] These caravans across Siberia offered nothing like the fantastic profits that Crusoe reaps in *Farther Adventures*. Yet however fanciful his hero's "wild ventures" may seem, Defoe evidently was fascinated by the narrative possibilities that such an epic trek offered. Having sent Crusoe 5,000 miles across Asia, the novelist has Singleton lead a shipwrecked band of pirates across Africa on foot, and, in *A New Voyage*, fifty sailors walk from Peru, across South America, to Brazil. In the latter two novels, these improbable treks allow the sailors to accumulate vast amounts of gold in regions which are free from competition: the natives in Africa are relatively few; the Amazon basin is a bucolic and unpopulated countryside of verdant hills, abundant game, and rivers of gold. While all three novels fantasize about trading opportunities with "savages" eager to exchange gold for brass pots and rusty hatchets, *Farther Adventures* makes Crusoe an improbable agent in rendering

Siberia a comparatively safe byway for British merchants. In brief, the anxieties provoked by China are displaced onto the nomadic "Tartars"; railing that has no consequences in China becomes a righteous – and violent – vindication of Christian belief on the borders of the Czar's dominions where the few "profess'd Christians" are outnumbered by "meer pagans" (440). In this regard, the fear and desire provoked by China can be unleashed as holy indignation against nomadic tribesmen and backward villagers who can be pigeonholed, albeit with some difficulty, as the colonized subjects of a Christian empire.

Crusoe seizes the opportunity to reaffirm his faith when he encounters a village where the "pagans" worship an idol. After seventy years of hardship, isolation, and danger, Crusoe declares, "I was more mov'd at their stupidity and brutish worship of a hobgoblin, than ever I was at any thing in my life" (441). His response to this "brutish worship" both recalls and exceeds those moments in *Robinson Crusoe* when he fantasizes about killing scores of cannibals. On Madagascar, earlier in the novel, Crusoe had tried to stop his sailors from slaughtering villagers as grim retribution for the death of a shipmate, and his ceaseless upbraiding had led them to put him ashore in India. Now, confronted by the specter of idolatry, he describes to one of his Scots companions how his shipmates "burnt and sack'd the village there, and kill'd man, woman, and child . . . and when I had done, I added that I thought we ought to do so to this village" (443). The excesses of "so bloody and cruel an enterprise" on Madagascar leave Crusoe, at the time, "pensive and sad" (386); now idolatry provokes in him thoughts of genocide. Fortunately, his Scots comrade, Captain Richardson, "famous for his zeal [against] devilish things," points out that because the idol is carried from village to village in this region, it is more cost-effective to destroy it rather than wage war against every settlement that the caravan encounters. The episode which follows is a displaced revenge fantasy for the imagined insults of Dutch torturers and shrewd Chinese merchants.

Although Crusoe declares that his vengeance is intended "to vindicate the honour of God, which is insulted by this devil worship" (442), his language of nearly chivalric honor is compromised by his actual escapade. He, Richardson, and another Scots merchant raid the village at night, tie up several pagan priests, and force them to watch their idol burn. Having struck this blow for their faith, Crusoe and his fellows hurry off with their caravan, never acknowledging to the Russian governor or their fellow-travelers that they are responsible for an incident which provokes a major confrontation between the Czar's officials and the "Tartars" who are "thirty thousand" strong (446). The nomads then pursue the caravan across the steppes, and what follows is an eighteenth-century chase scene across a "vast nameless desert" (447), a strategic standoff in a wood, and yet another narrow escape for the British merchants. The flight across Siberia, in one respect, is a flight from the consequences of cultural and theological conflict and the difficulties of colonial administration: burn the idol, play dumb, and leave the Czar's governor to deal with thousands of angry Mongols. As acts of Christian faith, burning the idol and then fleeing seem uncomfortably similar to the logic behind flying false colors at sea: vindicating the honor of God looks suspiciously like vandalism. In effect, Crusoe has adopted the strategy of the Jesuit missionaries who, according to the English translator of Le Comte's *Memoirs and Observations*, assume "the Characters of Physicians, Painters, Merchants, Astrologers, Mechanicians, &c. and are receiv'd as such in the Courts of *Asia*, which are too fine to suffer openly the propagation of a strange Religion."[41] Like the Jesuits, Crusoe preaches, it seems, only to the credulous and unarmed. He does not converse with the Siberian nomads; they do not assume Friday's posture of submission before western technology and theology; he rescues no one; and he asserts no theological or political authority. Instead *Farther Adventures* offers the prototypical logic of the action-adventure genre: the reconfirmation, through juvenile acts of "heroism," of moralistic denunciations of alien cultures, the imposition of western standards of morality as universal truths, and violence as a means to an end. At the age of seventy-one, Crusoe re-establishes the hyper-masculinity of the merchant adventurer by burning a phallic log and claiming a symbolic victory. Such declarations ultimately pose no threat to the safety of the caravan or the hero's profits because we recognize that, once outside the borders of China, providence smiles on Christian merchants who use deception as a basic strategy of survival, profitability, and self-definition, who adopt, in effect, the characteristics and strategies of their Chinese counterparts.

If *Farther Adventures* disorients readers who may expect another tale of "man's" triumph over "nature," it also reorients the values and assumptions which tradition-ally have defined *Robinson Crusoe* and the realist "rise" of the novel. It is significant, in this regard, that the *Crusoe* trilogy concludes with a set piece that harks back to the medieval dream vision, the hero's imaginative ascent to the "angelic world." Crusoe's vision is the generic form to which "realism" tends: if zealotry is the form that fantasy takes to obscure the weakness of Protestant England in an Asian-dominated world, the hero's transcendence of the material world ironically reveals the artificiality of his "serious reflections" on his experiences. All along, this dream vision suggests, readers have been assured by the generic certainty of a faith-based memoir, Crusoe's after-the-fact *apologia* for the engaging literary strategies that shape his adventures. In one sense, *Serious Reflections* reads like the moralizing passages left out of the second half of *Farther Adventures*, belated efforts to bridge the gaps and resolve the inconsistencies within the Eurocentric ideologies of selfhood, economic individualism, and colonialist appropriation. If Defoe's moral and aesthetic imperatives remain the same in the first two volumes, as the novelist claims, *Farther Adventures* represents a broader range of narrative possibilities that Defoe exploits throughout his career: the protean self whose integrity can be guaranteed only by protestations of faith; the balance sheet that shows only profits, and not the costs or consequences of money-making; and a nationalism that picks its fights very carefully. Both the "profitability" and "diver-sion" of this sequel depend on a dialogic interaction among competing genres: the moral apology, the administrative treatise, the travel narrative, the trade embassy, and what I might call the Protestant revenge fantasy. After 1724 Defoe ceased writing novels, and his last years produced an astonishing array of polemical texts ranging from *The Complete English Tradesman* (1726) to *Conjugal Lewdness* (1727); these works are anticipated more by the literary experimentation of *Farther Adventures* than they are by the "realism" of its predecessor. In this sequel, Defoe sketches the beginnings of an alternative – and as yet unwritten – history of the eighteenth-century novel, one that depends on adventure, profit, and Protestant fanaticism to turn readers' thoughts from the fate of Crusoe's nameless island. Defoe in 1719 had already done with his island; and his desire to chart the conditions for an infinitely profitable trade demands that the second installment of his trilogy assuage the "anxieties and perplexities" that such fantasies produce.[42]

See also: chapter 2, Fiction/Translation/Transnation; chapter 3, Narrative Transmigrations; chapter 4, Age of Peregrination; chapter 16, An Emerging New Canon; chapter 19, Racial Legacies.

Notes

1. See Ian Watt, *The Rise of the Novel* (1957; repr., Berkeley and Los Angeles: University of California Press, 1965); J. Paul Hunter, *The Reluctant Pilgrim: Defoe's Emblematic Method and the Quest for Form in Robinson Crusoe* (Baltimore, MD: Johns Hopkins University Press, 1966); John Richetti, *Defoe's Narratives: Situations and Structures* (Oxford: Clarendon Press, 1975); Michael McKeon, *The Origins of the English Novel 1600–1740* (Baltimore, MD: Johns Hopkins University Press, 1987); Nancy Armstrong and Leonard Tennenhouse, *The Imaginary Puritan: Literature, Intellectual Labor, and the Origins of Personal Life* (Berkeley and Los Angeles: University of California Press, 1992); James Thompson, *Models of Value: Eighteenth-Century Political Economy and the Novel* (Durham, NC: Duke University Press, 1996); Sandra Sherman, *Finance and Fictionality in the Early Eighteenth Century: Accounting for Defoe* (Cambridge: Cambridge University Press, 1996); and Wolfram Schmidgen, "Robinson Crusoe, Enumeration, and the Mercantile Fetish," *Eighteenth-Century Studies* 35 (2001): 19–39.

2. See Peter Hulme, *Colonial Encounters: Europe and the Native Caribbean 1492–1797* (1986; repr., New York: Routledge, 1992), 184–222; Aparna Dharwadker, "Nation, Race, and the Ideology of Commerce in Defoe," *The Eighteenth Century: Theory and Interpretation* 39 (1998): 63–84; and Roxanne Wheeler, " 'My Savage,' 'My Man': Racial Multiplicity in *Robinson Crusoe*," *ELH* 62 (1995): 821–61.

3. *The Farther Adventures of Robinson Crusoe* (New York: Peebles Classics, 1927), 250. All citations are from this edition.

4. Recent critics who have dealt with the second and third installments of the *Crusoe* trilogy include Anna Neill, "Crusoe's Farther Adventures: Discovery, Trade, and the Law of Nations," *The Eighteenth Century: Theory and Interpretation* 38 (1997): 213–30; Jeffrey Hopes, "Real and Imaginary Stories: *Robinson Crusoe* and the *Serious Reflections*," *Eighteenth-Century Fiction* 8 (1996): 313–28; and Minaz Jooma, "Robinson Crusoe Inc(corporates): Domestic Economy, Incest and the Trope of Cannibalism," *Lit: Literature Interpretation Theory* 8 (1997): 61–81.

5. Hans Turley, "Protestant Evangelism, British Imperialism, and Crusoian Identity," in Kathleen Wilson, ed., *A New Imperial History: Culture, Identity, and Modernity in Britain and the Empire, 1660–1840.* (Cambridge: Cambridge University Press, 2004); and *Rum, Sodomy, and the Lash: Piracy, Sexuality, and Masculine Identity* (New York: New York University Press, 1999).

6. Lydia H. Liu, "Robinson Crusoe's Earthenware Pot," *Critical Inquiry* 25 (1999): 757.

7. Daniel Defoe, *Vindication of the Press* (London, 1718), 4.

8. See Robert Markley, "Riches, Power, Trade, and Religion: The Far East and the English Imagination, 1600–1720," *Renaissance Studies* 17 (2003): 433–55.

9. On the dominance of China before 1800, see Andre Gunder Frank, *ReOrient: Global*

Economy in the Asian Age (Berkeley and Los Angeles: University of California Press, 1997); Kenneth Pomeranz, *The Great Divergence: Europe, China, and the Making of the Modern World Economy* (Princeton, NJ: Princeton University Press, 2000); Jack A. Goldstone, *Revolution and Rebellion in the Early Modern World* (Berkeley and Los Angeles: University of California Press, 1991); R. Bin Wong, *China Transformed: Historical Change and the Limits of European Experience* (Ithaca, NY: Cornell University Press, 1997); and Geoffrey Gunn, *First Globalization: The Eurasian Exchange, 1500–1800* (Lanham, MD: Rowman and Littlefield, 2003), 170–80.

10. *Serious Reflections during the Life and Surprising Adventures of Robinson Crusoe*, introd. by G. H. Maynadier (Boston: Beacon Classics, 1903), 260. All quotations are from this edition.

11. See O. H. K. Spate, *The Pacific Since Magellan.* Vol. 2, *Monopolists and Freebooters* (Minneapolis: University of Minnesota Press, 1983), 155–65, 205–12; Glyndwr Williams, *The Great South Sea: English Voyages and Encounters 1570–1750* (New Haven, CT: Yale University Press, 1997).

12. Robert Markley, "Violence and Profits on the Restoration Stage: Trade, Nationalism, and Insecurity in Dryden's *Amboyna*," *Eighteenth-Century Life* 22 (1998): 2–17. On the English–Dutch rivalry in Southeast Asia, see Holden Furber, *Rival Empires of Trade in the Orient, 1600–1800* (Minneapolis: University of Minnesota Press, 1976); Jonathan I. Israel, *Dutch Primacy in World Trade, 1585–1740* (Oxford: Clarendon Press, 1989); and Neils Steensgaard, "The Growth and Composition of the Long-Distance Trade of England and the Dutch Republic before 1750," in *The Rise of Merchant Empires*, ed. James D. Tracy (Cambridge: Cambridge University Press, 1990), 102–52.

13. [Defoe], *Atlas Maritimus & Commercialis; or a General View of the World* (London, 1728), 202, 226.

14. Ibid., 226.

15. See Hosea B. Morse, *The Chronicles of the East India Company Trading to China 1635–1834.*

5 vols. (Oxford: Clarendon Press, 1926–29), 1:308; 1:122–23.

16. Daniel Defoe, *A New Voyage Round the World by a Course Never Sailed Before*, ed. George A. Aitkin (London: Dent, 1902), 155–56. I discuss this novel in "'So Inexhaustible a Treasure of Gold': Defoe, Credit, and the Romance of the South Seas," *Eighteenth-Century Life* 18 (1994): 148–67.

17. See Steensgaard, "The Growth and Composition of the Long-Distance Trade of England and the Dutch Republic," 104–10.

18. Jonathan D. Spence, *The Chan's Great Continent: China in Western Minds* (New York: Norton, 1998), 67.

19. Frank, *ReOrient: Global Economy in the Asian Age*, 111.

20. Louis Le Comte, *Memoirs and Observations Topographical, Physical, Mathematical, Natural, Civil, and Ecclesiastical, Made in a Late Journey through the Empire of China* (London, 1697), A3r (translator's preface). On European literature about China in the seventeenth and eighteenth centuries, see Donald Lach and Edwin J. van Kley, *Asia in the Making of Europe.* Vol. 3: *A Century of Advance. Book One: Trade, Missions, Literature* (Chicago: University of Chicago Press, 1993).

21. Rachel Ramsey, "China and the Ideal of Order in John Webb's *An Historical Essay*," *Journal of the History of Ideas* 62:3 (2001): 483–503; and David Porter, *Ideographia: The Chinese Cipher in Early Modern Europe* (Stanford, CA: Stanford University Press, 2001).

22. Daniel Defoe, *The Consolidator* (London, 1705): 60–61, 13.

23. Ibid., 12–13, 13–14.

24. Ibid., 14.

25. See David E. Mungello, *Curious Land: Jesuit Accommodation and the Origins of Sinology* (Stuttgart: F. Steiner Verlag, 1985); Lionel Jensen, *Manufacturing Confucianism: Chinese Traditions and Universal Civilization* (Durham, NC: Duke University Press, 1997); and Joanna Waley-Cohen, *The Sextants of Beijing: Global Currents in Chinese History* (New York: Norton, 1999), 55–128.

26. Le Comte, *Memoirs and Observations* (translator's preface), A1r.

27. Evret Ysbrants Ides, *Three Years Travels from Moscow Over-Land to China* (London, 1706). On Ides, see Markley, "Civility, Ceremony, and Desire at Beijing: Sensibility and the European Quest for 'Free Trade' with China in the Late Seventeenth Century," in *Passionate Encounters in a Time of Sensibility*, ed. Anne Mellor and Maximilian Novak (Newark: University of Delaware Press, 2000), 60–88.

28. Ides, *Three Years Travels from Moscow*, 108–9.

29. Le Comte, *Memoirs and Observations*, 75.

30. See Alexander Hamilton, *A New Account of the East Indies*. 2 vols. (Edinburgh, 1727), 2: 220–35.

31. Both works appeared in English translation in Awnsham and John Churchill's collection of previously unpublished manuscripts or untranslated foreign accounts, *A Collection of Voyages and Travels*. 4 vols. (London 1704–5).

32. Francis Gemelli Careri, *A Voyage Round the World*. In *Collection of Voyages and Travels*, (London, 1704–5), 4:363.

33. Domingo Fernandez Navarette, *An Account of the Empire of China, Historical, Political, Moral and Religious*. In *Collection of Voyages and Travels* (London, 1704–5), 1:52.

34. Ibid., 1:58.

35. Ibid., 1:60.

36. Careri, *A Voyage Round the World*, 4:372.

37. Le Comte, *Memoirs and Observations*, 237.

38. Ibid.

39. Mark Mancall, *Russia and China: Their Diplomatic Relations to 1728* (Cambridge, MA: Harvard University Press, 1971). See also C. Pat Giersch, "'A Motley Throng': Social Change on Southwest China's Early Modern Frontier, 1700–1880," *Journal of Asian Studies* 60 (2001): 67–94.

40. Mancall, *Russia and China*, 201.

41. Le Comte, *Memoirs and Observations*, A3r–A3v.

42. This essay is adapted from chapter five of my study, *The Far East and the English Imagination 1600–1730* (Cambridge: Cambridge University Press, 2005).

FURTHER READING

Frank, Andre Gunder. *ReOrient: Global Economy in the Asian Age*. Berkeley and Los Angeles: University of California Press, 1997.

Goldstone, Jack A. *Revolution and Rebellion in the Early Modern World*. Berkeley and Los Angeles: University of California Press, 1991.

Lamb, Jonathan. *Preserving the Self in the South Seas, 1680–1840*. Chicago: University of Chicago Press, 2001.

Pomeranz, Kenneth. *The Great Divergence: Europe, China, and the Making of the Modern World Economy*. Princeton, NJ: Princeton University Press, 2000.

Porter, David. *Ideographia: The Chinese Cipher in Early Modern Europe*. Stanford, CA: Stanford University Press, 2001.

Williams, Glyndwr. *The Great South Sea: English Voyages and Encounters 1570–1750*. New Haven, CT: Yale University Press, 1997.

2

Fiction/Translation/Transnation: The Secret History of the Eighteenth-Century Novel

Srinivas Aravamudan

A unitary language is not something given [*dan*] but is always in essence posited [*zadan*] – and at every moment of its linguistic life it is opposed to the realities of heteroglossia. But at the same time it makes its real presence felt as a force for overcoming this heteroglossia, imposing specific limits to it, guaranteeing a certain maximum of mutual understanding and crystallizing into a real, although still relative, unity – the unity of the reigning conversational (everyday) and literary language, "correct language." [. . .] Thus a unitary language gives expression to forces working toward concrete verbal and ideological unification and centralization, which develop in vital connection with the processes of sociopolitical and cultural centralization.

Mikhail Bakhtin, *The Dialogic Imagination: Four Essays*

As a country became civilized, their [*sic*] narrations were methodized, and moderated to probability.

Clara Reeve, *The Progress of Romance*

The second epigraph, from *The Progress of Romance*, Clara Reeve's 1785 tract on the novel/romance distinction, intuits a link between cultural advancement and narrative order. Cultural advancement is linked to the methodical and moderating effects of probability, even as fantastic excesses are reined in to accord with this valuing of realism. The methodical is to ensure the sociologically probable as the repeatable, even as the narratively repeatable is to enshrine the characterologically predictable as the civilizational advance of the country concerned. But what better admission than this sentence that, eventually, a unitary language – whether of novels and narrations or of a particular country – as Bakhtin has it, is "not something given but is always in essence posited"? If countries didn't exist, novels of national realism would need to invent them, or perhaps, as some accounts have it, they actually imagined them into existence.[1]

Mikhail Bakhtin's writings document a history of Western prosaics that has bedeviled twentieth-century novel theory. Despite warnings to the contrary by the most acute of his readers, Bakhtin has been popularized as an unqualified celebrator of the novel's "rise," and often his literary archaeology of prose genres has been read as an unabashed teleology of progress resulting in the apotheosis of *the* novel as a particularly versatile inheritor of all that went before. It is, therefore, worth recalling that "'novel' is the name Bakhtin gives to whatever force is at work within a given literary system to reveal the limits, the artificial constraints of that system."[2] In other words, "novel" puts a static hierarchy of genres into dynamic and transformative inter-relationships. However, why is it that historians of the English novel are often gleefully willing to use Bakhtin to document those aspects of the incipient novel that are polyglot and transgeneric in their subversion of epic, romance, and poetic modes, but suddenly partisan and forgetful when the novelistic usurper is installed on the throne in full regalia and declared the legitimate heir? If Bakhtin's admonition were to be carried through to its logical conclusion, "novel" might well end up meaning those subversive forces and also-rans that reveal, just as much, the artificial constraints generated by a posthumous system that erects a specific account of the novel at its center to the exclusion of various other texts and modes that are retroactively deemed anti-canonical, or subsequently cast out of the realm of the story of this kind of literature. Revisionist history of autochthonous creation, whether of the English novel or that of Romanticism's emphasis on originality, is a modern reflex, whereas epic was all too willing to circulate stories of bastardy, usurpation, and rival claimants to the throne. Homer Brown has an article on this contradiction whose title reveals very clearly the generic irony at the heart of the problem: "Why the Story of the Origin of the (English) Novel is an American Romance (If Not the Great American Novel)."[3]

The quotation from Bakhtin in the first epigraph could be read as an indication of how "novelization," initially linked to the concepts of "heteroglossia," and "unfinalizability," could at some times be posed as a force against the recently institutionalized form of the novel itself. This is especially so when novels have been established as a "unitary" language opposed to the heteroglossia from which they came, centralized around a particular national culture, and reiterating the parochial versions of domestic realism that Margaret Doody has described cogently as "Prescriptive Realism," a formula that "emerges not as a suggestion but as a kind of ideology."[4] It is further relevant that this unitariness is not given but posited; while heteroglossia is the shape of reality, a particular regime establishing *the* novel within the literary canon is ideological in its impersonation and obfuscation of the much vaster heteroglossia out there, whether linguistic or sociological. Bakhtin's ambivalent identifications of carnival, laughter, and the various genres of irreverence could just as well be his recognition of the prophylactic power of institutionalized ritual and the interplay between a unitary discourse of "sociopolitical and cultural centralization" and the heteroglossia that this unity ends up at times dominating.

While for Bakhtin the novel has largely been the heroic vehicle of heteroglossia against poetry and the epic, it will be the burden of this essay to demonstrate that the voluntary parochialization of the vast fictional and nonfictional archive – what other Bakhtinian critics have named his "creation of a prosaics" – into the artificial unity of a so-called eighteenth-century English or British novel is a nationalist and xenophobic project. In contrast to celebratory accounts about the English novel, I propose that various fictions, including oriental tales and surveillance chronicles, are provisional instances of the translational and transnational aspects of the multitudinous outside excluded by acts of enclosure around the novel.[5] Against the protocols of a national realism that renders the domestic novel centripetal and unitary, the oriental tale or the surveillance chronicle paradoxically indicates (but does not fully exhaust) the translational and transnational possibilities of centrifugality, heteroglossia, and unfinalizability, and it is also, therefore, a subordinate guarantor to the stability and clarity of the internal and interning (or as Margaret Doody mischievously puns, the "nationally in-turned") logic of the English novel.[6] In particular, I would like to single out for discussion a subgenre between the oriental tale and the early novel which I call the surveillance chronicle (a type of writing more commonly known as spy fiction).

Realism/Beyond/Nation

It is necessary to introduce one of Bakhtin's most effective conceptual inventions, the "chronotope," to realize how particular genres, considered *ex post facto*, generate dispositionally habitual ways of understanding experience even as they preclude others. The interrelation of space-time in the chronotope saturates the novelistic event. However, rather than coming forward as a figure, the chronotope "provides the ground essential for the showing-forth, the representability of events."[7] Needless to say, by this measure, a geography of novelization appears very different from a history of a specific national fictional genre, deemed *the* novel. Much has been said regarding the anachronism of the retroactive naming of early English fiction as the novel, even though several practitioners, including Behn, Defoe, Fielding, and Smollett, produced polemics about various versions of "romance" against which they claimed to write "true histories," "adventures," "fortunes and misfortunes," "lives," "comic-epic poems in prose," and "a large diffused picture, comprehending the characters of life, disposed in different groups, and exhibited in different attitudes, for the purpose of an uniform plan."

It is also relevant that the term "novel," used in the sense of a fiction dealing with familiar and realistic everyday events, in contrast with the idea of romance as distant, idealized and fantastical, was first used by William Congreve in his preface to *Incognita* in 1692, but not followed up until Clara Reeve latched on to roughly the same definition almost a century later in 1785.[8] Of course, the tautology of "the" (English) novel as celebrated by recent critics is worth pondering, especially as some things have not moved very far since Congreve or Reeve, having just edged forward to Walter Scott. One venerable critic's common sense has it that a novel is "a long prose narrative about largely fictional if usually realistic characters and plausible events."[9] Note the hedging and balancing – largely fictional, usually realistic. "Plausible" adds some more ballast on the side of realism, just in case an equal dose of the fictional in relation to the realist were about to take our readers off to the heady lands of Cockaigne. Another well-known critic approaches the topic from a different kind of tautology: the novel is "the story of a present-day individual in a recognizable social and cultural context."[10] Recognizable to whom? And why should it be so wedded to the singular subgenre of (pseudo)biography, when Bakhtin lists biography and autobiography as just one of at least eight types of novel?[11] And even if those problems were resolved (in an unsatisfactorily conservative fashion) as nationally, linguistically, sociologically, and culturally overdetermined, do all novels then fall from grace and become romances as times change and the recognizability of contexts vanishes? It has also been pointed out, time and again, that the novel/romance distinction is much harder to make in terms of any major European national tradition other than the English, where *le roman, der Roman,* or *il romanzo* designates continuously from the past to the present what in English is termed the novel. Therefore, going backward in these other non-English traditions, one can still document generic change. That would have to be discussed much more in terms of divergent continuities, rather than the sharp discontinuities that novel-promoters are wont to make in order to justify the shift toward the parochial descriptive realism of the English novel when contrasted with the most full-blown and antirealist romances.

In a recent anthology, entitled *The Literary Channel: The Inter-National Invention of the Novel*, contributors have also argued that the novel was more properly a Franco-British affair rather than an exclusively English one. But this concession appears to be still somewhat cautious and partial, when earlier Renaissance English fiction included major influences from Spanish and Italian sources, not to mention the internal dialogue with ancient Greek and Roman fiction and Near Eastern sources as well. All the same, it is revealing that about 36 percent of all novels read in Britain between 1660 and 1770 were translations of French fictions. The category of the novel was, until quite late in Britain, indifferent to the question of national origin.[12]

The first full-fledged European treatise on the history of prose fiction, *Traitté de l'origine des romans,* by the bishop of Avranches, Abbé Pierre Daniel Huet, serves as a corrective point of departure that potentially inflects later Anglocentric teleologies with a transnational spin. I invoke Huet not in order to forget the English novel, but to view it within a much larger frame. Huet provides a breathtakingly wide genealogy of genres. Appended to Madame de Lafayette's novel, *Zayde,* in 1670, the treatise was also subject to polemic attack for its xenotropism by various critics – even as it was motivated by Nicolas Boileau's attack on the *roman bourgeois.* A lot depends on how one translates Huet's central term, *Roman* (always capitalized in his text). Novel aficionados, who like to argue that the novel was not yet fully invented until the 1740s, would prefer to call his subject *romance,* whereas Margaret Doody, who argues for continuity from ancient times, prefers to translate Huet's references to *le Roman* as *the novel,* and especially so as the term in French never underwent the shift that the

English tradition has decreed retroactively. I have chosen to translate it as *Romance* but leave it in italics. Most significant regarding Huet's approach is his wide and lateral geography of the genre, imposing a solution for the origin of *Romance* that could very well be characterized as anatopian (or as a spatial displacement) but that is nonetheless refreshing compared to the more frequent resorts to anachronism made by the backward projections and false expectations of novel criticism. "The first beginnings of this pleasant amusement of idle innocents," according to Huet, "have to be found in faraway countries and in remote Antiquity."[13] It is worth attending to Huet's formulations as methodologically interesting for the manner in which they provide a refreshing alternative to what has become a rarely questioned national paradigm for novel criticism.

Huet's definition of *Romances* makes them out to be "fictions of amorous exploits written in Prose with artistry, for the pleasure and edification of their readers" (4). He teeters between the descriptive and the prescriptive, adding that if it is not clear whether these works are about love or in prose, they certainly ought to be amatory and prosaic (5). Huet distinguishes fictions from true histories (*Histoires véritables*), but this distinction is more one of degree than of kind, with histories being "largely true and only partly false, whereas, on the contrary, *Romances* are true in some parts but false on the whole" (*dans le gros*) (8). Just as the difference between *Romans* and *Histoires* is relative, the distinctions made between prose and poetry reveal definitional moves made later between novel and romance:

> Petronius says that poems signify through indirection, by divine intervention, and by free and strong expressions, so much so that they are mostly taken to be Oracles that come forth full of fury rather than as an exact and faithful narration; *Romances* are simpler, less elevated, less figurative in their invention and expression. Poems have more of the marvelous, and contain as well the verisimilar; *Romances* have more of the verisimilar, even though they also have sometimes [elements of] the marvelous. Poems are more rule-bound, and more constrained in their ordering, and contain less subject matter, events, and episodes; *Romances* contain more, because being less elevated and figurative, they affect the mind less, and give it room to load up with a much larger number of different ideas. (7)

In this vein, clearly foreshadowing the novel/romance debates in Britain in the middle of the eighteenth century and later, but anchoring them into verse/prose differences, Huet follows Aristotle, who argued that tragedy was more plausible if based on historical accounts of the fall of the high and mighty, but that this was not a necessary condition. So too *Romances* are more credible (*la fiction totale de l'argument est plus recevable*) when their characters are of middling status (*de mediocre fortune*), as in the *Romans comiques*, rather than when princes and conquerors are the protagonists whose distinguished and memorable exploits are recorded by the high *Romances* (9–10). For Huet, the exploits of the great do not pass muster as credible in these narratives because readers wonder why these actions had been hidden from the historical record so far, whereas the depiction of the lives of the less important appears more verisimilar. Of course, the desire to document everyday realism, ordinary life, and common folk is not something that only eighteenth-century Britons invented; Huet (and Bakhtin later) sees this expressed very early in Lucius Apuleius's *The Golden Ass*. Fables, however, are described as entirely without verisimilitude, along with allegories and parables. These earlier fictional forms are identified with a raft of peoples who are responsible for the non-European origins of fiction, ranging through the Egyptians, the Arabs, the Persians, the Medes, and the Syrians, as well as others.

Huet's treatise is speculative and progressive. From a vast geography of a world teeming with various forms of pleasurable lying, the Greeks and the Romans improved on the materials they were given. Sometimes, history degenerated into fiction for want of evidence. The eventual goal for Huet's treatise is to affirm a world that is composed of multiple forms of fiction that are universally desired, arrived at through different routes, but none of which is inherently superior to any other. In one of the most evocative passages of the treatise, Huet argues that mimetic fictions are needed whether in poverty or plenty:

> As when in need, we feed our bodies with roots and herbs when we lack bread; just so, when the knowledge of truth, which is the natural and proper food of the human mind, is lacking, we feed it with lies, which are imitations of truth. And as in plenty, to sate our appetites, we often forgo bread and everyday meats and search for ragouts; so even when our minds know truth, they leave study and contemplation in order to be entertained by the picture of truth, which is lies, because the picture and the imitation are, according to Aristotle, often more satisfying than the truth itself. (80–81)

According to Huet, the mind has a natural desire for fiction as well as for new knowledges. The moral work of these stories takes place through readers' identification and psychological processing of the actions; while some naïve readers are taken in by the shell of the narration, the sophisticated, who can penetrate beyond the surface, nonetheless savor the pleasure of the fictional framework (86). Ultimately, Huet commends *Romances* as "silent teachers [*precepteurs muets*] who continue the work of schoolteachers; they instruct us to speak and live in a much more practical and persuasive manner than the schoolteachers did; and in the manner of Horace's view of Homer's *Iliad*, that taught morality better and more solidly than the best Philosophers were able to" (96). In like fashion, turning to Madame de Lafayette's *Zayde*, to which this treatise was appended, he concludes with the suggestion that posterity would not know if this work was "a History or a *Romance*" (99).

From this consideration of Huet's early speculative essay, we learn that the study of modern fictions could (and maybe always should) involve the consideration of narrative and cultural interchange among a variety of people, sources, languages, and epochs; that geography and spatial models of horizontal cross-connections could be just as effective and persuasive as vertical national history or notions of temporal influence and succession; that realism, truth, verisimilitude, mimesis, history, and various other referential terms are always put into play relationally among various literary genres to favor prose over poetry and fiction over fable, but much less polemically so than was done later when particular brands of novelistic national realism were deemed to transcend all that went before. If these pointers are kept in mind, students of fictional genres who embark on the materials of the late seventeenth and early eighteenth century are less likely to make the errors of selection, omission, and validation that are absolutely necessary to create a national(ist) canon in realist fiction, a project that has as its single-minded objective the consolidation of citizen-subjects in full narcissistic contemplation of their own idealized images (and those of others). Eschewing the dead end of such intransitivity, we should return to the transitive multiplicity of the generic protocols involved in the fictional work of reading. In fact, a fuller awareness of Renaissance prose fiction in English, including William Painter's *The Palace of Pleasure* (1566–7), John Lyly's *Euphues: The Anatomy of Wit* (1578), and Philip Sidney's *New Arcadia* (1590), demonstrates the English high tradition's involvement with xenotropism. In addition to this investment, there are also popular pamphlet genres including the early native rogue tradition, the picaresque, and the criminal biography – all of which intersperse the domestic with the foreign and the realist with the fanciful, but not necessarily lining those oppositions up neatly with each other. However, theorizing prose fiction was not much of a priority for the writers and readers of these Elizabethan genres, whereas the anxious genre definitions insisted on by authors who wrote realist eighteenth-century English fictions eventually paid off with institutional recognition by nationalist culture.[14]

Fiction is certainly about new ways of discovering "truth" through "the image of truth," as Huet also acknowledges, and methodological and narrational innovations ought not to be forgotten, but at the same time, the crucial elements of transport, transformation, and translation cannot be underemphasized. The classical mode of the *translatio* documents the way cultural transmission followed political and military lines – hence, according to Huet, Spaniards learned *l'art de romaniser* from the Arabs, and the *translatio studii* followed the *translatio imperii*. In what follows, it will be my argument that it is important to understand the particular genre of the surveillance chronicle in the period from 1684 to 1724, especially because such a *translatio emissicii* stages a range of intercultural translations of the tropes of exploration, speculation, and circumspection. In fact, a recent study by R. W. Maslen has argued strongly that Elizabethan prose genres were systematically involved in structures of espionage and counter-espionage, making for standard themes of treachery, code-breaking, infiltration, confidentiality, surveillance, letter-writing, and physical mobility. A consideration of a text such as John Lyly's *Euphues* (1579; and a sequel in 1580) should make us realize the flamboyant morphing of genres involved in the exercise. If we consider the two volumes of *Euphues*, Maslen points out, "the first begins as an Italianate novel and ends as a series of letters, becoming an educational treatise and a theological dispute along the way; the second shifts from novel to fable to patriotic eulogy, and closes as a marriage guidance pamphlet."[15] Therefore, it is worth considering if what has normally been presented as a progress narrative of the development of the national-realist English novel is actually a fixing and a delimiting – a hegemonic stabilization of genre rather than the transgeneric voraciousness of a fictional structure such as that of *Euphues*.

In the rest of this article I explore the surveillance chronicle as a particularized pan-European *translatio*, first in the case of the most celebrated instance of the work of a Genoese refugee to the French court of Louis XIV, Giovanni Paolo Marana. Entitled *The Turkish Spy* in English, Marana's work and its continuations had a major impact in both France and Britain during this period. In the final section, I evaluate the relevance of this text as contextually determinative for an understanding of famous works by two early novelists who wrote in English and also worked as governmental spies – Aphra Behn and Daniel Defoe. Just as spies traffic with uncertain information in foreign lands to further the objectives of their state sponsors, novels written in English later become members of that inheriting proprietary class, *the* English novel.

Spying/Alienating/(Dis)orienting

The adventure novel of everyday life goes back to the classical period, when in the case of Apuleius's *The Golden Ass*, Lucius can spy on people's private affairs because he has been converted into an animal whose big ears allow even greater scope for eavesdropping. However, if eavesdropping and voyeurism are age-old tropes for spying, the notion of the private as the political secret in the early modern period is also thoroughly confused with the idea of subversion and conspiracy. The rise of diplomatic networks, faster communications, commissioned histories, and efficient commercial channels resulted in the activities of rival European states that recruited informers, spies, and agents to keep track of each other's military, economic, and political activities. The use of manuscript journalism, printed *gazettes à la main*, and early newspapers signaled a greater interest in current events and also much greater sophistication and skepticism regarding the interpretation of information through the cross-checking and dating of multiple sources. At the same time, these multiple sources allowed for the appreciation of several perspectives, through which readers and agents could realize opposing objectives, share or disagree about similar information, but also recognize their own limitations and biases within a collective universe of references. Skepticism about others could go hand-in-hand with being confronted by cultural relativism; other points of view sometimes cut the ground from under one's own feet and at other times solidified it.[16]

Spying is one of the chronotopic motifs that saturates British and French fiction, especially since the publication of *The Turkish Spy* in French in 1684 and then in English in 1687, after which there were numerous attempts at continuations and imitations for at least another century. Marana's initial Italian 30-letter original, *L'esploratore turco* (1684) had become a French 102-letter multivolume *L'espion turc*

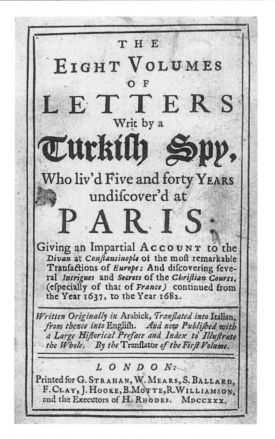

Plate 3.   Title page to the 1730 edition of *The Turkish Spy* by G. P. Marana.

by 1687. The vogue expanded drastically in London and avoided censorship by designating the place of publication as "Cologne," whereby *The Turkish Spy* ended up becoming an eight-volume, 632-letter *L'espion dans le cour des princes chrétiens* by 1696–7, by this point a large miscellaneous compendium in multiple editions that speculated on "present wars, transactions, and intrigues of Christian courts, states, and kingdoms."[17] Amid these political commentaries, the text also contains the protagonist's "immethodical falling upon philosophical, divine, and moral contemplations" that form some of the substance of the ongoing psychodrama of the spy's life, featuring paranoia and fear of exposure (1: iii). The eponymous Turkish spy is "Mahmut the Arabian," ironically described as "the vilest of the Grand Signior's slaves." The fiction contains letters written by him from Paris to Constantinople in the years 1637 to 1682. Under deep cover as a spy, Mahmut goes by the identity of Titus the Moldavian (where his knowledge of Slavonic is itself perhaps a hint of sympathy with Deism, Socinianism, and Hussitism).[18] While he alternately laughs

Mahmut The Turkish Spy *Ætais suæ* 72.
F. H. van Hove. sculp

Mahmut the Turkish Spy *Ætatis Suæ* 72

J. Basire Sculp.

Plate 4. Frontispieces to *The Turkish Spy*, 1730 (left) and 1770 (right) editions.

and weeps as half Democritus and half Heraclitus, Mahmut is a homely, ordinary
personality, "being of low stature, of an ill-favored countenance, ill-shaped and by
nature not given to talkativeness" (4:176; 1:1).

Over the course of the letters it comes out that Mahmut has fallen deeply in love
with Daria, a Greek matron married to someone else, who heartlessly betrays and
exposes Mahmut's erotic interest in her more than once (1:214–21, 272–76; 7:38–39,
60–63). Hence the letters run a gamut from the satirical to the sentimental, the
political to the religious, and the social to the personal; the reader is "assured of an
exact history, abounding in considerable events" (1: xxxix). Mahmut's advice is also to
"be conversant in histories"; histories "open the graves, and call forth the dead . . . they
introduce us into the closets of princes, revealing their most secret counsels; they
make us familiar with the intrigues of politicians" (1:9; 3:119–22). In addition to the
focus on history, the work delivers "proper and useful remarks [and] pleasant and
agreeable stories" (3:14–15). It is perhaps no surprise that Langlet du Fresnoy, in his
eighteenth-century treatise on the use of novels, characterizes the work as *roman*

historique.[19] The genre of personal advice and psychological counseling is under construction here in some letters (this impulse would later be perfected by Samuel Richardson). At the same time as it counsels, the text also teases readers into the possibility that they are privy to political letters that contain hidden information subject to special coding or ciphers, "Art's Master-piece." Mahmut says, "a letter of an ordinary style, of domestic affairs, of love and compliments, may contain secrets of the greatest importance" (1: 80–81). Decipherment is also subject to the vagaries of linguistic equivalence: "it is impossible to screw up the dull phrases of Europe to the significant idioms of Asia" (4: 46). The text discusses the possibility and the difficulty involved in the reciprocal transcoding of political and private fictions. Marana was implicated in the Savoy-inspired political conspiracy of Raphael della Torre against the Genoese state and had to suffer imprisonment for four years. Asked to write a pro-government history of the conspiracy that was all the same suppressed upon its submission, Marana fled to France, where he published his revised account of the conspiracy.[20] Nonetheless, this genre inspired by the need for political decipherment would classify a veritable flood of texts from the 1680s to the 1710s, in the surveillance and spy novels of Aphra Behn, François de Fénelon, Delarivier Manley, Eliza Haywood, and others.

There continues to be a controversy about the authorship of the volumes subsequent to Marana's first, based on a series of speculations that range from the possibility of the author being Marana himself for the most part, to a number of English replacement candidates including Daniel Saltmarsh, William Bradshaw, John Sault, Roger Manley (father of surveillance chronicler Delarivier Manley), John Midgley, and an unnamed English Jacobite in exile with James III's court in St. Germain-en-Laye. Meanwhile, French critics predictably favor the candidacy of a number of French authors including Bayle, Cotolendi, Marana's translator François Pidou de St. Olon, and the intriguing possibility of an unidentified French Huguenot refugee intellectual exiled in London after the Revocation of the Edict of Nantes in 1685. Even as there is a "continuity of design, characterization, and style" throughout the letters, the spy's political position also changes from that of a liberal Catholic to that of a rationalist Deist (and he is therefore sometimes accused by hostile reviewers of atheism). One of the most convincing source studies, by Jean-Pierre Gaudier and Jean-Jacques Heirwegh, describes the matter of the author as flatly equivalent to that of the text, in other words, "a network of plausibilities" rather than a fixed identity.[21]

However, this critical controversy imposes a different set of concerns in order to disambiguate the possibilities of a delirious transmission and circulation. The text itself is resolutely placed in a destabilizing web of found manuscripts, translation, and secret information from various elsewheres. The author's preface is about discovering a packet of Mahmut's writings that are thereupon being edited and made available to the public – indeed a standard trope in fiction from the mid-seventeenth- to the mid-eighteenth century – to reveal authorial fragmentation and the vagueness and hybridity of multiple sources. The ironical fact remains that a work that began with an

Italian-language original morphed into a French project and ended up as a prominent English-language venture (with the likelihood that the later volumes were retranslated from English back into French). What better model could be provided of the multi-directional passage of fiction – whether novel or romance, satire or epistle – across the Continent and through a mechanism of transmission that involved exchanges between a putative observer who had experienced Ottoman cosmopolitanism and also French (and implicitly English) provincialism? Mahmut translates texts for Cardinal Richelieu even as he reports on the purport of these same translations to Visier Asem (1: 140). Mahmut is more than a match for the churchman's legendary surveillance techniques, saying "though Cardinal Richelieu be an Argus, he is blind as to what concerns me" (1: 276). Mixed in with much late seventeenth-century political history there are also frequent redactions of ancient Assyrian, Persian, and Roman history as well as accounts of Germany, Italy, Africa, and France. The translational frame of the work enables the retailing of political news, moral reflections, and subjective emotions serially, through the form of the familiar letter that also anticipates the periodical essay and the novelistic chapter.

Frontispieces published with this text (see plates 3 and 4) emphasize the solitary and contemplative life of Mahmut, depicted as a scholar at his desk in his study. Present around him are the traveler-scholar's topoi including manuscripts, maps, a globe, timepieces, and other measuring instruments. Three of the books on his library shelves are singled out with titles: "Al-Coran," "Tacitus," and "St. Austin," perhaps signaling the perspective of the Muslim observer fused with the classical political rhetoric of Tacitus's observations of the Germans, and the religious confessional aspects of Augustinian interiority. If these attributes make Mahmut into something of a Renaissance humanist, the bag of gold coins, the lit lamp, his bearded appearance, the curtains, and some disarray among his documents also suggest the precarious, nocturnal, and secretive status of the spy. The transparency exuded by the props of rational humanism is delicately balanced by the subterfuge implied by the instruments of secret correspondence. Making visible the fact that information can be purchased and that the portrait is of a spy under an assumed identity, the visualizations generate the contradictory impression of self-revelation alongside imposture. Perhaps the discerning reader is made aware that the spy's careful cultivation of disinterestedness is potentially subject to a hidden agenda that could entirely reverse appearances.

The status of the spy's disinterestedness took off in terms of direct imitations, even as the motif of spying collapsed into that of innocuous voyeurism. In terms of the spinoffs, there are the cases of Gatien de Courtilz's *The French Spy* (1700); Ned Ward's *The London Spy* (1698–1700); Charles Gildon's *The Golden Spy* (1709); Captain Bland's *The Northern Atalantis: or York Spy* (1713); the anonymous *The German Spy* (1738); *The Jewish Spy* (1739); Eliza Haywood's *The Invisible Spy* (1755), and many more. In the meantime, by 1776 there had accumulated at least twenty-six different editions of *The Turkish Spy*. It has been argued that Addison and Steele's *Spectator* essays are at least generally beholden to Marana, who can be therefore credited not just with having invented the genre of the surveillance chronicle (or alternately, that of pseudo-ethnographic fiction) but with having inspired the later genre of the periodical essay as well. This type of fiction involves the featuring of distanced social and cultural observations about people who are described as culturally different from an observer who is often in disguise or passing through. The spy is a vehicle for satire and ethnographic commentary as well as a device to exonerate the author from the opinions of the naïve observer. There is always danger inherent in such activities, as it is normally better to attend to one's own affairs: "he that peeps in at his neighbour's window may chance to lose his eyes" (3:14–15). There is also present in Mahmut's commentary the bare beginnings of more innocuous forms of voyeurism, with the detailed touristic descriptions of great cities that would later become a flood when systematized by the publication of memoirs about the Grand Tour: "Constantinople and Paris are indeed two of the greatest cities in the world" (1:53; 2:199–204; 7: 241–48). However, he later expresses "a natural aversion for great and populous cities" which are "magnificent sepulchres of the living" (6:292). The city, a place of refuge, turns dangerous to its inhabitants: "cities, first designed for sanctuaries of the distressed, should become worse than desarts, and more inhospitable than the purlieus of dragons, or the dreadful haunts of lynxes, crocodiles and other animals of prey" (7:22).

Yet, at the same time, there is the inevitable absorption of the observer into the world he observes, and Mahmut agonizingly becomes more French as the volumes proceed: "I am in France, yet cannot call it a foreign country, since innocence and virtue naturalize a man in all parts of the world" (2:146). For theoretical clarity, Mahmut follows Descartes, who recommends that he who wishes to perfect his reason must "shake off the prepossessions and prejudices of his infancy and youth, [and] wipe, brush, or sweep his soul clean of the very dust and relics left behind on our faculties by those first foreign invasions and encroachments on our minds" (1:xvi). Keeping with this martial imagery of the triumph of reason that goes against Mahmut's duplicitous status as a spy, the objective of the treatise is proclaimed to be that of "building a fortress or stronghold from where attempts of open enemies and sly secret interlopers can be resisted" (1:xviii). At the same time, Descartes is also praised for giving women emancipatory potential; the Turks ought to follow suit in liberating their women in the manner of the French. As ladies apply themselves to the study of philosophy in France, "the pen has almost supplanted the exercise of the needle; and ladies closets, formerly the shops of female baubles, toys, and vanities, are now turned to libraries and sanctuaries of learned books" (2:26). Printing and translation into the vernacular are praised for the manner in which "the lowest sort of people who can but read, have the privilege to become as knowing as their superiors, and the slave may vie for learning with his sovereign." At the same time, from "this depraved indulgence of printing … what sacrileges, massacres, rebellions and impieties have overflown most parts of the west in this licentious age" (3:120–21). There is also another dark underside to this blinding light of reason: Mahmut's increasing melancholy (2:144–47; 6:74–78, 122; 7:241; 8:1–3). This fear of the loss of identity and also its counterpart, the fear of exposure whereby a "true" identity would be revealed, leads to Mahmut's ultimate disappearance – or perhaps unsolved murder – at the end of the eighth volume. While *The Turkish Spy* is a prime exhibit for the early expression of Enlightenment values, its complexity suggests also the irrational repercussions and violent rupture that Enlightenment has always been unable to vanquish.

The reader can be regaled with information about various manners and customs when seen from a decentered perspective and hear of Mahmut's interviews with Cardinal Richelieu (1:137–40, 165–76, 254–55; 2:89–91). Mahmut's observations range from those on political figures such as Richelieu, Mazarin, or the Queen Mother, to speculations on the status of women, advice about state policy, and major interventions in controversies about religious doctrine and their consequences. Mahmut "hope[s] to see in open light the naked form of things" even though this often takes the form of establishing national stereotypes, especially of the French, the Spanish, the Italians, and the Germans – which would later in the eighteenth century form the raw matter of novelistic national realism (8: 44, 75–81). By the last volume, Mahmut develops a very sophisticated notion of impressionistic accuracy that might well be at home with nineteenth- and twentieth-century debates around narrative realism. Speaking of Istanbul, he says:

> In describing this imperial city, I have imitated the painters, who, when they would draw a beauty to the life, do not go arithmetically to work, or observe any order in their rough drafts; but following the conduct of a wild and strong fancy, they dash their pencil here and there, as that volatile faculty inspires them, regarding only the symmetry of the picture, without preferring one part to another, or being curious in delineating every little singularity: So I, in pourtraying this queen of cities, this superlative beauty of the whole earth, draw my strokes at random, not designing to present thee with an anatomy-lecture over her, or to unveil all her interior secrets, but only to give thee a transient view of those parts which appear most eminent, and attract the eyes of all travellers; and this I do not perform all at once, (it were too great a task) but even like them, by fits and starts, as I find my opportunities. (8: 100–101)

Various modes of realism are compared in the above passage, even as the purposive use of one kind (presciently suggestive of Impressionism?) is both justified and enacted. At the same time, the pressing realities around these set pieces are about a European seventeenth century that has been reeling from various religious wars. The hermeneutic rift between the alienated spectator and his two worlds (because the world he reports to is quite different from the one he reports on) results in conflict, anguish, and deviousness, and indeed a third possibility for subjectivity that is neither that of the spy's disguise nor that of his deeper affiliation. The many class levels of the spy's interlocutors and addressees makes for a social cross-section that can cut across the boundaries between social elites and anonymous individuals. Readers can revel in information about the Sultan's seraglio in Constantinople, details of the cost of necessaries in Paris, and discussion concerning the numbers of coaches to be seen in the streets. Mahmut's foreign letters form individual elements in a medley or miscellany, mixing surveillance-related objectives with disinterested observation.

Perhaps the most famous novel of the eighteenth century that uses the ethnographic observer to telling effect is Charles Louis Secondat, Baron de Montesquieu's *Lettres persanes* (1721), which has often been identified as indebted to the pseudo-epistolary genre invented by Marana. The devices of cultural relativism and the distancing powers of satire in the novel produce something like Enlightenment absolutism (even though what is under critique is the French political absolutism of the seventeenth century). The Marana–Montesquieu combination of pseudo-ethnography alongside satire, critique, and reflection has a longer European genealogy, going back to Baltasar Gracián's *El Criticon* (1650–3) and other lesser-known texts.[22]

These types of literary letters written by foreign observers culminate with Montesquieu who owes much to Marana's surveillance chronicle. *The Persian Letters* moves this genre forward into becoming a self-enclosed fiction as well as satirical vehicle. By the time we get to later examples, such as Charles Dufresny's *Amusemens sérieux et comiques* (1734), George Lyttelton's *Persian Letters* (1735), Oliver Goldsmith's *Citizen of the World* (1762), or Elizabeth Hamilton's *Translations of the Letters of a Hindoo Rajah* (1796), the aspects of the surveillance chronicle have been shed or so naturalized as to get a version of the pseudo-ethnographic novel. These peculiar types of mixture, where fiction and non-fiction rub up against each other (books which never sit easily with the label of novel) derive from the innovations of Marana and Montesquieu. Mahmut's role allows for a centralized observation through his perspective even as individual letters function paratactically; in this regard, the epistolary compendium mirrors older story cycles that feature frame-narrators and individual stories, even as it narratologically manages the "abruptness and obscurity and frequent changes of subjects" that the preface apologizes for (1:iii).[23] Marana can therefore be cited as a common source for the oriental tale and the *Spectator* papers; for epistolary satire and the periodical essay; for fiction and social commentary.

From Surveillance Chronicle to Secret History

Although histories of the eighteenth-century English novel could sometimes pay lip-service to Cervantes's *Don Quixote* (1604) or Bunyan's *Pilgrim's Progress* (1684), many courses on the subject often begin with Aphra Behn, and especially her *Oroonoko* (1688), which features colonial, romance, and anti-slavery motifs along with the notions of "true history" and "natural Intrigues" opposed to those of "adorn[ment]" or "the Addition of Invention" involving a "feign'd *Hero*, whose Life and Fortunes Fancy may manage at the Poet's Pleasure."[24] The novel's insistence on the authenticity of the events it narrates and the transparency of the title character and the Peeie Indians are combined with a parallel undercurrent of subterfuge, espionage, and political manipulation referencing three continents. The unnamed female narrator observes, narrates, and also steps into the action, bridging the diegetic and nondiegetic worlds and the status of author, narrator, and character, generating epistemological and narratological uncertainty. Yet she is the focus of much political hostility and interpersonal slipperiness. Conspiracy and betrayal seem to be integral aspects of the novella – whether in the Ottoman-inflected Coromantien of Oroonoko's kingdom or the English- and Dutch-settled Surinam of the Americas to which Oroonoko is brought as a slave. Speculation as to whether Behn might have actually visited Surinam has never been fully resolved; although, as evidence strongly suggests, she probably did go there. The capacity in which she might have traveled ranges through that of daughter, mistress, husband-hunter, servant, agent, courier, or spy, perhaps with several of these identities overlapping each other. Behn, who subsequently had a full-blown career as a governmental spy for Charles II's Secretary of State, Lord Arlington, as "Agent 160" in Holland in 1666, was fully aware of the multiple protocols of secret and coded communications. Correspondingly, the text has been subject to multiple allegorical interpretations that are very suggestive, despite remaining insufficient for a full understanding of its scope.[25]

Oroonoko stakes a strong claim as a new global fiction that triangulates Africa, Europe, and America in equal measure – in this respect, it is a work that is arguably much closer to the disposition of Huet's followers than Ian Watt's.[26] A convergence of several different continents, races, political regimes, and gender dynamics makes this text a favored origin for a postcolonial eighteenth century and a symptomatic critical investment in it, which I have discussed and critiqued elsewhere.[27] In many ways, however, the assumed secrecy of the narrator and the surveillance to which Oroonoko and other characters are subjected, whether in Surinam or Coromantien, thematically unite the disparate parts of the text. The chronotope of the spy carries over as the appropriate organizing principle of a fiction of global relevance with various paratactical elements. Marana's text was translated and published in England by 1687, a year before Behn published *Oroonoko*. Turkish themes were not all that foreign to Behn, whether in her plays or in shorter fictions such as *The Dumb Virgin* (1700).

Charles II's extensive "harem" of mistresses was recognized during the Restoration as loosely resembling Turkish practices. For instance, in *The Turkish Spy*, Mahmut compliments Charles II's "concubines . . . most of them nobly extracted" even as he empathizes with this prince's being "harassed at home by domestic seditions, factions, plots, and conspiracies of his own subjects" (8: 144). Mahmut equates Charles's position with that of a Turkish Sultan, even as he refers to the range of controversies from the Popish Plot to the Exclusion Bill and Monmouth's Rebellion. Keeping such a comparison in mind, it is obvious that the Coromantien section in *Oroonoko* is a harem fiction with convergent allusions to the mistresses that Charles had left behind after a 25-year reign. When the separation of Imoinda from Oroonoko through the institution of the "Royal Veil" occurs in Coromantien, Oroonoko is reunited with his mistress with the help of Aboan's romantic intrigue with a "cast-mistress" of the King's, Onahal. Onahal's assignations with Aboan help Oroonoko to get secret audiences with Imoinda. Onahal's role is indeed reminiscent of harem intrigue as a stereotypical form of court politics; Mahmut in *The Turkish Spy* will recognize that spying and the veiled woman are equivalents, and therefore he too "converse[s] (like our women in Turkey) under a veil" (5: 89–90). Onahal could well be yet another allusion to Behn's predicament – unpaid by Charles II for her spying activities in Antwerp and perhaps Surinam, an unpaid agent if not quite a "Cast-Mistress" – although, as I have also suggested, there is considerable evidence in the text to argue for at least an indirect fantasy identification on Behn's part with some of Charles's aristocratic mistresses.[28]

The roles played by the narrator in the Surinam sections are multiple – as minder, manager, keeper, and entertainer of Oroonoko on the estate of the governor-proprietor, Lord Willoughby of Parham, during his absence. The narrator entertains the African prince with stories of Romans (and Imoinda with stories of nuns), and also admits (if somewhat inadvertently) that her role was utterly compromised. The narrator has to distract Oroonoko from political activity and thoughts leading to rebellion and freedom. The faction-ridden context of a Surinam of the early 1660s, where Cromwellian Parliamentarians were still at large, is also evocative of much of the local intrigue dividing the Royalists from each other, involving Deputy Governor Byam and his Irish agent Banister who actually organized Oroonoko's execution. In keeping with the slippery evasion of authority and accountability that spies possess, the narrator can report on the execution through surrogates who were present, including her mother and sister. However, she secretes herself: "I, taking Boat, went with other Company to Colonel *Martin*'s, about three Days Journy down the River."[29] It is worth asking, if somewhat uncharitably, for a discussion of the unstated secrets in the text. If Behn was indeed sent as a spy (a very precocious recruit in her early twenties) were there other political intrigues that she was fomenting, which demanded the surveillance of Colonel Martin, the brother to "*Harry Martin*, the great *Oliverian*"?[30] This explanation in the novella is ironical, as the Parliamentarian Henry Martin was a bitter opponent of Cromwell's; subsequently Behn will become a friend and admirer of Colonel Martin, naming him the hero of her play, *The Younger Brother, or, The Amorous Jilt* (1696). It is also an interesting coincidence that the narrator is "apt to fall into Fits of dangerous Illness upon any extraordinary Melancholy," just in the manner of the Turkish spy Mahmut.[31]

While *Oroonoko* conforms to aspects of the surveillance chronicle, its investment in questions of cultural translation and fictional genre makes it a text conversant with issues already discussed. Behn accurately writes down one of the rules of this genre in the context of discussing the innocence of the natives of Surinam: "where there is no Novelty, there can be no Curiosity." In this regard, the travelogue function of the text furnishes "curious" accounts of marvels and words from the native language.[32] It might be added as a corollary to the saying that if there is novelty where there is curiosity as its prerequisite, surveillance will likely be the technique that will have to generate that novelty. That information, processed by a hermeneutics – whether of credulity or suspicion – involves the genre of surveillance in domestic desires and also foreign affairs, transcolonial voyages and also translational interpretations. *Oroonoko* is a text where different kinds of secrecy cohabit, requiring multiple modes of translation. Early on, the natural language of the courtship among the Indian lovers observed by the narrator is a sign of the "absolute *Idea* of the first State of Innocence, before Man knew how to sin." At the other extreme, there is the violent inter-animation and translation of three very different kinds of bodily mutilation featured in the novella – the ritual scarification of the Coromantees, the competitive self-mutilation of the Indian generals, and the violent decapitation of Imoinda and attempted suicide by Oroonoko. To understand these acts fully, the reader cannot resort to meanings residing within any specific culture – English, Peeie, or Igbo – but needs to attend to the novelistic hybridization, citationality, and translation from bodily practice to narrative decoding. Much in the novella requires contextual decipherment and explanation – whether the system of the slave lots being devised at the early stages of plantation slavery, or the "Ceremony of Invitation" whereby Imoinda is sent the "Royal Veil," or the religious fetishism and indigenous healing practices of the Peeie Indians who "cure the Patient more by Fancy than by Medicines."[33]

This recognition of native healing as fraudulent legerdemain has some bearing on the function of the material context, itself producing a "romance effect" rather than the practices themselves. As Behn says in the epistle dedicatory to Lord Maitland, "If there be any thing that seems Romantick, I beseech your Lordship to consider, these Countries do, in all things, so far differ from ours, that they produce unconceivable Wonders; at least, they appear so to us, because New and Strange."[34] This particular sentence is a stunning reversal of the usual genre accusation also sounded against romance, that it produced implausibilities out of the formulary of chivalric conventions. Rather than romance producing false novelties, it seems to be that empirical novelties create romance effects. Truth is stranger than fiction then, and the novel is not necessarily the recognition effect of the familiar as opposed to the literarily fanciful. The experientially unfamiliar is the true outside, new and strange, that one kind of novelistic realism aims to capture; while Michael McKeon has termed this belief "naïve empiricism," such an understanding of it can only be from a retroactive and informed perspective that is not that of the original teller, who is not necessarily naïve. Behn was a translator of Bernard de Fontenelle's *A Discovery of New Worlds*, and it is not surprising that in her hands, the surveillance chronicle aims to map the outside and bring it home for translation and analysis, along with other elements of the defamiliarized familiar, such as the political happenings among the colonists and the slaves. In a preface to the Fontenelle translation, entitled "Essay on Translated Prose," Behn suggests that the point of translation is to make the unfamiliar empirically available, and thereby the translator is justified in staying as close as possible to the author's true meaning.[35]

When we take these lessons forward from a surveillance-oriented reading of *Oroonoko* and move chronologically to a consideration of Delarivier Manley's scandal chronicles and Eliza Haywood's masquerade novels, something different begins to emerge. Rather than treating all these morphings of identity as feints behind which some essential Englishness or womanliness can be found, these novels testify to a fictional and a historical space that is still profoundly unfixed, featuring fictional "fantasy machines," as John Richetti has called them. Talking of a "New Atalantis" as an island in the Mediterranean or a "Countess of Caramania" within a sea of European royalty can mean an inter-animation between the looseness of transcultural trafficking as well as the fixity of specific national context. The *roman à clef* aspect of fictions by Behn, Manley, and Haywood – increasingly referred to as secret histories – also reveals the ideology behind the later realism as itself an arms-length reaction formation to these earlier tell-all forms that are, as scandal sheets, *too close to truth to be realist*. The royalist ideology of these women writers makes them also cosmopolitan and xenotropic, rather than parochially English in the manner of the Whiggish novelists of several decades later. It is only to be expected that the tropes of translation and found manuscripts feature prominently in many of these early novels that are still obsessed with the relationality between here and there, now and then, domestic and foreign. Ros Ballaster sees four dominant fictional subgenres imported from France in this earlier period – the heroic romance, the *petite histoire* or *nouvelle*, the *chronique scandaleuse*, and the love-letter. However, the idea that these genres are feminocentric is debatable.[36]

William Warner suggests that the early novel instantiates the inauguration of a media culture of entertainment rather than high art, and that the "novels of amorous intrigue" written by the trio of Behn, Manley, and Haywood are formula fiction but also sophisticated responses to the anti-novelistic discourse of the early period. The later national realism of the mid-eighteenth century is a Whiggish counter-response (continued in a Marxist strain by Watt and others) that enshrines secondary English characteristics as primary realist features. Warner argues for a resituating of the novel in terms of the genre's perpetually defensive self-definition against puritanical anti-novelism, and this embattled position partly explains Richardson's and Fielding's self-promotion even as they both disavow and recycle their female predecessors. We should therefore realize that the focus on justification, nationalism, and realism makes for a navel-gazing institutional history of the English origins of the English novel, which, at the very least, ought to be decentered.[37]

This recognition of a later nation-centered gate-keeping function by literary history would ultimately revise the origins of the early English novel as "nobody's story," but in a much more expanded sense than Catherine Gallagher has defined it – in other words, as a multi-sited translational utopianism, a clearinghouse for multiple languages, polities, religions, and ethnicities rather than just a specific gynotropism dealing exclusively with the literary commodification of English women writers.[38] And even though there are certainly national realist strains that claim pre-eminence by mid-century and after, these are deified at the expense of counter-currents that still pull away from the dominant "posited essence" of realism – whether these be the later oriental satire, adventure tale, or gothic romance.

Daniel Defoe is the likely author of sixty-three letters of a spurious ninth volume of *A Continuation of the Letters of a Turkish Spy* in 1718, thereby using the fictional vehicle to discuss the political history of Europe from 1687 to 1693.[39] Clearly an admirer of the Marana text, Defoe justified his predecessor's fictional plain style:

The best Rule in all Tongues [is] to make the Language plain, artless, and honest, suitable to the Story, and in a Stile easie and free, with as few exotick Phrases and obsolete Words as possible, that the meanest Reader may meet with no Difficulty in the Reading, and may have no Obstruction to his searching the History of things by their being obscurely represented.[40]

As a piece of Williamite and anti-French as well as anti-papal propaganda, the continuation is written in a brisk style with no digressions, touching on the various aspects of military news, moral advice, and political stability without much experimentation in terms of a textual model which by that point had been tried and tested and proven spectacularly successful. The book's tone is less confessional than Marana's and national characteristics do not appear as extensively as they do in the predecessor text. One interesting passage for our purposes is a reflection on the love of narrative falsehood among Europeans' accounts of non-Europeans:

These *Nazarens* [Christians or Europeans] are the most addicted to Fiction and Forgery of any People that ever I met with; it is a received Custom among them, that whenever they have to do with any Sect or Opinion of People, differing from their own, the first thing they go about is, to represent them as monstrous and unnatural, either in Person or in Principle, or perhaps in both; dressing them up in ridiculous Shapes, and imposing a Thousand Stories about them upon the Credulity and the Ignorance of the Vulgar, that they may entertain immoveable Prejudices and Aversions against the Persons and Principles they profess.[41]

The point that Defoe makes here through Mahmut is that "absurd romantic Tales," "imaginary Histories," "innumerable forged Stories," and "fabulous Miracles" told by Christians against Islam are thoroughly ideological and politically motivated. A deliberate non-realism, it is argued, is being used to narrate the European other into a parallel ethnographic time that Johannes Fabian later called "nonallochronic."[42]

Defoe had also modeled his volumes of *The Family Instructor* (1715–18) on Marana's potent mixture of moral dialogue generated as a reflection upon different scenes of human life; while Marana focuses on political history and Mahmut's advice as domestic counselor to various correspondents, Defoe alters the balance exclusively in favor of the concomitant duties of participants in family life. While Marana's work and its continuation appear so transparently to us as a device, Maximillian E. Novak suggests that "audiences unaccustomed to reading a form of fiction so imbued with history were ready enough to take the account as real."[43] Of course, it should be obvious that as a governmental spy and informer, a protofeminist, as well as a secret religious dissident, Defoe might have had more than a passing interest and identification with a character such as Mahmut. In his letters, Defoe characterizes *The Turkish Spy* as "the books I Take as They Are a meer Romance" but heartily approves of the idea of commentary from the perspective of a penetrating diplomatic intelligence.[44] Furthermore, Novak draws a direct line of influence from Mahmut's melancholic fits to the occasionally lunatic possessions undergone by Robinson Crusoe. Crusoe's final

"Vision of the Angelick" in the *Serious Reflections* (1720) bears a strong resemblance to Mahmut's "ramble through an infinite Space" and his encounter with comets in the last volume of *The Turkish Spy* (8: 26–29).[45]

However, while many of Defoe's other novels (especially *Captain Singleton* {1720}, *Colonel Jack* {1722}, and *Moll Flanders* {1722}) correspond to the Bakhtinian idea of a novel without emergence, featuring a hero as "a moving point in space," his fiction *The Fortunate Mistress* (otherwise known as *Roxana* {1724}) is of great significance for its realistic depiction of paranoid conspiracy within a transnational/translational plot. The title page manages to allude to Britain, France, Germany, and Turkey all at once; almost the first thing we hear from the protagonist is that she is the daughter of Huguenots and that she speaks French fluently, thereby having access to the lingua franca of seventeenth- and eighteenth-century Europe (37).[46] Some of the generic brilliance of *Roxana* derives from the joint power of the surveillance chronicle and the scandal chronicle. The fiction is a double-time throwback to the Restoration era and the activities of Charles II's court and his numerous mistresses, as well as a scandal chronicle alluding to the court of George I and his German mistresses, encouraging an overlay of early eighteenth-century bourgeois values and sharp dealing by Quakers, high-priced mistresses, and slippery spies.[47] It is also a reconstruction of a time when the Ottoman threat to Europe was still significant, as well as being a double-coded reference to the aristocratic excesses of the Age of Louis XIV. Terms such as "Intelligence" and "Information" feature prominently in this text. Political conspiracy, financial peculations, and sexual scandal are closely related. Sexual violence, indeed what appears to be an attempted strangulation, can be the subterfuge that hides the nobleman's gift of an expensive diamond necklace to the protagonist; on another occasion, the personal intimacy that Roxana has with the French jeweler turns out to be the actual prolegomenon to a long and arduous attempt to secure his goods as hers upon his unsolved murder (73, 53–57). Roxana's profession demands perpetual disguise and the rejection of immediate family and genetic ties through escape, payoff, subterfuge, or murder, whether in familiar or unfamiliar circumstances. The difficulty caused by running into her brewer husband in Paris is solved by her close confidante and servant Amy, as is that caused by her discovery by her daughter Susan in London.[48]

Roxana's Turkishness is a domestication of the foreign as a delightful and exotic artifice. This novel is perhaps typical of the foreign-oriented fictions we have been considering, embodying what William Warner has called a "fantasy of the fungibility of identity."[49] Indeed, we might also ask if this is the beginning of the end of the open-network transnational novel, when the gates of domestic realism begin to clang shut, and a generic price will have to be paid to exit the moated castle of the bourgeois Englishman's fantasy of domestic realism. A previous Roxana was the wife of the Turkish Sultan, Amurath, and the legendary oppressor of Amurath's heir Bajazet. Roxana (or Roxolana) was already famous as a name for multiple literary and historical characters with Turkish provenance. The name of the wife of Alexander the Great and also of Suleiman the Magnificent, in the period Roxana becomes a "generic name for an oriental queen, suggesting ambition, wickedness, and exoticism" in texts such as William

Davenant's *The Siege of Rhodes* (1656); Nathaniel Lee's *The Rival Queens* (1677); Roger Boyle's *Mustapha* (1665); Jean Racine's *Bajazet* (1672); and Charles Johnson's *The Sultaness* (1717).[50] Most famous of all literary Roxanas was Usbek's favorite wife, who rebels against his sexual authority and breaks off the Enlightenment project of Montesquieu's *Persian Letters* with her suicide note, which is also a metaphorical letter bomb. However, by profession and reputation, Defoe's Roxana has, in her own description, become "a meer Roxana," a public woman, an actress, and a counterfeit of the real thing (182). This is why Roxana earns her name by sheer chance and contingent public acclaim, when she finishes her pretended Turkish dance before the King, "and one of the Gentlemen cry'd out, *Roxana! Roxana!* by –, with an Oath; upon which foolish Accident I had the Name of *Roxana* presently fix'd upon me all over the Court End of Town, as effectually as if I had been Christen'd *Roxana*" (176). As a result, Roxana's Turkishness is more style than substance, based on a tourist encounter and acquisitions enabled by her French nobleman during their Grand Tour through Italy together for two years. In Naples (or at Leghorn as she says later), "my Lord bought me a little Female *Turkish* Slave, who being Taken at Sea by a *Malthese* Man of War, was brought in there; and of her I learnt the *Turkish* Language; their Way of Dressing, and Dancing, and some *Turkish* or rather *Moorish* Songs" (102, 173). However, the actual dance interpreted by Roxana is "a Figure which I learnt in *France* when the Prince *de* – desir'd I wou'd dance for his Diversion; it was indeed, a very fine Figure, invented by a famous Master at *Paris*, for a Lady or a Gentleman to dance single" (175). Taken in, one of the gentleman in the audience swears he had seen that very dance in Constantinople; on another occasion, Roxana holds her own with two Persian ladies who danced Georgian and Armenian dances respectively (176, 179–80). Yet the faux-Turkish dance, performed yet again on this occasion, has her hint that it wins her the biggest prize of all – the status of mistress to the king himself for a period over three years. In the sexual union of British monarch and faux-Turkish French-speaking mistress, we could find the subordination, if not the dissolution, of the foreign into the national.[51] Yet Roxana will have to pay the exaggerated and scapegoat price for her inspired *turquerie*, which is discovery and fear of exposure at the hands of her daughter, Susan. Therefore, when an exasperated Roxana declares after the marriage to her Dutch merchant toward the end of the narrative that she would not care to be "known by the Name of *Roxana*, no, not for ten Thousand Pounds," it indicates that the foreign can barely survive, but only as an unacknowledged and hidden scandal within bourgeois conventionality. Being exposed at this point "wou'd have been enough to have ruin'd me to all Intents and Purposes with my Husband, and everybody else too; I might as well have been the *German Princess*" (271). This is the ultimate irony – Roxana is first of all not referring to a foreign royal, but the famous bigamist and impostor Mary Carleton who claimed to be a "Maria von Wolway," and therefore of German royalty. Carleton's confidence trick was exposed in the 1660s and she was finally hanged for theft in 1674, but only after she fully exploited the "serial subjectivity" that, according to Mary Jo Kietzman, gave her agency in the shadowy underworld of crime.[52] Yet, this is also a palpable hit at George I's German mistresses; the Duchess of Kendal had very recently bilked the nation during the South Sea scandal. Imposture and foreignness, roguery and royalty come very close to each other in a manner that cannot be ultimately disambiguated. If the claim to the foreign turns out to be a badly disguised form of roguery, speaking the French of Stratford-atte-Bowe in the manner of Chaucer's Prioress, or the German of George I's carpetbagging retinue, it is an indication that the interest in geographical horizontality is being trumped by a fear of vertical social porousness. Roxana, for all her Frenchness, Germanness, and Turkishness is nothing but a costume for a high-class English whore.

In the meantime, the Quaker with whom Roxana takes refuge to hide from her daughter Susan turns into another surrogate agent in the manner of her servant Amy. Roxana refers to the Quaker as her "faithful SPY, (*for such my* QUAKER *was now, upon the meer foot of her own Sagacity*)" (309). In the manner of many of Defoe's Quakers, Roxana's surrogate misleads Susan and plots Roxana's removal even as she manages not to tell an outright lie. There is the additional problem of Dutch intrigue that also comes to the surface as it did in Behn's transnational spy chronicle. It is possible that the Dutch connection, through Roxana's husband, serves as a placeholder for economic globalism in the novel, especially as there was fierce competitiveness between the British and the Dutch for Asian trade at this moment.[53]

By the end, all that is left of the structure of the Turkish themes of the surveillance novel is Roxana's inexorable guilt, identity crisis, and immitigable melancholy. Indeed, this sense of impending doom and imminent danger is how *The Turkish Spy* also concludes: Mahmut's Jewish correspondent, Nathan ben Saddi, has been mysteriously murdered, and Mahmut is increasingly fearful of whether he is likely to meet the same fate. Is it possible that both Marana and Defoe are uncannily revealing to us the dead end of the domestication of the foreign with Mahmut and Roxana, and their conversion of external spying into internal solitude? Both Marana's and Defoe's tales break off with news of the recent murder of an intimate, and the corresponding foreboding generated in the minds of their respective protagonists. I have raised the theme of foreignness only to show the eventual disposal of it. This underside is nonetheless important to excavate and hold up for examination, rather than simply giving in to the forgetfulness that argues that early novelists were merely interested in bourgeois domesticity. The surveillance chronicle and the secret history are not opposed to bourgeois domesticity and its putative autonomy. Rather, they present a world of heteronomies and divergences that speaks of the centrifugality of the transnational and the translational. By underwriting all these confusing morphings in terms of continuous narratives and stable identities, the *English* novel ideologically recuperates fiction for the nation, thereby becoming the precise and monolingual *opposite* of what Bakhtin means by *heteroglossia*.

Conclusion

In keeping with this volume's emphasis on "material context, not history," I have proposed that the pseudo-ethnographic fiction of the period can prompt us to place literary productions within the context of a horizontally integrative "geography" of transnational influence and exchange, rather than the more familiar vertical and genealogical "history" of the national model. The latter was itself a product of later eighteenth-century and Romantic models of national culture that retroactively synthesized "the novel" as a particularity arising from a range of disparate genres and modes. In this respect, the agency ascribed to "the novel" is a displaced function of the teleological project of constructing national culture.

To reinvestigate the fictional circulations of the period as a series of transnational/translational chronotopes rather than as a national ideology, this essay has taken us to the consideration of different theoretical models and other kinds of archival evidence. I have sought to demonstrate that self-reflexive fiction arises as an inter-genre – achieving translational/transnational power through performative characteristics such as "prosaics," "novelization," and "unfinalizability" as defined by Mikhail Bakhtin – rather than by the establishment of "one" genre that defeats various literary competitors – such as romance – through monolingualism. Reading fictions – even just English and French fictions – as provisional translations is to understand them as cultural transportation devices that carry something over from an elsewhere, in the etymological sense of metaphor, and also in the documentary manner of metonymy.

To pluralize these contexts into the "other realisms" of early eighteenth-century fiction is also to dissent from accounts that propagate "the" novel as self-same. It has been argued in this article that there is novelty in this world of the early eighteenth century, but that this novelty stages itself as inherently translational rather than one in the business of producing identity. Within this interpretive framework, how can the supposedly realist developments of the early English novel be rethought in relation to important bestsellers from the Continent, including Marana's *The Turkish Spy*, Antoine Galland's translation, retranslated as *Arabian Nights' Entertainments*, and Montesquieu's *Persian Letters*? What impact do these fantastic fictions have, if studied further, alongside the scandalous "fantasy machines" constructed by Behn, Manley, and Haywood? How does fiction look when it is defined as transnational currency rather than as national particularism? Why is it that only later English literary criticism invests exclusively in this word, "novel," while literary critics in most other European languages are content with cognates of words, or concepts, that link back to the many strands of "history" and "romance"? These questions need to be thought through, just as it is also very important to attend to the importance of the oriental tale that proceeds in parallel fashion with the early novel, especially after the huge popularity of Galland's *Mille et une nuits*, which began to be translated in 1704 and almost immediately made its way across the Channel.[54]

Interpreting the period's fiction as emblematic of an era of scientific empiricism and moral didacticism, novel-promoters often favor the triumph of one kind of fiction over others, which they see as occurring because of their favoring of particular elements of sociological accuracy that streamlined inchoate desires, morals, and pleasures. It's almost as if this national realist fantasy fulfills a subsection of one of the categories that Bakhtin identifies – the idyllic chronotope that restores the immanent unity of folkloric time – except that here it is an advance from the rural idyll to the empty time of nationalist narcissism.

See also: chapter 3, NARRATIVE TRANSMIGRATIONS; chapter 10, THE ORIGINAL AMERICAN NOVEL; chapter 23, LITERARY CULTURE AS IMMEDIATE REALITY.

NOTES

1. See Benedict Anderson, *Imagined Communities: Reflections on the Origin and Spread of Nationalism*, (rev. ed. London: Verso, 1983; repr., 1991).

2. Michael Holquist, "Introduction" to Mikhail Bakhtin, *The Dialogic Imagination: Four Essays*, ed. Michael Holquist, trans. Caryl Emerson and Michael Holquist (Austin: University of Texas Press, 1981), 31.

3. See Homer Brown, "Prologue," in *Cultural Institutions of the Novel*, Deidre Lynch and William B. Warner, eds., (Durham: Duke University Press, 1996), 11–43.

4. Margaret Anne Doody, *The True Story of the Novel* (New Brunswick, NJ: Rutgers University Press, 1996), 287, 288.

5. See Gary Saul Morson and Caryl Emerson, *Mikhail Bakhtin: Creation of a Prosaics* (Stanford, CA: Stanford University Press, 1990).

6. Doody, *The True Story of the Novel*, 292.

7. Bakhtin, *The Dialogic Imagination*, 250.

8. See J. Paul Hunter, "The Novel and Social/Cultural History," in *The Cambridge Companion to the Eighteenth-Century Novel*, John Richetti, ed. (Cambridge: Cambridge University Press, 1996), 9. The term was also used sporadically to signal the *nouvelle* or *petite histoire*.

9. Richetti, "Introduction," *The Cambridge Companion to the Eighteenth-Century Novel*, 1.

10. Hunter, "The Novel and Social/Cultural History," 9–10.

11. Autobiography and biography form one of three types within "Novels Without Emergence," the other two being "the travel novel," and "the novel of ordeal." There are five more types listed as "Novels of Emergence," including "the idyllic-cyclical chronotope," "the *Bildungsroman*," "didactic-pedagogical novels," "novels of historic

emergence," and an unnamed type that includes *David Copperfield* and *Tom Jones* as examples. See Mikhail Bakhtin, "The *Bildungsroman* and its Significance in the History of Realism (Toward a Historical Typology of the Novel)," in *Speech Genres and Other Late Essays*, ed. Caryl Emerson and Michael Holquist, trans. Vern W. McGee (Austin: University of Texas Press, 1986), 10–59; Morson and Emerson, *Mikhail Bakhtin*, 412–13.

12. See Mary Helen McMurran, "National or Transnational? The Eighteenth-Century Novel," in *The Literary Channel: The International Invention of the Novel*, Margaret Cohen and Carolyn Dever, eds. (Princeton, NJ: Princeton University Press, 2002), 53.

13. Pierre Daniel Huet, *Traitté de l'origine des romans* (Paris: Claude Barbin, 1670), 4. Huet's text was published twice in English, in 1672 and 1715, as *A Treatise of Romances and Their Originals*. Page numbers of the French edition are cited in parentheses. All translations are mine.

14. For a full survey, see Paul Salzman, *English Prose Fiction 1558–1700* (Oxford: Clarendon Press, 1985).

15. See R. W. Maslen, *Elizabethan Fictions: Espionage, Counter-Espionage and the Duplicity of Fiction in Early Elizabethan Prose Narratives* (Oxford: Clarendon Press, 1997), 12.

16. See Brendan Dooley, *The Social History of Skepticism: Experience and Doubt in Early Modern Culture* (Baltimore, MD: Johns Hopkins University Press, 1999); and also Lennard Davis, *Factual Fictions* (New York: Columbia University Press, 1985).

17. "General Preface," *Letters Written by a Turkish Spy Who Lived Five-and-Forty Years Undiscovered at Paris*, 8 vols. (London: Vernor and

Hood, 1801), 1: iii. Later references are cited in parentheses in the text.

18. Jan Lavicka, "*L'espion turc*, le monde slave, et le hussitisme," *XVIIe Siècle* 110–11 (1976): 75–92.

19. Langlet du Fresnoy, *De l'usage des romans* (Amsterdam, 1734), 2: 84–85.

20. See "Marana" in Louis Moréri, Claude-Pierre Goujet, and François Drouet, *Le grand dictionnaire historique* (1759), 7:188–89; S. F. Shimi, "Portrait d'un espion du XVIIè siècle," in *Les Lettres Romanes* 35:1–2 (February-March 1981): 129–43; and Guido Almansi and Donald Warren, "'L'Esploratore Turco' di Giovanni Paolo Marana," in *Studi Secenteschi Rivista Annuale* 9 (1968): 159–83 (Florence: Leo S. Olschki, 1969).

21. William H. McBurney, "The Authorship of *The Turkish Spy*," *PMLA* 72:5 (December 1957): 928; Joseph E. Tucker, "On the Authorship of *The Turkish spy*: An 'État Présent'," *Papers of the Bibliographical Society of America* 52 (1958): 44; Jean-Pierre Gaudier and Jean-Jacques Heirwegh, "Jean-Paul Marana, *L'Espion du Grand Seigneur*, et l'histoire des idées," *Études sur le XVIIIe Siècle* 8 (Brussels: Université Libre de Bruxelles, 1981): 25–51; Joseph Tucker, "*The Turkish Spy* and Its French Background," *Revue de Littérature Comparée* 32 (1958): 74–91; Gwyn A. Williams, "Prince Madoc and the Turkish Spy," *Times Literary Supplement* (December 24, 1982): 1415–16; and Donald Warren, "The Turkish Spy," *Times Literary Supplement* (July 1, 1983): 701.

22. See G. L. Van Roosbroeck, *Persian Letters Before Montesquieu* (New York: Publications of the Institute for French Studies, 1932). Other candidates are Ibn Tofaïl's 12th-century "Original Man," or *Philosophus Autodidacticus*; Honoré Bonet's 14th-century *Apparicion Maistre Jehan de Meun*; and Ferrante Pallavicino's *Il courriere svalligiato* (1643).

23. Josephine Donovan has identified this combination of hypotaxis and parataxis in the protofeminist *novelle* of Christine de Pisan and Marguerite de Navarre. See Josephine Donovan, *Women and the Rise of the Novel, 1405–1726* (New York: St. Martin's Press, 1999), 132–41.

24. Aphra Behn, *Oroonoko*, ed. Janet Todd, in *The Works of Aphra Behn* (Columbus: Ohio State University Press, 1995), 3: 51, 57.

25. See, for instance, the suggestively titled biography by Janet Todd, *The Secret Life of Aphra Behn* (London: André Deutsch, 1996), 41, 37–52, 417–21.

26. See, for instance, William C. Spengemann, "The Earliest American Novel: Aphra Behn's *Oroonoko*," *Nineteenth-Century Fiction* 38 (1984): 384–414.

27. Srinivas Aravamudan, "Petting Oroonoko," in *Tropicopolitans: Colonialism and Agency, 1688–1804* (Durham, NC: Duke University Press, 1999), 29–70.

28. Ibid., 41–42.

29. Behn, *Oroonoko*, 118.

30. Ibid., 97, 111.

31. Ibid., 117.

32. Ibid., 59.

33. Ibid., 59, 66, 92, 102.

34. Ibid., 56.

35. For a discussion of Behn's Cartesianism and interest in Fontenelle, see Todd, *The Secret Life of Aphra Behn*, 396–400.

36. Ros Ballaster, *Seductive Forms: Women's Amatory Fiction from 1684–1740* (Oxford: Clarendon Press, 1992), 42–66.

37. William B. Warner, *Licensing Entertainment: The Elevation of Novel Reading in Britain, 1684–1750* (Berkeley and Los Angeles: University of California Press, 1998), 1–44.

38. See Catherine Gallagher, *Nobody's Story: The Vanishing Acts of Women Writers in the Marketplace, 1670–1820* (Berkeley and Los Angeles: University of California Press, 1994).

39. While the authorship of this text by Defoe has not been established beyond doubt, I have followed Geoffrey Sill's suggestion that there is a demonstrable but not ironclad link between *A Continuation of the Letters Written by a Turkish Spy* and *Robinson Crusoe*. See Geoffrey Sill, "The Source of Robinson Crusoe's 'Sudden Joys,'" *Notes and Queries* 45:1 (March 1998): 67–68. Of course, I also follow the lead of Defoe's principal modern biographers, Paula R. Backscheider and Maximillian E. Novak, both of whom identify the text as Defoe's.

40. [Daniel Defoe], *A Continuation of the Letters Written by a Turkish Spy* (London, 1718), v.
41. Ibid., 270.
42. Ibid., 270–71; see Johannes Fabian, *Time and the Other: How Anthropology Makes Its Object* (New York: Columbia University Press, 1983).
43. Maximillian E. Novak, *Daniel Defoe* (Oxford: Oxford University Press, 2001), 529.
44. *The Letters of Daniel Defoe*, ed. George Harris Healey (Oxford: Clarendon Press, 1955), 38; cited in Novak, *Daniel Defoe*, 234.
45. Ibid., 563.
46. Daniel Defoe, *The Fortunate Mistress: Or, A History of the Life and Vast Variety of Fortunes of Mademoiselle de Beleau, Afterwards Call'd The Countess de Wintselsheim, in Germany. Being the Person Known By the Name of the Lady Roxana, In the Time of King Charles II* (London: T. Warner, 1724). Page numbers in parentheses refer to Daniel Defoe, *Roxana: The Fortunate Mistress*, ed. Jane Jack (Oxford: Oxford University Press, 1964).
47. See David Blewett, *Defoe's Art of Fiction: Robinson Crusoe, Moll Flanders, Colonel Jack, and Roxana* (Toronto: University of Toronto Press, 1979), 121–27, and his "Introduction" to Daniel Defoe, *Roxana: The Fortunate Mistress* (Harmondsworth, UK: Penguin, 1982), 13–14.
48. William Warner suggests that the novel continues the serialization of fiction begun by the female novelists discussed, dividing the novel into five discrete episodes. See Warner, *Licensing Entertainment*, 153. This aspect also matches the epistolary structure of *The Turkish Spy*.
49. See Warner, *Licensing Entertainment*, 164.
50. See *Roxana*, ed. David Blewett, 395 n. 191.
51. One reading suggests that Roxana's later relationship with an older nobleman is on the basis of granting him anal intercourse, which was often seen as an Italian or Turkish predilection. See *Roxana*, 228; Maximillian E. Novak, "The Unmentionable and Ineffable in Defoe's Fiction," *Studies in the Literary Imagination* 15 (1982): 85–102; and *Daniel Defoe*, 622 and 622 n. 54.
52. For the influence of Mary Carleton's biography on Defoe's fictions, see Mary Jo Kietzman, "Defoe Masters the Serial Subject," *ELH* 66 (1999): 677–705.
53. I thank Robert Markley for making this suggestion.
54. See Srinivas Aravamudan, "In the Wake of the Novel: The Oriental Tale as National Allegory," *Novel: A Forum on Fiction* 33 (Fall 1999): 5–31.

FURTHER READING

Aravamudan, Srinivas. "In the Wake of the Novel: The Oriental Tale as National Allegory." *Novel: A Forum on Fiction* 33 (1999): 5–31.

Cohen, Margaret, and Carolyn Dever, eds. *The Literary Channel: The Inter-National Invention of the Novel*. Princeton, NJ: Princeton University Press, 2002.

Doody, Margaret Anne. *The True Story of the Novel*. New Brunswick, NJ: Rutgers University Press, 1997.

Maslen, R. W. *Elizabethan Fictions: Espionage, Counter-Espionage and the Duplicity of Fiction in Early Elizabethan Prose Narratives*. Oxford: Clarendon Press, 1997.

Richetti, John J. *Popular Fiction Before Richardson: Narrative Patterns 1700–1739*. 1969. Repr. Oxford: Clarendon Press, 1992.

Warner, William B. *Licensing Entertainment: The Elevation of Novel Reading in Britain, 1684–1750*. Berkeley and Los Angeles: University of California Press, 1998.

3

Narrative Transmigrations: The Oriental Tale and the Novel in Eighteenth-Century Britain

Ros Ballaster

In 1908, Martha Pike Conant commented that: "Historians of English fiction have insufficiently recognized the fact that the oriental tale was one of the forms of literature that gave to the reading public in Augustan England the element of plot which, to a certain extent, supplemented that of character."[1] Subsequent histories remained, despite Conant's intervention, wedded to the exploration of the "English-ness" of the novel in Britain. While the influence of a small number of French and Spanish fictions (Marivaux's *La Vie de Marianne* {1731–42}, Cervantes's *Don Quixote* {1605}) is acknowledged, the novel continues to be cast as an expression of national identity, especially the increasing dominance of empirical philosophy and mercantile values within the national culture. Ethnocentric accounts of the rise of the novel in England have seen it as a product of indigenous traditions (in news reporting, ballads, history writing) or at best an imitation of other European traditions (the Spanish/Italian *novella* or the French romances and *nouvelles*).[2] An honorable exception is found in the work of Margaret Anne Doody who argues for the importance of Greek and Roman classical fictions in shaping the modern novel in her *True Story of the Novel* (1998); she complains that "A certain chauvinism leads English-speaking critics to treat the Novel as if it were somehow essentially English, and as if the English were pioneers of novel-writing."[3] Although William B. Warner accurately diagnoses the history of the eighteenth-century novel as an ongoing struggle between the absorptive pleasures of reading and the mission to ensure that it would provide a vehicle for the transmission of virtue, he nowhere considers the importance of the narrative frame of the *Arabian Nights Entertainments* (1704–17) as a model in this struggle.[4]

In returning to a consideration of the contribution of "oriental" or "pseudo-oriental" sources to the development of the novel in Britain, we can also move beyond Conant's simple understanding of these texts as a rich source of plot, to a broader consideration of the way fiction came to be conceptualized in the period: as a kind of fabricated import, a hybrid construction similar to other commodities in demand and imported from the Orient in the period, such as Indian muslin or Chinese porcelain. This is not to abandon the argument about the "national" character of the novel in Britain, but rather to recognize that it could be taken as a measure of the strength and adaptability of an emergent "Britishness" that it could speak from and of the place of the "other." Moreover, the influence of oriental narrative derives from its staging of the reading process as a form of imaginative "transmigration" on a number of different levels. First, oriental fiction consists of "shifting shapes" on the level of narrative content: Arabic djinns, lives of the Buddha, animals that become human and vice versa in Indian fable. Second, narrators and addressees in oriental fiction learn to inhabit different identities: the two most influential oriental fictions of the early eighteenth century, the *Arabian Nights Entertainments* and the *Letters Writ by a Turkish Spy* (1687–94) are narrated by figures whose survival rests upon the continuing production of textual credit. Third, the European reader must engage in acts of transmigratory identification, projecting himself or herself into the place of the eastern interlocutor. And finally, on the level of metanarrative, oriental fiction is also a shape-shifter, undergoing powerful transform- ations when it migrates in diverse and numerous forms to a new continent in the eighteenth century, never wholly or entirely a fictional invention of the East by the West nor a colonizing or observing traveler maintaining its "native" dress.

This essay highlights changes in the relationship between the oriental tale and "English" fiction from the late seventeenth to the late eighteenth century. Far from being displaced by the modern "English" novel with the huge success of Samuel Richardson and Henry Fielding in the mid-century market, the oriental tale, I suggest, "transmigrates" to incorporate elements from conduct/domestic fiction and generate a hybrid form. By the 1760s, English fictions were not only adopting plots and structures from oriental tales, but also incorporating plots, structures, themes from the "English" novel into oriental tales, whether translations or imita- tions. Through the century, there is a discernible shift from the oriental tale mediated by French translations and understood to provide a critique of political absolutism and religious authoritarianism in the "foreign" spaces of Catholic France and the Islamic East, to a "native" oriental tale with more direct relevance to English and Protestant values. These latter narratives incorporate elements of conduct fiction into the oriental tale, and shift from the idea that the sequence of tales is addressed to a ruler or a prospective ruler to correct his tendency to despotism to the idea of an address to a bourgeois, particularly female, community encouraged to regulate and examine its own desires. Despotic and tyrannical modes of masculinity associated with the Orient are increasingly displaced by models of "reformed" masculinity and heroic femininity. These were the models of colonial identity that were to gain the most ideological credit for British rule in India through the eighteenth and nine- teenth centuries. The novel can thus serve the twin purpose of acting as a vehicle for the exploration of the nature of imperial/colonial and domestic rule.

What links the fortunes of the oriental tale's contribution to the novel in the first and second halves of the eighteenth century is its evident feminization of political agency. However, the understanding of the *nature* of that agency changes dramatically through the period so that the novel can continue to serve the "syncretic" function outlined by Michael McKeon, negotiating transformations of political and moral hierarchy in the wider culture.[5] In the early eighteenth century, the *Arabian Nights Entertainments* and the *Letters Writ by a Turkish Spy* could be received in Britain as critiques of the aristocratic and religious absolutism of French Catholic monarchy and Ottoman Islamic empire. In these narrative sequences, British readers encountered a *précieuse* femininity which tempered the excesses of despotism implicit in absolutist government. By the second half of the century, narratives are more likely to show how a domesticated and feminized spirit fostered within British Protestant contractual monarchy could temper and civilize distant "eastern" spaces or be mapped onto the private relations between "oriental" men and women.

This article charts this transformation/transmigration through consideration of a small number of key texts. In order to indicate the general outline of a relationship in Britain between imported oriental fiction (largely from France) and the indigenous novel, I have had to overlook much fiction in both genres. I do not consider here the role of Joseph Addison's popularization of oriental fable in his periodical writings nor the similarly philosophical and moral directions taken by Samuel Johnson's *Rasselas* (1759). I have not had space to look in detail at the large number of translations, pseudo-translations, and imitations translated into English from French in the wake of Antoine Galland's *Arabian Nights Entertainments* (especially the works of Thomas-Simon Gueullette and François Pétis de la Croix). I do not view William Beckford's French/English/oriental hybrid, *Vathek* (1786), as the zenith of the interaction of oriental and English genres, but rather as a late and eccentric example. My concern here is rather to map the shape(shift)ing influence of the oriental tale in the formation of the novel in Britain as a form of what William Warner has termed "licensed entertainment" with a particular moral and political agency, a power to foster identification and empathy between reading self and narrated/narrating "other."

Loquacious Women, Speculative Men: The *Arabian Nights Entertainments* and *The Turkish Spy*

We cannot overestimate the combined influence on the development of British fiction of the eight volumes of fictional letters purportedly by a Turkish spy living in seventeenth-century Paris, invented by the Italian francophile journalist, Paolo Marana, and the 12-volume "translation" by Antoine Galland of numerous tales drawn from a variety of Arabic sources, manuscript and oral. Although the former has now disappeared from modern print altogether and the latter was overtaken in the nineteenth and twentieth centuries by a more shocking translation (Sir Richard Burton's *The Book of the Thousand Nights and One Night* of 1885–8) and later a more accurate one (Husain Haddawy's 1990 translation of the fourteenth-century Arabic manuscript which was Galland's principal source), throughout the eighteenth century Marana's and Galland's texts went into multiple reprints[6] and generated countless imitations. These texts, one drawn from genuine Arabic sources and the other an act of occidental ventriloquism, made significant contributions to the development of English fiction despite their diffuse and compendious character. What I concentrate on here is their metafictional awareness of the power of narrative, even when delivered from a subaltern position, to engage, direct, and correct the imaginative sympathies of its consumer.

The context of the "Orient" and especially the Ottoman empire (no longer a territorial threat to the borders of western Europe after the defeat at Vienna in 1683, but still a physical reminder of the expanse and wealth of "oriental empire") was vital to this construction of verbal agency. The eighteenth-century ideological construction of oriental despotism, itself drawn from sources such as Galland and Marana, casts the state as organized around the blind and self-interested whim of a single man, apparently all-seeing and all-powerful but in fact an "absent center," a symbolic presence/phallus rather than a genuinely expansive authority.[7] Both Scheherazade and Mahmut address themselves, if always obliquely, to their sultan and master; both use narrative accounts to secure their own survival, but also seek to correct the blindness and willfulness of the despotic reader, promoting identificatory and analogical interpretation in their addressee.

Significantly, it is a moment of shocking epiphany of vision that prompts Schahriar's decision to execute each new wife the morning after he has enjoyed her. His brother Schahzenan, King of Tartary (who has retreated to Schahriar's court after discovering his own wife's infidelity) shows him his queen and her women consorting with a number of black slaves in his garden. Schahriar's reign of terror is halted with his marriage, at her request, to the clever vizier's daughter, Scheherazade. She arranges that her sister Dinarzade sleep at the foot of their bed and instructs Dinarzade to wake before dawn and request her to continue with a series of tales which are really devised to attract her husband's interest. Schahriar listens in and, finding himself curious to hear each tale's continuation/conclusion, defers his wife's execution for another day. Many of the tales Scheherazade tells to defer her fate are tales about the withholding of arbitrary and tyrannical punishment in exchange for further story-telling, so that narrative content parallels narrative frame. Scheherazade figures not only the enclosing and constraining power of despotism but also resistance to it. In so doing, she represents an axis of temporality (the narrative time of story-telling and deferral of its conclusion, the keeping of her head quite literally) which counters the axis of space and looking associated with the oriental male. Her agency is that of the tongue and of time, his of the eye and of the masterful control of space.

However, the stories Scheherazade tells are by no means feminist in their import. They are peopled by unchaste women, enchantresses who turn men into birds and animals and stones, sultans' wives who attempt to murder rivals. And women's unchastity is often demonstrated by their loquacity, their virtue by silence; the closed female mouth signifies the intact and defended female body. Galland's wholly invented conclusion points to a way of understanding Scheherazade's risky strategy of inscribing an ambivalence about female speech into her own:

The Sultan of the Indies could not but admire the prodigious memory of the sultaness his wife, who had entertained and diverted him so many nights, with such new and agreeable stories, that he believed her stock inexhaustible.

A thousand and one nights had passed away in these agreeable and innocent amusements; which contributed so much towards removing the sultan's fatal prejudice against all women, and sweetening the violence of his temper, that he conceived a great esteem for the sultaness Scheherazade; and was convinced of her merit and great wisdom, and remembered with what courage she exposed herself voluntarily to be his wife, knowing the fatal destiny of the many sultanesses before her.

These considerations, and the many rare qualities he knew her to be mistress of, induced him at last to forgive her. I see, lovely Scheherazade, said he, that you can never be at a loss for these sorts of stories to divert me; therefore I renounce in your favour the cruel law I had imposed on myself; and I will have you to be looked upon as the deliverer of the many damsels I had resolved to have sacrificed to my unjust resentment.[8]

Both the motive behind and the nature of Schahriar's decision are purposefully confused here, suggesting that perhaps the one lesson learned from his consumption of so many tales is the agency of ambivalent statement. When we are told that he has chosen to "forgive her" we must necessarily ask what crime it is that he forgives: the crime of all women, of unchastity, which has not in any case been proved against her, or the crime of speaking out in his presence, of daring to "teach" an absolute ruler and question the absoluteness of his decisions? Moreover, the reason for his reversal of intention (the decision to "forgive") is not clear. He nowhere suggests that the stories themselves have proved the possibility of female virtue. It is the fact that they amuse and divert him, rather than returning him to the obsessive jealousy which had preoccupied his thoughts before the sequence commenced, which has "contributed so much towards removing the sultan's fatal prejudice against all women." How can one woman telling many stories prove to the listener that all women are not unchaste? What they have proved is that their teller is clever, entertaining, and a fit, if not superior, intellectual companion.

Indeed, Scheherazade's greatest success as story-teller may be in her delivery of stories which have nothing to do with "proving" or "disproving" female virtue. Sinbad's voyages, for instance, like Robinson Crusoe's adventures, prove the resilience of the protagonist while his fortune magically accrues without much positive action on his part. "The Story of Cogia Hassan Alhabbal," in which the rope-maker loses a vast fortune given to him by the rich Saadi but succeeds in turning a vast profit from a simple bar of lead given by the poor Saad, demonstrates the same magical power of profit without intention. Scheherazade's stories similarly appear to succeed by their circulation alone; their producer need not husband or manage her resources particularly well, but rather simply keep them in circulation and her symbolic capital magically grows.

This may be why the *Nights* remained from their first appearance onward the touchstone and paradigm of the oriental tale, the sequence ever burgeoning and expanding, but always retaining its magical power as a sign of the East for its western readers. The *Nights*, like the woman who tells them, transform the world around them by repetitive acts of simple accretion. It is not what they tell that matters so much as the stubborn vitality of their matter itself, which continues to survive and grow, requiring only assent to their continuance rather than complex acts of interpretation or organization on the part of their auditor(s).

Galland's translation repeats in the frame the narrative trajectory of the stories, capturing and converting male violence and action associated with the gaze into a pleasurable subjection to narrative deferral associated with the ear. Schahriar is "captured" by Scheherazade's control of narrative and speech, and sublimates his scopophilia to the new auditory pleasures she offers. The transformation of male gazer and female speaker is mutual, each testing out and performing each other's positions within narrative itself. This might also be understood to be the pleasure of the oriental sequence for the occidental reader, a game of fictional metamorphosis where s/he can test out a series of "exotic" roles, male and female, safely distanced by being placed in a historically and geographically remote "East," in order to adjust her or his own mental horizons.

An equally strong tradition in eighteenth-century prose centered the oriental male as both character and narrator. To return to the gender dynamic of eighteenth-century representations of the Near and Middle East – the loquacity of female and feminized positions challenges the despotic gaze of the oriental male – it should be noted that the dominant genre in this tradition was that of the "observing" or "speculating" oriental male, who appears in the West as either spy or "curious" traveler. In other words, the same gendered economy underpins writings which ventriloquize the role of the male oriental speaker, who privileges the power of the look over that of the voice.

One of the most familiar "oriental" voices for readers in eighteenth-century prose was that of the male "reverse" or pseudo-traveler, a fictional correspondent who travels from East to West and writes of his experiences in the West. The *Letters Writ by a Turkish Spy* extended to 600 letters over eight volumes, describing from Paris events in Europe between 1637 and 1682. The first volume in an English translation of 1687 was compiled from four slim volumes published in Paris (and the last in Amsterdam) between 1684 and 1686 by a Genoese author named Giovanni Paolo Marana (1642–93) in French under the title *L'espion turc*. The second English volume appeared with the first in 1691 and was claimed to be translated from an Italian edition of the work brought to England by a Mr. Saltmarsh; the same edition was claimed to be the basis for the remaining six volumes. This English translation was the source of the first French version of the last seven volumes, which appeared to have been published in Cologne in 1696 though it was printed in London.

The fictional narrator of all the *Letters* is an Arabian named Mahmut, raised in Sunni Islam, who spent four years held captive by Christians in Sicily, where he learned Greek and Latin and acquired a taste for ancient history, before arriving in the seraglio at Constantinople. From there he is sent by Sultan Amurath (Murat IV) as a spy to report on western European affairs from Paris, where he passes himself off as "Titus the Moldavian," expert in oriental languages. The experience is not a happy one, and the authority of the spy's "gaze" is consistently undermined by his terror of discovery; from being the one who looks, he may become the one who is looked at and exposed. He repeatedly requests that he be allowed to return to the "Porte" or to his native "Arabia" to take up a contemplative life, a different kind of "speculation" from the one in which he is employed. Mahmut is an advocate of Cartesian rationalism, as well as a member of an Islamic sect with a belief in transubstantiation, and he is a great "speculator" on the larger mysteries of life, revealing a sense of confinement because his remit from his employers is limited to peering into the secrets of political cabinets. When Mahmut is recognized by his old Sicilian master at Notre Dame, he realizes he has been too sanguine about his anonymity, his "unseen-ness":

> One would think it an easie Matter, for a Stranger to conceal himself in so vast and Populous a City as is *Paris*. Especially, one who makes so mean and contemptible a Figure, as does the supposed *Titus of Moldavia*. I little thought, that the *Lowness* of my *Stature*, and the *Deformity* of my *Body*, would have attracted any Curious Eyes, but, that my very *Habit*, would have prevented me from all Suspicion, and, that I might have pass'd an Age undiscovered, amongst the Infinite Crowds of People, who throng both the Houses and Streets of *Paris*.[9]

Mahmut's survival is dependent on his narrative "credit" with his masters in Constantinople and his ability to conceal his secret purpose in Paris. Indeed, Mahmut reveals a powerful identification with western and eastern women, especially those who use disguise and cross-dressing. He returns often to the cross-dressing figure of Queen Christina of Sweden, whom he admires for her learning; he compares her with Semiramis, Queen of Assyria, who dressed as her son in order to rule during his infancy. He tells the story of Joan of Arc to the Aga of the Janissaries as an example of a national heroine. Mahmut suggests a parallel between these women, who adopt male disguise in order to serve their nation and maintain its status and authority, and his own "passing" activity of living as a Christian in Paris in order to gain information for the Porte. He also equates his situation with that of veiled women in the East, confiding to his brother Pesteli Hali, "Thou art he, to whom I can unmask. With others I converse (like our Women in *Turkey*) under a Veil."[10]

In the concluding letters of the eighth volume the analogy between the spy at the French court and the female or feminized/eunuch inhabitant of the seraglio at Constantinople becomes even more explicit. Mahmut receives dispatches from a fellow spy at Vienna named Nathan Ben Saddi, not written in his familiar hand or style, and suspects that there is a plot against him in Constantinople. A messenger he sends to Vienna returns with news that Nathan disappeared eight weeks previously and that a dead body of a man found in the Danube has been so facially disfigured that he cannot be recognized. The evidence of neither the verbal or visual text can be trusted and Mahmut falls into a state of panic. His final letter is to his close friend Dgnet Oglou asking him to act as a spy at the Ottoman court on Mahmut's behalf: "I have not One Friend in the *Serrail*, whom I dare trust with such a Secret: Thou art my only Refuge at a Juncture which requires Fidelity, Prudence, and a dexterous Conduct in diving and searching into a certain Mystery, which, for ought I know, may concern my Life."[11] By the conclusion of the letters, Mahmut has turned the tables and appointed his own spy, but it is an act of paranoia and fear, rather than one of authority and expansionism. The despotic authority of the oriental male embodied in the gaze is revealed to be itself a disguise or fiction propped up by a chain of verbal and narrative dissemination and dissimulation. If Marana's text aspires to the status of existential parable, it does so through suggesting that the fiction of authority is simultaneously maintained and undermined by a web of language, the circulation of stories that give or withhold "credit" to those that speak them and those they "represent". This narrative agency is always imperiled, always vulnerable, but always necessary to survival.

Oriental Traces: *Robinson Crusoe* (1719) and *Pamela* (1741–2)

The stout Protestant heroism of Defoe's *Robinson Crusoe* and Samuel Richardson's *Pamela* may seem unlikely places to look to demonstrate the importance of oriental fiction to the development of the novel in Britain. However, the use of narrative as survival strategy, the notion of the "otherness" to be found within the self, especially in the act of consuming story, and the casting of epistolarity as an unstable and volatile alienation of the self, can all be traced to the influence of the oriental tale.

Oriental sources have been identified in *The Life and Strange Surprizing Adventures of Robinson Crusoe* before now: in 1671, the first professor of Arabic at Oxford, Edward Pococke, supervised a translation by his son of ibn Tufayl's story about the life of Hayy ibn Yaqzan; the narrative concerns a shipwrecked child who grows to spiritual and philosophical maturity on a desert island, and seems to have appealed because it confirmed the premises of John Locke's philosophy.[12] It probably provided one of many sources for Defoe's allegorical novel, including the mercantile and naval providential successes of Sinbad in the *Arabian Nights Entertainments*. But there was a more direct engagement with the *Turkish Spy* on the part of Crusoe's author. Defoe had published only a year previously to this novel *A Continuation of Letters Written by a Turkish Spy at Paris* (1718), which took Mahmut's correspondence up to the year 1693 and expressed the spy's sympathies with French Huguenots and dissent in general.[13] Defoe's experience in establishing a network of spies across Britain for the Tory minister, Robert Harley, may also have led him to a more than passing interest in the fictional spy, Mahmut. While he chose not to imitate the epistolary form in his novel *Robinson Crusoe*, Defoe's presentation of a subjectivity in crisis, thrown into intense isolation in a "new" world where he has to learn to negotiate new dangers, as well as the extraordinary length of his hero's exile, suggest a connection with the *Turkish Spy.*

By contrast, *Pamela*'s overt debt to the *Turkish Spy* in terms of the heroine's struggle to keep her correspondence secret, its interception, manipulation, and incendiary effects, conceal a perhaps more significant debt to the figure of Scheherazade and the *Arabian Nights Entertainments.* Pamela's text, which Mr. B. forces her to deliver into his hands, proves the means to reform her master from rapacious libertine to domestic head of household.

Toward the close of the novel, when Pamela has returned voluntarily to her repentant lover and he has proposed honorable marriage to her, the two exchange confidences as they take a turn in Mr. B's chariot. Pamela shows him a letter she received during the period of her imprisonment with Mrs. Jervis, warning her that Mr. B. planned to offer her marriage and engage a false parson for the purpose. Mr. B. looks at the letter and recognizes the handwriting of his Bedfordshire steward, Mr. Longman. Pamela confesses:

> I will tell you all the Truth. And then I recounted to him the whole Affair of the Gypsey, and how the letter was put among the loose Grass, &c. And he said, The Man who thinks a thousand Dragons sufficient to watch a Woman, when her Inclination takes a contrary Bent, will find all too little; and she will engage the Stones in the Street, or the Grass in the Field, to act for her, and help on her Correspondence. If the Mind, said he, be not engag'd, I see there is hardly any Confinement sufficient for the Body. You have told me a very pretty Story; and, as you never gave me any reason to question your Veracity, even in your severest Trials, I make no doubt of the Truth of what you have now mentioned. And I will in my turn give you such a Proof of mine, that you shall find it carry Conviction with it.[14]

Mr. B. goes on to confess that he had fostered such a plan but then abandoned it out of respect for Pamela's virtue. Mr. B.'s choice of fable to illustrate women's cunning associates him with the oriental despot even as his choice to live honorably in marriage with Pamela contrasts with oriental concubinage. After he has uncovered his wife's perfidy, Schahriar and his equally cuckolded brother leave the kingdom, only to encounter a lovely woman enslaved to a vast genie who forces them, by threatening to reveal their presence to her sleeping master, to have sex with her. The two conclude that all men face a similar fate at the hands of lustful women and their experiences have not been exceptional. Mr. B. marks both his proximity to and his distance from Schahriar by concluding that if women will always find a means to evade confinement, it is better to give them their liberty and intellectual freedom. His comment that Pamela has told him a "pretty story" suggests that he, like Schahriar, has fallen under the enchantment of a woman's narrative skill, although he frames his "reformation," like Schahriar again, as the discovery of a woman's sexual purity.

Reforming Gender/Genre:
Domesticating the Oriental Tale, 1760–1785

Robinson Crusoe and *Pamela* reveal traces of the oriental tale, but it continued through the eighteenth century to be a vital and popular form in its own right. I turn here to consider some lesser-known oriental tales, written or translated with great freedom by British writers, which illustrate the harnessing of oriental political allegory to the emergent domestic, colonial, and mercantile ideologies of the period. These oriental fictions respond to the popularity of the domestic fiction exemplified in *Pamela*, creating a hybrid syncretic form which speaks both to debates about the nature of emergent British empire and domestic virtue. They demonstrate that the novel, far from becoming an increasingly parochial exploration of domestic concerns, of private relationships and the inward self, understood those concerns as precisely the ideological ground on which the success of the move "outward," and especially to the East, would be premised. The transmigration of genre is effected through the transformation of the traditional gender conflict of oriental fiction: despotic and tyrannical modes of masculinity associated with the Orient are displaced by models of "reformed" masculinity and heroic femininity.

Nourjahad (1765) and *Charoba* (1785)

Two short fictions by Frances Sheridan and Clara Reeve illustrate the transmigration of oriental fiction into the domestic novel or novella. While Frances Sheridan's *The History of Nourjahad* (1765) depicts the reforming magic worked by homosocial love and heterosocial community on despotic masculinity, Clara Reeve's *The History of Charoba, Queen of Egypt* (1785) celebrates a chaste and heroic femininity resistant to despotic foreign incursion. In both cases the weaving of fictions is associated with a feminine agency of resistance to and transformation of a masculine desire for gratification and dominance.

The History of Nourjahad introduces us to the newly crowned 22-year-old Sultan of Persia, Shemzeddin, who is troubled about whether his dearest friend, Nourjahad, has the necessary qualities to adopt the role of his closest advisor. Shemzeddin asks Nourjahad to confide his greatest wish and, when Nourjahad says he wants inexhaustible wealth and immortality, Shemzeddin is angered. That night, Nourjahad is visited by a golden-haired youth, his "guardian genius," who allows him to choose between this wish and being restored to the sultan's favor. Nourjahad selects the wish and is given access to a room full of treasure, which he secretes in a cave in his own home. He proceeds to indulge a life of pleasure, immersing himself in "a tide of luxurious enjoyments" which make him "lazy and effeminate."[15] He falls passionately in love with one of his wives, Mandana, and secures the loyal services of one Hasem to act as his steward. However, Nourjahad falls prey to the punishment threatened by his "genius" (genie), that he will experience bouts of sleep lasting long periods if he succumbs to evil. After a banquet in which he has assumed "the pomp of an Eastern monarch"[16] and drunk to excess, he sleeps for four years and twenty days, waking to be told that Mandana is dead and has left a young son fathered by him. His attempts to console himself through dissipation result in a mock-ceremony where he presents himself as Mahomet and his favored mistress as Cadiga (Mahomet's favorite wife). Again he falls asleep, this time for forty years and eleven months. He wakes to find his seraglio full of aged hags and his son fled after trying to obtain his father's wealth. Now he "grew peevish, morose, tyrannical; cruelty took possession of his breast; he abused his women and beat his slaves, and seemed to enjoy no satisfaction but that of tormenting others."[17] When Cadiga chastises him, he stabs her in the side. Once again he falls into a sleep, this time of twenty years' length, and wakes to find his only attendant is Cozro, brother to Cadiga, who has been charged by the latter with watching over him. Cozro's advice leads to Nourjahad's repentance and he now decides to use his wealth benevolently, but thereby breaks a prohibition passed by Shemzeddin's newly ascended son, Shemerzad, against the pursuit of business in the city for twenty days to observe the passing of the sultan. Cozro, who has been acting as Nourjahad's emissary, is imprisoned with him and executed. Nourjahad is called before the sultan, where he willingly embraces his punishment of death. The execution is averted, however, by the disclosure that he has been the victim of a trick orchestrated by Shemzeddin. It has been only fourteen months since the visit from his genie. The latter is revealed to be Mandana in disguise, a Persian lady who had fallen in love with Nourjahad unbeknown to him and sought Shemzeddin's assistance in winning him. Cadiga is not in reality dead, and Shemzeddin had adopted the role of Cozro to bring him to virtue. Shemzeddin concludes with the moral:

> Let this dream of existence then be a lesson to thee for the future, never to suppose that riches can ensure happiness, that the gratification of our passions can satisfy the human heart; or that the immortal part of our nature, will suffer us to taste unmixed felicity, in a world which was never meant for our final place of abode.

Nourjahad is given Mandana as a wife and becomes the sultan's first minister, a role he conducts virtuously so "that his name was famous throughout the Eastern world."[18]

Sheridan proves herself an adept parodist of genre. Just as in her better-known *Memoirs of Miss Sidney Bidulph* (1761) she had converted the Richardsonian romance of *Pamela* into a darker form of domestic realism, here she turns the eastern tale into a conduct fiction. Rational virtue replaces superstition, magic, and Faustian ambition, largely through the agency of female and feminized characters: Mandana, Cadiga, Shemzeddin/Cozro. The heart of the story is a homosocial (if not explicitly homoerotic) relation between the two male friends, but it is Nourjahad who behaves as the tyrannous despot, and his friend, the sultan, who exercises the wiles of fiction to "correct" his craving for personal absolutism. Sheridan efficiently marries two traditions of fiction associated with female voice and the regulation of transgressive subjectivity: domestic fiction and the oriental tale. From this hybrid form emerges a parable about the formation of modern Enlightenment subjectivity, self-regulating, subservient only to moral rather than arbitrary authority, and, as Nancy Armstrong has persuasively argued, characterized as female.[19] Mandana – cross-dressed beautiful boy, eastern genie, chief mistress of the seraglio, but also virtuous wife – represents this hybridity most powerfully in the novel. Here too, then, the oriental tale is captured by an Anglicized version of revolution as domestic reform led by virtuous mothers, wives, and feminized companionship.

Hybridity of genre and the translation of the Orient into an allegory of English culture is at the heart of Clara Reeve's eastern tale also. *The History of Charoba, Queen of Ægypt* is an allegory of a battle between narrative genres discussed explicitly in the critical work to which it was appended, *The Progress of Romance* (1785). In the latter, a woman reader, Euphrasia, on the request of her fellow romance-lover Sophronia, offers a defense of the romance to a male critic, Hortensius, who considers the "Genus" to be "a kind of writing . . . generally exploded."[20] Reeve exploits the etymological connections between the terms "Genus," "Genre," "Genius," and "Genie" in the two texts. The metaphor of building also links *The Progress of Romance* and *Charoba*. The Egyptian Queen Charoba prevents her suitor, the foreign giant Gebirus the Metaphequian, from forcing her into marriage by persuading him to use the stones he has brought to dam up the Nile to build a palace in her honor on its banks; nightly, Penelope-like, sea spirits or genii dismantle the work he has completed during the day. In the critical text, Hortensius describes Euphrasia as "laying a deep foundation" but he is puzzled as to "what kind of building you will raise upon it," to which she responds that she "propose[s] to trace Romance to its Origin, to follow its progress through the different periods to its declension, to shew how the modern Novel sprung up out of its ruins."[21] Significantly, the eastern tale is early identified as central to the tradition and proof that the romance is as exalted as epic works: Euphrasia directs Hortensius to read the story of Sinbad the Sailor in the *Arabian Nights Entertainment* and note the similarities with Homer's *Odyssey*.[22]

The battle in both critical and narrative text is won, however, not through the force traditionally deployed in epic, but through stratagem, specifically the kind of dilatory verbal agency associated with the romance and with Scheherazade. Reeve herself, like Scheherazade, appropriates an Arabic story and dilates it to serve her own instructional purposes. Charoba and her nurse, like Scheherazade and Dinarzade, are wily manipulators of reality: Charoba has been blessed by Abraham as a result of her generosity to him and Sarah with "subtilty to deceive her enemies," and she is described as "a young and blooming Virgin, handsome, ingenious, and of a generous spirit."[23] Charoba's father, Totis, is presented in the mold of the eastern tyrant, "more feared than beloved in his own Country, for he did many unjust and cruel actions," and it is implied that Charoba may have conspired in his death for the sake of her people.[24]

On her accession, Gebirus plans to marry Charoba in order to gain possession of Egypt. He arrives with 5,000 Gadites carrying huge stones on their heads and threatens to dam the Nile. Charoba's nurse persuades him to build a great city as proof of his love and to assuage the suspicions of the Egyptian nobility. However, sea-spirits in Charoba's service are nightly dismantling the city, and it is only when he enlists the assistance of a sea-nymph in love with one of his shepherds that he acquires the magic lore to prevent them. Throughout the story, epic and tyrannical force in the giant shape of Gebirus, and associated with the earth, stone, and material objects, is proved powerless without the romancing assistance of women, associated with the watery elements.

When Gebirus has completed his city, built on the ruins of an ancient one begun by his own ancestor, Sedad, Charoba is forced to take more drastic action, having "meant only to weary out the King, and to reduce him to an impossibility."[25] The nurse instructs him to send his forces to Charoba in three parts, and as each arrives they are duly poisoned. When Gebirus arrives he is poisoned by a regal garment thrown over his shoulders, having been weakened by fumes blown into his face and water sprinkled over him by the nurse. On his deathbed he asks Charoba to engrave his dying words on a pillar of the palace he has built. A long account of his wondrous actions is concluded with the comment, "I have been circumvented by the wiles of a woman; weak, impotent and deceitful; who hath deprived me of my strength and understanding; and finally hath taken away my life," and a warning, "beware of the craft and subtilty of a woman." Appropriately enough, Charoba does not allow him the last word, enclosing his statement with her own, which reads: "This is the fate of such men as would compel Queens to marry them, and kingdoms to receive them for their Kings."[26] If romance overcomes epic and women's words overcome and redirect male speech, it is also the case that Charoba's language is that of dynastic conflict, lineage, and monarchical authority (more often associated with the epic) and Gebirus's are the complaint of the victim of women's romancing activities. Reeve thus relocates epic heroism as female agency, incorporating epic into romance as a hybrid rather than simply replacing one with the other.

Reeve's tale is one of virgin heroism (rather than the wifely or homosocial instruction found in Sheridan) used as a means of defeating masculine tyranny/absolutism. However, in both cases, fictions are woven in order to overcome egotistic desire and material ambition, and those fictions are understood to be the special artillery of women. Central to the agency of fiction in the stories is the communal activity of feminine or feminized protagonists; Scheherazade requires her sister Dinarzade to act as cover in addressing Schahriar with her tales. Charoba conspires with her nurse; Shemzeddin enlists the help of Mandana, Cadiga, and his vizier. Sheridan and Reeve offer visions of ameliorative reform in line with Enlightenment ideals of civil humanism, a new model of personhood which, according to J. G. A. Pocock, privileges "commerce, leisure, cultivation" over the older model of civic humanism with its stress on property, leisure, and politics.[27] The cultivation of the private man as significant in the maintenance of public political order newly foregrounds the responsibilities of women as educators of children in the home and as supportive wives, if it cannot conceive of them as political agents in their own right.

Hau Kiou Choaan (1761) and *Tales of the Genii* (1764)

Two oriental collections of the 1760s "translated" by men also indicate a turn to the presentation of a reformed masculinity and a heroic femininity in line with the "new" novel and the "new" trading and imperial ambitions of British Protestantism: Thomas Percy's *Hau Kiou Choaan* (1761) and James Ridley's *Tales of the Genii* (1764). These texts illustrate an attempt to incorporate the morality and sentimental appeal of Richardsonian domestic fiction into the traditionally more plot-driven and parabolic oriental tale.

Percy's four-volume work was the only genuine Chinese fiction to be translated into English in the eighteenth century and, like the *Arabian Nights Entertainments*, it was routed through another European language. Thomas Percy, an Anglican antiquary and later Bishop of Dromore in Ireland, received a manuscript partially translated into English in 1719 by one James Wilkinson, a British East India Company man based in Canton, who had undertaken the work as an exercise in learning Chinese under instruction from a Portuguese tutor; Percy had to learn Portuguese to translate the remaining sections which the tutor had completed in that language.[28] Percy may have thought the novel would appeal to English readers because of its similarity to popular novels of domestic courtship and embattled virginity, such as Samuel Richardson's *Pamela* and *Clarissa* (1747–8).

Delivered in the third person, the novel primarily concerns the fastidious but passionate love between a clever young son of an influential Peking mandarin, Tieh-chung-u, and the wise daughter of a disgraced military commander of Tsee-nan, Shuey-ping-sin. The latter is left unprotected when her father is exiled to Tartary and her devious uncle tries to marry her off to the son of a mandarin of the privy council, one Kwo-khé-tzu. Shuey-ping-sin repeatedly avoids the marriage despite leading officials of the city conspiring with Kwo-khé-tzu to trick her into compliance, so that she is praised as a miracle of cunning. When Tieh-chung-u and Shuey-ping-sin meet, the former saves her from abduction. He then falls victim to a plot led by Kwo-khé-tzu, aided by the corrupt Bonzes who provide housing for travelers, to poison him through his tea, which Shuey-ping-sin uncovers. She engineers his removal to her own house where he is nursed back to health. However, this brief cohabitation becomes the impediment to plans later in the novel for them to marry in that the fastidious lovers consider it may imply an illicit relation prior to marriage. Eventually, all is resolved; Shuey-ping-sin's father is restored to favor through the good offices of Tieh-chung-u, and the Emperor himself gives his blessing to their union, punishing the conspirators against them.

Like Galland's Scheherazade and Richardson's Clarissa, the heroine is the indulged daughter of a powerful man: "the darling of her father, who loved her with an affection, equal to that he would have had for a son of the same accomplishments, and gave her the entire management of his house: where she governed the family with... admirable skill."[29] However, Percy fears that her cleverness may be misunderstood

Plate 5. Frontispiece to Thomas Percy's *Hau Kiou Choaan, or, The Pleasing History* (1761).

by English readers as artifice and in this respect she runs the risk of appearing lacking in virtue by contrast with the eighteenth-century English ideal (a risk Richardson's *Pamela* also runs, of course). A footnote explains that:

> The Chinese, who are the most subtle crafty people in the world, may naturally be supposed to esteem and admire subtilty and craft. The reader must have observed that these qualities are predominant in the character of *Shuey-ping-sin*; who is yet set forth by the Chinese author, as a perfect exemplar of all virtue. The Chinese morals, notwithstanding their boasted purity, evidently fall short of the Christian, since they know not how to inspire that open and ingenuous simplicity, void of all guile, which more elevated principles of morality propose to our esteem and imitation.[30]

To be a "pleasing history," then, Percy's translation must carefully balance the familiar and the strange. He encourages his readers to identify with the position of the hero and heroine, especially the heroine, so that the novel becomes a Chinese variant on mid-eighteenth-century domestic fiction, but also uses footnotes to remind readers of a different set of cultural values.

His stress throughout is on the possibility of fiction mediating a more "true" account of a culture than eyewitness accounts. His preface criticizes collections of voyages and travels, universal histories and accounts of the present states of other countries, complaining that:

> *Those writers may give a dead resemblance, while they are careful to trace out every feature, but the life, the spirit, the expression will be apt to escape them. To gain a true notion of those we must see the object in action. There is not a greater difference between the man who is sitting for his portrait, stiffened into a studied composure, with every feature and limb under constraint; and the same person unreserved, acting in his common sphere of life, with every passion in play, and every part of him in motion: than there is between a people methodically described in a formal account, and painted out in the lively narrative of some domestic history. A foreigner will form a truer notion of the genius and spirit of the* English, *from one page of* Fielding, *and one or two writers now alive, than from whole volumes of* Present States of England, *or French Letters concerning the English Nation.*[31]

Not only does Percy's comment here remind us of the special power ascribed to fiction to produce in its readers hybridity and identification across cultures, but the metaphor he uses of the painting of a portrait, by contrast with that of a scene or narrative, returns us to that insistent slippage between China the country, and china the porcelain commodity so craved by consumers of oriental fiction and other products. Europe had little contact with Chinese high art, such as calligraphy and painting, in this period; however, the Chinese exported porcelain, lacquerware, furniture, and wallpaper, crafts of fairly low status, in abundance. After 1709, when Johan Gottfried Böttger discovered how porcelain was made, high-temperature kilns were built in European centers and vast amounts of blue and white porcelain in imitation of the Chinese were produced. Percy's achievement can be paralleled with that of the Delft producers of blue and white china; a simulacrum of Chineseness which retains a balance of strangeness and familiarity, exoticism and domestic morality.

Eighteenth-century accounts of China, such as Percy's, presented this part of the Orient as a secular and ancient territory which, despite its absolutism, could offer positive models of moral value. Fictions derived from India were more concerned to displace the legacy of Islam and imagine European Christian government as a convincing alternative. The sequence of tales by James Ridley, an Oxford-educated clergyman who did not in the end take up the chaplaincy with the East

Plate 6. Frontispiece to *The Tales of Genii: or, The Delightful Lessons of Horam, the Son of Asmar* by James Ridley (1764).

India Company he was offered, uses the transformation of the oriental tale into domestic fiction to illustrate the succession of Christian from Islamic empire in "Hindostan."

The tales in Ridley's collection are repeated by the Iranian Muslim "sage," Horam, to the English ambassador Sir Charles Morell, when Horam is forced to flee his employment as tutor to the Mughal emperor Aurangzeb's (1658–1707) vicious son, Osmir. Horam's tales were devised to bring Osmir to a sense of virtue, and he uses a relevant fictional frame in which two children of an imam, Patna and Coulor, are spirited by a female genie to a council of twenty-eight genii who are receiving reports from their fellows about how they have instructed mortals in the path of Islamic morality. The longest tale in the collection is "The Inchanters of Misnar the Sultan of India," the only tale of nine to take India as its location. The tale pits a virtuous young Sultan of India, the woman he loves (the Princess of Kashmir, Hemjunah), and the Sultan's wise counselor, also called Horam, against seven evil genii and Misnar's ambitious younger brother Ahumal. Hemjuna flees from her father's court to the arms of a rich young merchant called Bennaskar in order to escape the marriage her parents plan for her with a Prince of Georgia. Like that of Shuey-ping-sin, Hemjunah's tale is an oriental version of *Clarissa*; she is driven to trust a stranger when her mother's protection is not forthcoming and succumbs to the offer of a female slave to help her to "fly from [her] father's court"[32] to avoid an unwanted marriage. This slave proves to be a disguised enchantress, Ulin, in the service of Bennaskar, but this Clarissa is saved from rape by the presence of her guardian genius, Macoma. Misnar liberates his beloved with the help of Macoma and the two unite in their marriage their two kingdoms. Misnar and Hemjunah represent a new order of Muslim government in India, driven by their sympathies, protective of their people, and monogamous in their loves.

At the conclusion of the tales, the presiding genius Iracagem pronounces that "Our mansion totters on its mouldering base! The fleeting scene rolls far away, and all the visionary dream dissolves!"[33] The genie council is revealed to be an elaborate fiction for the promotion of virtue, an analogy with the text itself. The troubled distinction between disturbing illusion and prophetic dream, deceit or falsehood or fakery and the improving fiction, which characterizes every tale in the collection but especially the tale of Misnar, is resolved for Ridley by the transcendent and unifying vision of the global dominance of Christianity. A long passage in conclusion, written in the voice of a Christian narrator, presumably Ridley in the persona of Sir Charles Morell, triumphantly imagines Christ's body on the cross as the point where the ineffable and the divine become flesh, and humankind no longer requires the mediation "of departed souls or ministering spirits" to have contact with the divine:

> In friendly guise these sheets were written to lead thee unto virtue; and the proud, gaudy trappings of the *East*, with all its wide romantick monsters, have risen far above their usual sphere, to serve the cause of moral truth. But then perchance you'll ask, what shall that truth avail, now all the beauteous wildness is no more, which was the spring and mover of this pagan virtue? The *Genii* all are fled, who watched attendant the

virtuous mind, and crown'd it with success; and the reward ceasing, the incentive to noble actions ceases with it . . .

Behold the moral veil rent in twain, and from thick clouds of darkness, the sun of righteousness arise! Behold death nailed on the cross, and mercy springing from the grave! Redemption brought to man by an heavenly being, far superior to angels or ministering spirits; and the voice of God declared to us by his son, whom he hath appointed heir of all things; by whom also he made the worlds . . .

We then may make an happy exchange from pagan blindness to Christian verities, and look upon ourselves as creatures dignified with heaven's peculiar grace.[34]

Ridley here announces the death of the oriental tale as a vehicle for morality, ostensibly severing the analogical connection between Islam and Christianity as moral monotheisms. Islam is revealed to be itself a fiction by contrast with Christianity's truth. Like Misnar, readers must see through the deceit to reach the revelation of the "true" God, and not be tempted by worldly pleasures or retreat in fear from moral challenge.

The Dangers of Excess Consumption

Oriental fiction's influence upon the emergent novel in eighteenth-century Britain contributes to the construction of both producer and consumer of narrative fiction as either female or feminized. Scheherazade, after all, is ostensibly telling her tales to entertain her younger sister, with her intended addressee, the male ruler, concealed behind this front. The mutual activity of producer and consumer is that of imaginative projection into the place of an "other" or an "other" place. This kind of activity, however, runs risks. Such projection can result in an "excess" which declines into self-indulgent sensibility, enthusiasm, or commodity fetishism, tendencies that were explicitly associated with female consumers in the eighteenth century.[35]

The hybrid interchange between Orient and Occident, often imagined as a smooth "succession" of one empire by another in prose fictions, can also be viewed as a form of contamination and corruption from within. This is perhaps most evident in the increasing criticism of the English "nabob" in India, culminating in the impeachment trial prosecuted by Edmund Burke of the first British Governor-General, Warren Hastings, between 1788 and 1795. Burke characterized Hastings "as a Soubahdar, as a Bashaw of three tails."[36] The British ruler is seen as imitating the despotic tendencies of his Islamic predecessors in India. The nabob appropriates indigenous culture and can slide into a perilous imitation of its vices: luxury, venality, despotism.

The late eighteenth century saw a similar characterization of the experience of immersion in the world of the "novel." The reader of fiction can become addicted to or sated with the pleasures of fictionality itself, and fail to respond to its regulatory and moral intentions. The sentimental trajectory outward of the traveler encountering "others" can become an inward pursuit of sensuous pleasure through vicarious experience, as it does in Lawrence Sterne's famous *A Sentimental Journey through France and Italy* (1768). That the link between the encounter with the Orient and the encounter with the novel is not merely fanciful can be defended by a brief mention of the importance of Sterne's epistolary love-affair with the young wife of an East India Company official, Eliza Draper, in the history of the invention of the *Sentimental Journey*. Sterne casts Eliza as his "Bramine," a female sage/muse whose picture presided over his writing of the work after she returned to India just before its composition.[37]

Eliza marries in her (fictionalized) person the imaginative authority of the different figures common to the oriental tale: Scheherazade, the oriental tale-teller (she sends her journal entries to Yorick/Sterne but they are not reproduced in the manuscript *Continuation of the Bramine's Journal*); Mahmut, the oriental informant in Europe; the sage or brahmin who tells instructive tales of morality and virtue to correct the vices of the young and enthusiastic. And most importantly, she plays the role of Dinarzade, youthful recipient/conduit of narrative pleasure. Sterne casts the female consumer as the necessary ground of narrative production, but also the sign of its dissolution. Her capacity to project herself into the place of the "other," which makes possible the pleasures of the novel, also undermines narrative progress and completion, leading to the indulgence of fictional pleasure for its own sake rather than for its ostensibly moral end. It is this struggle – between reading for the pursuit of virtue and reading for more inchoate and disturbing pleasures of consumption, identification, and absorption – that continues to dominate the history of the novel through the eighteenth and nineteenth centuries. And it was a struggle that the political, moral, and exotic allegories of the popular oriental tale had made especially visible to producers and consumers of "English" fiction.

See also: chapter 1, Crusoe's *Farther Adventures*; chapter 2, Fiction/Translation/ Transnation; chapter 15, The Eighteenth-Century Novel and Print Culture.

Notes

1. Martha Pike Conant, *The Oriental Tale in England in the Eighteenth Century* (New York: Columbia University Press, 1908), 242.

2. For the former see Lennard Davis, *Factual Fictions: The Origins of the English Novel* (New York: Columbia University Press, 1983), and Robert Mayer, *History and the Early English Novel: Matters of Fact from Bacon to Defoe*, (Cambridge: Cambridge University Press, 1997). For the latter see Ros Ballaster, *Seductive Forms: Women's Amatory Fiction from 1684–1740* (Oxford: Clarendon Press, 1992).

3. Margaret Anne Doody, *The True Story of the Novel* (London: HarperCollins, 1997), 1–2.

4. William B. Warner, *Licensing Entertainment: The Elevation of Novel Reading in Britain, 1684–1750* (Berkeley and Los Angeles: University of California Press, 1998).

5. Michael McKeon, *The Origins of the English Novel, 1600–1740* (Baltimore, MD: Johns Hopkins University Press, 1987).

6. The *Arabian Nights Entertainments* went into nineteen editions by 1798 and the *Letters Writ by a Turkish Spy* went into fifteen editions by

1801 (the last edition of all eight volumes complete).

7. See Alain Grosrichard, *The Sultan's Court: European Fantasies of the East*, trans. Liz Heron (London: Verso, 1998).

8. *Arabian Nights Entertainments*, trans. Antoine Galland, ed. Robert L. Mack (Oxford: Oxford University Press, 1995), 892.

9. Giovanni Paolo Marana, *The Eight Volumes of Letters Writ by a Turkish Spy at Paris*, trans. William Bradshaw, 8th ed., vol. 2, book 3, letter 18 (London, 1707), 221.

10. Ibid., vol. 5, book 1, letter 7, 25.

11. Ibid., vol. 8, book 6, letter 18, 279.

12. See G. A. Russell, "The Impact of the *Philosophus Autodidactus*: Pocockes, John Locke, and the Society of Friends," in *The "Arabick" Interest of the Natural Philosophers in Seventeenth-Century England*. Brill's Studies in Intellectual History, ed. G. A. Russell, 47 (Leiden: Brill, 1994), 224–65.

13. P. N. Furbank and W. R. Owens list this work as "probably" by Defoe as it has a number of close parallels to his known writings. See their *A Critical Bibliography of Daniel Defoe* (London: Pickering and Chatto, 1998), 182–83.

14. Samuel Richardson, *Pamela, or, Virtue Rewarded*, ed. Thomas Keymer and Alice Wakely (Oxford: Oxford University Press, 2001), 268.

15. *Oriental Tales*, ed. Robert L. Mack (Oxford: Oxford University Press, 1992), 131.

16. Ibid., 136.

17. Ibid., 162.

18. Ibid., 194.

19. Nancy Armstrong asserts that "middle-class authority rested in large part upon the authority that novels attributed to women and in this way designated as specifically female." Nancy Armstrong, *Desire and Domestic Fiction: A Political History of the Novel* (New York: Oxford University Press, 1987), 4.

20. Clara Reeve, *The Progress of Romance: and the History of Charoba, Queen of Aegypt*. Facsimile Text Society Series 1: Literature and Language, vol. 4 (New York: Facsimile Text Society, 1930), 8.

21. Ibid., 8.

22. Ibid., 24–25.

23. *Oriental Tales*, 198, 196.

24. Ibid., 199.

25. Ibid., 207.

26. Ibid., 209–10.

27. J. G. A. Pocock, *Virtue, Commerce, and History: Essays on Political Thought and History, chiefly in the Eighteenth Century* (Cambridge: Cambridge University Press, 1985), 49.

28. The Portuguese trading base established on Macao from the 1550s meant that Portuguese was the first language to provide an orthography for transliterating Chinese texts and terms.

29. Thomas Percy, *Hau Kiou Choaan: or, the Pleasing History*, vol. 1 (London, 1761), 70–71.

30. Ibid., 129.

31. Ibid., xvi–vxii.

32. James Ridley, *Tales of the Genii* (1764; 3rd ed., London, 1766), 2: 39.

33. Ibid., 363.

34. Ibid., 365, 363–64.

35. For critical accounts of the "feminization" of these vices see Catherine Ingrassia, *Authorship, Commerce, and Gender in Early Eighteenth-Century England: A Culture of Paper Credit* (Cambridge: Cambridge University Press, 1998); Erin Skye Mackie, *Market à la Mode: Fashion, Commodity, and Gender in the Tatler and the Spectator* (Baltimore, MD: Johns Hopkins University Press, 1997), and John Mee, *Romanticism, Enthusiasm, and Regulation: Poetics and the Policing of Culture in the Romantic Period* (Oxford: Oxford University Press, 2003).

36. Edmund Burke, *India: The Launching of the Hastings Impeachment 1786–1788*, in *The Writings and Speeches of Edmund Burke*, ed. Peter J. Marshall, vol. 6 (Oxford: Clarendon Press, 1991), 267.

37. Laurence Sterne, *A Sentimental Journey through France and Italy and Continuation of the Bramine's Journal: The Text and Notes*, ed. Melvyn New and W. G. Day, vol. 6 of *The Florida Edition of the Works of Laurence Sterne*, ed. Melvyn New (Gainesville: University Press of Florida, 2002).

FURTHER READING

Conant, Martha Pike. *The Oriental Tale in England in the Eighteenth Century.* New York: Columbia University Press, 1908.

Grosrichard, Alain. *The Sultan's Court: European Fantasies of the East.* Translated by Liz Heron. London: Verso, 1998.

Said, Edward. *Orientalism.* London: Routledge and Kegan Paul, 1978.

4

Age of Peregrination: Travel Writing and the Eighteenth-Century Novel

Elizabeth Bohls

It is scarcely possible to discuss the eighteenth-century novel without speaking of travel. Its protagonists' journeys so often give impetus and form to their stories, from the "mobile adventuress"[1] who narrates Aphra Behn's *Oroonoko* (1688) at the beginning of the long eighteenth century to Ann Radcliffe's peripatetic heroines at its end. The travels of Robinson Crusoe, Moll Flanders, Joseph Andrews and Tom Jones, Tristram Shandy and Yorick, Roderick Random and Matt Bramble come to mind. Even Pamela and Clarissa, so much indoors, move or are removed at key junctures, like the abducted heroines of so many sentimental and gothic novels later in the period. And prominent novelists wrote travel narratives as well: Defoe's *Tour Round the Whole Island of Great Britain* (1724–6), Fielding's *Journal of a Voyage to Lisbon* (1754), Smollett's *Travels Through France and Italy* (1766), Beckford's Continental journals (1787–8), and Radcliffe's *Journey through Holland and Germany* (1795).[2] The affinities between these two prose genres, one enjoying sustained popularity during the century, the other expanding its readership while fighting disrepute, are extensive enough to have given rise to a magisterial study, Percy G. Adams's *Travel Literature and the Evolution of the Novel.*[3]

This essay obviously cannot cover a fraction of the material that Adams surveyed. Instead, I will visit (in the manner of a tour) examples of modes of intersection between travel writing and the novel. In 1797 the *Critical Review* pronounced, "This may be called the age of peregrination; for we have reason to believe, that the desire of seeing foreign countries never before so diffusively operated."[4] Travel, driven by diffusively operating desire – epistemological, political, social, sexual – permeated the print marketplace of eighteenth-century Britain. The novels I have chosen to examine intersect with travel writing through shared epistemological, rhetorical, and stylistic strategies and through a common concern with inter-cultural encounters. Perhaps most importantly, each of these works contributes to the eighteenth-century novel's extended and troubled exploration of the meaning of Englishness in an age of overseas imperial expansion and intra-British negotiation and consolidation.

Before turning to novels, however, I ought to mention the upsurge of scholarly interest in travel writing since the publication of Adams's landmark book. This shift is congruent with familiar developments in literary study in recent decades. "One of the positive results of the poststructuralist critique . . . has been that we no longer fetishize so-called creative writing as something essentially separate from and superior to writing of other kinds," as Dennis Porter puts it. Challenges to the traditional canon and hierarchy of genres have made more room for interest in what Porter dubs "ignoble genres," once considered marginal to literary criticism.[5] New Historicism and cultural studies call for interdisciplinary, theoretically sophisticated analyses, in which the texts of law, politics, history, popular culture, and travel – as well as cultural practices such as mapping, tourism, collecting, shopping, or masquerade – are read alongside and on the same terms as literary texts in an attempt to approach an earlier culture as much as possible on its own terms, rather than through "presentist" categories of value whose history itself demands critical scrutiny. The issues addressed by colonial discourse theory – relationships of culture and power, western construction of non-European others, the impact of colonization and empire on all those involved – are clearly relevant to the novel as well as to travel writing, and have been extensively analyzed in both by critics such as Peter Hulme, Mary Louise Pratt, Jonathan Lamb, and Nigel Leask.[6]

Questions of Genre, Questions of Truth: *Oroonoko*

That the eighteenth-century novel was a genre in flux, marked by limited self-consciousness and even more limited agreement about its defining features, is perhaps the extent of current critical consensus about it. Among the contending accounts of the novel's emergence, J. Paul Hunter's pragmatic, non-dogmatic approach seems most useful for thinking about the novel's relation to travel writing. His erudite reconstruction of the early novel's historical context draws extensively on the "materials of everyday print." Who read early novels, and what did these kinds of readers read before novels were to be had? Clearly, the answer to Hunter's question includes travel books, along with "journalism, didactic materials . . . private papers and histories." What needs and desires, addressed by these earlier and coexisting forms, did the novel serve? *Before Novels* includes a welcome emphasis on the novel's "imperialism – its ability to take over features from other species and assimilate them into a new form." Hunter's discussion of travel writing is brief. He points to title pages: "The first novelists openly tried to capitalize on the contemporary popularity of travel books by suggesting the similarity of their wares." He also emphasizes the relation in the early novel between setting, or place, and thematic, even philosophical concerns. "Few eighteenth-century novels stay in one place; even the ones . . . set wholly in

Britain emphasize cultural comparisons between different regions or social groups that minister to similar curiosities." Unlike the romance, old or new (which he declines to treat as its predecessor), "the novel is a product of serious cultural thinking about comparative societies and the multiple natures in human nature."[7]

Formally, Hunter points out, the "similarity between novels and travel books consists mostly in their both being loosely constructed, capable of almost infinite expansion, and susceptible to a great variety of directions and paces. But just as important are the formal differences. Travel books almost never have or need a sense of closure, for example. Journeys in most travel books just end, they do not culminate in much of anything, nor do they bring to fruition some theme or series of themes set up earlier in the book" – except, he concedes, for a few of the better ones.[8] Some scholars of travel writing might question the idea that travel accounts are less structured than novels. Their thematic structure is generally less obtrusive, even as their narrative structure is in a sense more standardized than that of the novel – bounded by departure and return. But the symbolic repertoire of travel narrative, and its ideological power, is broad indeed. Since I am centrally concerned with the novel, however, I will leave the reader to test this suggestion.

One point of intersection between travel writing and the early novel is epistemological: both types of narrative (for at least part of our period) needed to claim to be true, and both faced damaging accusations of lying.[9] Although truth claims can be considered a standard feature of the genre, it should be clear by now that travel writing does not provide a transparently empirical record of fact to contrast with the novel's literary fiction. Mary Baine Campbell remarks, "A text that generically proffers itself as 'true,' as a representation of unaltered 'reality,' makes a perfect test case for analytical work that tries to posit or explain the fundamental fictionality of all representation."[10] Travel writing's features as a mode of representation are a prominent concern of recent scholarship.

But the early novel, too, trafficked in truth claims. Here is Aphra Behn's opening to *Oroonoko*:

> I do not pretend, in giving you the History of this *Royal Slave*, to entertain my Reader with the Adventures of a Feign'd *Hero*, whose Life and Fortunes Fancy may manage at the Poets Pleasure; nor in relating the Truth, design to adorn it with any Accidents, but such as arriv'd in earnest to him: And it shall come simply into the World, recommended by its own proper Merits, and natural Intrigues; there being enough of Reality to support it, and to render it diverting, without the Addition of Invention.
>
> I was my self an Eye-Witness to a great part, of what you will find here set down; and what I could not be Witness of, I receiv'd from the Mouth of the chief Actor in this History, the *Hero* himself.[11]

The narrator's elaborate protestation asserts not only the factual authenticity of her story, but also her intention to tell it in a simple, unadorned style appropriate to its truthfulness. Her need to protest so much arises most obviously from her story's exotic subject and setting in Africa and Surinam – features shared with travel writing. Her dedicatory epistle to Lord Maitland foregrounds this context:

> This is a true story... The Royal Slave I had the Honor to know in my travels to the other World... If there be any thing that seems Romantick, I beseech your Lordship to consider, these Countries do, in all things, so far differ from ours, that they produce inconceivable Wonders; at least, they appear so to us, because New and Strange.[12]

Whether or not it is deemed a novel, *Oroonoko* is widely considered a generic hybrid, deploying elements of travel writing, romance, and novel, to the extent that it was possible to separate these in 1688.[13] Early twentieth-century criticism of *Oroonoko* swung from enthusiastic praise for its "sincerity" and "factual truth" – pronouncing it valuable because true – to Ernest Bernbaum's influential and damaging 1913 essay damning Behn as a liar and plagiarist (adding to the opprobrium of various kinds, mainly moral or sexual, that had hounded her reputation since the mid-eighteenth century).[14]

Michael McKeon, in *The Origins of the English Novel 1600–1740*, discusses Behn's strategy in the context of what he calls "questions of truth" in pre-novelistic narratives. He characterizes the later seventeenth century as a period of transition from a traditional mode of recounting an individual life as an illustration of an overarching pattern of transcendent truth to an innovative "historicity" calling for fuller detail. Travel writing and the imaginary voyage are among the genres that characterize this period, marked by the "instability of narrative structures."[15] Even experienced compilers of travels like the Churchill brothers, McKeon notes, were occasionally taken in by a tall tale, because style rather than substance emerged during this period as a criterion of truth: "if a narrative observes the proper conventions, it demonstrates its own veracity." An "effect of disingenuousness or duplicity" in a given narrative

> results at least in part from the uncertainty of authors and readers alike about just what is required to establish narrative truth. And this is a problem that is felt equally by writers who are "sincere" in seeking to tell a "true history" and by those who are not, since in both cases the question of truth is accessible (although most contemporaries would not have seen it this way) only in terms of the choice between competing conventions.[16]

Behn espouses a plain or "anti-rhetorical" style in the wake of the Royal Society's 1666 directives to travel writers to cultivate accurate observation and "a natural, easy and intelligible style."[17]

Her self-defensive opening, quoted above, and her dedication exemplify what McKeon calls "naïve empiricism" – an attitude, or epistemology, for which "strange, therefore true" counts as a valid mode of authentication. Naïve empiricism risks toppling into self-parody, a risk dramatized by Swift's famous parody of travel writing in *Gulliver's Travels* (1720). But Behn's "naïve empiricism," McKeon maintains, "betrays no parodic intent.... Behn audaciously and unapologetically idealizes her Surinam as a prelapsarian Eden ... the lovers, after a separation in the Old World, are reunited in the New with all the miraculousness of a romance discovery."[18] In other words, its apparently (to us now) bold-faced passing off of romance as reality marks *Oroonoko* as the product of a time when narrative conventions were in flux and it was thus difficult or impossible for readers to discriminate among what we would now identify as travel narrative, romance, and novel. Behn's book is all of these and none of them. In Oddvar Holmesland's words, "Her narrative reveals the fissures to which her conception of verisimilitude is vulnerable."[19]

Holmesland has recently re-evaluated the significance of travel narrative within *Oroonoko*'s generic hybridity. The "early novel's individualist quest for truth and origins," he suggests, "expressed in first-person accounts of far-off places, is partly the legacy of an old travel-narrative genre" exemplified by Thomas More's *Utopia* (1516) and Walter Raleigh's *Discovery of Guiana* (1596). The latter's discovery of "a community freer and truer to nature because isolated from European civilization" gets overtaken by "the motive of conquest, expressed in the lofty and elaborate language of chivalric romance." The seemingly progressive, proto-scientific mission of travel and discovery thus intersects, in *Oroonoko* as in Raleigh's earlier travel account, with the feudal hangover associated with romance: "The verisimilitude of *Oroonoko* is not premised on the rejection of romance convention in all its aspects."[20] The "Roman-tick" appeal of travel poses travel narrative as a complex intermediary between the categories of romance and realism, so often opposed in discussions of the early novel – with a Janus face, looking both backward and forward in time.

Identity and Imperialism: *Robinson Crusoe* and *The Female American*

More than questions of truth and genre, however, recent criticism of *Oroonoko* has focused on another issue also central to travel writing: European exploration and colonialism, and the representation of non-European people and cultures. The stand-ard locus for these issues in canonical accounts of the novel's "rise" was Defoe's *Robinson Crusoe*.[21] Ian Watt argues as follows for *Crusoe*'s centrality to the rise of the novel:

> The plot's reliance on travel does tend to allot *Robinson Crusoe* a somewhat peripheral position in the novel's line of development, since it removes the hero from his usual setting in a stable and cohesive pattern of social relations. But Crusoe is not a mere footloose adventurer, and his travels, like his freedom from social ties, are merely somewhat extreme cases of tendencies that are normal in modern society as a whole, since, by making the pursuit of gain a primary motive, economic individualism has much increased the mobility of the individual. More specifically, Robinson Crusoe's career is based, as modern scholarship has shown, on some of the innumerable volumes

which recounted the exploits of those voyagers who had done so much in the sixteenth century to assist the development of capitalism by providing the gold, slaves and tropical products on which trade expansion depended; and who had continued the process in the seventeenth century by developing the colonies and world markets on which the future progress of capitalism depended.

Defoe's plot, then, expresses some of the most important tendencies of the life of his time, and it is this which sets his hero apart from most of the travelers in literature. Robinson Crusoe is not, like Autolycus, a commercial traveler rooted in an extended but still familiar locality; nor is he, like Ulysses, an unwilling voyager trying to get back to his family and his native land: profit is Crusoe's only vocation, and the whole world is his territory.[22]

Watt's reading of Crusoe as the type of the modern capitalist individualist, *Homo economicus*, subsumes his relationship with Friday in the commoditizing egocentrism of his general outlook. "A functional silence, broken only by an occasional 'No, Friday,' or an abject 'Yes, Master,' is the golden music of Crusoe's *île joyeuse*."[23]

To sustain this emphasis on the rationality of Crusoe's motives, however, Watt must overlook a significant dimension of Defoe's novel. More recent criticism corrects his skewed interpretation by calling attention to Crusoe's irrational behavior, especially in relation to the famous footprint which first intimates that he is not alone. Michel de Certeau's description is closer to my own reading of *Robinson Crusoe*:

> The conquering bourgeois is transformed into a man "beside himself," made wild himself by this (wild) clue that reveals nothing. He is almost driven out of his mind. He dreams, and has nightmares. He loses his confidence in a world governed by the Great Clockmaker. His arguments abandon him. Driven out of the productive asceticism that took the place of meaning for him, he lives through diabolical day after day, obsessed by the cannibalistic desire to devour the unknown intruder or by the fear of being devoured himself.[24]

The fear and desire evoked by the prospect of contact with an as yet immaterial Other, de Certeau contends, derail every aspect of Crusoe's exemplary northern European mentality: confidence, logic, "productive asceticism."

Peter Hulme's discussion of *Crusoe*, centered around cannibalism, foregrounds the geographical specificity of the island's Caribbean location. Hulme contextualizes Crusoe's "ungrounded," "psychotic" fear of cannibals within "the existence of such a psychosis at the heart of European perceptions of Amerindian culture in the Caribbean," starting with Columbus. Crusoe's drawn-out, painstaking "composing" of a self during his time alone on the island before Friday's arrival, threatened by his successive discoveries of the footprint and the remains of the cannibal feast, culminates, according to Hulme, in a crucial moment when Crusoe "finally knows who he is."[25] After having discovered the gnawed remains, then "vomited with an uncommon violence," he walks away, "and then recovering my self, I looked up with the utmost affection of my soul, and with a flood of tears in my eyes, gave God thanks that had cast my first lot in a part of the world where I was distinguished from such dreadful creatures as these."[26] Constructing his identity through distinction from an abjected non-European Other, the fictional Crusoe, Hulme argues, reiterates a procedure performed by travel writers, fictionists, and anthropologists ever since the "discovery" of the New World and the concomitant definition of "cannibal" as a supposed eater of human flesh who was a native of the Antilles, or a Carib. "Through the connection made [by Columbus] between that people [the Caribs] and the practice of eating the flesh of their fellow-creatures, the name 'Cannibal' passed into Spanish (and thence to the other European languages) with that implication welded indissolubly to it."[27] Hulme's critical method, crossing genres and disciplines to analyze colonial discourse, exemplifies a powerful strain in recent scholarship on travel writing and the novel.

The astonishing popularity of Defoe's book secured a place in the history of the novel for transatlantic travel and encounters with Amerindians. Of his many imitators, at least twenty-six "Robinsonades" put a woman in the place of the hero.[28] One of these, *The Female American* (1767), is of particular interest for my account of the interrelations between travel writing and the novel. Drawing on travel accounts such as Thomas Hariot's *Brief and True Report of the New Found Land of Virginia* (1590), George Percy's "Discourse of Virginia" (1606), and John Smith's *Generall History of Virginia* (1624), the pseudonymous author of *The Female American* constructs a narrative of a woman of mixed race, Unca Eliza Winkfield, born in Virginia to an English father and a Pocahontas-like Indian mother. Unca Eliza is educated in England and subsequently shipwrecked on a deserted island visited, like Crusoe's, by local Indians. Instead of hiding when the Indians arrive, Unca Eliza audaciously takes it upon herself to convert them to Christianity, using for this purpose the massive idol to which they have come to pay homage. "This image, particularly the head of it, it seems, was so wonderfully constructed as to increase the sound of even a low voice to such a degree as to exceed that of the loudest speaker." Speaking from within the idol, she instructs the Indians to await the coming of a female teacher, who will bring holy writings and instruct their priests in "the knowledge of the true God, and the way to be happy for ever." Her knowledge of their language (which just happens to be that of her mother's tribe) first allows her to talk to them. As she develops her plan, she considers "that if I should hereafter judge it prudent to ... go and live among them, my tawny complexion would be some recommendation."[29]

Michelle Burnham, editor of the recent Broadview Press edition of *The Female American*, interprets this fiction of hybrid identity and intercultural negotiation as centrally concerned with "the fantasy of female power exercised within and by means of a Christian colonialist utopia." *The Female American*, she suggests,

> revises the narratives of capitalist accumulation, colonial conquest, and political imperialism that have been associated with Defoe's book. Winkfield's story engages instead in fantasies of a feminist utopianism and cross-racial community, both of which are enabled, however, by a specifically religious form of imperialism.[30]

Like the narrator of Behn's *Oroonoko*, Unca Eliza is an equivocal heroine, problematic for feminist critics. Although Burnham points out that her behavior complicates "the traditional dichotomy between male adventure and female domesticity,"[31] throughout her vicissitudes, Unca Eliza clings as closely as she can to the passive virtues of a Richardson heroine, deviating only when this docile paradigm threatens her survival. At the end of the novel her cousin, an Anglican clergyman, arrives on the island (he is in love with her and has been traveling in search of her). Though she has previously refused his proposal and shows little romantic interest in him, she agrees to marry him for the convenience of their missionary work — so her delicacy won't be hurt by having to spend time alone with him — in an arrangement similar to the one that Brontë's Jane Eyre rejects with her cousin St. John.[32]

Adrienne DuVall questions Burnham's emphasis on the transgressive and utopian elements of the novel, arguing instead:

> In reaffirming her identity as a proper woman according to British norms of behavior when possible, Unca Eliza chooses to identify herself along patriarchal lines, allying herself with her father and her father's (Western) culture. [Her] choice to conform to British ideals is problematic, because, as a biracial person and the daughter of a Native American princess, she has other cultural ideals to draw from. Her mother's culture provides an alternative femininity, one that allows Unca Eliza the option of claiming female autonomy without conforming to religious precepts or deferring to male authority figures.[33]

Indeed, when the island Indians invite her to be their queen, she declines: "I will come and live among you, and be only your instructor."[34] This decision, along with her later acceptance of her cousin's marriage proposal, echoes her mother's earlier choice to convert to Christianity in order to marry William Winkfield, whom she has saved from execution by taking him under her protection. The conversion of the princess (also named Unca) "necessitates," DuVall points out, "a new understanding of the power structure of her relationship with Winkfield," since Christian theology and ideology of the time understood women as naturally subordinate to men.[35] "The novel . . . moves between . . . different kinds of worlds and people: colony and 'wilderness,' pagans and Christians, Indians and Englishmen."[36] Both mother and daughter are presented by the novel's plot of transatlantic travel and cultural encounter with choices between autonomy and subordination, ruling and being ruled. Both choose imperial, patriarchal British culture — despite their subordinate place within it, and despite the resolve of Unca Eliza and her husband, at the novel's close, "never . . . to have any more to do with Europe."[37]

Internal Itineraries: *A Sentimental Journey*

If the eighteenth-century novel could represent far-flung exploration, adventure, and colonial rule, it could also ramble closer to home. The most institutionalized of trips

in this period was undoubtedly the Grand Tour of Europe. Its itinerary was standardized by the late seventeenth century, and its place in aristocratic British culture as the
finishing touch on a gentleman's education equally well established – if also subject to
debate. Richard Hurd's 1763 essay, "On the Uses of Foreign Travel," takes the form of
a dialogue between a fictional "Shaftesbury," advocating such travel, and "Locke,"
arguing that young gentlemen were better off staying home, at least until they were
mature and fully formed men. At that point, the philosopher argues, "to study
HUMAN NATURE to purpose, a traveler must enlarge his circuit beyond the bounds
of Europe. He must go, and catch her undressed, nay quite naked, in *North America*,
and at the Cape of *Good Hope*."[38]

Hurd's gendered division between the male traveler and the personified, feminine
object of his journey, "HUMAN NATURE," is echoed with a difference in Laurence
Sterne's *A Sentimental Journey* (1768). The protagonist, Yorick, is conversing in
Versailles with a French Count whom he has asked for help in getting a passport,
especially important since his journey takes place during the Seven Years War
between England and France. *"Heh bien! Monsieur l'Anglois!"* the count jokes. "You
are not come to spy the nakedness of the land – I believe you – *ni encore*, I dare say,
that of our women – But permit me to conjecture – if, *par hazard*, they fell in your
way – that the prospect would not affect you." Yorick protests the decency of his
intentions:

> Excuse me, Monsieur le Count, said I – as for the nakedness of your land, if I saw it,
> I should cast my eyes over it with tears in them – and for that of your women (blushing
> at the idea he had excited in me) I am so evangelical in this, and have such a fellow-
> feeling for whatever is *weak* about them, that I would cover it with a garment, if I knew
> how to throw it on – But I could wish, continued I, to spy the *nakedness* of their hearts,
> and through the different disguises of customs, climates, and religion, to find out what
> is good in them, to fashion my own by – and therefore am I come.
>
> It is for this reason, Monsieur le Compte, continued I, that I have not seen the Palais
> royal – nor the Luxembourg – nor the Façade of the Louvre – nor have attempted to
> swell the catalogues we have of pictures, statues, and churches – I conceive every fair
> being as a temple, and would rather enter in, and see the original drawings and loose
> sketches hung up in it, than the transfiguration of Raphael himself.
>
> The thirst of this, continued I, as impatient as that which inflames the breast of the
> connoisseur, has led me from my own home into France – and from France will lead me
> through Italy – 'tis a quiet journey of the heart in pursuit of NATURE, and those
> affections which rise out of her, which make us love each other – and the world, better
> than we do.[39]

Yorick's effusive protest becomes a manifesto for a new kind of travel, taking as its
object not the conventional sights and cultural monuments visited by the tourist or
connoisseur, but interpersonal encounters, the feelings they evoke, and the moral

development these catalyze. His itinerary, as is often remarked, is driven from within, rather than externally.

Sterne's book, now considered a novel, was received at its first publication as a travel account.[40] The ambitious and financially needy author had already taken advantage of the popularity of travel books in volume VII of his masterpiece, *Tristram Shandy* (1765), which takes the narrator on a comically eccentric, parodic tour of France.[41] According to Dennis Porter, *A Sentimental Journey* "was a highly influential work, which by the end of the century contributed to the breakdown, in the genre of literary travel accounts, of [the] balance between entertainment and enlightenment."[42] More to the point of my discussion, Sterne's little book brought travel writing closer to the novel, structured not by an externally imposed itinerary, but by the demands of the protagonist's moral and psychological development. After a piece of gratuitous rudeness to a begging monk, Yorick mounts a parody/tribute to the educational agenda of the traditional Grand Tour that could also be plot summary for a *Bildungsroman*: "I have only just set out upon my travels; and shall learn better manners as I get along."[43]

"Sterne's originality in this matter, however," notes Jean Viviès, "should not be too categorically defended." Other published travel writers of Sterne's day, such as Smollett (parodied as "Smelfungus," the "Splenetic Traveler," in *A Sentimental Journey*) similarly forgo describing sights they assume readers can find in guidebooks.[44] Sterne's contemporary, James Boswell – recording his Grand Tour not for publication, but in journal form – often foregrounds his internal temptations and struggles in a confessional vein reminiscent of Rousseau, whom he sought out in Geneva (and went on to seduce the philosopher's companion, Thérèse). Boswell's travel, like Yorick's, is driven by a curiosity whose worldliness encompasses the erotic as well as the moral, and whose egotistical focus is frequently his own psychology. "What a curious, inconsistent thing is the mind of man!" he muses in his London journal after catching himself planning for sex in the middle of a church service – "and yet I had the most sincere feelings of religion."[45] The women of the Continent, of course, were part of its charm for randy Grand Tourists from the start; this was part of what made the Tour controversial. As *A Sentimental Journey* recounts Yorick's serial flirtations with Frenchwomen, from shop-girls to aristocrats, alongside his moral education in true charity and benevolence, it literalizes and at the same time disavows this erotic agenda. Sterne ambiguously sublimates sexuality in the purported service of benevolence, while exploring the psychological connection between the two.

Transgression – crossing boundaries, literal and symbolic – has preoccupied some of the best recent scholars of travel writing.[46] Eighteenth-century travelers through Europe overwhelmingly registered the Alps as a "major geographical and symbolic boundary." *A Sentimental Journey through France and Italy* (planned as four volumes, but cut short at two by the author's death) never actually makes it, Chloe Chard points out, across the Alps. Never getting there, she contends, increases the "effect of suspense ... the reader is left to speculate indefinitely as to what might take place once the boundary is crossed." Volume II of *A Sentimental Journey* ends with a double "attempted traversal": two interrupted boundary crossings. His road blocked by a great stone rolled down from the mountains, Yorick makes an unscheduled stop at an inn, where he must share the only available bedroom with a Piedmontese lady and her maid. Sterne gives an "elaborate description of the spatial relation between the two beds, both mapping out the liminal space between them and emphasizing that their proximity must ineluctably raise the possibility of a transgression of this boundary."[47] The book ends, teasingly, in mid-sentence:

> – But the Fille de Chambre hearing there were words between us, and fearing that hostilities would ensue in course, had crept silently out of her closet, and it being totally dark, had stolen so close to our beds, that she had got herself into the narrow passage which separated them, and had advanc'd so far up as to be in a line between her mistress and me –
> So that when I stretch'd out my hand, I caught hold of the Fille de Chambre's

END OF VOL. II.[48]

Of course, should the reader imagine that anything "not the most delicate in nature" ensues, Yorick has already set him (or her) up to take the blame: "'tis the fault of his own imagination – against which this is not my first complaint."[49]

Chard's is the most persuasive and thought-provoking account I have seen of the structure of Sterne's travel novel. By reading *A Sentimental Journey* in the context of travel writing by Sterne's contemporaries, she does justice to both its genres.

> As a result of the structure of *mise-en-abyme*, according to which the narrative in the bedchamber echoes the narrative of crossing the Alps in which it is set, the danger, excitement, and unpredictability of this smaller liminal space are deflected back onto the larger liminal space of the Alps, within which the whole episode unfolds. The crossing of the geographical boundary, in other words, is elided with the crossing of other limits. . . . Through the elision between geographical and behavioral transgressiveness, Sterne ironically endorses the role of the Alps in travel writing, as the beginning of a domain where the limits established by behavioral and moral rules are more easily disregarded than within the familiar.

Southern Europe inspires in British travelers, from Boswell to Byron and beyond, an "adjustment of manners" in the direction of sexual permissiveness.[50]

Jane Austen's *Northanger Abbey* also ironically connects this standard imaginative geography of Europe with the relation between Gothic novels, so often set in southern Europe, and everyday English life as Austen's heroine Catherine Morland "innocently employs the trope of zeugma to bracket together the imaginative pleasures of landscape and the forbidden."[51] Disillusioned, Catherine resolves never again to confuse "the alarms of romance" with the "anxieties of common life." "Of the Alps and Pyrenees, *with their pine forests and their vices*," Ann Radcliffe's novels "might give a faithful delineation; and Italy, Switzerland, and the South of France, might be as fruitful in horrors as they were there represented. . . . Among the Alps and Pyrenees, perhaps, there were no mixed characters. There, such as were not as spotless as an angel, might have the dispositions of a fiend. But in England it was not so."[52] Radcliffe famously fantasized her characters' elaborately scenic journeys through a southern Europe that she never really got a chance to see. I will turn now to the significance of tourism in her last published novel, titled for its southern setting.[53]

Tourism, Taste, Nation: *The Italian*

Any serious interpretation of Gothic fiction needs to account for displacement. Starting with Walpole's *Castle of Otranto*, the eighteenth-century Gothic overwhelmingly prefers southern Europe as the setting for its narratives of "vice" and terror. The highly aestheticized imaginative world of Radcliffe's novels begins with a strategy of displacement. A semiotics of exoticism governs her choice of settings, from the Scottish highlands of *The Castles of Athlin and Dunbayne* (1789) to the Alps, Pyrenees, and Apennines in *The Mysteries of Udolpho* (1794) and the Bay of Naples, with Vesuvius in the background, in *A Sicilian Romance* (1790) and *The Italian* (1797).[54] Her French and Italian landscapes contain elements of both fairytale and eighteenth-century opera: Arcadian vistas, glowing in jewel-like tones from Radcliffe's luxurious treatment of color and light, with sparkling afternoons, sensuous sunsets, and endlessly hazy twilights.[55] Poetry, painting, and aesthetic theory, as well as travel writing, prepared these exotic yet strangely familiar zones for Radcliffe's educated readers. Her densely allusive presentation opens each chapter with an epigraph from Milton, Shakespeare, Thomson, Collins, or some other currently beloved poet. Her insistent pictorialism conjures with the names of painters – Claude Lorrain, Salvator Rosa, Poussin, Domenichino – well enough known to England's tasteful elite that their names evoked a visual style. The novels are usually set in a vague, relatively ahistorical past (for example, the "1584" of *Udolpho*), though, as we shall see, *The Italian* is an exception. All this elaborate stylization can conspire to give the reader the feeling of having entered a microcosm, a self-enclosed aesthetic universe remote, as one critic has put it, "from the commonplace world of the present," governed by "an alternative logic resembling that of dream."[56]

But we must also understand Radcliffe's displacement (and that of other Gothic novelists) as a ruse, a cover – conscious or not – for working through issues highly pertinent to 1790s England, but too volatile to be dealt with openly, especially in a decade of revolution and conservative reaction. A number of critics have recognized this, Claudia Johnson for example:

> National and religious difference . . . functions in *The Italian* much as historical difference did in *The Mysteries of Udolpho* – both to establish a safely removed context in which to represent civil disorder without coming too close to home and to give a shape to anxieties that are felt precisely because civil disorder already is close to home.

But Johnson goes on to complicate this assertion: "the unwonted specificity of Radcliffe's dating in the opening section indicates that distance could hardly have been her only design."[57] I want to consider this opening, in which English tourists in a church in Naples in 1764 are shocked to find out that a mysterious figure lurking on the portico is an assassin, given sanctuary by the unfamiliar laws and customs of Catholic Italy. He enters a confessional, which turns out to be at the center of the events of the novel (whose full title is *The Italian, or the Confessional of the Black Penitents*). The Italian friar who has guided their tour of the church offers them a manuscript relating the "extraordinary circumstances" surrounding a "horrible confession" made there a few years back, though not by the assassin they saw.[58]

Diego Saglia has recently complained that critics of the Gothic novel, though copiously analyzing its landscape descriptions, have neglected the significance of specific place. He reads *The Italian* "as an explicit example of how Gothic novelists conceive geographic place as a unity with the cultural and human landscape and develop specific ideological issues and dilemmas within such distant locales." Radcliffe's prologue, he points out, "plunges into the mysteries of present-day Italy and into the conventions of the Grand Tour with its peculiar modes of observation and evaluation." The visual – the traveler's gaze – is at the center of *The Italian*'s strategy of posing and then unsettling the "distinction between a viewing subject and a visually dominated object."[59] This starts in the prologue, when the English tourists look curiously at the assassin – and he looks back: he "had an eye, which, as it looked up from the cloke that muffled the lower part of his countenance, seemed expressive of uncommon ferocity."[60] The English gentleman is shocked out of his smugness and scared away.

The issues raised in the prologue, Saglia argues, are renegotiated throughout the novel. The prologue announces that Radcliffe's representation of Italy will use different modes of travel, juxtaposing, in particular, Grand Tourism with the quest structure of romance. She creates "an imaginative geography of Italy," a "realm of otherness" through which her characters travel. The heroine Ellena and her suitor Vivaldi take on the role of English tourists, characterized by their cultural competence in the aesthetic language of the picturesque, "the diction of sentimental travelers and the referential tone of travel guidebooks." The villain, Schedoni, inhabits the domain of difference, Italian and sublime.[61] Like the assassin in the church, he looks back at Vivaldi with "piercing" eyes,[62] manifesting "the alien nature of Italy and … the dangers that impend over the characters' individual and cultural identities."[63] The Inquisition, that quintessentially Roman Catholic institution, looks at Vivaldi through the "piercing eye" of an Inquisitor with a "black turban" and ferocious visage.[64] It wields vision, knowledge, and power, and thus

> extends and deepens the power of Schedoni's gaze to unsettle the self-assured cultural positioning of the English characters. In other words, it pursues the strategy of "cultural chastening" sketched in the prologue. … Vivaldi, like the curious tourist in the prologue, is a voyeur [who] by a quick turning of the cultural focus becomes an object of both vision and power.[65]

Eventually, with the hero rescued from the Inquisition, the mystery of the heroine's birth resolved, and the villain poisoned, the happy couple retire to a picturesque villa on Lake Celano, complete with English-style landscape garden. But although "the sublime and its agents have been apparently defeated or neutralized, the home as haven of familiarity still exists in an island of difference."[66]

Saglia incisively explains the way Radcliffe's displaced Gothic intersects with travel writing to function as a "technology of nationality." Imperialistically assimilating characteristic features and strategies of travel writing, the novel at the close of the eighteenth century continues to need travel formally, thematically, and at the level of language. It would take a broader survey than has been possible here to refute Watt's assertion, quoted above, that travel is peripheral to the novel's development. Among the "social relations" that the novel takes upon itself to represent, test, and stabilize, national identity is surely not the least significant.

Bogs and Prospects: Maria Edgeworth and Arthur Young

The British novel's preoccupation with national self-definition continued into the early nineteenth century, and travel writing continued to be a powerful model for novelists such as Maria Edgeworth, whose *Castle Rackrent* (1800) was the first of her novels set in Ireland (followed by *Ennui* in 1809, *The Absentee* in 1812 and *Ormond* in 1817). The extremely popular *Castle Rackrent* paved the way for the subsequent popularity of local or provincial fiction. "'Tales and Sketches' of the life of a particular locality became an important nineteenth-century form," and "much of the best modern fiction," as Marilyn Butler points out, is still "provincial fiction, located anywhere from Bengal to Montana."[67] Local fiction clearly has a great deal in common with travel writing: both take up the task of cultural translation, explaining the manners and customs of a region foreign to their readers.

In her concluding remarks to *Castle Rackrent*, in the persona of its "Editor," Edgeworth pays tribute to the travel writer Arthur Young, calling her story

> a specimen of manners and characters which are, perhaps, unknown to England. Indeed, the domestic habits of no nation in Europe were less known to the English than those of her sister country, till within these few years.
>
> Mr. Young's picture of Ireland, in his tour through that country, was the first faithful portrait of its inhabitants. All the features in the foregoing sketch were taken from the life, and they are characteristic of that mixture of quickness, simplicity, cunning, carelessness, dissipation, disinterestedness, shrewdness, and blunder, which, in different forms, and with various success, has been brought upon the stage, or delineated in novels.[68]

This way of describing her fiction assimilates *Castle Rackrent* to the didacticism that characterizes most of Edgeworth's writing: it sets out to teach ignorant English readers about the manners of their "sister country." Published in the midst of the heated debate over the Union between Ireland and England, the novel clearly intervenes – despite its humorous, light-hearted tone – in national politics. As Brian Hollingworth argues, "To publish an Irish story in January 1800 was a political act."[69] Maria Edgeworth's father, Richard Edgeworth, was an Anglo-Irish landowner and Member of Parliament whose reformist agenda his daughter shared. But the passage above points to an important ambiguity in the intention of *Castle Rackrent*. The allusion to Young suggests that Edgeworth aspires to be taken as seriously as Young, a prominent agricultural reformer who traveled and wrote in the service of "improvement." But her subsequent mention of novels and plays that stereotype the Irish as cunning, dissipated, shrewd, and so forth implicitly align her with a very different tradition, one she elsewhere castigates as the "Teague and Dear Joy" school of literature.[70]

Situating her story ambiguously, Edgeworth occupied an ambiguous position in relation to its native Irish characters and narrator. As a member of the Anglo-Irish Ascendancy, she was both committed to Ireland – she lived there all her adult life – and necessarily detached from its Catholic majority. This detachment enters her text in the figure of the Editor, who provides a preface, conclusion, footnotes, and glossary. "His" authoritative voice is strongly reminiscent of Arthur Young's, or those of any number of eighteenth-century travel writers, advancing their observations of manners and customs in the areas they toured. Katie Trumpener argues that Edgeworth's Irish novels "assume a Youngian detachment in order to reopen the fractious questions of cultural difference and political domination which preoccupied Elizabethan commentators" on Ireland, beginning with Edmund Spenser's 1596 *View of the Present State of Ireland*. Trumpener also sets Irish nationalist novels, including those of Sydney Owenson and Charles Maturin as well as Edgeworth's, in dialogue with travel writing, illuminating the concerns and strategies the two genres share. "For Edgeworth, the travelogue (or fictions based on travelogue forms) can potentially explain, to a distant and differently situated audience, just how national circumstances have been shaped by internal and external forces, and thus why national character is formed as it is." *Castle Rackrent* in particular, Trumpener argues, with its unreliable vernacular narrator, Thady Quirk, registers the "tension . . . between Youngian political economy and an ethnographic analysis sensitive to cultural and linguistic tradition."[71] One prominent locus of this tension is that prototypically Irish landscape feature, the bog.

For a line of Anglo-Irish commentators stretching back to Spenser, the bog served as an emblem of "Ireland's intractable national character" or "Irish resistance to . . . Anglo-Irish rule." For Irish nationalists, the bog likewise took on material and discursive significance.[72] Arthur Young devotes an entire section in volume 2 of his 900-page *Tour in Ireland* to bogs, setting forth their types (black and red) and speculating on their origin. "But the means of improving them," he emphasizes, "is the most important consideration. . . . Fortunately for a bog-improver, drains are cut at so small an expense in them, that that necessary work is done at a very moderate cost. But in spungy ones it must be repeated annually . . . Whatever the means used, certain it is that no meadows are equal to those gained by improving a bog."[73] Maria

Edgeworth's father, Richard, exemplified Young's wisdom when he successfully drained bog land on his estate.[74]

The bog in *Castle Rackrent* becomes a metonym, as critics have noted, for the Enlightenment project of land reform, or social progress in general.[75] Viewed in contrasting ways by Sir Kit Rackrent and his new English bride, the bog serio-comically exposes the mismatch between English expectations and Irish realities. With her lack of understanding and imported criteria for judging land, "my lady" occupies the position of the stranger or traveler, condescending to Ireland and the Irish in ways for which she is later richly punished.

> Then, by-and-bye, she takes out her glass, and begins spying over the country. "And what's all that black swamp out yonder, Sir Kit?" says she. "My bog, my dear," says he, and went on whistling. "It's a very ugly prospect, my dear," says she. "You don't see it, my dear," says he, "for we've planted it out, when the trees grow up in summer time. . . . But, my lady, you must not quarrel with any part or parcel of Allyballycarrick-o'shaughlin, for you don't know how many hundred years that same bit of bog has been in the family; we would not part with the bog of Allyballycarricko'shaughlin upon no account at all. . . ." Now one would have thought this would have been hint enough for my lady, but she fell to laughing like one out of her right mind, and made me say the name of the bog over for her to get it by heart a dozen time – then she must ask me how to spell it, and what was the meaning of it in English.[76]

The metropolitan idiom of landscape aesthetics – "prospect" – applies incongruously to this characteristically Irish feature. Landscape aesthetics, in particular the aesthetics of the picturesque (enormously popular in the 1790s), shared with aristocratic English landscape gardening the improver's mentality. The lover of the picturesque was always trying to determine, in the words of its chief pundit, William Gilpin, "what would amend the composition; how little is wanting to reduce it to the rules of our art."[77] The language of aesthetics was by 1800 a standard feature of travel writing. Even Arthur Young, that eminently practical traveler, indulges frequently in aesthetic description, as in his remarks on Shanes Castle: "The Castle is beautifully situated on the Lake, the windows commanding a very noble view of it; and this has the finer effect, as the woods are considerable, and form a fine accompaniment to this noble inland sea."[78]

Imposing English values on an Irish "prospect," the new Lady Rackrent renders a judgment that betrays her utter lack of understanding or sympathy for local circumstances, attachments, or history. Ironies sprout around this comic moment: the bride is no entitled member of the English upper classes, but, as the old retainer Thady forthrightly remarks, "little better than a blackamoor . . . a *Jewish* by all accounts."[79] And her condescension is repaid when Sir Kit, miffed at her refusal to hand over her valuable diamond cross, locks her in her room for seven years as his neighbors turn a blind eye. Critics diverge on the interpretation of the bog passage. Hollingworth reads Sir Kit's indifference to improvement as an indictment of Irish "lethargy," or "parasitic inertia": "Edgeworth constructs *Castle Rackrent* as the deliberate antithesis of all that Young advocates." Trumpener finds her attitude more ambivalent, edged with a defensive, "implicitly nationalist" response to the condescending outsider.[80] But however we read Allyballycarricko'shaughlin, it is clear that novels and travel writing, at the outset of the eighteenth century, were entangled in a politicized contest over the meanings of landscape, language, and history on Britain's Celtic periphery.

The eighteenth-century novel, as all these examples suggest, intersected with travel writing in a number of ways that have increasingly preoccupied recent scholarship. Both genres struggled with epistemological issues, intertwined with questions of style and conventions of representation, which became especially acute when confronted with the exotic horizons opened by exploration and colonization. Both genres sought means of representing encounters with peoples, cultures, and ways of life that were different – subtly or dramatically – from English life, and of defining an English self in relation or opposition to these. Both genres worked, in the course of the century, to refine the relation between travel plots and the development of a central character or persona, negotiating between external environment (setting) and internally generated affective or moral agendas. For both genres, character and landscape took on national dimensions and representational force as both travel writing and the novel contributed importantly to nation formation. And both, in the hands of Scottish and Irish writers, became instruments for testing and challenging English hegemony in the British Isles. My examples have illustrated the diverse connections between the two genres during this historical period. My brief synopses of important recent work on travel writing and the novel cannot, of course, do justice to the complexities of each scholar's argument. Rather, I hope to send readers back to the sources – secondary and primary, including the wealth of travel writing the eighteenth century produced – to experience the pleasures of peregrination for themselves.

See also: chapter 1, Crusoe's Farther Adventures; chapter 3, Narrative Transmigrations; chapter 19, Racial Legacies.

Notes

I am grateful to the students in my Spring 2003 seminar, "Novel, Travel, Nation," for their searching engagement with these materials and thought-provoking discussions.

1. Oddvar Holmesland, "Aphra Behn's *Oroonoko*: Cultural Dialectics and the Novel," *ELH* 68 (2001): 69.

2. Not to mention travel writings by Addison, Swift, Boswell, Johnson, Hester Thrale Piozzi, Dorothy Wordsworth, and Mary Shelley.

3. Percy G. Adams, *Travel Writing and the Evolution of the Novel* (Lexington: University Press of Kentucky, 1983). Adams treats French as well as English literature.

4. Quoted in Katherine Turner, *British Travel Writers in Europe 1750–1800* (Aldershot, UK: Ashgate, 2001), 2.

5. Dennis Porter, *Haunted Journeys: Desire and Transgression in European Travel Writing* (Princeton, NJ: Princeton University Press, 1991), 19.

6. Mary Louise Pratt, *Imperial Eyes: Travel Writing and Transculturation* (New York: Routledge, 1992); Peter Hulme, *Colonial Encounters: Europe and the Native Caribbean 1492–1797* (London: Routledge, 1986); Nigel Leask, *Curiosity and the Aesthetics of Travel Writing, 1770–1840* (Oxford: Oxford University Press, 2002); Jonathan Lamb, *Preserving the Self in the South Seas 1680–1840* (Chicago: University of Chicago Press, 2001).

7. J. Paul Hunter, *Before Novels: The Cultural Contexts of Eighteenth-Century English Fiction* (New York: W. W. Norton, 1990), 5, 58, 353.

8. Ibid., 353.

9. Adams, *Travel Writing*, 81–102.

10. Mary Baine Campbell, "Travel Writing and Its Theory," in *The Cambridge Companion to Travel Writing*, Peter Hulme and Tim Youngs, eds. (Cambridge: Cambridge University Press, 2002), 263.

11. Aphra Behn, *Oroonoko*, in *The Works of Aphra Behn*, ed. Janet Todd (Columbus: Ohio State University Press, 1995), 3: 57.

12. Ibid., 56.

13. Holmesland, "Aphra Behn's *Oronooko*," 57.

14. George Guffey, "Aphra Behn's *Oroonoko*: Occasion and Accomplishment," in *Two English Novelists: Aphra Behn and Anthony Trollope* (Los Angeles: William Andrews Clark Memorial Library, 1975), 5–6.

15. Michael McKeon, *The Origins of the English Novel 1600–1740* (Baltimore, MD: Johns Hopkins University Press, 1987), 91.

16. Ibid., 110.

17. John Braithwaite, *The History of the Revolutions in the Empire of Morocco . . .* , Preface (1729), quoted by McKeon, *Origins of the English Novel*, 103. See also McKeon, 101–103, on the Royal Society's influence on prose style.

18. Ibid., 112.

19. Holmesland, "Aphra Behn's *Oronooko*," 75.

20. Ibid., 66–67.

21. See e.g. Arthur Secord's account of Defoe's sources in travel writing, *Studies in the Nar-rative Method of Defoe* (Urbana: University of Illinois Press, 1924).

22. Ian Watt, *The Rise of the Novel* (London: Chatto and Windus, 1957; rpt. Berkeley and Los Angeles: University of California Press, 1965), 67.

23. Ibid., 69.

24. Michel de Certeau, *The Practice of Everyday Life*, trans. Steven Rendall (Berkeley and Los Angeles: University of California Press, 1984), 154.

25. Hulme, *Colonial Encounters*, 176, 193–94, 198.

26. Quoted in Hulme, *Colonial Encounters*, 198.

27. Ibid., 15.

28. Michelle Burnham, "Introduction," Anonymous [Unca Eliza Winkfield, pseud.], *The Female American*, ed. Michelle Burnham (Peterborough, Ontario: Broadview, 2001), 13.

29. [Winkfield], *The Female American*, 80, 111, 84.

30. Burnham, "Introduction" to *The Female American*, 19, 11.

31. Ibid., 12.

32. [Winkfield], *The Female American*, 139.

33. Adrienne DuVall, "A Problematic Utopia: Feminine Autonomy and Subordination in *The Female American*," unpublished paper, 2.

34. [Winkfield], *The Female American*, 115.

35. DuVall, "A Problematic Utopia," 5.

36. Kristi Funch Lodge, "Colonial Self-Fashioning: Color, Race, and Religion in *The Female American*," unpublished paper, 2.

37. [Winkfield], *The Female American*, 154.

38. Quoted in Porter, *Haunted Journeys*, 27.

39. Laurence Sterne, *A Sentimental Journey*, in *The Florida Edition of the Works of Laurence Sterne*, ed. Melvyn New and W. G. Day, vol. 6 (Gainesville: University Press of Florida, 2002), 110–11.

40. Adams, *Travel Writing*, 198.

41. Ian Campbell Ross, *Laurence Sterne: A Life* (Oxford: Oxford University Press, 2001), 315–17.

42. Porter, *Haunted Journeys*, 57–58.

43. Sterne, *A Sentimental Journey*, 11.

44. Jean Viviès, *English Travel Narratives in the Eighteenth Century: Exploring Genres*, trans. Claire Davison (Aldershot, UK: Ashgate, 2002), 73.

45. Quoted in Porter, *Haunted Journeys*, 38.

46. Porter, for example.

47. Chloe Chard, "Crossing Boundaries and Exceeding Limits: Destabilization, Tourism, and the Sublime," in *Transports: Travel, Pleasure, and Imaginative Geography, 1600–1830*, Chard and Helen Langdon, eds. (New Haven, CT: Yale University Press, 1996), 117, 121.

48. Sterne, *A Sentimental Journey*, 165.

49. Ibid., 164.

50. Chard, "Crossing Boundaries," 124–25.

51. Ibid., 125.

52. Jane Austen, *Northanger Abbey*, ed. Claire Grogan (Peterborough, Ontario: Broadview, 2002), 198, 197.

53. Chard's essay connects transgression to the sublime, an aesthetic category also of tremendous importance to Radcliffe's traveling protagonists, as well as to other women travel writers of the 1790s. See Elizabeth A. Bohls, *Women Travel Writers and the Language of Aesthetics, 1716–1818* (Cambridge: Cambridge University Press, 1995).

54. J. M. S. Tompkins, "Ramond de Carbonnières, Grosley and Mrs. Radcliffe," *Review of English Studies* 5 (1929): 294–301.

55. Emily's bookshelf in *The Mysteries of Udolpho* holds a copy of Ariosto, source of Handel's opera *Orlando*.

56. Marilyn Butler, "The Woman at the Window: Ann Radcliffe in the Novels of Mary Wollstonecraft and Jane Austen," in *Gender and Literary Voice*, ed. Janet Todd, (New York: Holmes and Meier, 1980), 129.

57. Claudia Johnson, *Equivocal Beings: Politics, Gender, and Sentimentality in the 1790s* (Chicago: University of Chicago Press, 1995), 124.

58. Ann Radcliffe, *The Italian* (Oxford: Oxford University Press, 1998), 3–4.

59. Diego Saglia, "Looking at the Other: Cultural Difference and the Traveler's Gaze in *The Italian*," *Studies in the Novel* 28 (1996): 13–14.

60. Radcliffe, *The Italian*, 1.

61. Saglia, "Looking at the Other," 15, 18, 23, 28.

62. Radcliffe, *The Italian*, 35.

63. Saglia, "Looking at the Other," 19.

64. Radcliffe, *The Italian*, 201.

65. Saglia, "Looking at the Other," 31.

66. Ibid., 34.

67. Marilyn Butler, "Introduction" to Maria Edgeworth, *Castle Rackrent and Ennui* (New York: Penguin, 1992), 2–3.

68. Edgeworth, *Castle Rackrent*, 121.

69. Brian Hollingworth, *Maria Edgeworth's Irish Writing* (Basingstoke: Macmillan, 1997), 73.

70. Ibid., 86.

71. Katie Trumpener, *Bardic Nationalism: The Romantic Novel and the British Empire* (Princeton, NJ: Princeton University Press, 1997), 50, 60.

72. Ibid., 47, 48, 46.

73. Arthur Young, *Arthur Young's Tour in Ireland (1776–1779)*, ed. Arthur Wollaston Hutton (London: George Bell, 1892), 2:102–103.

74. Hollingworth, *Maria Edgeworth's Irish Writing*, 28.

75. Ibid., 82–83, Trumpener, *Bardic Nationalism*, 42.

76. Maria Edgeworth, *Castle Rackrent and Ennui*, ed. Marilyn Butler (New York: Penguin, 1992), 77–78.

77. Quoted in Bohls, *Women Travel Writers and the Language of Aesthetics, 1716–1818*, 94.

78. Young, *Tour in Ireland*, 1:149.

79. Edgeworth, *Castle Rackrent*, 76.

80. Hollingworth, *Maria Edgeworth's Irish Writing*, 85–86, Trumpener, *Bardic Nationalism*, 62.

Further Reading

Adams, Percy G. *Travel Writing and the Evolution of the Novel*. Lexington: University Press of Kentucky, 1983.

Batten, Charles L., Jr. *Pleasurable Instruction: Form and Convention in Eighteenth-Century Travel Literature*. Berkeley and Los Angeles: University of California Press, 1978.

Chard, Chloe. *Pleasure and Guilt on the Grand Tour*. Manchester: Manchester University Press, 1999.

Clifford, James. *Routes: Travel and Translation in the Late Twentieth Century*. Cambridge, MA: Harvard University Press, 1997.

Pratt, Mary Louise. *Imperial Eyes: Travel Writing and Transculturation*. New York: Routledge, 1992.

Turner, Katherine. *British Travel Writers in Europe 1750–1800*. Aldershot, UK: Ashgate, 2001.

5

Milton and the Poetics of Ecstasy in Restoration and Eighteenth-Century Fiction

Robert A. Erickson

Dissolve me into ecstasies,
And bring all Heav'n before mine eyes.
> Milton, "Il Penseroso"

In liquid raptures I dissolve all o'er
Melt into sperm and spend at every pore.
> Rochester, "The Imperfect Enjoyment"

Till all dissolving in the Trance I lay,
And in tumultuous Raptures dy'd away.
> Pope, "Sapho to Phaon"

The critical extasy, the melting flow, into which nature, spent with excess of pleasure, dissolves and dies away.
> Cleland, *Memoirs of a Woman of Pleasure*

In the two years after *Paradise Lost* (1667) first appeared, a large number of people, "fit or unfit, satisfied or unsatisfied," as William Riley Parker puts it, from all classes of society, were reading the poem (or trying to read it), or having it read to them (or trying to listen to it), for Milton designed his literary epic as a work not simply to be read silently in the "closet" (i.e. in a study or small bedroom) but aloud, and with feeling, to as many as would listen, and the popularity of the poem increased dramatically in the eighteenth century.[1] This was a long *narrative* poem, it had a story, and the story was a Bard's retelling of the most ancient and resonant of all stories in the Christian West, that of Adam and Eve and the Fall. But equally important to the story is Milton's fashioning and positioning of highly dramatic, histrionic scenes or moments within the narrative, such as Satan's first encounter with Sin and Death, and the opening of Book V with Eve's recounting of her dream and Adam's attempt to interpret it. Milton's brilliant combination of narrative with dramatic moments may be the chief feature his epic shares with early modern fiction. "*Paradise Lost* is from the outset, admittedly didactic – but with a difference. It rarely preaches, rarely argues. 'This great argument' is for Milton 'this significant story.'"[2] Built into early narrative, and this includes romance, "novels," and everything we call early fiction, is the element of dramatic story-*telling* itself. What I want to stress at the start is that Milton's great poem was read first, by most people, even the best-educated and most "literary," more as an oral narrative than as what we think of as "poetry." The strict and conventional boundaries we observe between "poetry" and "prose" and "fiction" and "drama" were more permeable in the early modern period by virtue, in large part, of the speaking-enacting voice and body of the performer of the work. As Margaret Doody has said, "Augustan poetry" (and she includes Milton under this rubric) "frets against boundaries."[3] I wish also to emphasize at the start that Milton's representation of human sexual relations and eroticism in terms of ecstasy, imagination, and confession became a kind of ur-text or model for plotting hetero-sexual eroticism in early fiction, culminating with Cleland and Richardson in the mid-century novel. We shall focus on Aphra Behn's *The Fair Jilt* (1688), Eliza Haywood's *Fantomina* (1725), and, especially, Daniel Defoe's *Roxana*.

Eve, Adam: Ecstasy, Fancy

My earlier writing on the structures of feeling in *Paradise Lost* focused, in *Mother Midnight*, on Milton's Eve as both a beautifully "pre-eminent" and a credulous "fallen" prototype of Richardson's Clarissa and, in *The Language of the Heart*, on Satan's assault upon Eve's "head," "hand," and "heart" in Books IV to IX of *Paradise Lost*.[4] Here my concerns are related but take quite different directions. In Books VIII and IX of *Paradise Lost*, Milton establishes, primarily in his rendering of Adam's sexual response to Eve, a pattern and interplay of ecstasy and confession that is acted out in a variety of ways in early modern fiction. Nearly all the young, beautiful, intelligent, and spirited young women who abound in this fiction owe a debt to *Milton*'s Eve, who combines all of these attributes.[5] In *The Language of the Heart* I suggested that Eve is the most interesting character in *Paradise Lost*, and I agree with the contention that "the most revolutionary thing that the early novel did was make women the central protago-nists."[6] In this essay, I am not arguing so much for Milton's influence on these writers as for the potency of Milton's epic poem (and his other poetry of ecstasy) to inspire and stimulate them in their rendering of the language of erotic love, female fancy, and amorous intrigue. In *Regaining Paradise*, the most recent full-scale study of Milton's "influence" on the eighteenth century, Dustin Griffin argues, against W. J. Bate and Harold Bloom, that far from stifling or oppressing writers who came after him, "the record of the eighteenth-century's attitudes toward Milton and its own literary achievement suggests . . . that Milton helped to stimulate some of the best poetry of the century."[7] In his book Griffin concentrates on poetry, but I believe his argument can also be shown to apply to Milton's stimulus on the writing of fiction.

The example of *Paradise Lost* did more than inspire; it also protected. In his own inimitable way, Milton was creating a highly charged poetics of nakedness, eroticism, and ecstasy, translating into a verbal medium some of the erotic features of Renaissance and Baroque painting, in the name of sacred art. These early writers of prose narrative thus had the sanction of Milton's poetic and virtually sacred authority – and of his bold version of "poetic license." If Milton could do this, what could they not do? They knew better than to imitate Milton's style, but under his covering wing, they could create all manner of sexual discourse, including "pornography,"[8] and attempt to go beyond even his masterly portrayal of feminine *power*, in all its visual and moral registers of sexuality, sin, and confession. When a milestone narrative achievement bursts upon a cultural scene, like *Paradise Lost* (or *The Godfather*), it generates all kinds of responses and reverberations that can't be accounted for under the conventional category of "influence." Milton's epic narrative poem came to attain for these writers, and for nearly all early modern readers, something like the authority and status of sacred writ (and the story was much more exciting, intricate, and involving than its original in Genesis), but always with the *license* of poetic fiction, of sheer imaginative play. The ideals of liberty Milton fought for all his life had strange rebirths and a fascinating legacy in the fiction of his admiring and often uninhibited successors.

Let us begin our examination of how Milton represents Eve's and Adam's sexuality with the lake scene in Book IV. The divine voice, referring to Adam, says to Eve, "him thou shalt enjoy"[9] (4.472), suggesting mutual enjoyment, giving and receiving. One did not have to be a reader of Rochester to know that "enjoy" meant not only to experience sexual pleasure, but to experience orgasm. The voice concludes by calling her "Mother of human race," a definition in terms of function and use, not unique personhood. She is humankind's "general Mother" (4.492). "What could I do, but follow straight" (4.475–76) suggests not choice but its opposite.[10] The voice had said I will bring you "where" no reflection waits for you, and your "soft imbraces" (4.470–71). The indefinite "where" is Milton's first evocation of the sexual body, the first suggestion of the mysterious, numinous bodily place in which the rites of erotic love are performed, a magical *space* around the body with enormous potential for excitement, for "bliss," "transport," "rapture," "passion," Milton's synonyms for ecstasy. "Bliss" is the primary term for the erotic ecstasy Eve and Adam enjoy in Paradise, culminating in the "blissful Bower" described in the embedded epithalamion toward the end of Book IV (4.598–775).

In the famous "Hail wedded Love" passage (4.750–75), a digression by the Narrator that became a much-studied set piece for eighteenth-century readers, from female novelists to American schoolchildren,[11] Milton contrasts the holy, mysterious marriage bed of Adam and Eve in their bower – a "Perpetual Fountain of Domestic sweets" (4.760) — with "the bought smile / Of Harlots, loveless, joyless, unindear'd, /

Casual fruition," and with "Court Amours, / Mixt Dance, or wanton Mask [masquerade], or Midnight Ball" (4.765–68),[12] all the paraphernalia of the routine, casual set of socially ritualized sexual practices of the Restoration – an early version of Swift's "mechanical operation of the spirit" – bemoaned by Artemiza to her friend Chloe in Rochester's brilliant poetic ventriloquizing of the new role of the woman writer. Employing language reminiscent of his friend Aphra Behn, Rochester's Artemiza extols the godlike power of erotic love, "Love, the most gen'rous passion of the mynde, / The softest refuge Innocence can fynde / . . . / This onely Joy for which poore We were made" (lines 40–50), and notes that it has grown, like gambling, into an "errant trade," like the low female libertinism of prostitution:

> But what yet more a Womans heart would vexe,
> 'Tis cheifely carry'd on by our owne Sexe,
> Our silly Sexe, who borne, like Monarchs, free,
> Turne Gipsyes for a meaner Liberty,
> And hate restraint, though but from Infamy.
>   . . .
> To an exact perfection they have wrought
> The Action, Love, the Passion is forgot.[13]

Eve's question, "What am I?" (4.451–52) here becomes, "What is a woman's heart?" Significantly, Jane Barker's Galesia would remember Artemiza's lines when pondering whether her lover Bosvil was indeed more sincere in his love than complacent Mr. Brafort, only she transposes the pronouns from the female to the male sex.[14]

It is important to note that the word "ecstasy," from its very beginnings, has had the double and conflicting connotations of rapture as supreme, overpowering pleasure, and madness, or overpowering grief and sorrow. Ecstasy is the condition of being overpowered by some strong emotion, either of joy or grief, but the earliest uses of the term, beginning with *ekstasis* (the prefix *ek* means "out," "away from"), suggest a violent transition from one state of being to another, the state of being "beside oneself," or "outside of oneself," effected by some internal or external force. This is the fundamental sense of ecstasy as *dis-placement*. One is thrown into a frenzy or a stupor with anxiety, astonishment, fear, or passion.[15]

Robert Burton, in *The Anatomy of Melancholy*, has surprisingly little to say about "ecstasy" as such, but the whole work is in some sense about ecstasy or mental illness as a species of "melancholy." Burton first defines "Madness" as:

a vehement *Dotage*, or raving without a feaver, farre more violent than *Melancholy*, full of anger and clamor, horrible lookes, actions, gestures, troubling the Patients with farre greater vehemency both of body and Mind . . . . Of this fury [madness] there be divers kinds: *Extasie*, which is familiar with some persons, as *Cardan* saith of himselfe, he could be in one when he list [wished to]; in which the *Indian* priests [i.e. yogi] deliver their Oracles, and the witches of *Laplande*, as *Olaus Magnus* writeth . . . *Exstasi omnia praedicere*, answere all questions in an *Extasis* you will aske . . . . The other *species* of this Fury are

Enthusiasmes, Revelations, & Visions... Obsession or Possession of divels, Sibylline Prophets, and Poeticall Furies.[16]

Burton, like many early modern definers of ecstasy (including Samuel Johnson), stresses the violent, mindless fury of ecstasy as madness but adds the important element of *manipulation*, as practitioners like the great Italian polymath Cardano and "shamanic" Lapland witches, male and female, can induce the ecstatic state and use it to prophesy or for other purposes. We have here the sense of calculated or controlled ecstasy, a self-induced state that may be anything but violent or mindless. Perhaps the best-known example in English of this kind of non-violent, controlled, willed ecstasy is Donne's love poem by that title. The sense of calculation or manipulation in Burton's definition of ecstasy suggests the deliberate psychic split of a person "playing a part," an impersonation (and here we recall the basic Latin meaning of "person" from *persona*, or mask), an act that invokes the whole spectrum of motivations for dissimulation, from entertainment and therapeutic role-playing to deceit and betrayal. In his essay "Of Simulation and Dissimulation," Francis Bacon defines "Simulation, in the affirmative; when a man industriously and expressly feigns and pretends to be that he is not."[17] This definition would apply to characters as different in motivation as Edgar feigning to be Tom o' Bedlam in *King Lear* and Iago in his cold, brilliantly concealed and restrained fury (in one interpretation) explaining to Rodrigo, "I am not what I am" (*Othello*, I.i.62). Such extreme examples also come under the category of early modern "ecstasy."

To appreciate more fully the importance of Milton's Eve to the writers of early modern fiction, we must pause to consider her relationship to "Fancy" or Phantasia, one of the three major components of the mind (the other two were Ratio or reason and Memoria or memory) in the paradigm of faculty psychology that prevailed in the West from the Middle Ages into the eighteenth century. We remember that the mind or "psyche" itself, and its three major components, and even the "soul" (often equated with the mind) were almost always feminized, as were the arts and sciences in the Muses. The words "fancy" and "fantasy" (fancy is a contraction of fantasy, and was sometimes spelled "fant'sy") are virtually synonymous in the early modern period, and they derive from the Greek and Latin *phantasia* (appearance, idea, or notion), with more the sense of "mental image" in Latin. "Fancy" as a faculty of the mind was the equivalent of imagination, but it could also mean, in psychological terms, an unfulfilled desire, and in ordinary terms, a whim or caprice, or more deeply, a wild or visionary idea, an unnatural or bizarre mental image, an illusion, even a delusion. The words "phantom" (cf. "Fantomina") and "phantasm" also derive from the root for fancy/fantasy. This cluster of words appears over and over again in early modern poetry and narrative, often in association with the feminine. Now Adam associates Eve with Fancy from the time of her dream of eating the forbidden fruit, the first disruption of their harmonious existence together. Satan's violation of Eve through his refashioning of her dream and his attempt to engender something new in her mind – the primary sin of "pride" – might also be seen as the prototype of numerous subsequent representations of a dangerous imaginative object, a book or a painting, impressing itself on the all too receptive female mind or heart in Restoration and eighteenth-century fiction.[18]

When Adam attempts to interpret Eve's dream to her (and to himself) after she describes it, he gives a shortened outline of faculty psychology, and then says that in sleep, Reason retires into her private cell and often "mimic Fancy wakes / To imitate her," taking her place like one actress for another on the mental stage, and often produces "Wild work," an exaggerated rendition of the original performance. This is not only wild work but bad work, "Ill matching words and deeds long past or late" (5.110–13). Fancy is capable of getting things wrong long before Eve and Adam fall. Fancy is slippery, coy, wanton, wild, like Chaucer's Alisoun in *The Miller's Tale*, like Milton's own Mirth in "L'Allegro," like Nature in innocent paradise, described by the Narrator a few lines later: "for Nature here / Wanton'd as in her prime, and play'd at will / Her Virgin Fancies, pouring forth more sweet, / Wild above Rule or Art; enormous bliss" (5.294–97). Can Nature produce bad work in innocent Paradise? Adam lovingly and considerately encourages Eve not to be sad, but he knows that something "Evil" (5.117) has been added to this dream; it is not all Eve's invention. At the same time, he seems to be saying that the Eve of the dream was a version of wild Fancy, and even though this Eve abhorred eating the fruit, he seems to have his first doubts about Eve's ability to withstand temptation.

Pondering the powerful role of Fancy in the poem helps us realize that Adam and Eve, in their "woody Theatre" (4.141), share with the Narrator the role of ecstatic poets. After their conversation in the blissful bower, Adam and Eve move on to their morning orisons, praising their Maker in "holy rapture … such prompt eloquence / Flow'd from their lips, in *Prose* or numerous Verse" (5.147–50; my emphasis). Adam and Eve themselves, the original poets and performers, do not make a sharp distinction between prose and verse. What they sing is a continuous discourse of rapture, an earthly version of angelic song, the same kind of thing Monteverdi, Palestrina, William Byrd (and even Milton's father) were trying to do in their polyphonies. Eve and Adam replicate the holy rapture of the Narrator, "rapt above the pole" (7.23) in singing the first half of his epic.[19] Their "Unmeditated" (5.149) songs also link them to the resigned but assured poet of the fourth invocation of the Muse (at the start of Book IX) singing his "unpremeditated Verse" (9.24) for the tragic denouement of his story.

In Book VIII, just after the sociable Archangel Raphael (with whom Adam seems to have an almost trance-like homosocial conversational bond) has told him to "joy" in paradise and his fair Eve (as if Eve and Paradise are one) and not "Dream" of other worlds, Adam professes himself "satisfied" but proceeds to note that the mind or fancy (he virtually equates the two terms now) is apt "to rove / Uncheckt, and of her roving is no end; / Till warn'd, or by experience taught, she learn" that what lies before us "in daily life, / Is the prime Wisdom" (8.188–94). In two lines, Adam gives Aphra Behn a cue for the female "Rover," proleptically outlines the plot of Haywood's *Fantomina*, and provides a rationale for the content of the eighteenth-century novel from Defoe to

Sterne. Perhaps owing to his infatuation with Raphael's discourse, and despite his avowed concern to pay attention to what happens in ordinary life, he also seems strangely unaware that Eve has quietly exited the scene to visit her flowers in a prologue to her own "strange Desire of wand'ring" (Adam's post-lapsarian words, 9.1135–36), her own pre-enactment of the role of the female Rover.

Let us take a closer look at Adam and his own Fancy as he relates his "Story" (8.205) to Raphael, one that corresponds to Eve's story of her first day in Book IV. Like Eve, Adam awakes to consciousness upon a bank of flowers. After pensively sitting down, he goes back to sleep. We recall that Adam was formed for valor and contemplation. His contemplative questioning and pensiveness are far more evident in the poem than his courage; interestingly, the early female novelists, like Behn and Haywood, often fashion their male heroes, usually men "of Quality," if not royalty, in a passive, thoughtful, receptive posture (a pose going back at least as far as the second stanza of Thomas Wyatt's "They flee from me"), in various modes of reverie, from trance-like conversation to misgivings of the heart, as we see in Adam waiting for Eve to return (9.845–46). In recounting for Raphael his first moments of experience, Adam feels himself "passing to [his] former state / Insensible, and forthwith to dissolve" (8.290–91). He is like the speaker in "Il Penseroso" who implores his Melancholy goddess muse, "Dissolve me into ecstasies, / And bring all Heav'n before mine eyes" (lines 165–66). This altered state leads to various kinds of rapture, reverie, and for Adam, a dream state. As Eve was defined as "Mother," Adam is defined as "First Father" (8.298). After his colloquy with God the Father, "As with an object that excels the sense," he sinks down, spent. But God left open "the Cell of Fancy my internal sight," and Adam, "Abstract as in a trance" (8.460–62), sees through the lens of his fancy, untainted by any outside influence, the creation of Eve from the left side of his own body. What Adam describes in his trance state is another version of ecstasy, "the exalted state of feeling which engrosses the mind to the exclusion of thought; rapture, transport," as the *OED* writer eloquently defines it (sense 4). For Adam, Eve "in her looks . . . infus'd / Sweetness into my heart, unfelt before, / And into all things from her Air inspir'd / The spirit of love and amorous delight" (8.474–77). She is not "uninform'd of nuptial Sanctity and marriage Rites" (8.486–87), a veiled way of saying that she knows innately, intimately, inimitably, the arts and techniques of amorous intercourse and erotic ecstasy.[20] Adam concludes his narrative for Raphael with the couple's walk to the nuptial bower, and Adam is "at the sum of [his] earthly bliss" (8.522).

It is at this point that Adam confesses to Raphael that all other sources of delight for him, all sensory response to herbs, fruits, flowers, Nature herself, do not work any change "in the mind" or generate "vehement desire." But "here" – and this is his word for the almost ineffable experience of being in her presence, of looking at her, and then touching her – here he is "Transported," here he first feels "passion" (8.528–30).[21] Eve is an agent of transport, "Commotion strange" (8.531), and ecstasy for Adam. Moreover, he describes Eve as a virtual goddess upon whom "Authority and Reason . . . wait" and there is an "awe / About her, as a guard Angelic plac't" (8.554, 558–59).[22] Adam's attempt to describe his feelings to Raphael is the culmination of the rich subgenre of what I call "the poetry of ecstasy" in the seventeenth century, a tradition exemplified by poets as diverse as Donne, Wroth, Vaughan, Crashaw, Carew, Cavendish, and Traherne.[23] Has Fancy for Milton become the most powerful mental faculty? Certainly it was for many eighteenth-century poets, like Thomson and the Americans Phillis Wheatley and Philip Freneau before the elevation of the imagination in Wordsworth and Coleridge and Keats. And the female protagonist in much early fiction, ranging from "Furies" like Behn's Miranda in *The Fair Jilt* to the all too mortal goddess of Wisdom, Richardson's Clarissa, is often represented, like Milton's Eve in the eyes of Adam, as a semi-divine being in the eyes of the narrator or other main characters in the work.

Raphael is deeply disturbed by Adam's revelation, and reminds him that Eve "sees when thou art seen least wise" (8.578). Totally intent upon her flowers when the serpent enters her nursery, Eve is "mindless the while" (9.431), "engrossed to the exclusion of thought." And when she eats the fruit she is again mindless in this sense: "Intent now wholly on her taste, naught else / Regarded" (9.786). But she is now intent on gratifying her *self*, whereas before she was intent on nurturing her flowers – and Adam. A momentous change occurs in Eve, though it has been gradually prepared for. It is a transformation of one kind of *ekstasis* into another, reminiscent of Burton's discussion of Cardano's manipulation of "Extasie." We see a transition from unconscious, mindless transport to a calculated and rehearsed putting oneself out of one's place, the birth of the actress: "But to *Adam* in what sort / Shall I appear?" (9.816–17). The word "sort" means manner or fashion; she will now improvise her fate, but it involves risky choices. The actress becomes the gambler, willing to risk everything on what she sees and knows about Adam when he is "least wise." But Adam knows when he sees her in her heightened state, bringing to him the newly gathered bough of fruit, and "in her face excuse / Came Prologue, and Apology to prompt," that she has become "Defac'd, deflow'r'd, and now to Death devote" (9.853–54, 901). This line might serve as an epigraph (or epitaph) for many of the beautiful, fallen heroines of early modern fiction, and Eve is the first fallen woman, as Satan is the first libertine.[24] The burden of her three confessions to Adam (10.967–1006; 11.163–80; 12.610–23) is that "by sad experiment" she knows she is vile, unworthy, the transgressor, and the snare for Adam, and yet in her fallen condition the source of new life and restoration for the human race.

It cannot be emphasized enough that Milton's fusion in fallen Eve of the metaphor of theatricality with that of gambling and risk-taking, always saturated with the erotic language of the heart, will emerge as a primary scenario for much of the fictional plotting of male/female sexual relations in the early novel. At the same time, all this is compounded with the rhetoric of sexual ecstasy, confession, and inflamed, even pathological sexuality, a sense of boundless excess, self-consuming desire, and passion born of fancy.

> As with new Wine intoxicated both
> They swim in mirth, and fancy that they feel

> Divinity within them breeding wings
> Wherewith to scorn the Earth . . . .
> [the false fruit]
> Carnal desire inflaming, hee on *Eve*
> Began to cast lascivious Eyes, she him
> As wantonly repaid; in Lust they burn
> (9.1008–15).

Compare Fanny Hill: "Giddy and intoxicated as I was with such satiating draughts of pleasure, I still lay on the couch, supinely stretch'd out, in a delicious languor diffus'd over all my limbs . . . . I abandon'd myself entirely to the ideas of all the delight I had swam in. I lay stretching out, glowingly alive all over, and tossing with burning impatience for the renewal of joys that had sinn'd but in a sweet excess."[25] Adam begins to sound and act like a Restoration libertine: " . . . never did thy Beauty . . . / . . . adorn'd / With all perfections, so inflame my sense / With ardor to enjoy thee . . . . / . . . well understood / Of *Eve*, whose Eye darted contagious Fire. / Her hand he seiz'd, and to a shady bank, / . . . / He led her nothing loath. . . . / There they their fill of Love and Love's disport / Took largely" (9:1029–32, 1035–40, 1042–43).[26] This is "love in excess," and they are beginning to die. The language of fire, burning, toxicity, contagion tells us they are now mortal.[27] Satan, the first "murderer" according to the Gospel of John (8.44), wants to kill Adam and Eve, and he succeeds. He renders them mortal. Fire is the ultimate metaphor of finitude, and "intoxication" and "contagion" suggest that the venom Satan communicated to Eve has been passed on to Adam and to their posterity.[28] The mutual, creative, unhurried lovemaking of their innocence has become mutually exploitative, and calculated, lovetaking. "Much pleasure we have lost, while we abstain'd / From this delightful Fruit" (9.1022–23). We have entered fully into the complicated world of Milton's Sin and Death, with all of its entanglements and hazards, and at the same time into the sexual world of early modern English fiction, the subject of the second half of this essay. I will discuss examples of the ecstasy/confession binary under the aspect of the power of female Fancy in two works, first (as a kind of prelude), Behn's novella or short story, *The Fair Jilt, or, The History of Prince Tarquin and Miranda*, then Defoe's last and greatest narrative, *Roxana*, focusing on the experience of Behn's and Defoe's vivid female protagonists.

The Fair Jilt

Behn presents her beautiful, intelligent, and brilliantly histrionic 18-year-old protagonist, Miranda, as a proof case for the power of Eros to rule the ungoverned female heart like "*a Fury from Hell*"[29] and her delicate male protagonist Henrick, a prince in the disguise of a Franciscan monk, as the passive male "confessor" par excellence. Though Behn presents Miranda as a case of early modern "possession," her protagonist is also a mistress of ecstasy as calculated histrionics. When Miranda discovers that the young father is "a man of quality," she begins to indulge an elaborate sexual fantasy about him. As in so many of Behn's dramatic sexual role reversals, Miranda is the sexual initiator; she is the one imagining, embracing, transforming him from unrobed friar to naked prince, lavishing "In the Bed" a thousand dalliances on his youthful body. "Some Moments she fansies him a Lover," in others "he had a Youth to be fir'd, as well as to inspire" (18–19). He becomes the passive ravisher of her heart and soul. She takes fire from his eyes, and all unaware he gives her "Wounds." She makes the further feminine transgression of writing to him, letters that become a kind of third-person narrative in which she gives him a "Character" of her beauty and allows him to judge her love "by the Extremity of the Passion she profess'd" (20). The metaphor of erotic fire and flame plays all through the confession scene, Lucretian fire projected from his eyes and face into her whole sensibility. But she is the ravisher and predator. The "lovely," passive friar makes no return to these advances except to respond in writing that he has dedicated his life to Heaven. She finally resolves to show him her "Person," that is, her living body (see *OED* III.4).

There is a complex and fascinating motif in Behn's imaginative writing about women that elaborates the gradual disclosure of the sexual body, evident in *The Rover* (1677) in the characters of both Hellena and Angellica Bianca, in Lady Fulbank in *The Lucky Chance* (1686), in Imoinda in *Oroonoko* (1688). Miranda will present her person to Father Henrick in his sacristy, a room for vestments which also serves as a confessional, but she will enter veiled. In the age-old ritual of confession, as Foucault has reminded us and to which Behn gives brilliant dramatic testimony, there are two "confessors": the father confessor (to whom one confesses), and the "confessor" (the speaking subject). And in the intimacy of the confessional space, the two confessors often share a sexual linguistic bond. "It is . . . a ritual that unfolds within a power relationship, for one does not confess without the presence . . . of a partner who is not simply the interlocutor but the authority who requires the confession. . . . the agency of domination does not reside in the one who speaks (for it is he who is constrained), but in the one who listens and says nothing."[30] Behn completely reverses this dynamic of power and reinforces the ambiguity of the "confessor" relationship. In the sacred space of the sacristy, Miranda kneels down before Father Henrick's "Confession-Chair," turns up her veil, "and discover'd to his View the most wond'rous Object of Beauty he had ever seen . . . and question'd whether he saw a Woman or an Angel at his feet. . . . he confess'd, he had never seen anything in Nature so perfect, and so admirable" (22).

Like Eve (*PL* 9.533), she is a "Wonder" – "Miranda" – and he is the one "confessing" before she makes her confession – of her violent love for him. She appropriates the language of the male libertine: "*'Tis you will have me die . . . when I complain of Tortures, Wounds and Flames. O cruel Charmer, 'tis for you I languish*" (22). He tries to rise from his chair, but allows her "to force him" back into it as his words of dissuasion gain the same "passionate" force of her revelation and he is prevailed upon to "own" or confess that he has a real tenderness for her. One confession continues to extort another as the ambiguity of subject/subject is replaced by the ambiguity of confessor/confessor in an escalation of contrasting mutual passion. But she remains the dominant figure, and finally becomes the virtual rapist. In a conflicted "agony of passion" and "full of rage," she threatens to "ruin" him, to take away his life and honor; he trembles in fear and anguish, and demands what she would have him do: "*Do that which thy Youth and Beauty were ordain'd to do*"; she snatches him in her arms and accosts him with a thousand kisses (23–24). After his final confession that he is "*frail Flesh and Blood*" ... ("*I own your power*"), and his final resistance, she throws *herself* into the confessional chair, pulls the friar down violently into her lap, and screams "*Help, help: A Rape!*" so loudly that she is heard all over the church (24).

The sacristy is not only a room for confession; it is the friars' private dressing room in which they put on their vestments, a sacred male space which Miranda invades, violates, usurps. When the other "Fathers" come into the room, they see the two confessors struggling "very indecently" and naturally misinterpret "as *Miranda* desir'd" (24–25). She describes in rapturous detail the violent sexual assault she was trying to provoke and convinces them of the truth of her false confession, relying securely on the force of social convention to convict the silent Henrick. She makes her accusation all the more convincing by not actually saying she was violated. The fact that this was the outcome she desired is confirmed by the subsequent arrival of the aptly named Prince Tarquin: "She was resolv'd to be the *Lucretia*, that this young *Tarquin* shou'd ravish" (28). Hence, in a stunning final fantasy drawing upon her own considerable narrative and dramatic powers, and then employing another script drawn from the Roman classics, Miranda succeeds in ravishing herself both figuratively and in actuality. In a final reversal typical of Behn, she becomes the Lucretia who engineers her own rape. After her final true confession of her crimes (including the attempted murder of her sister by poison), Father Henrick is reprieved. In its elaboration of the crimes and punishment of a beautiful and powerful female protagonist, this brief novella itself makes an intriguing preface to the female-centered novels of Defoe, *Moll Flanders* and *Roxana*.

Roxana

In the mid-1720s, novel readers were presented with Defoe's *The Fortunate Mistress* (*Roxana*), his first novel of amorous intrigue and its labyrinthine consequences, and *Fantomina, or, Love in a Maze*, by the even more prolific writer of amatory fiction, Eliza Haywood. Haywood's novella is a brief, brilliant exploration of female fancy/fantasy in a self-dramatizing young lady who embodies the virtual paradigm of birth, beauty, wit, and spirit going back to Milton's Eve. Her curiosity and "humour" lead her to dress up as a prostitute and convince her lover, Beauplaisir, that she is, over a period of time, four different women. Beauplaisir is "transported to find so much Beauty and Wit" in a woman who seemed to be a whore.[31] Fantomina describes the "unspeakable Ecstasy of those [lovers] who meet with equal Ardency" (237) while she moves through increasingly challenging tests of her histrionic genius towards a final confession forced by the "Rack of Nature" (247), childbirth, and by the return of her implacable mother when she is finally forced to acknowledge that life is not simply a "Masquerade novel."[32] It is as if a retributive Nature arranges her mother's return to coincide with the fact of her own impending motherhood.

Roxana is Defoe's deepest exploration of the female paradox of passive sexual attraction and active maternal rejection. Here we have a mature female retrospective narrator, long past childbearing age, whose narrative is almost a continual confession of sin ("whoredom"), regret, hypocrisy, wrong choices, and crime, the whole "dirty History of my Actings upon the Stage of Life."[33] The complicated specter of Milton's self-revelatory Sin hovers over and behind the protagonist, especially toward the end of the narrative. "It was well, *as I often thought*, that I was not a *Roman-Catholick* [like so many of Behn's female characters]; for what a piece of Work shou'd I have made, to have gone to a Priest with such a History as I had to tell him? And what Pennance wou'd any *Father-Confessor* have oblig'd me to perform? especially if he had been honest and true to his Office" (265). So the reader becomes her confessor and her intimate companion through over 300 pages of unbroken self-revelation that leads not to a qualified affirmation of the self as in *Robinson Crusoe* (1719) or *Moll Flanders* (1722), but to "a dreadful Course of Calamities" (329) that even for Roxana are unspeakable as, in a tone of fatigue and disgust, she recedes at the end further into the depths of her deceit, always deferring, ever unresolved.

How might the concept of "ecstasy" as an interpretive tool help shape our reading of this novel? At the very beginning of her narrative, Roxana says, "Being to give my own Character, I must be excus'd to give it as impartially as possible, and as if I was speaking of another-body" (6). Roxana attempts, with varying degrees of success, the fundamental ecstatic gesture of stepping outside the body and then recording what happens to that body, but there is no question that Roxana is an essentially passive protagonist, as Terry Castle has argued,[34] delegating agency over and over again to her servant Amy, receiving a procession of men in her static spatial interiors, luxuriating in "the most profound Tranquility" while "the Tide of Pleasure continues to flow, or till something dark and dreadful brings us to ourselves again" (69). It also needs to be said, however, that Roxana (like Milton's Eve and so many of the female protagonists of early modern fiction), is "tall, and very well made" (6), well aware (unlike Milton's Eve) of her "own Vanity, for I was not ignorant that I was very handsome" (57), by her own modest estimate quick, smart, and satirical in conversation and repartee, witty and bold (6) like Miranda and Fantomina, an accomplished dancer and singer from her youth, and for the most part she controls the freedom of her body as if it were a sovereign state. The first sentence of the preface emphasizes her beauty and her verbal autonomy: "*The History of this* Beautiful Lady, *is to speak for itself*" (1). We might think of Roxana as the languidly dancing self, fluid, constantly displacing her body, transporting herself from one intricate sequential pattern to another in what I shall argue becomes a kind of eighteenth-century version of the dance of death.[35] Dance, dress, verbal agility, histrionics, fluidity (one is struck by all the nautical metaphors, the terrible storm on the Channel, that climactic, claustrophobic scene with her daughter Susan on the ship) are the metaphoric basis of the narrative, *ekstasis* as displacement, deferral, and finally, varied manifestations of madness. At the age of 10 she is displaced from France to England, and her adult life is a cycle of displacements between the Continent and England.

In all this coming and going, Roxana displays a remarkable combination of passivity with occasional assertive management. She is almost always intimately acted upon, mainly by Amy "putting things into her head," recalling Satan's manipulation of the organs of Eve's fancy. In her joy at the prospect of their being saved from economic ruin by the Landlord/Jeweller, "the Girl was so transported, that she got up two or three times in the Night, and danc'd about the Room in her Shift" (32). Eve's "sweet, reluctant, amorous delay," and its power to hold (or "entertain" Adam) is in Roxana's behavior with the importunate Landlord a crude form of holding out, of deferring sexual favors ("However, I stood out a little longer still," 42). And then, after Amy taunts her about her not yet being pregnant ("what have you been doing?" 45), Roxana becomes a violent Mother Midnight to Amy, bawd and bully in one figure, when she strips the girl, a virgin, and forces her to have sex with the Landlord against her will.[36] "*Amy* . . . the next Morning . . . cry'd, and took on most vehemently . . . that she was a Whore, a Slut . . . . A Whore! says I, well, and am not I a Whore as well as you? No, no . . . you are not, for you are Marry'd" (47). Amy is Roxana's young, volatile, shadow self, her mistress's displacement of herself into the physical agent of her morbid desires, and she serves her mistress with disciple-like devotion: "I will be a Whore, or any thing, for your sake" (28).

If Roxana can "do" this to Amy early in the narrative, what may she not do, or condone the doing of, to her persistent daughter Susan, despite Roxana's violent disclaimers when Amy twice suggests murdering the girl (270, 272)? It is Amy who is carried away by periodic "transports" of delight or rage, not Roxana. The protagonist has her own forms of ecstasy, but mostly in the earlier and more prevalent pathological sense of the word applied to all morbid states characterized by some form of "lethargy," or loss or impairment of consciousness, often in swoon, trance, catalepsy (from *OED* sense 2), and Roxana's "dark Intervals," "Vapours," "Vapourish Fancy" (53), "Stupidity," and later more extreme forms of depression, "madness," "melancholly" (264), "Distraction" (161), are closer etymologically to the radical meanings of *ekstasis*, to be beside oneself, to be two persons at once, to be psychically "drawn apart," the literal sense of "distraction."[37] But in Roxana's case, the psychic split is further complicated. After the Landlord/Jeweller is robbed and killed in Paris, she exhibits two contradictory forms of ecstasy at the same time, a calculated displacement of herself into the fiction of her being a Catholic (54), and her claim to have suffered a deep psychic "Wound" (54): "I think I almost cry'd myself to Death for him; for I abandon'd myself to all the Excesses of Grief" (54). Again, I would suggest that Milton's Eve, in her first unrestrained and "hightened" state after eating the fruit, then her moments of calculating the odds of knowledge now in her power, and finally her deep sorrow, is a possible inspiration for Defoe's conception of Roxana's psychic evolution. In all this, Defoe gives an even deeper and more complex representation of female "Fancy" and disordered "Imagination" than he did in *Moll Flanders*, and Milton's Eve, as we have seen, is a paradigm for such representations.

Roxana achieves the zenith of her social and sexual power, and her fullest "Measure of Wickedness . . . [becoming] a standing Monument of the Madness and Distraction which Pride and Infatuations from Hell runs us into" (159, 161), when she decides to leave the honest Dutch merchant (with a "Bastard in her Belly," 163) and move from Paris to London where, after giving birth, she sets herself up in fine lodgings on the south side of Pall Mall with a private door into the King's Garden next to St. James's Palace: "I was rich, beautiful, and agreeable, and not yet old; I had known something of the Influence I had on the Fancies of Men, even of the highest Rank; I never forgot that the Prince *de*—had said with an Extasie, that I was the finest Woman in *France*; I knew I could make a Figure at *London*. . . . I thought of nothing less than being Mistress to the King himself" (161). This exclamation by the Prince has further poignancy when we observe that the word ecstasy could also be a synonym (not noted in the *OED*) for orgasm. Consider the ethnographic observation of another kind of calculated ecstasy by Swift's enthusiastic virtuoso in *The Mechanical Operation of the Spirit* (1704): "The Art of *See-Saw* on a Beam, and swinging by Session upon a Cord, in order to raise Artificial Extasies, hath been derived to Us, from our *Scythian* Ancestors, where it is practiced at this Day, among the Women."[38] We must pause to take notice at this point that of all the displacements in the novel, not the least is Defoe's prudent removal of the action of his narrative of Roxana (the name is a variant of Roxolana, the term for an expensive whore in Congreve's *The Way of the World* {1700}) to the seventeenth century, and at this moment in Roxana's history, to the reign of Charles II.[39] The last decades of the seventeenth century are also the chief era relevant to Swift's early satires. Swift's allusion to the Scythians, an actual people who moved from central Asia to southern Russia in the eighth century BC and who survived until about the second century AD, is more relevant to Lady Roxana's sojourn in Pall Mall than may at first appear.

In her Grand Tour with the Prince, Roxana had traveled to Naples (a city known for its loose women {102}, and also the setting for Behn's *The Rover*), where he had bought her a little female Turkish slave. Roxana, in her own peculiar ethnographic style, says she at this time learned the Turkish language and a good deal about the Turkish way of dressing and dancing, as well as several "*Turkish*, or rather *Moorish* Songs" (102). With the slave girl came rich clothes, particularly a fine dress, with a robe in fine Persian damask, "the Habit of *a Turkish Princess*" (173). Roxana's grand apartments consist of a large dining room and five other rooms, the last of which (a kind of theatrical fifth act) is reserved for her reception of the most eminent male visitors. In these semi-royal apartments, on her own semi-royal dramatic stage, Roxana achieves her most resplendent makeover ("I knew I cou'd make a Figure") as a gorgeous mystery woman (in Amy's accompanying public-relations fiction, the rich widow of a French aristocrat) who, with the help of her servants, manages her own gambling tables and presides over her own balls and masquerades. As Charles II re-created the Restoration theater, so Roxana in her much narrower sphere of influence ("now I began to act in a new Sphere" {172}), creates her own feminine theater in his very backyard (or "Gardens"), and the King and his courtiers enter in masquerade disguise to play their parts. She aspires to be the most powerful kind of woman she can be in her social world, "and seeing Liberty seem'd to be the Men's Property, I would be a *Man-Woman*; for as I was born free, I wou'd die so" (171). She will be a woman who has all the power and freedom of a wealthy and influential man while retaining her uniquely feminine powers of beauty and attraction as a "Modern" androgyne.[40] I "was possess'd with so vain an Opinion of my own Beauty, that nothing less than the KING himself was in my Eye" (172). No doubt Defoe had taken Rochester's satirical measure of the King's influence and transfers it to Roxana's wish to be a royal mistress in the sense of mastering the King: "His Scepter and his Prick are of a Length; / And she may sway the one, who plays with th'other."[41] As Swift created the first "media event," complete with an interview, in the Bickerstaff Papers' annihilation of the astrologer John Partridge (1708–9), so Defoe creates the first complex, arriviste female "celebrity" in Roxana.

At a second masquerade of Roxana's managing, and while she is "a-dressing" in her new Turkish dancing costume, two ladies, unknown to her, come into her apartment below (apparently her dressing room, as in a theater, is near the main "stage"), both dressed as virgin ladies of quality, one from Russian Georgia and one from Armenia. They each have richly dressed, bare-headed, female slaves attending them, as beautiful as their mistresses. None of the four is masked. Roxana is worried that she might be "out-done" by these beautiful creatures. The ladies dance three times around the room all alone: "The Novelty pleas'd, truly, but yet there was something wild and *Bizarre* in it, because they really acted to the Life the barbarous Country whence they came" (179). Now Georgia and Armenia made up part of ancient Scythia, as did parts of northern Greece, Thrace (the homeland of mythic Orpheus), Russia, and Persia. For Swift, the myth of Scythia was a convenient satirical ethnic conglomerate with which he could bludgeon the hated enthusiastic preachers, "*Roundheads*," and religious cult leaders of the late seventeenth and early eighteenth centuries, as well as the Scots and Irish.[42] For Defoe, these ladies in their exotic, bizarre, and wild masquerade costumes and unique dances are meant to evoke associations with the barbarous Scythian women (known also for blinding male prisoners of war to use them sexually), and act as a foil to Roxana, who wants to be thought exotic, but not too exotic: "as [my costume] had the *French* Behavior under the *Mahometan* Dress, it was every way as new, and pleas'd much better, indeed." And she reminds us that she is also "Queen of the Day" (179).

The function of ecstasy in *Roxana* is involved significantly with the huge effort she makes to dis-place herself from the rather prosaic young English woman we first see married to the Brewer into the exotic Other. There is always something Roxana prefers to the ordinary, and coming back to her actual everyday self is always a dreadful experience for her. She wants to think she is most powerful when most outside of herself, but even at her most independent and "free," she desires to be kept by a man. In one sense, Roxana's link with the "barbarous" women and their beautiful female slaves (what is the relationship of these women to their slaves?) is an indication of her longing for the *ekstasis* of total displacement into a fantasy realm of unknown, perhaps forbidden pleasures; paradoxically, she seems to fear such a radical displacement. She once had a Turkish slave girl of her own, and it seems she has always had Amy. By invoking "French" behavior, and recalling the French tunes and dances she is expert in (175), she presents herself as exotic and extraordinary, but still civilized and fashionable. She also presents herself, self-servingly and without apparent irony, as having "had the Day of all the Ladies that appear'd at the Ball, I mean, of those that appear'd with Faces on" (180). Roxana has made a point, all along, of her being a natural beauty; the Prince is overpowered by the natural luster of her skin, and here she says she had no mask, nor did she paint, as the other women with their "faces on" obviously do. Here again is a subtle fictional variant on the innocent but erotic nakedness of Eve (and Adam). But Roxana's naked, unpainted beauty is belied by the layers of damask and jewels she displays in her costume, at the same time "being somewhat too thin in that Dress, unlac'd, and open-breasted, as if I had been in my Shift" (181). And her constant use of "it must be confess'd" or variants of that expression always seems self-congratulatory, contrasting with the hollowness of many of her more dramatic "confessions."

The culminating moment in this Pall Mall "chapter" is the arrival of the King himself, the only one with his hat on, who comes across the room to her side and says, "Madam *Roxana* you *perform to Admiration*; I was prepar'd, and offer'd to kneel to kiss his Hand, but he declin'd it, and saluted me, and so passing back again thro' the Great Room, went away" (180). The King does not let her kiss his hand, but kisses *her*. Whether or not she becomes the King's mistress, this transient kiss is the acme of Roxana's account of her high life in Pall Mall, and of her career as self-fashioned celebrity incognita. And this kiss is contrasted with another at the low point of her final, complicated, external (and internal) *ekstasis*, in the disguise and as the protégé of the "Quaker" woman (she looks ten years younger, says Amy, 211), the total antithesis of the Restoration "man-woman" with all her wealth and power.

Her vacillation between choosing the Dutch Merchant to marry and fantasizing about life as a "Princess" generates Roxana's most extended meditation on female Fancy and Imagination, and sets the stage for her final ecstasy of madness in her confrontation with her daughter Susan: "During this time, I had a strange Elevation upon my Mind...pleasing my Fancy with the Grandeur I was supposing myself to enjoy" as a Princess (234). Her rude treatment of the merchant (who "began with a kind of an Extasie upon the Subject of finding me out," 224) had "the Effect of a violent Fermentation in my Blood"; she develops "a kind of Fever," and no longer thinks it strange that people can become "quite *Lunatick* with their Pride, fancy[ing] themselves Queens, and Empresses" (235). In all this echoes the language of Satan's compliments to Eve as queen, empress, goddess as well as the language of ecstasy as madness: "[N]othing is so chimerical, but under this possession we can form *Ideas* of, in our Fancy, and realize to our Imagination...a Man or Woman...may as easily die with Grief, or run-mad with Joy...as if all was real, and actually under the Management of the Person" (238–39). Roxana characterizes these delusions as her "weakest Part" (231), her "Disease" (239).

As her daughter Susan gradually comes closer to the truth about "Lady Roxana" being her true mother, the girl is perceived by Roxana (and Amy) in increasingly hostile, disparaging, and animalistic terms: she is "mad," "a sharp Jade," "positive" (313), "violent," given to "Fits, and she cry'd ready to kill herself," "a passionate Wench" (268). Amy concludes, "I think the D—l is in that young Wench, she'll ruin us all, and herself too" (272), a "Fool" persisting obstinately in her quest (274). The pathology of fallen sex in *Paradise Lost* has here been deflected into the symptoms of "Third-Day Ague" her mother now suffers from Susan's passionate pursuit, and Roxana says "had she died of any ordinary Distemper, I shou'd have shed but very few Tears for her" (302). The moment of Roxana's greatest success and mastery of her glamorous world, her sojourn as Lady Roxana of Pall Mall, epitomized in her Turkish costume and dance, is of course the moment that links her with Susan, who, along with Charles II and the courtiers, witnessed the dance. But for me the most compelling connection between that moment and the Susan we (and Roxana and Amy) see now is her kinship with the "barbarous," "wild," Scythian dancing girls. Susan is truly her mother's daughter, restless, "in a . . . Passion" (266), "mad" (267), but she is now something more. She is Roxana's wild *retributive* daughter.[43] A few pages earlier, Roxana had described her present state of mind as "a secret Hell within . . . I had such a constant Terror upon my Mind, as gave me every now and then very terrible Shocks" (260) . . . "[my] Reflections [had] gnaw'd a Hole in my Heart" (264). She is now about to receive perhaps her greatest psychic shock, one all the more terrible when seen under the aspect of Milton's Sin, and the murder of Susan. Indeed, it could be said that Roxana begins as a protagonist inspired in part by Milton's fallen Eve, and ends as one whose dance of deferral and displacement becomes entangled in the folds of Milton's Sin and Death.

When Susan comes on board ship into the Captain's room, the last of Roxana's interior dramatic stages (which have become more and more constricted since Pall Mall), a confined, claustrophobic, liminal space which rocks gently, queasily on the quiet Thames between sea and land, mirroring Roxana's deeply troubled mind and perhaps recalling her experience in the storm at sea in which she first confessed her sins to God, Roxana kisses her daughter in what must be the most intense and desperate moment of her life:

> there was no room to escape. . . . notwithstanding there was a secret Horror upon my Mind, and I was ready to sink when I came close to her, to salute her; yet it was a secret inconceivable Pleasure to me when I kiss'd her . . . my own Flesh and Blood, born of my Body. . . . I felt something shoot thro' my Blood: my Heart flutter'd; my Head flash'd, and was dizzy, and all within me . . . turn'd about, and much ado I had, not to abandon myself to an Excess of Passion at the first Sight of her. . . . with infinite Uneasiness in my Mind, I sat down. . . . I had a Complication of severe things upon me . . . . I trembled, and knew neither what I did, or said; I was in the utmost Extremity. . . . there was no retreat; no shifting anything off. (277–78)

For once, Roxana has no hope of deferring, and the moment has the inevitability of childbirth – or death. This account of her symptoms as her lips come closer to her daughter's face have an uncanny congruence with Satan's symptoms at the birth of his daughter Sin, *as described by Sin*, a mother, lover, daughter, and retrospective narrator whose experience intimately fuses the rapture of sex and the horror of rape:

> All on a sudden miserable pain
> Surpris'd thee, dim thine eyes, and dizzy swum
> In darkness, while thy head flames thick and fast
> Threw forth . . .
>
> . . .
>
> . . . but familiar grown,
> I pleas'd . . .
>
> . . .
>
> Thyself in me thy perfect image viewing
> Becam'st enamored, and such joy thou took'st
> With me in secret, that my womb conceiv'd
> A growing burden. (*PL* 2.752–67)[44]

Sin goes on to describe – after this act of lovetaking – the birth of her son Death, who rapes his mother and engenders a crew of monstrous hell hounds, "hourly conceiv'd / And hourly born, with sorrow infinite / To me," who creep, whenever they wish, back into her womb and "gnaw / My Bowels" (a word that also meant emotions), then burst forth and "with conscious terrors" vex their mother round without intermission (2.796–801). It is a scene of primal female terror, and it hovers over Roxana's terror at her unceasing, obstinate daughter's quest to learn the secret of her mother's womb. Susan has become the physical agent of Roxana's morbid "Reflections" (264); the girl is not only "a sharp Jade," connoting a loose woman, a "young Slut" (270, 288), but one with sharp claws, like a mythical Harpy. She becomes Roxana's own intimately personal hell hound: "the Perplexity of this Girl, who hunted me, as if, *like a Hound*, she had had a hot Scent" (317), finally drives her mother over again to Holland and to ever-increasing, endless ecstasies of self-reproach and anguish.

See also: chapter 6, Representing Resistance; chapter 9, The Erotics of the Novel; chapter 14, Joy and Happiness; chapter 23, Literary Culture as Immediate Reality.

Notes

1. William Riley Parker, *Milton: A Biography*, revised by Gordon Campbell (Oxford: Clarendon Press, 1996), 1: 603. "Milton was first and foremost the property of the popular culture, with editions of *Paradise Lost* numbering over one hundred, many of them illustrated, and just as often illustrated the more than seventy editions of his com-

plete poems. In 1796 an anonymous writer asked, 'Who has not . . . read Paradise Lost and Paradise Regained?' . . . *Paradise Lost* and *Paradise Regained* were now generating epic cycles." Joseph Wittreich, *Feminist Milton* (Ithaca, NY: Cornell University Press, 1987), 44–45. I concur with his argument that Milton's wide early female readership, a kind of "counter-culture" to the prevailing male elitist readership, in general revered his epic poems and his portrait of Eve. On Milton's reception in the eighteenth century see also the two volumes compiled by John T. Shawcross, *Milton: The Critical Heritage* (London: Routledge and Kegan Paul, 1970–2). I wish to thank Paula Backscheider for many helpful suggestions during the long genesis of this essay, and thank Cassandre Gniady, Annaliisa Trulio, and Brian Reynolds for unstinting research and technical assistance.

2. Parker, *Milton*, 1: 594.

3. Margaret Anne Doody, *The Daring Muse: Augustan Poetry Reconsidered* (Cambridge: Cambridge University Press, 1985), 62. "Poetry" could refer to imaginative literature in general (*OED* 2.).

4. Robert A. Erickson, *Mother Midnight: Birth, Sex, and Fate in Eighteenth-Century Fiction: Defoe, Richardson, and Sterne* (New York: AMS Press, 1986), 128–31, 136–37; "The Heart of Eve: Satan and Eve in *Paradise Lost*," in *The Language of the Heart 1600–1750* (Philadelphia: University of Pennsylvania Press, 1997). I extend in the present essay my "Lucretian" reading of *Paradise Lost*.

5. Milton's first description of Adam and Eve stresses their noble shape, "erect and tall," their "naked Majesty," the truth, wisdom, sanctitude, and freedom that radiates from their godlike image, and their difference from each other: "For contemplation hee and valor form'd / For softness she and sweet attractive Grace" (*PL* 4.288–98). The beauty and softness (compassion) of Milton's Eve, and her "Grace" and "Dignity" (5.827, 8.489), are perhaps her chief legacy to the representation of young women in the fiction and poetry written by women in the eighteenth century. Clara Reeve's the "soft sex" had by 1756 become

more the sex of loose superficiality than compassion and sympathy; see *Eighteenth-Century Women Poets*, ed. Roger Lonsdale (Oxford: Oxford University Press, 1989), 248. Besides the well-known examples of "extraordinary beauty" and sensuousness in Fielding's Fanny Goodwill with her "swelling breasts" (echoing *PL* 4.495) in *Joseph Andrews*, Lennox's beautiful Arabella with her "sweet and insinuating Voice, and an Air so full of Dignity and Grace, as drew the Admiration of all who saw her" in *The Female Quixote*, and Burney's *Evelina*, whose name and beauty link her with Eve, there are the less well-known Eve-like figures in the lively Amoranda of Davys's *The Reformed Coquet*, and Ardelisa in Aubin's *The Strange Adventures of the Count de Vinevil*. See *Popular Fiction by Women 1660–1730: An Anthology*, ed. Paula R. Backscheider and John J. Richetti (Oxford: Clarendon Press, 1996), 116.

6. Paula Backscheider in a private communication. See her elaboration of this point with respect to the emergence of women characters in the imaginative literature of the early eighteenth century in "The Novel's Gendered Space," in *Revising Women: Eighteenth-Century "Women's Fiction" and Social Engagement*, ed. Paula Backscheider (Baltimore, MD: Johns Hopkins University Press, 2000), 6–15.

7. Dustin Griffin, *Regaining Paradise: Milton and the Eighteenth Century* (Cambridge: Cambridge University Press, 1986), ix.

8. I am using the term "pornography" in its literal sense as writing about prostitutes. That's obviously not the only sense, but in the much vexed controversy over what constitutes "pornography," this definition seems the most significant one when talking about early modern literature and culture. See James Grantham Turner, *Libertines and Radicals in Early Modern London: Sexuality, Politics, and Literary Culture, 1630–1685* (Cambridge: Cambridge University Press, 2002), xii.

9. John Milton, *Paradise Lost*, in *John Milton: Complete Poems and Major Prose*, ed. Merritt Y. Hughes (New York: Odyssey Press, 1957), 281 (Book IV, line 141). References are to this edition by book and line number.

10. Eve displays whimsy, playfulness, caprice, traits associated with Fancy (discussed

below). Her playfulness also fits with the other adjectives of her innocent demeanor, "wanton" and "coy" (*PL* 4.306, 310), and with her "sweet, reluctant, amorous Delay" (*PL* 4.311), a trait often echoed in early modern fiction (e.g. he "held to his burning Bosom her half-yielding, half-reluctant Body." Haywood, *Fantomina*, in *Popular Fiction by Women 1660–1730*, 235). She is Milton's final conception of "Mirth." Eve is also a woman who gives and receives "pleasure," erotic, aesthetic, intellectual: "Yet went she not, as not with such discourse / Delighted, or not capable her Ear / Of what was high: such pleasure she reserv'd, *Adam* relating" (8.48–50). For a very different feminist reading of Eve and the pool scene, and how it might relate to Defoe's Roxana, see Robyn Wiegman, "Economies of the Body: Gendered Sites in *Robinson Crusoe* and *Roxana*," *Criticism* 31 (1989): 33–51.

11. See George Sensabaugh, *Milton in Early America* (Princeton, NJ: Princeton University Press, 1964), 98–109.

12. On the basis of this passage, Terry Castle can assert that "eighteenth-century writers [on masquerade] . . . implicitly followed Milton." *Masquerade and Civilization: The Carnivalesque in Eighteenth-Century English Culture and Fiction* (Stanford, CA: Stanford University Press, 1986), 66 note. Compare also the still pervasive notion of what I call the "Galenic body" underlying the "Fountain" image here, and my initial epigraphs (see *The Language of the Heart*, 6–11, 14, 18, 22, 154).

13. "A Letter from Artemiza in the Towne to Chloe in the Countrey," in *The Poems of John Wilmot, Earl of Rochester*, ed. Keith Walker (Oxford: Blackwell, 1984), ll. 54–63. References are to this edition.

14. Jane Barker, *Love Intrigues* ("To an exact Perfection he had brought / The Action Love, the Passion be [sic] forgot") in *Popular Fiction by Women 1660–1730*, 91.

15. *Oxford English Dictionary*, sense 1. The word *pathos* and its linguistic relatives, especially "passion," will play a large part in this essay. Pathos as feeling, especially as suffering and disease, is akin to *pathein*, to suffer, to feel, and the basic meaning of passion is suffering.

16. Robert Burton, *The Anatomy of Melancholy*, ed. Thomas C. Faulkner, Nicolas K. Kiessling, and Rhonda Blair (Oxford: Clarendon Press, 1989), 1: 132–33.

17. *Selected Writings of Francis Bacon*, ed. Hugh G. Dick (New York: Modern Library, 1955), 18.

18. In this regard, see *The Whole Duty of Woman* (1737) which warns, "Those amorous Passions, which it is [the novel's] Design to paint to the utmost Life, are apt to insinuate themselves into their unwary Readers, and by an unhappy Inversion a Copy shall produce an Original," quoted in William Beatty Warner, "Staging Readers Reading," in *Reconsidering the Rise of the Novel*, ed. David Blewett, a special issue of *Eighteenth-Century Fiction* 12 (2000): 402.

19. For Milton's literary affinities with Nordic shamanism, see my "'Rapt Above the Pole': Milton and Shamanism," in *Shamanhood: Symbolism and Epic*, ed. Juha Pentikainen (Budapest: Akademiai Kiado, 2001), 221–35. See also my "Words of Power: *Paradise Lost*, Shamanism, and the *Kalevala*," in *Styles and Positions: Ethnographic Perspectives in Comparative Religion*, ed. Heikki Pesonen, Tuula Sakaranaho, Tom Sjöblom, Terhi Utriainen, (Helsinki: University of Helsinki, 2002), 98–124.

20. Adam's lines immediately following, "Grace was in all her steps, Heav'n in her Eye, / In every gesture dignity and love," were often quoted by Milton's female readers, including Haywood in her *Female Spectator* of 1745, cited by Wittreich, *Feminist Milton*, 58. Wittreich goes on to note that "Lady Mary Wortley Montagu had spoken early (in 1717) of the 'majestic Grace which Milton describes of our General Mother,' a Milton who from her point of view is committed to freeing poetry of its 'Monkish Chain' and to 'reform[ing] the taste of a degenerate Age'" (p. 58). Eighteenth-century women readers of Milton, like Haywood and Montagu, were acutely conscious of the erotic element in Eve's "Love" for Adam, before and after the Fall. Compare Martha Sansom (Haywood's bête noire) in "To Cleon's Eyes" (1720): "Or when in nobler language dressed / With Milton's spirit they [the eyes] are

blessed: / Thus Adam tenderly surveyed / With guiltless looks the blushing maid, / Who met his eyes unskilled in art: / They were no prudes but spoke her heart," *Eighteenth-Century Women Poets*, 87. The stress on "dissolution" and "infusion" in this paragraph suggests the Galenic, as opposed to the Harveian body, as discussed in the introduction to *The Language of the Heart*.

21.   Compare Ovid, *Amores* III.vii.39: "*At qualem vidi tantum tetigique puellam!*" ["What a girl I saw, and what a girl I was touching!"] Ovid, *The Art of Love*, trans. Rolfe Humphries (Bloomington: Indiana University Press, 1957), 81. Compare Pope: "Her I transported touch, transported view, / And call her *Angel*! *Goddess*! *Montague*!" "Sober advice from Horace, to the Young Gentleman about Town," lines 165–66. Alastair Fowler notes "vehement" (1.526) from *vehe-mens*, "lacking in mind." *The Poems of John Milton*, ed. John Carey and Alastair Fowler (London: Longman, Green & Co., 1968), 843. The most significant analogue to Adam's "passion" and confession here is Satan's great soliloquy near the opening of Book IV. "Thus while he spake, each passion dimm'd his face" (4.114), and the whole speech (his first without an interlocutor) – Satan's confession that "Heav'n's matchless King" created him and that he seduced the other angels with vain promises of victory – originates in a state of mental conflict or "distraction" ("horror and doubt distract / His troubl'd thoughts" [4.18–19]). He is beside himself, in a state of psychic *ekstasis* as his "conscience" self (4.23) struggles with his "Hell" self ("myself am Hell" [4.75]), and fails. As we shall see, the conclusion of Defoe's *Roxana* is an exploration of this basic sense of ecstasy as madness.

22.   Compare Lysander to Cleomira in Haywood's *The British Recluse* (1722): "Thou loveliest—wisest—Best of all created Beings! . . . To be permitted to adore you, is Ecstasy too great to bear in Silence!—O give my impetuous Transports leave to vent themselves" (*Popular Fiction by Women 1660–1730*, 167–68). Cf. Adam's inner exclamation after Eve's fall: "O fairest of Creation, last and best / Of all God's Works" (9.896–97).

23.   A useful distinction can be made between poetry of "stasis" (from the Greek word for

"standing"), which as in Ben Jonson's "To Penshurst" and the "country house" poetic genre celebrates the virtues of stability, permanence, social equilibrium, family tradition, the regenerative human bonds with nature and myth, and the poetry of "ekstasis," which explores all the varieties of erotic and religious rapture, trance, transport, transcendence, ecstasy, and madness.

24.   The word "Defac'd" recalls the mutilation of prostitutes as described in Turner's *Libertines and Radicals In Early Modern London*, 24–29. Turner does not make the connection with Milton's Eve. Compare *Mother Midnight* on Clarissa and Eve, 137. The word can apply equally to "a Man enslav'd to the Rage of his vicious Appetite; how he defaces the Image of God in his Soul." *Roxana, The Fortunate Mistress or, a History of the Life and Vast Variety of Fortunes of Mademoiselle de Beleau, Afterwards call'd The Countess de Wintelsheim, in Germany. Being the Person known by the Name of the Lady Roxana in the Time of Charles II*, ed. Jane Jack (London: Oxford University Press, 1964), 75. References are to this edition. Compare also the excellent Penguin edition (1986) edited by David Blewett. I am indebted to his notes and his discussion of Roxana's mental history in the introduction. See also William B. Warner, *Licensing Entertainment: The Elevation of Novel Reading in Britain, 1684–1750* (Berkeley and Los Angeles: University of California Press, 1998): 149–75.

25.   John Cleland, *Memoirs of a Woman of Pleasure*, ed. Peter Sabor (Oxford: Oxford University Press, 1986), 78–79. References are to this edition.

26.   Compare Michael Wilding, "*Paradise Lost* and *Fanny Hill*," *Milton Quarterly* 5 (1971): 14–15.

27.   This entire process owes much to Milton's reading and remembrance of Lucretian epistemology, psychology of perception, and erotics of physical desire, especially in the fourth book of *De rerum natura*. See *The Language of the Heart*, 19–22, 50, 91–92, 101, 116, 135.

28.   And conversely the ambivalent image of fire in the fallen world may also have holy, inspirational, and purgative virtues, as in Peter Bembo's ecstatic description in *The Courtier*

(translated by Sir Thomas Hoby) of how the soul, "kindled in the most holy fire of heavenly love," achieves ultimate union with God, perhaps the greatest mystical vision of heaven articulated in the Renaissance. Baldassare Castiglione, *The Book of the Courtier* (London: J. M. Dent, 1928), 319. The image of holy fire recurs constantly in the literature of ecstatic mysticism. Martin Buber was the first to combine "ecstasy" and "confession." See his *Ecstatic Confessions*, ed. Paul Mendes-Flohr, trans. Esther Cameron (San Francisco: Harper and Row, 1985). Willis Barnstone was the first to use the phrase "poetics of ecstasy." See his *Poetics of Ecstasy: Varieties of Ekstasis from Sappho to Borges* (New York: Holmes and Meier, 1983).

29. Aphra Behn, *The Fair Jilt, or the History of Prince Tarquin and Miranda* in *The Works of Aphra Behn*, ed. Janet Todd (Columbus: Ohio State University Press, 1995), vol. 3, *The Fair Jilt and Other Short Stories*, 9. References are to this edition.

30. Michel Foucault, *The History of Sexuality.* Vol. 1: *An Introduction*, trans. Robert Hurley (New York: Random House, 1980), 61–62.

31. Haywood, *Fantomina: or, Love in a Maze* in *Popular Fiction by Women 1660–1730*, 228. References are to this edition.

32. From the title page of Haywood's novella in *Secret Histories, Novels and Poems*, 2nd ed., 4 vols., 1725, reprinted in *British Literature 1640–1789: An Anthology*, ed. Robert DeMaria, 2nd ed. (Oxford: Blackwell, 2001).

33. Daniel Defoe, *Roxana, The Fortunate Mistress* ed. Jane Jack (London: Oxford University Press, 1964), 75.

34. Terry Castle, "'Amy, Who Knew My Disease': A Psychosexual Pattern in Defoe's *Roxana*," in *The Female Thermometer: Eighteenth-Century Culture and the Invention of the Uncanny* (New York: Oxford University Press, 1995), 44–55.

35. In the critical ur-text on this novel, Maximillian E. Novak calls attention to the importance of the dance motif in Roxana's narration: "Crime and Punishment in Defoe's *Roxana*," *Journal of English and Germanic Philology* 65 (1966): 460, 464.

36. See John Dunton's description of how a "Bully" (a professional rapist), after four hours spent in bed with the bawd who employs him, attempts a young woman who has been lured into the bawd's house. When the girl resists him, the bawd gets out of bed and with the bully's assistance, ties the girl's hands behind her back, gags her with a handkerchief, and holds down one of her legs while the bully rapes her (see *Mother Midnight*, 274, note 26). Novak says that Roxana is "the only protagonist in Defoe's fiction who intentionally forces evil on another character" ("Crime and Punishment in Defoe's *Roxana*," 450).

37. It is telling that Roxana, deeply averse to marrying the Dutch merchant, defines marriage as a form of negative *ekstasis*: "that a Woman gave herself entirely away from herself, in Marriage" (Defoe, *Roxana*,147–48).

38. Jonathan Swift, *A Discourse Concerning the Mechanical Operation of the Spirit. In a Letter to a Friend. A Fragment in A Tale of a Tub To which is added The Battle of the Books and the Mechanical Operation of the Spirit . . .*, ed. A. C. Guthkelch and D. Nichol Smith, 2nd ed. (Oxford: Clarendon Press, 1958), 272. The speaker concludes, "I have been informed by certain Sanguine Brethren . . . that in the Height and *Orgasmus* of their Spiritual exercise it has been frequent with them *****," 288. In Cleland's *Memoirs of a Woman of Pleasure*, nearly all of the many uses of the word "extasy" are as a synonym for female orgasm. Compare Thomas Carew's "The Rapture" (1640): "souls entranced in amorous languishment . . . shoot into our veins fresh fire / Till we in their sweet ecstasy expire" (ll. 52–54)

39. See David Blewett, "Roxana and the Masquerades," *Modern Language Review* 65 (1970): 499–502, and his commentary on Roxana's masked ball in *Defoe's Art of Fiction* (Toronto: Toronto University Press, 1979), 127. See Novak's discussion of previous occurrences of the names "Roxana" and "Roxolana" in "Crime and Punishment in *Roxana*," 461–62.

40. "Instead of violently appropriating the masculine . . . [Roxana] aspires to a new category and actually declares that her ultimate ambition lies in a powerful androgyny," John Richetti, *Defoe's Narratives:*

Situations and Structures (Oxford: Clarendon Press, 1975), 195. In this role, and in her calculated theatricality, she also recalls the business woman Aphra Behn's famous assertion, in the preface to *The Lucky Chance* (1686): "All I ask is the Priviledge for my Masculine Part the Poet in me . . . to tread in those successful Paths my Predecessors have so long thriv'd in."

41. Rochester, "[A Satire on Charles II]" in *The Poems of John Wilmot*, 74.

42. "[William] Temple, *Introduction to the History of England*, believed [the Scythians] came from Norway and were the ancestors of the Scots." Swift, *A Tale of a Tub and Other Works*, ed. Angus Ross (Oxford: Oxford University Press, 1986), 210, note to p. 47; Swift links the Scythians to the modern Irish in *The Mechanical Operation of the Spirit*, 272. Early modern sources for Scythian lore were the fourth book of Herodotus' *Persian Wars* and Montaigne's *Essays*, book 3, chapter 5.

43. "Roxana's many changes cause her to fear being Proteus without a shape of her own; but now Susan defines her as a mother. What has previously been altogether too easy for Roxana – the shifting of identities – has become impossible. Susan is all the abandoned children in Defoe's novels. They have been ignored or bought off, and now they claim their relationship . . . Susan wants nothing of Roxana but to be acknowledged. 'She is my Mother; and she does not own me,'" Everett Zimmerman, *Defoe and the Novel* (Berkeley: University of California Press, 1975), 163.

44. Satan's symptoms are remarkably similar to those of lethargy, or stroke. Defoe was reported in the newspapers to have died of a lethargy. Long before he wrote *Roxana*, he adapted Milton's unholy trinity of Satan, Sin, and Death into his own verse allegory in *The True-Born Englishman*; see Paula Backscheider, *Daniel Defoe: His Life* (Baltimore, MD: Johns Hopkins University Press, 1989), 527, 75. See also Paul Alkon's discussion of Defoe's view of *Paradise Lost* with respect to anachronism in *Defoe and Fictional Time* (Athens: University of Georgia Press, 1979), 44–45.

FURTHER READING

Backscheider, Paula R. *Daniel Defoe: His Life*. Baltimore, MD: Johns Hopkins University Press, 1989.

Griffin, Dustin. *Regaining Paradise: Milton and the Eighteenth Century*. Cambridge: Cambridge University Press, 1986.

McColley, Diane Kelsey. *Milton's Eve*. Urbana: University of Illinois Press, 1983.

Parker, William Riley. *Milton: A Biography*. Revised by Gordon Campbell. 2 vols. Oxford: Clarendon Press, 1996.

Turner, James Grantham. *One Flesh: Paradisal Marriage and Sexual Relations in the Age of Milton*. Oxford: Clarendon Press, 1987.

Warner, William Beatty. *Licensing Entertainment: The Elevation of Novel Reading in Britain, 1684–1750*. Berkeley and Los Angeles: University of California Press, 1998.

6

Representing Resistance: British Seduction Stories, 1660–1800

Toni Bowers

Seduction stories obsessed British writers and readers between the Restoration of the Monarchy in 1660 and the end of the eighteenth century. Plots featuring coercive heterosexual relations, where questions about force and complicity loom large, recurred in virtually all genres; they were a language that everyone spoke, a focusing point for popular fantasy across social divides.[1] Precisely because seduction tales dealt with intimate matters and seemed far removed from politics, they could be used as "cover stories" for otherwise dangerous or incendiary ideas. In Dryden's *Absalom and Achitophel* (1681), for instance, a seduction tale functioned as a parable about monarchical succession, intervening in pressing public questions. And as we shall see, seduction stories also entered debate over the possible meanings of that odd legislative invention of 1707, "Great Britain."

The eighteenth century produced much of its most memorable seduction writing in prose fiction, where subtleties of inner motivation could be represented in detail, in ordinary language, by non-elite writers (including women) and in what could feel like real time. Stories of coercive sexual relations offered readers recognizable narrative rubrics: familiar plot devices, character types, and themes. These included the naïve young woman who is coerced, deceived, and ultimately "ruined," and the older, more knowing man who preys expertly on her unconscious desires. The predatory male character is more powerful than the woman he defrauds: of a higher social station, sexually experienced, and often his prey's relative or legal guardian – a circumstance that makes his behavior especially shocking, puts the woman in an intensely vulnerable position, and allows for suggestions of incest. The seducer orchestrates the woman's downfall with considerable cunning. Promising everlasting love, he instead abandons his unfortunate quarry once she has yielded. Most important, perhaps, sexual initiative is *his* prerogative in these stories, not hers. Only degraded women act first, out of their own desire. A virtuous woman's role is limited to that of respondent, and her choices are consent or resistance – though often female characters manipulate this binary to achieve indirect sexual agency.[2]

Along with these familiar topoi, we witness in eighteenth-century seduction stories an effort to imagine for the first time the now familiar (though still problematic) distinction between *courtship*, supposedly a process of mutual consent, *seduction*, which involves the gradual achievement of female collusion with primary male desire, and *rape*, an act of force defined by female resistance or non-consent.[3] From the Middle Ages until the seventeenth century, "rape" (*raptus*) denoted what we today understand as two separate actions, abduction and elopement. A man who carried a woman off from her father's home could be accused of rape whether she went willingly or not, and his victim in any case was not the woman herself, but her father. Rape was, in effect, a property crime between men. Though not entirely new, the notion that a clear distinction might be drawn between rape and seduction, as sexual acts defined according to female response, gained new power in our period.[4] During the eighteenth century, differentiating courtship, seduction, and rape became a central feature of popular fiction, although the same tales often demonstrated the difficulty of maintaining such distinctions. Seduction stories almost always included scenes where what is presented as legitimate courtship overlaps with (usually sexual) coercion; likewise, in many scenes putatively consensual sex can be hard to tell apart from what may now look like sexual violence. In the particulars, courtship, seduction, and rape tended to overlap, like the consent, complicity, and resistance that supposedly distinguished them.

Feminist theorists have long argued that when force is eroticized, when sexual arousal and satisfaction are routinely, as if necessarily, linked with domination – as is often the case today and was certainly the case in eighteenth-century British writing – a stable distinction between consent and non-consent becomes illusory. Under such conditions, the two models for consensual sexual relations – courtship and seduction – implicitly take place within the possibility of rape's violence and degradation.[5] The persuasions of courtship and seduction often contain in reserve the violence assigned (as if exclusively) to rape, while rape is not necessarily void of complicity and even consent. Indeed, the assumption that rape and seduction can be distinguished on the basis of female response – that a woman consents in seduction and resists in rape – presupposes more fundamental assumptions that demand examination. These include the assumption that pursuit and response are distinct acts in the first place, generated by coherent, unequivocally gendered subjects; and the related assumption that consent and resistance are necessarily categorically distinct.

Eighteenth-century writers of seduction fiction, a disproportionate number of whom were women, were among the first to represent convincingly female subjectivity as something in its own right, beyond mere abjection, vacancy, or complement.[6] Furthermore, seduction fiction offered readers ways to imagine agency – the ability to make effective choices – not only for women but for other "others" as well.[7] It is not too much to say, in fact, that the central preoccupation of seduction stories during the eighteenth century was less seduction *per se* than the effort to define the relative agencies of persons in relations of power and subordination. In particular, they were concerned with the agency of less powerful partners – those who have to say yes or no, but whose ability to choose is limited by dependence, social subordination, even physical vulnerability. So when seduction writers recycled familiar plots and rubrics, they were not just repeating themselves. They were doing something urgent for their time: struggling to find satisfactory ways to demarcate possible agencies available to unequally empowered persons.

Not only was there a great deal of seduction fiction produced in Britain between 1660 and 1760. More remarkable, seduction fiction was the special province of Tory writers during those decades, a period when Tories were largely disenfranchised from public politics (between 1715 and 1760, even officially "proscribed").[8] More remarkable still, after Tory proscription was lifted in 1760 the ideological location of seduction fiction shifted dramatically. Outsider Tories had dominated seduction writing until then; thereafter seduction paradigms beckoned writers of other partisan persuasions. By the 1790s, seduction fiction had become the specialty of radical writers – including British supporters of the French Revolution and outspoken feminist apologists. In short, the partisan locations and functions of seduction fiction shifted over the course of the century. Why?

This essay considers the changing ideological and partisan functions of seduction fiction across the eighteenth century. It examines the implication of seduction stories in one of the largest projects of British culture at that time: the effort (or refusal) to imagine difference within "British" identity – difference of gender, ethnicity, partisan identity, or political ideology, for example – and to mark out (or deny) possible agencies for Britons marked as "other" and subordinated by those in positions of dominance.[9] Women were marked and subordinated throughout the century; so were the ethnic and religious minority groups being problematically bundled into a new "British" identity, Scots prominent among them; so, before the 1760s, were Tories; and so, at the end of the century, were political radicals. Representing the complex subjectivities and agencies of these and others at once inside and outside a British identity still under construction became a necessary, but difficult, undertaking. Considering eighteenth-century Britain's obsession with seduction plots, it is not surprising that such stories were enlisted in the struggle, becoming crucial parts of an effort to imagine possible British identities at a formative moment, to understand "Britishness" as something realizable from within multiple social and cultural positions.

Seduction Stories and Scottish Resistance to "Great Britain"

The Union of 1707, one of the century's most important events in Britain, was not achieved without considerable struggle. Especially between 1705 and 1707, debate raged over the Articles of Union, a 25-point treaty that attempted to describe the new relationship that would pertain between England (and Wales) and Scotland after their merger into a single nation.[10] At stake were the line of monarchical succession, the future of constituent identities (what it would mean to be Scottish, English, or Welsh *while* British), and Scotland's relation to England's imperial pretensions, of which it was both object and subject. Seduction stories were indispensable to these debates, and revealed tangled relations among many categories of difference within eighteenth-century "British" identity. Ethnicity overlapped with gender, as writers argued questions of state formation and dissolution using the codes of seduction fiction.

In the years immediately preceding Union, for instance, resistant Scottish writers told powerful stories where sexual coercion stood unmistakably for the bullying tactics of Queen Anne's pro-Union ministers. Their stories demonstrate the attraction of seduction paradigms for those struggling to imagine autonomy within connection and agency within subordination, and allow us to observe how available sexual metaphors both permitted and delimited options for imagining resistant agency. Once Scotland and England were cast as partners in a seduction story, the forms and degrees of sovereignty resistant writers could imagine for Scotland were directly influenced by reigning assumptions about heterosexual agencies. Available plots and language placed limits on imaginable political relations; sexual metaphors exposed injustice, gave voice to resistance, and restricted the forms resistance could take, all at once.

In countless sexual stories told to debate the Union Articles, England appeared as the male agent, Scotland the female respondent. But the stories told by pro-Union writers, mostly English, were quite different from those told among resistant Scots. Even what to call the proposed merger was debatable. Pro-Union pamphleteers insisted that the Articles of Union were best imagined as marriage articles, the negotiations as a courtship remarkable for the generosity displayed by a wealthy and attractive suitor (England) who stoops to offer his hand to an impoverished old maid (Scotland).[11] Resistant interpreters told stories of coercion and deceit that emphasized the difficulties involved in creating a just union between a stronger party and a weaker one. For those with Jacobite leanings, the most appropriate story was often a tale of rape, the brutal cancellation of Scottish sovereignty and identity.[12]

What distinguished these opposing stories was the way each imagined the responsive agency of a feminized Scotland when faced with English overtures of Union. In the courtship story promulgated by Queen Anne's agents, Scotland was an autonomous respondent freely consenting to a good "Contract of Marriage."[13] In the seduction story, Scotland's agency was complicated and her consent compromised; at once resistant and colluding, her responses defied easy categorization. In the rape story, she is denied effective agency altogether: England forces "himself" upon Scotland against "her" will. But actually the distinctions between the three plots were never so clear. Courtship, seduction, and rape overlapped in stories about the Union as in much other fiction of the time, undermining the supposed differences between the three and casting doubt on the possibility of real choice or consent for Scotland.

We can watch this happening in a representative resistant pamphlet, *The Comical History of the Marriage Betwixt Fergusia and Heptarchus* (1706), a hybrid that combines imaginative fiction, historical review, political essay, drama, and dialogic debate.[14]

Scotland is personified in Fergusia, "a Lady of Venerable Antiquity, of a Competent Estate and Fortune, and a Sovereign over a Bold and Hardy People," England in Heptarchus, a "Gentleman . . . young, and Lusty, very opulent and rich, and upon that account a great Contemner of his Neighbours," on whom he "did nothing but commit Rapes" (3, 7). The pamphlet details the long, brutal "courtship" Heptarchus's forebears have offered over several centuries (a courtship at many points indistinguishable from sexual assault), and brings readers to the present moment of decision. Despite the "rough wooing"[15] she has undergone, Fergusia recognizes that some kind of "marriage" has become essential, and declares herself willing enough in principle. What is at issue, then, is not union itself – which both parties consider inevitable – but its configuration. Heptarchus wants "an entire Union"; Fergusia insists that she will consider only a union that "preserves my Independency and Sovereignty, as well as yours" (11).

The distinction had enormous importance at the time. Debaters on both sides saw theirs as a choice between two potential forms of Union, "federal" and "incorporating." "Federal" suggested a combination where uniting entities need not lose their constituent features, their essential differences. A federal union between England and Scotland, its supporters said, would be a limited arrangement, whereby the two states would unite only so far as union would be profitable to both – in certain aspects of trade or for mutual defense, for instance. In essentials such as national identity, state religion, and forms of governance, each would remain separate and sovereign.[16] "Incorporation," at that time an easier concept to grasp, had since at least the sixteenth century denoted a "melting down" of separate entities into an entirely new form.[17] To this traditional meaning had been added, by the early eighteenth century, the understanding that "incorporation" entailed the subsumption of a weaker entity into a stronger – "a smaller partner swallowed by a larger," as one critic has recently put it.[18]

The Articles of Union that were drawn up by the Queen's Commissioners and presented to the Scottish Parliament for ratification in 1706 were explicitly articles of incorporation, not federation. They entailed the dissolution of Scotland's Parliament in Edinburgh and the absorption of a fraction of its members into London's existing Westminster Parliament, where representatives of England and Wales would outnumber Scottish representatives by a ratio of more than eleven to one. Many Scots found the proposal intolerable, tantamount to a demand that they abdicate autonomous self-governance and national identity.[19]

In *Fergusia and Heptarchus*, the debate over federalism and incorporation is transposed, as it were, into the realm of sexual politics. Heptarchus equates incorporation with consensual marriage, and insists that anything less would not really be a "compleat Marriage" at all; "I can never be happy," he declares, "till you and I become one Flesh, and be entirely Incorporated" (12). But Fergusia insists on exposing the overlap between this proposal and Heptarchus's previous brutality and violence. She demands, "What Credit can You have to Marrie one whom You have so abused?" (14). The pamphlet ends without resolving the dispute. More important here, it foregrounds the problematic, overlapping relation of the metaphors it relies on: courtship, seduction, and rape. Heptarchus insists that he is now courting Fergusia, but Fergusia argues that there is little to separate his new approach from the rapes of old, especially since Heptarchus will turn to violence if the "courtship" is refused.[20] Fergusia reluctantly concurs with Heptarchus's plan, but one cannot really say that she is seduced or that she consents, since she has no viable alternatives. In *Fergusia and Heptarchus*, practices supposedly distinct – courtship, seduction, rape – are conflated uncontrollably. Any one of the three terms offers at once too little and too much; none can adequately name what is going on.

Furthermore, in exposing the built-in bad faith of the Articles, the pamphlet also exposes the injustices built into marriage as it was practiced across eighteenth-century British society – an "incorporating union" if there ever was one – and the poverty of existing frameworks of heterosexual relation to create justice. Heptarchus's arguments were clearly intended by the pamphlet's federalist author to invoke outrage in readers, outrage fueled by a nearly exact overlay between the patriarchal marriage that Heptarchus proposes to Fergusia and the incorporating Union that England was proposing to Scotland; but that outrage was only supposed to extend to the "real" meaning of the allegory, England's putative "courtship" of Scotland. Ironically, when the pamphlet damns the structure of incorporating Union by making clear how closely it parallels the structure of patriarchal marriage, it cannot but reveal (and assume readers who understand) that marriage too is what Fergusia calls the proposed Union: "a State of Politick Slavery." *Fergusia and Heptarchus* makes only too visible the contradiction involved in opposing the injustice of incorporation in one context (state formation) while practicing it in another (marriage).

Perhaps this explains why Fergusia can advocate a federal union but is not able to say with much specificity what such a relationship between sovereign nations would look like or how it would work (an inability shared by most federalists at the time). The problem may have been the difficulty for eighteenth-century writers of imagining a "federal" relationship between a man and a woman. Courtship, seduction, and rape were all models for sexual relation that made male desire primary while denying female desire (or rendering it deviant). Once these became the reigning models for relations between unequally empowered agents, the varieties of relation that could be constructed, or even thought, were limited. Union not dependent on domination and erasure, like marriage not built on the subordination of women or "Britishness" that did not entail the silencing and disenfranchisement of some, seems to have been difficult for eighteenth-century writers to imagine.

It would be a mistake, though, to see the strategies of *Fergusia and Heptarchus* as entirely unsuccessful. The pamphlet is undeniably powerful, not only because it pushes its own metaphors to their limits, but also because it exemplifies a peculiar, historically specific form of resistance. As we've seen, Fergusia does not practice out-and-out resistance to Union *per se*, but a more limited resistance to a specific form of Union, incorporation. In fact, Fergusia enacts a limited form of resistance much like that on display in seduction novels of the period: complicit, conciliatory, partial, strategic. Hers is the resistance of a woman who knows that "courtship" can be a codeword for force, but who has also learned that manipulating the codeword might be safer than calling down the force; who has discovered forms of resistance outside the reductive economy that assumes *either* passive acquiescence *or* active resistance; who knows that neither her consent nor her resistance need be a monolithic, all-or-nothing affair. Her response epitomizes a carefully calibrated *resistance that partakes in complicity* – what we might call "collusive resistance."

Stories like *Fergusia and Heptarchus* attacked the fiction of consensual incorporating Union and the assumptions on which that fiction relied – particularly the assumption that in unequal relationships, courtship's consent can be reliably separated from seduction's coercion and rape's force. *Fergusia and Heptarchus* is the story of a courtship that is also a seduction and a rape, a story that exposes pro-Union myths of egalitarian agency, to be sure. But it also (perhaps unintentionally) exposes other equally reductive myths: of Scotland's helpless victimization, of Scottish exceptionalism (the presence of Ireland in the pamphlet, not discussed here, does much to complicate the picture), of Scotland as always the object and never the agent of imperialism. Illusory binaries fail, and their failure suggests new possibilities: non-dominant agencies beyond mere "consent or resistance," originary desire for the subordinated, autonomous subjectivity within relations of dependence.

Unfortunately, the Union stories that prevailed were not nuanced tales of collusive resistance like *Fergusia and Heptarchus*, but the more palatable courtship myths promulgated by Queen Anne's agents. Still, the unsettling questions raised in resistant writing threatened for decades to undermine any emergent consensus over the meaning of "Britain" – particularly questions about the possibility of consensual participation in relationships of inequality underpinned by force. A tradition of complicated resistance continued to fester below the surface of nationalist self-congratulation. In the years to come, Scots both infiltrated the new British infrastructure and took the lead in successive Jacobite rebellions, while seduction stories pursued the connection between the disenfranchised (women, Tories) and collusive resistance.

That tradition continued even beyond the eighteenth century. Fergusia's collusive resistance, her attempt to retain a measure of autonomous sovereignty by means of strategic partial capitulations to imperialist aggression, was mirrored not only in Tory seduction stories during the first half of the century, but also in carefully calibrated attitudes toward Union still on display in the nineteenth-century fiction of Walter Scott, where famously – or infamously – ardent Scottish patriotism combined with a refusal to disparage the 1707 Union, indeed with a marked *approval* of the changes it brought to Scotland. For Scott, "British" was a valuable identity that need not exclude "Scottish."

Nowadays, Scott's attitudes toward the Union come in for strong disapproval from some Scottish nationalist critics. Scott's collusive habits, they argue, have led directly to a debilitating sentimentalization of Scottish nationalism, and to a vision of Scotland too easily incorporated into Great Britain rather than upheld in opposition to that fiction. In his willingness to embrace British identity, the argument goes, Scott is too willing to keep Scottish difference safely in the past, a matter for elegy and antiquarian curiosity but not a living political struggle. And this weakness, significantly, is labeled "Tory."[21] "Tory" emerges from such criticism less as the marker for an ideology than as a way to suggest what is somehow beneath ideology – "sentimental," "ambivalent," "diluted," and " compromising" – an oddly *a*partisan partisan position, insufficiently committed and without practical political agency.[22] Lacking a resistant agenda of its own and failing to mount any real resistance, "Tory," by such accounts, necessarily plays into the hands of other, more authentic, agendas. It is seducible: it does not effectively resist.

What such writing does not acknowledge is the practical, if often covert, power of strategic compromise, the resistance that can be achieved by means of collusion. In condemnations of Scott's "Tory" tendencies, there is at work an oddly impoverished notion of what counts as resistance: when faced with force, we are to believe, the only response worthy to be called resistance is counter-force. The kind of subtle, collusive, and strategically capitulative resistance at play in *Fergusia and Heptarchus* and in many Tory seduction stories, the notions that "British" need not eliminate "Scottish" and that "yes" and "no" are not mutually exclusive responses, the possibility of *resisting while colluding* – all these are never considered by critics for whom authentic Scottish identity necessarily exists against, rather than within, British identity. The possibility of collusive resistance flies under the radar, just as it does in the masculinist definitions of "rape" and "seduction" that developed during the eighteenth century and continue to feature in today's contests over sexual agency. "Rape," according to those definitions, requires absolute resistance uncontaminated by the presence of any capitulation, and "seduction" magically excludes violence.

The inability of many interpreters to recognize resistance except in obvious, force-oriented forms has made it difficult for collusive resistance to register as resistance at all, both in the eighteenth century and now. Seduction stories offer a chance to understand resistance differently. For what is most fundamentally at issue in eighteenth-century seduction fiction is precisely the complexity of resistant agency – its many potential locations, forms, meanings, and effects. Collusive resistance, though often represented with difficulty, becomes visible in seduction stories as the defining feature of resistant agency. We see it not only in the Union struggle, where resistant-while-complicit Scots refused to let rape go by the name of courtship, but also in eighteenth-century British politics before the 1760s (cut-throat and partisan as they famously were), where the outside-yet-inside position was the Tory position – uneasily collusive, never fully consenting. In the hierarchy of genres, prose fiction was distinctly subordinated at this time; and nowhere were the possibilities and limitations of collusive resistance more constantly in evidence than there.

Seduction Stories and Tory Resistance: *Pamela* and *Clarissa*

Available meanings of "British" changed over the course of the eighteenth century, and so did the shifting connections between familiar seduction topoi, the phenomenon I am calling "collusive resistance," and Tory ideology. Samuel Richardson held a pivotal mid-century position in the changing history of Tory seduction writing. The ideological heir of his Tory predecessors L'Estrange, Behn, Manley, and Haywood,[23] Richardson deployed and revised seduction rubrics for the 1740s in *Pamela* (1740) and again in *Clarissa* (1747–8), offering his generation not partisan polemic *per se*, but seduction stories where besieged heroines enact resistance by means of paradoxically virtuous collusions. And in the following decade, as we shall see, a shift in Richardson's Tory preoccupations heralded an ideological relocation of seduction paradigms.

In *Pamela*, Richardson introduced a new kind of heroine, a 15-year-old servant girl. But he put her in a position only too familiar from earlier Tory seduction writing: virtuous but disadvantaged, Pamela resists the sexual enticements/threats of an older, richer, better-educated, and well-connected man with legal authority over her. She eludes both Mr. B.'s seductions and his attempts at rape, insisting on courtship instead. But the distinction has struck generations of readers as containing little difference. Pamela continues calling B. "Master" after their marriage, and he continues his tyrannical ways.

Still, the quality of Pamela's resistance is significant. Pamela never resists so far as actually to end B.'s pursuit, though this is sometimes within her power (she could go home without finishing an embroidery project, for example, or refuse to return to B. when he is ill). The scorn that has been heaped on Pamela, on *Pamela*, and on Richardson as a result of this apparently half-hearted (if not actually fraudulent) resistance can hardly be exaggerated. Pamela's compromised resistance is routinely presented to students as an index of the failures of Richardson's novel and the duplicities of his false morality. But this reading, time-honored though it may be, shares all-too-familiar habits of mind that make it difficult to recognize resistance when it appears in other than direct forms – for instance, to see a woman who is not injured or killed in the course of a sexual assault as really having been raped. We must learn to think differently. I suggest that in Pamela's oddly acquiescent refusals Richardson enunciates a version of collusive resistance, a balancing act consistent with Tory *praxis* in his day.

Perhaps the least rebellious of literary rebels, Pamela is pious, modest, eager to oblige, and content in her role as a domestic servant; she constantly repeats her desire to be subordinate to Mr. B.'s will. But his demands are inconsistent with other submissions she longs to make – for instance, to the will of God and to the virtuous expectations of her father and mother. Richardson is at pains throughout the novel to make it clear that Pamela is by no means willfully rebelling against her master's authority. Her resistance takes place in the context of a delight in submission, an approval of a social hierarchy where she herself is near the bottom. Pamela is forced to move outside her station because Mr. B. first moves outside his, and she is distressed by this disruption of traditional order. "It is very difficult," she complains, "to keep one's Distance to the greatest of Men, when they won't keep it themselves to their meanest Servants. . . . It is more my Concern than my Pride, to see such a Gentleman so demean himself."[24]

In this distress, Pamela had much in common with Tories of her time. Tories had long espoused the doctrine of non-resistance, the notion that obedience to one's superiors (monarch, father, husband, brother, magistrate, cleric, master, teacher, and so on) was the same as submission to God. But once the order of succession had been derailed at the so-called Glorious Revolution of 1688–9, this tenet came under serious stress. To whom did one owe obedience when the reigning monarch was not the hereditary heir? Whigs decided early on that heredity was less important than suitability to rule a Protestant nation; Jacobites remained loyal to the hereditary king despite his Catholicism (an attraction for many Jacobites anyway) and even despite the fact that he lived in exile and only civil war could restore him. In distinction to both of these extreme positions, Tories tried to take a middle way: they cooperated with what they saw as an unfortunate and disturbing but still unavoidable reality.[25] Loyal to the idea of absolute monarchy but suspicious of its Catholic personification in the deposed James and his male heirs "over the water," uncomfortable alike with Jacobite schemes for violent restoration and the famously corrupt government of the triumphant Whigs, Tories like Richardson could not bring themselves to choose irrevocably between the ousted Stuarts and the now established Hanoverians, whose lack of hereditary priority seemed balanced by their ability to preserve a Protestant peace. Instead, they turned to stories about seduction, telling and retelling tales of compromised virtue, ambiguously lost innocence, and false choices.

In Pamela's repeated refusals of Mr. B.'s often violent proposals, Richardson was at pains to mark out a Protestant resistant practice carefully located between disrespectful rebellion and unquestioning submission, to delineate the vital space between force and counter-force so important to Tory identity and survival. Both "Tory" and "woman" stood as epitomizing figures of a specific kind of duplicitous agency in eighteenth-century British culture; both became repositories for paradoxically enabling uncertainties and contradictions; and both are epitomized in *Pamela*.

A heated debate followed the publication of *Pamela*, a debate concerned partly with the gendered sexual agency of the protagonists (who is seducing whom?) and partly with the novel's ideological agenda. (Does *Pamela* advocate resistance? Would that make it an apology for the Glorious Revolution?) This is not the place to go far into these questions, important though they were at the time.[26] But we can acknowledge that the ferocious 1740s debates over *Pamela* constituted a series of attempts to control the novel's ideological suggestions. The struggle over *Pamela* was a struggle for correct interpretation not of a single work, but of the relation between those in power and those subordinate. Among its stakes were the meaning and legitimacy of Tory ideology in a Whig world. *Pamela* mattered as much as it did because its representation of competing sexual agencies re-presented broader issues still troubling to the heirs of the Glorious Revolution. By attending to the debate over *Pamela* as a manifestation of partisan anxieties, we can perceive the ideological stakes of the century's most influential novel, and begin to understand the eighteenth century's obsession with seduction.

Richardson's dismay when readers failed to interpret *Pamela* as he intended has become a critical truism. But Richardson was not only troubled by readers' failures to place correct *moral* interpretations on Pamela's actions; his was also a *partisan* dismay over the discovery that his novel was vulnerable to Whiggish exploitation. Readings such as Henry Fielding's in *Shamela* (1741), though consistent enough with the largest outlines of *Pamela*'s plot, obscured crucial nuances: the great unwillingness with which Pamela resists the authority of her master, the oddly non-revolutionary aspects of her rebellion. These details shift the ideological weight and reveal *Pamela*'s implication with Tory sensibility – a sensibility that acquiesced, as it were, to resistance. Indeed, Richardson's driving need to revise *Pamela* for the rest of his life is attributable largely to his concern over the novel's vulnerability to ideological misreadings (he produced no less than fourteen editions as well as a novel-length "continuation" where the original story is painstakingly recounted and interpreted by a variety of characters). A partisan focus also helps us to understand another much-remarked phenomenon, the fact that Richardson's revisions tamed the text in important ways and attempted, often with some strain, to reduce its ambiguities.[27] Over the course of the century, a constantly revised Pamela became less low-class, less revolutionary in her language, and ever less willing to cross or humiliate Mr. B. – indeed, altogether more Tory. The 1741 continuation, too, worked hard to establish the heroine as an approving part of class and gender systems inherited from a time before the Glorious Revolution.

Even Richardson's masterpiece *Clarissa* (1747–8) can be seen as an attempt to rewrite his first novel so as better to communicate the peculiar complexities of a Tory ideological stance at mid-century. *Clarissa*, after all, was composed in the context of the final Jacobite rebellion (1745), and was published in that rebellion's immediate wake. At that climactic moment, Richardson offered not a simple tale of force, but a meditation on the complexities of desire and resistance. In *Pamela* the would-be seducer and inept rapist dwindled by degrees into a husband, his stagey sexual assaults mutating into a disturbingly violent courtship. In *Clarissa* the suitor/seducer is always also a rapist; an undertow of violence constantly exposes the bogus, overdetermined "choice" he offers his prey. Clarissa exercises autonomous agency within brutally dehumanizing circumstances not by choosing to be courted rather than to be seduced or raped, but by refusing to choose among those false alternatives at all; even rape is dignified with neither resistance nor representation, nor is it permitted to leave a lasting stain.

In short, the darkest suggestions of seduction fiction's familiar rubrics come to life in *Clarissa*. The rape of the heroine becomes less an aberration than the ultimate manifestation of the structures of dominance and subordination that order the novel's world, making force inevitable not only between Lovelace and Clarissa but in virtually every human relationship. Lovelace's rape of Clarissa – which, famously, is never represented – is inseparable from the myriad acts and omissions that accommodate, approximate, and replicate rape, making it not merely thinkable, but ultimately unavoidable.[28]

Lovelace stands for all the misreaders, both of *Pamela* and of Tory resistant practice, when he exults that Clarissa, once no longer "corporately inviolate," will be able to "tell no tales" and "(be her resistance what it will) even her own Sex will suspect a yielding in Resistance."[29] His binary reading, according to which any yielding necessarily discredits resistance, reveals an impoverished moral imagination. Clarissa is raped, but not because she resists (at the moment of rape she is unconscious) and not even because she never capitulates. Along the way Clarissa's resistance does sometimes weaken: she corresponds with Lovelace despite her better judgment; she lets him talk her out of the garden gate; later, she actually contemplates marrying him. Examples might be multiplied. The point is that Clarissa achieves a triumph beyond Lovelace's conception, a triumph of collusive resistance that defeats courtship, seduction, *and* rape. The silenced woman *can* still "tell tales," and yielding by no means neutralizes or invalidates resistance – but rather, indeed, authenticates it.

After Seduction: *Sir Charles Grandison* and Later Tory Fiction

Tory proscription ended in 1760. By that time, the tensions that had defined public debate for the first half of the eighteenth century – English/Scottish, Church/Dissent, and Whig/anti-Whig tensions, primarily – had begun to alter. Both the Jacobite separatist political agenda and the discomfited and disenfranchised Tory opposition had to a large extent been subsumed or dismantled. True, elimination of the Jacobite threat was by no means as sudden as historians sometimes imply; it was years after the decisive Battle of Culloden before Britons could be certain that the Jacobites would not rise again, and degrees of security varied regionally. Nevertheless, as the realization dawned that Stuart hopes were at an end, it permanently altered Toryism in Britain. No longer were Tories driven to distinguish themselves from Jacobite extremism, and what "Tory" meant could develop along other lines.

By 1760, as well, the changes brought about at the Glorious Revolution had become distinctly less troubling. Many years had passed. The Hanoverian dynasty was familiar, its legitimacy less questionable merely because it was so long established. The violent divisions between Whigs and Tories that had characterized the first half of the century smoothed out during the 1760s, a decade when social unrest at home and in colonies abroad tended to draw the ruling classes together. Most importantly, "British" was becoming an increasingly powerful identity. Long-promised economic benefits of the Union were at last beginning to be felt in Scotland, and Scots increasingly began to establish themselves in positions of authority, especially in military and imperial posts. By 1763 a Scot had even risen to become Prime Minister.[30] British military victories of the century's early decades combined with those of the Seven Years War (1756–63) to produce unimagined wealth and imperial influence. In short, early-century crises were resolving: the Jacobite threat was disintegrating, Britain was growing ever richer at home and mightier abroad, and both Tory and Scottish assimilation were moving forward apace.[31]

A specifically Tory response to these developments is manifest in Richardson's final novel, *Sir Charles Grandison*, which appeared during the post-Culloden period of Tory redefinition. *Grandison* (1753–4) starts out as a typical Tory seduction story: Harriet Byron is kidnapped and nearly forced to marry a Lovelacean figure, Sir Hargrave Pollexfen. But this plot is hardly the center of the novel. Indeed, Richardson dispenses with the seduction story with surprising speed (for Richardson, that is) and goes on to replace it with a new kind of story with elements now associated with the "novel of manners."[32] Those elements would have enormous influence on subsequent eighteenth-century novelists, especially the ideological heirs of early-century Tory seduction writers – "conservative" authors such as Frances Burney, Jane Austen, and Susan Ferrier, in whose novels traditional seduction plots often form subplots or backstories. Burney's *Evelina* (1778), for instance, is literally a "second-generation" seduction story: the heroine is the offspring of an early-century-style seduction and abandonment. She learns to negotiate the social minutiae that were the stock-in-trade of polite society and polite fiction in the second half of the century, and eventually not only avoids her mother's fate but recuperates it, literally rewriting the earlier story. Burney's novel, like many to follow, owed much to *Grandison*'s move away from received Tory seduction paradigms.

But *Grandison* not only pointed to a new generic future for Tory novels. It also looked back on the pressures that since the seventeenth century had shaped Tory fiction into seduction fiction. In particular, Richardson's final novel recalled the anxious pull of divided loyalties felt by many Tories until well after Culloden, when a Stuart restoration finally seemed impossible. It is not too much to say, in fact, that the most important function of *Sir Charles Grandison* at its first publication may have been its sustained consideration of the central problem for Protestant Tories of Richardson's generation: the problem of negotiating a response to "the King over the water."[33]

For what occupied Richardson much more than Harriet's old-fashioned adventure with Pollexfen was another episode, one that tends to put off readers today: Sir Charles's prolonged struggle over whether to marry or repudiate his Italian fiancée, Clementina della Poretta.[34] Supremely virtuous, elegant, generous, intelligent, and deeply in love with Charles, Clementina seems precisely the woman he ought to marry. Their attraction is powerful and mutual, their fortunes commensurate; her family encourages the match and his father leaves him entirely his own master. Nothing, it would seem, is amiss. Yet despite all these perfections, Clementina is also clearly *not* the right woman for Charles, for a reason only too legible, too relevant, to Richardson's contemporaries: she is a devout Roman Catholic.

In the world of *Sir Charles Grandison*, Clementina's religion necessarily entails unreasonable bigotry, oppression by tyrannical priests and patriarchs, and the influence of false advisers. It is the reason why Clementina lowers herself to duplicity, caprice, and irrationality when her passion for Grandison is thwarted. Charles loves Clementina and wants to be faithful to her; but he often suffers the brunt of her excessive pride, and eventually he finds it impossible to negotiate her family's religious arrogance. Their courtship is characterized by near-Machiavellian intrigue: relatives hide behind doors and screens to eavesdrop on the young lovers; anonymous notes are secretly exchanged; there are late-night visits from maidservants in disguise. In short, while in Clementina's orbit in Bologna, Grandison is swept up in the repertoire of deceit and dissimulation that had long been associated in British fiction with Continental intrigues, the goings-on of benighted, sex-obsessed Roman Catholics. Ultimately, all this prevents Charles from fulfilling his obligation to marry Clementina. The tragic story of Charles and Clementina is a story of hopeless longing and misplaced, untenable commitments between a tormented British Protestant, representative of all that is best in his nation, and a woman ideal in all but her Catholicism. It is a Tory story.

Clementina, the luxurious and passionate Roman Catholic, Richardson carefully sets against her English Protestant counterpart, Harriet Byron. And the courtship between Charles and Harriet could not be more different. Its beginning marks not the commencement of intrigues, but their closure, as Grandison puts an early stop to Pollexfen's predatory ways. Henceforth the relationship proceeds through rational friendship to esteem and eventually to love, building slowly through a series of well-lit drawing-room encounters under the benevolent eyes of well-wishing chaperones, in conversations marked by delicacy, good sense, and a kind of easy, unforced harmony of minds. It is no surprise when at last Sir Charles bestows on Harriet the supreme gift, himself.

Still there is conflict aplenty, as Charles struggles to do the right thing by his first love. Richardson's great concern is to be sure that Clementina's loss is in no way attributable to negligence or unfaithfulness on Charles's part. The hero has to be able to abandon his first love without *seeming* to abandon her at all, but rather to submit sadly to the inevitable. Accordingly, much is made of Grandison's agonized soul-searching, complete with several trips across Europe to present the Porettas with detailed "proposals" – suggested compromises that would allow Clementina to retain her religion were she to become Charles's wife. Painstaking negotiations ensue; the characters tread and retread an increasingly dismal circuit of proposal, rejection, counterproposal, and stalemate. What is lost in novelistic pacing through all this is gained in the assurance of honorable dealing and pure intentions on the part of the hero, and in a sense of the inevitability and justice of his eventual union with Harriet. The story of Harriet and Charles after all (as Harriet is constantly fretting) is the story of a *second* love, a second choice embraced only because the first went terribly wrong. Yet the union that eventually takes place between these two Protestant paragons emerges as more right than the connection between Charles and Clementina could have been – more peaceful, more workable, more natural. Unconquerable religious difference ultimately gives a greater claim to the second love.

Grandison's partisan resonances are complicated. In the letters that trace Sir Charles's prolonged struggle over Clementina, Richardson variously rehearses the impossible choices available to the exiled Stuart kings, to their faithful followers the Jacobites, and especially to Tories who, while painfully aware of the Stuarts' prior claims, nevertheless, with considerable misgivings, defaulted to the new, Protestant dynasty. Sir Charles can be interpreted as a figure for Britain itself, struggling between the glorious Catholic and the less illustrious, less entitled, but more appropriate Protestant "spouse." At the same time, it is possible to see in Sir Charles a type of his namesake Charles Stuart, who alongside his military campaigns tried for years to achieve a negotiated return. Clementina is like the Jacobites, misled by error but faithful to a fault. Then again, Clementina also suggests Prince Charles, whose prior claim was indisputable and who espoused Roman Catholicism at great cost. The novel's tone toward Clementina is consistently reverential, affectionate, elegiac, even wistful. Indeed, in the strange mixture of repulsion, fascination, and painful tenderness that *Sir Charles Grandison* brings to the representation of its doomed Catholic heroine and a Protestant's love for her, Richardson reveals most clearly, when it is finally safe, the long-denied, equivocal, but always present sympathy for the Stuart cause that had been part of Tory sensibility since the seventeenth century. In contemplating the lovely, lost Clementina, *Grandison* mourns the resonant absence, the denied collective memory and possible futures refused, that the Stuarts would always represent in British history.

Alongside Richardson's generic innovations and indeed as part of their necessity, then, *Grandison* offers a reconsideration of the nation's recent history, with emphasis on the complex agencies of those struggling to mark space between outright resistance and abject capitulation. In *Grandison*, Richardson attempted to assuage anxieties that had divided Tory and Jacobite for all of his own lifetime (he was born, fittingly enough, in 1689). The novel is its author's great experiment with thinking beyond the violence common to both seduction/rape/courtship plots and partisan politics earlier in the century; it marks a turning point in attempts to imagine authentic political identity and agency for those in subordinate positions. By dispensing early with seduction paradigms and concentrating instead on Sir Charles's agonized choice, *Grandison* marks an end of Tory seduction writing in the tradition of L'Estrange, Behn, Manley, and Haywood and exemplifies a new beginning featuring a new kind of heroine. Harriet Byron, while virtuous, is also "openly desiring":[35] she does not wait for Charles's declaration to recognize her own desire for him. In Harriet's combination of rectitude, wit, and forthright desire, Richardson demonstrates the dwindling need for Tory collusive resistance, and gives birth to something new.

Resistance and the Problem of Collusion:
Seduction Stories after 1760

By the 1760s, new points of resistance were emerging in British culture (which now included distant, dissatisfied colonies, especially in North America), points of resistance no longer defined primarily by narrow partisan alignments. There was growing awareness and sympathy for what Mary Wollstonecraft called "the oppressed part of mankind," a broad category that included, but was not limited to, women.[36] Courtship/seduction/rape stories, which for a century had been the specialty of Tory writers, became powerful vehicles for writers with very different ideological alignments. In Horace Walpole's *The Castle of Otranto* (1764), an inaugural work of eighteenth-century Gothic fiction, an avid Whig author figures political tyranny as an overlapping series of attempted rapes, purported seductions, and bogus courtships. Written at a time of renewed Tory influence, the novel reveals a surprisingly unsure Whiggish sensibility; there is real anxiety in *Otranto* about the displacement of a rightful hereditary monarch generations ago and about the future of a government built on that usurpation. But of more immediate interest here are novels explicitly devoted to seduction plots and the pronounced shift in their ideological center of gravity.

During the century between 1660 and 1760, in the work of L'Estrange, Behn, Manley, Haywood, Richardson, and others, seduction fiction had been aligned with Tory experiences and values (as these were variously constituted over time). But by the 1790s, seduction fiction had become a chosen vehicle for writers with radical agendas who struggled for new ways to imagine consensual relations among unequals and autonomous difference within British society. These writers placed ever-more-critical emphasis on social hierarchies that earlier seduction fiction had taken for granted. They worked to expose the implication of overdetermined personal choices within a larger world of injustice. For them, the complicated logic of collusive resistance, its emphasis on the complex inside/outside position of resistant subordinates, made it an unsatisfactory strategy – too hesitant, too duplicitous, and unlikely to bring about material change.

Accordingly, these writers separated Tory fiction's seduction paradigms from its collusive practices, exploiting familiar plot lines for new purposes. They deliberately opted against the manners genre ("In writing this novel, I have rather endeavoured to pourtray passions than manners," Wollstonecraft declared in 1798[37]) and sought instead to use seduction stories directly to resist larger systems of injustice and exploitation that doomed women (and other "others") to responsive, dependent roles. "Asylums and Magdalenes are not the proper remedies for these abuses," was Wollstonecraft's famous comment about seduction. "It is justice, not charity, that is wanting in the world!"[38]

This new emphasis on the material and social causes of women's "ruin" is evident in Mary Hays's *The Victim of Prejudice*, a radical novel from 1799 that is in many respects a retelling of the Tory tradition of seduction writing (especially of *Clarissa*) from a new ideological vantage point. Like Burney's Evelina, Mary Randolph is a second-generation seduction heroine, the daughter of a woman seduced and abandoned according to traditional narrative paradigms. Evelina's life was shadowed but not determined by her mother's story, but Mary is "a helpless, devoted victim"; the "frailty" of her "wretched and ill-fated mother" "entailed" calamity on her daughter. "Reflect on the consequences in which ye are about to involve your innocent, devoted offspring," Mary grimly directs her readers.[39] The warning is puzzling, since women's ability to save themselves (and their daughters) is by no means assured in this novel, no matter what they do. Mary's mother is responsible for all Mary's trouble because she submitted to seduction; but that submission was hardly a free choice. As the mother herself puts it, "I perceive myself the victim of the injustice, of the prejudice, of society, which, by opposing to my return to virtue almost insuperable barriers, had plunged me into irremediable ruin ... [Society's] institutions compelled [me] to offend."[40]

Unlike her mother, Mary resists sexual transgression and remains "virtuous" to the end. But that distinction, crucial in Richardson, turns out to be largely beside the point here. Mary's vigorously defended virtue saves her from none of the disappointment, pain, disgrace, and loss that were supposedly her mother's due as a fallen woman. Nor, significantly, does virtue protect Mary from despair. "Desert not yourself in any situation," her guardian Mr. Raymond tells her, as if quoting Clarissa's friend Anna Howe, "however difficult and perilous: never be induced to despair ... ever bear in mind, that on *yourself* depends the worth and the dignity of your character" (102). "I will not desert myself," Mary declares (140), Clarissa-like, and she responds with similar heroism to Sir Peter's assaults, even to rape. Indeed, Mary is more certain of her own spotless virtue than Clarissa was. Richardson's heroine was always keenly aware of her own failings, but Mary insists on her own "purest intentions, ... unconquerable fortitude," and "most spotless innocence." Nevertheless, all these "have availed me nothing" (41):

> My spirit ... acquits me of intentional error. Involved, as by a fatal mechanism, in the infamy of my wretched mother, ... I have still the consolation of remembering that I suffered not despair to plunge my soul in crime, that I ... eluded the snares of vice ... with dauntless intrepidity. But *it avails me not!* I sink beneath a torrent, whose resistless waves overwhelm alike into common ruin the guiltless and the guilty. (168)

Unlike Clarissa, Mary is destroyed at heart, utterly demoralized by sexual exploitation and the failure of justice. "The sensibilities of my heart have been turned to bitterness," she cries, "the powers of my mind wasted, my projects rendered abortive, my virtues and my sufferings alike unrewarded, *I have lived in vain!*" (174). Mary's friend Mrs. Neville sums up the action of the novel with chilling words that would never have been found in Richardson: "Injustice has triumphed!" (172).

While both Mary and Clarissa are hunted, drugged, and raped by powerful seducers, only Clarissa is able to redefine rape's cancellation of her voice and agency as merely temporary, and to reassert her difference from Lovelace with greater power after the rape than before. Mary attempts to do the same. "My honour ... will break out ... from the temporary cloud which envelops it, with undiminished brightness," she proclaims (119). But the option of transcendence, still viable for Clarissa, has been canceled for Mary. "Reason derides" the effort to reimagine society's inequitable assignments of power; to hope for something else is to be what Mary herself in the final words of the novel calls a "visionary projector." Paradoxically enough, there is more hope at the end of *Clarissa* even though the heroine dies than at the end of *The Victim of Prejudice* though Mary lives, because Mary exists only to await extinction. She has lost hope for justice in this world, the novel's only world.

"Injustice has triumphed!" The words mark the great difference between seduction fiction at the end of the century and earlier, Tory, seduction fiction. Inhabiting a moral world of little nuance, denying her own implication in the "institutions" that defeat women, Mary operates without Clarissa's ability to construct alternative forms of resistance outside relentless either/or paradigms that make rape the default human interaction.[41] Assailed heroines from the first part of the century could be disgraced, suffer unfairly, and even die, but their complicated virtue, achieved in strategic collusion, remained a valid currency that could circulate outside the reductive economy of consent and resistance. Tory seduction novels had remained always keenly aware of the complicity of the oppressed, and deliberately complicated the categories of victim and victimizer. The radical seduction novels of the 1790s, by contrast, re-establish stark alternatives. Evil is clearly marked, unmistakable, and relentless. Virtuous resistance, we are repeatedly informed, must remain untouched by collusion.

Why the shift? I suggest that the explanation is a political one. The tradition of seduction stories that shaped collusive resistance to the Articles of Union and found its fullest manifestation in *Clarissa* was linked indissolubly to traditional patriarchal authority structures and to the practical experience of overt subordination. The paradoxes and subterfuges built into Tory seduction stories during the difficult decades before 1760, habits that gave those stories peculiar power, were developed largely in response to the strictures of proscription: Tories had to learn to speak indirectly or risk being silenced altogether. A keen awareness of paradox and ambiguity resulted, but not a viable foundation for singly directed revolutionary action. The assumptions at work in seduction novels at the end of the century, by contrast, are in many respects less complicated, more programmatic. These stories aim to expose injustice and contribute toward its immediate revision. Denying the practicality of collusive resistance, impatient with compromise, exploiting inherited seduction paradigms in order to call for material justice in the present or not at all, their stakes are high indeed. When all is to be won or lost, less can be salvaged.

In Tory seduction stories before 1760 and radical seduction stories from the century's end, in other words, we encounter two distinct claims about what counts as effective resistance to injustice. Tory seduction fiction exemplifies what I have called "collusive resistance"; radical seduction fiction at the end of the century insists that only direct resistance will do. The difference between these visions of resistance is not unlike the difference between, on one hand, the strategically accommodating resistance of Scottish federalists before 1707 and of Walter Scott's Scottish-while-British patriotism, and on the other, contemporary Scottish nationalist criticism that decries such compromises as "Tory." For both 1790s seduction writers and certain contemporary Scottish nationalists, the rejection of Tory ideology entails the rejection of collusive resistance in favor of more direct rebellion. And not without reason. After all, Clarissa dies and Mary lives; and though Scott's work made Scotland desirable and distinct around the world, his critics are correct when they say that Scott's Scotland is a fiction that as often as not reduces Scottish difference to tartan tea towels. At the same time, it is worth asking whether Mary Raymond's life at the end of the novel is preferable to Clarissa's death, or whether the Scottish Parliament, resurrected in a surge of nationalism in 1999 but disappointingly limited and underachieving ever since, has improved on what went before. These questions point to the larger problem confronted variously by seduction stories across the eighteenth century: what counts as effective resistance? How might resistance be imagined and practiced among those aligned simultaneously with both dominant and subordinate groups – both British and Scottish, both loyal subject and Tory, both human and woman?

The history of seduction fiction over the course of the eighteenth century offers a clue. For early and late, Tory and radical, the most consistent and surprising turn in eighteenth-century seduction fiction is the subversion and revision of its own rubrics. Received assumptions and narrative patterns shape the stories, to be sure, but time and time again are quietly supplanted by other less certain, more provisional, rubrics. Even in Manley, the least nuanced of the great Tory seduction authors, seduction's "victims" share responsibility. And even in the 1790s, seduction is never quite a simple matter of victimized innocence; despite loud claims to the contrary, women's "falls" are always dependent to some degree on victims' complicity. (Hays's Mary refuses even to consider going to work as a servant; she agrees *after the rape* to manage a farm dependent on Osborne's goodwill; she never writes to the Nevilles for help, and asks William only once; she returns Osborne's money carelessly, exposing herself to malicious misunderstanding – and so on. Despite her protestations, Mary is hardly "blameless.") At the same time, the collusions of the seduced, both in Tory and in late-century seduction stories, never fully satisfy as sufficient causes for devastating outcomes that seem far out of proportion to characters' complicities and errors. (Should Clarissa really have had to *die* for feeling "a conditional sort of liking" for a notorious rake? Should Mary suffer so greatly for comparatively venal transgressions?) Across eighteenth-century seduction writing, the clarity of supposedly changeless, diametrically opposed positions – power and powerlessness, rape and seduction, virtue and vice, subject and object, Scotland and England, consent and resistance, Tory and radical, male and female – turns out to be an illusion. Between the lines, as it were, both Tory and radical seduction stories offer hints that undermine their own assumptions, traces of new rubrics for stories where human relations, whether the most intimate sexual relations or the broadest international ones, are based not in a false choice between all-powerful force and helpless capitulation, but in the deconstruction of that grim and somewhat pretentious formula.

Despite the appearance of a clear alternative between collusive and non-collusive resistance, in other words, the more closely we look at eighteenth-century seduction fiction the more it appears that neither alternative is quite distinct from the other. In that case, perhaps the most productive response on the part of the coerced might be a refusal of "either/or" choices like that Richardson experimented with in *Clarissa*, an abandonment of the fiction of stable difference on which binary choices are founded. Effective resistance might begin in a seductive politics that deconstructs the consent/resistance binary itself, recognizing the collusions always present in resistance, the resistance often at work in consent, and the always crucial variable of specific material circumstances.

Eighteenth-century seduction stories are not merely artifacts of a bygone era. On the contrary, they shed light on anxieties within "British" self-definition that remain pertinent in our own day and have relevance for the study of national self-definition beyond British shores. They reveal connections between resistant practices of many kinds. And they continue to invite readers to think critically about a world where force and submission too often remain the destructive alphabet of erotic representation, gendered identity, and nationalist agency alike.

See also: chapter 5, MILTON AND THE POETICS OF ECSTASY; chapter 11, NEW CONTEXTS FOR EARLY NOVELS; chapter 17, QUEER GOTHIC; chapter 22, THE NOVEL BODY POLITIC.

NOTES

1. Cf. John Richetti, *Popular Fiction Before Richardson: Narrative Patterns 1700–1739* (1969; repr., Oxford: Clarendon Press, 1995), 125; Jean B. Kern, "The Fallen Woman, from the Perspective of Five Early Eighteenth-Century Women Novelists," *Studies in Eighteenth-Century Culture* 10 (1981): 457–68; Susan Staves, "British Seduced Maidens," *Eighteenth-Century Studies* 14 (1981): 109–34; Jane Spencer, *The Rise of the Woman Novelist: From Aphra Behn to Jane Austen* (Oxford: Blackwell, 1986); Frances Ferguson, "Rape and the Rise of the Novel," *Representations* 20 (Fall, 1987): 88–112; Ros Ballaster, *Seductive Forms: Women's Amatory Fiction from 1684–1740* (Oxford: Clarendon Press, 1992), 77–78; and Toni Bowers, "Sex, Lies, and Invisibility: Amatory Fiction from Behn to Haywood," in *The Columbia History of the British Novel*, ed. John J. Richetti (New York: Columbia University Press, 1994), 50–52.

2. Cf. Toni Bowers, "Collusive Resistance: Sexual Agency and Partisan Politics in *Love in Excess*," in *The Passionate Fictions of Eliza Haywood: Essays on Her Life and Work*, ed. Kirsten Saxton and Rebecca Bocchicchio (Lexington: University Press of Kentucky, 2000), 48–68.

3. See Katherine Sobba Green, *The Courtship Novel, 1740–1820: A Feminized Genre* (Lexington, University Press of Kentucky, 1991); Isobel Grundy, "Seduction by Other Means? The Rape in *Clarissa*," in *Clarissa and Her Readers: New Essays for the* Clarissa *Project*, ed. Carol Houlihan Flynn and Edward Copeland (New York: A.M.S. Press, 1999), 255–67. Cf. Ellen Rooney, "Criticism and the Subject of Sexual Violence," *Modern Language Notes* 98 (1983): 1269–78; Joan I. Schwarz, "Eighteenth-Century Abduction Law and *Clarissa*," in *Clarissa and Her Readers*, 269–308. Legal scholars struggle to distinguish rape from seduction. See e.g. Donald A. Dripp, "Beyond Rape: An Essay on the Difference between the Presence of Force and the Absence of Consent," *Columbia Law Review* 92 (1992); Robin West, "The Difference in Women's Hedonic Lives: A Phenomenological Critique of Liberal and Radical Legal Feminism," *Wisconsin Women's Law Journal* 3 (1987), esp. 101–106, and "Legitimating the Illegitimate: A Comment on Beyond Rape," *Columbia Law Review* 93 (1993). Cf. *Harvard Law Review* 99 (1985–6); Lynne Henderson, "Rape and Responsibility," *Law and Philosophy* 11 (1992); Patricia J. Falk, "Rape by Fraud and Rape by Coercion," *Brooklyn Law Review* 64 (1998); and Joshua Dressler, "Where We Have Been, and Where We Might be Going: Some Cautionary Reflections on Rape Law Reform," *Cleveland State Law Review* 46 (1998): 409–42.

4. See Nazife Bashar, "Rape in England between 1550 and 1700," in *The Sexual Dynamics of History: Men's Power, Women's Resistance*, ed.

London Feminist History Group (London: Pluto, 1983), 28–42; Susan Staves, "British Seduced Maidens," *Eighteenth-Century Studies* 14 (1980–1): 110, 125–32; Joy Kyunghae Lee, "Seduction and the Eighteenth-Century English Novel: Constructions of the Feminine in Defoe, Richardson, and Burney" (Ph.D. diss., University of California, Irvine, 1994) and "The Commodification of Virtue: Chastity and the Virginal Body in Richardson's *Clarissa*," *The Eighteenth Century: Theory & Interpretation* 36 (Spring, 1995): 38–54; Miranda Chaytor, "Husband(ry): Narratives of Rape in the Seventeenth Century," *Gender and History* 7 (1995): 378–407, esp. 384–85; Julia Rudolph, "Rape and Resistance: Women and Consent in Seventeenth-Century English Legal and Political Thought," *Journal of British Studies* 39 (2000): 157–84.

5.   Catharine MacKinnon, "Feminism, Marxism, Method, and the State: Toward Feminist Jurisprudence," *Signs* 8 (1983): 635, 644. Cf. MacKinnon, *Towards a Feminist Theory of the State* (Cambridge, MA: Harvard University Press, 1989), 180–83, 194–214, and "Reflections on Sex Equality Before the Law," *Yale Law Journal* 100 (1991). Cf. Carole Pateman, "Women and Consent," *Political Theory* 8 (May 1980): 149–68; Andrea Dworkin, *Intercourse* (New York, 1987), 133; Susan Estrich, *Real Rape* (Cambridge, MA: Harvard University Press, 1987); Elizabeth V. Spelman, *Inessential Woman: Problems of Exclusion in Feminist Thought* (Boston: Boston Press, 1988); James Scott, *Domination and the Arts of Resistance: Hidden Transcripts* (New Haven, CT: Yale University Press, 1990), 29; Emily Jackson, "Catharine MacKinnon and Feminist Jurisprudence: A Critical Appraisal," *Journal of Law and Society* 19 (1992): 203; Elizabeth Rapaport, "Generalizing Gender: Reason and Essence in the Legal Thought of Catharine MacKinnon," in Louise M. Anthony and Charlotte Witt, eds., *A Mind of One's Own: Feminist Essays on Reason and Objectivity* (Boulder, CO: Westview, 1993), 127–43; John D. Walker, "Liberalism, Consent, and the Problem of Adaptive Preferences," *Social Theory and Practice* 21 (1995): 457–71; Jessica Benjamin, *The Bonds of Love: Psychoanalysis, Feminism, and the Problem of Domination* (New York: Parthenon,

1988) and *Like Subjects, Love Objects: Essays on Recognition and Sexual Difference* (New Haven, CT: Yale University Press, 1995); David Archard, "'A Nod's as Good as a Wink': Consent, Convention and Reasonable Belief," *Legal Theory* 3 (1997): 273–90; Kimberly A. Yuracko, *Perfectionism and Contemporary Feminist Values* (Bloomington: Indiana University Press, 2003), 14–20, 118; Frances Ferguson, *Pornography, the Theory: What Utilitarianism Did to Action* (Chicago: University of Chicago Press, 2004), 34–56.

6.   Nancy Armstrong, *Desire and Domestic Fiction*; Backscheider and Richetti, eds., *Popular Fiction By Women 1660–1730: An Anthology* (Oxford: Clarendon Press, 1996), x; Spencer, *Rise of the Woman Novelist*, 112–13; Margaret Anne Doody, "*Clarissa* and Earlier Novels of Love and Seduction," in *A Natural Passion: A Study of the Novels of Samuel Richardson* (Oxford: Clarendon Press, 1974), 128–50.

7.   For eighteenth-century ideas about agency, see Scott Paul Gordon, *The Power of the Passive Self in English Literature, 1640–1770* (Cambridge: Cambridge University Press, 2002), 22–23.

8.   Linda Colley, *Britons: Forging the Nation 1707–1837* (New Haven, CT: Yale University Press, 1992), 21–24, 55–57; Eveline Cruickshanks, *Political Untouchables: The Tories and the '45* (London: Duckworth, 1979), 3–4; K. G. Feiling, *A History of the Tory Party 1640–1714* (Oxford: Clarendon Press, 1924), 178.

9.   For "ethnicity" during this period, see Colin Kidd, *British Identities Before Nationalism: Ethnicity and Nationhood in the Atlantic World, 1600–1800* (Cambridge: Cambridge University Press, 2000), introduction.

10. The ghostly presence of Wales, though seldom recognized, overshadowed the Union debates. Both Scottish and English primary documents refer to "England" in an imperialist re-enactment that complicates Scottish arguments against Union. See Gwyn A. Williams, *When Was Wales? A History of the Welsh* (Harmondsworth, UK: Penguin, 1985).

For "nation" and "nationalism," see Ernest Renan, *Qu'est-ce qu'une nation?* (Paris, 1882);

Ernest Gellner, *Nations and Nationalism* (Ithaca, NY: Cornell University Press, 1983); Benedict Anderson, *Imagined Communities: Reflections on the Origin and Spread of Nationalism* (London: Verso, 1983); and E. J. Hobsbawm, *Nations and Nationalism Since 1780* (Cambridge: Cambridge University Press, 1990). Scotland, however, "may...be held to contradict [the] model" (Gellner, 44). Cf. Michael Hechter, *Internal Colonialism: The Celtic Fringe in British National Development* (London: Routledge, 1975); Christopher Harvie, *Scotland and Nationalism*, 3rd ed. (London: Routledge, 1998); H. Kearney, *The British Isles: A History of Four Nations* (Cambridge: Cambridge University Press, 1989); Linda Colley, *Britons*, and "Whose Nation? Class and National Consciousness in Britain 1750–1830," *Past & Present* 113 (1986): 97–117; David McCrone, *Understanding Scotland: The Sociology of a Stateless Nation* (London: Routledge, 1992); Brendan Bradshaw and Peter Roberts, eds., *British Consciousness and Identity: The Making of Britain, 1533–1707* (Cambridge: Cambridge University Press, 1998); William Ferguson, *The Identity of the Scottish Nation* (Edinburgh: Edinburgh University Press, 1998); Colin Kidd, *British Identities Before Nationalism* and *Subverting Scotland's Past: Scottish Whig Historians and the Creation of an Anglo-British Identity 1689–1830* (Cambridge: Cambridge University Press, 1993); Murray G. H. Pittock, *Scottish Nationality* (New York: Palgrave, 2001). For links between British nationalism and prose fiction, see Deirdre Lynch and William Warner, *Cultural Institutions of the Novel* (Durham, NC: Duke University Press, 1996), introduction; Robert Crawford, *The Scottish Invention of English Literature* (Cambridge: Cambridge University Press, 1998); Janet Sorensen, *The Grammar of Empire in Eighteenth-Century British Writing* (Cambridge: Cambridge University Press, 2000); Katie Trumpener, *Bardic Nationalism: The Romantic Novel and the British Empire* (Princeton, NJ: Princeton University Press, 1997).

11. See Anon. [attrib. Francis Grant Cullen], *The Patriot Resolved. In a Letter to an* Addresser, *from his* Friend; *of the same* Senti-

ments *with himself; concerning the UNION* (Edinburgh, 1707), 8.

12. See George Lockhart of Carnwath, *Scotland's Ruine*, 1714 (pirated ed.), 1817, ed. Daniel Szechi (Aberdeen: Association for Scottish Literary Studies, 1995); Howard Erskine-Hill, "Literature and the Jacobite Cause: Was there a Rhetoric of Jacobitism?" in Eveline Cruickshanks, ed., *Ideology and Conspiracy: Aspects of Jacobitism, 1689–1759* (Edinburgh: John Donald, 1982), 49–69; Kathryn R. King, *Jane Barker, Exile: A Literary Career 1675–1725* (Oxford: Clarendon Press, 2000), 160; Murray G. H. Pittock, *The Invention of Scotland: The Stuart Myth and the Scottish Identity, 1638 to the Present* (New York: Routledge, 1991), 32.

13. Daniel Defoe, *The Review*, ed. Arthur Wellesley Secord. Facsimile Text Society (New York: Columbia, 1808), III: no. 153 (December 24, 1706), 609. Defoe used marriage as one of many metaphorical figures for the Union. In Scottish resistant pamphlets, by contrast, marriage was the metaphor *par excellence* for incorporation, though there were others, especially cannibalism. See John Hamilton 2nd Lord Belhaven, *The Lord Belhaven's speech in Parliament, the 15th Day of November 1706, on the Second Article of the Treaty*, 4; [William Wright], *The Comical History of the Marriage Betwixt Fergusia and Heptarchus* (1706), discussed below.

14. Attributed on the title page to "William Wright," but in the second (English) printing to "Mr. Ballendine, a presbyterian preacher."

15. The term originated in sixteenth-century English-Scottish relations. See James Fergusson, *The White Hind and Other Discoveries* (London: Faber and Faber, 1963), 12.

16. See Anon. [attrib. William Black], *A Reply to the Authors of the Advantages of Scotland by an Incorporate Union...* (1707), 9; Andrew Fletcher, *Speeches by a Member of the Parliament Which Began at Edinburgh the 6th of May, 1703* (Edinburgh, 1703), *Andrew Fletcher: Political Works*, ed. John Robertson (Cambridge: Cambridge University Press, 1997), 132–34; Anon., *An Essay upon the Union. Shewing, That...the best Security...is, to have Separate Parliaments* (Edinburgh, 1706); James Hodges,

*The Rights and Interests of the Two British Mon-
archies . . .* (1703) and *The Rights and Interests of
the Two British Monarchies . . . Treatise III*
(London, 1706).

17. For "melting down," see Francis Bacon, "A
    Brief Discourse on the Happy Union," in
    *The Union of the Two Kingdoms . . . Or, The
    Elaborate Papers of Sir Francis Bacon . . .* (Edin-
    burgh, 1670), 6.

18. Susan Manning, *Fragments of Union: Making
    Connections in Scottish and American Writing*
    (New York: Palgrave, 2002), 9.

19. See Anon. [attrib. Andrew Fletcher], "State
    of the Controversy betwixt United and
    Separate Parliaments . . . Printed in the Year
    1706," ed. P. H. Scott. Saltire Society
    Pamphlets NS 3 (Edinburgh, 1982), 8.

20. Scots believed – and England strongly
    hinted – that if diplomacy should fail, Eng-
    land would go to war to secure union. See
    P. H. Scott, *Andrew Fletcher and the Treaty of
    Union* (Edinburgh: John Donald, 1992),
    147. Cf. the Earl of Mar's comment in
    P. H. Scott, ed. *1707: The Union of Scotland
    and England: in Contemporary Documents*
    (Edinburgh: Chambers, for the Saltire Soci-
    ety, 1979), 57; James Hodges, *War Betwixt
    the Two British Kingdoms Consider'd . . .*
    (London, 1705); [George Ridpath], *The Re-
    ducing of Scotland by Arms, and Annexing it to
    England as a Province, Considered* (London and
    Edinburgh, 1705).

21. Edwin Muir, *Scott and Scotland: The Predica-
    ment of the Scottish Writer* (London: Rout-
    ledge, 1936; Edinburgh, 1982), 86–87;
    Tom Nairn, *After Britain: New Labour and
    the Return of Scotland* (London: Granta,
    2000), esp. 230, 250–53. For "Tory" as de-
    scriptor for Scott's collusions, see Pittock,
    Invention of Scotland, 60–61.

22. Pittock, *Invention*, 54, 61.

23. For Richardson's partisan identifications, see
    Margaret Anne Doody, "Richardson's Polit-
    ics," *Eighteenth-Century Fiction* 2 (1990):
    113–26.

24. Samuel Richardson, *Pamela, or Virtue
    Rewarded* (1740), ed. Thomas Keymer
    (Oxford: Oxford University Press, 2001),
    35, 54.

25. Cruickshanks, *Political Untouchables* 3.

26. See Thomas Keymer and Peter Sabor, eds.,
    *The Pamela Controversy: Criticisms and Adap-
    tations of Samuel Richardson's Pamela, 1740–
    1750* (London: Pickering & Chatto, 2001).
    Cf. Richard Gooding, "*Pamela, Shamela*, and
    the Politics of the *Pamela* Vogue," *Eight-
    eenth-Century Fiction* 7 (1995): 109–30;
    Stephen Raynie, "Hayman and Gravelot's
    Anti-Pamela Designs for Richardson's
    Octavo Edition of *Pamela* I and II," *Eight-
    eenth-Century Life* 23 (1999): 77–93; James
    Grantham Turner, "Novel Panic: Picture and
    Performance in the Reception of Richard-
    son's *Pamela*," *Representations* 48 (1994):
    70–96; and William B. Warner, *Licensing
    Entertainment: The Elevation of Novel Reading
    in Britain, 1684–1750* (Berkeley and Los
    Angeles: University of California Press,
    1988), introduction.

27. See Keymer's fine introduction to the
    Oxford *Pamela* (2001).

28. Cf. Terry Castle, *Clarissa's Ciphers: Meaning
    and Disruption in Richardson's Clarissa*
    (Ithaca, NY: Cornell University Press,
    1982).

29. Samuel Richardson, *Clarissa: or, The History
    of a Young Lady* (1747–8), 3rd ed., 1751, ed.
    Florian Stuber et al. 8 vols. (New York:
    A.M.S. Press, 1990), 5: 283 (Letter LXXIV).

30. John Stuart, 3rd Earl of Bute (1713–92).

31. For Tory and Scottish assimilation, as well as
    significant remaining points of difference,
    see Colley, *Britons*, chapters 3–5.

32. See Bege K. Bowers and Barbara Brothers,
    *Reading and Writing Women's Lives: A Study of
    the Novel of Manners* (Ann Arbor, MI: UMI
    Research Press, 1990).

33. Cf. Kathryn King, *Jane Barker, Exile*, ch. 4,
    Howard Erskine-Hill, "Literature and the
    Jacobite Cause," and Toni Bowers, "Jacobite
    Difference and the Poetry of Jane Barker,"
    ELH 64 (1997): 857–69.

34. Cf. Wendy Jones, "The Dialectic of Love in
    Sir Charles Grandison," *Eighteenth-Century
    Fiction* 8 (1995): 15–34; repr. in *Passion and
    Virtue: Essays on the Novels of Samuel Richard-
    son*, ed. David Blewett (Toronto: University
    of Toronto Press, 2001), 295–316.

35. Doody, "Saying 'No,' Saying 'Yes': The
    Novels of Samuel Richardson," *Tennessee*

Studies in Literature 29 (1985): 67–108, at 98, 100.

36. Mary Wollstonecraft, *The Wrongs of Woman: Or, Maria. A Fragment* (1798) in Wollstonecraft, *Mary, A Fiction and The Wrongs of Woman*, ed. Gary Kelly (New York: Oxford University Press, 1976), 73.

37. Wollstonecraft, *The Wrongs of Woman*, preface.

38. Mary Wollstonecraft, *A Vindication of the Rights of Woman* (1792), ed. Janet Todd, in *Mary Wollstonecraft: Political Writings* (Toronto: University of Toronto Press, 1993), 150.

39. Mary Hays, *The Victim of Prejudice*, ed. Eleanor Ty (Peterborough, Ontario: Broadview Press, 1994), 1: 135–37.

40. Ibid., 66, 69.

41. The work of post-colonial critics is pertinent here, particularly the insight that "subalterns' resistance" can never "simply oppose power" but is always "also constituted by it" (Gyan Prakash, "Subaltern Studies as Postcolonial Criticism," *American Historical Review* 99 (1994): 1475–90, at 1480).

FURTHER READING

Archard, David. *Sexual Consent*. Boulder, CO: Westview, 1998.

Ballaster, Ros. *Seductive Forms: Women's Amatory Fiction from 1684–1740*. Oxford: Clarendon Press, 1992.

Bowers, Toni. "Seduction Narratives and Tory Experience in Augustan England." *The Eighteenth Century: Theory and Interpretation* 40 (1999): 128–54.

Doody, Margaret Anne. "Richardson's Politics." *Eighteenth-Century Fiction* 2 (1990): 113–26.

Kidd, Colin. *British Identities Before Nationalism: Ethnicity and Nationhood in the Atlantic World, 1600–1800*. Cambridge: Cambridge University Press, 2000.

Rooney, Ellen. "Criticism and the Subject of Sexual Violence." *Modern Language Notes* 98 (1983): 1269–78.

Part Two
The World of the Eighteenth-Century Novel

7

Why Fanny Can't Read: *Joseph Andrews* and the (Ir)relevance of Literacy

Paula McDowell

> How simple are our notions about literacy. How directly and linearly we conceive its consequences. How stark and inflexible are our assumptions and expectations about it. And how deeply we hold our faith in its powers.
>
> Harvey J. Graff, *The Legacies of Literacy*[1]

Should everyone learn how to read and write? Many eighteenth-century authors did not think so, for it was not yet taken for granted that literacy was an inherent good for all social groups. Schooling made sense for those who were likely to obtain careers that required specific educational qualifications or who needed it to govern or rule. But it was not only unnecessary but undesirable for those "born to poverty, and the drudgeries of life,"[2] wasting time that should be devoted to the larger social good. As Bernard Mandeville wrote in 1723:

> Reading, Writing and Arithmetick are very necessary to those, whose Business require such Qualifications, but where Peoples Livelihood has no dependence on these Arts, they are very pernicious to the Poor, who are forc'd to get their Daily Bread by their Daily Labour. Few Children make any progress at School, but at the same time they are capable of being employ'd in some Business or other, so that every Hour those of poor People spend at their Book is so much time lost to the Society. Going to School in comparison to Working is Idleness.[3]

In England, there was little support for state-sponsored public education, and in rural areas as much as half the population could not read.[4] Yet older assumptions about literacy as an occupational tool were increasingly challenged by arguments anticipating the modern Western assumption that literacy is a universal good. These shifts are reflected in the gradual transformation of the most common understanding of the term "literate," from the older meaning of literate as "learned" (*litteratus*: a person who knew Latin, or was learned) to the most common definition today: that is, having a basic ability to read and write.[5] In 1699, the Society for Promoting Christian Knowledge began promoting a system of privately supported charity schools primarily intended to socialize the poor. These schools would teach children the Bible, catechism, and basic arithmetic, and so "save souls, impart moral discipline, and relieve suffering."[6] Hopes for personal elevation through increased schooling were encouraged by popular narratives. In his best-selling novel *Pamela; Or, Virtue Rewarded* (1740), printer-author Samuel Richardson represented female servants' literacy as an intangible personal property that, properly invested, could turn a bountiful profit.[7] Another phenomenal bestseller, *The History of Little Goody Two-Shoes* (1766), published by children's bookseller John Newbery, relates "the Means by which [little Margery Goodwife] acquired her Learning and Wisdom, and in consequence thereof her Estate."[8]

Henry Fielding's novel, *The History of the Adventures of Joseph Andrews, And of his Friend Mr. Abraham Adams* (1742), was written in the midst of these debates concerning literacy and schooling, and tells us much about the eighteenth century as a key transitional period with links both to modernity and to the past. This essay reads *Joseph Andrews* as a sustained engagement with contemporary debates concerning education, especially the type of education befitting the "lower Orders of Mankind." Echoing Mandeville's "Essay on Charity-Schools" as well as John Locke in *Some Thoughts Concerning Education* (1693), Fielding challenges key assumptions of arguments for broader schooling. By means of his central characters in both *Joseph Andrews* and *Shamela* (1741), he systematically shows that there is no necessary causal relationship between literacy and (i) virtue (his virtuous country lass Fanny Goodwill, the future wife of his hero, can neither read nor write); (ii) moral improvement (the corrupt Shamela Andrews devours books sent to her by her bawd mother and tutor in immorality, Parson Arthur Williams); or (iii) socioeconomic elevation (Parson Abraham Adams, the most "literate" character in *Joseph Andrews*, is patriarch of the most "ragged Family in the Parish,"[9] and subject to every kind of humiliation and contempt).

Many of the seemingly incidental episodes of *Joseph Andrews* participate in a broader sociocultural debate on education. One of the first things Fielding shows us about his footman hero is his contentment with his minimal schooling. By ten years old, Joseph's "Education was advanced to Writing and Reading" (1.2.21), but the same year, when he entered into the service of Sir Thomas Booby, his formal education ceased. What additional learning he has gained is the product of his few "Hours of Leisure" and of minutes stolen from his work when he reads "without being perceived":

> Ever since he was in Sir *Thomas*'s Family, he had employed all his Hours of Leisure in reading good Books; that he had read the Bible, the *Whole Duty of Man*, and *Thomas à Kempis*; and that as often as he could, without being perceived, he had studied a great good Book which lay open in the Hall Window. (1.3.24)

Yet when Parson Adams asks Joseph "if he did not extremely regret the want of a liberal Education, and the not having been born of Parents, who might have indulged his Talents and Desire of Knowledge?" Fielding's hero responds:

> he hoped he had profited somewhat better from the Books he had read, than to lament his Condition in this World. That for his part, he was perfectly content with the State to which he was called, that he should endeavour to improve his Talent, which was all required of him, but not repine at his own Lot, nor envy those of his Betters. (1.3.24–25)

Of this scene, critic Judith Frank observes: "One of the novel's first acts is to deny Joseph 'Instruction in *Latin*' ... imagining Latin as the engine of social mobility, the novel concertedly refuses him that mode of literacy that would enable a rise in station." Frank suggests that Fielding "imagines literacy as the engine of upward mobility,"[10] but my argument here is exactly the opposite. *Joseph Andrews* does *not* suggest that literacy or Latin are "engine[s] of upward mobility"; rather, it exposes these as *false* assumptions. Neither literacy or higher learning ensures socioeconomic advancement (as the example of Parson Adams shows). In fact, a surprisingly sustained argument of *Joseph Andrews* is that literacy and/or education – in itself – will get you nowhere.

Frank reads *Shamela* and *Joseph Andrews* "in light of the pressures exerted upon them by ambivalence over lower-class literacy."[11] While I agree that the issue of lower-class literacy exerts special "pressures" on these texts, I would suggest that they do not show Fielding himself to have been "ambivalent" about this issue. Rather, they suggest that he viewed laboring-class literacy much as Mandeville did: as largely irrelevant, either to the personal happiness of the poor or to the larger social good. In *Joseph Andrews*, education can actually be *detrimental* to the "lower Orders"; one benevolent character, a retired "Sea-Faring Man" of great worldly experience, tells two pointedly similar stories of farm boys tragically educated beyond their rank. Fielding's satire on those who naïvely link schooling and social advancement works partly through the character of Parson Adams. Fielding's pedagogue parson is immune to careerism on his own account, but even he is caught up in new-fangled modern foibles concerning schooling. Despite his own and his eldest son's failure to obtain a secure living through advanced education; despite the stories he hears of unfortunate youths ruined by "over"-education; and despite the many characters he encounters whose schooling seems only to have made them more corrupt, Adams persists in imagining a direct causal relationship between learning, social advancement, and moral improvement, and has grand educational ambitions not only for Joseph but also for his own sons whom he aims to make scholarly parsons like himself.

While Fielding himself was an accomplished Latinist who knew Greek and loved learning, he did not assign unvarying values either to advanced learning or to the basic ability to read and write. Ironically, in refusing our modern faith in the "consequences" of literacy, Fielding anticipated recent revisionary arguments by major theorists of literacy – challenges to what Harvey J. Graff calls the "literacy myth":

> Until recently, scholarly and popular conceptions of the value of the skills of reading or writing have almost universally followed normative assumptions and expectations of vague but powerful concomitants and effects presumed to accompany changes in the diffusion of literacy. For the last two centuries, they have been intertwined with post-Enlightenment, "liberal" social theories and contemporary expectations of the role of literacy and schooling in socioeconomic development, social order, and individual progress. These important conjunctures constitute what I have come to call a "literacy myth."[12]

Models of "literacy effects" in twentieth-century development literature and related scholarship attempt to isolate literacy as a variable, then measure its consequences. Growth in literacy is linked to desirable outcomes such as modernization and democratization and to cognitive consequences such as enhanced reasoning and analytic powers.[13] Yet recently, scholars of literacy have observed a worrying "disparity between theoretical assumptions and empirical findings" in arguments about "literacy-as-a-path-to-development." This troubling gap has led to questioning of "the grander claims for the radical shift supposedly entailed by the acquisition of literacy" and to heightened efforts to distinguish broad claims for the consequences of literacy from its real significance for particular social groups. Literacy in itself is not necessarily an "agent of change"; rather, "its impact is determined by the manner in which human agency exploits it in a different setting."[14]

Recent challenges to widespread modern assumptions about literacy can help us to understand eighteenth-century debates concerning education in new ways. In turn, eighteenth-century *non*-assumptions about literacy can provide an essential historical dimension that is often lacking in these twentieth-century debates. At the very moment when modern ideas about the "consequences" of literacy first began to be articulated, Fielding challenged assumptions about a *necessary causal relationship* between schooling and any particular outcome whether moral, social, economic, or cognitive. In his fiction, Fielding does not necessarily take one 'side' or the other in contemporary debates; while a deeply conservative social thinker himself, he lays out the issues at stake as competing positions, then uses the antithesis he creates as a powerful means for the analysis of complex questions. This essay will read *Shamela* and *Joseph Andrews*, along with Fielding's social pamphlet *A Proposal For Making an Effectual Provision For the Poor, For Amending their Morals, and for Rendering them useful Members of the Society* (1753), as part of the prehistory of our modern cultural construct of "literacy." Fielding's texts provoke a valuable – and for us, counter-intuitive – questioning of the meanings and consequences of literacy at a time when "literacy" was not yet a stable cultural construct with universally agreed meanings.

Fielding and the Emergent Myth of Literacy

In addressing the "Distraction the Nation has labour'd under for some time, the Enthusiastick Passion for Charity-Schools," Mandeville argued that the withholding of education from the poor was fundamental to national advancement. While twenti-eth-century development discourse has traditionally linked economic growth to increased literacy, this is the opposite of widely held eighteenth-century views. Most eighteenth-century elites held that the acquisition of literacy by too many would hurt the economy. National "Welfare" was dependent on a large body of cheap laborers ready to work:

> The Welfare and Felicity...of every State and Kingdom, require that the Knowledge of the Working Poor should be confin'd within the Verge of their Occupations, and never extended (as to things visible) beyond what relates to their Calling. The more a Shepherd, a Plowman, or any other Peasant knows of the World, and the things that are Foreign to his Labour or Employment, the less fit he'll be to go through the Fatigues and Hardships of it with Chearfulness and Content.[15]

Fielding's *A Proposal For Making an Effectual Provision for the Poor* (1753), a product of his first-hand observation of the "Misdeeds" and "Sufferings"[16] of the lower classes during his tenure as a justice of the peace, suggests that he shared Mandeville's view of the poor as "a vast store of potential energy."[17] As Fielding theorizes, "among a civilized People," all members of society "are obliged to contribute a Share to the Strength and Wealth of the Public"; therefore, because the poor have "nothing but their Labour to bestow," this labor rightfully belongs to the social good.[18] Outlining a program of "universal employment" for the able-bodied poor, Fielding calls for the erection of workhouses – not schools – for the poor of the entire country. Especially concerned to eliminate all opportunities for wasteful idleness, he details an agenda for workhouse time management, ten hours a day, six days a week. While the inculcation of religion was essential, Fielding's program for reform says nothing about literacy instruction. Religion was to be imparted orally by means of mandatory twice-daily attendance at chapel and twice-weekly lectures on morality. The conspicuous absence of any provision for literacy instruction reflects conventional elite opinion that educating the poor was not only economically unwise but against God's divine design.[19] As poet, essayist, and Member of Parliament Soame Jenyns would write four years later:

> Ignorance, or the want of knowledge and literature, the appointed lot of all born to poverty, and the drudgeries of life, is the only opiate capable of infusing that insens-ibility which can enable them to endure the miseries of the one, and the fatigues of the other. It is a cordial administered by the gracious hand of Providence; of which they ought never to be deprived by an ill-judged and improper Education.[20]

Proponents of so-called "Charity" schools had it backwards. It was not education but the *withholding* of education from those "born to ... the drudgeries of life" that was the truly wise and benevolent act of Christian charity.

In outlining the "Necessity there is for a certain Portion of Ignorance in a Well-order'd Society," Mandeville anticipated that the only groups *certain* to benefit from increased literacy were printers and stationers. He expected that these groups would vocally object to his critique of charity schools:

> I cannot but smile when I reflect on the Variety of uncouth Sufferings that would be prepar'd for me, if the Punishment they would differently inflict upon me, was Emblematically to point at my Crime. For if I was not suddenly stuck full of useless Penknives up to the Hilts, the Company of Stationers would certainly take me in hand, and ... have me buried alive in their Hall under a great heap of Primers and Spelling-books, they would not be able to sell.[21]

As the examples of Samuel Richardson and John Newbery show, printers and stationers were indeed foremost among those who promoted the spread of literacy. Richardson's awareness of potential new markets is evident in his *Familiar Letters on Important Occasions* (1741),[22] a collection of sample letters designed to serve as a model for "Country Readers ... unable to indite for themselves."[23] In his most successful textual commodity, *Pamela*, Richardson provocatively represents female servants' literacy as cultural capital. Pamela has been described as "a pioneer capitalist, a middle-class entrepreneur of virtue, who looked on her chastity not as a condition of spirit but as a commodity to be vended for the purposes of getting on,"[24] but her real "commodity" is arguably her literacy. Pamela represents her ability to read and write as a perquisite of her employment in an aristocratic household. Her deceased mistress, she explains, "overpaid me ... in Learning."[25] Her literacy sets her apart from other servants, catches her employer's eye, and, by means of her letters revealing her true chastity and worth, ultimately wins his heart.

Richardson's novel resonates with a key word of contemporary debates concerning the education of the poor, "improvement." In the opening letter, Pamela records how Mr. B. noticed she can "write a very pretty Hand, and spell tolerably too" and gave her permission to "look into any of [his mother's] Books to improve yourself," and she later thanks him for "the Opportunities I have had of Improvement and Learning; through my good Lady's Means, and yours" (12–13, 36). Yet Richardson's novel also echoes Mandevillian discourses of lower-class reading as a waste of time that rightfully belongs to employers. Pamela notes how Mr. B. unjustly accuses her of "mind[ing] [her] Pen more than [her] Needle" and declares that he does not want "such idle Sluts" in his house (48). Yet like Mr. B., she assumes that her reading and writing are activities that must never interfere with her "work." They are luxuries for which she will have little time when she returns to her parents' cottage: "If I can but get Work, with a little Time for reading, I hope we shall be very happy" (77). Indeed, Pamela once concedes to Mandevillian arguments about the irrelevance of laboring-class literacy. On the brink of being fired from her job, she acknowledges of her deceased mistress, "all her Learning and Education of me, as Matters have turn'd, will be of little Service to me now; for it had been better for me to have been brought up to hard Labour" (80). Richardson's text sometimes undermines its platform of social mobility through education. While Pamela's own "investment" in literacy is ultimately a success, her father's similar investment has failed. Mr. Andrews has laboriously managed to acquire exceptional reading and writing skills for a man of his rank, yet his hard-won skills have not improved his position. As Pamela writes to her father, it is a shame that "you ... who are so well able to teach, and write so good a hand, succeeded no better in the school you attempted to set up; but was forced to go to such hard labour."[26] Nor does clergyman Arthur Williams gain the rewards he expects through advanced learning. Williams's college education means nothing in terms of social advancement without the patronage of the great. Williams admits that his "whole Dependence is upon the 'Squire" (128). Nonetheless, anticipating Parson Adams in *Joseph Andrews*, Williams persists in seeing a causal relationship between education and social mobility. Like Pamela's father used to do, he runs a school – in his case, "a little *Latin* School in the neighbouring Village, ... and this brings him in a little Matter, additional to my Master's Favour, till something better falls" (111–12).

Fielding detects and widens these fault lines already present in *Pamela*. In the opening pages of both *Joseph Andrews* and *Shamela*, he immediately demonstrates the false logic of arguments that reading necessarily teaches virtue. Both texts open with an explicit discussion of the *bad* things to be learned through reading. (Indeed, the full title of *Shamela* itself makes this point: *An Apology For The Life of Mrs. Shamela Andrews. In which, the many notorious Falshoods and Misrepresentations of a Book called Pamela, Are exposed and refuted* {my emphasis}.) Reading is not inherently good or bad; the outcome depends on who is reading, what they're reading, and how. Shamela is a determined reader of books ranging from *Venus in the Cloyster* to *The Whole Duty of Man*, while her brothel-keeping mother sends her books and encourages her to read. Bad human beings can appropriate even good books for immoral ends: Shamela reads *The Whole Duty of Man* to compensate for her adultery, noting, "I read in good Books, as often as I have Leisure; and Parson *Williams* says, that will make amends."[27] Conversely, bad books can lead even good men astray – and waste their time. As the temporarily misguided clergyman Thomas Tickletext observes of *Pamela*, "I have done nothing but read it to others, and hear others again read it to me, ever since it came into my Hands; and I find I am like to do nothing else, for I know not how long yet to come" (2).

Similarly, the opening chapter of *Joseph Andrews* debunks assumptions that literacy and reading promote morality. Fielding opens his novel with the declaration, "It is a trite but true Observation, that Examples work more forcibly on the Mind than Precepts. .... A good Man therefore is a standing Lesson to all his Acquaintance, and of far greater use in that narrow Circle than a good Book" (1.1.17). While this truism needs to be taken with a grain of salt, Fielding suggests the negative lessons to be learned from books such as "the Lives of Mr. *Colley Cibber*, and of Mrs. *Pamela Andrews*" (1.1.18–19). He then raises another thematically central issue, the question of readers' "Capacity." He parodically praises those biographies "of excellent Use and Instruction, finely calculated to sow the Seeds of Virtue in Youth, and very easy to be comprehended by Persons of moderate Capacity": that is, popular chapbooks such as *The History of Jack and the Giants* (1.1.18). Is it worth learning to read, Fielding asks in the opening pages of *Joseph Andrews* and *Shamela*, if one does not have the "capacity" to read beyond chapbooks; if one cannot discriminate between *The Whole Duty of Man* and *Venus in the Cloyster*; if one does not have *evaluative* and *interpretive* skills as well as the technical ability to read?[28]

One of the first acts of *Shamela* and *Joseph Andrews*, Frank suggests, is to "defuse the scandal of Pamela's literacy.... The first thing we know about Shamela, when she asks her mother to 'commodate [her] with a ludgin,' is that she cannot spell." In *Shamela*, "lower-class literacy is aggravatedly eroticized and utopian"; accordingly, one of the "main projects" of *Joseph Andrews* is to "detach literacy from the eroticism it produces in *Shamela*, or to decathect literacy."[29] This "decathecting" is apparent in the character of Fanny Goodwill. In response to the amazingly literate Pamela, Fielding supplies a virtuous servant-girl who can neither read nor write. Like Pamela, Fanny is "a poor Girl, who had formerly been bred up in" an aristocratic household, but unlike Pamela, she has not been unwisely educated by her employers. In introducing Joseph's future wife, Fielding goes out of his way to explain why his hero has not communicated with his beloved for a year:

> The Reader may perhaps wonder, that so fond a Pair should during a Twelve-month's Absence never converse with one another; indeed there was but one Reason which did, or could have prevented them; and this was, that poor *Fanny* could neither write nor read, nor could she be prevailed upon to transmit the Delicacies of her tender and chaste Passion, by the Hands of an Amanuensis. (1.11.48–49)

Frank argues that Fielding explains Fanny's "radical disqualification from literacy as an effect of her feminine modesty," but there is in fact nothing "radical" about Fanny's inability to read or write. What Frank calls Fanny's "illiteracy"[30] was the norm, not the exception, for a female servant. (Indeed, that is arguably Fielding's point.) Fielding never suggests that there is anything problematic about Fanny and Joseph's inability to correspond; the devoted couple share "a mutual Confidence in each other's Fidelity, and the Prospect of their future Happiness" and "content... themselves... with frequent Enquiries after each other's Health" (1.11.49). Fanny, Fielding's comic fiction suggests, will live a good and happy life even though she will never be able to teach her children to read. The example of this happy pair suggests that Fielding would also share Mandeville's view, "we shall find Innocence and Honesty no where more general than among the most illiterate, the poor silly Country People."[31]

In contrast to Fanny, Frank continues, we have Mrs. Slipslop:

> Shamela's other double, in whom an avid semiliteracy is linked with a hideous corporeality and tainted sexuality.... In Fanny...the absence of writing is linked with

chastity, while the figure of Slipslop combines the letter with its concomitant social rebelliousness and sexual promiscuity.... Slipslop's "slip" is literacy itself.[32]

But there is also a problem with Frank's argument that Fielding contrasts the "illiterate" Fanny with the "literate" Slipslop. For in fact, Fielding never tells us whether or not Slipslop can read or write:

> Mrs. *Slipslop* the Waiting-Gentlewoman, being herself the Daughter of a Curate, preserved some Respect for *Adams*; she professed great Regard for his Learning, and would frequently dispute with him on Points of Theology; but always insisted on a Deference to be paid to her Understanding, as she had been frequently at *London*, and knew more of the World than a Country Parson could pretend to.
>
> She had in these Disputes a particular advantage over *Adams*: for she was a mighty Affecter of hard Words, which she used in such a manner, that the Parson . . . was frequently at some loss to guess her meaning. (1.3.25–26)

Fielding notes that Slipslop takes great pride in her "Understanding" but also explains that the source of this "Understanding" is that "she had been frequently at *London*." He tells us she "professe[s] great Regard for . . . Learning" and uses "hard Words," but he never once depicts her reading or writing or even quoting from a book.[33] Any assumption of Slipslop's literacy is our own, not the text's. The point is, Fielding simply doesn't bother to tell us one way or the other.[34]

In sharp contrast to these minimally educated characters, Fielding introduces Adams as:

> an excellent Scholar. He was a perfect Master of the *Greek* and *Latin* Languages; to which he added a great Share of Knowledge in the Oriental Tongues, and could read and translate *French*, *Italian*, and *Spanish*. He had applied many Years to the most severe Study, and had treasured up a Fund of Learning rarely to be met with in a University. (1.3.22–23)

Adams has "treasured up a Fund of Learning," yet this is not a stock that can be exchanged for social advancement. At 50 years old, he struggles to support a large family by preaching regularly at four churches. His tattered cassock – and good nature despite of it – makes him appear "foolish," "ridiculous," "pitiful," and "shabby" to many observers (4.9.311; 3.13.276). Describing Adams to her genteel companions, Lady Booby states:

> if they pleased she would divert them with one of the most ridiculous Sights they had ever seen, which was an old foolish Parson, who, she said laughing, kept a Wife and six Brats on a Salary of about twenty Pounds a Year; adding, that there was not such another ragged Family in the Parish. (4.9.311–12)

Early in the novel, Adams quizzes young Joseph on his memorization of seemingly extraneous details concerning the Bible. He asks, "how many Books there were in the

New Testament?" and "how many Chapters they contained?" Surprised by the boy's abilities, he is "wonderfully sollicitous [*sic*] to know at what Time, and by what Opportunity, the Youth became acquainted with these Matters." Joseph explains that he did not gain this knowledge by attending a charity school. Instead:

> he had very early learnt to read and write by the Goodness of his Father, who, though he had not Interest enough to get him into a Charity School, because a Cousin of his Father's Landlord did not vote on the right side for a Church-warden in a Borough Town, yet he had been himself at the Expence of Sixpence a Week for his Learning. (1.3.23–24)

Joseph's relation to literacy, books and learning is that of an exemplary *servant*, not a gentleman. His reading is functional rather than comprehensive, he reads books in snippets without fully understanding their subjects, and he absorbs part of his "reading" aurally rather than visually, by eavesdropping on his "betters" while serving them at the table (3.6.235). Supporters of charity schools aimed to reconcile the laboring ranks to their estate rather than to stimulate social discontent, and while Joseph's father "had not Interest enough to get him into a Charity School," Joseph appears to have been an exemplary student. He is not without *any* desire to improve his situation, but his desires befit his station. When he hears a rumor that his sister Pamela is about to be married to Williams, he suggests that his reading and writing

Plate 7.   An attempt to encourage subscriptions for a foundling hospital to be built on Guilford Street, St. Pancras; this 1739 print features children who would benefit from the mission of education for "exposed and deserted young Children."

abilities might qualify him to be his clerk, "for which you know I am qualified, being able to read, and to set a Psalm" (1.6.31).

It is the learned Adams who has grander ambitions for Joseph. Adams applauds Joseph's contentment with his position in the social order, but he then immediately conceives a plan to teach this footman Latin, "by which means he might be qualified for a higher Station" (1.3.26). Adams urges Mrs. Slipslop to recommend Joseph to Lady Booby as "a Youth very susceptible of Learning, and one, whose Instruction in *Latin* he would himself undertake" (1.3.26). Parson Adams in this instance views Latin as an engine of social mobility, but in the terms of Fielding's fiction, his desire to teach a footman Latin is as "Ridiculous" as his later expression of regret that Mrs. Adams does not know Greek (3.4.227). The debate that follows between Adams and Slipslop is part of this novel's larger engagement with debates concerning not only literacy but also the question of who should undertake the study of classical languages. In *Some Thoughts Concerning Education* (1693), Locke observed, "what a-do is made about a little *Latin* and *Greek*, how many Years are spent in it, and what a noise and bustle it makes to no purpose." Latin and Greek were an essential part of the education of a gentleman, but in most instances a "waste [of] Money, and . . . time" for everyone else:

> Custom . . . has made it so much a Part of Education, that even those Children are whipp'd to it, and made spend many Hours of their precious time uneasily in *Latin*, who, after they are once gone from School, are never to have more to do with it, as long as they live. Can there be any thing more ridiculous, than that a Father should waste his own Money, and his Son's time, in setting him to learn the *Roman Language*, when at the same time he designs him for a Trade.[35]

Similarly, Mandeville suggested that for the majority of the population, the time-intensive study of classical languages was a "Loss of . . . Time and Money":

> It is a Vulgar Error that no body can spell or write *English* well without a little smatch of *Latin*. This is upheld by Pedants [masters of petty schools] for their own Interest, and by none more strenuously mantain'd than such of 'em as are poor Scholars in more than one Sense. . . . to Youths who afterwards are to get a Livelihood in Trades and Callings, in which *Latin* is not daily wanted, it is of no Use, and the learning of it is an evident Loss of just so much Time and Money as are bestowed upon it.[36]

Latin was essential for the governing classes and "Learned Professions," but for everyone else it was a foolish investment. Echoing these arguments, Slipslop rejects Adams's proposal. She asks, "why is *Latin* more *necessitous* for a Footman than a Gentleman? It is very proper that you Clargymen [*sic*] must learn it, because you can't preach without it: but I have heard Gentlemen say in *London*, that it is fit for no body else" (1.3.26). Latin and Greek, Fielding would suggest, are a deep repository of human wisdom and sympathy available to persons genuinely seeking virtue, but they are no easy "ticket" to social elevation or moral improvement. Furthermore, even when this kind of learning is attained, in modern society its true value is often misunderstood. As Shamela exclaims of Parson Williams's classical learning as cultural capital, "*O! What a brave Thing it is to be a Scholard, and to be able to talk Latin*" (21).

Parson Adams's own deep knowledge of the classics, it is frequently noted, is of little assistance in daily life. His immersion in his Aeschylus sometimes seriously inconveniences his friends. His erudition bears no relation to critical self-examination; he is unable to apply to himself the lessons he learns from his reading and is no smarter at the end of his "Adventures" than when he started out. Conversely, the minimally schooled Joseph quickly learns through his experiences. When he and Adams are tricked by pretended offers of hospitality from a duplicitous gentleman, Adams is "greatly confounded," but Joseph, drawing on prior experience, immediately understands that they have been deceived. Adams asks why the gentleman would gratuitously trick them, to which Joseph responds, "It is not for me... to give Reasons for what Men do, to a Gentleman of your Learning." Adams responds, "You say right... Knowledge of Men is only to be learnt from Books, *Plato* and *Seneca* for that; and those are Authors, I am afraid Child, you never read" (2.16.176). Yet Joseph has, in fact, already done plenty of hard learning from traveling with Adams, and he politely suggests that a disquisition on learned authors is not what is needed at this time, "for the generous Gentleman... hath left us the whole Reckoning to pay" (2.16.176–77).

Adams observes, "he had never *read* of such a Monster" (2.16.177, my emphasis), and especially notes that the duplicitous gentleman had an honest face. Overhearing Adams, the retired "Sea-faring Man" of great worldly experience interjects, "Ah! Master... if you had travelled as far as I have... you would not give any Credit to a Man's Countenance." Adams, whose vanity is nettled, responds, "Master of mine, perhaps I have travelled a great deal farther than you without the Assistance of a Ship.... the travelling I mean is in Books, the only way of travelling by which any Knowledge is to be acquired" (2.17.180–82). The two men debate whether more learning is acquired through experience or reading and whether men of business or learning provide the most valuable service. The host asks, "Of what use would Learning be in a Country without Trade? What would all you Parsons do to clothe your Backs and feed your Bellies? Who fetches... all the... Necessaries of Life?" to which Adams responds, "there is something more necessary than Life it self, which is provided by Learning; I mean the Learning of the Clergy." While there is truth in Adams's position, his claims are hyperbolic and dismissive. Books are not "the *only* way of travelling by which *any* Knowledge is to be acquired" (2.17.183, 182, my emphasis).

The noble and worthy Adams, it is also often acknowledged, is not without his faults. He can be irascible, pompous, and vain, and he is most often so when it comes to his abilities as a scholar and a teacher. When Joseph tells him, "you must be allowed by all the World to be the best Teacher of a School in all our County," he responds, "Yes, that,... I believe, is granted me... nay I believe I may go to the next County too – but *gloriari non est meum*" (3.5.230). In *Some Thoughts Concerning*

Education, Locke anticipated his reader's surprise that he thought "Learning" the "least part" of a gentleman's education. He explains, "Reading, and Writing, and *Learning*, I allow to be necessary, but yet not the chief Business. I imagine you would think him a very foolish Fellow, that should not value a Vertuous, or a Wise Man, infinitely before a great Scholar." He advises, "when you . . . are looking out for a School-Master, or a Tutor," do "not have . . . *Latin* and *Logick* only in your Thoughts."[37] Fielding's erudite country parson fails to recognize that what makes him an exemplary educator is not his great learning but his *goodness*. And the truly "Vertuous" things about Adams, Fielding suggests, he never needed to learn from books.

As Martin C. Battestin has shown, Fielding's depiction of Parson Adams was part of his "campaign . . . to reform the popular contempt of the clergy."[38] Adams suffers both the material deprivations of poverty and also the social snubs. His noble resignation to his poverty is a Christ-like virtue. Yet as Fielding's anxious remarks concerning Adams in the preface to *Joseph Andrews* acknowledge, there are aspects of his handling of this character that elude any neat moral agenda. Fielding assures us that Adams is a portrait of Christian idealism and charity, "notwithstanding the low Adventures in which he is engaged" (*Preface*, 11). Yet he makes his country parson undergo relentless, physical humiliations of the most slapstick kind. Among other "low Adventures," Adams is scalded with soup, covered with hogs' blood, set on fire with a candle, tumbled in the mud, and chased and pulled about by hounds. Fielding tells us how we are *supposed* to read Adams's character, but as Simon Dickie has reminded us, Fielding's contemporaries seldom followed his instructions:

> Many readers seemed incapable of seeing [Adams] as anything but the object of ridicule. It was almost impossible, Sarah Fielding complained in defense of her brother, to convince readers that an eccentric idealist like Adams was not a figure of contempt: most readers fixed their thoughts on his oddities of dress and behaviour, or "the hounds trailing bacon in his pocket," and entirely overlooked "the noble simplicity of his mind, with the other innumerable beauties in his character."[39]

As if to anticipate and debunk modern cognitive theories of literacy which associate advanced literacy with advanced reasoning powers, Fielding gleefully shows his most erudite character as worryingly devoid of common sense. When Adams and Fanny are brought before a drunken magistrate on false charges, a spectator observes Adams's cassock and challenges him to a schoolboy's game of "*cap{ping}* Verses." This "witty Fellow" offers as the first verse a line from his Latin schoolbooks, then waits for Adams to take his turn. At this moment when Adams is on the brink of being committed to a prison, we expect him to chastise the wit for not understanding the gravity of the situation, but instead he gives him "a Look full of ineffable Contempt," telling him "he deserved scourging for his Pronuntiation" (2.11.146). The "witty Fellow" admits that he has forgotten most of what he learned at college. Yet Adams's own much deeper learning also fails him, for he is wholly unable to put matters of Latin pronunciation into perspective. Having now completely forgotten his imminent imprisonment, he responds, "I have a Boy not above eight Years old, who would instruct thee, that the last Verse runs thus: *Ut sunt Divorum, Mars, Bacchus, Apollo, virorum*" (2.11.147). Fielding could not be more pointed as to what this chapter is about. He ironically titles it *"A Chapter very full of Learning"* (2.11.145). Significantly, the only person who is *not* satirized in this chapter can neither read nor write. When Adams begins to argue with the drunken justice concerning matters of learning, it is the uneducated Fanny who saves him from his foibles. The dispute between the Justice and the parson

> had most probably produced a Quarrel, (for both were very violent and positive in their Opinions) had not *Fanny* accidentally heard, that a young Fellow was going from the Justice's House, to the very Inn where the Stage-Coach in which *Joseph* was, put up. Upon this News, she immediately sent for the Parson out of the Parlour. *Adams...* found her resolute to go. (2.11.151)

Critics routinely note that Fielding parodies Adams's *pedantry* and *vanity* concerning his learning, but does Fielding ever satirize the *extent* of Adams's learning as incongruous or irrelevant for a country parson of his rank? As Claude Rawson suggests, "there is a hint of patronage in Fielding's own treatment of [Adams]."[40] Adams has high hopes for his sons' advancement through higher learning, and aims to make them parsons like himself. His love for his sons is benevolent paternalism, but his unitary faith in the outcome of their education becomes problematic when read in light of the novel's larger arguments concerning schooling. Adams's benevolent plan misfires from the beginning, for his eldest son's education does not bring the expected material returns. Although several gentlemen have promised Adams "to procure an Ordination for a Son of mine, who is now near Thirty, [and] hath an infinite Stock of Learning," unfortunately, as this son "was never at an University, the Bishop refuses to ordain him" (2.8.135). In terms of social advancement, Adams's son's "Stock of Learning," like his own "treasured up ... Fund of Learning," gets him nowhere, for as we have seen in *Pamela* with Parson Williams, this kind of "Stock" cannot be exchanged for advancement without the sustained patronage of the great.

Recall too the seemingly gratuitous scene of reading instruction at the end of *Joseph Andrews*, where Adams drills his nearly drowned, still dripping wet 8-year-old son in Latin grammar. Adams has been lecturing Joseph on the sin of excessive attachment to earthly things (4.8.308). Unfortunately, mid-sermon Adams is informed that "his youngest Son was drowned." Instead of heeding his own advice concerning the conquest of the passions, "He stood silent a moment, and soon began to stamp about the Room and deplore his Loss with the bitterest Agony" (309). Adams particularly laments the loss of a future "Scholar":

> Had it been any other of my Children I could have born it with patience; but my little Prattler, the Darling and Comfort of my old Age. . . . It was but this Morning I gave him his first Lesson in *Quae Genus*. This was the very Book he learnt, poor Child! it is of no

further use to thee now. He would have made the best Scholar, and have been an Ornament to the Church – such Parts and such Goodness never met in one so young. (4.8.309)

Fortunately, Dick suddenly comes running towards his father, "in a wet Condition indeed, but alive" (4.3.309). Dick sits by the fire to try to dry his clothes, when Lady Booby unexpectedly makes a visit. "She then seeing a Book in his Hand, asked 'if he could read?'" (4.9.314). Adams answers, "a little *Latin*, Madam, he is just got into *Quae Genus*." But Lady Booby appears to share Locke and Mandeville's conviction that Latin is a waste of time for poor country "Brats." "A Fig for *quere genius*," she exclaims, "let me hear him read a little *English*." Accordingly, Adams encourages his son:

> "*Lege, Dick, Lege*," said *Adams*: But the Boy made no Answer, till he saw the Parson knit his Brows; and then cried, "I don't understand you, Father." "How, Boy," says *Adams*. "What doth *Lego* make in the imperative Mood? *Legito*, doth it not?" "Yes," answered *Dick*.—"And what besides?" says the Father. "*Lege*," quoth the Son, after some hesitation. "A good Boy," says the Father: "And now, Child, What is the *English* of Lego?"—To which the Boy, after long puzzling, answered, he could not tell. "How," cries *Adams* in a Passion,—"What hath the Water washed away your Learning? Why, what is *Latin* for the *English* Verb *read*? Consider before you speak."—The Child considered some time, and then the Parson cried twice or thrice, "Le—, Le—."—*Dick* answered, "Lego."— "Very well;—and then, what is the *English*," says the Parson, "of the Verb *Lego?*"—"To *read*," cried *Dick*.—"Very well," said the Parson, "a good Boy, you can do well, if you will take pains. —I assure your Ladyship he is not much above eight Years old, and is out of his *Propria quae Maribus* already." (4.9.314–15)

Parson Adams puts his nearly drowned, still dripping wet son through a semi-public display of Latin learning without questioning his own motives. In *Some Thoughts Concerning Education*, Locke advises that whenever young boys "are at a stand . . . help them presently over the Difficulty, without any Rebuke or Chiding, remembering, that where harsher Ways are taken, they are the effect only of Pride or Peevishness in the Teacher." He adds of the experience of learning Latin grammar, "I believe there is no body, that reads this, but may recollect what disorder, hasty or imperious words from his Parents or Teachers have caus'd in his Thoughts."[41]

Of this scene, Frank observes: "Dicky may be unpromising, or recalcitrant, but Fielding's text stutters and repeats the words – *lego, I read* – that will, perhaps, guarantee the eight-year-old a better life than service."[42] But as the situation of Dick's father and older brother has already shown, the acquisition of Latin will not "guarantee" this son of a poor country parson anything – nor should it, many contemporary readers would assume. The universal education of children in morality was one thing, but the time-consuming education of all children in Latin or Greek was quite another. And even with regard to morality, critics seldom note, even Adams is not always a successful tutor. While he does an exemplary job with the moral education of his sons, he fails miserably with his wife and daughter. When Lady Booby chastises Adams for concerning himself with Joseph and Fanny, Mrs. Adams concurs: "Indeed, Madam, your Ladyship says very true . . . he talks a pack of Nonsense, that the whole Parish are his Children." His daughter then scolds him for bringing home "Strangers . . . to eat your Children's Bread," noting of Fanny, "I would not give such a Vagabond Slut a Halfpenny, tho' I had a Million of Money; no, tho' she was starving." Adams bids his wife prepare the travelers a meal, and "quoted many Texts of Scripture to prove, *that the Husband is the Head of the Wife*," but he ends up having to take his guests to an alehouse to get them fed (4.11.321–23).

Joseph Andrews contains numerous pointed stories of misfired education. The same innkeeper who argues with Adams concerning the value of experience also tells two stories of farm boys tragically educated beyond their rank. As Mandeville observed, "Those who spent a great part of their Youth in Learning to Read, Write, and Cypher, expect and not unjustly to be employ'd where those Qualifications may be of use to them . . . the longer Boys continue in this easy sort of Life, the more unfit they'll be when grown up for downright Labour."[43] The innkeeper tells how the local squire promised one boy's parents that he would make their son an exciseman:

> The poor People, who could ill afford it, bred their Son to Writing and Accounts, and other Learning, to qualify him for the Place; and the Boy held up his Head above his Condition with these Hopes; nor would he go to plough, nor do any other kind of Work; and went constantly drest as fine as could be, with two clean *Holland* Shirts a Week. (2.17.178)

But the squire failed to follow through on his promise, and the "young Fellow," despite his knowledge of "Writing and Accounts," could not find employment, "So that being out of Money and Business, he fell into evil Company, and wicked Courses; and in the end came to a Sentence of Transportation, the News of which broke the Mother's Heart" (178). The host then tells Adams of another parent who "over"-educates his son. This farmer allows the squire to convince him that his boy should become a parson – a sentiment with which the listening Adams would surely concur:

> There was a Neighbour of mine, a Farmer, who had two Sons whom he bred up to the Business. Pretty Lads they were; nothing would serve the Squire, but that the youngest must be made a Parson. Upon which, he persuaded the Father to send him to School, promising, that he would afterwards maintain him at the University; and when he was of a proper Age, give him a Living.

But this boy's over-education also turns out to be his undoing:

> 'But after the Lad had been seven Years at School, and his Father brought him to the Squire with a Letter from his Master, that he was fit for the University; the Squire, instead of minding his Promise, or sending him thither at his Expence, only told his Father . . . it was pity he could not afford to keep him at *Oxford* for four or five Years more, by which Time, if he could get him a Curacy, he might have him ordained.' The

Farmer said, "he was not a Man sufficient to do any such thing." "Why then," answered the Squire; "*I am very sorry you have given him so much Learning*; for if he cannot get his living by that, it will rather spoil him for any thing else; and your other Son who can hardly write his Name, will do more at plowing and sowing, and is in a better Condition than he." (2.17.178–79, my emphasis)

Like the other farm boy with his "clean Holland shirts," this youth comes to a desperate end: "the poor Lad not finding Friends to maintain him in his Learning, as he had expected; and being unwilling to work, fell to drinking . . . fell into a Consumption and died." Schooling not only gets these boys nowhere in terms of the desired social advancement, but also "spoil[s]" them "for anything else." The boy who spent "seven Years at School" (the time it would have taken him to complete a useful apprenticeship) "fell to drinking, though he was a very sober Lad before" (2.17.179). Fielding is not anti-education in these pointed passages and he is certainly not anti-clergy. Rather, he is addressing some of the potential human risks at stake in contemporary proposals for educating the poor. Later we learn of a more privileged young man whose schooling failed him in a different way. Now older and wiser through experience, Mr. Wilson notes that he obtained what by conventional standards was an excellent education: "My Education was liberal, and at a public School, in which I proceeded so far as to become Master of the *Latin*, and to be tolerably versed in the *Greek* Language" (3.3.201–202). Yet Wilson's mastery of Latin failed miserably to prepare him for the realities of the world. Despite his genteel birth, he soon ended up no better than the farm boys, "out of Money and Business," and most ironically, living "the Life of an Animal, hardly above Vegetation" (3.3.204–205).

But Fielding's most sobering suggestion concerning the necessity of caution in assuming any particular "outcome" to education comes in the chapter, "*A Disputation on Schools, held on the Road between Mr.* Abraham Adams *and* Joseph" (3.5.229). This "curious Discourse," while ostensibly a debate on private vs public education, is in reality a profound reflection on the issue of whether or not any kind of schooling can teach virtue or correct vice. Having just listened to Mr. Wilson's story of his useless schooling, Adams suddenly exclaims:

> I have found it; I have discovered the Cause of all the Misfortunes which befel him. A public School, *Joseph*, was the Cause of all the Calamities which he afterwards suffered. Public Schools are the Nurseries of all Vice and Immorality. All the wicked Fellows whom I remember at University were bred at them. . . . you may thank the Lord you were not bred at a public School, you would never have preserved your Virtue as you have. (3.5.230)

Joseph once again politely notes that it does not become him to argue with a man of Adams's learning, then goes on to express an alternative view:

> My late Master, Sir *Thomas Booby*, was bred at a public School, and he was the finest Gentleman in all the Neighbourhood. . . . It was his Opinion . . . that a Boy taken from a

public School, and carried into the World, will learn more in one Year there, than one of a private Education will in five. (3.5.230)

Echoing Locke on the secondary significance of "Learning" in relation to morality, Adams objects, "Who would not rather preserve the Purity of his Child?" But Joseph persists in arguing that public schools are equally effective – *or ineffective* – as private ones:

> [A boy] may get as much Vice [in a private school], witness several Country Gentlemen, who were educated within five Miles of their own Houses, and are as wicked as if they had known the World from their Infancy. I remember when I was in the Stable, if a young Horse was vicious in his Nature, no Correction would make him otherwise; I take it to be equally the same among Men: if a Boy be of a mischievous wicked Inclination, no School, tho' ever so private, will ever make him good. (3.5.231)

Joseph's suggestion of the possibility of innate virtue and vice recalls Locke's assessment of "*Learning*" as "a great help" to virtue "in well dispos'd Minds; but yet it must be confess'd also, that in others not so dispos'd, it helps them only to be the more foolish, or worse Men."[44] It also anticipates Fielding's sentiments in "An Essay on the Knowledge of Characters of Men" (1743), where he describes certain "original," apparently innate inclinations in children:

> This original Difference will, I think, alone account for that very early and strong Inclination to Good or Evil, which distinguishes different Dispositions in Children, in their first Infancy...and...in Persons who from the same Education, &c might be thought to have directed Nature the same Way; yet, among all these, there subsists, as I have before hinted, so manifest and extreme a Difference of Inclination or Character, that almost obliges us, I think, to acknowledge some unacquired, original Distinction, in the Nature or Soul of one Man, from that of another.[45]

If vice is innate in certain individuals, then education can at best only "cover" the inclination to evil. Mr. Wilson too echoes contemporary "ruling passion" theory when he suggests that education cannot "weed out" man's natural "Malignity" but only cover it up: "there is a Malignity in the Nature of Man, which when not weeded out, or at least covered by a good Education and Politeness, delights in making another uneasy or dissatisfied with himself" (3.3.217).

Fielding's social pamphlets of the 1750s suggest that he eventually came to believe that strict government was the only preservative of civilization. As Martin C. Battestin observes, Fielding's detailed plans for the regulation of the poor most clearly reveal his "final, disturbing vision of human nature and the tenuous grounds of order in society...Like Mandeville...he became convinced that reason and the will, the agents of morality in classical moral philosophy, were powerless to regulate man's emotional nature."[46] In his fiction, Fielding is less interested in offering detailed solutions to social problems than in laying out competing positions to clarify the issues under debate. Still, Fielding's position in *Joseph Andrews* on *both* public and private education is less than optimistic: there is no guarantee that *either* a public or private education will produce the desired result.

On a more positive note, however, in certain individuals virtue rather than vice may be innate. As Joseph suggests hopefully, if a boy "be of a righteous Temper, you may trust him to *London* . . . he will be in no danger of being corrupted" (3.5.231). The possibility of innate virtue is suggested most eloquently in the character of Adams, whose goodness is spontaneous or "natural" rather than learned. Not coincidentally, Fielding illustrates Adams's innate goodness most powerfully in the farcical episode where his book is burned – a scene seemingly straight out of stage comedy, but one that nevertheless resonates deeply when considered in light of the novel's arguments concerning education. Adams and Fanny are resting at an inn, when all of a sudden, Fanny faints. "*Adams* jumped up, flung his *Æschylus* into the Fire, and fell a roaring to the People of the House for Help." The voice turns out to be Joseph's, and the happy couple are reunited, whereupon Adams "danc[es] about the Room in a Rapture of Joy . . . the happiest of the three" (2.12.154–55). Unfortunately, however, he soon "cast his Eyes towards the Fire, where *Æschylus* lay expiring; and immediately rescued the poor Remains, to-wit, the Sheep-skin Covering of his dear Friend, which was the Work of his own Hands, and had been his inseparable Companion for upwards of thirty Years" (2.12.155). While Fielding's subversive comic impulses burn Adams's precious manuscript book with pleasure, Fielding the moralist also delivers a serious message: to a good man, no book, however irreplaceable, is as important as the happiness of the people he loves.

Conclusion

This essay has used Fielding's sometimes surprisingly fierce critique in *Joseph Andrews* of contemporary arguments for educating the poor to explore changing understandings of "literacy" and rationalizations for wider schooling in eighteenth-century England. Confronting Fielding's skepticism concerning the expected "outcomes" of education illuminates the eighteenth century as a transitional period that looked backwards to the past as well as forward to our modern assumptions and hopes. By the turn of the nineteenth century, what Graff calls an "epochal shift" would take place in elite attitudes toward mass education. But the new *expectation* of universal literacy should not be confused with actual reality, for throughout the eighteenth century, "despite Enlightenment rhetoric . . . relatively little was accomplished, especially in elementary (or literacy) education." Furthermore, new arguments for universal literacy were not necessarily more "enlightened" than older arguments *against* teaching the poor to read and write. Arguments both *for* and *against* popular education were commonly motivated by fear. Whereas authors like Mandeville suggested that mass literacy would weaken society by creating discontent, by the 1780s, "fear was spreading that *without* the security of mass education, social order, morality, and productivity were increasingly threatened." Political and religious leaders "concluded that [mass] literacy, if provided in carefully controlled, formal institutions, could be a useful force."[47] When it comes to the history of literacy and education, we need to recognize the inseparability of new humanitarian initiatives and older fears concerning the "lower Orders of Mankind." What appears to us an "epochal shift" in attitudes toward literacy also had certain crucial continuities with older ways of thinking.

Today, our trust in literacy places "a great burden...on a single attribute." In development discourse, "The assumption is that literacy, development, growth and progress are inseparably linked."[48] Yet as I have tried to show, "faith in the power and qualities of literacy is itself socially learnt."[49] Fielding challenged modern assumptions concerning the presumed "consequences of literacy" at the very moment when these modern ideologies of literacy and models of "literacy effects" were first being formulated. In *Joseph Andrews*, there is no causal relationship between literacy and "progress"; the most "literate" character in the novel, Parson Adams, is associated not with the future but with the classical and humanist past. Just as Fielding questioned the assumption that increased literacy would itself lead to progress, so today we cannot assume that schooling in itself leads to socially progressive outcomes. As Parson Adams's rote drilling of his 8-year-old in Latin grammar suggests, literacy instruction can be restrictive and hegemonic, concerned with imparting social values, instilling discipline, and maintaining social hierarchies rather than stimulating a desire to challenge the status quo.

The meanings and consequences of literacy are vitally dependent on sociohistorical context. The main task for historians and literary scholars seeking to understand the consequences of literacy is reconstructing the uses to which literacy has been put "and the real and symbolic differences that emanated from the social condition of literacy among the population."[50] Eighteenth-century novels can serve as a powerful analytic lens on historic transitions. Equally important, they can help us to recognize our *own* assumptions concerning literacy – a seemingly urgent task given how much recent scholarship on eighteenth-century "print culture" and the "public sphere" fundamentally depends on assumptions about dramatically increased literacy at a time when as much as half the population could not read. But ultimately, perhaps the most important lesson taught us by Fielding's Fanny Goodwill is that in seeking to generalize about what the "lower Orders of Mankind" have historically thought about access to literacy or education, we literary historians will always be at something of a loss, for the written texts we rely on can only tell us so much.

See also: chapter 8, MEMORY AND MOBILITY; chapter 12, MOMENTARY FAME; chapter 14, JOY AND HAPPINESS.

NOTES

1. Harvey J. Graff, *The Legacies of Literacy: Continuities and Contradictions in Western Culture and Society* (Bloomington: Indiana University Press, 1987), vii.

2. [Soame Jenyns], *A Free Inquiry Into the Nature and Origin of Evil*, (1757; Rpt. New York: Garland, 1976), 34.

3. Bernard Mandeville, "An Essay on Charity, and Charity-Schools," *The Fable of the Bees, or Private Vices, Public Benefits*, ed. Philip Harth (Harmondsworth, UK: Penguin, 1970), 294–95. *The Fable of the Bees* was first published in 1714. An expanded edition containing the "Essay on Charity, and Charity-Schools" was published in 1723.

4. What figures we have on early modern literacy remain far from definitive. In his synthesis of existing historical studies of literacy, J. Paul Hunter estimates that at mid-century as many as four out of ten adult men and six out of ten adult women could not read. Urban men and women were more likely to be literate than their rural counterparts, and men were more likely to be literate than women. See *Before Novels: The Cultural Contexts of Eighteenth-Century English Fiction* (New York: W. W. Norton, 1990), 61–88, and also "The novel and social/cultural history," in *The Cambridge Companion to the Eighteenth-Century Novel*, ed. John Richetti (Cambridge: Cambridge University Press, 1996), 9–40.

5. Such a definition, while convenient, necessarily sets aside the question of what level of skill an individual needs to be categorized as literate. Today theorists such as Brian V. Street suggest "we would probably more appropriately refer to 'literacies' than to any single 'literacy'" (*Literacy in Theory and Practice* Cambridge: Cambridge University Press, 1984}, 8).

6. See M. G. Jones, *The Charity School Movement* (Cambridge: Cambridge University Press, 1938). This quotation is from Jonathan Brody Kramnick, "'Unwilling to be Short, or Plain, in Any Thing Concerning Gain': Bernard Mandeville and the Dialectic of Char-

ity," *The Eighteenth Century: Theory and Interpretation*, 33 (1992): 148–75, at 150.

7. Catherine Ingrassia, in *Authorship, Commerce, and Gender in Early Eighteenth-Century England: A Culture of Paper Credit* (Cambridge: Cambridge University Press, 1998), notes Richardson's "personal investment in the idea of ... personal improvement" (147) and traces the ways Pamela "invests in herself for herself by creating her own negotiable paper or 'paper credit', letters and a journal which act as an indicator of her worth" (139). Building on Ingrassia's argument, I suggest that Richardson's text also represents *literacy itself* as an intangible commodity.

8. In thinking about this text I have benefited from Patricia Crain's talk in the Rutgers University History of the Book Lecture Series, "Spectral Literacy: The Case of *Goody Two Shoes*," 26 March 2003.

9. Henry Fielding, *The History of the Adventures of Joseph Andrews, And of his Friend Mr. Abraham Adams*, ed. Martin C. Battestin (Middletown, CT: Wesleyan University Press, 1967), 4.9.312. All further references to *Joseph Andrews* are to this edition and will be cited in parentheses by book, chapter, and page number.

10. Judith Frank, *Common Ground: Eighteenth-Century English Satiric Fiction and the Poor* (Stanford, CA: Stanford University Press, 1997), 51, 166. See also "Literacy, Desire, and the Novel: From *Shamela* to *Joseph Andrews*," *Yale Journal of Criticism* 6 (1993): 157–74.

11. Frank, *Common Ground*, 31.

12. Graff, *Legacies of Literacy*, 3.

13. Street points to anthropologist Jack Goody as an influential proponent of this line of thinking, but these assumptions are very widely held, and Goody himself often seems careful to disclaim such attitudes. See in particular Goody, *The Domestication of the Savage Mind* (Cambridge: Cambridge University Press, 1977) and Goody, ed., *Literacy in Traditional Societies* (Cambridge: Cambridge University Press, 1968).

14.   Graff, *Legacies of Literacy*, 4; Street, *Literacy in Theory and Practice*, 10.

15.   Mandeville, "Essay on . . . Charity-Schools," 275–76, 294.

16.   Henry Fielding, *A Proposal For Making an Effectual Provision For the Poor*, (1753, Repr. in *An Enquiry into the Causes of the Late Increase of Robbers and Related Writings*, ed. and intro. Malvin R. Zirker, Middletown, CT: Wesleyan University Press, 1988), 230.

17.   Zirker, intro., *An Enquiry into the Causes of the Late Increase of Robbers and Related Writings*, lxiii.

18.   Henry Fielding, *Proposal for the Poor*, 226, 228.

19.   Martin C. Battestin suggests that Fielding's views of the poor as expressed in his *Proposal* are "entirely representative of his age" (Martin C. Battestin with Ruthe R. Battestin, *Henry Fielding: A Life* {London: Routledge, 1989}, 514).

20.   [Jenyns], *Free Inquiry*, 34. In his review of Jenyns's work, Samuel Johnson exposes Jenyns's platitudes yet acknowledges the complexity of the question of educating the poor in a society where the majority were expected to labor for the few: "Concerning the portion of ignorance necessary to make the condition of the lower classes of mankind safe to the public and tolerable to themselves, both morals and policy exacts a nicer enquiry than will be very soon or very easily made" (*The Literary Magazine*, nos. xiii–xv, April–July 1757, repr. in *The Oxford Authors: Samuel Johnson*, ed. Donald Greene {Oxford: Oxford University Press, 1984}, 522–43, 528).

      Views like Jenyns's continued to be held throughout the century, including by Enlightenment *philosophes*. Voltaire held that "the children of laborers" need "know only how to cultivate, because you only need one pen for every two or three hundred arms" (*Questions sur l'Encyclopédie*, "Fertilisation," *Oeuvres complètes*, 19: 111, quoted in Harry C. Payne, *The Philosophes and the People* {New Haven, CT: Yale University Press, 1976}, 97).

21.   Mandeville, "Essay on . . . Charity-Schools," 324, 297.

22.   The full title of this work, now usually referred to as *Familiar Letters*, is *Letters Written To and For Particular Friends, On the most Important Occasions, Directing not only the Requisite Style and Forms To be Observed in Writing Familiar Letters; But How to Think and Act Justly and Prudently, In The Common Concerns of Human Life* (1741).

23.   Richardson, Letter to Johannes Stinstra, 2 June 1753, in *Selected Letters of Samuel Richardson*, ed. John Carroll (Oxford: Clarendon Press, 1964), 228–35, at 232.

24.   Maynard Mack, "*Joseph Andrews* and *Pamela*," intro. to Mack, ed., *Joseph Andrews* (New York: Holt, Rinehart and Winston, 1948), repr. in *Fielding: A Collection of Critical Essays*, ed. Ronald Paulson (Englewood Cliffs, NJ: Prentice-Hall, 1962), 52–58, at 52–53.

25.   *Pamela: Or, Virtue Rewarded*, 1st ed. 1741, ed. Thomas Keymer and Alice Wakely; intro. Thomas Keymer (Oxford: Oxford University Press, 2001), 46. Except where otherwise indicated, further references to *Pamela* are to this edition and will be cited in parentheses by page number.

26.   This quotation, which does not appear in the 1741 edition, is taken from the 1801 edition edited by Peter Sabor with an introduction by Margaret A. Doody (Harmondsworth, UK: Penguin, 1980), 48. As is well known, Richardson made extensive revisions to the first edition of *Pamela*, especially toning down Pamela's "lowness" by making her language more refined. More subtly, he also heightened her concern with "improvement" through reading and gave her father, a laborer, an earlier (failed) career as a schoolmaster. Even in her darkest hours, while confined at Mr. B.'s Lincolnshire estate, Pamela records that she "picked out some books from the library . . . and from these I hope to receive improvement" (1801 ed., ed. Sabor, 150). I have chosen to quote chiefly from the 1741 edition because it is the version of the text that Fielding would have read. But as Thomas Keymer acknowledges in his introduction to the 1741 edition, the 1801 edition is also valuable in that "by superimposing defensive revision on the original version" it "incorporates within itself, if properly decoded, a history of its own reception" (Keymer, intro., xxxi).

27. Henry Fielding, *An Apology For The Life of Mrs. Shamela Andrews* (London, 1741; facsimile ed. New York: Garland, 1974), 12. All further references to *Shamela* will be cited in parentheses by page number.

28. Fielding repeatedly suggests the dubious usefulness of literacy skills in readers of "moderate Capacity." Parson Adams's own wife can read but not correctly interpret Scripture. When Lady Booby chastises Adams for concerning himself about Fanny and Joseph, Mrs. Adams concurs, stating, "I can read Scripture as well as he; and I never found that the Parson was obliged to provide for other Folks Children" (4.1.322). Is it worth learning to read, Fielding seems to ask, if this is the message one gleans from the central text of Christianity?

29. Frank, *Common Ground*, 48, 47, 50.

30. Ibid., 52, 55, 58, *et passim*. I use Frank's word here with caution, as our modern term "illiteracy," in the sense of a condition of being unable to read or write, was not commonly used before the nineteenth century – most likely because what we identify as a special condition was still the norm. Well into the eighteenth century, a common definition of "illiterate" (from the Latin *illiteratus*) was someone who did not know Latin.

31. Mandeville "Essay on . . . Charity-Schools," 277.

32. Frank, *Common Ground*, 53–54.

33. Fielding's women of the "Lower Orders" are typically associated with tongues and mouths, not paper and pens. Slipslop's sexuality is linked not to literacy but to orality – her unbridled mouth. Even Fanny, who speaks only rarely, is still associated with the mouth. Early in the work, under threat of rape, she defends herself with shrieks. Later, again under threat of rape, she cries aloud for assistance, but her ravisher informs her, "if she persisted in her Vociferation, he would find a means of stopping her Mouth" (3.12.268). In the same chapter we meet another woman of the "lower Orders" who rambles on before lawyer Peter Pounce as if she is deposing before a magistrate. She complains about her husband, "a very *nonsense* Man," and "would have proceeded in this manner much longer, had not *Peter* stopt her Tongue" (3.12.271–72).

34. Even at the end of the century, female servants' literacy could not be assumed. If it existed in any significant degree in fiction, it had to be "explained" by authors. In *Maria or The Wrongs of Woman* (1792), Mary Wollstonecraft goes out of her way to explain how Jemima, a servant, learned to read and even acquired a "taste for literature." Significantly, with respect to Jemima, Wollstonecraft makes the same point that I am arguing Fielding makes in *Joseph Andrews*: without other opportunities, even the most hard-won literacy will not necessarily lead to socioeconomic elevation. Despite her exceptional learning for a woman of her station, Jemima ends up in wretched circumstances doing hard labor. Wollstonecraft suggests that Jemima's education actually makes it *worse* for her when she has to return to her laboring origins: "I had acquired a taste for literature . . . and now to descend to the lowest vulgarity, was a degree of wretchedness not to be imagined" (*Maria or The Wrongs of Woman*, ed. Moira Ferguson {New York: W. W. Norton, 1975}, 63).

35. John Locke, *Some Thoughts Concerning Education*, ed. John W. Yolton and Jean S. Yolton (Oxford: Clarendon Press, 1989), 207, 217.

36. Mandeville, "Essay on . . . Charity-Schools," 301–302.

37. John Locke, *Some Thoughts Concerning Education*, 207–208.

38. Martin C. Battestin, *The Moral Basis of Fielding's Art: A Study of Joseph Andrews* (Middletown, CT: Wesleyan University Press, 1959), x.

39. On the competing impulses of satire and sentiment in mid-eighteenth-century fiction and the problems of celebrating the eighteenth century as a polite and enlightened age of humanitarian initiatives, see Simon Dickie, "In the Mid-Eighteenth Century: Hilarity, Pitilessness, Narrative Fiction," Ph.D. diss., Stanford University, 2000. This quotation is from 255.

40. Claude Rawson, "Henry Fielding," in *The Cambridge Companion to the Eighteenth-Century Novel*, ed. John Richetti (Cambridge: Cambridge University Press, 1996), 120–52, at 136.

41. Locke, *Some Thoughts Concerning Education*, 220, 222.
42. Frank, *Common Ground*, 62.
43. Mandeville, "Essay on . . . Charity-Schools," 295.
44. Locke, *Some Thoughts Concerning Education*, 208.
45. "An Essay on the Knowledge of Characters of Men," in *Miscellanies by Henry Fielding, Esq.*, Vol. 1, ed. Henry Knight Miller (Oxford: Clarendon Press, 1972), 153–78, at 154.
46. Battestin, *Henry Fielding: A Life*, 517.
47. Graff, *Legacies of Literacy*, 177, 184, 177, 14.
48. Ibid., vii, 8.
49. Street, *Literacy in Theory and Practice*, 1.
50. Graff, *Legacies of Literacy*, 4.

FURTHER READING

Anon. [Soame Jenyns]. *A Free Inquiry Into the Nature and Origin of Evil*. 1757. Rpt. New York: Garland, 1976.

Fielding, Henry. *A Proposal For Making an Effectual Provision For the Poor*. 1753. Rpt. in *An Enquiry into the Causes of the Late Increase of Robbers and Related Writings*, ed. and intro. Malvin R. Zirker. Middletown, CT: Wesleyan University Press, 1988. 219–80.

Graff, Harvey J. *The Legacies of Literacy: Continuities and Contradictions in Western Culture and Society*. Bloomington: Indiana University Press, 1987.

Johnson, Samuel. Review of Anon. [Soame Jenyns], *A Free Inquiry Into the Nature and Origin of Evil*. In *The Literary Magazine*, nos. xiii–xv, April–July 1757. Rpt. in *The Oxford Authors: Samuel Johnson*, ed. Donald Greene. Oxford: Oxford University Press, 1984. 522–43.

Jones, M. G. *The Charity School Movement*. Cambridge: Cambridge University Press, 1938.

Locke, John. *Some Thoughts Concerning Education*, ed. John W. Yolton and Jean S. Yolton. Oxford: Clarendon Press, 1989.

Mandeville, Bernard. "An Essay on Charity, and Charity-Schools." 1723. In *The Fable of the Bees, or Private Vices, Public Benefits*, ed. Philip Harth. Harmondsworth, UK: Penguin, 1970. 261–325.

Street, Brian V. *Literacy in Theory and Practice*. Cambridge: Cambridge University Press, 1984.

Thomas, Keith. "The Meaning of Literacy in Early Modern England." In *The Written Word: Literacy in Transition*, ed. Gerd Baumann. Oxford: Clarendon Press, 1986. 97–131.

8

Memory and Mobility: Fictions of Population in Defoe, Goldsmith, and Scott

Charlotte Sussman

Recent scholarship on eighteenth-century fiction has established the cultural work of the novel in consolidating the important social structures of the family, the nation, and the public sphere. Little attention, however, has been paid to the relationship between the novel and another emergent concept of the period: the population. Demographic theory developed in England during the 1660s through the work of early Royal Society members, inspired by the mercantile conviction that "people are the wealth of the nation." Scholars like John Graunt and William Petty devised the science of "political arithmetic" – what the eighteenth-century economic theorist Charles Davenant called "the art of reasoning by figures, upon things related to government."[1] These scientists attempted to quantify each individual's cash value to the nation, and to conceptualize population as a natural resource. This turn towards valuing persons in economic terms, rather than in terms of religious or regional affiliations, often has been understood, following Marx, as the invention of "the value-form of the product of labor."[2] A less recognized implication of political arithmetic, however, is that when persons are considered valuable in terms of their labor power, rather than their regional or religious affiliations, they can be thought of as portable and deployable. Thinking about people as resources in the field of imperial and mercantile expansion in this way, early theorists often counted them for the purpose of conceptualizing their movements. This theoretical preoccupation coincided with the actual mass migrations of the eighteenth century: from country to city; from old world to new; and from Africa to the Americas.

In tandem with the new discourse of demography, some eighteenth-century novels addressed the question of how best to represent aggregates of people as they moved through both space and time. As awareness of the transience of whole communities, as well as individual lives, heightened over the course of the long eighteenth century, these novels struggled to capture communal memory in the face of large-scale human mobility. This problematic provoked the question of memory's relationship to space, as well as time, the question of memory's capacity to travel, and to link disparate locations as well as eras. This essay examines three different narrative strategies for dealing with this issue: the realism of Daniel Defoe's *A Journal of the Plague Year* (1722); the sentimental narrative of Oliver Goldsmith's *The Vicar of Wakefield* (1766); and the Gothic historicism of Walter Scott's *Guy Mannering* (1815). The chronological span of these novels reveals aspects not only of the development of British fiction, but also the history of population theory, as a mercantilist view is replaced by a mid-century anxiety about luxury and the limits of imperial expansion, and then by a post-Malthusian concern with "redundant" population. We have long thought of novels as telling the stories of individuals or of cultures through representative individuals; yet these novels take on a different task – telling collective stories, fictions of population.

A Journal of the Plague Year

A Journal of the Plague Year can be considered a fiction of population in that it narrates the story of a corporate entity – the city of London – under a threat to population – the epidemic of 1665. The novel's narrator, H. F., insists that he is describing the experience of what he calls "the people," "the generality," and "the multitude." We can see the effort he exerts to do so early on:

> The Face of *London* was now indeed strangely alter'd, I mean the whole Mass of Buildings, City, Liberties, Suburbs, *Westminster, Southwark* and altogether; for as to the particular Part called the City, or within the Walls, that was not yet much infected; but in the whole, the Face of Things, I say, was much alter'd; Sorrow and Sadness sat upon every Face, and though some Part were not yet overwhelm'd, yet all look'd deeply concern'd; and as we saw it apparently coming on, so everyone looked on himself, and his Family, as in the utmost Danger... *London* might well be said to be all in Tears.[3]

In the shifting pronouns of this passage – as the face of London dissolves into every face, as those faces become a "we" and then shift back to a personification of the city – we can see the difficulties involved in a communal portrait. The outlines of London as a collective subject are also in question. London here is the "whole mass of buildings" spreading westward and on the south side of the Thames to ill-defined borders.

A Journal of the Plague Year often has been considered a novel of stasis, as it records the rule of individual and metropolitan quarantine necessitated by the plague. John Bender argues that "H. F. considers the whole of London as a place of confinement bounded by hostile villages whose citizens allow no passage by road."[4] Yet, the novel's concern with the mechanics of containment can be read as a response to the heightened human mobility both evidenced and triggered by the plague. Observers were fascinated by the growth of London during the eighteenth century; the metropolis held 400,000 people in 1650, and almost a million by 1801. It was the largest city in Europe, and ten times larger than any other English city. Many contemporary observers attributed its growth to migration from other parts of England during the upheavals of the seventeenth century. William Petty, for example, points out that:

> from 1642 to 1650 . . . men came out of the country to London, to shelter themselves from the outrages of the civil wars, during that time: from 1650 to 1660, the royal party came to London, for their more private and inexpensive living: from 1660 to 1670, the King's friends and party came to receive his favours after his happy restoration: from 1670 to 1680, the frequency of plots and parliaments might bring extraordinary numbers to the city.[5]

Defoe appears to agree with this analysis, and notes that after the Restoration, "this Conflux of the People, to a youthful and gay Court, made a great Trade in the City, especially in everything that belong'd to Fashion and Finery; So it drew by Consequence, a great Number of Work-men, Manufacturers, and the like, being mostly poor People, who depended upon their Labour" (19). The Bills of Mortality, Defoe's documentary source for the number of deaths caused by the plague, provided only a partial picture of this newly expanded metropolis. As M. Dorothy George points out, "the Bills . . . stood for the greater London of the seventeenth century . . . Though they included the parishes of Bethnal Green, Bermondsey and Hackney . . . they did not cover the extensions of London in the west, notably Marylebone and St. Pancras."[6] Thus, the ill-defined borders of London are caused in part by a new flood of people into the city from the country. This mobility troubles the coherence of the corporate subject.

The arrival of the plague serves to emphasize the connection between movements of people within Britain and the movements of people on a global scale. Its introduction into London seemingly results from the expansion of trade: "some said" it was brought "from *Italy*, others from the *Levant* among some Goods, which were brought home by their Turkey Fleet; others said it was brought from *Candia*; others from *Cyprus*" (1). This evidence of the global movement of traders is mirrored in the microcosm of London by the mobility of plague victims themselves, who are reputed to run "about the streets with the Distemper upon them without any control" (124). This continuous movement, of course, exacerbates the shifting nature of London's population as an aggregate subject. Once the plague comes to London, it initially inspires the same movement out of the city that the Restoration inspired into it: "the City it self began now to be visited too, I mean within the Walls; but the Number of People there were indeed extreamly lessen'd by so great a Multitude having been gone into the Country; . . . In August, indeed, they fled in such a manner, that I began to think, there would really be none but Magistrates and Servants left in the City" (15).

Rather than condemning this mobility, H. F., like a political arithmetician, urges the state to step in and manage it. For, if "the best Physick against the Plague is to run away from it," too many Londoners have run too late, after they have already been infected by the disease. H. F. suggests these "Measures for managing the People" (198): "separating the People into smaller Bodies, and removing them in Time farther from one another, and not let such a Contagion as this, which is indeed chiefly dangerous, to collected Bodies of People, find a Million of People in a Body together" (198). Underlining the idea that persons are units with differing values to the state, H. F. continues:

> I could propose many Schemes, on the foot of which, the Government of this City, if they should ever be under the Apprehensions of such another Enemy [as the plague], (God forbid they should), might ease themselves of the greatest Part of the dangerous People that belong to them; I mean such as the begging, starving, labouring Poor, and among them chief those who in Case of a Siege, are call'd the useless Mouths; who being then prudently and to their own Advantage dispos'd of, and the wealthy Inhabitants disposing of themselves, and of their Servants, and Children, the City, and its adjacent Parts would be . . . effectually evacuated[.] (198)

H. F. does not imagine that human mobility can be halted, only that it can be rationally regulated. The government takes the greatest control over bodies that have become simply mouths – consumers of resources who contribute nothing to the state. The imagery of the city itself as a corporate subject – the bodies of people that are a Body of People – recurs here. In H. F.'s fantasy of the procedures to be followed in future plagues, however, the boundaries of that body will be clearly delineated, and its movements easily surveyed.

A Journal of the Plague Year also asks how "the people" can recognize itself as a collectivity when most forms of group interaction – public worship, theaters, markets – have become life-threatening, if not actually prohibited. During the epidemic, sociability itself is pathologized. Although H. F. takes pains to deny it, the desire to infect others is supposed to be a symptom of the plague; some doctors say there is "a wicked inclination in those that were infected to infect others . . . a malignity not only in the Distemper to communicate itself, but in the very Nature of Man" (154). Sociability is only possible when the living imagine themselves to be dead. At the height of the plague, "looking at themselves all as so many dead corpses, they came to the Churches without the least caution" (175). Self-imposed isolation turns out to be the best way to escape the disease – and H. F. celebrates those individuals and families able to confine themselves to their own houses or ships (although, notoriously, he finds himself unable to emulate them).

The plague thus both isolates persons and brings them back together as undifferen-tiated, decaying flesh.[7] Defoe's novel, as much as Swift's "Modest Proposal," published in the same decade, is preoccupied with the tendency of persons to revert back into undifferentiated physical material. H. F.'s talismanic word for this dynamic is "heaps," a word he uses with great frequency: to describe dead bodies – as in "they died by Heaps, and were buried by Heaps" – but also to depict living moving bodies – "sometimes Heaps and Throngs of People would burst out" of places like plague-ravaged Harrow Alley (177) – and supplies of coal – "ships deliver'd great Quantities of Coals in particular Places . . . in vast Heaps, as if to be kept for Sale" (220). The

Plate 8. Defoe's *Journal of the Plague Year* remained popular throughout the nineteenth century. This painting, *Rescued from the Plague*, was done by Frank Warwick Topham in 1898.

word points disturbingly to the way these agglomerations seem piled, not ordered, and emphasizes that their significance resides in their quantity, not their quality. The continuity between animate and inanimate matter is not merely rhetorical; at the height of the plague, there is not much distinction between those bodies in heaps of the living, and those in heaps of the dead: "many People had the Plague in their very Blood . . . and were in themselves but walking, putrified Carcasses." These images of heaps of flesh – a nightmarish double to the idea of a communal identity – signal the limits of representation. Faced with the plague pit, H. F. can only stammer, "it was indeed very, very, very dreadful, and such as no tongue can express" (60).

Here, we can see another crucial problem in the narrative's struggle to represent London as a communal subject. While H. F. can record his conversations with those living, as he does, through the plague, he struggles with how best to make visible, and affecting, the absence of the dead. As much as it is a journal — a day-to-day account of life lived during the plague — the novel is also a record of absent bodies — those lost to disease, and consequently lost to time. Thus, *A Journal of the Plague Year* is a novel of memory both because it looks back to 1665 from 1722, and because it works to remember the bodies lost to the plague. One of Defoe's strategies for making that absence visible is the inclusion of many actual London Bills of Mortality, the best records of the numbers and causes of deaths in the city until the first British census in 1801. For many, the Bills seemed to hold the key to London's history and identity; John Graunt, for instance, attempted to sum up the condition of the city in his *Natural and Political Observations . . . made upon the Bills of Mortality,* published in 1662. Graunt believed that the information derived from the Bills would not only represent London, but also help manage it. He concluded that it was "necessary. . . to know how many People there be of each Sex, State, Age, Religion, Trade, Rank, or Degree, &c. by the knowledge whereof Trade, and Government may be made more certain, and Regular."[8]

Throughout Defoe's narrative, H. F. relies on the Bills, including many in the narrative itself to illustrate the scope of events. And yet, the sheer scale of the epidemic escapes statistical representation: "When the violent Rage of the Distemper in *September* came upon us, it drove us out of all Measures: Men did no more die by Tale and by Number, they might put out a Weekly Bill, and call them seven or eight Thousand or what they pleas'd: Tis certain they died by Heaps, and were buried by Heaps, that is to say, without Account" (237). The structure of this passage, in which H. F. simultaneously decries the inaccuracy of the Bills, and registers their dogged attempt to keep track of the inhabitants of London (they continued to come out every week), is typical of the narrative. Yet, we should not confuse the narrator's refutation of the Bills' accuracy with a dismissal of their value and force. Instead, his refusal to view statistics as neutral facts emphasizes their representational and affective power — their capacity to shape "reality" rather than "realistically" represent it. Indeed, discovering the inaccuracy of the Bills has the paradoxical effect of revealing their representational potency — a potency that Defoe's narrative envies and hopes to share.[9] In a world where all gatherings are gatherings of the dead, the Bills of Mortality hold out the promise of making a community of isolates visible to itself, and to make the absent members of that community visible again.

As the plague decreases in strength, the narrator depicts a complementary dynamic between the Bills and individual behavior: "As soon as the first great Decrease in the Bills appear'd, we found that the two next Bills did not decrease in Proportion; the Reason I take to be the People's running so rashly into Danger. . . the audacious Creatures were so possess'd with the first Joy, and so surpriz'd with the satisfaction of seeing a Decrease in the weekly Bills, that they were impenetrable by any new Terrors" (226–27). In this case, the Bills first reflect the city's condition (the decrease in deaths), but then affect it, as people feel encouraged by the numbers to socialize without caution; this causes the Bills to reflect behavior once again, as that interaction increases the death toll again. The best example of the Bills' capacity to represent London itself comes near the end of the plague year: "It is impossible to express the Change that appear'd in the very Countenances of the People, that *Thursday* morning when the Weekly Bills came out; it might have been perceived in their Countenances, that a secret Surprize and Smile of Joy sat on every Bodies Face; they shook each other by the Hands on the Streets, who would hardly go on the same side of the way with one another before" (245). Here, the statistical tables not only produce an emotional effect worthy of a theatrical performance or a great sermon, but they also seem literally to reforge the bonds of community, as the happy people begin to touch each other again. This capacity to affect the city's behavior as a whole is something the narrative envies. Acknowledging the limit of his own persuasive power, H. F. asks, "who am I that I should think myself able to influence either one Side or other?" and wonders, "why we cannot be content to go Hand in Hand to the Place where we shall join Heart and Hand without the least hesitation" (176). His narrative lacks the power to produce the spontaneous earthly handholding he attributes to the Bills of Mortality.

Yet even as he records the power of statistical representation, H. F. acknowledges that it is an influential fiction, rather than a transparent reflection of the city's experience. In one of the most poignant moments of the novel, H. F. describes the way in which the recorders of Bills are under the same pressures as the writers of *Journals*:

> Now when, I say, that the Parish Officers did not give in a full Account, or were not to be depended upon for their Account, let any one but consider how men could be exact in such a time of dreadful distress, and when many of them were taken sick themselves, and perhaps died, in the very time their accounts were being given in . . . Indeed, the Work was not of a Nature to allow them leisure to take an exact Tale of the dead bodies, which were all huddled together in the Dark into a Pit. (99)

H. F. suggests that novelists and statisticians share the same material difficulties, and aspire to the same goal: not merely to reflect, but to create a corporate subject. The homology between "tale" and "tally" is brought home.

The uneasy relationship between the narrator and the Bills helps define the work of realist fiction in relation to the contemporaneous emergence of statistics. Ian Watt points to something "implicit in the novel form in general: the premise, or primary convention, that the novel is a full and authentic report of human experience."[10] Yet, Watt is careful to emphasize that this completeness is a representational convention, and that narratives shape our perception of the world as much as they reflect it. By drawing so heavily on the Bills of Mortality, *A Journal of the Plague Year* stages an implicit comparison between demography and novel-writing as representational forms. Indeed, the novel's engagement with the Bills suggests that Defoe learned something from early forms of statistics about the way descriptions of "reality" shape the reality they describe. The parallel is particularly pointed in this case because the novel and the statistics have the same goal: to imagine London as a collective subject. The realist novel of population, then, faces its greatest challenge in the shifting human shape of its aggregate subject, but imagines its greatest triumph in uniting with the statistical apparatus of the state to record the history of a mobile "Body" of people.

The Vicar of Wakefield

Oliver Goldsmith's consideration of population and mobility is best known through *The Deserted Village* (1770). In *The Vicar of Wakefield*, however, he is also concerned with problems of population, particularly in the family as a unit and producer of population. Dr. Primrose declares in the first pages of the novel: "I was ever of the opinion, that the honest man who married and brought up a large family, did more service than he who continued single and only talked of population . . . in this manner, though I had but six [children], I considered them as a very valuable present made to my country, and consequently looked upon it as my debtor."[11] Here we can see evidence of Michel Foucault's argument that during this period, the family became a "segment," rather than a "model" for government: "prior to the emergence of population, it was impossible to conceive the art of government except on the model of the family, in terms of economy conceived as the management of a family; from the moment when . . . population appears absolutely irreducible to the family, the latter becomes of secondary importance compared to population, as an element internal to population."[12] That is, the family is less often imagined in an allegorical relationship to the state, and instead comes to be seen, as the Vicar sees it, as part of a larger whole, the British nation. The family is necessary in the continued prosperity of the nation, and it is through the family that the nation is able to both cohere and expand. Although the Vicar also calls his family "that little republic to which I gave laws" (50), its allegorical quality is eventually overshadowed by its instrumental value.

The belief that "people are the wealth of the nation" persisted into Goldsmith's day; in 1773 the *York Chronicle* stated: "the number of people constitutes the most valuable treasure of a nation."[13] Jonas Hanway, in an appeal for a "regular, uniform, Register of the parish poor" proclaims: "increase alone can make our natural strength in Men correspond with our artificial power in riches, and both with the Grandeur and Extent of the British empire."[14] Thus, the family must be managed so as to benefit that greater aggregate, and produce population as a resource. Dr. Primrose sees his family management (faulty as it may be) as directed toward that goal; his use of the vocabulary of finance – "present," "debtor" – marks his children as a national economic resource. In this way, *The Vicar of Wakefield*, like *A Journal of the Plague Year*, can be considered a fiction of population.

The novel's emphasis on the importance of marriage and procreation to the nation needs to be read in relation to contemporaneous anxieties about luxury, which was seen to threaten population growth through its encouragement of extravagant, non-domestic lifestyles, and its desire for exotic commodities, dissipating national strength in the pursuit of frivolity.[15] Thus, at mid-century, the greatest danger to population in city life was no longer the brutal assault of plague, but rather the seductions of luxury. As one writer puts it, "Luxury is not only a Vice, but another great impediment to marriage . . . Some, viewing city expenses in a married life, look upon entering into that state as chaining themselves down to perpetual Slavery, Poverty and Distress, and therefore avoid it."[16] In *The Vicar of Wakefield*, while Mrs. Primrose imagines that positions for her daughters as the paid companions in London for the "ladies" visiting Squire Thornhill will give them the opportunity to marry well, the scheme is eventually revealed to have the opposite consequences; it is a plot to "introduc[e] infamy and vice into retreats where peace and innocence have hitherto resided" (77). Those "retreats" were understood to be corporeal as well as moral: the city was seen as a place where even virtuous married women, and the children they bore, would be exposed to venereal diseases, another consequence of "luxury."[17] In the novel, as well as in popular imagination, luxury and vice thrive in the city, while happy marriages and healthy children are made in the country.

Yet, if Goldsmith shares with Defoe the anxiety that city life threatens the (re)production of population as a national resource, in Goldsmith's era that danger is coupled with that of another kind of mobility: that demanded by colonial expansion. Thus, the period's critique of luxury is often joined to opposition to emigration. As one of the same writers against luxury continues: "Instead of being solicitous to people America in haste, it should be our ceaseless endeavour to cultivate or improve every waste spot of Ground in this Island, and by affording the greatest scope and encouragement to honest industry and useful arts, to extend home population to the utmost degree possible, because therein lies the only Source of all Riches and Power" (166). We can trace the connections between this opposition to luxury, its limiting effect on Britain's population, and the issue of colonial expansion in an ongoing controversy over the territorial gains of the Seven Years War, in which Goldsmith participated. Political commentators debated whether it was in Britain's best interest to acquire so many new possessions through conquest. Such new lands would need inhabitants, and while some thought that new acquisitions to the west would expand Britain's trading empire, others believed the effort to people them posed too great a threat of leaving a vacancy at home. As one writer says of Canada, "if Possession of the country should ever lead us to the thought of settling it, we shall become still greater sufferers by draining our own of its inhabitants."[18]

Goldsmith joins the fray in opposition to expansion, writing in *The Weekly Magazine* in 1759:

I see no reason why we should aggrandize our colonies at our own expense; an acquisition of new colonies is useless, unless they are peopled; but to people those deserts that lie behind our present colonies, would require multitudes from the home country; and I do not find we are too populous at home. All that are willing or able to work in England can live happy, and those who are neither able nor willing, would starve on the banks of the Ohio, as well as in the streets of St. Giles's; it is not the lazy or the maimed that are wanted to people colonies abroad, but the healthy and the industrious, and such members of society, I think, would be more usefully kept at home. To enlarge our territories, there in America, should not be the aim of our ministry, but to secure those we are already in possession of: Aye, but perhaps an opponent will say, if we people those countries, we shall have more tobacco, more hemp, and we shall be able to procure prodigious quantities of raw silk! Away then with thousands of our best and most useful inhabitants, that we may be furnished with tobacco and raw silk; send our honest tradesmen and brave soldiers to people those desolate regions, that our merchants may furnish Europe with tobacco and raw silk.[19]

Like Defoe, Goldsmith distinguishes between useful and useless population, and argues that populating America with the former will damage the parent country. Furthermore, Goldsmith joins the question of emigration to a critique of luxury by arguing that colonial expansion replaces people with luxury goods: labor disappears into the west and only commodities return. Such an exchange is a further threat to population, since those very goods create the way of life that leads young people to shun marriage and children. Thus, the energy that should be directed towards biological reproduction, and the aggrandizement of the nation, is channeled into a process that merely transmutes useful people into useless products. Goldsmith includes in *The Vicar of Wakefield* a brief glimpse of the office of a Mr. Crispe (a real person), who "offers all his majesty's subjects a generous promise of 30 l. a year, for which promise all they give in return is their liberty for life, and permission to let him transport them to America as slaves" (115). When George Primrose, at the nadir of his fortunes, encounters Crispe, he acknowledges, "I knew in my own heart that the fellow lied, and yet his promise gave me pleasure" (115–16). He is only saved from selling his labor and freedom for colonial expansion by a chance encounter with an old friend.

Yet, although George is tempted, no one in *The Vicar of Wakefield* emigrates to North America. Instead, the novel's concern with mobility is played out in the Primrose family's forced travels around rural England. Like *A Journal of the Plague Year*, *The Vicar of Wakefield* has been read as concerned with questions of confinement, since the Vicar eventually ends up in jail.[20] Its plot, however, is closer to another mid-century comic novel, Smollett's *Humphry Clinker* (1771), which follows a family group as it tours England and Scotland. Yet, while Matthew Bramble and his family are essentially tourists, traveling from place to place in search of health and romantic happiness, moving on whims, Goldsmith is more interested in *The Vicar of Wakefield*, as he would be in *The Deserted Village*, in forced migration. The Primroses are forced by bad luck (and/or incompetence) from one habitation to another until Dr. Primrose's final imprisonment. Along with these "migrations" (43), the novel includes accounts of his daughters' abductions, Dr. Primrose's journey after Olivia, and his son George's travels in London and Europe. And, whereas Smollett deploys the epistolary form to emphasize the differences in perspective within any family structure, Goldsmith uses the Vicar's first-person narration to bind the Primrose family to a shared vision of happiness.

The force that the novel relies on to hold the family together is sentiment. In particular, sentiment seems to ensure that members of the family remember each other, something that is ever more necessary in an increasingly peripatetic world. George's letter home from his military post recounts the way that memory and sentiment allow the family to remain intact over distance:

> I have called off my imagination a few moments from the pleasures that surround me, to fix it upon objects that are still more pleasing, the dear little fire-side at home. My fancy draws that harmless groupe as listening to every line of this with great composure. I view those faces with delight which never felt the deforming hand of ambition or distress! . . . But it is my fate to remember others, while I am myself forgotten by most of my absent friends. (157)

His ability to imagine his family reading his letter with interest, his capacity, through memory and sentiment, actually to draw the scene, inspires George to write home, keeping family ties intact. This emotional dynamic echoes a similar moment in Goldsmith's long poem of 1764, *The Traveller*, in which the speaker imagines that "The pensive exile, bending in his woe, / To stop too fearful, and too faint to go, / Casts a long look where England's glories shine, / and bids his bosom sympathize with mine" (lines 419–22). Here, too, sympathy has the power to maintain social bonds over great distances. This belief in sentiment seems to offer a supplement to Goldsmith's earlier critique of emigration. Imagination and sympathy can hold communities – perhaps even nations – together across space.

As is characteristic of the novel, however, George's letter directly precedes a remarkable coincidence: George's own arrival in prison in chains for challenging Thornhill to a duel. Yet, even within the hopeless environs of the prison, the novel imagines the emergence of sentimental community. When the Primrose family finally is reunited and restored to happiness, "a burst of pleasure now seemed to fill the whole apartment; our joy reached even to the common room, where the prisoners themselves sympathized" (179). And, at the end, after happy marriages are made for two of the Primrose children, the Vicar brings to life the scene from George's letter. He has "the pleasure of seeing all my family assembled once more by a cheerful fireside. My two little ones sat upon each knee, the rest of the company by their partners" (184). Sentiment secures the family as a unit, and connects them to a larger whole. Thus, Foucault's description of the place of the family within the economy of the state is augmented in Goldsmith's novel by an account of familial sentiment. Sympathetic bonds, strongest between family members, but potentially extended to other kinds of community, have the potential to mitigate the emotional entropy associated with mobility. Sentiment, nurtured in memory, focused on the family, allows the far-flung members of the population to imagine themselves as part of a coherent unit. In this way, too, the family may be instrumental in the coherence and expansion of the empire.

In the novel, however, sentiment only assumes this power in confluence with a particular aspect of its narrative form. The family is brought together and expands through marriage through a series of coincidences so remarkable that Dr. Primrose feels called upon to comment on it. When George's former fiancée Arabella Wilmot appears at the prison with her new fiancé Squire Thornhill, believing that George has indeed emigrated to America, the Vicar reflects: "Nor can I go on, without a reflection on those accidental meetings, which, though they happen every day, seldom excite our surprise but upon some extraordinary occasion. To what a fortuitous concurrence do we not owe every pleasure and convenience of our lives. How many seeming accidents must unite before we can be cloathed or fed. The peasant must be disposed to labour, the shower must fall, the wind fill the merchant's sail, or numbers must want the usual supply" (174). The peasant is presumably forced to labor, rather than "disposed," because he needs food, money, or both. But in this passage, the economic forces that power production are equated with natural forces, such as rain or sun, and all designated "accidents." This view of the world allows the Vicar to concentrate on the sentimental reactions provoked by such meetings – Arabella's "compassion and astonishment" (174) – and relegate the actions that have led to them to "fortuitous concurrence." The passage articulates an economic theory, but it can also be seen as a description of sentimental narrative form, in that it imagines the forces of the world, economic and natural, as something that *happen to* the sentimental psyche, subordinating action to reaction. Of course, we are probably meant to look slightly askance at the Vicar's undeniably skewed view of the world. At the same time, however, this narrative form, by subordinating the reasons behind human mobility to the power of sentiment to overcome them – as it appears to do for George and Arabella in this instance – provides one way of managing the anxiety surrounding the management of population, particularly through emigration, during this period.

We should note, however, that Goldsmith was later to envisage a world in which coincidence does not intervene to prevent familial and cultural diaspora. In *The Deserted Village* (1776), he describes a village emptied out by emigration to both the city and the American colonies. Unlike the emigrant in *The Traveller*, these colonists have no sentimental ties to the world they leave behind. Asked to "participate the pain" of a young woman lost to city vices (lines 326–38), they seem to answer, "Ah, no":

> . . . To distant climes, a dreary scene,
> Where half the convex world intrudes between,
> Through torrid tracts with fainting steps they go,
> Where wild Altama murmurs to their woe. (lines 343–46)

The distance of "half the convex world" seems to break the possibility of backward looks or sentimental ties. This severing is signaled by the relative silence of the scene. The voices of the emigrants are displaced by the river that "murmurs to their woe," in "Those matted woods where birds forget to sing, / But silent bats in drowsy clusters cling." This silence contrasts with the remembered sounds of the village's past (lines 351–52), its "cheerful murmurs fluctuat[ing] in the gale" before "the sounds of population fail[ed]" (lines 128, 127). Now, their village is an empty landscape, presided over by a single, "wretched matron": "She only left of all the harmless train, / The sad historian of the pensive plain" (lines 131, 135–36). Here the power of memory to hold travelers to the places they have left is extinguished. Imagination needs what George Primrose has, the assurance that the scene it paints might actually exist, in order to remember home; this is how memory works across space. When that possibility is evacuated, when the remembered space is empty, all that remains is history, a sad gathering of scraps, as the sad matron picks her "wintry faggot from the thorn."[21]

Guy Mannering

There are several possible historical reasons for Goldsmith's loss of faith in familial sentiment to preserve the British nation, including the end of the Seven Years War, and intimations of American Independence. By the end of the eighteenth century, however, channeling "redundant population" into the colonies began to seem a necessary evil, and by the early nineteenth century, Britain was preoccupied with the problem of redundant population. After the agricultural revolution, and the increasing reliance on potatoes in Scotland and Ireland, after Malthus, and after the return of discharged veterans of the Napoleonic wars, the rhetoric surrounding "useless" population grew stronger. With the advent of the concept of redundant population, moreover, the anxiety surrounding Britain's numbers shifted from the waste or dispersal of population, as we see in Defoe and Goldsmith, to the disruption of Britain's social structures by an excess of "useless mouths."

Published in 1815, *Guy Mannering* describes events in Scotland in the 1770s, explicitly taking up the issues of population displacement and mobility that occupied Goldsmith's poetry of that decade. The novel recounts two parallel instances of involuntary mobility, one individual, one communal. An entire Gypsy village is evicted by the improving landlord, Godfrey Bertram, and, shortly thereafter, seemingly as a result of a Gypsy curse, Bertram's son is kidnapped by smugglers. Eventually, that son, Harry Bertram, who like George Primrose constructs an independent identity through military service, returns to claim his title, but the Gypsies remain dispersed, their village a haunted ruin. Readers have noted the novel's connections to several historically specific instances of displacement and diaspora: the Highland clearances of the early nineteenth century, and the concurrent displacement of indigenous peoples in India, along with the seemingly eternal homelessness of the Gypsies.[22] I would like to add another figure to the novel's consideration of homelessness and vagrancy: the veteran. The two former soldiers in the novel both have served well, and act heroically in the novel. Guy Mannering is identified as "he who relieved Cuddieburn, and defended Chingalore, and defeated the great Mahratta chief, Ram Jolli Bundleman"; Harry Bertram (the lost heir) is one "whose genius has a strong military tendency; and was the first to leave what might have been the road to wealth, and to choose that of fame."[23] The narrative, however, structurally connects these veterans to the peripatetic, unruly Gypsies, alluding, in this linkage, to the disruption feared from returning soldiers – a formerly useful, now useless segment of the population. Using the Gypsies as uncanny doubles for the soldiers allows the novel to solve the problems of mobility and "uselessness" associated with veterans in the early nineteenth century by displacing those problems onto the Gypsies; erasing the anxiety of mobility when the Gypsies disperse or die.

While both the novel's veterans find happy homes by the narrative's end, the returning veterans of the Napoleonic wars were imagined to be one of the principal elements of "surplus population" in the early nineteenth century. Patrick Colquhoun, writing in 1814, proclaims: "There cannot be a greater calamity than that which exhibits a surplus population, who must be clothed and fed – willing to labour, but without the means of finding employment."

> That such a crisis is to be apprehended in this country no person will deny, who has looked accurately into the state of society, in all its intricacies and ramifications, and contemplates at the same time the period which has arrived when vast numbers must cease to receive the wages of the state, and when others whose support depended on the continuance of war, can no longer find the means of subsistence.
>
> In this situation, the multitude become desperate, – criminal delinquency pervades every part of the country; the demand for punishment increases; and the general happiness and comfort of the nation are abridged. The privileges of innocence are everywhere invaded, and the persons and property of the subject are rendered insecure.[24]

The usual remedy proposed for this influx of redundant population was emigration, now seen as a cure, rather than the national bloodletting it had seemed to many in Goldsmith's day. As the anonymous author of "Memoir on the Necessity of Colonization at the Present Period" writes in 1817: "War has, of late years, thinned the ranks of mankind; but, inasmuch as the destructive sword is sheathed, and long it is hoped to remain undrawn, other means of provision and employment must be made out. The most obvious is that of colonizing, and at the present moment, can only be looked to as the means of salvation to the kingdom of Great Britain."[25] Veterans, who had been useful servants of the nation by leaving it to fight, became "useless mouths" on their return home, redundant population trained for violence, without a rooted home. Indeed, former soldiers are often figures of vagrancy and homelessness in late eighteenth- and early nineteenth-century novels, from Lismahago in *Humphry Clinker*, to the peripatetic naval officers of *Persuasion*. Wordsworth's image of the "Discharged Soldier" in Book IV of the *Prelude* exemplifies this trope: "His arms were long, and bare his hands; his mouth / Shewed ghastly in the moonlight ... / ... He was alone, / Had no attendant, neither Dog, nor Staff, / Nor knapsack; in his very dress appeared/ A desolation, a simplicity / That seemed akin to solitude" (IV. 408–19). Although this soldier is a solitary being, rather than part of an unruly horde re-entering England,

Plate 9. *The Gipsey Mother*, steel engraving by E. Portbury after a picture by David Wilkie RA, published in *The Wilkie Gallery*, about 1850.

his Gothic appearance, his seeming rootlessness, his detachment from his own history ("Remembering the importance of his theme / But feeling it no longer" (lines 477–78), connects him with the anxiety raised by veterans for population management.

The soldiers of *Guy Mannering* return not from the Napoleonic wars, but from the British Empire's first military interventions in India. Yet, while the eighteenth century viewed such "nabobs" with distrust, Scott's novel presents them as upstanding citizens.[26] The association with India, however, is the first connection between soldiers and Gypsies. The Gypsies' roots in India had been discovered in the late eighteenth century, and Meg Merrilies, their leader in the novel, incorporates Indian elements into her dress.[27] While the Gypsies were believed to have left India in a perpetual diaspora, the soldiers in the novel have journeyed there and back, their own mobility in the service of patriotism. Gypsies also embodied a threatening mobility, rejecting the link between settlement and coherent communities implicit in early forms of nationalism. According to Katie Trumpener, the "rise of European nationalism, in identifying peoples in historical relationship to place, would redefine civil society to exclude Gypsies from being part of the nation, or forming a distinct nation themselves … The Gypsies' perennial 'homelessness' thus became at once an innate failing and a virtually irreparable state."[28] Both veterans and Gypsies thus figured in the problem of "redundant" population in early nineteenth-century British culture: Gypsies because they refused to settle and work "productively"; veterans because they had lost their use value to the state by returning from foreign wars. Both were "useless mouths," over which the state had no control. By making figures from these representative groups central to his narrative, Scott engages with contemporary concerns about population, and attempts to resolve them. The question *Guy Mannering* implicitly raises, therefore, is whether, like the Gypsies, the soldiers coming from India will disrupt emerging ideas of nation by remaining peripatetic, or whether they will bolster those ideas of nation by settling down.

The connection between the soldier and the Gypsy is set up in the first chapters of the novel, when both Mannering and Meg are represented as soothsayers, prophets whose predictions turn out to be accurate. Mannering, a young man and not yet a soldier, accidentally shows up on Godfrey Bertram's estate the night his heir is born. He does not know the family, and in compensation for their generosity in letting him stay the night, he uses astrology to predict the child's future.[29] Meg Merrilies, an old retainer who helps with the birth, also predicts his future, using the charms of her culture (43). Meg's power as a prophet, however, is most fully demonstrated by her curse after the expulsion of the Gypsies. As Godfrey Bertram passes them leaving the area, Meg "unexpectedly present[s] herself" (64):

> She was standing upon one of those high banks, which, as we before noticed, overhung the road; so that she was placed considerably higher than Ellangowan, even though he was on horseback; and her tall figure, relieved against the clear blue sky, seemed almost of supernatural stature … Her attitude was that of a sibyl in frenzy, and she stretched out, in her right hand, a sapling bough which seemed just pulled. (43–44)

From this position, like the Welsh Bard in Gray's poem of 1757, Meg accurately prophesies the fall of the house of Bertram, although she, unlike that earlier image of an "avenger," does not then throw herself to her death (1.46). She casts the Bertrams' doom as retribution for displacing the Gypsies: "ride your ways, Godfrey Bertram! – This day have ye quenched seven smoking hearths – see if the fire in your ain parlour burn the blyther for that. Ye have riven the thack off seven cottar houses – look if your own roof tree stand the faster. – Ye may stable your stirks in the shealings at Derncleugh [the Gypsies' village] – see that the hare does not couch on the hearth-stone at Ellangowan" (44). The force of Meg's statement here is emphasized by her relation to the landscape. She emerges suddenly from its most imposing features, capitalizing on the intimidating power of the overhanging banks. Thus, the enforced mobility of the Gypsy community, their mutable connection to the land they inhabit, is contrasted to Meg's intimate relationship with her environment, her ability to emerge from it, and to merge back into it.

This uncanny relationship to the landscape is one of the tropes that unites Meg and the other returning soldier of the narrative: Harry Bertram, now known as Vanbeest Brown. Though he does not prophesy, Brown also "presents himself unexpectedly" several times during the narrative, reappearing to Julia Mannering after their court-ship in India, for example, by serenading her with her favorite "Hindu air" in the middle of the night. Thus, while at the beginning of the novel, Meg and one soldier, Mannering, are linked through their capacity to turn up out of nowhere and predict the future, in the second part of the novel Meg and another soldier are linked in their capacity to turn up out of nowhere and stir up the past. Indeed, Bertram is as much a haunting figure as Meg, constantly popping up and triggering violent events. For example, during a winter's walk around a frozen lake with Lucy Bertram and her suitor Charles Hazlewood, Julia Mannering records: "Such was our position, when, at once, and *as if he had started out of the earth*, Brown stood before us at a short turn of the road! He was very plainly, I might say coarsely, dressed, and his whole appearance had in it something wild and agitated" (168, emphasis added). In the ensuing struggle, Brown accidentally shoots Hazlewood and sets in motion the events that restore him to his heritage. Meg's final appearance, as she leads Brown to the events that will unravel his past, repeats the terms of Brown's appearance, even as it duplicates the scene of her prophecy:

> And immediately Meg Merrilies, *as if emerging out of the earth*, ascended from the hollow way and stood before them.
>
> "I sought ye at the house," she said, "and found but him (pointing to Dinmont;), but ye are right, and I am wrang. It is *here* we should meet, on this very spot." (324, first emphasis added)

These Gothic entrances, tinged with violence and terror, present both Gypsy and soldier as if they had never left the land they were born to inhabit. The time between Meg's prophecy and its fulfillment disappears, as she replicates the circumstances of her

Gypsies

Plate 10.   A gathering of Gypsies, detail from a woodcut, "Five Street Sellers."

announcement. In these instances, it seems that the land itself holds so much memory that it conjures up the figures "emerging" from it. Bertram and Meg seem to have been hidden by vertical space (under the earth) rather than horizontal (India, Meg's travels).

Like *A Journal of the Plague Year*, *Guy Mannering* is a novel of memory in a double sense; it both remembers the 1770s from the vantage point of 1815, and represents, within the novel, Bertram's efforts to remember his infancy and kidnapping.[30] As in *The Vicar of Wakefield*, events in *Guy Mannering* are foretold by uncanny figures, allowing the novel to explore the relationship of memory to space, as well as time. Yet, while Goldsmith's plot wanders, or migrates, all over rural England, the space with which Scott's novel concerns itself is quite circumscribed: the estate of Ellangowan (events in India are not represented, except in retrospect). *Guy Mannering* employs two ways of exploring the question of mobility and displacement without following its characters on many of their journeys. First, as we have seen, it continually re-enacts the surprising reappearance of characters who have been forcibly removed from the estate, emerging from the earth as if they had never left it. Second, it examines how a piece of ground can itself hold memory.

The possibility that a landscape could hold the memory of the events that had transpired there was deeply felt in Britain during the years in which Scott wrote the first Waverley Novels, and in a way inextricably connected to war and soldiers. The same year that *Guy Mannering* was published, Scott visited Waterloo, and wrote:

To recollect, that within a short month, the man whose name had been the terror of
Europe stood on the very ground which I now occupied . . . that the landscape, now
solitary and peaceful around me, presented so lately a scene of such horrid magnificence . . . oppressed me with sensations which I find it impossible to describe. The scene
seemed to have shifted so rapidly, that even while I stood on the very stage where it was
exhibited, I felt an inclination to doubt the reality of what had passed.[31]

Here, as Stuart Semmel notes, "the physical landscape offered the tempting prize of
communion with history . . . but then snatched it away."[32] This kind of empty
landscape, whose very vacancy, its dearth of living bodies, signified its historical
importance, fascinated the eighteenth and early nineteenth centuries, from Defoe's
plague pits, to Goldsmith's "Deserted Village," to Scott's Derncleugh. While the
soldiers of Waterloo have disappeared into death, not cities or faraway colonies, the
dilemma posed by the battlefield is similar to the representational problem posed by
depopulation due to mass migration: how to preserve the memory of communal
events without the evidence of living bodies in a landscape.

Guy Mannering manages the problem of making visible the memory of a departed
community with the same Gothic strategies that allow representative figures to
emerge suddenly from the earth, drawing on the trope of haunted ruins to both
eliminate the problem of time, and represent the traces left by people on the
landscape. As Ian Duncan says, "history is troped in terms of place or setting."[33]
The most striking instance of this is the unexpected narrative reappearance of
Derncleugh, the village the Gypsies are forced to leave. Unknowingly returning to
his birthplace, Ellangowan, Bertram finds himself lost in a snowstorm, and goes to
find help. At the bottom of a deep dell, "he next found himself embarrassed among
the ruins of cottages, whose black gables, rendered more distinguishable by the
contrast with the whitened surface from which they rose, were still standing; the
side-walls had long since given way to time, and, piled in shapeless heaps, and covered
with snow, offered frequent and embarrassing obstacles to our traveller's progress"
(143). Here, the sharp outlines of the past rise up to perplex and entangle – to
embarrass – our protagonist. Finding a larger deserted building, Bertram encounters
Meg Merrilies tending to a dying man.

> She moistened his mouth from time to time with some liquid, and between whiles
> sung, in a low, monotonous cadence, one of those prayers, or rather spells, which, in
> some parts of Scotland, and the north of England, are used by the vulgar and ignorant to
> speed the passage of a parting spirit, like the tolling of the bell in Catholic days. (144)

Like Goldsmith's "sad historian of the barren plain," Meg both shelters the remains of
the living knowledge of the place, and ushers it into oblivion. The scene is liminal in
many ways – inside and outside history, between life and death, part of the landscape,
and removed from it. Structurally, the scene replays an earlier scene of Meg singing to
Bertram during a childhood illness: "she lay all night below the window, chanting a
rhyme which she believed sovereign as a febrifuge, and could neither be prevailed

upon to enter the house, nor to leave the station she had chosen, till she was informed that the crisis was over" (40). Here too, Meg and her singing are on the borders of life and death. Yet Meg and Harry are also connected by their shared mobility – they have left Ellangowan only to return at just this point – and by their uncanny relationship to the landscape – their capacity to rekindle memory by popping up out of nowhere. This scene serves to cement their bond: Meg exacts a promise from Bertram to obey her summons the next time they meet.

The novel solves the problem of mass displacement, figured in the forcible removal of the Gypsies, and, more obliquely, in the wanderings of the novel's veterans, through a fantasy of individual restitution; Harry Bertram's soldierly wanderings come to an end, and his ancient right to Ellangowan is reasserted. His tie to this particular plot of ground is figured through his body. While Meg's appearance, as readers have noted, seems to combine elements of many displaced groups (the Gypsies are compared to Red Indians, Caribbean maroons, and East Indians, along with a number of figures from literature and mythology), expanding the resonance of the narrative to multiple forms of modernizing and colonial displacement, Bertram's stabilizes the situation through its exact repetition of his father's. The inhabitants of Ellangowan finally recognize the missing heir in this way:

> Our friend, Jock Jabos, the postilion, forced his way into the middle of the circle; but no sooner cast his eyes upon Bertram, than he started back in amazement, with a solemn exclamation, "As sure as there's breath in man, it's auld Ellangowan arisen from the dead!" . . .
> "I have been seventy years on the land," said one person.
> "I and mine hae been seventy years and seventy to that," said another; "I have the right to ken the glance of a Bertram."
> "I and mine hae been three hundred years here," said another old man, "and I shall sell my last cow, but I'll see the young laird placed in his right." (338)

In contrast to the scene of forcible and arbitrary displacement near the beginning of the novel, in this episode the villagers reiterate, perhaps excessively, the length of their tenure on the land, producing a fantasy of continuous habitation.[34]

While Lukács, in his famous etiology of the rise of the historical novel, exemplarily that of Scott, sees veterans as the agents of a new attitude toward history, the early nineteenth century often actually saw them as those outcasts of "nation" – redundant population.[35] Yet, the form of the historical novel allows Scott to work through the issues of the "necessary" mobility of "redundant" populations in the wake of the Napoleonic wars, displacing the disturbing mobility, lack of productivity, and propensity to theft and violence feared from discharged soldiers first onto virtuous nabobs of the late eighteenth century (oxymoronic as that concept would have been at the time), and then onto the Gypsies. Meg Merrilies' dying words both facilitate Bertram's reinstatement as heir and accomplish this displacement: "When I was in life, I was the mad randy gipsy, that had been scourged, and banished, and branded –

that had begged from door to door and been hounded like a stray tike from parish to parish – wha would have minded her tale? – But now I am a dying woman, and my words will not fall to the ground, any more than the earth will cover my blood" (399). Revealing the truth about Bertram's abduction, she ends her own wandering with the singular, immobile mark of her bloodstains and her grave. Her final stasis allows her words to be heard, and Bertram to be recognized. The same transition from wandering Gypsy to stable veteran occurs in the ruins of Derncleugh. The novel implies that the "Bungalow" Bertram builds for Mannering (now his father-in-law) will be built on that haunted site of the past.

In his *Journey to the Western Islands of Scotland*, published in 1775, Samuel Johnson recounts his visit to a ruined site of ancient learning: "Inch Kenneth was once a seminary of ecclesiastics, subordinate, I suppose, to Icolmkill. Sir Alan had a mind to trace the foundation of the college, but neither I nor Mr. Boswell, who *bends* a keener *eye on vacancy*, were able to perceive them."[36] The 1770s, the decade of Goldsmith's "Deserted Village," and the decade Scott remembers in *Guy Mannering*, were a focal point for considerations of how memory and imagination might combat the vacancies left by the depopulation of parts of rural Britain. Johnson alludes to *Hamlet*, Gertrude's words to her son as he sees his father's ghost approaching: "how is't with you, / That you do bend your eye on vacancy, / And with th'incorporal air do hold discourse?" (III.iv). Johnson's casting of Boswell as the melancholy Dane is comical, but his application of this familial revenge drama to the problem of seeing a vanished culture, one that might only appear to us as a ghost, is telling. In their own ways, each of the novels I have discussed here "casts an eye upon vacancy," trying to see not the ghost of a single powerful patriarch, but the afterimage of a community that has moved on, or disappeared. They ask what forms of representation might allow us to see communities that are no longer there, that have vanished into time, or across vast distances. More concerned with the collective – city, village, or family – than with the individual, Defoe, Goldsmith, and Scott arrive at different strategies – statistics, sentiment, and the uncanny – for filling that vacancy with powerful images. They point to the power of literature to act as the supplement of memory, and remind us of the growing necessity for the novel to remember populations during the long, and increasingly mobile, eighteenth century.

See also: chapter 4, AGE OF PEREGRINATION; chapter 20, HOME ECONOMICS; chapter 21, WHATEVER HAPPENED TO THE GORDON RIOTS?; chapter 22, THE NOVEL BODY POLITIC.

NOTES

1. Charles Davenant, "Discourse on the Public Revenues and the Trade of England, Part II," in *The Political and Commercial Works of that Celebrated Writer, Charles Davenant . . . collected and revised by Sir Charles Whitworth*. 5 vols. (London: 1771), 1: 128.

2. Karl Marx, *Capital*, trans. Ben Fowkes (Harmondsworth, U.K.: Penguin, 1976), 1: 174.

3. Daniel Defoe, *A Journal of the Plague Year*, ed. Louis Landa (Oxford: Oxford University Press, 1969), 16. Further page references will be to this edition.

4. John Bender, *Imagining the Penitentiary: Fiction and the Architecture of Mind in Eighteenth-Century England* (Chicago: University of Chicago Press, 1987), 73.

5. William Petty, "Another Essay in Political Arithmetic concerning the growth of the city of London" (1683; London, 1757), 72.

6. M. Dorothy George, *London Life in the Eighteenth Century* (1925; reprt. Harmondsworth, UK: Penguin, 1966), 36.

7. See Carol Houlihan Flynn, *The Body in Swift and Defoe* (Cambridge: Cambridge University Press, 1990) and Scott Juengel, "Writing Decomposition: Defoe and the Corpse," *Journal of Narrative Technique* 25 (Spring 1995): 139–53.

8. John Graunt, *Natural and Political Observations made upon the Bills of Mortality*, ed. with an introduction by Walter F. Wilcox (Baltimore, MD: Johns Hopkins University Press, 1939), 78–79.

9. Some critics who argue that H. F. dismisses the Bills are Benjamin Moore, "Governing Discourses: Problems of Narrative Authority in *A Journal of the Plague Year*," *The Eighteenth Century: Theory and Interpretation* 33 (1992): 133–47; and Richard Rambuss, "'A Complicated Distress': Narrativizing the Plague in Defoe's *A Journal of the Plague Year*," *Prose Studies* 12 (Sept. 1989): 115–31.

10. Ian Watt, *The Rise of the Novel* (Berkeley and Los Angeles: University of California Press, 1957), 32.

11. Oliver Goldsmith, *The Vicar of Wakefield*, in *The Collected Works of Oliver Goldsmith*, ed. Arthur Friedman (Oxford: Oxford University Press, 1966), 4: 18. Further page references will be to this edition.

12. Michel Foucault, "Governmentality," in *The Foucault Effect*, ed. Graham Burchell, Colin Gordon, and Peter Miller (Chicago: University of Chicago Press, 1991), 99.

13. Quoted in Bernard Bailyn, *Voyagers to the West* (New York: Alfred A. Knopf, 1986), 52.

14. Jonas Hanway, "Serious Considerations on the Solitary Design of the Art of Parliament for a regular, uniform Register of the Parish Poor in all the Parishes within the Bills of Mortality" (London, 1762), 26.

15. For a history of luxury, see John Sekora, *Luxury: The Concept in British Thought, Eden to Smollett* (Baltimore, MD: Johns Hopkins University Press, 1977).

16. Thomas Short, *A Comparative History of the Increase and Decrease of Mankind in England and Several Countries Abroad...* (London: W. Nicoll, 1767), 33. On Goldsmith's opposition to colonial expansion, see Laurence Goldstein, *Ruins and Empire: The Evolution of a Theme in Augustan and Romantic Literature* (Pittsburgh: University of Pittsburgh Press, 1977).

17. See *The Secret Malady: Venereal Disease in Eighteenth-Century Britain and France*, ed. Linda E. Merians (Lexington: University of Kentucky Press, 1996).

18. "Letter from a Gentleman in the Country to his Friend in Town. On his perusal of a Pamphlet addressed to two great men" (London, 1760), 12–13.

19. Oliver Goldsmith, *The Collected Works of Oliver Goldsmith*, ed. Arthur Friedman (Oxford: Clarendon Press, 1966), 3: 33.

20. John Bender, "Prison Reform and the Sentence of Narration in *The Vicar of Wakefield*," in *The New Eighteenth Century: Theory, Politics, English Literature*, ed. Felicity Nussbaum and Laura Brown (New York: Methuen, 1987), 168–88.

21. I am drawing on the distinction made between "memory" and "history" by Pierre Nora in "Between Memory and History: *Les Lieux de mémoire*," *Representations* 26 (Spring 1989): 7–25.

22. See Graham McMaster, *Scott and Society* (Cambridge: Cambridge University Press, 1981), 155–62; Peter Garside, "Meg Merrilies and India," in *Scott in Carnival: Selected Papers from the Fourth International Scott Conference, Edinburgh, 1991*, ed. J. H. Alexander and David Hewitt (Aberdeen: Association for Scottish Literary Studies, 1993), 154–71; Katie Trumpener, "The Time of the Gypsies: A 'People without History' in the Narratives of the West," in *Identities*, ed. Kwame Anthony Appiah and Henry Louis Gates, Jr. (Chicago: University of Chicago Press, 1995), 338–79.

23. Walter Scott, *Guy Mannering*, ed. Peter Garside (Edinburgh: Edinburgh University Press, 1999), 66, 97. All further quotations are from this edition.

24. Patrick Colquhoun, "A Treatise on the Wealth, Power, and Resources of the British Empire, in every quarter of the World, including the East Indies" (London, 1814), 420–21.

25. "Memoir on the Necessity of Colonization at the Present Period" (London, 1817), 1.

26. On perceptions of nabobs, see Philip Lawson and Jim Phillips, "'Our Execrable Banditti': Perceptions of Nabobs in Mid-Eighteenth-Century Britain," *Albion* 16 (Fall 1984): 225–41; on the transmutation of that image in *Guy Mannering*, see Tara Ghoshal Wallace, "The Elephant's Foot and the British Mouth: Walter Scott on Imperial Rhetoric," *European Romantic Review* 13 (2002): 311–24.

27. See Garside, "Meg Merrilies and India."

28. Trumpener, "The Time of the Gypsies," 359.

29. Scott, *Guy Mannering*, 39.

30. See Katie Trumpener, *Bardic Nationalism: The Romantic Novel and the British Empire* (Princeton, NJ: Princeton University Press, 1997), 221–22.

31. Quoted in Stuart Semmel, "Reading the Tangible Past: British Tourism, Collecting, and Memory after Waterloo," *Representations* 69 (Winter 2000): 14.

32. Ibid.

33. Ian Duncan, *Modern Romance and Transformations of the Novel: The Gothic, Scott and Dickens* (Cambridge: Cambridge University Press, 1992), 111.

34. It's significant, though, that this recognition does not allow Bertram to actually repossess Ellangowan, which has been sold to pay his father's debts. Only after Glossin, the villainous new owner, dies, is he able to pay those debts and regain his inheritance. Even then, he needs the assistance of "a few bags of Sicca rupees" from Mannering, his wealthy father-in-law. The spoils gained from displacing Indians on the subcontinent pay for the replacement of the heir at home.

35. For Lukács, a new attitude toward history was enabled by the experience of so many in great national armies, *The Historical Novel*, trans. Hannah Mitchell and Stanley Mitchell (Lincoln: University of Nebraska Press, 1983), 24.

36. Samuel Johnson, *Selected Writings*, ed. Patrick Cruttwell (Harmondsworth, UK: Penguin, 1968), 369.

FURTHER READING

Bailyn, Bernard. *Voyagers to the West*. New York: Alfred A. Knopf, 1986.

Bender, John. "Prison Reform and the Sentence of Narration in *The Vicar of Wakefield*." In *The New Eighteenth Century: Theory, Politics, English Literature*, ed. Felicity Nussbaum and Laura Brown. New York: Methuen, 1987. 168–89.

Foucault, Michel. "Governmentality." In *The Foucault Effect*, ed. Graham Burchell, Colin Gordon, and Peter Miller. Chicago: University of Chicago Press, 1991.

Nora, Pierre. "Between Memory and History: *Les Lieux de mémoire*." *Representations* 26 (Spring 1989): 7–25.

Semmel, Stuart. "Reading the Tangible Past: British Tourism, Collecting, and Memory after Waterloo." *Representations* 69 (Winter 2000): 9–37.

Trumpener, Katie. "The Time of the Gypsies: A 'People without History' in the Narratives of the West." In *Identities*, ed. Kwame Anthony Appiah and Henry Louis Gates, Jr. Chicago: University of Chicago Press, 1995. 338–79.

9

The Erotics of the Novel

James Grantham Turner

In Denis Diderot's *Les Bijoux indiscrets* (1748), the genie Cucufa reaches into his pocket and finds a mess of everyday objects – a half-sucked candy, toy pagodas made of lead, wheat crumbs, "images," and a silver ring (chapter 4). In this assemblage I find a miniature history of the novel. Here is exactly the "reality-effect" most valued as novelistic, the rendering of everyday, insignificant objects through which an entire character streams, for example the waistcoat that Richardson's Pamela embroiders for her employer and future husband Mr. B., or Uncle Toby's fragile clay pipe in Sterne's *Tristram Shandy* (1759–67). These objects are tucked away and have to be fished out. Novelistic truth is buried in pockets (as here), in packets – as in epistolary novels that involve purloining and breaking open private letters – and in plackets, as in the famous scenes where Pamela sews her journal into her underwear "about her Hips," forcing Mr. B. to search her (120, 198). In Diderot's case the pocket location is especially apt, since the collection of random objects includes the famous magic ring that generates the entire novel and the entire "discourse of sexuality" according to Foucault – the ring that makes the genital organs speak.

Genies and magic rings are not supposed to feature in the canonical "realistic" novel as defined by Ian Watt and the Anglo-monoglot school, though preposterous coincidences are considered legitimate by historians who want Fielding to fit their narrow definition of the genre. Even at the time, Richardson repudiated "the French Marvellous" while insisting on the truthfulness and the non-fictional origins of his text.[1] But quotidian realism is only half the story. Magic must still work, and intimate crevices must still speak, only not through supernatural agents. Like the famous confession of the Princesse de Clèves to her husband, events in the novel must be completely understandable in terms of psychology and yet utterly "singular" and "without example" (122, 125). The sober realist Richardson might seem the opposite of the libertine fabulist Diderot, but he too tells his tale of a magic ring that provides an unwitting paradigm of the novel. He asks Elizabeth Carter in a letter:

Did you never, madam, wish for Angelica's Invisible Ring, in Ariosto's Orlando? I remember when I first read of it, having then more faith in romance than I had afterwards, I laboured under a real uneasiness for a whole week, from the strong desire I had to be master of such a one. I was a very sheepish boy, and thought I should make a very happy use of it on a multitude of occasions. (*Selected Letters*, 235–36)

Even after the literal belief in "romance" fades, the "strong desire" persists to acquire quasi-supernatural depths of knowledge. And since so much eighteenth-century fiction focuses on sexual manipulation and amorous self-realization, we can speculate that the two magic rings of Diderot and Richardson are one and the same.

Another anecdote from Richardson's youth suggests a crucial step between romantic myth and novelistic practice. By the age of 13 (though still bashful) he had developed the skills of story-telling and infiltrating intimate female space. "The young Women of Taste and Reading" not only "revealed to me their Love Secrets" but employed him to write love-letters that often contradicted what he could perceive from his vantage: "I have been directed to chide, and even repulse, . . . at the very time that the Heart of the Chider or Repulser was open before me, overflowing with Esteem and Affection, and the fair Repulser dreading to be taken at her Word" (*Selected Letters*, 231). Acting as a "Secretary" in several senses, the future novelist has already reached the point where unsuspected truths pour over him from the "open" cleft between apparent discourse and inner feeling.

We should no more reduce the novel to sex than we should reduce it to the ordinary. But there does seem to be a deep affinity between these two realms of secrecy. My stories of magic rings and intimate revelations suggest that an ostensibly rational age longed for a different kind of talk, less mediated by appearances, and a different scene of human life, less inhibited by the presence of a visible stranger. Sexuality provided such a world, and the novel provided the device to make it talk in public. Scholars have proposed new histories of the novel based on prostitution, arousing entertainment, amorous intrigue, transvestism, Sapphism, or "desire" in general.[2] But vast, overarching theories of desire may not help the reader of this *Companion*, who wants to know what particular desires drove the eighteenth-century novel, and what particular forms satisfied them. I propose instead to illustrate some concrete connections among canonical novels, scandalous or sexually explicit fiction, descriptions of reading, and methods of policing sexual transgression. As in my parallel of Diderot and Richardson, my examples will be both French and English. It is most important to remember that English readers devoured French writing in the original and in translation, and that – contrary to the impression given by monoglot histories of "the rise of the novel" – prose fiction retained a Continental, amorous, and gallant aura.

Espionage and Libertinage

A significant number of novels are in fact *about* devices for making secret feelings and discourses visible. Some affinity between the novel of private life, the prurient observation of secret matters, and the techniques of espionage must have occurred to any reader scanning the titles of an eighteenth-century library: *The London Spy, La Mouche, L'Espion dévalisé, The Invisible Spy*. Hidden scandals are narrated by a sofa, or a guinea coin, or the vulvas of apparently respectable ladies, as in *Les Bijoux indiscrets*. Ferrante Pallavicino's *Corriere Svaligiato* (1642) produces stories from stealing and opening the mail, as do Charles Gildon's translation *The Post-Boy Robb'd of His Mail, or The Pacquet Broke Open* (1692) and imitations such as *The Unknown Lady's Pacquet of Letters* (1707). These truths are not *necessarily* sexual, but sexuality tends to become their paradigm. *A Spy on Mother Midnight* (1748) is only the most explicit of many tales in which the male narrator infiltrates the private space in which women speak the truth about sex.

The eighteenth-century novel should be placed within a complex network of clandestine reading, looking, and reporting. I would illustrate this with an episode in Casanova's memoirs, ostensibly true though drenched in fiction throughout (and written, of course, in French). A high-born nun in Murano, known only by the initials "M. M.," invites him to a secret *casino* where they browse in, and re-enact, the erotic texts and pictures that line the room – a definitive library of Enlightenment libertinism. (All the books he mentions, interestingly enough, Casanova himself denounced to the Venetian authorities in his own secret police reports.) In this private space, sex becomes not an expression of intimacy but a self-conscious performance, as if staged for a larger audience; Casanova seems to display himself to an external presence for approval, a parallel in the sexual realm to the "presumed spectator" that contemporary moralists posited as the source of ethical behavior (notably Adam Smith in his 1759 *Theory of Moral Sentiments*). And indeed, this turns out to be literally true. M. M. explains that she and Casanova will be watched in the act by her regular lover, the Abbé (later Cardinal) de Bernis, French Ambassador to the Venetian Republic. Her *casino* has been designed precisely with such voyeurism in mind, literalizing a scene ubiquitous in the fiction she owns. Each flourish of the rococo decoration conceals an eyehole, so that one entire wall becomes a screen of perforated flowers, behind which lies an invisible duplicate apartment with its own furnishings and its own separate entrance. Casanova poses M. M. "so as to afford a most voluptuous vision for our hidden friend," and imagines himself being watched even when Bernis is not actually concealed in his viewing-box. Sometimes the Ambassador watches Casanova performing with M. M., and at other times he and the nun dine together in the invisible flat and enjoy the spectacle of Casanova with his younger mistress; what better opportunity, as Bernis remarks, to "know the human heart"? Meanwhile, the Doge's secret police watch Casanova and the Ambassador – who was also under investigation back home in Paris – and the reader observes the entire dizzying multiplication of spectacle within spectacle.[3]

The secretive "library-boudoir" of libertinism – its double-shelled and multiple-entried design reiterated in novels as far apart as *Thérèse philosophe* (1748) and *Clarissa* (1747–9) – can serve as a paradigm for a much broader interest in those truths about the "human heart" made available by invisibility. Countless scenes in novels, memoirs, and art hinge upon watching someone else read silently and projecting oneself (mentally and in some cases physically) into her private thoughts. As in M. M.'s *casino*, the space as well as the act of reading becomes sexualized. The "Closet" – not a cupboard but a small room off the chamber that could serve as a study – appears in the King James Bible as the place of solitary prayer, in political gossip as the "cabinet" where cabals are formed, in the history of private life as the site of introspection, and in literary history as the quiet recess that allowed women to become readers or writers; but it could also be interpreted as the space of sex. (I have found no trace of its modern meaning, the concealment of homosexuality.) This association of interior space and sexuality is so close, in fact, that one critic of *Pamela* (1740) can use the phrase "the *Closet Commerce* between the Sexes" as a euphemism for copulation, without further explanation.[4]

Diderot's famous praise of Richardson presents the whole spectrum of fiction in terms of claustrophobic interiors and far-flung landscapes. Unlike most authors, Richardson does not "splash the panelling with blood," transport you to remote climes to be "devoured by savages," "seal himself up in the clandestine places of debauchery," or "lose himself in Fairyland"; instead, he renounces all escapism and engages with "the world where we live," the truths common to "all the well-policed nations." Diderot uses the spatial-textual continuum to contrast the openness of contemporary realism with hermetic, derivative genres such as pornography, Gothic romance, and the exotic thriller. But this realism itself depends on penetration into a remote, sealed space occupied by the terrifying Other: Richardson "carries the torch into the depths of the cavern" of family life, dispels the "phantom" of civilization and respectability, and reveals the "hideous Moor" at the centre of the Western psyche.[5]

Investing significance in partitions puts a premium on broaching them. The clear demarcation of social meaning – dividing serious from pleasurable, male from female, public from private – seems to provoke a desire to perforate the wall that enforces the distinction. It is not a question of demolishing categories and boundaries, but of crossing them at will, slipping through a concealed door or devouring nudity through a keyhole while staying hidden from those who guard that space. This concentration of significance at the aperture helps to explain the preoccupation with what Diderot called the "lieux clandestins de débauche," widespread in moral and sentimental fiction as well as libertine memoirs. The purpose of "clandestine debauchery" is rarely just to enjoy physical pleasure without detection, but to bring knowledge back through the aperture and "publish" it in a form that captures some of the original secretive thrill. The invisible communicating doors, listening-closets, and decorative eye-holes that proliferate in every representation of the libertine – in Richardson's *Pamela* as in Cleland's *Fanny Hill* (1748–9) – let the secrets of a luxuriously insulated space escape into the domain of public knowledge.

These manipulations of space and visibility are nicely exemplified in the stories told about, and possibly by, the Maréchal-Duc de Richelieu (1696–1788). Memoirs of this "French Lovelace" show him forever pursuing clandestine affairs by concealing himself in bedrooms or behind "pierced partitions," or by designing secret doors that allow him entry.[6] In one anecdote, supposedly passed down by word of mouth from the participants/victims themselves, the teenage Don Juan gained access to the heavily guarded Mlle. de Valois by cutting a door through the party wall and mounting on swivels the furniture that conceals it – the cupboard where the princess keeps her jam; as a modern interpreter puts it, she had only to open the door and "from behind the preserves, in their place, the elegant Duke appears."[7] Perhaps this story reached England in time to influence *Pamela*, where Mr. B. observes an intimate conversation between the heroine and his housekeeper concealed, by prior arrangement, in a sash-doored closet used for storing jam (78).

We may classify Richelieu's hidden doorways and revolving fireplaces among other devices to command the subjectivity of women and produce the truth about their sexuality, like the magic ring of *Les Bijoux indiscrets*, which forces the vagina to speak for itself, or the concealed apartment contrived by M. M. and the Cardinal de Bernis. In the visual realm the goal is to pierce the *cloison* with the eye, without knocking down bricks and mortar; we might almost say that the keyhole becomes the point of the door, the peephole the focus of the decorated panel. (One eighteenth-century invention typifies this desire to combine closure and transparency, the internal door glazed and curtained like a window; in Richardson's novels, Mr. B. uses this device to spy on Pamela, but Clarissa uses it conversely to shut her family out of her closet.) The seemingly closed interior becomes a camera, made up of a "hide" or clandestine means of access, an obscure space that accommodates the viewer without intruding on the viewed, an aperture that frames the action and allows it to be grasped as a scene, and a means of "fixing" the result as an object for memory. After a lifetime of scandal-writing, Eliza Haywood introduces her last fiction with an allegorical tale that sums up her conception of authorship; shown a range of miraculous contraptions, she chooses the magic belt that makes her invisible and the "Wonderful Tablet" that captures every conversation and turns it into print (and can be wiped clean only by a virgin certifiably pure in mind as well as body).[8] In a sense all writers on sexuality in this period want to own those powerful objects, to become what Haywood calls herself in this collection: the *Invisible Spy* (1755).

We should be careful not to reduce these clandestine observations to a single Foucauldian "gaze," however. Voyeurism is not the same thing as spying, since one tries to obtain pleasure leading to orgasm, the other evidence leading to conviction. We should further distinguish the voyeuristic (sexual pleasure derived from the act of seeing alone, without introjection into the scene), from the seductive (observing another's arousal in order to intrude at the crucial moment). And we should recognize other motives, less erotic than experimental or inquisitional. Concealment allows the adolescent Richelieu to hear what is really said about him, to adjust his weak identity to the reputation that circulates in the world without him (*Vie privée*, 337). It allows the sentimental *philosophe* to study the "human heart" in its true, private form, away from the false world of appearances (an impulse equally strong in the Cardinal de Bernis and the Reverend Laurence Sterne). And of course the peephole focuses darker impulses – intrusion and violation, surveillance with intent to control, blackmail, or impeach.

Nevertheless, the same techniques of observation and narration serve to titillate the reader of erotica and to report on a foreign envoy, a dangerous author, or a private sexual indulgence. Indeed, the secret agent and the author of scandalous fiction may be one and the same person. Aphra Behn, a founding figure in the new literary history that includes "novels of amorous intrigue," actually worked as a secret agent before turning to drama and fiction as a more reliable source of income. Defoe was likewise a spy as well as a novelist. Another Grub Street entrepreneur, John Dunton, went under cover as a fashionable rake in order to penetrate the London brothels and expose them to vigilante policing – generating sensational descriptions that turn out to be plagiarized from the same bawdy fiction that corrupted morality in the first place.[9] Charles de Fieux, chevalier de Mouhy, was famous for gathering and writing up everything he overheard in the cafés and streets of Paris, converting it into successful novels like *La Paysanne parvenue* (the most striking antecedent to Richardson's *Pamela*) and *La Mouche* (*The Fly*), narrated by the secret agent of the title. Police files reveal that his daily report went straight to the Inspector, and that Mouhy was in fact one of the most important secret informants or *mouches* in Paris.[10] No wonder we refer to the omniscient narrator as a fly on the wall.

Richardson's preoccupation with revealing the "secret purposes" of "professed Libertines as to the Fair Sex"[11] invites comparison with official surveillance of prostitution, an increasing concern in England and in France – where the Police and the Poste instigated a program of reporting from brothels and opening mail. Government leaders were accused of extracting "licentious stories" as well as danger-ous secrets this way.[12] Diderot may praise Richardson for never "closing himself" into *lieux clandestins de débauche*, but in fact the first two novels largely take place within such claustrophobic spaces: Mr. B. jokes about setting Pamela up in London "Lodgings," then later shuts his victim in a lonely country house guarded by a vulgar bawd who sounds like a "vile *London* Prostitute" (69, 180); Lovelace imprisons Clarissa in a hermetically sealed and custom-made *petite maison* concealed within the heart of London, staffed by a whole nightmarish team of whores under the direction of "Mother" Sinclair. Mr. B. associates female sexuality with secret correspondence as he boasts of the "Stays" and "Garters" he will penetrate in search of hidden letters (234, 235), but Lovelace seems to invest his entire sexual imagination in the letter, so that he can barely distinguish the erotic and the epistolary; even after Clarissa has escaped him, he longs to recapture her private letters, dreaming that "the Seal would have yielded to the touch of my warm finger (perhaps without the help of the Post Office Bullet) and the folds, *as other plications have done*, opened of themselves, to oblige my curiosity" (*Clarissa*, 6: 310–11). Mr. B. was a relatively unsophisticated country squire, but in Lovelace Richardson has created a walking embodiment of high libertine culture, trained "at the French Court" in the secretive arts of infiltrating correspondence and suborning servants (2: 106). Lovelace sees himself as the monarch of his little court, its Lieutenant de Police, and its Intendant de la Poste. He dreams of a phallic power so pervasive that letters, like labia, open of themselves even without the Post Office Bullet, the device that removes seals undetectably.

But how can the author himself acquire the knowledge to construct such a character, researching in those clandestine texts that constitute the libertine identity, without exposing himself to the accusations leveled against Shamela? Surely knowing and handling the forbidden text, rendering the seducer's private thoughts, makes him complicit in those secret pleasures? Richardson constantly proclaimed his abhorrence of indecent fiction, however – refusing to read a novel as shocking as *Tom Jones* – and when his friends asked where he found his material, resolutely denied any first-hand knowledge of illicit sexuality. The solution lies in the fable of the ring and the anecdote of the "Secretary," those two episodes in Richardson's early life that antici-pate his mysterious infiltration of a world he refuses to enter in person, and his compulsion to utter its secrets. They suggest an imagination inspired by clandestinity and a readiness for secret service. The "strong desire to be master" of the ring that makes its wearer invisible led to the invisibility conferred by fiction. In writing up the "Love Secrets" of women, soaking in the discourse that "overflowed" from their "open" hearts, the 13-year-old Richardson "learned important lessons in the erotics of intimacy, the contradiction between words and feelings, and the power of writing for others."[13]

In his own account, the novelist adopts the stance and the acuity of the *mouche* or informant, a carefully cultivated pose of marginality and invisibility, slipping un-detected through the spaces of the city, "a sly sinner, creeping along the very edges of the walks . . . afraid of being seen." "I have been always as attentive to the communi-cations, I may say, to the profligate boastings, of the one sex, as I have been to the disguises of the other."[14] He makes himself inconspicuous in masculine company and becomes all ears. What he gathers – not truth in any factual sense, but the "profligate boastings," the projections and fictions that stand for truth in a phallocratic world – he then distills into a narrative at once diverting and instructive, a fiction that half the world found "lascivious" and the other half reformatory. It seems appropriate, then, that the author of *Les Bijoux indiscrets* should shortly become Richardson's most eloquent champion, praising his ability to "carry the torch into the depths of the cavern," his preoccupation with entering the secret places of human nature to bring back reports more real, more inimitable, than any before.

The Erotics of the Novel

The English words *novel* and *romance* were in fact wildly unstable during this period. Sometimes they were used interchangeably as if synonymous, reflecting the practice of those European languages that enjoyed only one term for prose fiction (*novella* in Italian, *roman* in French, *novela* in Spanish); thus Richardson denounces "such Novels and Romances as have a Tendency to inflame and corrupt" (*Selected Letters*, 46–47). At other times they were diametrically opposed. But the criteria for definition also fluctuated, sometimes referring to length, sometimes to probability, sometimes to frivolity, sometimes to class. "Romance" might denote impossible or supernatural fiction and "novel" domestic, quotidian realism, though even this distinction dissolves when Richardson boasts that *Pamela* eschews "the improbable and marvellous, with which novels generally abound" (41). English moralists often use "Romance" to disparage French upper-class narratives (Madeleine de Scudéry's in the seventeenth century, innumerable eighteenth-century "Mémoires" by anonymous *marquises* and *comtes*); Hazlitt sums up a long tradition when he declares the "vices" and "miseries" of "the great" a theme antithetical to the true novel of middle-class folk.[15] By this criterion, however, Richardson's *Clarissa* is not so much innovating as returning to the vast length and absolutist morality of Scudéry's *Clélie* (1654–60) and *Grand Cyrus* (1649–53), re-establishing the focus on microscopic analyses of emotional crises and libertine eruptions within the aristocracy.

The erotic provides a common thread in this bewildering variety of definitions. The expanded 1737 edition of *The Whole Duty of a Woman* assumes that even virtuous "Romances" will wreak havoc on the libido: "those amorous Passions, which it is their design to paint to the utmost Life, are apt to insinuate themselves into their unwary Readers, and by an unhappy Inversion a Copy shall produce an Original" (74). Nathaniel Ingelo had likewise disparaged the novel because its "chief Design" is "to put fleshly Lust into long Stories."[16] Even the preposterous definition in Johnson's *Dictionary* – "a small tale, generally of love" – assumes that the novel is to lovers as the pastoral is to shepherds. This amorous association creeps in even when the ostensible focus is elsewhere. To emphasize the contrast between solid fact and flimsy fiction the word "mere" may be attached, as in Richardson's insistence that *Clarissa* not be taken for "a mere *novel* or *romance*," or Milton's assurance that the myth of Eros and Anteros invented for his divorce tract is "no mere amatorious novel."[17] In this case the word carries its obsolete meaning of "novelty" or "piece of news," but the association with sex and fiction still governs Milton's word choice, as it does in another striking instance: when the hero and heroine of *Oroonoko* (1688) are suddenly reunited in the slave plantation, Behn tells us that Trefry, the sympathetic planter who first "designed" to write Oroonoko's biography, "was infinitely pleas'd with this Novel" (92). Behn's curious usage suggests a sudden change in real-life lovers' fortune that feels as if it is already fiction, approximately the same thing that Mr. B. means when he ironically, and proleptically, predicts that he and Pamela will make "a pretty Story in Romance" together (32).

Margaret Doody declares in the opening line of *The True Story of the Novel* that "Romance and the Novel are one," flying in the face of all those parochial, Anglocentric anachronists who want to separate the terms, indeed to polarize them into self-excluding and self-defining opposites. But seventeenth- and eighteenth-century usage did polarize them at times, particularly when defining genres in terms of their sexual effect. *The Whores Rhetorick* (1683) discourages the courtesan from reading high-flown "Romances" because they promote sexual virtue and constancy, recommending instead the cynical comedy and the aphrodisiac "Novel"; this pornographic text anticipates the new literary history by hinting that the sexual adventures of Charles II and his son Monmouth might "afford matter for a Novel" and obviate the need for "translating daily such numbers of *French* ones, that are in my mind fitter for the necessary House than the Closet."[18] (Three years later Behn realized this possibility for nationalizing the Novel and raising it above the disposable level when she made *Love-Letters between a Nobleman and His Sister* [1686] out of the scandals of Monmouth and his co-conspirator Lord Grey.) Also in the 1680s, the severe moralist Jane Barker promotes a similar distinction when she blames the "Novel" for debauching the nation's morals, encouraging "Interest and loose Gallantry": "How far this has been an Inlet to that Deluge of Libertinism which has overflow'd the Age, the many unhappy Marriages, and unkind Separations, may inform us." As an antidote she champions (and exemplifies) Romance, which endorses "Heroick Love" and "con-fin[es] the Subject to such strict Rules of Virtue and Honour" that the fashionable libertines hate it.[19] For these contemporary experts the all-important difference lay not in length or probability but in sexual ideology.

This dichotomy runs deep in eighteenth-century conceptions of fiction. Elizabeth Boyd, agreeing with Barker's polarity but speaking from the opposite camp, boldly accepted the term *novel* for her own work, arguing for a morality that tolerated female as well as male frailties, and creating male characters whose linkage of new sexuality and new language foreshadows the Age of Sensibility: "Tis most certain, when we come to a true Notion of Life, we have a more refin'd Taste of Love. La Motte felt every Word like a new Being" (*The Happy-Unfortunate* {1732}, 19). We are not dealing with a conflict between sexual vice and asexual virtue, but rather between differing conceptions of sexuality; each party to this polemic claims refinement for themselves and caricatures the opponent as either gross and whorish or impossibly virtuous and irredeemably artificial. The French word *roman* inspired similar debates, even though no contrasting term for realistic fiction had arisen: in *Les Égarements du cœur et de l'esprit* (1736–8) by Crébillon *fils*, the cynical libertine Versac destroys the last remnants of amorous idealism in the narrator by dismissing talk of the heart as "jargon de Roman" (502); Diderot's "Éloge" claims that after Richardson the frivolous term *roman* no longer applies, though no new name has been found (1089).

"Novels" convey a carnal frisson, and yet the virtuous countertext is also a novel. Richardson assails the "mere Novel" and the trivial age of "Story-Lovers and Amuse-ment-Seekers," yet still promotes the "good novels" of Penelope Aubin (who like Jane Barker and Elizabeth Rowe tried to use fiction in the cause of Virtue). And he admits while defending *Clarissa* that he does write "in the humble guise of a *Novel*," even if it is "a Religious Novel," "a new Species of Novel" devised "by way of Accommodation to the Manners and Taste of an Age overwhelmed with a Torrent of Luxury, and abandoned to Sound and senselessness."[20] This bizarre notion – that a novel disguised as real letters is really a moral tract pretending to be a novel – derives from his friend Aaron Hill's rash defense of *Pamela*, much derided by opponents like Henry Fielding. Hill's raptures over this tract in "the modest disguise of a Novel," where "the *Thought* is everywhere exactly *cloath'd* by the *Expression*, and becomes its Dress as roundly, and as close, as *Pamela* her Country-habit," sounded embarrassingly close to Mr. B.'s excitement when the silk-clad Pamela puts on the modest disguise of a country wench.[21] An even more expert witness complains that "Romances [and] Novels, especially the *French* ones," have corrupted the age by encouraging in its male readers the "Fashion" for "debauching as many Women as they could come at." And yet again the solution, a critical program of moral reform, must itself be conducted through the medium of the "Novel-Memoir" – a uniquely effective medium since in the hands of a master like Charles Duclos it gives a "Form, Connexion, and Consistence" to "Love and Gallantry."[22] These remarks come from John Cleland himself, the creator of Fanny Hill.

Hogarth's engraving *Before* illustrates the sexual association of the novel with unusual simplicity. The woman's face and gesture present a genuinely horrified Pamela-figure struggling against an aggressive Mr. B., but the left and right foreground point to an "inward" reality that negates this resistance. Hogarth proposes a symmetry and equivalence between underwear and books, the stays removed beforehand and the true reading matter revealed at this moment of ruin, crudely labeled ROCHESTER and NOVELS (plate 11). These contradictory signs suggest Hogarth's collusion with the attacker, who has clearly caught her with "Rochester" out on the dresser, and who obviously bases his hopes on what contemporary moralists feared – that reading "Novels" will somehow turn the respectable maid into a cauldron of uncontrollable desire. Discovering the lewd text proves her already "open" to clandestine pleasure, whatever her external demeanor might announce. In private female space the book becomes a surrogate lover, as in the memoirs of Richelieu and in the Coulommiers scene in *La Princesse de Clèves* (1678) where the heroine is secretly observed gazing on a picture of the lover she has rejected (154–56). We find the same assumption in the revealingly titled *A Spy on Mother Midnight* of 1748. The hero, disguised as a woman to infiltrate private female space and witness the free sexual conversation that accompanies childbirth when no men are present, throws down his virtuous mistress's resistance upon discovering that she owns two intimate representations of the sexuality she denies in public: a dildo ("Representative" of himself) and the poems of Rochester.[23]

Fielding's attack on *Pamela* is hardly any subtler, foreclosing even the slightest character development by presenting Shamela as a tart from the beginning. Mr. Booby commits no fundamental error when he catches "Pamela" reading and taunts her with "I warrant you *Rochester's* Poems" (*Shamela*, 328). Like Fielding's friend Hogarth, he assumes that if he can stick the label ROCHESTER onto the space occupied by the ambiguous or incomprehensible female, he will mark her definitively as sexual prey. Richardson's B. himself starts with a similar assumption, trying to soften the waiting-maid with bawdy jokes and indecent epithets as well as suggestive gestures – but he changes his approach once Pamela convinces him of her integrity. Fielding wants to rewrite this conviction as a failure to detect fraud, and so to endorse Booby's original approach (aggressive lechery combined with dismissive skepticism) as the right one. Booby is not so much wrongheaded as dimwitted, insufficiently skilled at "penetrating" (in both senses) Shamela's façade of "VARTUE." The reader privy to the "authentick" bawdy letters passed between the daughter and the mother (325, 356), and the

Plate 11.   This protesting lady in William Hogarth's *Before* has removed her stays and invited her lover into her bedroom, where she has been reading novels and Rochester's poems. *The Practice of Piety* lies open as an ironic comment on the scene.

"true" content of her little library, could never make such a category error. Her bundle of tattered books includes not only sermons, plays, and a conduct-book but "The Third Volume of the *Atalantis*" (by Delarivier Manley) and Edmund Curll's notorious translation of the pornographic *Venus in the Cloyster, or the Nun in Her Smock* (1725) (344). Owning the amorous novel and the hard-core dialogue *must* make her what Mr. Booby's clumsy hinting hopes, a sham and a whore. Naming the secret text makes all the difference.

Scenes of Reading

In one of the more jarring episodes of *Les Liaisons dangereuses* (1782) – the novel that most fully sums up eighteenth-century sexual intrigue – the libertine Valmont writes a long, serious letter to the Présidente de Tourvel. He describes a stormy night of emotion, the depth of his feelings, the frequent moments when he is so overcome that he must break off writing (letter 48). She is supposed to receive this letter in what Jane Barker calls the Romance mode, sincere and devoted, but we readers perceive it differently because Valmont (imitating the English rake Viscount Bolingbroke) actually writes it on the naked back of an actress with whom he is spending the night in Paris. As he boasts to Mme. de Merteuil, everything is a cruel double entendre, a miniature version of the deception that Lovelace practices when he shuts Clarissa into a house that she believes respectable and he gloatingly reveals to be a brothel. I find in this scene yet another paradigm, this time not of writing but of reading the novel. The vast majority of novels in the century before Jane Austen depict virtuous women engaged in respectable if troubled courtships – definitely on the Romance side of amorous discourse. But the vast majority of critics and journalists assume that novels, like Valmont's letter, emanate from the lewdest pleasures of the flesh and lure their victims into seduction whatever their surface message.

The idea of the book as inherently seductive has a long history, of course. Long before print, Ovid's *Sappho to Phaon* stages its own scene of arousal-through-reading, as Sappho remembers her lover's reaction to her poetry. The episode of Paolo and Francesca in Dante's *Inferno* V can hardly be bettered as an account of the book as erotic mediator. Sir Philip Sidney's Astrophil recognizes that readers fall in love with a fictionalized representation while rejecting the supposed original, begging Stella in sonnet 45 to "pity the tale of me." But these apprehensions seem to become institutionalized in the seventeenth century, presumably responding to changes in women's education, significant if fitful expansion of the print market, and a dramatic increase in the number and visibility of women novelists like Scudéry and Lafayette in French, Maria de Zayas in Spanish, and Aphra Behn in English.

The French lawyer and educator Alexandre Louis Varet, for example, denounces a group of monks who tried to infiltrate a convent by distributing erotic literature, including novels and the famous pornographic dialogue *L'Escole des filles* (1655); the goal was "insensibly to ingage" the nuns "in vitious inclinations," making them "susceptible of the Affections [*des mouvements*] which they endeavoured to cherish in them." (The 1676 English translation fictionalizes and trivializes the whole episode by calling the "*innocent Gallantry* of the *Nunns* and *Fryars* . . . very agreeable divertisement.") *L'Escole des filles* itself instructed the sexually awakened woman to read the novel (*le roman*), to "let herself be captivated" by those narratives "that can most insinuate love into the heart," to "make her mind supple to the fine passions represented there." In Varet's educational handbook (1669) he particularly warns young ladies about the effects of novels, which "redouble the ardors of their passions" and translate the "movements of fictitious heroines" directly into the mind and the body. Such books are interactively "dangerous," provoking in their female readers "the desire to raise in men who look at them" the same passions "expressed so agreeably" on the page.[24] As another seventeenth-century moralist argued, "since Mothers cannot look at certain paintings without affecting their children, why should we not think that lascivious Histories and Novels may have the same effect on our imagination and always leave some stain on our soul?"[25]

In the decade of the *Pamela* sensation, reading itself was eroticized, even sexualized. Bodily reaction becomes an essential badge of true sensibility, as when Richardson responds to Aaron Hill's *Art of Acting* with "such Tremors, such Startings, that I was unable to go thro' it." Hill replies that the author of *Clarissa* "fill[s] all you reach with tremblings!" When Hill murmurs "All you think, and all you do, is *beautiful*," Richardson crosses the passage out with heavy ink, finding him "too warm" – exactly the complaint leveled against *Pamela* itself.[26] Hill had gone over the top in his praise of that first novel ("We are All on Fire"), yet Richardson had published most of these eulogies in the second edition, inspiring merciless parodies by Fielding and other Antipamelists. As we have seen, Pamela's disingenuous self-display in the "modest disguise" of a country girl becomes the model for readerly response. Hill amplifies this still further: "when modest Beauty seeks to hide itself by casting off the *Pride* of *Ornament*, it but displays itself without a *Covering*" (508). (Fielding needed to change only a few words in this passage to create the autoerotic letter by Tickletext that prompts the story of Shamela: "Oh! I feel an Emotion even while I am relating this; Methinks I see *Pamela* at this Instant, with all the Pride of Ornament cast off!" {*Shamela*, 322}.) Hill even proclaims that "this Author has prepar'd an enamouring *Philtre* for the Mind, which will excite such a *Passion* for Virtue, as scarce to leave it in the Power of the *Will* to neglect her" (513). Exactly the same aphrodisiac assumptions were made by hostile critics:

> Interspersed throughout the Whole, there are such *Scenes* of *Love*, and such *lewd Ideas*, as must fill the Youth that read them with *Sentiments* and *Desires* worse than ROCHESTER can. . . . It is impossible to read it without endeavouring to gratify the Passion he hath raised; let us view *Pamela* then, divested of the Drapery in which she is enclos'd, tho' not hid, and then her Charms will appear thus: The wise Father will never think it proper for his Son's Closet, and the careful Mother banish that with other Novels and Romances from her Daughter's Cabinet. (*Pamela Censured* {1741}, 24–25)

The anonymous *Pamela Censured*, like Fielding's *Shamela* (1741), rests on the idea that the representation of subjectivity operates on the young and susceptible reader "almost without the Intervention of the Will." (The phrase comes from Johnson's famous essay on fiction {*Rambler* 4}, a reminder of how widespread was this fear of novel-induced automatism.) According to the Censurer, the images interspersed throughout *Pamela* "must necessarily," "directly," "infallibly" inflame the young reader, who cannot help being aroused by "the Idea of peeping thro' a Keyhole to see a fine Woman extended on a Floor in a Posture that must naturally excite Passions of Desire."[27] The "novel panic" induced by *Pamela* "led partisans to characterize the reader or spectator as an automaton, overwhelmed by passions beyond her control or programmed by subliminal messages from the concealed author. Inexorably, both sides equated this textual response with sexual arousal, valorized according to the polemic as genial warmth or onanistic frenzy."[28]

Fielding's Old Etonian approach to sex imposed a strong class division. A servant can only be a whore, as conveyed in *Shamela* and in *Joseph Andrews* (1742) (I: xviii), where the kindly chambermaid Betty avoids pregnancy by taking several lovers at once (in the medical myth of the day, the sperm of multiple partners lost its fertility when mingling in the prostitute's vagina). Elsewhere in *Joseph Andrews*, however, Fielding treats erotic responsiveness more sympathetically. Introducing his heroine Fanny, he warns (or promises) that his description will be dangerously captivating: "Reader, if thou art of an amorous Hue, I advise thee to skip over the next Paragraph; which to render our History perfect, we are obliged to set down, humbly hoping, that we may escape the Fate of *Pygmalion*" (II: xii). (Varying the myth, he then equates the love-struck reader with Narcissus.) Male author and male reader converge in this Pygmalionic-Narcissistic lust for the female artifact. Richardson too exploits this trope in his teasing correspondence about Clarissa: "I find," from the passionate letters he receives, "that I have drawn her too amiable. Nor can I go thro' some of the Scenes myself without being sensibly touched. Did I not say, that I was another Pygmalion?" The sexual association deepens as *Clarissa* moves toward the climactic rape scene: the same correspondent, Lady Brad-shaigh, tells Richardson, after reading that installment, "you now can go no farther" – the very words that Lovelace uses to announce the outrage itself.[29]

The text-within-a-text features widely in fiction and memoirs, as we might expect. Casanova performs according to the books he finds in M. M.'s library-boudoir, and Richelieu seduces his duchess by intruding into her reverie about him, induced by reading a novel in bed (*Vie privée*, 345–46). Pamela's reading-matter and writing-matter are contested and manipulated, not only by Mr. B., but increasingly by Pamela herself, who places crucial letters in her stays, or about her hips, or in sight of a keyhole. Full-blown versions of this topos had been developed in the "novels of amorous intrigue" that have only recently been readmitted into the canon, after languishing for centuries in Shamela's library. Delarivier Manley, for example, creates several seduction-in-the-library scenes, and advertises them in her audacious work of metafiction, the autobiographical *Adventures of Rivella, or the History of the Author of the Atalantis* (1714).

In the introduction to *Rivella* two young gentlemen – one English, one French – lock themselves into a garden to enthuse over their favorite passages in Manley's novels. Bonding through the female text, they confess their erotic excitement and long to experience the same raptures in the arms of the author herself – a perfect paradigm of the masculine reader's desire to blur the boundaries of fiction and reality. Far from degrading sexuality à la Fielding, Manley's erotic fictions (according to Manley) "raise high Ideas of the Dignity of Human Kind, and inform us that we have in our Composition wherewith to taste sublime and transporting Joys." The Chevalier d'Aumont particularly loves the scene in *The New Atalantis* (1709) where "Her *Young and innocent Charlot*, transported with the powerful *Emotion of a just kindling Flame, sink{s} with Delight and Shame upon the bosom of her Lover in the Gallery of Books*." D'Aumont's vicarious enjoyment of this library-seduction scene presumably depends upon identification with the triumphant male, but in the situation of reading it is D'Aumont who takes the "female" position and Manley the male; *he* becomes Charlotte, swooning in the gallery of fictions Rivella has herself composed, while the female author becomes the imperious seducer.[30] *Rivella* deliberately reverses the usual gendered scenario, in which men invent fictions of women reading fictions that imagine women imagining men, allowing the male character and the male reader to triumph over this supposed evidence of women's "true" susceptibility.

Reading-scenes like Manley's, self-consciously posing the nubile heroine with a book that prepares for her fall, have been interpreted as constituting a passive, addicted "novel reader" reduced to the repetitive trash of mass entertainment. But the reading scenes of Manley and Haywood, which William Warner analyzes at length to show how this aroused yet stupefied novel reader is thematized within the novel itself, are not quite as regressive. When she yields to the Duke, Charlotte in the *New Atalantis* is reading not a novel but Ovid's *Metamorphoses*; her surrender comes, not when she breaks out in erotic rapture, but when she *weeps* over the fate of the incestuous daughter that her father-like seducer wishes her to become. (As we learn from the *Pamela* craze and later from Sterne's novels of sensibility, tears are the eighteenth century's favorite sexual lubricant.) In Haywood's 1719 *Love in Excess*, again, Melliora slides into acquiescence when reading, not a novel, but Ovid's poetry of amorous "Misfortune."[31] In this case the original, the heroic epistle from Sappho to Phaon, is itself highly medium-conscious: Sappho wonders how Phaon will react to her "litteras," points to the lines blotted by her own tears as she writes to the minute, and recalls how she seduced him by reciting her own poetry, leading him from verse to bed. Haywood reminds us that the novel inherits a long and deep history of imitative erotic reading.

"Virtuous" authors tried to emulate these scenes of deliquescent reading. Richardson's Mr. B., improving on what he overheard in the closet and what he read in the letters he stole even before Pamela surrendered them willingly, creates a similar library-scene in an attempt to regain control over erotic space and erotic discourse. Pamela recoils in terror on being invited into his "Closet," understandably afraid of coerced "closet commerce," but relents when she sees that the room could be described in a different vocabulary; it is in fact "his Library, and full of rich Pictures besides" (83). Here he declares his "Love" explicitly for the first time, having been "quite overcome with your charming manner of Writing, so free, so easy, and so much above your Sex." B. obviously hopes that mutual excitement over "free" and "easy" discourse will lead to surrender and consummation, as in Manley and Haywood, so he asks Pamela to consider an experiment whereby they live together for two weeks in "Kindness," setting aside the master-servant relationship. Indeed Pamela's heart does "give way" most alarmingly (84) – her first admission that she is seriously tempted by his attentions.

When Fielding sneers at Shamela's little library, or shows the oafish Fitzpatrick reading "one of Mrs. *Behn*'s Novels" to improve his chances with the ladies (*Tom Jones*, X.ii), he is transcribing the erotic-book topos from the "sublime" to the abject and whorish stratum. Sterne recovers the motif in a subtler way, when Parson Yorick observes an attractive chambermaid in a bookshop, buying Crébillon's *Wanderings of the Heart and Mind*, the libertine memoir of a young man propelled into amorous adventures by something "lacking in my heart," only to end up with "a void in my soul" (*Égarements*, 382, 537). This racy French book serves as a large-scale parallel to the *Sentimental Journey* itself – that "quiet journey of the heart in pursuit of NATURE," intended "to spy the *nakedness*" of France's "hearts" rather than her bodies or her military defenses – and a suggestive pocket tool à la Diderot. When Yorick slips each volume into the maid's loose pocket he initiates a series of double entendres that leads to his bedroom and to the very brink of the bed – only to interrupt this classic "French" seduction-memoir at the last minute, substituting a sermon on the divine nature of passion (89–91, 108–109, 115–18). The high priest of sensibility recapitulates the "Dignity" of Manleyesque eroticism, without the actual surrender.

The Hard Core and the Soft

"Scandalous and flagitious Books," one moralist observed in 1751, "are not only privately but publickly handed about for the worst Purposes ... to inflame the Passions, to banish all Sense of Shame, and to make the World, if possible, more corrupt and profligate than it is already."[32] This is another of John Cleland's gratuitous comments, here added to his translation of a sensational case-history of lesbianism. It might seem strange that the leading English pornographer of the 1740s, the inventor of Fanny Hill, should complain about the kind of "inflaming" book that got him out of debtors' prison. But Cleland expertly sensed that the same reader could feel prurience and indignation, that only thin partitions separated the policing and the enjoying of sexuality. This age of "callous Appetites" and "debauched Readers" – to quote another pornographer-cum-moralist – was also an age of crusading reform.[33] The reformer and the libertine shared one central belief – in the intense transforming power of the book, for better or worse. Cleland's warnings about the power of pornography exactly concur with his explanation of how Catarina Vizzani came to be a lesbian: even before any "Incitements from her Constitution," her "Imagination" was "corrupted . . . either by obscene Tales that were voluntarily told in her Hearing, or by privately listening to the Discourses of the Women." The "tales" and "discourses" that women tell among themselves – which men need magic rings and invisibility to discover – inevitably shape Vizzani's mind and body to "preternatural" lusts and "venereal Fury" (54–56), as much by their "form, connection, and consistence" as by their literal content.

The magic ring was working hard in the 1740s; the decade that launched major British novels such as *Pamela, Joseph Andrews, David Simple, Clarissa, Tom Jones,* and *Roderick Random* also saw a peak in the production of clandestine erotica. In France the favored genres of the 1720s and 1730s – the secret memoir, the Oriental tale, the anti-clerical scandal narrative – mutate into full-length erotic fictions like *L'Histoire de Dom B——, ou le Portier des Chartreux, Les Bijoux indiscrets,* and *Thérèse philosophe,* which emulate the libertine dialogues of the seventeenth century in their vast amplification of pornographic detail, their attempt to reconstruct the inmost truth of female sexuality, and their self-conscious articulation of a "philosophical" eroticism.[34] Thus a worldly protagonist of *Bijoux* names the seventeenth-century "*Aloysia*" as the source of his sexual expertise (chapter 44), and the educated Thérèse surrenders like Manley's Charlotte in a library-boudoir like M. M.'s, lined with this and other canonical works that define the sexuality she is enacting. In England, the full-blown philosophical-pornographic narrative took longer to develop, but the publishing mechanism had been set in motion by Edmund Curll. In the 1720s Curll launched a flurry of works like Shamela's translation of *Vénus dans le cloître* (1683), which itself included a review of its own predecessors, *L'Escole des filles* and *L'Académie des Dames, ou Les Sept Entretiens satyriques d'Aloïsia.* In the 1740s he commissioned the lewd *New Description of Merry-land* (by "Roger Pheuquewell") and the censorious *Merryland Displayed,* both from Thomas Stretser.[35]

Motifs of espial and arousal pass freely between this hard-core fiction and more recognizable novels. Monique in *Le Portier des Chartreux* falls asleep in the nunnery chapel, dreaming of the dashing Verland, until "the excess of pleasure woke me" and she finds a "real" man embracing her sleeping body: "I thought that my happiness was changing illusion into reality," but when she opens her eyes she sees the novice Martin, who had been watching her and who now completes the "real" act (66–67). "Thérèse the *philosophe*" likewise drifts into an erotic-pictorial reverie in the Count's library, a space both closed and transparent, sealed off from the world yet shot through with one-way apertures for the invisible spectator. The Count secretly watches her, materializing in person the moment she cries out in soliloquy "Appear, my Lord, I no longer fear your dart!" (146–49). Mr. B. wishes for exactly this surrender when he ushers Pamela into his library, and after his reformation he continues to spy on her there, though she is praying and not masturbating (468).

Viewing-scenes naturally proliferate in the memoirs of Fanny Hill, evolving from crude scenes glimpsed through knot-holes into elaborate staged tableaux. Mrs Cole's house, the setting for these more advanced couplings, resembles M. M.'s *casino* in its simply respectable exterior and complicated libertine interior, which allows scenes of voyeurism to be themselves watched by concealed observers. The narrative develops even more layers than Casanova's memoir: while Fanny and her lover copulate on the sofa (a scene reconstructed in her memory for a female friend), the other rakes and courtesans gather round to gaze and applaud, the proprietress watches from her private viewing-place, the reader devours the whole spectacle with his eyes, and the police scour London looking for copies of Cleland's illicit book. At times, however, Fanny's language takes on a policing tone, for example in a painful flogging routine that she performs cheerfully because she "knew Mrs *Cole* was an eye-witness from her stand of *espial*" (148). She herself "stands" and "spies" in a later scene where her motive is explained as the exposure of criminality rather than the induction of pleasure: in a local tavern, she climbs on a chair and stares through the crumbling plaster as two Sodomites go to work, then turns away burning with indignation and intent on having them arrested. But just as the language of vigilantism creeps into the discourse of pleasure, so vice versa the attitude of horrified denunciation dissolves in the lush, familiar style of Fanny's description: the younger man's penis becomes an "ivory toy," anal penetration becomes a "carpet-road" – a phrase associating smooth passage with luxury fabrics as well as calm waters (158).

Cleland's goal, like Mrs. Cole's, was to "reconcil[e] even all the refinements of taste and delicacy with the most gross and determinate gratifications of sensuality" (94). To achieve this "refinement" he replaces the old dirty words with a luxuriant, genteel, periphrastic vocabulary of "velvet tip," "double ruby pout," and "sweet miniature, such as not *Guido*'s touch or colouring could ever attain to the life or delicacy of" (220, 44, 30). To this "decent" diction he adds a shift in narrative form; in what might seem like an impossible hybrid, the career of sexual adventure is enclosed within a happy-ever-after marital ending. Even *Les bijoux indiscrets* and *Thérèse philosophe* achieve closure by lodging the heroine in a stable, companionate, and sexually faithful bond. Once again we sense a congruence between the virtuous and the wicked, between those who feared, and those who hoped, that reading equivocal fictions could turn women into erotic fictions themselves: both parties aspire to confine women to a feminized realm dominated by the sexual body – the family home, or the still more isolated *petite maison*. Just as the sentimental novel sexualizes domesticity, hard-core fiction domesticates sexuality.

Libertine and virtuous critics could agree, whether they approved or not, that the text's capacity to arouse constituted its most impressive feature, and that it increased in proportion to what Elizabeth Boyd called "a more refined taste of love." Aaron Hill praised *Pamela* as a philter or aphrodisiac for the mind, whose "warmly-pleasing moral Scheme / Gives livelier Rapture, than the Loose can *dream*" (513, 518). Richardson himself declared *Tristram Shandy* "too gross to be inflaming," retrospectively admitting the possibility that refinement (which he championed *ad nauseam*) and aphrodisiac power (which he denied *ad infinitum*) were closely linked (*Selected Letters*, 341). It has been argued that Richardson and Fielding create the elevated, literary novel by "over-writing" the scandalous novels of Behn, Manley, and Haywood, obliterating their cheap sexuality. But this elevating process seems oddly ineffective, since these great reformers were themselves condemned as dangerous fiction-mongers who corrupt youth by implanting imitative desires. For Mary Wortley Montagu Richardson's confusing mélange of "tenderness" and impropriety "will do more general mischief than the Works of Lord Rochester." Catharine Macaulay found Richardson "totally unfit for the perusal of youth." Isaac Watts the hymnodist reported that ladies could not read *Pamela*'s attempted-rape scenes without blushing; Anna Barbauld cites this approvingly and goes further, declaring them "totally indefensible." Vicesimus Knox banned the supposedly "elevated" works of Richardson and Fielding entirely from schoolboy reading.[36] Even now they induce the same fear of imitative passion that the anti-novel discourse ascribed to Behn and Haywood: I know one professor, accused of sexually harassing her students, who was grilled by lawyers at some length because she taught a course on *Clarissa*.[37]

See also: chapter 2, Fiction/Translation/Transnation; chapter 3, Narrative Transmigrations; chapter 6, Representing Resistance; chapter 17, Queer Gothic.

Notes

1. Samuel Richardson, *Selected Letters of Samuel Richardson*, ed. John Carroll (Oxford: Oxford University Press, 1964), 54.
2. I refer to books by Bradford K. Mudge, William Warner, Ros Ballaster, Madeleine Kahn, Lisa Moore, and Nancy Armstrong.
3. Jacques Casanova de Seingalt, *Histoire de ma vie* (Wiesbaden, 1960), 4: 57, 65–70, 77, 118–20; cf. Casanova, *Mémoires* (Paris: Gallimard, 1960), 3: 1124–5, 330 n. 2; and Robert Darnton, "A Police Inspector Sorts His Files," in *The Great Cat Massacre and Other Episodes in French Cultural History* (New York: Basic Books, 1984), 164.
4. *Pamela Censured, in a Letter to the Editor* (London, 1741), facsimile ed. Charles Batten (Los Angeles: Clark Library, 1976), 45.
5. All citations from Denis Diderot, "Éloge de Richardson," in *Oeuvres*, ed. André Billy (Paris: Gallimard, 1946), 1090–91.
6. *La Vie privée du Maréchal de Richelieu*, in *Mémoires du Maréchal Duc de Richelieu*, ed. François Barrière (Paris: Firmin Didot, 1868–9), 337–46; Hubert Cole, *First Gentleman of the Bedchamber: the Life of Louis-François-Armand, Maréchal Duc de Richelieu* (New York: Viking

1965), 160–63, 170–71, 174–75, 294; cf. Alexandre Duval, *La Jeunesse du duc de Richelieu, ou le Lovelace français* (Paris, 1796), cited in Benedetta Craveri, "Fatti della vita del maresciallo di Richelieu," *La Vita Privata del Maresciallo di Richelieu* (Milan: Adelphi, 1989), 214 n. 172.
7. Patrick Wald Lasowski, *Libertines* (Paris: Gallimard, 1980), 94; Pierre-Victor Besenval, *Mémoires*, ed. Saint-Albin Berville and François Barrière (Paris: Baudouin Frères, 1821), 1: 105–13; Cole, *First Gentleman*, 37–38, 40–41, 294.
8. Eliza Haywood, *The Invisible Spy, by Exploralibus*, in *Selected Fiction and Drama of Eliza Haywood*, ed. Paula Backscheider (New York: Oxford University Press, 1999), 10–11.
9. See my "Pictorial Prostitution: Visual Culture, Vigilantism, and 'Pornography' in Dunton's *Nightwalker*," *Studies in Eighteenth-Century Culture* 28 (1999): 55–84.
10. Darnton, "Inspector," 188.
11. Samuel Richardson, *Clarissa, or, The History of a Young Lady*, ed. with an intro. and notes by Angus Ross (Harmondsworth, UK: Penguin Books, 1985), preface, vol. 1, f. A3.

12. See D. A. Coward, "Eighteenth-Century Attitudes toward Prostitution," *Studies on Voltaire and the Eighteenth Century* 189 (1980): 371–72; *Mémoires de Richelieu*, 1: 180–85; Jacques Peuchet, *Mémoires tirés des Archives de la Police* (Paris: Levavasseur, 1838), 2: 124–25, 146; *Mémoires de Madame de Hausset sur Louis XV et Madame de Pompadour*, ed. Jean-Pierre Guicciardi (Paris: Mercure de France, 1985), 35.

13. As I said in "Richardson and His Circle," in *The Columbia History of the British Novel*, ed. John Richetti (New York: Columbia University Press, 1993), 75.

14. Richardson, *Selected Letters*, 172, 297.

15. Cited in William Warner, *Licensing Entertainment: The Elevation of Novel Reading in Britain, 1684–1750* (Berkeley and Los Angeles: University of California Press, 1998), 24.

16. Nathaniel Ingelo, *Bentivolo and Urania* (London, 1669), f. b3.

17. Richardson, *Clarissa*, 1498; John Milton, *Complete Prose Works* ed. Ernest Sirluck, vol. 2, (New Haven, CT: Yale University Press, 1959), 256.

18. Ferrante Pallavicino, *The Whores Rhetorick* (London, 1683), 182–83; cf. my "*The Whores Rhetorick*: Narrative, Pornography, and the Origins of the Novel," *Studies in Eighteenth-Century Culture* 24 (1995): 297–306, and "Pornography and the Fall of the Novel," *Studies in the Novel* 33 (2001): 358–64.

19. Jane Barker, *Exilius, or the Banish'd Roman*, facsimile introduced by Josephine Grieder (New York: Garland, 1973), ff. A2r–v.

20. *Selected Letters*, 117; preface to Aubin's novels, cited in Warner, *Licensing Entertainment*, 186; "Hints of Prefaces," in *Clarissa*, 4, 7.

21. Samuel Richardson, *Pamela, or Virtue Rewarded*, ed. Thomas Keymer and Alice Wakeley (Oxford: Oxford University Press, 2001), 506, 508, 55–57.

22. John Cleland, "Translator's Preface," to volume 2, Charles Pinot-Duclos, *Memoirs Illustrating the Manners of the Present Age* (ca. 1753), ix, vi, xiii.

23. *A Spy on Mother Midnight* (London, 1748), 33; *A Continuation ... the Second Part of the Spy on Mother Midnight* (London, 1748), 22.

24. All cited in my *Schooling Sex: Libertine Literature and Erotic Education in Italy,* France, and England, 1534–1685 (Oxford: Oxford University Press, 2003), 112–13, 155.

25. Jacques Du Bosc, cited in Natalie Zemon Davis and Arlette Farge, eds., *A History of Women in the West* (Cambridge, MA: Harvard University Press, 1993), 272.

26. T. C. Duncan Eaves and Ben D. Kimpel, *Samuel Richardson: A Biography* (Oxford: Oxford University Press, 1971), 170; Aaron Hill, *The Works of the Late Aaron Hill* (London, 1753–4), 4: 388–400, 2: 169; Forster MS XIII.2, f. 50, and cf. f. 35.

27. *Pamela Censured*, title page, 21, 31, 60 (and see Tassie Gwilliam, *Samuel Richardson's Fictions of Gender* (Stanford, CA: Stanford University Press, 1993), 38–41).

28. As I say in "Novel Panic," *Representations* 48 (1994): 73.

29. Richardson, *Selected Letters*, 90; Anna Laetitia Barbauld, ed. *Correspondence of Samuel Richardson*, (London, 1804), 4: 207.

30. Delarivier Manley, *Novels*, facsimile ed. Patricia Köster (Gainesville, FL: Scholars' Facsimiles and Reprints, 1971), 2: 740; cf. *The New Atalantis* (1709), 1: 59–60 (*Novels*, 2: 331–32).

31. Warner, *Licensing Entertainment*, 104–105, 117–19, 212–13.

32. John Cleland, "Remarks upon the Foregoing Dissertation," in *An Historical and Physical Dissertation on the Case of Catherine Vizzani* (London, 1751), 63–64.

33. Thomas Stretser, *Merryland Displayed* (Bath, UK: J. Leake, 1741), 3.

34. See my *Schooling Sex*, chapters 3–4.

35. Jean Barrin, *Venus in the Cloister* (London, 1725), 125–29; cf. David Foxon, *Libertine Literature in England, 1660–1745* (New Hyde Park, NY: University Books, 1965), 14–15, 17.

36. Lady Mary Wortley Montagu, *Complete Letters*, ed. Robert Halsband, vol. 3 (Oxford: Oxford University Press, 1965–7), 9; Catherine Macaulay, *Letters on Education*, facsimile ed. Gina Luria (New York: Garland, 1974), 145; Barbauld, ed. *Correspondence of Samuel Richardson* 1: lxvii; Warner, *Licensing Entertainment*, 10.

37. For legal reasons the identity of this acquaintance cannot be revealed, nor has the case ever been discussed in print.

FURTHER READING

Armstrong, Nancy. *Desire and Domestic Fiction: A Political History of the Novel*. New York: Oxford University Press, 1987.

Ballaster, Ros. *Seductive Forms: Women's Amatory Fiction from 1684–1740*. Oxford: Oxford University Press, 1992.

Cusset, Catherine. *No Tomorrow: The Ethics of Pleasure in the French Enlightenment*. Charlottesville: University of Virginia Press, 1999.

DeJean, Joan. *Tender Geographies: Women and the Origins of the Novel in France*. New York: Columbia University Press, 1991.

Wahl, Elizabeth Susan. *Invisible Relations: Representations of Female Intimacy in the Age of Enlightenment*. Stanford, CA: Stanford University Press, 1999.

10

The Original American Novel, or, The American Origin of the Novel

Elizabeth Maddock Dillon

Colonial Origins

William Hill Brown's novel, *The Power of Sympathy*, published in Boston in 1789, is often accorded the title of the "first American novel."[1] The historical coincidence of the publication of *The Power of Sympathy* and the adoption of the US Constitution in 1789 has implicitly given currency to literary-critical understandings of the link between the political form of the nation and the literary genre of the novel. Accounts of the early American novel have taken the nation–novel connection as axiomatic: the tales of sympathy, seduction, incest, and captivity that typify early American novels have been primarily interpreted as allegories of American nationhood – as narratives that thematize the vicissitudes of citizenship and national identity in the new polity. This allegorical view is pithily embodied in John Adams's 1804 statement: "Democracy is Lovelace and the people are Clarissa."[2] Adams indicates that the politics of American nationhood play out as a seduction narrative: a virtuous people, like the virtuous woman, must be prepared to rebuff the advances of a libertine or suffer destruction. Adams' example has been duly followed by literary critics who have elaborated in compelling fashion the connections between particular early American novels and the state of the early republic, yet the proclivity for this model of reading has had the effect of foreclosing a range of alternative readings. In this essay I step away from the neat conjunction of nation and novel that has guided critical work in this field; I do so in order to examine the form and meaning of the novel in relation to a distinctively different frame – a frame better characterized in terms of an eighteenth-century nascent global market shaped by the forces of colonialism, mercantile capitalism, and imperialism.

The developing world market and its cultural relays and divisions informed both the production and the reception of the eighteenth-century novel; as I argue below, the formal innovation of the realist novel as well as its nationalist associations emerge against the ground of the colonial world market. Indeed, attention to the transatlantic trade in texts, culture, and persons that marked eighteenth-century life in North America has made the title of "first American novel" an increasingly vexed one to assign: *The Power of Sympathy* was certainly not the first novel to be read, printed, or even written in colonial North America.[3] As Cathy Davidson points out, a "convergence" of criteria has seemed to point to Brown's novel as worthy of such a title: the novel was "written in America, by an author born in America, published first in America, set in America, [and is] concerned with issues that are specifically grounded in the new country and not simply transplanted from England."[4] The narrative of seduction and unwitting sibling incest that comprises *The Power of Sympathy* is thus one that Davidson takes to be grounded in the newly nationalized soil of the United States rather than England. Yet in this article I suggest that the insistently domestic and familial content of the early novel – in its very emphasis on *formulating* the domestic – speaks to the social, economic, and cultural effects of colonialism rather than the particularity of national identity. More specifically, I turn to scenes of incest and miscegenation that appear in eighteenth-century novels (both "English" and "American") in conjunction with landscapes and thematics of coloniality.

Christopher Flint argues that the eighteenth-century English novel is marked, above all, by its concern with "narratives dealing with the affective experience of young adults seeking conjugal bliss in a domestic environment" – with, that is, formulating the nuclear family.[5] While the same might be said of the early American novel, literary critics have told quite different stories about the novel in each case. In an English critical tradition, much attention has been paid to the way in which novelistic concerns with "family fictions" involve reshaping the family (together with related discourses of gender) in terms congenial to an ascendant bourgeoisie over and against those of a feudal and status-based society.[6] In American literary criticism, similar fictions concerning courtship and family formation in the novel have been primarily read in terms of American politics: the travails of negotiating consensual marriage have been viewed as allegorical of the politics of consent at stake in the formation of the early Republic.[7] Without collapsing all distinction between English and American novelistic traditions or concerns, I nonetheless aim to indicate the shared interest of British and American eighteenth-century novels in issues of family formation, and, more broadly, to point to the relation between colonialism and domestic fictions. I argue that issues of nationhood and the nuclear family appear against a larger, transatlantic scene of colonialism and market expansion and that this scene is visible in the limits of family formation that appear repeatedly in the novel in the forms of incest (excessive endogamy) and miscegenation (excessive exogamy). Incest and miscegenation are not simply invoked in these texts but are created and given meaning as marking the limits of familial arrangement; the very terms of incest and miscegenation thus emerge in the eighteenth century as indices of concern with the circulation of persons and relationships in the shifting terrain of a globalizing economy.[8] Rather than viewing the early American novel as the *effusion* of a new nation, then, I describe nationalism as more after-effect than origin of the novel and view the inward-turning domestic plot lines of the novel (seduction, marriage, incest) as standing in relation to the expansiveness of eighteenth-century commerce and Anglo-American imperialism.

The conjunction of nation and novel has been succinctly and influentially formulated by Benedict Anderson, in whose felicitous phrasing the nation constitutes an "imagined community" – a community most readily imagined in the print vehicles of newspaper and novel. According to Anderson, the novel and the nation serve as analogues insofar as both operate within an "empty, homogeneous" time – a time in which a variety of persons (citizens of a nation, characters in a novel) pursue their own lives yet understand themselves to stand in relation to others whom they don't know – other individuals who occupy a narrative/national "meanwhile." Like the covers of a novel, the borders of the nation hold these discrete individuals – despite their diverse engagements and plot lines – in a bounded relation to one another. The *form* of the novel is thus the focus of Anderson's thesis: rather than addressing the content of particular narratives that appear in novels, Anderson is interested in the bounded yet fictive space the novel conjures for its readers. Yet as Jonathan Culler points out, Anderson's claims concerning the formal analogy between nation and novel have been regularly confused with assertions that the novel is the purveyor of nationalist content:

> The power of Anderson's thesis about the novel is that it makes [the novel] a *formal* condition of imagining the nation – a *structural* condition of possibility. Critics, who are interested in the plots, themes, and imaginative worlds of particular novels, have tended to transform that thesis into a claim about the way some novels, by their contents, help to encourage, shape, justify, or legitimate the nation – a different claim, though one of considerable interest.[9]

The novel, one could posit, is a genre conducive to the articulation of nationalism insofar as its structure mirrors the invisibly bounded relation of individuals and events that characterizes the nation. Yet this is a claim distinct from the suggestion that the novel is the *product* of the nation or nationalism: indeed, the novel may aim to imagine a community (like the nation) precisely because such a community does not exist.

In the larger exploration of the phenomenon of nationhood undertaken by Anderson in *Imagined Communities*, the linkages between and among nation, novel, and newspaper clearly emerge from the historical ground of colonialism and early capitalism. Indeed, Anderson's specific focus is on post-colonial versions of nationhood – those of Mexico, Peru, the Philippines – rather than European nation-formation. And a closer examination of his claims concerning the novel indicates the importance of this historical ground to the genre. Consider, for instance, his account of the colonial newspaper which, like the novel, links disparately located individuals in a shared imaginary space:

What were the characteristics of the first American newspapers, North or South? They began essentially as appendages of the market. Early gazettes contained . . . commercial news (when ships would arrive and depart, what prices were current for what commodities in what ports), as well as colonial political appointments, marriages of the wealthy, and so forth. In other words, what brought together, on the same page, *this* marriage with *that* ship, *this* price with *that* bishop, was the very structure of the colonial administration and market-system itself. In this way, the newspaper of Caracas quite naturally, and even apolitically, created an imagined community among a specific assemblage of fellow-readers, to whom *these* ships, brides, bishops and prices belonged. In time, of course, it was only to be expected that political elements would enter in.[10]

Anderson thus indicates that the technology of communication that developed in relation to capitalism and the administration of empire (the newspaper, reporting initially on shipping and imperial administration) determined the shape of an imagined community that would eventually assume concrete political dimensions as the post-colonial nation. In broader terms, Anderson argues that vernacular linguistic communities grew up around absolutist imperial states as men who worked as administrators within such states moved from one peripheral location to another: the very *distance* that marked their relation to the metropole shaped their forms of communication and the nature of their imagined rather than proximate community. For Anderson, then, the administrative structure of empire is decisive with regard to the "imagined community" of the nation that will follow colonialism: "why was it precisely *creole* [colonial] communities that developed so early conceptions of their nation-ness? . . . The beginnings of an answer lie in the striking fact that each of the new South American republics had been an administrative unit from the sixteenth to the eighteenth century" (50, 52). As Anderson's more specific historical account of the development of "imagined communities" indicates, the fact of colonial expansion across an increasingly far-flung geographical area was the enabling condition of new forms of communication and newly imagined relations of community that formed the structural possibility of post-colonial nationalism.

As attentive as Anderson is to the effects of colonial expansion on communicative norms in the creole community, he does not explore how the structure of colonial diaspora served to shape the community of the imperialist national community as well as the post-colonial one. In other words, while Anderson offers a plausible account of the Filipino novel *Noli Me Tangere*, further elaboration of the relation of nationalism to empire would be needed to account for British novels such as *Tom Jones* (1749) or *Pamela* (1741). If the novel is not the effusion of the nation but a form associated with the long-distance communicative norms of creole colonial administration, how, precisely, does the *English* novel "rise" in the eighteenth century? Using Anderson's framework, Nancy Armstrong and Leonard Tennenhouse have proposed that creole colonial experience does, indeed, inform the eighteenth-century British novel. Specifically, Armstrong and Tennenhouse suggest that the colonial captivity narrative served as an enabling precursor of the English novel insofar as it presented a

formal innovation in the literary expression of nationalized and individualized subjectivity. English colonials in North America were required to "reinvent" Englishness
for themselves in their absence from English ground and they did so through writing.
For instance, in its heightened emphasis on the distance between home and foreign
ground, the captivity narrative relies upon literary production to preserve attachment
to Englishness: "The captivity narrative requires the captive to ward off the threat of
another culture by preserving the tie to her mother culture through writing alone."[11]
As a result of this effort, new models of being English and of imagining Englishness
appeared before a metropolitan readership: "New World nationalism allows us to
imagine how eighteenth-century readers back in England began to reconceive that
nation as a readership."[12] For a metropolitan audience, writing becomes a mode of
producing English subjectivity that eventuates in the novel. In their bold formulation
of the connection between colonial captivity narrative and novel, Armstrong and
Tennenhouse argue that the captivity narrative finds its English novelistic incarnation
in *Pamela*, a novel in which an individual (bourgeois) subjectivity is paradigmatically
produced entirely through literacy – a novel in which the central character produces
her freedom from captivity through the act of writing.

  Anderson together with Armstrong and Tennenhouse thus points toward the
colonial origins of the novel, yet significant questions with respect to this account
nonetheless remain. Individuated subjectivity is important to Armstrong and Tennenhouse, as is the imagined or fictive community invoked by the individual who
writes to remain part of a national community, but neither Anderson nor Armstrong
and Tennenhouse place specific emphasis on what literary critics have defined as the
hallmark of the eighteenth-century novel: namely, what Ian Watt has described as the
"formal realism" of the genre – an innovation linked by Watt and subsequent critics
to fundamental shifts in philosophy and epistemology occurring in the eighteenth
century. Furthermore, we might ask what the link is between the imagined community of the novel and the colonial ground that might be seen as giving rise to this
fictive entity. Does the tension between empire and nation, or colony and nation,
inscribe itself within the novel in formal or thematic terms? More broadly, how might
an understanding of the coloniality of the novel change existing understandings of the
genre as an expression or allegory of nationhood?

The Episteme of Contract

If the novel is not the effusion of national spirit, then the history of the early
American novel might be revised considerably. Indeed, as William Spengeman has
suggested in his classic essay, the title of "first American novel" might be accorded not
to Brown's *Power of Sympathy*, but to a novel set in the British colonial holding of
Surinam: namely, Aphra Behn's *Oroonoko* (1688).[13] Spengeman's analysis of *Oroonoko*
dispenses altogether with the equation of nation and novel, suggesting that the
American novel might best be defined as a work that takes "literary cognizance of

America, incorporating some idea of that place into its very form of words" (387). The "America" of this sentence (namely, the setting of *Oroonoko*: Surinam in 1688) is clearly a *geographical* rather than a political formation. Yet Spengeman indicates that the Americanness of *Oroonoko* can be located in its linguistic form and not simply its geographical setting. How might a place register as a distinctive *linguistic* form? Spengeman associates the American continent with the form of writing first generated by Europeans there: specifically, the travelogue or "Brief True Relation" which is characterized by its empiricist and experiential account of the New World. In *Oroonoko*, he argues, Behn combines the narrative structure of romance with that of the colonial relation, thereby creating a hybrid form that, in its blend of fact and fiction, is recognizably novelistic *and* distinctively American: in *Oroonoko*, Behn "employed a narrative form that had been devised specifically to register those changes, in the shape and meaning of the world and in the concepts of human identity and history, that were prompted by the discovery, exploration, and settlement of America" (407–408). Spengeman's provocative claim for the colonial origin of the novel thus turns in a sharply different direction from that of Anderson or Armstrong and Tennenhouse: rather than linking the form of the novel to the sociological or political conditions of colonialism, Spengeman associates the novel with an epistemic shift that he correlates with the discovery of the New World: namely, the development of a discourse of empiricism entirely absent from the logic of romance. Spengeman's claims are intriguing insofar as they begin to address the question of the "formal realism" of the novel left aside by the "imagined community" model. Yet he is unable to offer a convincing account of just why Behn might have turned from romance to true relation: did the very facticity of the American continent generate an empiricist mode of writing that somehow elbowed its way into Behn's romance once she set it in America? Or, as Spengeman also seems to suggest, did Behn attempt to cater to a middle-class audience that had begun to be interested in new forms of narration and "useful information"?

Spengeman is not alone among critics in pointing to the generic instability of *Oroonoko* or to Behn's use of the travelogue as a means of sustaining the authority of her own narrative voice.[14] The opening pages of Behn's text offer a taxonomy of the Surinam flora and fauna, cataloguing "Marmosets," "*Cousheries*," "*Parakeetoes*," and "*Muckaws*." The narrator reports, moreover, that she has collected the skin of a "prodigious Snake" as well as rare butterflies for display in "His Majesty's *Antiquaries*," indicating her participation in the cataloguing aims of the "New Science" promoted by the Royal Society.[15] Indeed, as Michael McKeon indicates, the "naïve empiricism" of *Oroonoko* partakes of the "epistemology of the travel narrative" promoted by the Royal Society – an epistemology that locates truth in the authority of the observer rather than in the force of tradition.[16] The travelogue thus stands as a precursor of the novel, according to McKeon, insofar as it participates in an epistemological shift away from scholasticism and/or romance toward empiricism. Spengeman's emphasis on the function of the Brief True Relation as the narrative of "individual contributions to the accumulating store of human knowledge about the world" (393) thus pinpoints one way in which the writing of the New World intersects with the formal realism of the novel. Yet the colonial context of the Brief True Relation points not simply to empiricism as a new mode of knowledge, but to the function of the travelogue as a discursive tool for appropriating the objects, land, and peoples of the New World. Two genre-founding examples of the Brief True Relation are Sir Walter Raleigh's 1596 account, *The Discoverie of the Large, Rich, and Beautiful Empire of Guiana*, and Thomas Harriot's 1588 *A Brief and True Report of the New Found Land of Virginia*. Both of these texts have been subject to extensive critical attention aimed at demonstrating that the Brief True Relation was far from (simply) empiricist in its aims, but rather served as a crucial means of effecting the project of colonial possession of the New World in tandem with the discourse of the New Science. Gesa Mackenthun thus argues that Harriot's *Brief and True Report* relies "on a new formal mode for the representation of reality" in which "Harriot...throws overboard all scholastic cargo and concentrates on the mercantile aspect of American nature. He emphasizes the various possibilities of its commodification and reveals his own identity as one of the main exponents of the new empirical science."[17] While the true report may rely on the category of individual experience to assert its claims to veracity, that experience must be understood as framed by the aims of colonial expansion and developing market relations. I would thus argue that we do, indeed, find an important (and novelistic) shift of epistemes within Behn's narrative that is related to the discovery of the New World, but this shift is the result of the new norms of a market-oriented colonial growth rather than the geographic fact of the American continent. The episteme of the novel that registers here, then, is less empiricist than *contractual* – less the effect of the discovery of the New World than of the mercantile logic fueling colonial expansion and imperialism.

Where, then, does contractual logic appear in *Oroonoko*? And what does *Oroonoko* tell us about the contractual episteme of the novel? The generic shift from the logic of romance to that of realism ("naïve empiricism") clearly occurs when Oroonoko arrives in Surinam, translated from the royal African court of Coramantien to the plantation economy of colonial America: a close look at this shift indicates the role that contractual relations play in establishing the language that replaces romance. When Oroonoko arrives in Surinam, his identity as romance hero remains intact: despite his new status as a slave (dubbed "Caesar" rather than "Oroonoko" by a colonial administrator), his innate royalty is recognized by all those around him – both white and black – and he proceeds to discover Imoinda (now dubbed "Clemene") and wed her: "From that happy Day *Caesar* took *Clemene* for his Wife, to the general Joy of all People; and there was as much Magnificence as the Country wou'd afford at the Celebration of this Wedding: and in a very short time after she conceiv'd with Child; which made *Caesar* even adore her, knowing he was the last of his Great Race" (93). While this sentence constitutes closure with respect to romance, Behn's narrative continues past the end-point which would represent full knowledge – full elaboration of divine principle – in romance. In the sentence following the one above we are thus introduced to a new set of concerns and epistemic norms best characterized as colonial and contractual:

> This new Accident [the conception of his child] made [Oroonoko] more Impatient of Liberty, and he was every Day treating . . . for his and *Clemene's* Liberty; and offer'd either Gold, or a vast quantity of Slaves, which shou'd be paid before they let him go, provided he cou'd have any Security that he shou'd go when his Ransom was paid: They fed him from Day to Day with Promises, and delay'd him, till the Lord Governor shou'd come; so that he began to suspect them of falshood, and that they wou'd delay him till the time of his Wives delivery, and make a Slave of that too, For all the Breed is theirs to whom the Parents belong: This Thought made him very uneasy, and his Sullenness gave them some Jealousies of him. (93)

The conception of his child-to-be shifts from serving as a sign of narrative fulfillment (the child as the continuation of Oroonoko's "Great Race") in the first sentence cited above to a sign of Oroonoko's deeply distressing situation as a slave embedded within the colonial economy in the next sentence. While Oroonoko is accustomed to a system of honor (the logic of romance) he finds himself located in a system of contract instead: whereas honor is innate and essential, contract is situational and depends not upon recognition of a god-given interior status but instead upon the accurate prediction of commercial return. Contractual logic is *actuarial* in both the vernacular and etymological senses of the word – predicated, that is, upon the Latin *actum*, "things done" in the world, and linked to the capacity to aggregately predict, on the basis of empirical observation of such acts, what may unfold in the future.

In the passage cited above, we see Oroonoko respond to the contractual economy of Surinam with an attempt to construct contracts that are more favorable to him: he thus offers gold and slaves in return for the promise of his manumission. Yet his efforts seem to founder on the breach that divides slave from master within the colonial economy as he is offered apparently empty promises in return rather than a viable contract. His very difficulty in securing a new contract points to another significant aspect of contractual logic in the novel, namely, that the limits of contractual engagement repeatedly appear to be defined as racialized and nationalist within *Oroonoko*. Thus, for instance, contracts habitually fail or evaporate between Oroonoko and whites, not simply because the whites are untrustworthy but because they do not see Oroonoko as someone who lives within the realm of their contractual world – as someone with whom they must keep promises. Oroonoko, on the other hand, views his honor as innate rather than circumstantial and repeatedly insists upon his honor as the guarantor of his conduct.

Further evidence of the distinction between a system of honor and one of commercial contract is evident in Oroonoko's own views of slavery – views that initially may seem contradictory. When he foments rebellion among his fellow slaves in Surinam, he argues less that slavery is wrong than that colonial race slavery is wrong:

> And why, said he, *my dear Friends and Fellow-sufferers, shou'd we be Slaves to an unknown People? Have they Vanquish'd us Nobly in Fight? Have they Won us in Honourable Battel? And are we, by the chance of War, become their Slaves? This wou'd not anger a Noble Heart, this*

wou'd not animate a Souldiers Soul; no, but we are Bought and Sold like Apes, or Monkeys, to be the Sport of Women, Fools and Cowards. (105)

Oroonoko here criticizes the slavery of the colonial commercial economy that sells Africans like animals or commodities and does not recognize their diverse human capacities or inner natures; in contrast, he suggests that forms of slavery practiced in Africa, in which individuals become slaves on the basis of having lost battles, are more acceptable – this is so because the outcome of a battle will reflect the innate status of the fighter; one who loses in battle may well be fit to be a slave rather than a warrior. Oroonoko's views on slavery as a potentially justified status hierarchy appear again when the slaves he has urged to rebel later desert him in battle: he calls these men "Dogs, treacherous and cowardly" (109) and contends that they deserve to be en-slaved. Oroonoko suggests then, that the status of slave may be justified if it corresponds to a divinely calibrated truth. As we have seen, this is precisely the logic of romance and is a logic that founders in the face of contractual colonialism.

Michael McKeon argues that the romance often proceeds by way of a succession of acts of naming, each of which is increasingly revelatory of divine truth: "If romance names are the outward embodiment of an inner or essential truth, romance character development tends to proceed by discontinuous leaps between states of being – by 'rebirths' – and to be signified by the successive divergence or alteration of name."[18] In ironic terms, Behn's narrative does follow this structure though I would suggest that it finally inverts its meaning, overturning the logic of romance. We have seen that Oroonoko's name shifts to Caesar when he reaches the New World and becomes the possession of a white master. According to the narrator, this name is appropriate or revealing of Oroonoko's inner nature, "for 'tis most evident, [Oroonoko] wanted no part of the Personal Courage of that *Caesar*, and acted things as memorable, had they been done in some part of the World replenish'd with People, and Historians, that might have given him his due" (88). She laments, in effect, that only she herself, "a Female Pen," is able to write his story. Yet while the narrator attempts to lend romance – which is to say, an inner logic – to the name of Caesar, she cannot ultimately do so since this nomination is fundamentally commercial: "the *Christians* never buy and Slaves but that they give 'em some Name of their own, their native ones being likely very barbarous, and hard to pronounce . . . For the future, therefore, I must call *Oroonoko, Caesar*, since by that Name only he was known in our Western World" (88–89). To insert Oroonoko into the colonial economy – "our Western World" – he must be easily appropriated and rendered exchangeable (commodified) in the word and the flesh, and his renaming enacts this appropriation. While the narrator gestures toward the nobility of Caesar's name, it is worth noting that Caesar was a name often given to dogs in England. Indeed, Srinivas Aravamudan points to the iconography linking pets and slaves in eighteenth-century England; both were represented as possessions that served to increase their owner's status. In *Oroonoko*, Aravamudan argues, the narrator's friendship with Oroonoko may partake more of her interest in his status as Caesar the dog than as Caesar the Roman leader: the "narrator's

befriending of Oroonoko could mean establishing his loyalty not only as a vassal or
slave, but also as pet . . . Her access to Oroonoko increases her prestige and establishes her social superiority through his metonymic proximity to her."[19] The multi-
valence of the name "Caesar" thus embodies the split within the narrative itself, and
although the narrator seems to endorse the romance account of the name, it is the
commercial or contractual valence of the name that she will ultimately turn to her
own account.

That Oroonoko himself does not fully accede to his colonial renaming is evident in
his later statement that "Oroonoko *scorns to live with the Indignity that was put on
Caesar*" (112). Interestingly, however, one final act of naming occurs in the text to
which Oroonoko does accede. A villainous but wealthy Irishman, Banister, renames
Oroonoko once more at the close of the narrative as he is about to burn Oroonoko at
the stake on behalf of the administrators of the colony: "[Banister] told him, he shou'd
Dye like a Dog, as he was. *Caesar* replied, this was the first piece of Bravery that ever
Banister did; and he never spoke Sence till he pronounc'd that Word; and, if he wou'd
keep it, he wou'd declare, in the other World, that he was the only Man, of all the
Whites, that ever he heard speak Truth" (118).[20] While one might read this to
indicate that Oroonoko welcomes his death and that the significant word in Banister's
statement is "Dye," I would suggest that the act of naming Oroonoko a "Dog" is
perversely welcomed by Oroonoko as well insofar as it names the very truth of
his condition within the world he now inhabits – a world which is not that of
romance but of contract. In the world of contract, Oroonoko has no standing as
human but is instead reduced to a dog: in his honorable fashion, Oroonoko recognizes
that he has been properly "named" by Banister in the new world beyond romance.
Like Shakespeare's Caliban, then, his insertion into the language and economy of the
colonial world market is one that has taught him that his status will always be that of
the non-human, the dog. Whereas before he believed that dogs were fit to be slaves,
he here understands that slavery has dubbed him a dog and that he must die in this
state. This is both the fulfillment of McKeon's logic of romance nomination and its
abrogation, since the essential truth revealed in Oroonoko's death is that his status as
an honorable hero of romance has been finally eradicated by the fact of New World
slavery.

As we have seen, the contractual relations established in Surinam do not grant
Oroonoko a nationalized identity or a new status in the imagined community of the
colony: rather, a newly nationalized identity is established for the British female
narrator of the novel as her white identity and her narrative voice emerge with
increasing authority across the text. As critics have argued, Behn evidently speaks
with ambivalence about the role of the slave trade in producing contractual relations
and destroying hierarchical ones: one might, for instance, see her deployment of
romance as elegiacal and thus as fundamentally critical of a colonialist discourse in
which innate honor no longer counts as valuable. On the other hand, the discourse of
imperialism enables the narrator, however reluctantly, to establish and consolidate her
own power as an author/observer of empirical fact on a distant continent, and as a

white Englishwoman who uses the written word to produce her own identity and her link to an imagined national community as well. While Oroonoko is dubbed "Caesar" and then "Dog" within the colonial economy, the narrator emerges with a new name as well, as a "Female Pen," writing to an imagined community of white, British readers. The narrator cannot keep her "word" to Oroonoko despite her attempt at honor, but she can produce the authoritative word and verisimilitude of the novel – the authority of the true relation – which relies upon her successful navigation of colonial contractual relations. *Oroonoko* thus displays not only the dominance of the logic of contract in the colonial setting, but the limits of contract as they appear in explicitly racialized terms: the white, colonial community with whom the narrator does keep her word and the imagined national community to whom she directs the words of her narrative clearly exclude the racialized, dehumanized, and finally dismembered foreign prince, Oroonoko.

What makes *Oroonoko* a novelistic text, then, is its deployment of the episteme of contract, an episteme that I have defined as *actuarial* but that might also, in the words of Irene Tucker, be seen as "primarily *probabilistic*."[21] According to Tucker, the kind of knowledge that the novel concerns itself with is empiricist but also contingent and deliberative. Linking the novel to political liberalism, Tucker argues that liberal subjectivity (and the novel) concern "one's capacity to know and predict the contingent particularities of the material world – including the particularities of other people in specific social, political, and economic relations to one."[22] As recent critical work on the eighteenth-century novel has demonstrated, the horizon of probability explored in the novel – namely, the *speculative* nature of fictional realism – is linked to the development of the world market and new forms of capitalist investment and credit-based finance that evolved during England's financial revolution. With the advent of credit and paper notes issued by the new Bank of England, financial relations became associated with forms of speculation, probability, and fictionality.[23] To invest funds in the speculative contracts of this new economy required imagining what the future might hold in the form of a return on investment. The promising, yet uncertain nature of this imaginative calculus caused a great deal of anxiety as well as real financial losses and gains. In 1720, for instance, the "South Sea Bubble" ruined many investors who had placed money in the South Sea Company. The Whig writer "Cato" describes credit as based in "gilded clouds [and] . . . fleeting apparitions" which may well be scuttled by the "story of a Spanish frigate . . . or the sickness of a foreign prince, or the saying of a broker in a coffee-house."[24] Credit, here clearly linked to the growing global economy, thus involves an explicitly *fictive* element – stories, sayings, and apparitions are all forms of the imaginative work upon which contract and credit rely. As Catherine Ingrassia argues, the logic of credit thus mirrors the logic of the developing genre of the novel: "Reading a novel, like investing in a speculative financial venture, demanded readers' imaginative participation in a narrative that could potentially be a vehicle with which early modern subjects could reinvent themselves and envisage their lives differently."[25] The fictional world of the novel has meaning not insofar as it is actual but insofar as it is *realistic* or probable, a claim linking the aesthetic form of the novel with a world in which contractual relations dominate. Contract thus entails an epistemic shift toward a belief in probability – not simply toward empiricism, but toward a kind of deliberative intelligence oriented toward navigating future (and thus fictive) possibilities.

Yet if the task of fictional realism is to create a predictable and knowable world in which ties of understanding create bonds and enable contracts, the global context of contractual relations would seem to introduce a distinct risk of uncertainty and unpredictability. Accounts of both the novel and the contract tend to emphasize the democratizing or destratifying effects of the new commercial world of the eighteenth century, yet the equalizing force of contractual relations brings with it the weakening of certainty grounded in status relations.[26] J. G. A. Pocock in particular has described the anxiety that the new world of finance and mobile property generated, especially among a land-holding elite: "the revolution of public credit . . . generated the idea that political relations were becoming relations between debtors and creditors . . . and this was seen as leading not merely to corruption, but to the despotism of speculative fantasy."[27] As both Pocock and Ingrassia emphasize, credit was viewed by its critics as feminizing those who heeded its siren song: "The 'moneyed' or economic subjects, in contrast to the paternal, stable, and rational figure of the landed citizen, were perceived as symbolically indulging their desires and displaying their 'feminized' tendencies."[28] Efforts were made, writes Pocock, for "the stabilisation of this patho-logical condition" including those of novelist Daniel Defoe to describe credit as linked to more predictable terms, such as reputation and opinion, rather than unfettered fantasy. Thus the concern with credit that generated charges of feminiza-tion also generated other (ultimately successful) strategies to stabilize and masculinize credit. I would suggest that one such strategy of stabilizing credit involved the rhetorical deployment of racialization. For instance, if we return to Cato's anxieties about overseas trade, we see that he implicitly suggests that the sickness of a *foreign* prince is far from predictable and thus not solid ground upon which to base contracts; epistemological claims grounded in probability meet their limit in foreign (and hence unpredictable) cultures and persons. Cato's claims thus echo the logic of *Oroonoko* in which the foreign prince is excluded from contractual exchange. In *Oroonoko*, the limits of the known (and knowable) community are redrawn in the colonial American section of the novel in implicitly national and racial terms, thereby containing or warding off the threat posed to contractual relations by the unknown or unpredict-able. In related terms, Daniel Defoe outlines a project for world trade, including trade with Africa, that invokes both race and nation as means of stabilizing the speculative nature of such an endeavor. For instance, while promoting trade with Africa, Defoe also argues against relying upon African merchants to engage in this trade: Africans, he argues, are "Wild, Barbarous, Treacherous, and perfectly intractable as to Com-merce." Only by building fortresses and "keeping the Natives at a Distance" can trade be preserved. Defoe concludes, "Experiments have taught us, *if we please to learn* this Maxim in the *African* Trade, that it is no way to be carried on but by Force: for a mere Correspondence with the Natives as Merchants, is as impracticable, as it would be if they were a Nation of Horses."[29] Here Defoe echoes the racial and nationalist logic of Behn's novel, in which Oroonoko became a dog rather than a contractual partner to white colonials: dogs or horses do not register as viable trading partners. As Aparna Dharwadker argues, Defoe "practices an economic nationalism thoroughly qualified by a poetics of race and religion."[30] The strongly nationalist aims of Defoe's vision of English global trade delimit risk through a discourse of racialization. Defoe's strategy of nationalizing (and thus stabilizing) engagements in the world market is one that the novel more generally seems to follow as well. Indeed, one might argue that precisely because the global horizon creates a loss of intelligibility, the novel restores the reader to the limited, comprehensible frame of a national community. In creating a circumscribed national horizon, inside of which equitable and intelligible relations obtain, the novel reconstructs, as it were, a culturally "flat earth" at the very moment when, geopolitically, the earth has become round.

Domestic Drama and Incest

Paradoxically, then, the novel is a genre reflective of a colonial and commercial economy that opens the way to expansive relations of trade and exchange *and* a nationalism that forecloses the horizon of exchange by way of newly codified social identities and relations. The newly codified relations are particularly pronounced at the domestic level, where they are visible in terms of marked shifts in class structure and kinship systems. As historians have demonstrated, eighteenth-century England saw the waning authority of kinship systems in organizing political, economic, and social power in favor of the authority of the bourgeois family, individualism, and, I would add, nationalism. As Ellen Pollak argues, the increased importance of mobile over landed property was associated with new models of marriage and revisions to the social rules governing the exchange of women: as property became mobile, so too did women as conveyors of property, and women thus began to circulate upon different terms, according to new norms.[31] While Pollak emphasizes that the new rules of social exchange and marriage turn to a large degree upon the increased weight placed upon a binary model of sex and gender, Franco Moretti, in turn, suggests that a geographical set of constraints is also important with respect to the new forms of social identity and exchange that are the focus of the eighteenth-century novel. According to Moretti, marriage plots in the British novel can be mapped primarily in terms of the boundaries of the nation-state: by literally mapping the geographic movement of marriage partners in Jane Austen's novels, Moretti makes visible a "National Marriage Market," which "is new . . . a mechanism that crystallized in the course of the eighteenth century, which demands of human beings (and especially of women) a new mobility."[32] The novel, for Moretti, is the "symbolic form" which enables this imagined community of potential marriage partners to exist. For Moretti, then, the boundaries of the nation-state enable mobility – they open up possibilities for the exchange of women between men at disparate locations that were previously not possible. Yet we might also see the horizon of the nation-state as *delimiting* the borders of this exchange – as closing off some forms of mobility as well as opening others. For example, Moretti argues that colonialism is not an essential component of the national marriage market, yet in novels from Maria Edgeworth's *Belinda* (1801) to Charlotte Brontë's *Jane Eyre* (1847), characters who are born beyond the boundaries of the nation-state but very much within the commercial system of the British empire – creole characters such as Mr. Vincent or Bertha Rochester – are entertained and rejected as suitable marriage partners for English-born men and women. Read as a boundary that renders plausible certain forms of mobility (around class and gender) but that renders implausible other forms of mobility (particularly with respect to race) the nationalized horizon of the novel can be viewed within the context of empire and broader forms of market expansion than solely British national ones.

If a concern with policing the boundaries of the nation-state – a concern with the limits of exogamy that typically appears in the guise of miscegenation and a refusal to contract across racial lines – appears in the eighteenth-century novel as evidence of the novel's relation to the commercial effects of empire, I would argue that representations of incest – of the internal limits of kinship defined in terms of endogamy – are also very much related to the expansive horizon of the global market. In other words, while the rules governing the marriage market shifted away from lineage and an evident system of kinship, rules of kinship or the exchange of women in marriage were reinscribed in two new locations: at the horizon of the nation (often marked as racial), and in the very internal location of the nuclear family (marked in terms of gender). Just as the borders of the nation become an invisible horizon of intelligibility for the novel and the marriage market, so too do the nuclear family and the heterosexual couple of man and wife become an increasingly important unit of structural meaning with respect to kinship rules. Specters of miscegenation and incest thus haunt the national boundaries of the novel, bringing into occasional focus the boundary-drawing acts needed to sustain the coherence of the nation.

Eighteenth-century novels seem to be concerned in particular with one specific form of incest: namely, *unwitting* sibling incest.[33] As Ellen Pollak remarks: "incest is possibly always present in not knowing where one belongs"; in other words, the violation of the basic rules of kinship might be seen as a result of dislocation and loss of structure, an effect of the loss of a kinship system and an increase in social mobility. Daniel Defoe's *Moll Flanders* (1722) begins with the condition of not knowing that Pollak links with incest: Moll is born to a mother who is imprisoned in Newgate for theft and who is transported to Virginia shortly after Moll's birth, thus leaving her daughter with no visible support system or social affiliations. Significantly, Moll's first memory is of living with a band of Gypsies in a heightened state of mobility that bespeaks the complete rupture of social ties and a resultant lack of place and position. The mobility of colonialism (the deportation of her mother) thus immediately stands as destructive rather than enabling of sustaining forms of social identity – her mother's mobility robs her of any place in the world. Yet the novel as a whole is about nothing so much as the success of social mobility figured as primarily commercial; Moll moves from her unpromising start in Newgate, through a series of marriages and a criminal career, eventually attaining a repentant and wealthy state: in the narrative of her rise to respectable and propertied English citizenship, however, both incest and coloniality are key elements.

The shift away from kinship or lineage to a social space defined by commercial contract is thus writ large in Moll's narrative, and Moll is typically seen as exemplary of the self-made individual who flourishes in such a world. Indeed, in the opening sentence of the novel, Moll begins her narration by stating that she will not set down her "True Name" (her patronym), thereby implying that the truth of her identity lies in the story and name that she constructs for herself rather than that which was given her at birth. Commercial contract and profit thus appear to be the guiding forces within the novel and behind Moll's actions, particularly with respect to marriage, and are, moreover, crucial to establishing her individualism and subjectivity. As Amit Yahav-Brown contends, "Moll's ingenuity lies in her deliberative capacities" which are an expression of her agency and will; indeed, according to Yahav-Brown, the novel as a whole seeks to emphasize the deliberative (or contractual) capacities of Moll as the grounds of her English citizenship and subjectivity.[34] In her deliberative capacity, Moll demonstrates her right to the political freedom and identity of liberal citizenship. Yahav-Brown's claims accord well with a model of the novel as both national and contractual: those who engage in contracts within the novel (who master its contractual episteme) also properly inhabit a national space and thus attain citizenship in the nation. And indeed, Moll's ability to assess the probable relations among individuals and events – her predictive and deliberative capacity to shape these events to her will – is nowhere more evident than in the marriage contract she secures with her third husband, the Virginia planter. Posing as a woman of fortune (despite her lack of one), she aims and succeeds at marrying a propertied man. Moreover, when she reveals her lack of financial estate to him, she nonetheless also evinces the more important bourgeois capacity to labor and circulate geographically with her husband in order to increase their estate: she readily agrees to move to Virginia with him in order to extract more money from his property there. Yet her deliberative (as well as contractual and capitalist) capacities meet their limit in the "most unexpected and surprizing thing that perhaps ever befel any Family in the World," namely, the discovery that her Virginia husband is her half-brother.[35] Incest as the result of excessive circulation in the colonial economy – the effect of her mother's transportation to Virginia – has resulted in the ruin of her deliberative efforts to lay up an estate with her husband. As such, incest would seem to mark the failure of deliberative citizenship and commercial circulation.

Far from dismissing kinship entirely in favor of autonomous individualism, then, Defoe at this point indicates a concern for displaced forms of kinship – specifically, as I argue below, for kinship forms embodied in the relation of the marital couple to the nation. Whereas Moll has been independent of parentage previously in the novel, her successful, independent circulation is brought up short by the revelation of her patronym on the lips of her husband's (and her own) mother. Moll realizes she is wed to her half-brother when her mother relates her history and arrives at "one Particular that requir'd telling her Name" (88). Though no specific mention of Moll's biological father is made, the name that Moll and her mother share functions structurally as the patronym that locates Moll within a kinship system. While Moll's mother subsequently seeks to collaborate with Moll in forgetting and amending the personal history that has revealed the incestuous nature of her relation with her husband, Moll herself is unwilling to ignore the "real" of this patronym despite her pronounced capacity for self-fashioning and speculation. The revelation of incest and of Moll's patronym shifts the action in the novel decisively and in a direction that moves away from the autonomous and deliberative commercial circulation Moll has thus far pursued. Moll chooses to leave her husband and return to England to look for another husband, yet the "choice" of exogamy seems rather to be a concession to the rules of kinship than a considered selection between two possibilities. Moreover, Defoe represents her decisions regarding incest as driven less by judgment than by gut instinct. Her response to the incest taboo is thus portrayed as less rational than innate, a move by which Defoe naturalizes the "real" of the patronym and erases the cultural contingency of Moll's location within kinship structures. Thus while Moll does not object to incest "in point of Conscience" she finds the thought of sex with her husband "the most nauseous thing ... in the World" (98). Moreover, when she finally does devise a plan for her future, she concedes that "I might perhaps have Marry'd again there [in Virginia], very much to my Advantage, it had been certainly my Business to have staid in the Country [Virginia], but my Mind was restless too, and uneasie; I hanker'd after coming to *England*, and nothing would satisfie me without it" (104). In short, her innate rather than rational desires lead her away from incest as well as away from marriage with another creole; her innate desires lead her, instead, to return to England and to the national (and seemingly more *natural*) marriage market there. While it would benefit her, in financial terms, to remain in Virginia and find a husband there, she inexplicably *hankers* after returning to England. Insofar as Moll accepts (in her gut) the prohibition on incest, she retains her commitment to kinship rules that require her own circulation, as a woman, for the sake of fraternal ties between men. The traditional authority of patriarchy and kinship is certainly attenuated in the novel, yet it does not simply disappear: rather, Defoe reinscribes kinship rules within the heterosexual couple and the nation. At the moment when Moll's patronym is spoken by her mother, she is propelled away from her creole husband, back toward a specifically English marriage market that will ultimately enable her to re-establish her social identity and ownership of property (including the property she will finally accrue in Virginia).

The incest taboo, as many have argued, concerns primarily the circulation and exchange of women between men. Prohibiting excessive degrees of endogamy promotes forms of exogamy that establish ties between men of different familial groups. As Talcott Parsons argues, the incest taboo involves "the positive obligation to perform functions for the subunit and the larger society by marrying out. Incest is a withdrawal from this obligation to contribute to the formation and maintenance of supra-familial bonds on which major economic, political and religious functions of the society are dependent."[36] The supra-familial bonds at stake in *Moll Flanders* and the novel are clearly *national* ones. The move from kinship systems to the national marriage market requires a good deal of exogamy – indeed, marriage in this market seemingly occurs with little regard for kinship alliances. Yet if kinship is erased from the political horizon of the nation, the novel nonetheless underwrites national boundaries in terms of its concerns with miscegenation and incest taboos. While the novel opens with Moll's absolute lack of position as a foundling of empire, it nonetheless ends with a firm sense of her national identity: the novel closes not simply with her successful accumulation of property and social relations (husband, mother, son), but with her return to *England* and thus to the national space that property and social relations entitle her to comfortably inhabit. I mean to emphasize, then, the extent to which Moll's circulation among marriage partners and through colonial geographic spaces is ultimately recuperated to a stabilizing national narrative that enables a return on investment: Moll's investment in commercial and autonomous adventure is finally secured when she is located as married (and thus gendered) to an English man (and thus nationalized/racialized).

We might also note that unwitting sibling incest seems to mark a failure of or divergence from the novelistic form itself. While the novel aims to make the world probable, unwitting sibling incest seems a highly improbable event, particularly in the colonial context. What are the chances of marrying a colonial (indeed, a creole) who turns out to be one's brother? With the appearance of this improbable event in the midst of the novel, the logic of romance (divine truth revealed in events of mythic dimension) seems to reassert itself. Incest and miscegenation might, then, be seen to represent the return of romance within the novel: these violations of national space make evident the structural (and seemingly divine or mythic) limits of the probable and serve as the enabling exceptions of the imagined community of the nation-state. Moreover, these enabling exceptions institute kinship laws defined less as kinship than as the naturalized divisions of race and gender. Consider, for instance, Moll's language and treatment of her husband once she has discovered that he is her brother: she concurs that she "Treated him rather like a Dog than a Man, and rather like the most contemptible Stranger than a Husband" (93). Just as Oroonoko became a dog in the contractual economy of slavery, Moll's incestuous partner becomes a dog as well – an inhuman species with whom one cannot engage in contracts.

If unwitting sibling incest is the improbable consequence of commerce, colonialism, and circulation, it is nonetheless common in eighteenth-century novels on both sides of the Atlantic.[37] The centrality of incest to the "first" American novel, *The Power of Sympathy*, has led some critics to view it as representative of a particularly American set of concerns regarding nation-formation. Yet as I have suggested above, the literary genre of the novel and the political form of the nation remain in tension and dialogue with colonialism, the global market, and imperialism even as the nation gains political authority in England and the United States. Placed next to *Moll Flanders'* tale of unwitting incest, it becomes clear that *The Power of Sympathy* exhibits similar concerns about kinship that emerge in relation to post-colonial nationality and market relations that govern the exchange of women. Unlike Defoe's novel, however, Brown's *Power of Sympathy* exhibits little interest in commerce or property acquisition. Rather, the novel as a whole reads as a disquisition upon the education of women. Although the plot follows the incestuous relations between a young man named Harrington and his half-sister Harriot, the epistolary novel consists, in the main, of letters exchanged among a circle of friends, many of which are highly didactic in nature and focus in particular on the topic of female education and reading. The purpose of reading books, we are told, is not simply to gain knowledge about the world (books may, after all, misrepresent the world), but to learn to exercise judgment. As one Mister Holmes opines:

> There is a medium to be observed in a lady's reading; she is not to receive everything she finds, even in the best books, as invariable lessons of conduct; in books written in an easy, flowing style, which excel in description and the luxuriance of fancy, the imagination is apt to get heated – she ought, therefore, to discern with an eye of judgment, between the superficial and the penetrating – the elegant and the tawdry – what may be merely amusing, and what may be useful.[38]

While books may provide a variety of acceptable and unacceptable models for behavior, the correct way to read books is with a discerning eye: moreover, experience alone will not teach one discernment; rather, books themselves facilitate this capacity for deliberation. Reading, then, develops one's sense of what is probable in the world, and hence one's capacity to form sound judgments and, we might say, to deliberately enter into contracts.

The most crucial contract into which young, novel-reading women must enter in the early American novel is the marriage contract. The well-read woman might thus be expected to exercise informed judgment in attracting and selecting a marriage partner, avoiding, in particular, the pitfalls of seduction and coquetry. And indeed, when Harriot and Harrington first meet, Harriot's virtuous demeanor derails Harrington's initial intentions of seducing her and keeping her as a mistress rather than marrying her. In a letter to his friend Worthy, Harrington at first contends that he is "not so much of a republican as formally to wed any person of [Harriot's] class." An orphan working as a lady's maid, Harriot, as Harrington complains, "has no father – no mother – neither is there aunt, cousin, or kindred of any degree who claim any kind of relationship to her" (11). Yet Harrington's republican stripes soon emerge as he becomes a believer in the value of Harriot's intrinsic virtue rather than a seeker after her extrinsic familial relations; he quickly proposes marriage to her despite her lack of status and patronym. In identifying republican values with the rejection of status-based marriage (in favor of marriage based on individual internal worth), the novel thus seems to endorse social mobility, liberal models of political and marital consent, and the dissolution of kinship and patriarchal authority. Yet despite the relentless promotion of deliberative action and republican virtue in *The Power of*

Sympathy, the central trauma of the novel – unwitting sibling incest – is one that could not have been avoided with increased deliberation, increased virtue, or increased reading of novels. Harriot and Harrington act with virtue and sound judgment, yet only shortly before they are married do they discover that they have the same father. At a basic level, the novel seems deeply contradictory insofar as it promotes a solution (deliberative judgment and republican virtue) that will not address the problem at hand (unwitting incest).

Yet if neither Harriot nor Harrington, nor any lack of deliberative capacities on their part is to blame for the incestuous relation they enter into, the text does offer something of a villain in the figure of Harrington's father. Having seduced Harriot's mother, Maura Fawcett, while he was married to another woman, the senior Harrington's act of adultery – and his abdication of paternal connection with respect to Harriot – may be taken as the effective cause of the incestuous relation formed between Harrington and Harriot. Seduction rather than incest may thus be seen as the trauma the reader is asked to guard against by way of arming herself with sound judgment and deliberative capacities. As I argued at the outset of this article, the seduction narrative in early American fiction has served as the basis for a critical account of the allegorical relation between the US nation and the early novel. Specifically, the oft-repeated caution against seduction in novels of the period is read as evidence that the nation needed to protect itself against vice and immorality in order to survive as a political entity. Yet in a novel such as Brown's, the displacement of the act of seduction into a tale of incest raises some questions about the force of this particular message. Indeed, as Leonard Tennenhouse has argued, the nation-seduction allegory raises questions specifically concerning gender. Why is the victim of seduction always a woman and what does this mean with respect to national identity? Tennenhouse's own answer to this question marks a surprising reversal in the standard account of the seduction plot, particularly with respect to the libertine. According to Tennenhouse, the libertine is *enabling* of new forms of American identity rather than destructive of American virtue: specifically, the libertine disrupts patriarchal authority and, as such, attenuates kinship models for the exchange of women and property in favor of increased exogamy and new forms of social mobility. Tennenhouse writes: "Seduction is first and foremost a disruption of established relations between men ... The seduction plot of the elder Harrington in *The Power of Sympathy* suggests that the older, more traditional British notion of kinship as defined by established rank was far too limited for the new United States."[39] The actions of the libertine eradicate the authority of the patriarch, and specifically his ability to control the sexual commerce and exchange of daughters.

Tennenhouse thus argues that the libertine undermines the law of the father, and that this disruption of patriarchy and kinship is necessary in America in order to establish new models of familial and national identity. Like Moll Flanders, Harriot is a woman without patronym and without a fixed social status: this enables her to stand as an idealized autonomous agent. She is a woman who generates republican behavior in the man who loves her because of her very fitness for marriage based on virtue and labor rather than status. Yet the incest narrative in *The Power of Sympathy* points not only to the positive disruption of patriarchy and kinship systems, but also to the negative effects of this disruption and the need to reinscribe kinship forms in new locations. Where is kinship reinscribed in *The Power of Sympathy* if it is dislocated from older, patriarchal models? While the villainy of seduction is laid at the feet of the elder Harrington, a more specific account of his moral failing is offered in the text that offers some answers to this question. While long since reformed when the action of the novel occurs, Harrington senior explains that his early sexually licentious behavior was a result of a maxim he had adopted in his youth: "that *the most necessary learning was a knowledge of the world*" (69). This maxim, he explains, "hurried [him] down the stream of dissipation" where he "saw mankind in every point of view – from the acme of the most consummate refinement, to the most abject state of degradation" (70). Harrington senior's republican disregard for status evinced here, both in the act of mixing with men of all classes and in his cosmopolitan maxim, is clearly of a more dangerous variety than his son's republican courtship of Harriot. The association of knowledge of the world with forms of lawlessness points to an anxiety over cosmopolitanism or extra-national space and allegiances that appears in numerous texts of the 1790s in the United States. As the creole colonials of North America transformed themselves into the citizens of the United States, concerns over global trade and the limits of republican sympathy (particularly in relation to the French Revolution) erupted into arguments over national identity. Vitriolic debate over trade negotiations with England and France spilled into political squalls over immigration and naturalization policy, expatriation laws, shifts in franchise eligibility, and the controversial Alien and Sedition Acts of 1798.[40] Indeed, according to historian Chandos Michael Brown, the word "cosmopolitan" was a key term of opprobrium in anti-republican propaganda that circulated theories of a worldwide conspiracy linked to the French Revolution and the so-called "Bavarian Illuminati" – a conspiracy aimed at undermining national order, morality, and Christianity in the United States.[41]

Whereas a virtuous republicanism is associated with consensual marriage in the figures of Harriot and Harrington, a more dangerous *non-national* version of republicanism lies at the root of Harrington senior's immorality and ultimately causes the ruin of his children in their incestuous connection. The connection of cosmopolitanism with moral ruin and non-nationalized republicanism is perhaps more evident in a second novel by an American author that centers on unwitting sibling incest, Sally Sayward Wood's *Julia and the Illuminated Baron* (1800). Set in Europe rather than America, Wood's novel is centered on a virtuous, unpropertied young woman (lacking in family position and patronym) and an evil Baron who is a member of the "Illuminati" conspiracy. The Illuminati, while embracing Enlightenment philosophy (the fraternity and equality of republicanism) are immoral insofar as their embrace knows no bounds, enabling them to overstep the moral limits prescribed by religion, nation, and family. Thus the Baron reports to the virtuous Julia that the Illuminati have welcomed into their ranks "women...whose minds are too capacious, to be bound within the narrow and confined limits that the sex have been obliged to walk by."[42] Yet because the Illuminati reject all forms of limit, "they suppose," as one of their critics in the novel reports, "all relationship is dissolved; it is lawful and honorable in their opinion to form connections that we should think criminal with mothers or sisters."[43] Respecting neither national nor familial borders, the Illuminati endorse incest as enlightened behavior. Julia escapes the incestuous embrace of the Baron (who is, unbeknown to her, her half-brother) because she has chosen the unpropertied Francis Colwert for a future husband. Her partner of choice is also a man without a father, but he proves himself worthy of Julia's love by his labor and virtue, evidenced in a voyage to the United States, where he develops a friendship with George Washington after being shipwrecked on the Virginia coast. While the friendship with Washington is something of an aside in the novel, I would nonetheless suggest that it offers a model for nationalizing kinship relations: Colwert's absence of patronym – his lack of identity and property – is stabilized by his election of Washington as a substitute father. He writes to Julia that he is "fostered in the bosom of this virtuous and noble family, whose revered chief [Washington], is my protector, friend, and benefactor; he has put it in my power, to prosecute my voyage."[44] Electing Washington as a father enables him to prosecute the voyage that will return him to Julia as a suitable husband and enable him to rescue her from the incestuous embrace of the Baron. As a whole, Julia's rejection of the Illuminati and their incestuous aims is linked to a reformation of the aristocratic family into a bourgeois model in which virtue and labor, rather than status and kinship, determine consensual affiliation. This reformation, the novel suggests, is linked to understanding the value not only of proper marriage partners, but also of elective nationalism – of adopting fathers such as George Washington. While the failure of the patronym results in catastrophic boundary failure in the form of incest, the function of the patronym is here recuperated in the heterosexual couple who come together within a nationalized horizon of family formation.[45]

The limits of nationhood that the Illuminati conspiracy evoked were associated with both incest and miscegenation in the 1790s. As Jared Gardner has argued, Illuminati conspiracy theories in the United States were linked to anxieties about Jacobin revolution, but these concerns manifested themselves in relation to emerging ideas of the relation between race and nation. Thus, for instance, one Federalist writer describes republican conspiracy as a league of blacks and Irishmen that will pollute American racial purity: "Remove your wives far from the Infernal Fraternal embrace, or you may prove witness of their violation and expiring agonies, or if reserved for future infamy, may increase your families not only with a spurious, but a colored breed. Remove your daughters...unless you would be silent spectators of their being deflowered by the lusty Othellos."[46] Race becomes visible here as a term through which a consolidated (white) American national identity is created. Further, the threat to national identity described is also associated with the destruction of heterosexual, monogamous marriage. The "Infernal Fraternal embrace" refers to the secret brotherhood of Illuminati within the United States, but the imagery of the "fraternal embrace" suggests a clandestine, homosexual, physical contact that is also equated with an adulterous heterosexual embrace. Lawless sexuality is associated with promiscuous bodies and cosmopolitan (unbounded, interracial, incestuous) bodily identifications: in contrast, heterosexual marriage bespeaks proper boundaries and properly structured familial and national identifications.

The incest taboo, as Gayle Rubin has argued, serves to make sexual difference stand as an organizing social opposition. Thus, Rubin suggests, the incest taboo also enjoins against homosexual partnering: "the incest taboo presupposes a prior, less articulate taboo on homosexuality. A prohibition against *some* heterosexual unions assumes a taboo against *non*-heterosexual unions. Gender is not only an identification with one sex; it also entails that sexual desire be directed toward the other sex."[47] The dangerous cosmopolitanism of the "Infernal Fraternal embrace" may thus be referenced in both Harrington senior's adultery and Harrington junior's incest. Heterosexual marriage between exogamous partners, in contrast, secures fraternal relations among men through the exchange of women that is more carefully delimited, more clearly nationalized. As such, I would suggest that the patriarchal relations that the libertine disrupts find their new location in displaced kinship rules that appear as rules governing race (miscegenation), gender (incest and exogamous marriage), and national identity.

The British and American novels discussed in this essay – *Oroonoko*, *Moll Flanders*, *The Power of Sympathy*, and *Julia and the Illuminated Baron* – all include varied scenes of racialization, miscegenation, and incest. While miscegenation and incest are infractions of kinship rules that operate in opposite directions (exogamy versus endogamy), they are often paired within the novel and assume particular importance there insofar as they demarcate the possibility of a national, contractual space. In linking novels such as *Oroonoko* and *The Power of Sympathy* I mean to demonstrate that both texts – one set in colonial America and another in early national America – address the conditions of the expanding world market, early capitalism, and imperialism out of which discourses of nationalism developed. As a genre, the novel participates in articulating the contractual episteme of a world market – both in terms of its possibilities and its limits. While the novel is certainly linked to the development of national horizons and communities, the need to define the new rules of these communities occurs in the broader context of colonial expansion and early capitalism that links disparate sites such as London, Surinam, Virginia, and Boston. In its contractual concerns, the novel thus addresses the possibility and impossibility of the circulation of property and persons within this increasingly large world.

See also: chapter 6, Representing Resistance; chapter 15, The Eighteenth-Century Novel and Print Culture; chapter 22, The Novel Body Politic.

NOTES

1. See Carla Mulford, "Introduction," in *The Power of Sympathy by William Brown; and The Coquette by Hannah Webster Foster*, ed. Carla Mulford (New York: Penguin, 1996), xxxvii, and Cathy Davidson, *Revolution and the Word: The Rise of the Novel in America* (New York: Oxford University Press, 1986), chapter 5.

2. John Adams to William Cunningham, 15 March 1804, *Correspondence between the Hon. John Adams, Late President of the United States, and the Late William Cunningham, Esq.* (Boston: E. M. Cunningham, 1823), 19.

3. British novels circulated widely in colonial North America and were printed in American editions, see *A History of the Book in America*. Vol. 1, *The Colonial Book in the Atlantic World*, ed. Hugh Amory and David D. Hall (Cambridge: Cambridge University Press, 2000).

4. Davidson, *Revolution and the Word*, 85.

5. Christopher Flint, *Family Fictions: Narrative and Domestic Relations in Britain, 1688–1798* (Stanford, CA: Stanford University Press, 1998), 15.

6. Examples in this vein range from Ian Watt's influential study, *The Rise of the Novel: Studies in Defoe, Richardson, and Fielding* (Berkeley and Los Angeles: University of California Press, 1957) to Nancy Armstrong, *Desire and Domestic Fiction: A Political History of the Novel* (New York: Oxford University Press, 1987) and Catherine Gallagher, *Nobody's Story: The Vanishing Acts of Women Writers in the Marketplace, 1670–1820* (Berkeley and Los Angeles: University of California Press, 1994).

7. See, in particular, Jay Fliegelman's argument that consensual union (not union arranged by parents) mirrored the political liberation of the nation from the parental control of England in *Prodigals and Pilgrims: The American Revolution Against Patriarchal Authority, 1750–1800* (New York: Cambridge University Press, 1982). See also Elizabeth Barnes, *States of Sympathy: Seduction and Democracy in the American Novel* (New York: Columbia University Press, 1997); Julia Stern, *The Plight of Feeling: Sympathy and Dissent in the Early American Novel* (Chicago: University of Chicago Press, 1997); and Gillian Brown, *The Consent of the Governed: The Lockean Legacy in Early American Culture* (Cambridge, MA: Harvard University Press, 2001).

8. Although defined by Claude Lévi-Strauss as the founding taboo of civilization, incest is nonetheless culturally specific: relationships that might be considered incestuous in one culture are not considered so in another, such as sexual relations between individuals related through marriage (affinity) rather than by blood (consanguinity). Definitions of incest were shifting in Anglo-American culture in the eighteenth century, as were cultural norms and beliefs regarding marriage across racial lines: indeed, "miscegenation" is a term that did not exist in this period (originating later in the nineteenth century). Hence the *particular* forms of endogamy and exogamy at stake in the eighteenth-century novel warrant attention as historically determined formations. In this essay, I focus specifically on scenes of *unwitting* incest between biologically related siblings as well as representations of marriage across national/racial lines, both of which, I argue, are discursive constructions of endogamy and exogamy related to the economic and social effects of coloniality. For a useful history of debates over the definition of incest in England, see Ellen Pollak, *Incest and the English Novel, 1684–1814* (Baltimore, MD: Johns Hopkins University Press, 2003).

9. Jonathan Culler, "Anderson and the Novel," *Diacritics* 29 (1999): 37, emphases added.

10. Benedict Anderson, *Imagined Communities: Reflections on the Origin and Spread of Nationalism*, 2nd ed. (London: Verso Editions/NLB, 1991), 62.

11. Nancy Armstrong and Leonard Tennenhouse, *The Imaginary Puritan: Literature, Intellectual Labor, and the Origins of Personal Life*

(Berkeley and Los Angeles: University of California Press, 1992), 210.

12. Ibid., 213.

13. See William Spengeman, "The Earliest American Novel: Aphra Behn's *Oroonoko*," *Nineteenth-Century Fiction* 38 (1984): 384–414. Arguments have also been made for viewing Behn's *Oroonoko* as the first British novel: see Firdous Azim, *The Colonial Rise of the Novel* (New York: Routledge, 1993), chapter 2.

14. For discussion of mixed genres and historical sources upon which Behn draws see Joanna Lipking, "Confusing Matters: Searching the Backgrounds of *Oroonoko*," in *Aphra Behn Studies*, ed. Janet Todd (Cambridge: Cambridge University Press, 1996), 259–81.

15. Aphra Behn, *Oroonoko*, in *The Works of Aphra Behn*, ed. Janet Todd (Columbus: Ohio State University Press), 3: 58. Joanna Lipking notes that the term "Antiquaries" probably refers to "the new museum or repository of the Royal Society, which had published instructions calling on world travelers to contribute their natural history discoveries" (see Aphra Behn, *Oroonoko*, ed. Joanna Lipking {New York: Norton, 1997}, 9 n. 7). For discussion of the New Science and colonial women's roles as collectors for the Royal Society, see Susan Scott Parrish, "Women's Nature: Curiosity, Pastoral, and the New Science in British America," *Early American Literature* 37 (2002): 195–238. Parrish usefully defines the New Science as "the burgeoning of scientific activity beginning around 1650 in England, marked by the founding of the Royal Society of London (1662), its adoption of Baconian empiricism and experimentation and its inception of a global correspondence and collecting network as well as the mechanical philosophy," 224 n. 2.

16. Michael McKeon, *The Origins of the English Novel 1600–1740* (Baltimore, MD: Johns Hopkins University Press, 1987), 112, 101.

17. Gesa Mackenthun, *Metaphors of Dispossession: American Beginnings and the Translation of Empire, 1492–1637* (Norman: University of Oklahoma Press, 1997), 144.

18. McKeon, *The Origins of the English Novel 1600–1740*, 39.

19. Srinivas Aravamudan, *Tropicopolitans: Colonialism and Agency, 1688–1804* (Durham, NC: Duke University Press, 1999), 41.

20. My thanks to Robert Devlin for pointing out to me Banister's act of "dubbing" in this scene.

21. Irene Tucker, *A Probable State: The Novel, the Contract, and the Jews* (Chicago: University of Chicago Press, 2000), 26.

22. Ibid., 25.

23. See P. G. M. Dickson, *The Financial Revolution in England: A Study in the Development of Public Credit, 1688–1756* (New York: St. Martin's Press, 1967).

24. John Trenchard and Thomas Gordon, *Cato's Letters; or, Essays on Liberty, Civil and Religious, and Other Important Subjects*, ed. Ronald Hamowy (Indianapolis, IN: Liberty Fund, 1995), 56.

25. Catherine Ingrassia, *Authorship, Commerce, and Gender in Early Eighteenth-Century England: A Culture of Paper Credit* (Cambridge: Cambridge University Press, 1998), 2.

26. With regard to the contract, for instance, Brook Thomas writes, "If status-based societies are held together mostly by commitments that precede promises, promising has the potential to open these relatively closed communities to transactions with strangers by providing a mechanism for the ritual creation of new commitments," *American Literary Realism and the Failed Promise of Contract* (Berkeley and Los Angeles: University of California Press, 1997), 34.

27. J. G. A. Pocock, *Virtue, Commerce, and History: Essays on Political Thought and History, Chiefly in the Eighteenth Century* (Cambridge: Cambridge University Press, 1985), 112.

28. Ingrassia, *Authorship, Commerce, and Gender*, 3.

29. *Defoe's Review*, ed. Arthur Wellesley Secord (New York: Columbia University Press, 1938), 5: 560; cited in Aparna Dharwadker, "Nation, Race, and the Ideology of Commerce in Defoe," *The Eighteenth Century: Theory and Interpretation* 39 (1998): 68. Defoe's discussion occurs in the context of arguing for English trade with Africa; he contends that a nationalized trading com-

pany will be best able to protect itself in fortresses from the natives and better able to engage in the slave trade for the sake of English colonial interests in North America. Thus he advocates trade in Africa but not contractual relations with Africans.

30. Dharwadker, "Nation, Race, and the Ideology of Commerce in Defoe," 69.

31. Pollak, *Incest and the English Novel, 1684–1814*, 115.

32. Franco Moretti, *Atlas of the European Novel, 1800–1900* (New York: Verso, 1998), 15.

33. W. Daniel Wilson contends that unwitting sibling incest occurs in "almost thirty" eighteenth-century European literary works: see "Science, Natural Law, and Unwitting Sibling Incest in Eighteenth-Century Literature," *Studies in Eighteenth-Century Culture* 13 (1984): 249–70.

34. Amit Yahav-Brown, "At Home in England, or Projecting Liberal Citizenship in *Moll Flanders*," *Novel* 35 (2001): 26.

35. Daniel Defoe, *The Fortunes and Misfortunes of the Famous Moll Flanders*, ed. G. A. Starr (London: Oxford University Press, 1971), 102.

36. Talcott Parsons, "The Incest Taboo in Relation to Social Structure," in *The Family: Its Structures and Functions*, ed. Rose Laub Coser, 2nd ed. (New York: St. Martin's Press, 1974), 19; cited by Pollak, *Incest and the English Novel*, 122.

37. Examples of the plot of unwitting sibling incest in American novels include Brown's *Power of Sympathy* as well as his later novel, *Ira and Isabella* (1807); three novels by Susanna Rowson including *Mentoria* (1795), *Trials of the Human Heart* (1795), and *Lucy Temple* (1828, sequel to the best-selling *Charlotte Temple*); Sally Sayward Wood's *Julia and the Illuminated Baron* (1800); and several tales by anonymous authors including "The School for Libertines" (1789); *The History of Albert and Eliza* (1812); and *Margaretta* (1807). For further discussion of these novels see Anne Dalke, "Original Vice: The Political Implications of Incest in the Early American Novel," *Early American Literature* 23 (1988): 188–201.

38. William Hill Brown, *The Power of Sympathy*, in *The Power of Sympathy*, ed. Carla Mulford (New York: Penguin, 1996), 22–23.

39. Leonard Tennenhouse, "Libertine America," *Differences* 11 (1999/2000): 10, 14.

40. For useful discussion of these debates, see the volume, *Federalists Reconsidered*, ed. Doron Ben-Atar and Barbara B. Oberg (Charlottesville: University of Virginia Press, 1998) and in more literary terms, Jared Gardner, *Master Plots: Race and the Founding of an American Literature, 1787–1845* (Baltimore, MD: Johns Hopkins University Press, 1998).

41. Chandos Michael Brown, "Mary Wollstonecraft, or, the Female Illuminati: The Campaign against Women and 'Modern Philosophy' in the Early Republic," *Journal of the Early Republic* 15 (1995): 389–424, 397.

42. Sally Sayward Barrell Keating Wood, *Julia and the Illuminated Baron* (Portsmouth, NH: Charles Peirce, 1800), 205.

43. Ibid., 243.

44. Ibid., 136.

45. The successful couplings and revelations of identity at the close of *Julia and the Illuminated Baron* result in the relocation of the extended family of French and Italian nobility (of whom both Julia and Francis turn out to be the heirs) in England. The novel thus points to an Anglo-American resolution of republican crisis insofar as it posits a reconstructed *English* identity for those who share in what are portrayed as essentially American values.

46. Cited in John C. Miller, *Crisis in Freedom: The Alien and Sedition Acts* (Boston: Little Brown, 1951), 6, from the *York General Advertiser*, Aug. 1, 1798. For further discussion of this passage see David Waldstreicher, "Federalism, the Styles of Politics, and the Politics of Style," in *Federalists Reconsidered*, 115, and Jared Gardner, *Master Plots*, 61.

47. Gayle Rubin, "The Traffic in Women: Notes on the 'Political Economy' of Sex," in *Toward an Anthropology of Women*, ed. Rayna Raiter (New York: Monthly Review Press, 1975), 180.

Further Reading

Amory, Hugh, and David D. Hall, eds. *History of the Book in America*. Vol. 1, *The Colonial Book in the Atlantic World*. Cambridge: Cambridge University Press, 2000.

Armstrong, Nancy, and Leonard Tennenhouse. *The Imaginary Puritan: Literature, Intellectual Labor, and the Origins of Personal Life*. Berkeley and Los Angeles: University of California Press, 1992.

Brown, Gillian. *The Consent of the Governed: The Lockean Legacy in Early American Culture*. Cambridge, MA: Harvard University Press, 2001.

Gardner, Jared. *Master Plots: Race and the Founding of an American Literature 1787–1845*. Baltimore, MD: Johns Hopkins University Press, 1998.

Spengeman, William C. "The Earliest American Novel: Aphra Behn's *Oroonoko*." *Nineteenth-Century Fiction* 38 (1984): 384–414.

Stern, Julia A. *The Plight of Feeling: Sympathy and Dissent in the Early American Novel*. Chicago: University of Chicago Press, 1997.

11

New Contexts for Early Novels by Women: The Case of Eliza Haywood, Aaron Hill, and the Hillarians, 1719–1725

Kathryn R. King

Edmund Gosse's confident portrait of the early reader of popular fiction by women – Ann Lang he calls her – should give pause to students of the eighteenth-century novel today. Ann Lang was the name Gosse found inscribed in some Haywood novels that came his way, and although he admits to knowing nothing about Ann Lang, really, he is certain she was not a person of quality – her hand reveals that much. She must have been a milliner's apprentice or a servant-girl. She was a cleanly girl, for she did not drip warm fat on the pages. She was young, all Haywood's earliest readers were, and was drawn "instinctively" to stories of passionate love. She learned to feign fainting spells and violent disorders by imitating Haywood's palpitating heroines: "I am positive," he affirms, "that Ann Lang practised this series of attitudes in the solitude of her garret."[1] Ann Lang has proven to be an enduring figure, as Christine Blouch has demonstrated in a witty and suggestive essay.[2] To this day much criticism tends to read amatory novels by women, Haywood's in particular, through the imagined reading experiences of heuristic readers generally supposed to be females of diminished cognitive ability.

Supposititious reading experiences loom large in recent accounts of early popular fiction. In *Popular Fiction Before Richardson* (1969), John Richetti portrays the early reader of amatory fiction as a woman "possessed of severely limited capacities" and thus unappreciative of complexities of style, plot, or psychological complication. His Ann Lang did not grapple with "moral ideas" but responded with a "moral-emotional sympathetic vibration."[3] Like Richetti, Ros Ballaster in *Seductive Forms* (1992) posits a female reader seeking erotic pleasures, but because she wishes to invest amatory fiction with a psychological complexity and feminist edge absent in Richetti's account, she uses psychoanalytic theory to construct a female reader whose interior responses are at once complicated and contestatory: the erotic fantasies engendered by Haywood's stories offer resistance to the unpleasant realities of actual female existence under patriarchy.[4] William Warner's revision of Richetti and Ballaster in *Licensing Entertainment* (1998) turns on a newly minted version of Ann Lang. She now belongs to a "diverse plurality of readers"[5] who go to Haywood for a new kind of reading experience, one that "incites desire and promotes the liberation of the reader as a subject of pleasure" (93). Amatory novels appeal not to women, as had been assumed, but to the pleasure-seeking "general reader" – a cross-gendered "perversely poly-morphous" Ann Lang, liable to be "hooked by many zones of readerly enjoyment" (89). The space given over to fictionalized reading responses in histories of the early novel is astonishing when you think of it, and in Haywood criticism Ann Lang is nearly inescapable. It is scarcely an exaggeration, in fact, to say that the story of Haywood's role in the making of the novel has been largely a story of Ann Lang: a narrative assembled out of historical circumstance, informed speculation, theory-derived complication, and out-and-out fabulation.

Ann Lang preoccupies me here because I have come to believe that concentration upon the fantasy life of a patently fictional reader is unhelpful at best and may actually inhibit a productive approach to Haywood and women writers more generally. I say this for three main reasons. First, attention to one or another fictive reader implies an unspoken but subtly damaging judgment: a Haywood (or a Delarivier Manley or Mrs. Rowe or Penelope Aubin) really *is* something of a lightweight; her texts are thin, "untalkaboutable" apart from the supposed effects on susceptible bosoms – and seldom, one notes, on the critic her- or himself. *We* do not get it, so we invent a reader who does. Too often the result is a failure really to engage the texts, and such failure does nothing to dispel the suspicion that these novels really are trashy and overblown after all. Second, the well-studied responses of Ann Lang may delude us into believing we know a good deal more than we actually do about who was reading women writers and why. The example of the Jacobite author Jane Barker shows us that some women novelists wrote to and for a politically attuned niche market, in Barker's case a readership of conservative dissidents.[6] But other novelists – Haywood, certainly, but also Manley and Rowe – were widely, it might even be said wildly, popular. That works such as Manley's *New Atalantis* (1709), Haywood's *Love in Excess* (1719–20), and Rowe's *Friendship in Death* (1728) went through multiple editions and remained points of reference throughout the century is a continuing source of perplexity and even, perhaps, embarrassment. (Richetti may speak for many when he calls the breakaway success of *Love in Excess* "one of the more appalling and therefore interesting facts of literary history."[7]) We are far from being able to account for the appeal of such "bestsellers," as they are sometimes called, and it seems unlikely that further attention to Ann Lang's fantasy life will do much to advance understanding of the baffling but undeniable resonance of much popular work by women writers in their own moment. Third, it is all too tempting to substitute accounts of Ann Lang in her garret for the archival spadework needed to dig out concrete evidence of actual reading practices, identify the responses of actual readers to new prose fictions, and reconstruct with imagination and historical respect the reading communities within which the early novel took shape. Mature criticism of early women writers must resist the fascination exerted by Ann Lang and focus instead upon modes of inquiry likely to produce more historically based accounts of the audience, aims, and artistry of early women novelists.

To show the benefits of this more historically grounded approach, I offer here a discussion of Eliza Haywood in the context of what appears to have been her earliest reading community: the circle of young artists and writers, men and women, who gathered around Aaron Hill (1685–1750) during the first half of the 1720s. My discussion reverses the customary approach to Haywood in two ways. First, in place of the fictive Ann Lang I focus upon the Hillarians, as Hill and his circle were called: a small, short-lived, but unusually well-documented community of readers in which Haywood's earliest novels were conceived and first read. Second, instead of reading Haywood through the innuendoes and vilifications of her detractors, I read her in relation to her literary friends and allies. The dual change of emphasis results in an intriguingly "defamiliarized" Eliza Haywood. She is still, to be sure, a figure for the scandal of the early novel and for the anxieties aroused by the encroachments of (in Swift's phrase) stupid and infamous scribbling women. But she is also – and it is a cultural contradiction that deserves deeper consideration than I can give it here – a promoter of politeness and refined taste. It is seldom recognized that her earliest works, elegantly produced and marketed for fashionable audiences, belong in important ways to the developing discourse of politeness and bourgeois refinement. By offering new readings of Haywood's early fiction and new assessments of her place in the development of the novel, I hope to encourage a more energetic pursuit of new contexts for the study of early women novelists more generally.

Haywood, Hill, and the Hillarian Sublime

This section argues that Haywood's early novels can usefully be read as experiments in the Longinian sublime, a mode of writing that excited the enthusiasms of Aaron Hill and his circle. First, though, a few words on Hill, until recently a figure of scholarly fun. Scholars are now coming to recognize that the multi-talented Hill – dramatist, poet, journalist, projector, and tireless promoter of young literary talent – was a major unifying force in British literary culture in the first half of the century. Brean Hammond, in his study of the professionalization of literary writing in this period, places Hill at the center of London literary life, stressing that his cultural projects brought together "elements of the Whig-derived ideology of politeness and the aesthetic canons that derive from it with elements of the Scriblerian politics of decline."[8] Christine Gerrard in a revelatory biography describes Hill as "perhaps the most important, certainly the most ubiquitous, man of letters in London literary life" in the period from 1720 to 1728.[9] Hill's importance in Haywood's writing life would be hard to overestimate. When they met, in or around 1719, Haywood, a failed actress, was a newcomer to the London literary scene. Hill, on the other hand, was a socially well-connected and culturally formidable figure, not to mention handsome, kindly, generous, charismatic, and genuinely devoted to the cultivation of new artistic talent. Among the young writers that he befriended and supported were the poets Richard Savage, Martha Fowke, John Dyer, Edward Young, David Mallet, and, a little later, James Thomson. He used various means, including hosting "polite," sexually mixed assemblies at his house, to promote the careers of a diverse range of young writers, women as well as men. Indeed, the Hill circle was one of very few coteries in London at this time known to have encouraged female talent.[10] The *Plain Dealer*, the twice-weekly essay paper Hill wrote (with William Bond) in part to spotlight "new young literary talent and neglected writers" (Gerrard 63), claims in its opening number to draw inspiration from assemblies "of both Sexes, very numerous and diversified."[11] The paper gave special attention to women writers, including an affectionate glance at Aphra Behn in the opening number, a tribute to Delarivier Manley, a sympathetic account of romances, and a promise, never fulfilled, to devote future papers to showing the superiority of living English female writers to the ancients. The ideal of polite conversation and mutual respect between men and women fostered by Hill and his circle may have given Haywood the confidence to address a fashionable audience. When she tried her own hand at recreating polite mixed conversation in *The Tea-Table* (1725) she included a character modeled on Hill, the "refin'd and polite" Philetus. A "Gentleman than whom there is scarce to be found one Master of more Accomplishments," he is also (with a wink to the cognoscenti) a "Plain-dealer without Bluntness."[12]

   Haywood's admiration for the man she considered her friend, mentor, and patron glows in her verses to and about him. Her extravagant praise for the "majestic," "awful," and "godlike" Hill supports Gerrard's claim that "it would not be too extreme to say that Haywood adored Hill as a man" (70). But her adoration partakes not a little of the feelings of a student for her mentor. One poem testifies to her pride in Hill's approval of her writing. ("For who," she asks, "approv'd by thee, can stoop to take / The little Praises that the Vulgar make?"[13]) Another uses an extended sun metaphor to depict Hill's influence on the creative lives of his circle of admirers: his generous praise "inspire[s] them to *Excell*." He is the solar center of their literary universe. As the sun's "kindling Heat" blesses the green world with its "productive Influence," so does Hill enkindle the talents of the Hillarians: "o'er our Souls the Lov'd *Hillarius* reigns" and like Phoebus, the sun god, "his Sight Empowers."[14]

   Evident in this verse is Haywood's fascination with the sublime, with an aesthetic that courts excited states of mind in deliberate disruption of the canons of neoclassical poise. Her ecstatic response to Hill's sun-like wit – she is "Aw'd! charm'd! and dazled!", fired with "incoherent Extasies" – suggests an understanding of poetry as experience rather than artifact, less craft than exalted emotional state, something akin to an enraptured swoon or an ecstasy beyond language.[15] This trance-like state is the subject of "To Diana, On her asking me how I lik'd a fine Poem of Mr Hill's." Admiration for Hill's poem renders her speechless and transported: "The fault'ring

Tongue, the Use of Speech denies, / And Thought itself, in height of Rapture dies!" Like Saul on the road to Damascus she lies "lost, and o'er-whelm'd in Seas of Extasy."[16] Haywood's attraction to the poetic sublime doubtless owes something to Hill's Longinian enthusiasms, which can themselves be traced back to the critic John Dennis and forward to such Hillarian poets as James Thomson and David Mallet.[17] Haywood's literary affiliations with these practitioners of the sublime remain unstudied.

The notoriously exclamatory nature of Haywood's prose style, its melting and swelling tendency – features that have occasioned their share of ridicule – may be seen in this context as an attempt to translate into amatory fiction the effects of "the sublime," to represent the transporting effects of love in the medium of prose fiction. In one of the *Plain Dealer* essays, Hill praises Hebrew poetry for its capacity to stir the soul. Such poetry, he writes in No. 87, abounds in ideas "so *sublimely Enthusiastick*, that they transport and carry away the *Reader*, with a Power that is *resistless*" (2:256). In No. 40 he adapts ideas of the sublime to love in terms that may suggest Haywood's influence. Love is a "Passion, which is, of its own Nature, so violent, [that it] renders Men excusable, in a great measure, when they seem to misplace it" (1:338). Citing Plato's notion that love directs the soul to the object it dotes upon, he instances "this delightful Wandering of the Soul from its own mansion" as an illustration of the "Force of Love, and the Power, which those, who were created to charm, have to transport us . . . into their own absolute Dominion" (1:338). The marriage of Longinus and Plato evident here is found everywhere in Haywood's amatory fictions. In *Love in Excess*, to take a single example, love is a "spring that with a rapid whirl transports us from our selves, and darts our souls into the bosom of the darling object." Language, we learn earlier in the same paragraph, wants the "sublimity" and "softness" needed to "reach the exalted soaring of a lovers meaning!"[18]

Male poets in the Hillarian circle, Dyer and Thomson in particular, used verse to express an ecstatic sensory response to the natural world. Haywood used amatory fiction to express the ineffable bliss of sexual ecstasy. She moved the experience of the sublime into the realm of small, female, sexualized spaces, crafting melodramatic plots capable of projecting a range of extreme and unsettling states of mind – excesses (invoked in the aptly titled *Love in Excess*) that show ordinary women filled with and exalted by the sexualized sublime. Haywood's amatory fictions are sometimes associated these days with a Tory ideology, but attention to elements of the sublime in her early fiction suggests that it is a mistake to identify either the novels or their author too closely with any particular political orientation. On some level of generality these early fictions do indeed possess "the over-arching structure of a Tory ideology,"[19] but they also exhibit sympathy with what might be called emotive innovation, with Whiggish modes of narration that seek to articulate new registers of interior experience. Perhaps it is time to recognize that one of Haywood's achievements as a popular novelist is precisely her creation of politically multivalent texts that oscillate between Tory and Whiggish tendencies, that straddle Scriblerian and self-consciously modern cultural agendas.

Love in Excess, Delicacy, and Literary Reputation

Despite several decades of rehabilitative scholarship Haywood is still best known as the sexualized object of one of Alexander Pope's deadliest assaults and, more broadly, as a lightning rod for cultural anxieties about women and the "scandal" and "contagion" of the novel. There is no denying her notoriety – she did after all rank as the marquis prize in the booksellers' games in the 1728 *Dunciad*. But it is seldom noticed how far Haywood's disrepute is traceable to a rather thin scattering of public attacks – one from Pope, two from Savage, and some later roughing up from Henry Fielding; and not enough thought has been given to the fact that these attacks did not begin until 1725, after the publication of the first part of her earliest and most spectacular foray into scandal chronicling, *Memoirs of a Certain Island Adjacent to the Kingdom of Utopia*. It is no coincidence that *Memoirs of a Certain Island* included remarkably vicious attacks on two women, Martha Fowke and Martha Blunt, beloved by the two men destined to be her most vocal detractors, Savage and Pope. It is certainly true that, especially after 1725, a "popular perception of Haywood as a libidinous, scandalous, immodest woman actively circulated."[20] But other perceptions circulated as well, some of them laudatory, and about them we hear almost nothing.

Many will be surprised to learn, for example, that Haywood's first novel, *Love in Excess* (1719–20), enjoyed a special position in the *oeuvre* as signifier of the *non*-scandalous side of Haywood's literary production. The tendency today is to think of *Love in Excess* as a trashy page-turner or, in a more sophisticated formulation, as a prime breeder of "a new contagion of reading."[21] But in a fascinating study of Haywood's early career Al Coppola uses bibliographic evidence to show that Haywood's debut novel was produced and marketed to appeal to the elegant upper end of the literary marketplace. Its production values, as Coppola notes, were "far from mean." *Love in Excess* was finely produced on good stock paper with prestigious Elzevir letter, the pages "liberally graced with printers' ornaments and white space." The first part, a mere fifty-six pages plus prefatory matter, sold for a shilling. Format and pricing, in other words, announced suitability for a fashionable readership. Interestingly, her next prose work, a translation of *Letters from a Lady of Quality to a Chevalier* (1721), also printed in Elzevir on thick, glossy paper with "many elaborate printer's ornaments and a great deal of white space," was an even more elegant production. With two prestige publications to her credit, the author of *Love in Excess* seemed destined for an enviable place at the literary table. For some reason, though, these were followed by a string of cheaply produced, short amatory tales and secret histories. Published in rapid succession and printed in crowded lines on thin paper, these "Haywoods" were clearly targeted at a less culturally aspiring readership.[22] Although the reasons for the development are uncertain, it is clear that by 1725 there existed two Haywoods, one elegant and the other scandalous.

For the remainder of her career *Love in Excess* was the title her admirers used to evoke the "polite" side of her body of work. In a 1764 retrospective on her career,

David Erskine Baker uses *Love in Excess* to exemplify her special literary strengths. He concedes that the early novels were marred by the licentiousness of their moment but insists that, at their best, they exhibit "great Spirit and Ingenuity." *Love in Excess* (along with *Fruitless Inquiry*) demonstrates her "great inventive powers" and "perfect knowledge of the affections of the human heart." He is careful to distinguish her "inventive powers," by which he seems to mean her ability to create strong original stories (i.e., those containing no personal scandal), from her regrettable practice elsewhere of "exposing . . . the private errors of individuals" and catering to "the public Taste for personal Scandal, and diving into the Intrigues of the Great."[23] These two sides of Haywood – the author of elegant tales of inner experience and the scandalmonger – help us understand the ambiguities of her reputation after *Memoirs of a Certain Island Adjacent to the Kingdom of Utopia.* As Gerrard suggests in her biography of Hill, it was Haywood's vicious attack on Martha Fowke in *Memoirs* that turned the disgusted Hillarians against her. The assault on Fowke was "so flagrant that it backfired on her altogether," provoking "a backlash of criticism of Haywood which effectively ended her association with the circle" (Gerrard 94, 95). An off-the-record comment from David Mallet the following year hints at the way her former Hillarian friends talked about her in private: "I must tell you," he writes to Savage, "that if I judge by that Fury's writings, one that thoroughly knows her is acquainted with all the vicious part of the sex" (quoted in Gerrard 95). Even Aaron Hill, by Gerrard's account the gentlest of men, concludes an October 1724 *Plain Dealer* essay on detraction with a muted glance at "the *Unfair* Author of the *NEW UTOPIA*."[24] One has to wonder what the usually shrewd and heretofore respected Haywood was thinking when she composed the lively, teeming, boundlessly ill-natured and still largely unstudied *Memoirs of a Certain Island*. If any single early work by Haywood calls out for close attention, it would surely be this scandal chronicle. In any event the well-known public attacks were soon to follow, first Savage's in *The Authors of the Town* (1725) and then Pope's in *The Dunciad* (1728). From 1725 onwards, Haywood's reputation took on a strangely bipolar character.

A full study of Haywood's reputation is likely to confirm the circulation during her lifetime of a number of perceptions of Eliza Haywood, not all of them scandalous.[25] At least two Haywoods are now discernible.[26] The first, the execrated scandalmonger attacked by Pope in the *Dunciad*, is only too well known today. The other, the polite author of such fashionable works as *Love in Excess*, has been all but effaced, glimpsed only in passing references. Baker, as we have seen, called attention to the "great Spirit and Ingenuity" of *Love in Excess*, which displayed the author's inventive powers and insight into the human heart. A 1737 *Daily Advertiser* notice for a benefit performance at the Haymarket identifies her as "Author of Love in Excess, and many other entertaining Pieces."[27] In 1747 she is described as "made eminent by several Novels, called *Love in Excess*, &c. wrote by her, which were much approved of by those who delight in that Sort of Reading and had a great Sale."[28]

A reading of *Love in Excess* in its Hillarian contexts suggests that this novel was marketed for, and later associated with, a genteel readership in part because of its innovative treatment of the new virtues of "politeness." The novel is, to begin, a recasting of male and female relations along the self-consciously progressive lines promoted by the Hillarians. As Gerrard has shown, the writers and artists who gathered around Hill pursued in their own assemblies and friendships relationships "untainted by outmoded rituals of female coquetry and male pursuit" (76). They believed in the possibility of friendships between men and women and celebrated an ideal of high-minded heterosexual love guided by principles of sincerity, generosity, and openness. The complicated amatory plots in *Love in Excess* project these emerging bourgeois ideals at the same time that they critique older aristocratic values. The artfulness exhibited by such aristocratic women as Alovysa and Ciamara is exposed as grotesque and self-destroying. A new brand of heroine, Melliora – her name, as is often noted, means "better" – combines the capacity for sexual passion of her aristocratic female forebears with a decidedly bourgeois capacity for enlightened self-governance. Melliora even manages to arrange events in such a way as to dispose of herself in marriage at the end. The aristocratic male at the center of most of the sexual adventures, Count D'Elmont, is put through a course of education in polite behavior that fits him for marriage with Melliora. Attached at first to the masculinist, homosocial, and vaguely aristocratic ideals (honor, martial glory) that had flourished in the older heroic romances, D'Elmont is instructed over the course of the novel in the ways of bourgeois private virtues. He even discovers his own capacity for feminine "softness." (In his "softness," sexual charisma, and sweetness of disposition D'Elmont resembles Aaron Hill.) In the stagey, largely comedic world of the third part of *Love in Excess*, men reform, sexual interest survives consummation, virginity is not always the beginning and end of female virtue, and men and women alike aspire to companionate marriage. These generous possibilities are encapsulated in the uncharacteristically sunny (and thus, one might suspect, ironic) final sentence: "Both he [D'Elmont] and Frankville, are still living, blest with a numerous and hopeful issue, and continue, with their fair wives, great and lovely examples of conjugal affection" (LE 297). Arguably this benedictory closure cannot contain the excesses of the earlier parts of the novel, but it comes as close as the temperamentally pessimistic Haywood ever does to closing a plot in conformity with the progressive social ideals of the Hillarians.

The Hillarian context also alerts us to the importance of the polite ideal of delicacy in *Love in Excess*. Haywood is known, of course, for her ability to deliver "warm" effects, but in this she could hardly be regarded as singular. Behn and Manley, to take the two best-known examples, share her gift for closely detailed rendering of bodily responses to sexual stimuli. What is distinctive about Haywood in this regard is her practice of elevating sexual experience to the condition of the sublime and then making appreciation of its sublimity a signifier of refined taste and delicacy of perception: the narrator addresses herself to "the few who have delicacy enough to feel what I but imperfectly attempt to speak" (LE 134). Blessed with an exquisite fineness of perception herself, the narrator teaches her readers to recognize love as an all-stirring experience that unites body and spirit, sensuous pleasure and transports of the soul. The kisses of Melliora and D'Elmont are carnal and spiritual in equal measure, for example: they collect "every sence in one, exhale the very soul, and mingle spirits!" (LE 288). Sublime love is allied with the "nicer, and more refined delicacies of desire." It is appreciable only by the special few possessed of these "refined delicacies" (LE 182). She invites her readers to unite with her against the "*insipids*" who lack the "elegance of thought, delicacy, or tenderness of soul" to appreciate the force of love (LE 206). For Haywood the crucial distinction is neither moral (the virtuous and the wicked) nor social (the polite and the vulgar). It is aesthetic. The fine discriminations of the "delicate" are ranged against the insensibility of the "insipids." In writing narratives that come down on the side of eros *and* delicacy, Haywood in effect removes sexuality from its well-known patriarchal contexts and subjects it to the narratorial surveillance of those capable of finely sensitive modes of discrimination – her own narrators for example. Feminine consciousness is thus privileged and, in the process, sex and sexuality are positioned in a very odd space indeed, somewhere between the disruptions of desire and the regulatory effects of the Augustan refinement of manners.

Haywood's ability to evoke the intertwining of delicacy and desire garnered praise from commentators in the early 1720s. Savage's commendatory lines on *Love in Excess* – written, needless to say, before their falling out – stress elements of the sublime. The "*Soul-thrilling accents*" of her language "*all our senses wound*" (LE 88). A later poem by Savage praises her ability to stir the mind to elevated feeling: "*As Music charms, thy Language lifts the Mind.*"[29] A dedication to Haywood by the unidentified "Ma. A" emphasizes her heroines' delicacy (they possess "*so forcible, so natural a Delicacy*") as well as the refining tendency of her novels, which rouse the dullest minds to expansive generosity.[30] Read alongside the bibliographical evidence gathered by Coppola, comments such as these suggest that Haywood's early novels were received as uplifting offerings in the world of polite entertainment. The "scandal" of *Love in Excess* is, perhaps, an invention of our own critical moment.

Haywood, Savage, and *The Rash Resolve*

Examining Haywood's early novels in the context of her friendship with Richard Savage, the man frequently (and perhaps inaccurately) described as her lover and the father of one of her children, reveals another feature of her amatory fiction that has received little comment: its topicality. Speculation about relations between Haywood and Savage has developed into a narrative of sexual entanglement that may well turn out to be no more verifiable than Ann Lang's swooning palpitations: Haywood is routinely called Savage's "mistress," he is credited with the paternity of at least one illegitimate child, and Martha Fowke is regularly cast as a rival for Savage's sexual attentions. I have found little to substantiate this story and much to call it into question, but it is certainly true that Haywood had strong feelings for Savage and was eager to support with her pen his claim to noble birth – that he was the natural son of the late Earl Rivers who had been cruelly disinherited by his supposed mother, the former Lady Macclesfield, and denied his rightful paternal estate. In 1723 and 1724 she and Aaron Hill, separately or in partnership, mounted a public campaign on Savage's behalf. This meant, among other things, blackening the character and conduct of Lady Macclesfield, who for her part insistently denied any connection with Savage.

Mothers, cruel and exemplary, figure prominently in the writings of both Hill and Haywood during this time. Between May and November 1724, Hill espoused Savage's claims in a series of three *Plain Dealer* essays. The first, No. 15 (1 May 1724), finds Hill baffled to explain something "so *Shocking* and *Frightful* to *Human Nature*" as a "*Mother who can look with Indifference* (not to say with Aversion) *upon the Child of her Body.*" He calls for patrons for the shockingly ill-treated young poet. Later that year Haywood included in *Memoirs of a Certain Island* a sympathetic retelling of Savage's supposed birth in the History of Masonia, Count Marville, and Count Riverius (157–87). So much is well known.

Late in 1723 Haywood published a novel, *The Rash Resolve*, which would appear to be the first of the Hillarian printed efforts on Savage's behalf. The intensely idealized story of maternal tenderness contained in the final portions of this novel offers a fantasy version of the unsatisfying story that Savage – with the help of Haywood and Hill – sought to rewrite in his own favor. In sharp contrast to Savage's putatively cruel and unnatural mother, Haywood's Emanuella dotes on her illegitimate son, little Victorinus: "Never did maternal Tenderness reach to a height more elevated than her's."[31] This devotion sets Emanuella above the "generality of her Sex" and indeed from "the greatest part of my Female Perusers," who will wrongly imagine that "this unfortunate Lady could regard a Child whose begetting had cost her so many Tears but with Indifference" (95). "All the Ignominy which this Adventure, if divulg'd, would bring upon her, was now no longer a Concern to her – Even Virtue was become less dear; and she could scarce repent she had been guilty of a Breach of it, so much she priz'd the Effect" (96). The story ends in scenes of the most noble maternal self-sacrifice and a reconciliation with Emanuella's father and his new wife. The principals all behave with exemplary generosity, Emanuella dies of a broken heart, and every character with a fortune competes to lavish it upon young Victorinus. The bastard child, at last restored to his father and his inheritance, grows up to be, as the final sentence of the novel has it, "the greatest Ornament of the Kingdom which claims his Birth" (128). It is surely significant that Savage supplied this novel with commendatory verses.

Haywood pulled out all the stops when she created her exemplary mother. Not only does the incomparably beautiful, elegant, and witty Emanuella possess learning, superior understanding, greatness of spirit and courage, and an aptitude for public self-defense. She is also, arguably, the most exquisitely pathetic of Haywood's early heroines, supremely so in her role as unwed but selflessly devoted mother. Toni Bowers finds that Emanuella stands alone in Augustan fiction as an example of "successful, autonomous motherhood" and celebrates Haywood for offering a unique "vision of powerful, enabling, and independent motherhood."[32] Perhaps, but it strikes me that the figure of Emanuella is implicated in the particulars of time and space more deeply than this account would suggest. Indeed, I would suggest that Emanuella is less an exemplar of maternal autonomy than a ripped-from-the-headlines fantasy intended to generate support for Savage's claims.

Would readers outside the Hillarian circle have connected the doomed and un-friended Savage with his fortunate antithesis, Victorinus? Would the reading public look beyond the generous Emanuella to see her cruel antitype, the former Lady Macclesfield? It is impossible to say, but I am confident the Hillarians would have read the tissue of references to mothers and bastard sons in this way. Certainly Savage himself was anything but reluctant to invite such reflections. Why else would he supply *Rash Resolve* with commendatory verses calling attention to his cruel motherless plight? (He proclaims himself "*DOOM'D to a Fate, which damps the Poet's flame*" – the allusion is to the poverty attendant upon his cruel abandonment by his mother – yet his "*unfriended*" Muse manages to greet Haywood's rising name.[33]) Suggestive also is the little-discussed dedication to the 1724 novel *The Prude*, by one 'Ma. A.' (According to the *Monthly Catalogue*, *The Prude* was published July 1724, at the mid-point of the pro-Savage campaign.) The identity of the author, who proudly declares herself a friend of Haywood's, remains a tantalizing literary puzzle. After Ma. A. praises Haywood's easy flowing style and admires the generous pity aroused by her "*matchless Writings*," she calls special attention to Emanuella and her "*maternal Tender-ness for little* Victorinus." Especially noble is this heroine's self-sacrificing care, which makes him "*some amends for the Severity of Fortune, in the cruel Inhumanity of a Father, and her too fond Credulity.*"[34] It seems telling that a member of Haywood's circle, at the height of the public campaign on Savage's behalf conducted by Haywood and Hill, would use her dedication to call attention to the novel's maternal themes.

Did Haywood seek in *Rash Resolve* to capitalize on the public interest in the Savage story? Was she, perhaps at Savage's instigation, making an early contribution to the campaign on his behalf? Did she write what amounts to a coterie fiction intended to resonate in special ways within a tight little circle of friends? Was the maternal fantasy of *Rash Resolve* an attempt to win back Savage with whom, if her hostile treatment in *The Injur'd Husband* (1723) of Du Lache, thought to be based upon Savage, is any indication, she seems already to have been on rocky terms?[35] We can only guess at this point. But if *Rash Resolve* was intended as an olive branch to Savage, it failed. By late summer of that year, if not well before, their differences had gone beyond any hope of reconciliation, on Savage's part anyway. In the first part of *Memoirs of a Certain Island*, published in September 1724, Haywood plays the role of the injured friend who still bears her friend "a singular Respect" and could be persuaded to welcome him back. Savage would have none of it, and, as has been seen, the Hillarians more generally closed ranks after the attack on Martha Fowke and others in *Memoirs*.

Implications and Conjectures

The foregoing discussion suggests new contexts for investigations of other early women novelists. Since the publication of Ballaster's deservedly influential *Seductive*

Forms, the study of early prose fiction by women has been dominated by romance/ amatory models, and critics have extended in illuminating ways Ballaster's analysis of modes of sexuality/subjectivity as they challenge or subvert figurations of the feminine. *Love in Excess* certainly lends itself to such an analysis. With a complicated intrigue plot in which chastity and sexual passion blend and merge in dizzying ways, this novel puts the ideal of female virginity under considerable pressure. This is, after all, a story in which two lovers conduct their dalliance at the foot of a statue of Diana. But when *Love in Excess* is removed from its amatory contexts and read alongside the literature of taste and manners being produced by Dennis, Shaftesbury, Addison, and Steele, as well as in relation to poets of the "sublime" such as Dyer, Mallet, and Thomson, other elements emerge. The novel becomes more satiric – an exposure of feminine levity and artificiality on one hand, patriarchal heavy-handedness in conjugal arrangements on the other – and at the same time more ideological in the way it mobilizes support for modes of discrimination and refinement that privilege female perception and foster what we would today call a feminized masculine ideal. For all its melodrama and lubricity, pathos and eros, *Love in Excess* is at its core an expression of bourgeois self-definition from a slyly feminist point of view, its stress upon elements of delicacy, sublimity, and "polite" sexual behavior a contribution to the new middle-class regulation of manners. One wonders how other novels by women will look when viewed through the lens of other cultural projects and debates – the growing appetite for commerce and empire, for example.

We can never know how much scandal, gossip, and salacious immediacy made its way into Haywood's amatory fictions, but it seems clear that stories that strike readers today as "timeless tales of seduction and betrayal" possessed for their earliest readers a racy topicality now lost to us.[36] That the portrayal of motherhood in *Rash Resolve* is tied at four corners, like Virginia Woolf's spider-web, to local Hillarian circumstances suggests the strong likelihood that Haywood's other amatory fictions were embedded in local, immediate, and topical contexts in ways that have gone unrecognized. A good case can be made for *The Injur'd Husband* as malicious reflection upon Savage and Fowke. It is intriguing to discover that the shape-shifting protagonist of *Fantomina*, one of the best known and most interesting of the early amatories, has a rough analogue in the character of Clarismonda/Mrs. Molly in *Memoirs of a Certain Island*, identified in the key to the second edition as Lady H. Is Lady H. – whoever she may be – the original of Fantomina?[37] Did Haywood's earliest readers look for "real-life" reflections such as these? If, as seems likely, readers expected gossip in "a Haywood," it seems at least possible that topicality was a feature of the amatory writing more generally. Suggestive in this connection are two lively and little studied novellas by Mary Hearne, *The Lover's Week* (1718) and its sequel *The Female Deserters* (1719), which include closely specified London settings and such "real-life" figures as the poet and physician Samuel Garth, and which appear to celebrate the new Hanoverian order.[38] The tales of sexual disappointment that recur in Jane Barker's *Galesia Trilogy* (1713–26) resonate with longing for the "lost King," the Jacobite Pretender "James III." Examples such as these suggest the benefit of expanding our range of inquiry when it comes to early novels by women and remind us that novels by women, like all novels, exist in a complicated relationship to a plurality of contexts.

A final implication is that we are still untold archive-hours away from the kind of basic intelligence that permits reliable assessments of the lives, projects, and purposes of many early women writers. We would do well, then, to exercise a "controlling sense of uncertainty" when we approach these writers.[39] Much has been written, for example, about the scandal of Haywood's "babes of love" – a scandal textual, sexual or both – but I have come to believe that our own need to see Haywood as an object of cultural vilification has imparted to Pope's innuendo a solidity it may not deserve. Perhaps we should take Haywood's first biographer more seriously when he says that, though Haywood had acquired something of a reputation as "a lady of gallantry," he had been unable to confirm "any particular intrigues or connexions directly laid to her charge."[40] Much has been written too about the role of economic necessity in Haywood's writing life – the two hungry children, babes of love or no, she was obliged to feed. Necessity is indeed a spur to invention but impecuniousness in itself is no guarantee of literary success. If it were, the *Monthly Catalogue* would have teemed with best-selling women writers, and there is only one Eliza Haywood. To understand Haywood's success and accomplishments in her own time, to take a fuller measure of the meaning of her early novels in her own culture, I have sought here to approach Haywood's early novels through the shared concerns and cultural aspirations of one specific and well-documented community of readers, in this case the literary circle that formed around Aaron Hill. Doubtless other reading communities remain to be explored, and so I will conclude by urging scholars with a facility for the archival spade to look for ways to excavate and reconstruct some of the other reading communities in which the novels of early women writers were conceived, shaped, read, and understood.

See also: chapter 9, THE EROTICS OF THE NOVEL; chapter 12, MOMENTARY FAME; chapter 13, WOMEN, OLD AGE, AND THE EIGHTEENTH-CENTURY NOVEL; chapter 16, AN EMERGING NEW CANON.

NOTES

In addition to the editors of this volume, I wish to thank Al Coppola, Christine Gerrard, and Paula McDowell for their invaluable comments on an earlier version of this essay.

1. Edmund Gosse, "What Ann Lang Read," in *Gossip in a Library* (London: Heinemann, 1891), 163–64, 165.
2. Christine Blouch, "'What Ann Lang Read': Eliza Haywood and Her Readers," ed., Kirsten T. Saxton and Rebecca P. Bocchicchio, *The Passionate Fictions of Eliza Haywood* (Lexington: University Press of Kentucky, 2000), 300–25.
3. John J. Richetti, *Popular Fiction Before Richardson: Narrative Patterns 1700–1739* (1969; repr. with new introduction, Oxford: Clarendon Press, 1992), 127, 182.
4. Ros Ballaster, *Seductive Forms: Women's Amatory Fiction from 1684–1740* (Oxford: Clarendon Press, 1992), 153–95.

5. William B. Warner, *Licensing Entertainment: The Elevation of Novel Reading in Britain, 1684–1750* (Berkeley and Los Angeles: University of California Press, 1998), 89. Further references are indicated in parentheses in the text.

6. See my *Jane Barker, Exile: A Literary Career 1675–1725* (Oxford: Clarendon Press, 2000), especially chapter 4.

7. Richetti, *Popular Fiction Before Richardson*, 179.

8. Brean S. Hammond, *Professional Imaginative Writing in England, 1670–1740: "Hackney for Bread"* (Oxford: Clarendon Press, 1997), 240.

9. Christine Gerrard, *Aaron Hill: The Muses' Projector, 1685–1750* (Oxford: Oxford University Press, 2003), 62. Further references are indicated in parentheses in the text. For more on the tangled relations among Hill, Haywood, Richard Savage, and Martha Fowke (Sansom), see chapters 3 and 4. I am grateful to Gerrard for sharing with me these chapters in manuscript.

10. Ros Ballaster, "A Gender of Opposition: Eliza Haywood's Scandal Fiction," in *The Passionate Fictions of Eliza Haywood*, ed. Kirsten T. Saxton and Rebecca P. Bocchicchio (Lexington: University Press of Kentucky, 2000), 146.

11. Aaron Hill and William Bond, *The Plain Dealer: Being Select Essays on Several Curious Subjects*, 2nd ed. (London, 1734), 1:3. Further references to this edition are indicated in parentheses in the text.

12. Eliza Haywood, *The Tea-Table* (1725) in Alexander Pettit, ed., *Selected Works of Eliza Haywood*, set 1, vol. 1 (London: Pickering and Chatto, 2000), 10.

13. Eliza Haywood, "To Hillarius, On his sending some verses, sign'd *M. S.*" in *Poems on Several Occasions, The Works of Mrs. Eliza Haywood, consisting of Novels, Letters, Poems, and Plays*. 4 vols. (London, 1724), 14.

14. "A Pastoral Dialogue, between *Alexis* and *Clorinda*; Occasioned by *Hillarius*'s intending a Voyage to *America*," in *The Tea-Table . . . Part the Second* (1726), in Alexander Pettit, ed., *Selected Works of Eliza Haywood*, set 1, vol. 1 (London: Pickering and Chatto, 2000), 41, 42.

15. Eliza Haywood, "The Vision," in *Poems on Several Occasions*, 13.

16. Eliza Haywood, "To Diana," in *Poems on Several Occasions*, 15, 16.

17. See Robert Inglesfield, "James Thomson, Aaron Hill and the Poetic 'Sublime'," *British Journal for Eighteenth-Century Studies* 13 (1990): 215–21, especially 215.

18. Eliza Haywood, *Love in Excess; or, the Fatal Enquiry*, ed. David Oakleaf (Peterborough, Ontario: Broadview Press, 1994), 134, 133. Further references are indicated in parentheses in the text, and abbreviated LE.

19. Ballaster, *Seductive Forms*, 156.

20. Catherine Ingrassia, *Authorship, Commerce, and Gender in Early Eighteenth-Century England: A Culture of Paper Credit* (Cambridge: Cambridge University Press, 1998), 82.

21. Warner, *Licensing Entertainment*, 123.

22. Al Coppola, "The Secret History of Eliza Haywood's *Works*: A Study of the Book Trade." I am grateful to Coppola for sharing this unpublished essay with me.

23. David E. Baker, *Companion to the Play House*, reprinted in Christine Blouch, ed., *The History of Miss Betsy Thoughtless* (Peterborough, Ontario: Broadview Press, 1998), 635.

24. Aaron Hill, *Plain Dealer*, no. 63, 26 Oct. 1724. The allusion was deleted from the collected editions.

25. By 1785, when Clara Reeve published *The Progress of Romance*. 2 vols. (London, 1785), 1:120–21, *Love in Excess* had become unmentionable and was assimilated to the scandal chronicles. For Reeve the rehabilitative works – *Betsy Thoughtless, Female Spectator*, and *Invisible Spy* – were all published late in her career, after her putative atonement for her errors.

26. The duality of Haywood's early reputation is noticed in somewhat different terms by David Brewer in "'Haywood,' Secret History, and the Politics of Attribution," ed. Kirsten T. Saxton and Rebecca P. Bocchicchio, *The Passionate Fictions of Eliza Haywood*, 217–39. Brewer places early references to Haywood in "two broadly defined camps," one admiring her as a chronicler of erotic love and the other condemning her as "the epitome of scandal-writing" (223).

27. Quoted in Marcia Heinemann, "Eliza Haywood's Career in the Theatre," *Notes and Queries* NS 20, 1 (1973): 13.

28. Thomas Whincop, *Scanderberg, or, Love and Liberty* (London, 1747), 246.

29. Richard Savage, "To Mrs. Eliza Haywood, on her Novel Call'd The Rash Resolve," in Eliza Haywood, *The Rash Resolve: or, the Untimely Discovery* (London, 1724), xi.

30. Ma. A., dedication to *The Prude: A Novel* (London, 1724), iii.

31. Eliza Haywood, *The Rash Resolve: or, the Untimely Discovery* (London, 1724), 96. Further references will be indicated in parentheses in the text.

32. Toni Bowers, *The Politics of Motherhood: British Writing and Culture, 1680–1760* (Cambridge: Cambridge University Press, 1996), 125, 128.

33. Richard Savage, "To Mrs. Eliza Haywood, on her Novel Call'd The Rash Resolve," reprinted in Clarence Tracy, *The Poetical Works of Richard Savage* (Cambridge: Cambridge University Press, 1962), 50–51.

34. Ma. A., dedication, *The Prude*, iii, iv. 'Ma. A' reports having read portions of a Haywood play in MS, presumably *A Wife to be Lett* (1723), and closes with a reference to the *"affable Politeness"* of Haywood's conversation. One of few comments on early Haywood by a woman, the dedication needs to be better known.

35. For *The Injur'd Husband* as veiled commentary on Savage and Fowke, see Gerrard, *Aaron Hill*, 91–92.

36. Brewer, "'Haywood'," in *The Passionate Fictions*, ed. Saxton and Bocchicchio, 222.

37. For Clarismonda, a celebrated court beauty who initiates a sexual liaison dressed as a maid, see Eliza Haywood, *Memoirs of a Certain Island Adjacent to the Kingdom of Utopia*, 2nd ed. (London, 1725), 49–55.

38. See my "The Novel before Novels (with a Glance at Mary Hearne's Fables of Desertion)," in Dennis Todd and Cynthia Wall, eds., *Eighteenth-Century Genre and Culture: Serious Reflections on Occasional Forms* (Newark: University of Delaware Press, 2001), 36–57.

39. The phrase comes from Blouch, "'What Ann Lang Read,'" in *The Passionate Fictions*, 311.

40. Baker, *Companion to the Play House*, reprinted in Blouch, *Betsy Thoughtless*, 636.

FURTHER READING

Blouch, Christine. "Eliza Haywood." In Alexander Pettit, ed., *Selected Works of Eliza Haywood*, set 1, vol. 1. London: Pickering and Chatto, 2000. xxi–lxxxii.

Fergus, Jan. "Women Readers: A Case Study." In Vivien Jones, ed., *Women and Literature in Britain 1700–1800*. Cambridge: Cambridge University Press, 2000. 155–76.

Gerrard, Christine. *Aaron Hill: The Muses' Projector, 1685–1750*. Oxford: Oxford University Press, 2003.

Guskin, Phyllis J., ed. *Clio: The Autobiography of Martha Fowke Sansom (1689–1736)*. Newark: University of Delaware Press and Associated University Presses, 1997.

Saxton, Kirsten R., and Rebecca P. Bocchicchio, eds. *The Passionate Fictions of Eliza Haywood*. Lexington: University of Kentucky Press, 2000.

Tracy, Clarence. *The Artificial Bastard: A Biography of Richard Savage*. Toronto: University of Toronto Press, 1953.

12
Momentary Fame: Female Novelists in Eighteenth-Century Book Reviews

Laura Runge

In the judgment passed on her performances, she will have to encounter the mortifying circumstance of having her sex always taken into account, and her highest exertions will probably be received with the qualified approbation, *that it is really extraordinary for a woman*. Men of learning … are apt to consider even the happier performances of the other sex as the spontaneous productions of a fruitful but shallow soil.

Hannah More, *Strictures on the Modern System of Female Education*
(1799; repr., New York: Garland, 1974), 2:12–13.

In the last half of the eighteenth century, women novelists enjoyed a unique status that they unfortunately lacked the foresight to appreciate. Like every other author whose books were sold to the public, female novelists saw their works reviewed by comprehensive review journals that strove for both objectivity and universal coverage. The comprehensive project obliged reviewers to criticize novels by women however their own literary tastes or gendered ideologies might operate; so despite cultural imperatives for gallant condescension to women or assumptions about the catas-trophic effects of novel reading, reviewers were bound to assess novels by women.

Significantly, the number of novels by women increased at the same time that book reviewing became widespread. Judith Phillips Stanton demonstrates a tremendous rise in the numbers of published female authors in the last decades of the eighteenth century. The rate at which women entered the literary marketplace "far outstripped the population growth rate. Their numbers increased at around 50 percent *every decade* starting in the 1760s."[1] Of the genres in which women published, novels number second only to poetry. James Raven further determines that while "Novelists com-prised men and women in roughly equal numbers," the relative proportions shift during the period 1770–99 so that it appears that the number of women novelists outstrips the male counterpart by the end of the 1780s.[2] During the same time, book reviewing in England develops into a thriving, competitive critical enterprise. Beginning in 1749 with bookseller Ralph Griffiths's *Monthly Review*, the regular practice of reviewing books was established by 1760, with a total of nine venues, many of them short-lived. The trade expanded greatly in the 1780s and 1790s with the publication of several substantial and enduring new review periodicals. By the end of the century, nearly a dozen major journals, four major magazines carrying reviews, several more specialized review sections in magazines and countless short-lived critical endeavors offered the eighteenth-century reading public summaries, extracts, and opinions on the new books published.[3] As a result of this confluence of publishing trends, we have multiple first-hand accounts of the reception and critical treatment of hundreds of early books by women. This would not be the case when the nineteenth-century Reviews adopted a highly selective format which virtually erased the presence of female novelists. By analyzing the treatment of female novelists in the book reviews of the late eighteenth century, this essay opens a window on an isolated moment in literary history when the female novelist could not be ignored.

Gendered bias has a long history in literary criticism, and much feminist criticism demonstrates the ways in which the literary tradition fails to take women authors seriously. Recently, studies blame eighteenth-century gender codes for the exclusion of women from a sense of literary professionalism that developed in concert with the proliferation of writing and print technologies, which included the developing book-review trade and the rising number of published female authors. According to Clifford Siskin and Linda Zionkowski, for instance, critical discourses emerged at this time that elevated middle-class masculine literary labor over female or aristocratic amateurism, so that a professional male author might both earn a living by his writing and achieve a certain level of respect, but aristocratic men and women of any class entering the publishing world frequently faced charges of dilettantism or frivolity. More importantly, these discursive developments shaped the direction of literary values in the nineteenth and twentieth centuries in ways that excluded female authors from literary honors.

In *The Fame Machine: Book Reviewing and Eighteenth-Century Literary Careers*, Frank Donoghue links the establishment of professional reputations directly to the publicity provided by the main review journals, the *Monthly* and *Critical Reviews*. Far from being an organ of discrimination, Griffiths's *Monthly* began as a neutral, descriptive, and comprehensive review. He aimed to provide an announcement for every work that issued from the press, and he separated the notices into a section devoted to lengthy articles for the most noteworthy publications and a catalogue wherein all the rest could be mentioned. When the *Critical Review* began in 1756, Tobias Smollett objected to the blatant hypocrisy of a bookseller's pose as a neutral reviewer, and he proposed his periodical as a public censor with greater probity. He, nonetheless, adopted many of the conventions instituted by Griffiths, and the two Reviews essentially differed only in tone, Smollet's being more irascible.[4] These main competitors established the practice that would be copied and adapted by all the leading

Reviews of the period. While the Reviews professed standards of descriptive neutrality, they nonetheless contributed to the success or failure of the books published. The fact that many eighteenth-century authors expressed fear and malice toward book reviewers suggests the power of these Reviews and the perception that they controlled an author's fate.[5]

According to Donoghue, however, female authors had different cause for complaint than male authors. Critics, he claims, wrote of the categorically inferior work of women with indulgent condescension: the "major Reviews simply evaluated women's writing by a different, less demanding standard, and they thereby deprived female authors of the same fame they purported to confer upon men."[6] Donoghue's observations coincide with Hannah More's comment above – that a woman faced the liability of "having her sex always taken into account" – and both point to a critical attitude supported by notions of gallantry that prevailed during this era. Gallantry was a pervasive phenomenon during the eighteenth century, incorporating social, sexual, and linguistic behaviors in public and private throughout a range of classes. Such widespread practice was connected to the spread of politeness during this century and the progressive or enlightened model of patriarchy whereby men protected and exerted authority over compliant, elegant, but clearly subordinate women. These codes of civility incorporated a discourse of inflated and often absurd compliments that the men and women who parleyed them generally understood as conventional forms of address rather than expressions of sincere affect. These linguistic conventions and the gendered hierarchy from which they derive entered into the language and conventions of book reviewing. A man – and reviewers were generally men – was expected to protect a woman from injury or insult, which included bad reviews, or he failed to be a gentleman.

Critics, however, deal with this polite imperative in different ways to accommodate a range of quality among female authors. They rarely dismiss significant novels with frothy compliments, nor do they pass out purely positive evaluation. As Samuel Badcock writes of Frances Burney: "The Author of Cecilia [*sic*] asks no undue lenity: she doth not plead any privilege of her sex" (*MR* 67 {1782}: 456). To praise a less considerable work, critics often resort to a secondary tier of literary values that is remarkably consistent with idealized femininity. These literary values include sentimentality, propriety, agreeability, and above all virtue. Many accomplished authors, such as Clara Reeve, Charlotte Smith, and Burney herself, are at times subject to this form of condescension, though they are treated with significant evaluation elsewhere, especially after their preliminary work passes through the Reviews. Contrast Badcock's seriousness above with the brief notice that Burney's first novel *Evelina* (1778) receives from the *Monthly*: it is "one of the most sprightly, entertaining, and agreeable productions of this kind." The characters "are agreeably diversified, are conceived and drawn with propriety, and supported with spirit" (*MR* 58 {78}: 316). Sarah Fielding's *The History of Ophelia* (1760) likewise receives a specifically feminine form of compensatory praise; her novel "preserves that delicacy peculiar to female writers; and we may venture to say it affords as much entertainment, and harmless recreation, as most productions of this kind" (*CR* 9 {60}: 318). The *Critical Review* many years later minimizes the flaws of Clara Reeve's *Two Mentors* (1783) because the "fair author" has "succeeded in her attempt" to represent virtue (55 {1783}: 333–34). The *European Magazine* deploys its gallantry more explicitly: "This work is the composition of a lady; and of works by the fair sex we industriously avoid to exhibit any defects." He expresses his hope for its success "to promote the happiest interests of virtue" (3 {1783}: 208). The reviews testify to a set of critical alternatives shaped by gender. Women, unlike men, are ostensibly entitled to gallant protection or critical leniency, and so, in keeping with the objectives of criticism, reviewers construct a matrix of feminine literary values that allows them to praise the woman in the work. The questions of character, plotting, style, or intellect can be avoided altogether if the gallant critic can at least compliment the female writer on achieving a representation of the respected categories of womanhood. Sadly, this critical strategy survives the shift to the new format of Reviews in the early nineteenth century. It is precisely the language that William Hazlitt uses to dismiss Burney as a novelist in 1815; the author, he complains, is "a very woman" (*Edinburgh Review* 24 February 1815: 336).

All of this suggests that female novelists universally face critical condescension and that they fail to earn the acclaim bestowed on their male counterparts. If this were true, it would help to explain why so few female novelists survive in the canon-formation of the nineteenth century, a phenomenon that Siskin aptly calls "The Great Forgetting."[7] Yet, it would be a mistake to view the history of criticism of women's writing as a seamless continuum of condescension. When we consult the mass of reviews of women's novels, we learn a slightly different version of history. While gallant rhetoric persists in the reviews, critics distinguish among female novelists as they do among male novelists. Reviewers lay aside the mask of gallantry for the best female novelists who consequently achieve a respectable level of fame. Certainly the pages of eighteenth-century book reviews address a reading audience with minute knowledge and sincere admiration for a wide range of female novelists. Moreover, questions of character, plotting, style, and intellect do not remain neglected in reviews of women's novels. Spurred on by an anti-novel discourse that repeatedly claimed the debilitating effects of novel-reading on youthful minds, reviewers carry on a serious inquiry into the nature of the novel, and they find that some female authors contribute significantly to the development of the genre.

If the much-reviewed female novelist from 1750 to 1800 failed to anticipate the change in critical fortunes of the nineteenth century, later critics have not benefited from hindsight to understand its implications. Critics from Ian Watt to Nancy Armstrong consider the last quarter of the eighteenth century a veritable wasteland of novels, and most historians of the novel contentedly pass over the field with barely a nod at Frances Burney. "The majority of eighteenth-century novels," writes Watt, "were actually written by women, but this had long remained a purely quantitative assertion of dominance."[8] More recently, Terry Castle excoriated the field of BJ (Before Jane {Austen}) novels by women as sublimely bad and worth reading only for their insights on the trauma of coming-to-birth for female authors.[9]

Given this history of scholarship, it seems odd that the novel itself makes significant progress during these years. Whereas Richardson and Fielding both claim to be
inventing something new in the 1740s, Jane Austen knows exactly what a novel is
when she writes *Northanger Abbey* (1818) at the end of the century. Significantly, the
coming of age of the novel is a process that critics generally, albeit vaguely, associate
with women. Watt postulates that "feminine sensibility [is] in some ways better
equipped to reveal the intricacies of personal relationships and [is] therefore at a real
advantage in the realm of the novel."[10] As Austen suggests in *Northanger Abbey*, the
process that helped the genre reach its ontological form involves numerous women
authors:

> "It is only Cecilia, or Camilla, or Belinda;" or, in short, only some work in which the
> greatest powers of the mind are displayed, in which the most thorough knowledge of
> human nature, the happiest delineation of its varieties, the liveliest effusions of wit and
> humour are conveyed to the world in the best chosen language.[11]

Even allowing for hyperbole, Austen's tribute to Burney and Maria Edgeworth, whose
novels do not appear until 1800, marks women as the most significant contributors to
the genre.

Less recognized are the critical reviews that dialogically inform the creative process
and educate readerly tastes. Reviewers take seriously their didactic role and include
guidance and advice to writers and readers, perhaps, as Raven suggests, because so
many of the reviewers are clergymen.[12] As scholars such as Robert D. Mayo, J. M. S.
Tompkins, and Derek Roper have argued, book reviewers during these formative years
begin to take the novel seriously as an instrument of literary creativity and moral
instruction.[13] Far from puff-pieces and simple plot summaries, reviews frequently
revolve around formal assessment and generic questions. Certainly, the technology of
book reviewing is one of the remarkable developments of the period 1749–99, and
much evidence suggests that these journals set the standards of taste for the public's
broadening reading opportunities. Moreover, the Reviews are lucrative commercial
enterprises with enduring value.[14] According to Roper, "Numbers of the *Monthly* and
Critical were not meant to be read for entertainment and thrown away. They were
conceived as instalments of a continuous encyclopaedia, recording the advance of
knowledge in every field of human enterprise."[15]

As a fairly complete and ostensibly neutral record of the immensely expanding print
world, eighteenth-century book reviews offer an unparalleled compendium of data for
research on the professional and public representations of female authors. Because the
dictates of the reviews require the coverage of works by women regardless of the
attitudes of the reviewers, a requirement that would change after 1802, these reviews
offer a unique perspective on how women fit into a culture learning how to read and to
write novels. Though rarely consulted in a concerted way, the book reviews of novels by
women provide significant evidence for the contributions of female novelists and
convincingly challenge generalizations on women's amateurism and inferiority.

The Reviews, Novels, and Authors

Reviews of novels by women constitute a vast terrain not adequately mapped by previous scholarship. While studies by Roper and James Basker contribute significantly to our understanding of the origins and strengths and weaknesses of the distinct eighteenth-century form of the review, neither directly addresses the relationship between the Reviews and the phenomenon of the female novelist. This type of analysis has been considerably aided by recently published bibliographic tools by James Raven and Antonia Forster, who collectively provide detailed information about every novel published and the reviews that cover them from 1770 to 1829. In addition to reference material for reviews, their studies provide for the first time reliable, decade-by-decade statistics on titles, genres, individual authors, publishers, and reprints. This information corrects some of the misinformation floating about in criticism of novels from the period. For example, they show that from 1770 to 1799, the number of new novels by identified male authors (419) is *slightly greater* than those by identified female authors (407); however, the number of identified male novelists (292 or fifty-eight percent) is *significantly higher* than the number of identified female novelists (189 or thirty-seven percent). While this challenges claims, such as Watt's, that female authors are primarily responsible for novel production in the period between Smollett and Austen, these figures reveal an important fact in the development of the novel: "In total, individual women writers were more prolific than their more numerous male counterparts."[16] Whereas male novelists tend to write a single novel, female novelists frequently write more than one.

Because women are more likely to write more than one novel, they are more likely to receive serious critical treatment in the Reviews. The dictate of universal coverage for major Reviews means that all novels, regardless of the author, are to be read and at least mentioned. In the crush of new releases, reviewers sometimes overlook the merits of a first novel – *Evelina* offers a good example. Second and subsequent novels benefit from the established reputation of the author and garner more significant reviews. Furthermore, reviews of successive novels by novelists like Burney, Smith, and Radcliffe, provide generous amounts of information on the critical understanding of the genre. These multiple examples from the same pen prompt discussion about what a novel is, and more often than not a reviewer of these works prefaces his or her comments with a general statement on the nature of the novel. Although the critics differ as to what makes a novel – reviews of Charlotte Smith's *Desmond* (1792) provide an interesting test case for this – the collective sense suggests an increased awareness of the novel form in the general population of readers, a consensus that does not exist when the reviews begin in 1749. In this way, the more prolific female author advances the state of the art in novel-writing.

This article draws on some 325 reviews of eighty novels by more than twenty female novelists from the years 1749 to 1800. While the *Monthly Review* and the *Critical Review*, being the earliest, supply the greatest number of reviews, the scope of this analysis includes the other major reviews of the 1780s and 1790s (*English Review, Analytical Review, British Critic, Anti-Jacobin Review*), the magazines of a general nature that provided reviews (*Gentleman's, London, Town and Country*, and *European* magazines) and various specialized or short-lived periodicals (*New General Magazine, Monthly Mirror, Monthly Visitor, New Review, New Annual Register*). In total, the reviews derive from twenty different journal titles.

Like the Reviews, the included novelists range in fame and excellence of achievement. Those mainly considered are Frances Burney, Frances Brooke, Sarah Fielding, Eliza Haywood, Elizabeth Inchbald, Charlotte Lennox, Ann Radcliffe, Clara Reeve, Mary Robinson, Sarah Scott, Frances Sheridan, Charlotte Smith, and Mary Wollstonecraft. For contrast, reviews of work by Georgiana Cavendish, Amelia Opie, Annabella and Anne Plumptre, Mary Ann Radcliffe, Maria Elizabeth Robinson, and a few others are considered. For heuristic purposes, I construe the first list as the best female novelists of the period. This grouping intentionally draws attention to the need for specificity among the novelists of the last half of the eighteenth century and the desire – even tentatively – to apply labels of qualitative value to their work. I employ a double lens to determine the group, an historical lens focused on the period in which they first appeared, and the inevitable lens of my own historical context. The "best" or "most respected" signifies, in one measure of worth, those novelists whose works are considered significant enough to go through multiple printings during a period when the vast majority of novels have short press runs and a transient existence. From Raven and Forster we learn that among the sixty-four novels by identified novelists that go through five or more editions between 1770 and 1829, thirty (or nearly half) are written by female authors. This includes the first three of Burney's novels, Inchbald's two novels, five novels of Radcliffe's, Reeve's *Champion of Virtue* (1777), or *The Old English Baron*, Robinson's *Vancenza* (1792), two novels by Smith, and Wollstonecraft's *Original Stories* (1788).[17] While popularity is not a perfect index to literary quality, as a mark of enduring readability the figures suggest that these women produced works of substance. The group's elite status is underscored by its presence in the more liberal of the canon-making novelist series produced in the early nineteenth century. With the exception of Scott, Wollstonecraft, and Robinson, Anna Barbauld recognizes each of these authors either in her critical introduction to her *British Novelists* (1810) series or in the edited volumes proper.[18] Finally, all of the first-string authors enjoy classroom editions and scholarly discussion today.

This essay consequently draws on the majority of reviews for all of the novels by the most respected female novelists of the latter half of the eighteenth century, as well as those of a handful of less significant writers. Such a sample offers the most essential critical writing on these female novelists as a group, providing an accurate sense of their status in their own time as well as important information on their contributions to the genre.

Not all book reviews are equal in this study. Most of the reviews are no more than a paragraph; some are a single sentence or phrase. Of the substantially longer articles, the bulk generally consists of extracts or summaries from the novels themselves. This style characterizes the state of the art in book reviewing at that time. When Griffiths began the *Monthly*, he intended his enterprise to be an objective, descriptive account of the works issuing from the press. Over the course of five decades, various journals proposed varying opinions on the question of objectivity, and many reviewers took the opportunity to criticize and offer advice to the author in their reviews, but a stance of neutrality and description remained the status quo for Reviews until the arrival of the *Edinburgh* in 1802 and the *Quarterly* in 1809.

In tandem with purported objectivity, a mandate for universal coverage makes the eighteenth-century Review unique in an important way. While this requirement prompts critics to tedious complaints about the quantity of trash they must read, it conveniently provides for equitable coverage of female authors. In a very practical way the regular treatment of women authors in the eighteenth-century critical reviews gives women a public presence and offers a sanctioned iteration of female authorship that fosters the image of female professionalism. When historians of the novel overlook book reviews, they also overlook this fact of female visibility, a reality that late eighteenth-century readers would not or could not ignore.

Given the infant state of reviewing during the 1750s, the book reviews for Haywood's later works and the early novels of Lennox, Fielding, and Scott are slight by comparison with the review material from the 1780s and 1790s. After 1775 the world of critical reviews expanded enormously, with the addition of several substantial and long-lasting reviews.[19] Spurred on by multiple ideological debates, the 1790s witnessed an even greater proliferation of venues for book reviews, including the government-funded journal, the *British Critic*, and the adamantly conservative *Anti-Jacobin*. Whereas Lennox's *The Female Quixote* (1752) was reviewed in the *Monthly* and the *Gentleman's Magazine*, Burney's *Cecilia* (1782) was reviewed in seven additional periodicals, and Radcliffe's *The Italian* (1797) in a total of ten publications. As a result, the majority of the material for this study dates from the 1780s and 1790s.

Gallantry in the Reviews

One of the misconceptions contemporary critics – along with eighteenth-century readers – labor under concerns the idea that female authors receive preferential treatment from reviewers.[20] Certainly the impression is widespread. Raven reports a curious turn of gendered expectation, in which anonymous novels written by men adopt the tag "written by a lady" in order to avoid public humiliation at the critical tribunal. Critics, however, key into this deception and thwart its intended effect:

> We are not without suspicion that in anonymous publications, the words *written by a lady* are sometimes made use of to preclude the severity of criticism; but as Reviewers are generally churls and greybeards, this piece of *finesse* very seldom answers the purpose intended.[21]

This critic's supposition – that reviewers are churls and greybeards – coincides with the generality of the reviews of female novelists considered here and highlights one of the main findings to be developed in this chapter: While the conventions of gallantry certainly pervade the critical discussion, critics frequently refer to the practice of indulging the female author only to dismiss it out of hand. Critical gallantry by no means guaranteed female novelists protection from evaluation or censure. Rather than being treated with gallant condescension in the book reviews, the most respected female authors often receive judicious criticism and thoughtful advice.

It cannot be denied that the tone and rhetoric of gallantry pervade discussion of the novel from the time of its inception in England and France.[22] Book reviews evidence the residual effects of this convention in various ways. First of all, the earlier reviews of the 1750s and 1760s tend to invoke the codes of gallantry more than do the reviews of later decades. Thus the *Monthly* reviewers assert that Sarah Fielding, in her conclusion to *David Simple* (1753), will please her readers because she, "no less than her own *David*, would on all occasions chuse to pursue the unaffected simplicity she has a desire to recommend" (8 {1753}: 143). Similarly, the sex of the author promotes a gentle expression from the *Monthly* in their review of the anonymous *The Cry* (1754): "We write this with the more pleasure, as we believe we are doing justice to the production of a lady" (10 {1754}: 282). (The work is, in fact, jointly written by Sarah Fielding and Jane Collier.) Yet, a review of Lennox's *Harriet Stuart* (1751) raises the question of gallant expectations in a more complicated way:

> We are persuaded that this is really the produce of a female pen; and therefore some may think it intitled to our more favourable regard. However, without a compliment to the author, we may safely venture to pronounce her work to be the best in the novel way that has been lately published.

This pose, however, does not prevent the critic from closing his brief notice with the comment that "here are no striking characters, no interesting events, nor in short any thing that will strongly fix the attention, or greatly improve the morals of the reader" (*MR* 4 {1750–1}: 160). In the more extensive review article of Sheridan's *The Memoirs of Miss Sidney Bidulph* (1761), the reviewer retracts his criticism explicitly because the author is female:

> We had prepared a few slight criticisms on this performance; but being assured that it is the work of a Lady, we shall only add, that, in our opinion, it is, upon the whole, greatly superior to most of the productions of her *brother* Novelists. (*MR* 24 {1761}: 266)

Like others, this critic draws attention to the expectation for leniency, thereby highlighting the absence of proper criticism. These early examples – all coming before the growth in periodical reviews during the 1780s – suggest that gallant indulgence of the female author stands as a familiar option, but they also indicate the fact that such gallantry clearly interferes with the goals of the critic.

While gallant compliment arises from various motives, its presence never precludes negative, dismissive criticism of the same work or author. In fact, genuine gallantry runs in the face of the general trend of book reviewing. James Raven explains that "many reviews were extremely unfavourable, to the extent that reviewing a novel became something of a sport. Critics often seemed to compete for the most insulting or sarcastic dismissal."[23] The reviews of women novelists supply ample proof. *Town and Country* summarizes the whole of the anonymous *The Woman of Quality* (1786) as "one of the fluttering productions of the day, that neither afford instruction or entertainment" (18 {86}: 13), while Opie's *Dangers of Coquetry* (1790) is encapsulated in the solitary phrase, "Dull, insipid, and improbable!" (22 {1790}: 460). Haywood's name alone seems sufficient to inspire a reviewer's contempt in the posthumous 1768 review of *Clementina*: "This is a republication of a dull, profligate, Haywoodian production, in which all the males are rogues, and all the females whores, without a glimpse of plot, fable, or sentiment" (*CR* 25 {68}: 59). Haywood receives more considerable, though equally negative, evaluation of the earlier *The History of Miss Betsy Thoughtless* (1751):

> The *Insipid* chiefly marks the character of this work; tho' it is generally looked upon as the production of a female pen, which, for a long series of years, has been employ'd (often successfully) in the novel way. (*MR* 5 {51}: 394)

The *Critical Review*'s treatment of Maria Elizabeth Robinson's *Shrine of Bertha* (1794) assumes a higher tone:

> Other literary productions are valuable in different degrees, according to the proportion of truth or of utility which they contain; but *Novels*, as their sole purpose is entertainment, must either be the most amusing, or the most insipid of publications. We cannot say that the two volumes before us belong to the *former* class. (11 {94}: 468)

The exasperated reviewer of the anonymous *Georgina Harcourt* (1791) exclaims: "A trifling insignificant, improbable story. Will the labour of reviewing novels be never again compensated by a little rational entertainment?" (*CR* 2 {91}: 477). The churlishness on display suggests the seriousness with which the reviewers took up their task and the force of literary values exerting themselves despite ingrained codes of gallantry.

Both extremes of unctuous praise or venomous abuse fail the standards of objectivity the Reviews seek to maintain, and neither characterizes the reviews as a whole. By the late 1780s, reviewers declare themselves less willing to adopt the posture of the gallant altogether. In fact one reviewer identifies the change in treatment of female authors as a revolution in critical standards, thus tying it to greater political and social currents of the time:

> Among our ancestors it appears to have been thought a piece of gallantry to admire every thing that was the literary production of a lady.... At present, the case is altered; the fair sex has asserted its rank, and challenged that natural equality of intellect which

nothing but the influence of human institutions could have concealed for a moment. One of the good effects of this revolution is, that Criticism becomes once more the office of Reason, and Gallantry surrenders the sceptre to Justice and Truth. (*GM* 61 {91}: 255)

While the critic's enthusiasm for the equality of male and female writers – like so many early revolutionary endorsements – proves shortsighted, it nonetheless hails a significant change in the tone and content of book reviews for female authors, from gallantry to "Justice and Truth." Intriguingly, this change in criticism may also relate to the statistical increase in female-authored novels. Raven's data indicates a sharp upturn in the publication of new novels for the years 1788 to 1791, at the same time that named female authors and novels "by a lady . . . " are being published in greater numbers than ever before.[24] He argues that there seems to be a turning point in the relative presence of male and female novelists, when women appear to dominate the field. We can understand the shift away from critical gallantry as part of the recognized professionalism of the female novelist. Incidentally, Donoghue's study of fame excludes these final years of the century; contrary to his finding for the earlier period, the book reviews of this latter period as a whole convey respect for and establish the critical reputations of the best female novelists.

The Nature of a Novel

Concomitant with the revolution from gallantry to "Justice and Truth," critics at this time use reviews to articulate their own theories of the novel, launching a widespread defense of the novel into a culture versed in the hazards of novel-reading.[25] Regardless of the tenor of the criticism, it becomes conventional to open a lengthy review with a précis on the state of the modern novel. These epitomes frequently announce that the novel is, contrary to current anti-novel prejudice, a complex artistic enterprise: "Novel-writing having for its object a delineation of the manners and characters of men, is, necessarily, a difficult task" (*MR* 79 {88}: 241), a critic of Smith's *Emmeline* (1788) writes. A reviewer of *The Old Manor House* (1793) adds: "Among the various productions of literary genius, there is, perhaps, none that has a more legitimate claim to an ascendancy over the human mind than a well-written novel" (*CR* 8 {93}: 44). While claims for the novel range from imaginative genius to a moral hold over humanity, the reviews offer more than generic boosterism; they voice an increasing awareness of and interest in the novel's form and purpose.

While these discussions rarely introduce stunning innovation in novel theory, the regularity and detail of the arguments indicate a shared understanding of the features of the novel and a progressively more fixed set of standards by which the critics judge a novel's merits: unified, probable, and engaging plot; characters at once original and recognizable; natural and correct language; and a moral of truth and instruction. For example, the reviewer of Smith's *Old Manor House*, just quoted, articulates a broad agenda for the modern novel:

> To conduct a series of familiar events so as to rouse and preserve attention, without a violation of nature and probability; to draw and support the different characters necessary for an animated and varied drama in just and glowing colours; to hold up the mirror of truth in the moment of youthful intemperance, and to interweave amidst the web of fable, pictures to instruct, and morals to reform. (*CR* 8 {93}: 45)

While not straying far from the artistic and moral criteria Johnson set forth in *Rambler* 4, these critics hold modern novelists to a greater measure of realistic portrayal, narrative unity, and entertainment value. It is not surprising, therefore, that this particular critic limits the number of successful novelists to Cervantes, Le Sage, Rousseau, and Voltaire.

In these position statements, critics regularly distinguish the "immense lumber of trash that is hourly published" from what one critic calls the "genuine novel" (*GM* 61 {91}: 255; *MR* 22 {97}: 283). The bifurcation opens a discussion of the criteria and puts into play a variety of ideas as to what constitutes a good novel. Such theorizing sometimes clears the way for the female author in question to join the ranks of deserving novelists, as in the case of the *Monthly Review*'s treatment of Smith's *Celestina* (1791):

> The modern Novel, well executed, possessing the essential characters of poetry . . . certainly deserves a place among the works of genius. . . . Such distinction we judge to be due to the author of the novel now before us. (6 {91}: 287)

On the other hand, a critic might set the bar impossibly high so as to provide the rationale for a negative review, as in the case of the *Critical Review* of the *Old Manor House*. "Pre-eminence as a novelist" requires "superior qualifications, both mental and acquired. . . . such strength of genius, such stores of wit, humour, and original fancy; such nice discrimination of character, and such intimate and universal knowledge of the world" (8 {93}: 45). These forays into novel theory make diverse claims and adopt assorted values in an implicit recognition of the novel's popular form; in this historical window prior to the nineteenth-century elevation of the novel, criticism recognizes the multiple audiences and purposes for such fiction. For example, the reviewer of Smith's *Old Manor House* from the *Analytical Review* identifies three types of novel readers: those interested in the exciting plot, those interested in sentimental affect, and finally those who "value a fictitious tale in proportion as it exhibits a true picture of men and manners" (16 {93}: 60). Interestingly, this critic places Smith among novelists for the most exacting audience. Whether or not the reviewer includes the female novelist in the highest tier of the constructed hierarchy, these book reviews generate a critical discourse predicated on the novel's legitimacy as an art form.

As the examples above suggest, female novelists like Charlotte Smith play crucial roles as exemplars. Smith's multiple novels receive abundant critical attention, often inspiring debate about the nature of the novel. Reviews for her political novel *Desmond*, for instance, generate divergent opinions. The most generous, coming from the *Monthly Review*, uses *Desmond* as an example of the novel's improved capacity for educating women:

> Among the various proofs which the present age affords, that the female character is advancing in cultivation, and rising in dignity, may be justly reckoned the improvements that are making in the kind of writing which is more immediately adapted to the amusement of female readers. Novels, which were formerly little more than simple tales of love, are gradually taking a higher and more masculine tone, and are becoming the vehicles of useful instruction. (*MR* 9 {92}: 406)

All of the many extracts included in this lengthy review are taken from political sections of the novel and are duly appreciated. With slightly less admiration, the *European Magazine* also lauds the combination of novel skills and political subjects:

> The narrative, which is conveyed in the form of letters, is agreeably enlivened by discussions on the new face of affairs in France. It is not to be expected that much information is to be found here, but our Authoress has certainly vindicated the cause of French liberty with much acuteness. She has thought proper, however, to apologize for the introduction of political matter in a work professedly of another kind. To those who think an apology necessary, this will be sufficient. She is likewise supported by precedents by those of Fielding and Smollett, both of whom introduce more than *allusions* to the political state of their country. (*Euro Mag* 22 {92}: 22)

While the radical-leaning *Analytical Review* unsurprisingly celebrates Smith's pro-revolutionary stance – "the cause of freedom is defended with warmth, whilst shrewd satire and acute observations back the imbodied [*sic*] arguments" (*AR* 13 {92}: 428) – the *Critical* reviewer sagely, if conservatively, observes that the representation of affairs in France "will be differently judged of according to the taste, more properly according to the political opinions of the readers. . . . Her politics we cannot always approve of" (*CR* 6 {92}: 100). Even the least sympathetic review, however, recognizes Smith's success in the art of the novel: her skill in description, characterization, and plot receive universal praise. Her innovation in introducing a political subtext through the letters between Desmond and Bethel challenges the reviewers to assess the genre itself. Regarding the critic's political differences with the author, the *Critical Review* writes: "History may confirm her sentiments, and confute ours. The principal subject of enquiry is how far they ought to be introduced into a work of this kind" (100). Ultimately the pedagogical function of the novel prevails over aesthetic or political concerns, and this reviewer, like that of the *Monthly*, supports any opportunity for the female audience to learn about worldly affairs. Smith's experiment in novelistic content breaks new critical ground, as reviewers variously respond to the gendered and political implications of her fictional portrayal of radical causes. Her already established reputation as a novelist of merit secures the critical attention in the first place and perhaps predisposes even the politically hostile reader in her favor.

Other writers, such as Inchbald and Radcliffe, offer examples for models of novel form and style. Inchbald's *A Simple Story* (1791) is widely recognized as original in design, and for the critic of the *European Magazine* it represents an ideal of plot management:

> Uninterrupted by digressions of every kind, the tale never stops, either to hunt after ornament, or to narrate impertinent episodes, unconnected with the plan, and only of use to swell the volume, and enrage the reader. The scene is continually occupied by those of the *dramatis personae* for whom alone we are interested: they are never absent from our eyes, or thoughts; and in this respect, a more perfect whole was, perhaps, never exhibited. (19 {91}: 197)

Like many critics, this one bases his (or her) judgment on the experience of reading many, many novels. The critic underscores Inchbald's singularity with a hint of irritation toward the common flaws of other novels: digressions used to "swell the volume, and enrage the reader." Inchbald creates characters about whom the reader cares, and their continued presence creates the admired unity despite a radical narrative break of seventeen years between volumes II and III. Her originality garners praise, but her success in characterization, a notoriously difficult accomplishment, enables her to experiment with form.

Because of its difficulty, William Enfield identifies characterization as the central feature of "the higher novel." The achievement of balanced character development, for Enfield, distinguishes the best novels:

> The most excellent, but at the same time the most difficult, species of novel-writing consists in an accurate and interesting representation of such manners and characters as society presents; not, indeed, every-day characters, for the interest excited by *them* would be feeble; yet so far they ought to be common characters, as to enable the reader to judge whether the copy be a free, faithful, and even improved sketch from Nature. (*MR* 22 {97}: 282)

Significantly, he includes Frances Burney's *Cecilia*, with Richardson's *Clarissa* (1748) and Fielding's *Tom Jones* (1749), as examples of such sketches from nature. In this considered review of Radcliffe's *The Italian*, which Roper justly calls "excellent," Enfield establishes a hierarchy of novels based on the reader's continued pleasure in the text. In contrast to the success of Burney, Richardson, and Fielding, romances, which occupy a lower order of novel, "rivet the attention" through "high description, extravagant characters, and extraordinary and scarcely possible occurrences" (282). These novels cease to interest the reader after they "can no longer awaken our curiosity; while the other, like truth, may be reconsidered and studied with increased satisfaction" (283). In anticipation of Coleridge's criteria for good literature – "that to which we *return*, with the greatest pleasure" – Enfield distinguishes between the success of Burney and that of Radcliffe.[26] The productions of female novelists prompt inquiry into what comprises the art of the novel, and the reviews recognize artists like Smith, Inchbald, Burney, and Radcliffe in their own way, for their contributions to the genre.

Advice to Aspiring Female Novelists

Although reviewers clearly consider themselves put upon by the mass of poor fiction they are required to read, many also see themselves in the role of instructor, guiding the new novelist in practical requirements for success in his or her craft. The bits of advice interspersed throughout the reviews indicate both an accepted set of standards for the novel and a dialogic function for reviews – reviewers believe they have an impact on the evolution of an artist. Female writers attract such advice, perhaps, because of the avuncular stance of the critic – graybeards rather than churls – and because they are likely to produce more than one novel. This is explicitly the case for Anne Plumptre's 1796 novel, *Antoinette*:

> On the whole, this novel has considerable merit; and we think the writer might display her powers of description a little more freely.
>   The latter hint we drop, because we understand this is the production of a lady, who is likely to favour the world with another novel shortly...(*CR* 16 {96}: 221)

Much advice, as opposed to straightforward criticism, looks forward to forthcoming work by the same author. Thus the *Critical Review* foresees future editions of Inchbald's *A Simple Story*, in which the author ought to correct the flawed ending and the occasional grammatical solecism. A critic of *A Sicilian Romance* (1791) suggests that if Radcliffe "again engages in this task," she should avoid the introduction of "so many caverns with such peculiar concealments, or so many spring-locks which open only on one side" (*CR* 1 {91}: 350). Mary Robinson's "first prose essay," *Vancenza*, prompts the advice: "She will do well to study simplicity of expression, the sweetest charm of writing, and the truest characteristic of excellence" (*GM* 62 {92}: 553). And the respectful critic of *Desmond* ventures to wish that Smith "would devote some portion of her studious hours to the muse of comedy, whose gaiety she has frequently caught with success" (*ER* 20 {92}: 176).

The latter writers – Inchbald, Radcliffe, Robinson, and Smith – either are at this time or soon become established authors whom the critics clearly want to influence. Their advice reflects a practical understanding of the novel: proper denouement, judicious use of conventions, style appropriate for prose instead of poetry. The critics treat the writers as professionals who may benefit from the insight they have gained after reading and evaluating scores of novels, and their words may have had an effect. Inchbald's second (and third) editions of *A Simple Story* include numerous revisions to grammar, punctuation, and expression.[27] Radcliffe perfects the art of suspense in her later Gothic novels, and comes to be recognized by reviewers as the pre-eminent writer of that form of romance, and as *Walsingham* (1797) indicates,

Robinson limits the effusions of poetry and incorporates a more sensible prose style in her later novels.

As the request for more comedy from Smith suggests, the recommendations of critics also indicate their particular understanding of the role of novels: presumably as "faithful mirrors of modern life" Smith's narratives ought to be balanced between comic and tragic elements (*ER* 20 {92}: 176). The *Critical* reviewer of *Evelina* reveals a distaste for novels of high life because of the influence these portrayals have over the minds of middle-class readers: "We could wish [Evelina's] husband had not been a lord, and that her father had been less rich" (46 {78}: 203). The reviewer – using the customary first-person plural – worries that the uniform representation of high life in novels will leave readers dissatisfied with their more humble fortunes: "we wish, to see one novel in which there is no lord" (204). Intriguingly, Burney's next two novels follow this advice; Cecilia loses all her fortune when she marries into a distinguished but pointedly untitled family, and Camilla ultimately marries the local gentry heir.

Perhaps because the Gothic novel challenges so many of the "genuine" novel's standards, Ann Radcliffe receives a disproportionate amount of advice in her reviews. Apart from complaints about the tedium and improbability of suspense drawn out to four volumes, or the hope that she will avoid monosyllabic poetry in future volumes, Radcliffe's reputation and popular success garner her serious attention from the critics. Like Enfield's article on *The Italian* mentioned above, the *Critical Review's* treatment of the *The Mysteries of Udolpho* (1794) offers balanced and considered criticism. It opens with praise for Radcliffe's acknowledged expertise in evoking horror, terror, and suspense, but the critic warns against excessive sensationalism: "The trite and the extravagant are the Scylla and Charybdis of writers who deal in fiction" (11 {94}: 362). After making thoughtful comments on anachronisms in manners and lack of unity in a drawn-out plot, the critic offers, as is customary, long extracts to demonstrate the beauty of Radcliffe's writing. He concludes with an unprecedented challenge to the respected author:

> If, in consequence of the criticisms impartiality has obliged us to make upon this novel, the author should feel disposed to ask us, Who will write a better? we [*sic*] boldly answer her, *Yourself*; when no longer disposed to sacrifice excellence to quantity, and lengthen out a story for the sake of filling an additional volume. (372)

Radcliffe's next novel, *The Italian*, is considerably shorter than *Udolpho*, and it is justly praised for its greater "unity and simplicity" (*MR* 22 {97}: 283). While these reviews merit attention because they construct a dialogue between reviewer and author that indicates the significance of eighteenth-century literary reviews, these dialogic relationships underscore a more salient point for feminist criticism: literary critics recognize female novelists as creative authorities in the realm of fiction, and they treat them, for a moment in time, with critical rigor and professionalism.

Burney as the Model Female Novelist

In the process of analyzing the features and functions of the novel, providing advice to aspiring writers, and assessing the myriad novels issuing from the press, critics tend to rely on some failsafe examples from the past, constructing a de facto canon. Raven notes that Richardson is by far the most cited authority in reviews of novels, though Sterne has a presence, and Smollett and Fielding less. Among the women, Burney stands out as the one most cited and held up for imitation. Moreover, Burney's followers turn up in surprising numbers in Raven and Forster's bibliography: Raven writes in his introduction, "A still more remarkable feature of the following listings is the rediscovery of a flock of imitators of Frances Burney." He numbers at least eight novels from 1780 to 1792 – beyond what is included in this study – that are recognized as belonging to the Burney school of fiction.[28]

In reviews, critics frequently point to Burney's characters as exemplars for other writers, with differing implications. For example, in *Hermione* (1791) Lennox too closely follows Burney's lead: "we trace our author too often in the tracks of miss Burney's Evelina" (*CR* 2 {91}: 233);[29] whereas Radcliffe's Ellena and Vivaldi fail to live up to Burney's standard: "Compared with Mrs. D'Arblay's Deville and Cecilia they sink into insignificance" (*AJR* 7 {1800}: 29). Critics often yoke Smith to Burney in comparing their characters and plots. Smith's Sir Edward Nevenden from *Ethelinde* (1789) is called "a copy, *in the outline*, of Mr. Monckton" from *Cecilia* (*MR* 2 {90}:164); her Cathcart from *Celestina* is like Macartney from *Evelina* (*CR* 3 {91}: 320). Wollstonecraft in the *Analytical Review* somewhat curiously sees the happy ending of *Emmeline* modeled after *Cecilia* (1 {88}: 333). According to the *Critical Review*, Smith's Delmont, from *The Young Philosopher* (1798), commits the crime of beggaring himself for an unworthy brother, behavior he compares with that of Cecilia and Camilla, only excepting that such "conduct which accords with the timidity of their sex, is ridiculous in a man accustomed to think justly, and to act with manly decision" (24 {98}: 82).

Reviews of *Celestina* create a sense of competitive sisterhood between Smith and Burney, recognizing their achievements above and beyond other female novelists. The *Critical Review* puts Smith very "near" the first in rank of "the modern school of novel-writers":

> Perhaps, with miss Burney she may be allowed to hold 'a divided sway;' and, though on some occasions below her sister-queen, yet, from the greater number of her works, she seems to possess a more luxuriant imagination, and a more fertile invention. (3 {91}: 318)

Oddly, in a review of Smith's work, the reviewer addresses Burney directly:

> Let not miss Burney be angry at this remark; or, if she is, we will bear with pleasure the whole weight of her indignation, if it arouses her sleeping genius, and urges her to show that, in these respects also, she can excel. (318)

Like the earlier cited advice to writers, the critic aims to affect the development of fiction by spurring Burney on to more creative work. His address assumes that Burney reads the reviews of her fellow novelist, just as it assumes that Smith has read and appreciated Burney's novels. Such assumptions reveal a common understanding of the fame of both authors and a culture well read in the novels by women.

A critic from the *English Review* constructs a similar sorority, though he uncharacteristically includes Sophia Lee:

> A Gothic ignorance, similar to that which followed the subversion of the Roman empire must again occur, before the works of Miss Burney, Miss Lee, etc. will cease to be read and admired. Walking in the same path, the author of the present novel [*Celestina*] must be permitted with them to share the bays. (18 {91}: 259)

More overtly than the *Critical* reviewer, this critic establishes a coterie of female novelists who reign by virtue of their ability to join what he calls "l'utile et l'agréable" after the manner of Fielding and Smollett. These examples illustrate the ways in which Reviews grant female novelists fame. Even in reviews of works by other authors, the reiteration of certain names, Smith, Radcliffe, Lennox, or Lee, generally in connection with Burney, creates a category of authors who distinguish themselves from the teeming productions of the press.

Because of Burney's recognized authority, reviewers enlist her name or works in their individual campaigns to reform novel-writing. One reviewer, whose diatribe against the late fashion in reading resounds with commonplaces from the anti-novel discourse, singles out *Cecilia* as potential evidence of a positive change in taste:

> That dreadful deluge of novel-writing, which threatened some years ago to overwhelm the public with the grossest ribaldry and nonsense, has of late happily abated. Such at that time, indeed, was the general avidity for this deplorable species of reading, that little or no success attended any other mode of literary adventure. We very sincerely deprecate the relapse of a disease so fatal, so contagious, and so virulent, among those who attach themselves to books. May the celebrity of Cecilia have no such consequence. (*ER* 1 {83}: 419)

The work he considers here, Reeve's *Two Mentors* (1783), fails because while it inculcates solid morals it lacks energy and interest on every level. The "reformation so much wanted in this mode of composition" (419) – to make virtue attractive – will not result from Reeve's work, though presumably it may from the example provided by Burney.

Similarly, the critic from the *Anti-Jacobin Review* uses Burney to illustrate the novel's proper sphere. Unlike the more open-minded critics of *Desmond*, he charges Smith's *Young Philosopher* with meddling in things beyond a lady's ken, an error that Burney by comparison never commits:

> With her talents we think that [Smith] may still produce entertainment, and even advantage to society, if she will abstain from politics, concerning which, her views are

narrow and partial, her conclusions unjust, and her inculcations hurtful. The best of our female novelists interferes not with church nor state. There are no politics in Evelina or Cecilia [*sic*]. (1 {98}: 190)

With respect to current trends in feminist criticism that honor the political forays of early female novelists, the reviewer issues Burney a backward compliment; she clearly belongs among the best novel-writers – here, female novelists – but at the cost of eschewing certain worldly themes and events. Incidentally, a reviewer could not make the same claim about her final novel, *The Wanderer* (1814), which represents aspects of the French Revolution and pointedly illustrates England's hostility toward wage-earning women. In the reviews of Reeve's and Smith's works, Burney's novels operate as a normalizing paradigm, a proper blend of literary merit and topical decorum, be it moral or political. During her time, Burney's writing set the standard for novel achievement.

In a similar way, Burney enters the critical discussion of Robinson's *Walsingham* in two extended reviews. Following the pattern identified earlier, each critic opens his review of Robinson's work with a précis of the novel, although they emphasize different features. The *Analytical Review* (which merged with the *English Review* in 1797 and lost something of its radical edge) highlights consistency and unity as hallmarks of successful novels:

[T]o produce a work of fiction, in which an acquaintance with life and manners, a talent for observation, or a knowledge of the operation of the passions upon human character, and a vigorous creative fancy, should combine to form a consistent *whole*, harmonizing in all it's [*sic*] parts, is, we are inclined to suspect, one of the highest efforts of human intellect. (27 {98}: 80)

Robinson's novel fails because her noblemen act like stable boys and her fashionable ladies like "certain females who deal in aquatic productions at the east end of the town" (81). At this point, Burney's counterexample proves illustrative: "opposed to the brilliant pictures of Mrs. D'Arblay, those of our author bear the semblance of overcharged daubings" (81). The critic from the conservative *Anti-Jacobin Review* emphasizes the by then conventional attributes of "accurate observation, comprehensive understanding, the power and habit of marking moral causes and operations; genius for inventing a natural fable, and natural situations in which human character may manifest itself" (1 {98}: 160). Given this level of difficulty, he concludes that not all people of education and "lively ingenuity" – for example, the author – are equally capable of writing a novel: "Although the writer of this novel is . . . far from ranking in the same class with our Burneys and our Fieldings . . . , she still occupies a respectable situation among the inferior romance writers" (161). The critic implies, of course, that Burney as well as Fielding possesses the level of genius and knowledge of human nature to rank among the best novel writers.

Conclusions

As Siskin points out, "no single event illustrates so clearly" the changes in literary production at the turn of the nineteenth century and the cost for women writers "than the founding in 1802 of the *Edinburgh Review*."[30] Burney's status as an exemplary novelist would not survive the early decades of the nineteenth century. William Hazlitt's famous review of *The Wanderer* in the *Edinburgh* documents the turn in critical fortunes for the woman author, making gender the most significant criterion in the hierarchy of novelists. In that essay Hazlitt credits Burney with the power of observation, but nothing more. In marked contrast to earlier reviews that celebrate her development of character, Hazlitt detects failures in character, form, and sentiment, which he attributes to her being "a very woman" (24 February 1815: 336):

> Women, in general, have a quicker perception of any oddity or singularity of character than men, and are more alive to every absurdity which arises from a violation of the rules of society, or a deviation from established custom. This partly arises from the restraints on their own behaviour, which turn their attention constantly on the subject, and partly from other causes. The surface of their minds, like that of their bodies, seems of a finer texture than ours; more soft, and susceptible of immediate impression. They have less muscular power, – less power of continued voluntary attention, – of reason – passion and imagination: But they are more easily impressed with whatever appeals to their senses or habitual prejudices. (336–37)

Instead of ranking Burney among the best novelists – he identifies Cervantes, Fielding, Smollett, Richardson, and Sterne – Hazlitt groups Burney with unnamed and clearly unregarded women writers. In the process he articulates a gendered theory of the novel that associates literary criteria with the biological and social attributes of sex. Women's soft minds, like their soft bodies, are incapable of the sustained attention and inborn genius required to create the best novels, *pace* Cervantes et al. He attributes the minor successes of women, for he can hardly discount Burney entirely, to rote learning and obsessive scrutiny of their limited surroundings. Hazlitt's dismissal of Burney's novels underscores the very different critical climate created in the wake of a new form of book review. Because of the selective format in the quarterlies, a critic need only mention women novelists in extraordinary circumstances, and given the longer essay style, he could discourse at length on other – male – writers in lieu of detailed discussion of their work. Of the nineteen pages in this review, notice of Burney's work occupies only the last three. Even in a review of her own novel, the female novelist begins to disappear.

Hazlitt's essay signals a change in the status of the female novelist, one in which "female" takes on greater importance than "novelist." It closes that window of time in which the female novelist could not be ignored. The critical discussion prior to that point, however, provides a surplus of important and often overlooked information about the history of women writers, the formation of literary values, and the consolidation of the novel genre. The disappearance of so many female authors from the history of the genre to which they contributed so vitally remains one of the compelling mysteries in modern literary criticism. Their representation in the eighteenth-century book reviews offers new insights to correct that history.

There, the best female novelists enjoy fame and professional respect on a par with male novelists. Gender is never invisible in this criticism, but it does not yet confer exclusionary status. While the earliest reviews retain a gallant idiom of condescending flattery and frequently articulate a need to protect the female author from criticism, this stance eventually disappears. The increase in the numbers of female novelists toward the end of the 1780s corresponds to and perhaps motivates the change from critical gallantry to just and reasoned evaluation. It bears repeating that the universal coverage mandated by eighteenth-century Reviews means that women writers are as systematically reviewed as men, and this public critical discourse creates a powerful and sanctioned visibility for the female author. As the producers of multiple novels, female writers are more likely to be given longer reviews, and such considered treatment establishes their fame and professionalism. While the expectation that female authors would write further novels generates much advice from well-read critics, their multiple works also prompt inquiry into the nature of the novel. The resulting critical discourse locates authority and innovation in the genre with women writers, especially Burney, Smith, Lennox, Inchbald, and Radcliffe. These women may not have appreciated the fortunate timing of their critical debuts, but Burney, at least, witnessed the change in literary temper. While the pages of the late eighteenth-century book reviews provide evidence of a culture's appreciation and respect for female novelists of merit, the "great forgetting" that follows the shift in book-review format indicates the centrality of gender values to the emerging literary ethos. By their relegation to the margins of all that is feminine, the new Reviews register the importance of the female novelist as a threat to the elevated, nationally important, and insistently masculine novel form.[31]

See also: chapter 7, Why Fanny Can't Read; chapter 10, The Original American Novel; chapter 13, Women, Old Age, and the Eighteenth-Century Novel; chapter 15, The Eighteenth-Century Novel and Print Culture.

Notes

As is customary, throughout this chapter the word "Review" is used to signify a type of journal, whereas "review" indicates an individual article or essay. The following abbreviations have been used in the citations: *MR* for *Monthly Review*, *CR* for *Critical Review*, *ER* for *English Review*, *AR* for *Analytical Review*, *BC* for *British Critic*, *AJR* for *Anti-Jacobin Review*, *GM* for *Gentleman's Magazine*, *T&C*

for *Town and Country Magazine*, and *Euro Mag* for *European Magazine*, also known as the *London Review*.

1. See Judith Phillips Stanton, "Statistical Profile of Women Writing in English from 1660 to 1800," in *Eighteenth-Century Women and the Arts*, ed. Frederick M. Keener and Susan E. Lorsch (New York: Greenwood Press, 1988), 248.

2. James Raven and Antonia Forster, *The English Novel 1770–1829: A Bibliographical Survey of Prose Fiction Published in the British Isles*, vol. 1: *1770–1799* (Oxford: Oxford University Press, 2000), 17, 48.

3. Antonia Forster, *Index to Book Reviews in England, 1749–1774* (Carbondale: Southern Illinois University Press, 1990), 12–13, and *Index to Book Reviews in England, 1775–1800* (London: The British Library, 1997), xx–xxx.

4. James Basker, *Tobias Smollett: Critic and Journalist* (Newark: University of Delaware Press, 1988), 37–43.

5. See Forster, *Index to Book Reviews, 1775–1800*, xlii; Raven and Forster, *The English Novel*, 113–14; Joseph F. Bartolomeo, *A New Species of Criticism: Eighteenth-Century Discourse on the Novel* (Newark: University of Delaware Press, 1994), 109–11.

6. Frank Donoghue, *The Fame Machine: Book Reviewing and Eighteenth-Century Literary Careers* (Stanford, CA: Stanford University Press, 1996), 6.

7. Clifford Siskin, *The Work of Writing: Literature and Social Change in Britain, 1700–1830* (Baltimore, MD: Johns Hopkins University Press, 1998), 210–27.

8. Ian Watt, *The Rise of the Novel: Studies in Defoe, Richardson, and Fielding*, 2nd ed. (Berkeley and Los Angeles: University of California Press, 2001), 298.

9. Terry Castle, "Sublimely Bad," *London Review of Books*, February 23, 1995, 18–19.

10. Watt, *The Rise of the Novel*, 298.

11. Jane Austen, *Northanger Abbey and Persuasion*, vol. 5, *The Novels of Jane Austen*, ed. R. W. Chapman, 5 vols. (Oxford: Clarendon Press, 1923), 38.

12. Raven and Forster, *The English Novel*, 117–18.

13. Derek Roper, *Reviewing before the Edinburgh 1788–1802* (Newark: University of Delaware Press, 1978), 123.

14. Ibid., 32; Forster, *Index to Book Reviews in England, 1749–1774*, 9.

15. Roper, *Reviewing*, 36–37.

16. Raven and Forster, *The English Novel*, 48.

17. Ibid., 39.

18. See Brian Corman, "Early Women Novelists, the Canon, and the History of the British Novel," in *Eighteenth-Century Contexts: Historical Inquiries in Honor of Phillip Harth*, ed. Howard Weinbrot, Peter Schakel, and Stephen Karian (Madison: University of Wisconsin Press, 2001), 235–37.

19. Forster, *Index to Book Reviews in England, 1749–1774*, 14.

20. Donoghue, *The Fame Machine*, 6 and 160; Bartolomeo, *A New Species of Criticism*, 119–23.

21. Raven and Forster, *The English Novel*, 43, citing *Critical Review* 37 (1774): 317–18.

22. Laura L. Runge, *Gender and Language in British Literary Criticism, 1660–1790* (Cambridge: Cambridge University Press, 1997), 80–120.

23. Raven and Forster, *The English Novel*, 114.

24. Ibid., 27, 48.

25. See William Warner, *Licensing Entertainment: The Elevation of Novel Reading in Britain, 1684–1750* (Berkeley and Los Angeles: University of California Press, 1998), especially 4–19. Significantly, Warner overlooks the role of book reviews in the late eighteenth-century cultural debate over what type of novels should be read and written.

26. *Biographia Literaria*, vol. 7, *The Collected Works of Samuel Taylor Coleridge*, ed. James Engell and W. Jackson Bate, 16 vols. (London: Routledge and Kegan Paul, 1983), I.23.

27. See a note on the text, Elizabeth Inchbald's *A Simple Story*, edited with notes by J. M. S. Tompkins and introduction by Jane Spencer (1967; repr. with new introduction, Oxford: Oxford University Press, 1988).

28. Raven and Forster, *The English Novel*, 34–35.

29. Attribution of this anonymous novel to Lennox is questionable.

30. Siskin, *The Work of Writing*, 224.

31. See Warner, *Licensing Entertainment*, especially chapter 1, and Nicola Diane Thompson, *Reviewing Sex: Gender and the Reception of Victorian Novels* (New York: New York University Press, 1996).

Further Reading

Bartolomeo, Joseph F. *A New Species of Criticism: Eighteenth-Century Discourse on the Novel.* Newark: University of Delaware Press, 1994.

Corman, Brian. "Early Women Novelists, the Canon, and the History of the British Novel." In *Eighteenth-Century Contexts: Historical Inquiries in Honor of Phillip Harth*, ed. Howard Weinbrot, Peter Schakel, and Stephen Karian. Madison: University of Wisconsin Press, 2001.

Donoghue, Frank. *The Fame Machine: Book Reviewing and Eighteenth-Century Literary Careers.* Stanford, CA: Stanford University Press, 1996.

Raven, James, and Antonia Forster. *The English Novel 1770–1829: A Bibliographical Survey of Prose Fiction Published in the British Isles.* 2 vols. Oxford: Oxford University Press, 2000.

Roper, Derek. *Reviewing Before the Edinburgh 1788–1802.* Newark: University of Delaware Press, 1978.

Warner, William. *Licensing Entertainment: The Elevation of Novel Reading in Britain, 1684–1750.* Berkeley and Los Angeles: University of California Press, 1998.

13

Women, Old Age, and the Eighteenth-Century Novel

Devoney Looser

Jane Austen died in 1817 at age 41. Her death in middle age has led to some peculiar errors in grasping her position in literary history. In *A Room of One's Own* (1929), Virginia Woolf writes, "Jane Austen should have laid a wreath upon the grave of Fanny Burney."[1] As we should now recognize, this is an impossible admonition. Austen died twenty years before such an offering could have been made. Burney published her first novel when Austen was just 3 years old but lived to age 87. For years, many have read over Woolf's wish without doing the math. Maria Edgeworth, too, has been seen as a figure who "points forward to both Jane Austen and Sir Walter Scott," despite her substantial literary contributions long after the other two began – and stopped – publishing novels.[2] According to literary history, Burney and Edgeworth are before, rather than after, Austen. In reality, they – like many of her female contemporaries – were both.

Jane Austen did not have the opportunity to continue a novelist's career into old age. Burney and Edgeworth, like other long-lived women writers, negotiated sexism in the literary marketplace as the novel gained respectability and then encountered the obstacles of what we would now call ageism in their later years. There is a dearth of work documenting the frequency and scope of these challenges, which form a powerful and sometimes debilitating combination. Although "for a long time our image of the eighteenth century was dominated by males of advancing years," rarely was old age itself a category of analysis.[3] There has been a shortage of contributions considering age *qua* age. A fraction of existing scholarship on the subject specifically addresses gender as well.

Engrained and often invisible in literary histories, stereotypes of gender and old age have become difficult to contest. It is possible that, upon taking the category of old age seriously, we will determine that ageism was as powerful and prevalent a problem for women writers as was sexism. One obstacle in revisiting (or revising) our understandings is that even for well-regarded women novelists, late fiction is less likely to be accessible in modern editions. As Terri Premo observes, "most documents written by aging women remain uncollected, unpublished" – an especially unfortunate shortcoming because they may offer "a separate story requiring new sets of assumptions and different kinds of questions."[4] I argue in this essay for the importance of grasping the history of women and old age in order to apprehend with greater nuance the history of the novel. First, I describe the state of aging studies in the period. I then turn to Burney and Edgeworth to illuminate what we gain by exploring aging and authorship in histories of the novel. Examining these two authors' late works, I demonstrate new readings that might emerge if we attend to the eighteenth-century novel through the lens of women's aging.

Burney and Edgeworth were lionized in their early careers, gaining great popularity and critical acclaim. Later and posthumously, both lost some of that luster, although never entirely forgotten. They maintained positions as "minor" novelists throughout much of the twentieth century. Their reputations were based on their first works of fiction – for Burney, *Evelina* (1778) and for Edgeworth, *Castle Rackrent* (1800).[5] Their last published works appeared in 1832 and 1848 respectively, and their last novels appeared in 1814 and 1834. What does it mean to study a text from 1814, 1834, or 1848 as written by an "eighteenth-century novelist"? How were elderly authors received by a public that believed they belonged to a previous era? Although I do not have definitive answers, I propose ways we might approach these questions, as well as a rationale for what makes such approaches valuable.

Women Novelists who Outlived Jane Austen

Many of Jane Austen's contemporaries lived and wrote much longer than she did – well into their eighth decades.[6] As a result, 1800 may not serve as a strict or useful cutoff point for investigating eighteenth-century women writers' careers, a fact that Janet Todd's *Dictionary of British and American Women Writers 1660–1800* acknowledges. Todd notes that parameters of the dictionary are "arbitrary boundaries."[7] There are approximately 500 writers included in her *Dictionary*, not all of whose death dates are identified. One quarter of the 500 are known to have lived past 1800. Approximately 15 percent lived well past it, dying after 1820. More than a dozen lived to 1850. As a result, a large number of eighteenth-century women writers could also be reckoned as of the nineteenth.

Very few scholars have noticed that these women writers shared long lives. A few Victorian-era critics recognized the significant number of elderly among the previous generation's celebrated women. In 1864, one author observed:

> There is something remarkable in the longevity of literary women in modern times, even if we look not beyond our own country. Mrs. Piozzi and Mrs. Delaney perhaps scarcely enter within the conditions. . . . but Miss Edgeworth was above 80 when she died; Joanna and Agnes Baillie were older still; and Mrs. Trollope died the other day at 84.[8]

More extensive notice appeared in Jerome Murch's *Mrs. Barbauld and Her Contemporaries* (1877), which concludes with a chart of nineteen names, year of death, and age at death, sorted by the latter. Murch's chart began with Austen and ended with four women who died in their nineties and one said to have died at 103.[9] This chart succeeds a section he titled "How Long They Lived!" in which he writes, "The literary and scientific pursuits of Mrs. Barbauld and her contemporaries appear to have been largely conducive to the length of years" (175). He notes, "a considerable list might also be made of aged eminent men of the same period," but that "the average longevity in their case is not so high as the other" (175). He characterizes both groups as having enjoyed "calm and gentle old age" (175). One century later, these celebrated women writers' common longevity had become a little-discussed fact.

How did British women writers of the period fare in old age? Preliminary answers might be gathered from a sample of twenty-four women writers who lived beyond 70 years old, whose publication histories I compiled.[10] Collectively, their most prolific age was 50 years old, followed by a second peak at 30. The average age at first publication was 29, and the average age at last publication was 75. Although by 70 productivity fell to the levels seen during their twenties, many continued to find a mass audience. These conclusions, based on a small sample (and on the debatable premise that publication and productivity are linked), suggest that women writers were able to sustain professional careers up to, if not well into, old age. What it does not describe is whether or how the texture of careers changed over time. Future scholarship should seek to chart and explain variations from decade to decade, but broad brushstrokes provide an initial understanding of conditions for female authorship and old age.

Writing as an old woman was not without challenges. When an identifiably older woman published a novel, the fact of her age provoked comment. Novels dealing with love and romance posed a peculiar catch-22. If an older woman author pretended to youthfulness or to special knowledge about romance, she could be seen as sexually suspect, because proper older women were supposed to be asexual.[11] On the other hand, if an older woman author did not seem in touch with youth, her novel ran the risk of being labeled outdated – a problem in a genre that traditionally endorsed presentism in its content and/or moral lessons. A novel by an old woman was, like her body, in danger of being considered a faded beauty rather than a repository of mature wisdom. Women were "labeled old with reference to their reproductive rather than productive capacity," as Teresa Mangum argues.[12] An older woman writer who trafficked in romance could be belittled from any number of directions.

Old Age in Eighteenth-Century Great Britain

That Jane Austen died in "middle age" may come as a surprise to those who imagine that lives were far shorter two centuries ago. In a literal sense, the perception of lives foreshortened is accurate. Life expectancy remained at around 35 years old until 1800, but those who survived childhood stood a good chance of living into their sixties.[13] It is difficult to determine whether old age was considered a matter of chronological age, bodily decay, or some other factors. Peter Stearns defines the onset of old age in the eighteenth century as between 55 and 60, but emphasis was frequently placed on one's ability to perform tasks rather than on chronological age.[14] William Gordon's *The Plan of a Society for Making Provisions for Widows* (1772) supports the figures Stearns identifies, proposing that members be "not too far advanced in life" and setting an age limit of 60.[15] In the early nineteenth century, English females over 60 made up less than 8 percent of the population of women and men over 60 approximately 7 percent of the males.[16] Women fared better in terms of reaching old age, but the ideologies they faced were more cruel. Women "proved durable from a physiological standpoint in a culture which discouraged them from preparing for or accepting the results."[17]

A prediction was made two decades ago that "there will soon be a whole library on old age," but it has not yet come to pass in eighteenth-century studies.[18] David G. Troyansky's *Old Age in the Old Regime* considers representations of and conditions for the aged in eighteenth-century French literature and culture – research that remains needed in a British context.[19] When late careers of eighteenth-century writers have been examined, males traditionally provided the focus. Old age manuals noted that the very old – the centenarians – and the really creative among the elderly at any age were more likely to be male.[20] In what he calls the "geriatric enlightenment" of the eighteenth century, George Rousseau observes that many women lived extraordinarily long lives but that "they are less prominent in the literature because male lives were more often recorded."[21] The potential for a fruitful, productive old age was overwhelmingly viewed as a masculine privilege. Historians Susannah R. Ottaway and Janet Roebuck, among others, are adding to our knowledge of women's aging and social history, but the subject of eighteenth-century women, literature, and old age remains surprisingly undertheorized.[22]

British women writers of the late eighteenth and early nineteenth century provide a fascinating group through which to examine how women faced old age. They led far more public lives than many of their contemporaries and have left us, in many cases, with published and unpublished writings that document what it meant to continue to "speak" as elderly women. Although there were many ways that female old age was performed, it appears that the public received these performances through just a handful of recognizable patterns. Rich variety existed among the writers themselves, but the perceptions of readers and reviewers were far narrower. This led to strict determinations about whether women were performing old age appropriately or not. Of course, these determinations shifted as what old age could (or should) be changed. It seems possible that these shifts occurred in part because women writers challenged restrictive models, the documentation of which is beyond the scope of this essay.

Frances Burney: "Past the period of chusing to write a love-tale"

To the world, Edgeworth and Burney in old age seemed to be enduring periods of silence, inactivity, or stagnation. Each then published new fiction. Their last novels appeared after a long hiatus – for Burney, from 1796 to 1814, and for Edgeworth,

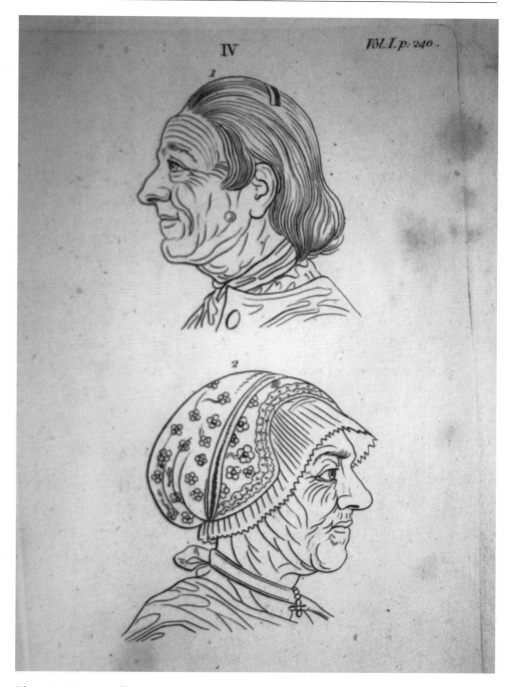

Plate 12. Drawing of two old women from Johann Casper Lavater's *Essays on Physiognomy: For the Promotion of the Knowledge and the Love of Mankind* (second edition, 1804).

from 1817 to 1834. (During these times, their previously published works continued to appear in new or reprinted editions.) The differences in Burney's and Edgeworth's writing in later life – and the differences in how they were written about – are just as instructive as their similarities. Where Burney pushed the envelope for women's aging, Edgeworth toed the line.

From the first, Burney showed an interest in women and old age, although in ways that are difficult to interpret. *Evelina*'s libertine Lord Merton quips, "I don't know what the devil a woman lives for after thirty; she is only in the other folks' way."[23] Lord Merton is a detestable character whose statements are of questionable use, but the novel also includes a notorious scene of illegal betting on a foot-race between two old women. The women – chosen because they are older than 80 and strong – fall from over-exertion, are plied with wine, and complain of injury. One ultimately slips and falls so badly that the other is declared the winner. A contemporary found that reading the account of the race "excited a roar of laughter," and a more recent critic called it one of the novel's "most delightful incidents."[24] Other readers have expressed horror. Burney's good characters deplore the race, so the novel would seem to expose the evils of exploiting the old. But the established pattern in Burney's fiction is one of using the pain faced by old women to provoke readers' laughter. (Mrs. Mirvan is another example.) Whether Burney endorsed or undermined such representations is unclear.

Later in her life, Burney was subject to similar representations. Her last years have been regarded as a footnote. The initial posthumous treatments she received virtually disregarded her final decades. In the first edition of Burney's journals and letters (1842–6), edited by her niece Charlotte Barrett, old age is sketchily represented. The publisher may be at fault, as it is said he came to fear the expense of bringing out the voluminous work. Burney's last years are accorded a handful of pages.[25] In the journals and letters published more than a century later, material from age 60 to her death spans six volumes – several thousand pages of text.[26] Barrett's compressed edition claims that from 1835 to 1838, Burney's "letters were now very few," stressing instead that Burney "lived to be a classic."[27]

Burney's novel-writing spanned five decades, but her late fiction has been overlooked at best and actively demolished at worst. In his famous essay on Burney, written shortly after her death, Thomas Babington Macaulay asserts that "the world saw and heard little of Madame D'Arblay during the last forty years of her life, and . . . that little did not add to her fame."[28] He sees in Burney's last works "no trace of dotage" but finds it "melancholy to think that . . . everything published during the last forty-three years . . . lowered her reputation" (5:60). He describes her decline (which he attributes to French immersion rather than decay of powers), concluding "That her later works were complete failures is a fact too notorious to be dissembled" (5:66). Macaulay praises *Evelina* as the first tale written by a woman that lived or deserved to live. He also names two women writers who have surpassed Burney, her "successors": Edgeworth and Austen. He writes, "in truth, we owe to her, not only *Evelina*, *Cecilia*, and *Camilla*, but also *Mansfield Park* and the *Absentee*" (5:67). For her part, editor Barrett, too, ends the journals and letters by praising Burney as "the Author of Evelina, Cecilia, and Camilla" without including *The Wanderer*.[29]

For years, few challenged these assertions. As Rose Marie Cutting has put it, "Later students of Fanny Burney, even partisans, usually scrutinize [*The Wanderer*] for evidence of her literary decline."[30] Joyce Hemlow and George Sherburn saw Burney's career as a novelist ending after *Evelina* and *Cecilia*, with her last two novels viewed as so inferior they were better understood as outside the genre, as essentially "conduct books – dull, and badly written" (quoted in Thaddeus, 3–4). Hemlow writes, "every reference to *The Wanderer* must serve to poke it further into the shadows."[31] It was not until the 1970s that Burney's last novel was considered an accomplished work of fiction. Though many theories have been proposed to explain why this novel "failed," one that has been only cursorily explored is how it was packaged (by Burney and her critics) as the work of an aging female author.

In the preface to *The Wanderer*, Burney declares that she writes as an older woman, who is "past the period of chusing to write, or desiring to read, a merely romantic love-tale, or a story of improbable wonders."[32] A year earlier, Burney made a similar statement in a letter to her brother. She asked that *The Wanderer* be called a work, because, as she put it, "I am passed the time to endure being supposed to write a Love-tale."[33] In her letter even more than in her preface ("being supposed to" versus "chusing to write"), Burney recognizes that the connection of old women and romance is not one her culture found palatable. In the preface she elaborates, not only on what she has left behind with age but on what she wishes to retain. She hopes she still has "the power of interesting the affections, while still awake to them herself, through the many loved agents of sensibility, that still hold in their pristine energy her conjugal, maternal, fraternal, friendly and . . . filial feelings" (9). Although her first statement disavows the idea that an old woman – Burney was, at this time, in her early sixties – should write a narrative of romantic love, her second undercuts it. She tells readers she remains "awake" to her "affections," not only as a mother, sister, daughter, and friend, but as a wife. An old woman who sought to interest the affections (particularly conjugal ones) was usually an object of derision. Burney was taking a chance in highlighting her romantic life.

Despite Burney's pronouncements, *The Wanderer* is, among other things, a love tale. It centers on an unnamed young woman – the Incognita, the Wanderer, L. S., or Ellis – later revealed as Juliet Granville. Raised in France, she becomes the victim of revolutionary corruption and is forced to flee her adopted country. When she arrives in England, she finds her purse gone and tries to convince others of her respectability, despite her financial need and her refusal to offer details about her "female difficulties" (the novel's subtitle). She is helped and harmed by a cast of characters, several of whom assume she is sexually available. She witnesses the world's benign and more serious evils – selfishness, criminal acts, and suicide attempts by a lovelorn proto-feminist "rival" among them. Juliet also discovers good, when she miraculously locates her French childhood friend in England; discovers another beneficent friend to be a sister; and is finally free to renounce a forced sham marriage in order to wed the hero. Though innocent, Juliet is not an innocent. She is worldly and has seen the world, perhaps more than a woman of her age and station "ought" – a far more mature character than the naïve, sheltered Evelina.

The Wanderer is not centrally concerned with old age, despite Burney's touting the book as by an older woman. Most of the older women characters, like the aptly named Mrs. Ireton, are unsympathetic. Mrs. Ireton is described by another character as in her fourth stage of existence, having passed through petted childhood, adored youth, forgotten and supplanted maturity, to reach "old age, without stores to amuse, or powers to instruct" (543). The man who thus criticizes her is an "old bachelor" of 75, Sir Jaspar Herrington (632; 532). He is a comic, likeable character, although he does make an unwanted proposal of marriage to Juliet. Later, he acknowledges that he could be her "great grandfather" (542). There is sparse commentary in the novel on old age. When it does appear, it is notable.

The novel's heroine is youthful, but one character speculates that her age, like her insistence that she is honest and virtuous, is a sham. While Juliet is applying to be Mrs. Ireton's humble companion, the old woman accuses her of pretending to be a young woman. Juliet refuses to reveal details about her background. The curious Mrs. Ireton reaches her boiling point and accuses Juliet of being supernaturally youthful looking:

> Pray, if I may presume so far, how old are you? – But I beg pardon for so indiscreet a question. I did not reflect upon what I was saying. Very possibly your age may be indefinable. You may be a person of another century. A wandering Jewess. I never heard that the old Jew had a wife, or a mother, who partook of his longevity; but very likely I may now have the pleasure of seeing one of his family under my own roof? That red and white, that you lay on so happily, may just as well hide the wrinkles of two or three grand climacterics, as of only a poor single sixty or seventy years of age. (485–86)[34]

The climacteric, as the novel's editors note, is "a critical moment in human life, occurring every seven years" (940). The grand climacteric refers to one's sixty-third year (seven times nine), so Mrs. Ireton sarcastically speculates that Juliet may be 126 or 189 years old (940).[35] Associating old age with vanity (laying on red and white make-up), with witchcraft or the supernatural, and with hiding its true number gives voice to then prevalent stereotypes about the elderly. One of the novel's most reprehensible characters repeats these stereotypes and provides the tongue-in-cheek speculation that Juliet is as old as (or even older than) her creator.[36]

The grand climacteric is again mentioned by Sir Jaspar, who lightheartedly reports that he will not fight a duel with one of Juliet's abusers. The young man has dismissed Sir Jaspar's challenge as coming from a superannuated goose, past his grand climacteric, who "ought not to meddle in affairs of which they had lost even the memory" (504). Sir Jaspar playfully banters with Juliet about his would-be gallantry, encouraging her to indulge his "garrulity of age" (504). Here a sympathetic character echoes another set of stereotypes about the old – that they are foolish, senile, and loquacious.

The only quality he assigns to himself is garrulity, a danger associated with aging during the period. Contemporary author Hester Lynch Piozzi, in her unpublished last work, poked fun at her own supposed talkativeness, subtitling the text, "A Granddame's Garrulity," and signing it "An Old Woman."[37] In *The Wanderer*, Sir Jaspar's "garrulity of age" is endorsed as a quality to be pandered to. An approval of garrulity may not be surprising in a novel that runs to five volumes and approximately 2000 pages.

It may be making too much out of several passages to suggest that *The Wanderer*'s discourse on aging unwittingly paved the way for the vituperative notice Burney faced at the hands of some critics. But from calling attention to her own affectionate old age, to indicating that her worldly heroine might be suspected of false youth, to suggesting we should indulge garrulity in old age, Burney and her novel risked associations with negative stereotypes of aging. The infamous notice in the *Quarterly Review* by the acerbic John Wilson Croker capitalized on all of these associations. From the first line of his review, Croker makes much of Burney's age:

> None of our female novelists (not even Miss Edgeworth) ever attained so early and so high a reputation as Miss Burney, or, as we must now call her, Madame D'Arblay. . . . we regret to say, that the Wanderer, which might be expected to finish and crown her literary labours, is . . . inferior to its sister-works.[38]

Croker finds the novel inadequate on several levels, the most notorious of which invoke the rhetoric of old age. The novel is "feeble" (124). It has a "total want of vigour, vivacity, and originality" (124). Because it is by the highly regarded Burney, it is especially disappointing: "during the thirty years which have elapsed since the publication of Cecilia, she has been gradually descending from the elevation which the vigour of her youth had attained" (124). The novel is called a "'lame and impotent conclusion'" to her career, although Burney nowhere names it her last (124). *The Wanderer* has no splendor, cannot dazzle, is not beguiling and is "increased in size and deformity exactly in the same degree that the beauties have vanished" (125).

Croker, damning the novel as repetitive and superannuated, leads up to this oft-quoted tour-de-force censure:

> The Wanderer has the identical features of Evelina – but of Evelina grown old; the vivacity, the bloom, the elegance, 'the purple light of love' are vanished, the eyes are there, but they are dim; the cheek, but it is furrowed; the lips, but they are withered. . . . We have completed the portrait of an old coquette author who endeavours, by the wild tawdriness and laborious gaiety of her attire, to compensate for the loss of the natural charms of freshness, novelty, and youth. (125–26)

A more pointed demonstration of the dangers of publishing a novel as an old woman would be difficult to locate. Female novelists, Croker suggests, had best not age. The power of their fiction fades, as does its beauty. The more authors try to deny the loss of bloom, the more ridiculous they become. The aging female novelist's body of work is like her own body. The Wanderer in Croker's comment may also refer to Juliet. Echoing the voice of Mrs. Ireton, Croker sees Juliet and Burney as painted, aged harridans. This review reveals a near obsession with old women. His description of the novel's plot begins (as the novel does not) with a description of elderly women: "Two cautious, selfish, ill-tempered, ill-mannered old ladies" introduce his summary (126). Croker twice more in his review refers to old ladies and holds a mock funeral for previous Burney heroines: "We have now done with this novel, on which we should not have been justified in saying so much, but that we conceived ourselves in duty bound to attend the lifeless remains of our old and dear friends Evelina and Cecilia to their last abode" (129). He rebukes Burney for implicitly capitulating to Napoleon, pronouncing *The Wanderer* dead on arrival and Burney's career over.

This review is telling about the treatment an aging woman author might endure. Seeing it alongside several others demonstrates an emerging pattern. William Hazlitt, writing in the *Edinburgh Review*, finds *The Wanderer* has little power:

> We are sorry to be compelled to speak so disadvantageously of the work of an excellent and favourite writer; and the more so as we perceive no decay of talent, but a perversion of it. There is the same admirable spirit in the dialogues, and particularly in the characters of Mrs. Ireton, Sir Jasper Herrington, and Mr. Giles Arbe.... But these do not fill a hundred pages of the work; and there is nothing else good in it.[39]

Hazlitt moves away from the rhetoric of aging that Croker employs but mentions the possibility of decay. Hazlitt instead implicates Burney's perversion of powers in the novel's "failure." He finds the novel garrulous; it includes just 100 pages of valuable material, while the rest is judged wild, chimerical, and perverse. Criticism of garrulity is made by several other reviewers. One suggests that the work is "unnaturally lengthened" and could have accomplished in three volumes what it did in five.[40] Another wants it reduced by half.[41] Yet another argues that five volumes could have been compressed into one and that "Madame D'Arblay has forgotten throughout too many of the pages that length of description should have some relation to the importance of the events related."[42]

Garrulity is not the only obstacle critics identify. Burney's age itself potentially limits her powers. The *British Critic*'s reviewer notes that public expectation is exceptionally high for a novel from an "old favourite," heightened by her "long silence" (374). The *Monthly Review*'s William Taylor emphasized that Burney was over the hill:

> Since the modest entrance of Evelina into the world, the sparkling triumphs of Cecilia, and the delicate embarrassments of Camilla, many years have elapsed, fertile not only in political but in moral revolutions. A new generation has grown up in the saloons [*sic*] of Great Britain ... an alteration insensibly progressive has effected considerable change in our idea of the gentleman and the lady. Whether a corresponding modification of the canon of propriety, or internal rule of excellence, has taken place in the mind of Madame

D'Arblay, during her long residence in France, may be liable to question: but we are glad to see depicted again such society as our matrons remember.[43]

Though Taylor finds *The Wanderer* "truly varied, original, and interesting" (413), he too asks whether a "matron" author can write an effective novel. The *Anti-Jacobin Review* wondered whether ten years in France "had the effect of incapacitating this lady from fixing the attention or exciting the interests, of an English reader" and says that the novel "falls very far short" in its "powers of attraction" (347). For the *British Critic*'s reviewer, *The Wanderer* demonstrates Burney's powers have declined because of her "long residence in France" during which she has "forgotten the common elegancies of her native tongue" (376) – implying that France corrupted her or possibly made her senile.

Reviewers concluded that the book was out of touch. Because of its proto-feminist character, Elinor Joddrel, *The Wanderer* is hopelessly out of date, according to the *British Critic*: "The revolutionary spirit . . . is, fortunately for a bleeding world, now no longer in existence: few of our female readers can remember the *égalité* mania" (385). Female readers, the reviewer assumes, are young, and Burney's age compels her to create an old-fashioned youthful heroine. The *Gentleman's Magazine*, in its positive review, also highlights the antiquated features of Elinor, despite viewing her as useful to "serve as an historical antidote to any lurking remnants of poisonous doctrine."[44] Burney's fascinating character is reduced to a historical remnant.

Burney straightforwardly explained in her preface that her novel was set in the 1790s and that it was composed beginning in 1802. Still, the critics questioned her ability to use "old" material to create successful new fiction. The *European Magazine*'s reviewer thought it was "doubtful whether the public will consider the subject sufficiently *modern*, though managed with the skill of a Burney."[45] The *Anti-Jacobin Review* believed Burney could not avoid "anachronism"; furthermore, "her farmer's sons and daughters are such as they were in *Evelina*'s days, but such as are not to be found at present. Madame D'Arblay does not seem to be aware of the change which has taken place . . . since she first began to write novels" (352–53). Taylor's review summed up the general assessment: "It is not enough that pictures of the *past* are executed with vital fidelity; they must be regarded with the eye of the *present*" (413).

As her first critics saw it, Burney's writing in old age did not lead to wisdom, affection, and truth, but to painting, decay, and falsehood. Brian Connery argues in his work on aging and Jonathan Swift that "The construction of the literary 'author' Swift has proven remarkably adaptable to those who wish to find in his later years . . . confirmation of their own views of the relation between middle adulthood and old age."[46] As we have seen, *The Wanderer* was for years downplayed if not omitted from discussions of the eighteenth-century novel and of Burney's career.[47] We must consider the possibility that early, ageist responses to Burney's late authorship may have played a role in that process.

Maria Edgeworth: "The voice of old experience"

Edgeworth's *Helen* (1834), "written in her sixties, long after her father's death, is so interesting because old age seems to have set her free to be, and write about herself," according to novelist Maggie Gee.[48] Finding in *Helen* evidence of "a new maturity," Marilyn Butler makes a similar claim, identifying a "strengthening of confidence that came in her sixties from years of self-reliance."[49] Studies of Edgeworth have been dominated by "the image of a daughter so timid that she has nothing to say for herself in her father's presence, so utterly devoted to him and his ideas that he speaks for her and through her."[50] Maria's father, Richard Lovell Edgeworth, was a noted inventor and educator, and with him, she co-authored several books. He took an active role in his daughter's writing career, was married four times, and fathered twenty-two children. After his death, Maria Edgeworth (like Burney after her) completed her father's memoirs.

Regardless of how the debates about Richard Edgeworth's influence are settled, we know from Maria Edgeworth herself that *Helen* was not an easy novel to write. She was "more anxious far (and for good reasons) about this book than any I ever sent into the world" because she did not want to "have lowered what my father took such pains to raise for me" – that is, his standards (quoted in Butler 463). Burney's last novel, written while her father still lived, took risks in its portrayal of gender, age, and aging. Edgeworth's last novel, published almost twenty years after her father's death, appears by comparison much more conventional in its treatment of women and old age.

The novel begins as heroine Helen Stanley gives up her small fortune to repay her recently deceased guardian uncle's business debts. She joins the household of a lifelong friend, the former Lady Cecilia Davenant, now wife to General Clarendon (10). Lady Cecilia's mother, Lady Davenant, is staying at Clarendon Park until she joins her husband, named ambassador to St. Petersburg. Helen greatly values (and is greatly valued by) Lady Davenant, even more so than Cecilia.[51] Daughter Cecilia is enthusiastic and coquettish, but her mother has "a sort of deep high character" of which Helen is in awe (13). Lady Davenant has flaws too, including an early, meddling interest in politics that led her to be nearly a stranger to her daughter. These three imperfect but likeable women form the heart of the story, and their strengths and weaknesses play out in a drama propelled forward by Cecilia.

Before her marriage, Cecilia swore to the General that he was her first love. When her love letters to another man resurface, Cecilia convinces Helen to take responsibility for them, at least until Lady Davenant leaves for Petersburg. Cecilia promises afterward to tell all to her husband. What starts as a series of white lies balloons as the novel proceeds. Cecilia's promised confession is repeatedly postponed until the material consequences increase exponentially. Because of her supposed authorship of the letters, Helen's engagement to the novel's generous and idealistic hero, Granville Beauclerc (ward to General Clarendon), is called off; the love-letters are bowdlerized, published, narrowly circulated, and suppressed; and General Clarendon refuses to shelter Helen any longer. Helen bears the brunt of the continued cover-up, until Cecilia is caught in another web of lies and is estranged from her husband. Finally, she confesses all. Helen is put back in the good graces of the General and the matrimonial path of her hero. The novel ends with the returned Lady Davenant, on her deathbed, witnessing her dying wish fulfilled – that Helen and Granville marry and that her daughter and son-in-law be reconciled, since all of the trouble arose out of a mother's early neglect.

Helen includes a great deal of commentary on old age, much of which comes from Lady Davenant, who calls herself the "voice of old experience" (46). She confesses to Helen her early mistakes, revealing a disappointed love from her youth, saying, "My identity is so much changed that I can look back upon this now, and tell it all to you calmly" (59). She presents herself as long past the age of inspiring (or being inspired by) passion, although the novel does not underestimate the magnitude of her errors. As Butler puts it, "Lady Davenant is the first of Maria's magisterial parent-figures to be subjected in her turn to impartial criticism" (477–78). Lady Davenant is, throughout the novel, a figure of perfectly acknowledged imperfection and hard-won wisdom.

Despite her early errors, Lady Davenant is presented as a model older woman not only in her just self-criticisms but in her love for the young. She is not jealous of their powers, though sometimes amused by their idealism. In an argument with her favorite, the hero Granville, she disabuses him of his sense of the new, bringing him "presently to see that he had been merely saying old things in new words" (93). She deems him "a resurrectionist of obsolete heresies, which had been gone over and over again at various long-past periods, and over and over again abandoned by the common sense of mankind" (93). She manages this transformation by "slow degrees," showing him that his systems are "old to older eyes" (93). Lady Davenant demonstrates that the voice of old experience need not be grating (or merely garrulous) to the ears of the young.

She is an equal opportunity critic of youth and age. When brought a book by the idealistic Beauclerc, she proclaims, "As we advance in life, it becomes more and more difficult to find in any book the sort of enchanting, entrancing interest which we enjoyed when life, and books, and we ourselves were new" (126). She says it is vain to try to determine "whether the fault is most in modern books, or in our ancient selves" (126). This is because the imagination cools and weakens with age, as the old become "too much engrossed by the real business and cares of life, to have feeling or time for factitious or imaginary interests," though she avers, "while they last, the imaginative interests are as real as any others" (126). Lady Davenant believes the old have an excess of care in the world's affairs and the young too great a desire to escape them through books of imagination. On her deathbed, she again contrasts them, finding weaknesses in both. The weaknesses she assigns to age – too little enthusiasm, benevolence, and confidence in self and others – seem not to be those of her own character (463–64). She locates imperfections and strengths in young and old alike, making her seem a reliable, rather than a one-sided or prejudiced, source for aphorisms about aging.

It is questionable how directly Lady Davenant's commentary should be allied with Edgeworth's, but Lady Davenant is not the novel's only repository of wisdom on old age. The novel's narrator reflects:

> There is a precious moment for young people . . . . a time, before the passions are awakened, when the understanding, with all the life of nature . . . is at once eager to observe and able to judge, for a brief space blessed with the double advantages of youth and age. This time once gone is lost irreparably; and how often it is lost – in premature vanity, or premature dissipation! (106)

The named advantages of old age – to observe and judge without awakened passions – resemble a novel's desirable, impartial narrator. Old age and novel-narrating would seem to go together in this formulation. *Helen*, by implication, heads off criticism that novel-writing (especially when it deals with the passions) does not belong in the hands of the old. Burney's attempt to forestall criticism of *The Wanderer* and old age was not nearly as effective, as it tried to link old age and passion, rather than distance these qualities.

Edgeworth was also more successful than Burney in showing the advantages of knowledge of the past and the present. *Helen*'s narrator reflects on past trends, emphasizing the differences between now and then: "Formerly in England, as still in every other country but England, a marked difference was made in the style of dress in the country and in town" (177). And, "Formerly, overdressing in the country was reprobated as quite vulgar; but now, even persons of birth and fashion are guilty of this want of taste and sense" (177). As the narrator's perceptions of the history of fashion and manners demonstrate, an "old" narrator has an advantage over a young one in that, if convincingly objective, she can offer access to what is now *and* what was then.

Setting her novel in the present and carefully highlighting cultural differences between past and present, Edgeworth avoids the charge that her novel is old-fashioned. One late nineteenth-century critic agreed, seeing Edgeworth as having kept up with the times. Emily Lawless takes the unusual step of placing *Helen* in a later time period: "In reading [*Helen*] we are aware that the eighteenth century has at last dropped out of sight, and that we are well out upon the nineteenth, not indeed as yet 'Victorian,' but in a sort of midway epoch" (194). Such a reading is made possible because *Helen* carefully draws distinctions between past and present, youth and age.

If Edgeworth is more skilled than Burney in maintaining the novel's appearance of being new-fangled, she also seems more savvy in her treatment of garrulity. As we have seen, Burney's wealthy old bachelor requests indulgence for his stereotypical garrulity. Edgeworth's novel also includes a garrulous unnamed old woman, featured in a handful of scenes with Granville and Helen. Though she is, like Sir Jaspar, indulged, the old woman occasions kind treatment because of her poverty. She allows Granville and Helen to demonstrate their respect for the poor aged. The old woman says to them, "'Well, well! I'm old and foolish. I'm old and foolish, and I should not talk'" (84). The narrator reports, "But still she talked on, and as this seemed her only comfort, they would not check her garrulity" (85). For Edgeworth, garrulity is not to be indulged for its own sake – or even for the sake of age – but because it is charitable. It is the "only comfort" of a poor, aging woman.

Helen does not ask readers to indulge novelistic garrulity either. Edgeworth and others worked to make her novel a radically shorter book. She had "resolved to keep *Helen* down to two volumes" and relied on her sisters to "cut back the narrative to the requisite length" (Butler 460). (It was publisher Bentley who later decided to make it three volumes {Butler 464}). Edgeworth felt that "Good books & precious stones are made by compression" (quoted in Butler 460 n. 3). One critic, expressing a minority opinion, finds that *Helen* exhibits "sprawling formlessness . . . that makes one almost wish for Mr. Edgeworth's supervisory cutting," but Edgeworth mainly escaped negative associations of authorship, old age, and garrulity.[52] Burney's last novel seemed to sanction garrulity over truth, but Edgeworth championed truth over garrulity.

Whereas Burney's novel stressed the necessity of keeping secrets through her mature, youthful heroine, Edgeworth's stressed the importance of telling secrets through the costs of her heroine's and friend's deceptions. Burney's older female characters in *The Wanderer* are unrepentant harpies. Edgeworth's most visible older female character in *Helen* demonstrates appropriate feminine strength, regretting her earlier ambitions outside the domestic sphere. Edgeworth's novel, in form and content, demonstrated a "good" old woman's aging; Burney's flirted with the "bad." Of course, this does not make one a good and the other a bad book. On the contrary, Burney's novel has as much to interest readers as does Edgeworth's. But the ways in which they negotiated (or anticipated) how old age would play to readers of their texts may have made a significant difference in their immediate, if not long-term, reception.

Critics were more generous in their assessments of *Helen*, but it received far less critical attention than did *The Wanderer*. *Helen* was financially successful, bringing Edgeworth an estimated £1100 (Butler 464).[53] Precisely how popular the book was is more difficult to gauge. Samuel Taylor Coleridge noted in a letter that *Helen* was making "noise" and exciting "great interest" (quoted in Butler 478). According to Butler, *Helen* was not a runaway success (479). Bertha Coolidge Slade concludes otherwise, considering *Helen* "not only well received and widely read, but one of Miss Edgeworth's most popular books."[54] Slade stresses that the novel was translated into Swedish, Danish, and French, and "probably went through more different English editions than any other of her books" (199). Lawless also believes that *Helen* "at the time it was written, was possibly the most successful of all her novels."[55] Late nineteenth-century critic Helen Zimmern would have it both ways: "Concerning *Helen* contemporary public opinion was much divided; some regarded it as a falling-off in power, others as an advance, but all agreed there was a change."[56]

The novel's initial critical success is even harder to judge. One major notice appeared in a British periodical, written by her friend and agent John Gibson

Lockhart. Lockhart's anonymous review reassures readers that Edgeworth's powers have not lessened: "If any of our readers had ever listened to the envious whispers, so indefatigably circulated among certain circles, to the effect that Miss Edgeworth's vein of creative fancy had been buried with her father – Helen will undeceive them."[57] After praising the work, he compares it to her earlier books, emphasizing that her age indeed has had an impact:

> As writers of a reflective and introspective turn advance in the walk of life, they are likely to detach their imagination more and more from the broad and blazing contrasts which delight the eye and heart of youth; and it is no wonder that the interest of this tale, put forth after an interval of, we believe, nearly twenty years, should be of a more sober cast than Miss Edgeworth chose to dwell upon in some earlier works. (483)

Because of the author's age, *Helen* is a more "detached" and "sober" work, but Lockhart believes the novel to be full of strengths. Because the novel is "already in everybody's hands," Lockhart does not make extracts. In contrast to Croker, who declares Burney's career as a novelist at an end, Lockhart wishes Edgeworth to publish more. He ends with a plea to her to complete and make public two novels that he understands she had begun "some years ago" (484).

Additional, favorable reviews appeared in North America, perhaps because there "literary fashions were slower to change" (Butler 478). Still, Edgeworth is talked about as if she were a relic. She is described as an author whom one is surprised to find still living:

> We know not when we have been more delighted, either as reviewers or as men, with any occurrence in the literary world, than with the opportunity of giving another welcome to Miss Edgeworth, the friend of our earlier years. And yet we must confess that our pleasure was mingled with many fears; for it was possible, that the recollection of the interest her writings used to inspire, might be stronger than the reality; there was a chance, too, that during her long silence she might have lost something of her power.... But ... the fears were uncalled for, and the hopes have been exceeded. We remember her as the morning star, whose radiance was lost for a time in the excessive brightness of the sun [i.e., Sir Walter Scott]; now we see her reappearing more beautiful than ever as the planet of evening, after that sun has left the sky.[58]

The reviewer, the Reverend W. O. Peabody, outlines the history of Edgeworth's published works and compares them to Scott's and to eighteenth-century novelists such as Samuel Richardson and Tobias Smollett.[59] When finally arriving at *Helen*, he again uses the language of age and aging to assess its value. He says that often authors "serve up old incidents and characters in new forms, while the reader, instead of being glad to meet his old acquaintance again, is vexed to see them endeavoring to hide their respectable antiquity under a youthful dress." Edgeworth, according to Peabody, is not pretending to youth. She is acting her age. He is grateful that she has proved "that the light within has not grown pale with age" (181). His assumption, nevertheless, is that authors do worsen with age.

In the short run, Burney's "badness" and Edgeworth's "goodness" as old women appear to have played a role in their critical reception. This may be because, as Margaret J. M. Ezell has argued, "The nineteenth-century valorization of 'the feminine' in its histories of women's writings ... led to the dismissal or the reduction of the reputation of most of the women writing before the Victorians."[60] In the long run, however, even those authors who benefited from the Victorian valorization of the feminine may have fallen into an undifferentiated mass as their old age itself (rather than its acceptable or unacceptable qualities) took center stage in evaluating their later works.

In 1823, Maria Edgeworth was already being referred to in an American periodical as "the great forgotten."[61] Her six-volume set of works is dubbed the work of an "old favorite," and she is classed with Richardson, Henry Fielding, and Smollett, in a historical sketch of novel-reading and readers. Her "little works" of 1800 to 1810 are appreciated as those produced "precisely at the time of life when the faculties possess their maturest vigor" (384). It is then bemoaned that she has "withdrawn from" the world of literature (389). When this review was written, Edgeworth was in her fifties, had published several novels and children's stories in the previous decade, and would live more than twenty-five years longer. Yet by this assessment, she was already a valuable antique.

After Edgeworth's death, *Helen*, like *The Wanderer*, was either glossed over in accounts of her authorship or highlighted as the work of an elderly woman. Zimmern (1883) gives it extensive treatment *because of* Edgeworth's age. She concludes, "A writer who can learn from criticism and experience, who can adopt a new method of writing when past the age of sixty, is a remarkable writer indeed" (266–67). Later editions of *Helen* also focus on Edgeworth's old age, rather than any notable qualities of the novel. In an 1893 edition, a one-page note begins, "Seventeen years elapsed between the publication of *Harrington* and *Ormond* ... and the issue of *Helen*." The rest of the note describes how Edgeworth published little from 1820 to her death.[62] A more extensive introduction by Anne Thackeray Ritchie in a 1903 edition also quickly moves to a discussion of old age:

> Age had not dimmed the author's brightness of intellect nor divided her from the interests of the generations which had followed upon her own. When Miss Edgeworth was getting to be quite an old woman, long after her father's death, after ten years of silence, she once more began to write a novel.[63]

The rest of the introduction focuses on Edgeworth's family members' deaths and on describing her old age.

When not celebrated as the work of an elderly woman, the novel has generally been ignored. In a forty-page review of Edgeworth's *Memoirs* (1867) that describes nearly all of her major writings, *Helen* receives nary a mention.[64] In her 1959 study, *The Great*

Maria, Elisabeth Inglis-Jones moves from a chapter titled "1831–1833" to one called "Epilogue," a once common biographical model when dealing with a woman author's old age.[65] Although some twentieth-century critics have given *Helen* its due, Mark D. Hawthorne's assessment (1976) is more typical. He says he omits the "very fine" novel *Helen* because it shows "no remarkable advance" over *Ormond* and because "a discussion of it would be anticlimactic."[66] For most critics, the old age of an eighteenth-century woman author has been described as a time of preparing for death or resting on her laurels, not for producing valuable new literary work. Authorship in old age, particularly for women, has been seen as a come down.

Conclusions

Edgeworth's and Burney's last novels have proven intriguing reading for and are considered significant contributions by today's critics. Their different early treatment may be due to changes in book-reviewing practices from 1814 to 1834, with Burney facing ageist criticism that became less venomous two decades later. (Perhaps we will even conclude that what Burney faced was peculiar to her or to Croker.) The differences may have been caused by changes in literary fashion – an explanation several critics have embraced. Butler notes that "Maria's name must have seemed quaintly old-fashioned beside those of Bulwer Lytton, the Countess of Blessington, Lady Charlotte Bury, and Mrs. Gore" (479). For Butler, Edgeworth "belongs to a more primitive stage of the novel's development" (480). Embedded in Butler's vocabulary is the suggestion that age may have played a part in what she identifies as *Helen*'s lackluster showing. Edgeworth's novelistic techniques were of a "primitive" sort compared to those writing in 1834. Contemporary readers might understandably devalue a novel that was perceived to deviate from current trends, but such judgments make little sense a century or two hence.[67] Surely Edgeworth and Burney belong to the entire era during which they wrote and published, rather than to a particular stage of the novel's development. Such authors should not necessarily be grouped only or even principally in the era demarcated by their youthful writings.

Toward the end of Edgeworth's first novel, *Castle Rackrent* (1800), Sir Condy Rackrent decides that he has "a great fancy to see my own funeral afore I die."[68] He longs to hear all of the things that his mourners will say about him at his staged wake but ends up disappointed. He is of a "sad order in the midst of it all, not finding there had been such a great talk about himself after his death as he had always expected to hear."[69] Edgeworth and Burney may well have experienced the reception of their last novels as Sir Condy did his mock funeral.[70] Both women were repeatedly declared forgotten or measured for faded powers. In response, Burney turned to writing a memoir of her father and Edgeworth to political causes and a short story published for charity. Few of the posthumous memorials or studies about them attend sufficiently to their later works. Because of such patterns, it is crucial to revisit late eighteenth-century women writers' last novels, not just to resuscitate them for their own sake but to ask the reasons why they may have been given short shrift.

In *The Work of Writing*, Clifford Siskin describes what he calls "The Great Forgetting" of women writers, enjoining us to remember that "there is much remembering to be done, and admirable progress has recently been made. But . . . we also need to find out how we forgot."[71] I would extend Siskin's question to ask how – and why – did we forget women writers in their old age? Perhaps it is because their later works are indeed inferior; because of the way literary history is periodized; because of how old age is represented, conventionally or unconventionally, in their texts; or because ageism prevented women authors from getting a fair reading by critics and audiences. The research I am undertaking suggests that the latter two reasons provide strong interpretive possibilities. Unless and until we weigh all of these factors together, however, we will merely recapitulate a woefully incomplete picture of eighteenth-century women novelists and their later (often nineteenth-century) productions.

See also: chapter 12, MOMENTARY FAME; chapter 18, CONVERSABLE FICTIONS.

NOTES

1. Virginia Woolf, *A Room of One's Own* (New York: Harcourt, Brace, 1929), 113.
2. Quoted from Samuel Chew's *The Nineteenth Century and After* (1948) in James Newcomer, "Maria Edgeworth and the Critics," *College English* 26 (1964): 216.
3. Pat Rogers, "Introductory Note," *Journal of Aging and Identity* 4 (1999): 55.
4. Terri L. Premo, *Winter Friends: Women Growing Old in the New Republic, 1785–1835* (Urbana: University of Illinois Press, 1990).
5. *Evelina* became the critical favorite in the twentieth century. See Janice Farrar Thaddeus, *Frances Burney: A Literary Life* (New York: St. Martin's, 2000), 189. Subsequent references are cited in parentheses in the text. In the mid-twentieth century, Edgeworth's *Castle Rackrent* was said to be the only of her novels then read, selling just 350 copies a year. See Newcomer, "Maria Edgeworth and the Critics," 215.
6. This fact is discussed in my essay, "'What the Devil a Woman Lives for After 30': The Late Careers of Late Eighteenth-Century British Women Writers," *Journal of Aging and Identity*

4 (1999): 3–11. Some arguments in this essay are revised and updated from that work.
7. Janet Todd, ed., *A Dictionary of British and American Women Writers 1660–1800* (Totowa, NJ: Rowman and Littlefield, 1985), xviii.
8. "Brainwork and Longevity," *Scientific American* X, no. 15 (1864): 226. It is odd that the author does not consider Piozzi (1741–1821) and Delany (1700–88) to have lived long lives.
9. Jerom Murch, *Mrs. Barbauld and Her Contemporaries: Sketches of Some Eminent Literary and Scientific Englishwomen* (London: Longmans, Green, 1877), 176. Subsequent references are cited in parentheses in the text.
10. The authors included in this sample were Elizabeth Craven (Lady Anspach), Joanna Baillie, Anna Laetitia Barbauld, Mary Berry, Elizabeth Bonhote, Frances Burney, Mme d'Arblay, Sarah Harriet Burney, Elizabeth Carter, Maria Edgeworth, Mary Hays, Harriet Lee, Sophia Lee, Charlotte Lennox, Hannah More, Amelia Opie, Sydney Owenson (Lady Morgan), Hester Lynch Piozzi, Jane

Porter, Clara Reeve, Regina Maria Roche, Sarah Trimmer, Priscilla Wakefield, and Jane West.

11. See Katharine Kittredge, "'The Ag'd Dame to Venery Inclin'd': Images of Sexual Older Women in Eighteenth-Century Britain," in *Power and Poverty: Old Age in the Pre-Industrial Past*, ed. Susannah R. Ottaway, L. A. Botelho, and Katharine Kittredge (Westport, CT: Greenwood Press, 2002), 247–63.

12. Teresa Mangum, "Growing Old: Age," in *Companion to Victorian Literature and Culture*, ed. Herbert F. Tucker (Oxford: Blackwell, 1999), 99.

13. Pat Thane, *Old Age in English History: Past Experiences, Present Issues* (Oxford: Oxford University Press, 2000), 19.

14. H. C. Covey, "The Definitions of the Beginning of Old Age in History," *International Journal of Aging and Human Development* 34 (1992): 328–30.

15. William Gordon, *The Plan of a Society for Making Provision for Widows, by Annuities for the Remainder of Life; and for Granting Annuities to Persons after Certain Ages* (Boston: Joseph Edwards and John Fleeming, 1772), 2. Gordon models his proposals on London societies.

16. Peter Laslett, *Family Life and Illicit Love in Earlier Generations* (Cambridge: Cambridge University Press, 1977), 194.

17. Peter N. Stearns, "Old Women: Some Historical Observations," *Family History* 5 (1980): 47.

18. Quoted in Georges Minois, *The History of Old Age: From Antiquity to the Renaissance*, trans. Sarah Hanbury Tenison (Chicago: University of Chicago Press, 1987), 4.

19. David G. Troyansky, *Old Age in the Old Regime: Image and Experience in Eighteenth-Century France* (Ithaca, NY: Cornell University Press, 1989).

20. Stearns, "Old Women," 46.

21. George Rousseau, "Towards a Geriatric Enlightenment," *1650–1850: Ideas, Aesthetics, and Inquiries in the Early Modern Era* 6 (2000): 32.

22. Jill S. Quadagno, *Aging in Early Industrial Society: Work, Family, and Social Policy in Nineteenth-Century England* (New York: Academic Press, 1982); and Susannah R. Ott-

away, "Providing for the Elderly in Eighteenth-Century England," *Continuity and Change* 13 (1998): 391–418.

23. Frances Burney, *Evelina; or, the History of a Young Lady's Entrance into the World*, ed. Edward Alan Bloom (New York: Oxford University Press, 1982), 275.

24. Quoted in Audrey Bilger, *Laughing Feminism: Subversive Comedy in Frances Burney, Maria Edgeworth, and Jane Austen* (Detroit: Wayne State University Press, 1998), 198; Earl R. Anderson, "Footnotes More Pedestrian Than Sublime: A Historical Background for the Foot-Races in *Evelina* and *Humphry Clinker*," *Eighteenth-Century Studies* 14 (1980): 56.

25. Fanny Burney and Charlotte Barrett, *Diary and Letters of Madame D'arblay* (London: H. Colburn, 1842–6), 7:378–85. See also Thaddeus, *Frances Burney*, 4.

26. Fanny Burney, Joyce Hemlow, and Althea Douglas, *The Journals and Letters of Fanny Burney (Madame D'arblay)* (Oxford: Clarendon Press, 1972), vols. 7–12.

27. Burney and Barrett, *Diary*, 7:378; 384.

28. Thomas Babington Macaulay, "Madame D'Arblay," in *Critical and Miscellaneous Essays* (New York: Dodd, Mead, 1880), 5:13. Subsequent references are to this edition and are cited in parentheses in the text.

29. Burney and Barrett, *Diary*, 7:385.

30. Rose Marie Cutting, "A Wreath for Fanny Burney's Last Novel: The Wanderer's Contribution to Women's Studies," *Illinois Quarterly* 37:3 (1975): 45–63, at 47.

31. Joyce Hemlow, *The History of Fanny Burney* (Oxford: Clarendon Press, 1958), 339.

32. Fanny Burney, *The Wanderer, or, Female Difficulties*, ed. Margaret Anne Doody, Robert L. Mack, and Peter Sabor (Oxford: Oxford University Press, 1991), 9. Subsequent references are to this edition and are cited in parentheses in the text.

33. Burney, Hemlow, and Douglas, *Journals*, 7:104.

34. On the figure of the wandering Jew, see George Kumler Anderson, *The Legend of the Wandering Jew* (Providence, RI: Brown University Press, 1965). On women and "painting," see C. Downing, "Face Painting in Early Modern England" [with a reply by

F. E. Dolan], *PMLA*, 109 (1994): 119–20.

35. Thaddeus describes the "grand climacteric" as the year in which Burney would "by tradition either change greatly or die" (148). When *The Wanderer* was published, Burney was nearing her grand climacteric. Later in the novel, Juliet is once more mistaken for an old woman, by her uncle, Admiral Powel (836).

36. Many have speculated that Juliet, the wanderer, has biographical resonances with her author. A contemporary anonymous poem identified Burney as a "lonely Wanderer." See "Addressed to Mrs. D'Arblay, on Reading Her 'Wanderer,'" *Gentleman's Magazine* 84 (1814): 373.

37. James L. Clifford, *Hester Lynch Piozzi (Mrs. Thrale)*, 2nd ed. (Oxford: Clarendon Press, 1952), 436.

38. John Wilson Croker, Review of *The Wanderer* by Frances Burney, *Quarterly Review* XI (1814): 123–24. Subsequent references are cited in parentheses in the text.

39. William Hazlitt, Review of *The Wanderer* by Frances Burney, *Edinburgh Review* 76 (1815): 338.

40. Unsigned review of *The Wanderer* by Frances Burney, *British Critic* NS 1 (1814): 385. Subsequent references are cited in parentheses in the text.

41. Unsigned review of *The Wanderer* by Frances Burney, *Anti-Jacobin Review* 46 (1814): 353. Subsequent references are cited in parentheses in the text.

42. Unsigned review of *The Wanderer* by Frances Burney, *Theatrical Inquisitor and Monthly Mirror* 4 (1814): 236–37.

43. William Taylor, Review of *The Wanderer* by Frances Burney, *Monthly Review* 76 (1815): 412. Subsequent references are cited in parentheses in the text.

44. Unsigned review of *The Wanderer* by Frances Burney, *Gentleman's Magazine* 84 (1814): 579.

45. Unsigned review of *The Wanderer* by Frances Burney, *European Magazine and London Review* 66 (1814): 426.

46. Brian A. Connery, "Self-Representation and Memorials in the Late Poetry of Swift," in *Aging and Gender in Literature: Studies in Creativity*, ed. Anne M. Wyatt-Brown and

Janice Rossen (Charlottesville: University Press of Virginia, 1993), 142.

47. Important reassessments of Burney's career and of *The Wanderer* have been published in recent years. See, for example, Pam Perkins, "Private Men and Public Women: Social Criticism in Fanny Burney's *The Wanderer*," *Essays in Literature* 23 (1996): 69–84; and George Justice, *The Manufacturers of Literature: Writing and the Literary Marketplace in Eighteenth-Century England* (Newark: University of Delaware Press, 2002).

48. Maria Edgeworth, *Helen* (London: Pandora, 1987), ix; xii.

49. Marilyn Butler, *Maria Edgeworth: A Literary Biography* (Oxford: Clarendon Press, 1972), 477–48. Subsequent references are cited in parentheses in the text.

50. Caroline Gonda, *Reading Daughters' Fictions, 1709–1834: Novels and Society from Manley to Edgeworth* (Cambridge: Cambridge University Press, 1996), 204.

51. Maria Edgeworth, *The Novels and Selected Works of Maria Edgeworth*. Vol. 9, *Helen*, ed. Susan Manly and Cliona O'Gallchoir (London: Pickering and Chatto, 1999), 12. Subsequent references are from this edition and are cited in parentheses in the text.

52. P. H. Newby, *Maria Edgeworth* (Denver, CO: A. Swallow, 1950), 89.

53. Despite the high price negotiated for *Helen*, Marilyn Butler claims "Maria probably reached her peak as a selling author in 1812–1814, before her reputation began to suffer from comparison with Scott and Austen," *Maria Edgeworth* (491–92).

54. Bertha Coolidge Slade, *Maria Edgeworth, 1767–1849: A Bibliographical Tribute* (London: Constable, 1937), 199.

55. Emily Lawless, *Maria Edgeworth* (New York: Macmillan, 1905), 194.

56. Helen Zimmern, *Maria Edgeworth* (Boston: Roberts Brothers, 1883), 260.

57. J. G. Lockhart, Review of *Helen* by Maria Edgeworth. *Quarterly Review* 51 (1834): 483.

58. Unsigned review of *Helen* by Maria Edgeworth, *North American Review* 39:84 (1834): 167. Subsequent references are cited in parentheses in the text.

59. The attribution to Peabody is made in Butler, *Maria Edgeworth*, 478.

60. Margaret J. M. Ezell, *Writing Women's Literary History* (Baltimore, MD: Johns Hopkins University Press, 1992), 103.

61. Unsigned review of *The Works of Maria Edgeworth, in Six Volumes*, by Maria Edgeworth, *North American Review* 17:41 (1823): 383. Subsequent references are cited in parentheses in the text.

62. Maria Edgeworth, *Helen* (London: J. M. Dent, 1893), iii.

63. Maria Edgeworth, *Helen* (London: Macmillan, 1903), vii.

64. Unsigned review of *A Memoir of Maria Edgeworth, with a Selection from Her Letters, Edinburgh Review* 126 (1867): 458–98.

65. Elisabeth Inglis-Jones, *The Great Maria* (London: Faber and Faber, 1959).

66. Mark D. Hawthorne, *Doubt and Dogma in Maria Edgeworth* (Gainesville: University of Florida Press, 1967), 4.

67. These assessments are certainly changeable and may be changing, as Cliona O'Gallchoir calls *Helen* "perhaps the author's most fluently written and best-plotted fiction." See "Gender, Nation, and Revolution: Maria Edgeworth and Stéphanie Félicité de Genlis," in *Women, Writing, and the Public Sphere: 1700–1830*, ed. Elizabeth Eger et al. (Cambridge: Cambridge University Press, 2001), 201. Another critic calls *Helen* one of Edgeworth's two most "effective and underrated novels." See Jacqueline Pearson, "'Arts of Appropriation': Language, Circulation, and Appropriation in the Work of Maria Edgeworth," *Yearbook of English Studies* 28 (1998): 212–34.

68. Maria Edgeworth, *The Novels and Selected Works of Maria Edgeworth*. Vol. 1, *General Introduction, Castle Rackrent, Irish Bulls, Ennui*, ed. Jane Desmarais, Tim McLoughlin, and Marilyn Butler (London: Pickering and Chatto, 1999), 46.

69. Edgeworth, *Castle Rackrent*, 47.

70. Thomas Babington Macaulay suggests this precise connection for Burney: "she survived her own wake, and overheard the judgment of posterity," "Madame D'Arblay" 5:14. He seems not to make the connection that, like Sir Condy, Burney could have been disappointed.

71. Clifford Siskin, *The Work of Writing: Literature and Social Change in Britain, 1700–1830*. (Baltimore, MD: Johns Hopkins University Press, 1998), 225.

FURTHER READING

Botelho, Lynn, and Pat Thane, eds. *Women and Ageing in British Society since 1500*. Harlow, UK: Longman, 2001.

Ezell, Margaret J. M. *Writing Women's Literary History*. Baltimore, MD: Johns Hopkins University Press, 1992.

Looser, Devoney. "'What the Devil a Woman Lives for after 30': The Late Careers of Late Eighteenth-Century British Women Writers." *Journal of Aging and Identity* 4 (1999): 3–11.

Ottaway, Susannah R. *The Decline of Life: Old Age in Eighteenth-Century England*. Cambridge: Cambridge University Press, 2004.

Thaddeus, Janice Farrar. *Frances Burney: A Literary Life*. New York: St. Martin's, 2000.

Thane, Pat. *Old Age in English History: Past Experiences, Present Issues*. New York: Oxford University Press, 2000.

14

Joy and Happiness

Adam Potkay

In this essay I situate two keywords of the eighteenth-century novel, "joy" and "happiness," within their broader discursive contexts – religious, erotic, ethical, and political.[1] My first section sketches genealogies of the terms "joy" and "happiness" as they evolve from Greco-Latin and medieval European cultural roots; in the several shorter sections that follow, I focus on selected eighteenth-century novels, chiefly English-language, in order to suggest the various and evolving contexts that inform invocations of joy and/or happiness from Bunyan and Defoe through to Mary Hays and Jane Austen. Invocations, representations, and dialogic examinations of joy and happiness, I will argue, are not incidental to most eighteenth-century novels after Defoe, but are, rather, fundamental to their mimetic and moral aims. A question that animates these novels is: in what does, or ought, an individual feel joy? Conversely, at what does one, or ought one, feel grief or distress? Teaching people to feel joy and grief at the right things is, as Aristotle observed (*Politics* 1339a–1340a) and the Gospels imply, the proper function of education, and this pedagogic lesson was not lost on long eighteenth-century prose-fiction writers as diverse as Bunyan and Austen. As Aristotle and the Hellenistic schools of philosophy also taught – but without Gospel sanction – our natural being's end or aim is happiness, and this was a lesson also conned by eighteenth-century novelists, particularly those of and after the 1740s.

Eighteenth-century novelists knew that some joys are compatible with happiness, and that some are clearly not. By the later eighteenth century many distinguished "joy" from "happiness" in a precise way – the precision, in *Sense and Sensibility* (1811), with which "Marianne's joy was almost a degree beyond happiness" in leaving for London with Mrs. Jennings, or, in Elizabeth Inchbald's *A Simple Story* (1791), "poor Matilda's sudden transports of joy, which she termed happiness, were not made for long continuance."[2] Yet even before the act of properly distinguishing between these terms became a criterion for assessing a young heroine's character, novelists, from Defoe onwards, apparently understood the distinction. Defoe, like Bunyan before him and many evangelical writers who followed him, is – to state the matter with a preliminary broadness – a novelist of joy and its antithesis, dejection, and not only in the religious stretches of his works; for Defoe's characters, the stability of worldly happiness is both practically unavailable and existentially unsatisfactory. Fielding, by contrast, is largely a novelist of neoclassical happiness, who nods in the character of Parson Adams to the Shaftesburian notion of ethical joy – the joy we experience in reflecting on benevolent acts, or through sympathy with those who feel a morally permissible delight. (Adams's excessive joys and sorrows, however, deprive him of the Christian-Stoic happiness to which he aspires, and towards which Fielding is only partly satiric.) Austen, especially in her first two published novels, *Sense and Sensibility* and *Pride and Prejudice* (1813), is also a novelist of happiness – or at least an inquirer into human happiness; the relation of romantic joys and sorrows to rational happiness is examined through the characters of Marianne and Elinor Dashwood. While Austen's dialogues concerning happiness partially fit the lineage of Fielding and Samuel John-son, Austen wrote, as recent critics have done well to remind us, on the far side of a revolution in France, and a Godwinian revolution at home, during which the term "happiness" acquired inescapably political overtones. The Jacobin leader Armand Saint-Just famously declared, "Happiness is a new idea in Europe";[3] in England, William Godwin – whose writings inspired the so-called "Jacobin" novelists of the 1790s – opposed "happiness" to "prejudice," with the latter referring to a host of Georgian ideas about gender roles, societal rank, and at the extreme, property itself. The happiness Godwin imagined at the end of *Political Justice and its Influence on Morals and Happiness* (1793) is that of the rationalist-anarchist Houyhnhnms, which might become available to humans raised under the proper political, social, and economic conditions. A version of Godwin's happiness serves as a philosophical aspiration in Mary Hays's *Memoirs of Emma Courtney* (1796), as well as a counterpoint to its heroine's sorrows in an adversely prejudiced society; it remains as the ghostly, negative image from which develop the profound unhappiness and evil joys of Mary Shelley's *Frankenstein* (1818).

Genealogies of "Happiness" and "Joy"

Even in our ordinary language, a sense of the distinction between happiness and joy persists – but "happiness," now the more muddied term, requires the initial geneal-ogy. Why, for example, does it make sense to say that Adolf Hitler may have experienced moments of joy (even if "evil joy"), but not to say, "Adolf Hitler had a happy life"? The degree to which possible claims about Hitler's happiness seem off-kilter, absurd, or offensive is the degree to which one implicitly believes that happiness is not simply a mental state or disposition. If we deny that "Hitler had a happy life" could be a true statement, regardless of Hitler's subjective experience, we concede three things: first, that happiness can be evaluated from a third-person perspective; second, that happiness entails ethical considerations; finally, that judg-ments about happiness are typically made within a whole-life frame of reference (the happy life doesn't end in an ignominious way).

Where this substantive notion of happiness comes from will be familiar enough to philosophy students. It derives from Greek notions of *eudaimonia*, which has traditionally been translated into English as "happiness," although scholars now prefer "(human) flourishing." *Eudaimonia* literally refers to the "good daemon" or "good genius" that was thought to accompany a successful or flourishing person, but Greek philosophy uses the term to refer to the sort of human flourishing that, independent of good demons, depends upon an individual's reason or will. Agreeing that happiness is the natural goal of life, moral philosophers after Plato also agreed that the best way to achieve a happy life was through the rational exercise of virtue. Even Epicureans, who construed happiness as pleasure, thought of virtue as a requisite means to pleasant living. Aristotelians and Stoics, agreeing that virtuous activity is a constituent of the happy life, disagreed chiefly on what role fortune or accident played in that life. For Aristotle, a virtuous life was made happier by the fortunate accidents of good health, moderate wealth, and an untarnished reputation; the Stoics, by contrast – counter-intuitively but with appealing *élan* – contended that virtue was sufficient for the happy life, and that a person was no less happy for being sick or poor, in disgrace with fortune and men's eyes. With evident swagger, Stoics liked to talk about their ability to be happy "on the rack." (Aphra Behn took heed: the conclusion of *Oroonoko* {1688} instantiates happiness undaunted by excruciating death.) But even Stoics spoke of external goods – such as not being on the rack – as "indifferents to be preferred."

When Shakespeare conjures eudaimonism he typically employs the term "philosophy," as in Romeo's exchange with Friar Laurence after his banishment from Verona: Laurence offers "Adversity's sweet milk, philosophy, / To comfort thee, though thou art banishèd"; Romeo replies, impetuously, "Yet 'banishèd'? Hang up philosophy!" (*Romeo and Juliet* III.iii). The noun "happiness" is a surprisingly recent coinage in English; although it can be found sparingly in Spenser, Shakespeare, and Milton, it does not fully take wing until the eighteenth century, as a translation of philosophical *eudaimonia*. Locke bequeathed to the age "the pursuit of happiness," a phrase from *An Essay Concerning Human Understanding* (1689); by the 1730s Pope could posit as self-evident that "happiness" is "our being's end and aim" (*Essay on Man* IV); in 1776, Thomas Jefferson enshrined "life, liberty, and the pursuit of happiness" among mankind's inalienable rights.[4] "Happiness" is primarily a neoclassical term, expressing a secular ideal of rational contentment through ethical conduct. Its Enlightenment usage is perfectly captured in a compliment paid to David Hume's *History of England* (1754–62) by the Comtesse de Boufflers: his history, she writes, "illuminates the mind, and in showing true happiness intimately tied to virtue, it discovers by the same light the one and only end of all reasonable beings."[5]

"Happiness," then – rooted, at least in part, in Hellenistic ethics – has taken on a meaning quite distinct from, and at times opposed to, "joy." The difference may first be approached analytically, before we turn to a consideration of the historical-contextual discourses in which "joy" has been embedded. In ordinary language, "happiness" refers either to a mental disposition or to an ethical evaluation, while "joy" refers either to a mental disposition or a transient mental state. Conceptually, "joy" is a trickier thing to talk about than "happiness," first because it is a responsive state or disposition often defined by category of stimulus – there is, as we shall see, spiritual joy, eschatological joy, erotic joy, ethical joy – and second because while happiness typically admits degree (i.e., one's happiness, whether understood subjectively or objectively, can be perfect or imperfect, lesser or greater), joy admits both degree *and*, in writing, a welter of adjectival qualifications: one finds in eighteenth-century verse, for example, "vulgar joy," "ethereal joy," "fatal joy," "unwieldy joy," and "consummate joy."

Joy refers, most basically, to an emotional response that ratifies something – often something that comes as a surprise – as a good; its opposite is grief or dejection. The novel, trading in surprise occurrences and sudden reversals of fortune, generates many simple joys: for example, when Defoe's Roxana recalls discovering the extent of her Dutch husband's riches, she declares: "I was equally pleas'd and surpriz'd; and it was with an inexpressible Joy, that I saw him so rich."[6] Quick pivots between dejection and joy are likewise common, as when Parson Adams hears "with the bitterest Agony" news that his son has drowned, and soon thereafter, "to his great Surprize and Joy," finds him alive: "The Parson's Joy was now as extravagant as his Grief had been before; he...danced about the Room like one frantick."[7] Edgar Allan Poe takes this plot device to its limit in the central, shipwreck scenes of *The Narrative of Arthur Gordon Pym* (1838), in which the crew's efforts at survival and hopes for deliverance are attended by a rapid, mechanized alternation between "great joy" (or "ecstatic joy") and, typically within a sentence or two, "inexpressible grief" (or "grievous disappointment"); the cumulative effect is, perhaps advertently, ludicrous.[8]

Pym's joys are of the type that an earlier shipwrecked character, Robinson Crusoe, categorized as "mere common Flight(s) of Joy" – as distinct from the true joy of Christian assurance.[9] Crusoe here adverts to the historical use of "joy" as a Christian shibboleth. "Joy," as Locke defines it, is "a delight of the Mind, from the consideration of the present or assured approaching possession of a Good"[10] – but for the Christian, joy pertains chiefly to the latter cause, the "assured approaching possession of a good." That good is, in Luke's account of the nativity, the birth of the messiah: as the angel of Luke 2:8 tells the shepherds, "I bring you good news of a great joy" (Greek *chara*, Latin *gaudium*). In the words of Isaac Watts's 1707 congregational hymn: "Joy to the world! the Lord is come: / Let earth receive her King; / Let every heart prepare Him room, / And heaven and nature sing." Yet the joy of Christ's birth lies, finally, in the promise of his death and resurrection, and their consequences for the believer's own future. Death, then, and the supernal good that lies beyond it are what Christian joy ever anticipates. In John's Gospel, Jesus says at the Last Supper, "These things I have spoken to you, that my joy may be in you, and that your joy may be full" (15:11).

Significantly, "happiness" is not a word that appears in English renditions of the New Testament. While the wisdom books of the Hebrew Bible, especially Proverbs and Ecclesiasticus, teach the way to worldly happiness – not surprisingly, it is largely through virtuous living – the King James Version of the New Testament conjures only "joy," the elation of receiving the Christ and anticipating his future kingdom. The essence of Christian life is the joyful desire for eternal joy. This desire is necessarily unsatisfied in life as we know it, its proper object, as Milton explains, being "New Heav'ns, new Earth, ages of endless date / Founded in righteousness and peace and love, / To bring forth fruits Joy and eternal Bliss" (*Paradise Lost* 12.549–51).

Christian desire, tensed against a future that does not arrive in time, discovers its erotic counterpart in courtly love (*fin'amor*), the other great context for "joy" in the Western tradition. "Joy" has a specialized sense in the *fin'amor* or troubadour tradition – and in erotic lyrics well into the eighteenth century – that requires unfolding. Troubadour songs concern a male speaker's ardent desire for an emotionally remote, typically married woman, whose very unavailability is key to her desirability. Whereas most desire seeks satisfaction, the troubadours reflexively desired, at least in part, the state of desire itself. Equating desire and love, the troubadours suggested that the satisfaction that ended desire would also put an end to love. Michel Zink formulates the paradox: "Love thus entails a perpetually unresolvable conflict between desire and the desire to desire, between love and the love of love. This is the explanation for the complex emotion unique to love, a mixture of suffering and pleasure, anguish and exaltation. The troubadours had a word for this complex emotion: they called it *joi*."[11] The yearnings at the heart of the lover and the Christian are drawn together in C. S. Lewis's definition of joy as "an unsatisfied desire which is itself more desirable than any other satisfaction."[12] I would only add – "than any satisfaction in life," as "dying" (of one sort or another) may afford possibilities for new joys.

All lovers are, in their joys, unhappy. In Horace Walpole's parodic rewriting in *The Castle of Otranto* (1764) of Romeo and Juliet's casement window scene, Matilda says to her garrulous maid, "Though he said he was unhappy, it does not follow that he must be in love"; the maid counters, "He tells you he is in love, or unhappy, it is the same thing."[13] In contrast to a happiness that involves, by definition, purposive activity and self-control, the lover is passive, acted upon, tossed between anguish and exaltation in his joy. In his splendid if monomaniacal study, *Love in the Western World* (1940, revised 1956), Denis de Rougemont claimed *tout court*, "Happy love has no history – in European literature."[14] Although a better acquaintance with eighteenth-century British novels may have led Rougemont to qualify this claim, it certainly does reflect on continental novels of the seventeenth and eighteenth centuries, and help explain some of their thematic *différence* from the rising novel in English. *Joi* provides the narrative motor for French novels such as Madame de Lafayette's *La Princesse de Clèves* (1678) and Rousseau's *Julie, ou la nouvelle Héloïse* (1761) – in both novels (for all their differences), the titular heroine's unsatisfied desire for her lover proves more desirable than the happiness of married life. In Goethe's 1774 novel *The Sorrows of Young Werther* (Werther experiences, we are told, "excessive joy" as well), Charlotte rightly observes to the title character: "I am afraid, very much afraid, that it is only the impossibility of possessing me that attracts you so much."[15]

Erotic love in the Western imagination involves a simultaneous assertion and loss of self through and in the need for another; this play of self and absence, of the lover's perception of his wholeness in wounds or "holes," is "joy" in erotic discourse. In other discourses as well, invocations of joy typically mark a point of tension between, or a paradoxical unity of, the assertion and negation of the self. In Protestant life-narratives "joy" refers to the sense of ecstatic relief felt by an individual when he or she gains a conviction of personal salvation – but that salvation is often envisioned as a deindividuated community with God or the saints. A structurally similar tension animates the Stoic-inflected philosophies of Spinoza and Shaftesbury, in which the joy of self-perfection is attained through recognizing oneself (in Spinoza, recognizing one's "self" stripped of memory or personal identity) as a part of God or nature.

These three senses of joy weave through eighteenth-century literature, often in tension or counterpoint with the rational self-assertion of happiness. I will turn first to the topic of joy in two quite different Protestant life-narratives, as one way into the world of the eighteenth-century novel.

Bunyan to Defoe: From the Joy of the Saints to the Joy of the Empowered Self

Between Bunyan and Defoe we move from a Calvinist Protestantism that, for all its introspective individualism, aims at a heavenly Jerusalem where the saints rejoice in unison, and towards a post-Protestant if not post-Christian sense of salvation joy, in which (to quote Coleridge) "we in ourselves rejoice." The paradox that we find in Bunyan's spiritual autobiography – that of personality obsessed with detecting assurances of its own future extinction before God – is not wholly absent from *Robinson Crusoe* (1719), but largely gives way in Defoe's novel to a new type of divine comedy: individual will manifestly destined by God to wider fields of worldly exertion.

In Bunyan's *Pilgrim's Progress*, Part I (1678), the joyful goal of life's pilgrimage is a divestiture of the self so anxiously examined and endured and advertised on earth, a putting on of other and shared clothing and melting into a choir of voices, finally anonymous:

> Now I saw in my Dream, that these two men [Christian and Hopeful] went in at the Gate; and loe, as they entered, they were transfigured, and they had raiment put on that shone like Gold. There was also that met them with Harps and Crowns, and gave them to them; The Harp to praise withal, and the Crowns in token of honour: Then I heard in my Dream, that all the Bells in the City Rang again for joy; and that it was said unto them, *Enter ye into the joy of your Lord* [Matthew 25:21]. I also heard the men themselves, that they sang with a loud voice, saying, *Blessing, Honour, Glory, and Power, be to him that sitteth upon the Throne, and to the Lamb for ever and ever* [Revelation 5:13–14].
>
> Now just as the Gates were opened to let in the men, I looked after them; and behold, the City shone like the sun, the Streets also were paved with Gold, and in them walked many men, with Crowns on their heads, Palms in their hands, and golden Harps to sing praises withal.... And after that, they shut up the Gates: which when I had seen, I wished my self among them.[16]

The song that is sung by the grammatically uncertain "men themselves" – Christian and Hopeful, or them "that met them," or the "many men" who follow, it seems no longer to matter – is, as Stanley Fish writes of the "inexpressive nuptial Song" of the heavenly Lamb in *Lycidas* (l.176), "not a communication at all, but a testimony to a joy which since it binds all need not be transmitted to any."[17] *The Pilgrim's Progress* ends with the visionary and solitary speaker peering in at a largely undifferentiated company that answers to the deepest desire of his heart, until the final shutting of the city's gates tolls us back to the narrator's sole self.

This corporate vision of the heavenly Jerusalem is what Robinson Crusoe neither attains to nor desires in Defoe's novel. Assurance of his own election is apparently his spiritual end, and the joy it brings the greatest he can imagine. As George A. Starr and J. Paul Hunter pointed out some time ago, we find in *Robinson Crusoe* (1719) the same contours of spiritual autobiography that we find in Bunyan – cycles of joyful assurance and backsliding, the intercession of biblical verses, active acquiescence in God's plan.[18] However, Crusoe's key difference from the churched Bunyan is that he feels little longing for any community greater than himself and God – or at most himself, God, and those who will tend his (God-given) possessions.

There is necessarily *some* self-transcendence in his joy of spiritual deliverance, inasmuch as it signals his surrender of at least a part of his self-determination – thus his ability to criticize his unconverted self for feeling "a mere common Flight of Joy," that is, the joy of more life, the satisfied desire for continued being. The converted Crusoe retrospectively narrates his shipwreck:

> It is true, when I got on Shore first here, and found all my Ship's Crew drown'd, and my self spar'd, I was surpriz'd with a Kind of Extasie, and some Transports of Soul, which, had the Grace of God assisted, might have come up to true Thankfulness; but it ended where it begun, in a meer common Flight of Joy, or as I may say, *being glad I was alive*, without the least Reflection upon the distinguishing Goodness of the Hand which had preserv'd me, and had singled me out to be preser'vd ... even just the same common Sort of Joy which Seamen generally have after they are got safe ashore from a Shipwreck, which they drown all in the next Bowl of Punch.... (89)

The didactic dimension of Crusoe's tale, as Geoffrey Sill has recently argued, can be seen as the progressive regulation of his passions, in which he passes from the "almost objectless desire" that makes him leave home, to the "government of temper" he achieves on the island, and achieves again after his turbulent experience of the irascible passions (fear, anger, revenge) stirred up by his discovery of a footprint in the sand.[19] I would add to Sill's fine analysis that Crusoe's progress of the passions is, finally, an arc from common joy in self-preservation to spiritual joy in deliverance from sin as well as from the island – although, as a sign of God's favor and by dint of his own prevalence, Crusoe gets to keep the island *in absentia*. Crusoe's narrative is set in motion by a desire as initially directionless as the young Augustine's, and his early joys are in the accidents of fortune: his "inexpressible Joy" at being delivered from the

sea by a Portuguese ship (33); or, once in Brazil, at receiving valuable English goods
and an indentured servant (37); or, shipwrecked on his island, on being alive. About a
third of the way through the novel, however, Crusoe's mobile desire – again like
Augustine's – finds its proper object in Jesus, the joy of man's desiring: "I was
earnestly begging of God to give me Repentance, when it happen'd providentially
the very Day that reading the Scripture, I came to these Words, *He is exalted a Prince
and a Saviour, to give Repentance, and to give Remission* [Acts 5:31]: I threw down the
Book, and with my Heart as well as my Hands lifted up to Heaven, in a Kind of
Extasy of Joy, I cry'd out aloud, *Jesus, thou Son of David, Jesus, thou exalted Prince and
Saviour, give me Repentance!*" Jesus obliges, and Crusoe finds "Deliverance from Sin a
much greater Blessing, than Deliverance from Affliction" (96–97).

After his passionate turmoil in the middle third of the novel – the fear he feels
at seeing a footprint; his thoughts of revenge against the cannibals; his desire
for society, only partly assuaged by Friday's arrival – Crusoe regains control of
himself and acquires an unprecedented control over his environment, exterminating
cannibals and liberating their intended victims (Friday's father and a Spaniard),
rescuing an English captain marooned on his island by mutineers and so gaining
his own passage back to Europe. With his deliverance from the island secured, Crusoe
– anticipating the paradoxical proverb, "God takes care of those who take care of
themselves" – credits his tactical self-deliverance to the "secret Hand of Providence
governing the World," and feels his greatest joy, a "Flood of Joy in my Breast,
that . . . put all my Spirits into Confusion; at last it broke out into Tears" (273).
This climactic joy effectively reconciles Crusoe's own agency with God's plan, or
indeed revisions God's plan as Crusoe's worldly empowerment. Once off his island,
Crusoe is not oriented toward the celestial city, but committed to continued proprietorship of the island and overjoyed by the accumulated capital from his Brazilian
plantations.[20]

Of course, *Robinson Crusoe* ends by forecasting Crusoe's further adventures, and by
doing so ends up, with at least apparent circularity, where the novel begins – with the
prospect of Crusoe leaving home. Crusoe was not, it seems, born for rational or
domestic happiness, the "true Felicity" of moderation and middle station that his
father had urged on the authority of the book of Proverbs (4). Crusoe's joys, like
Bunyan's – and, albeit in a quite different register, like those of many a heroine in the
coeval line of "amatory fiction" (e.g., Haywood's *Fantomina* {1725}) – are not,
ultimately, compatible with enduring worldly happiness. As the eighteenth century
progressed, however, novelists became increasingly interested in the possibility – or at
least the problem – of happiness.

Happiness and Ethical Joy: Shaftesbury and Fielding

Christian joy, as we have examined it, is not a joy that comes from doing good; it is
not, to coin a phrase, "ethical joy." In the Gospels it is not the Good Samaritan who

feels joy, but rather the disciples who have cut off their social ties, leaving the dead to bury the dead; in *The Pilgrim's Progress* Christian finds joy well after he has left his family behind in the City of Destruction, a deed he does with the full approval of Charity (42–43). Christian joy is incompatible with classical notions of the happy life insofar as the telos of human life – "our being's end and aim," as Pope put it – is no longer human flourishing in society, but anticipatory (or self-affirming) joy. Ethical joy, by contrast, is not only compatible with, but also a naturalistic argument for, an ethical conception of happiness.

Where does the concept of ethical joy come from? Ultimately, I believe, it derives from Aristotle: "No one is just who does not take joy in acting justly" (*Nicomachean Ethics* {350 BCE} 1099a); Aquinas later enshrined this tag in his section on the moral virtues in *Summa Theologiae* (1266–73). Yet neither Aristotle nor Aquinas is likely as an immediate source for British writers of the long eighteenth century, contempt for Scholastic philosophy having effectively consigned Aquinas to oblivion in Protestant Europe and Aristotle's reputation as a moral philosopher having suffered a decline through association with Scholasticism

R. S. Crane, in his classic article "Suggestions towards a Genealogy of the 'Man of Feeling'," claimed that the joy of doing good is a theme inherited from the sermons of late seventeenth-century Latitudinarian divines. Crane quotes, most strikingly, Richard Kidder's sermon of 1676, *Charity Directed*: "There is a Delight and Joy that accompanies doing good, there is a kind of sensuality in it."[21] Crane's thesis is threefold – first, that the Latitudinarian divines placed greater emphasis on works than on faith, on benevolence than on grace; second, that they recommended good works not only on scriptural grounds but also on the grounds of the delight and joy they brought to an ethical agent; third and finally, that the model of the feeling Christian fashioned in their sermons lies behind the "man of feeling" that emerges in mid-eighteenth-century fiction and moral philosophy.

I find the first two points of Crane's thesis unexceptionable; as for the Latitudinarians' influence on eighteenth-century fiction and philosophy, I would maintain, *pace* Crane, that it was largely mediated by the third Earl of Shaftesbury. I say this because although the notion of ethical joy makes *brief* appearances in the sermons of Whichcote, Kidder, Glanvill, Tillotson, and Barrow, joy was not a common term of practical ethics in either its classical or Christian modes before Shaftesbury.

Going back to Cicero (as early modern moralists almost always did), we find almost none of the ethical joy that Shaftesbury would promulgate under the banner of ancient philosophy. Cicero notes that the Stoics approved three affects, the rational versions of desire, delight, and fear: rational wishing, tranquil joy, and prudent caution (*voluntatem*, *gaudium*, and *cautio*, *Tusculan Disputations* 4:12–14); Cicero, however, goes on to say nothing of joy as a feature of the ethical life. Joy does feature in later Stoic-inflected works such as Boethius's *Consolation of Philosophy* (524) and Spinoza's *Ethics* (1677), but as an affect that attends the knowledge or intellectual love of an immanent and perfect God; it is not, at least explicitly, formulated as the "joy of *doing* good" or of "seeing good done."

Shaftesbury's eclectic philosophy, drawing perhaps on aspects of Spinoza's *Ethics* and certainly on a shared Greek and Roman philosophical heritage, particularly Stoic sources, became one of the most important influences on subsequent eighteenth-century literature.[22] Shaftesbury provided a post-Christian ground of authority, or at least a compelling extra-Christian motive, for virtuous conduct. According to Shaftesbury, we act virtuously, and generously, because in doing so we fulfill our natural essence, and in fulfilling our essence we not only make ourselves "happy" – i.e., we do not only flourish as human beings – but we experience conscious joy. Shaftesbury writes that "the Exercise of Benignity and Goodness" entails a "natural Joy" to the mind that reflects upon this "beautiful, proportion'd, and becoming Action" (*Inquiry Concerning Virtue*, *Characteristicks* {1711} 1:240). As a supplement to the joy that reflectively adheres to doing good, there are "in the next place" the communicated joys of "sympathy": "from the very Countenances, Gestures, Voices, and Sounds, even of Creatures foreign to our Kind, whose signs of Joy and Contentment we can any-way discern" (1:242).

Thus Shaftesbury's notion of ethical joy is a hybrid composed of (1) an intellectual emotion that attends rational reflection upon benign deeds, and (2) a socially communicated passion that depends on our bodily responses to benevolent acts or, more generally, any natural delight. Shaftesbury's conception of ethical joy, in both its rationalist and social-corporeal aspects, clearly opposes the selfish joys proposed by his *bête noire* (as earlier the beast of the Latitudinarians), Thomas Hobbes. Hobbes's chief "joy" is that of personal "glory" or ascendancy over others, and the "sudden glory... which makes those grimaces called laughter, and is caused either by some sudden act of their own that pleases them or by the apprehension of some deformed thing in another, by comparison whereof they suddenly applaud themselves" (*Leviathan* 1.6, "Of the Passions"). To eclipse the theoretical validity of this combative, triumphant joy seems one of Shaftesbury's chief aims – and for nearly a hundred years, at least, his program seems largely to have succeeded.

Shaftesbury is careful to exclude from the true nature of joy, or what he calls "original joy" (1:270), "that unnatural and inhuman delight in beholding Torments, and in viewing Distress, Calamity, Blood, Massacre and Destruction, with a peculiar Joy and Pleasure" (1:268). This adventitious, aberrant joy is, according to Shaftesbury, not a positive pleasure, but only a temporary alleviation of some inward pain (Shaftesbury may here be recalling the *schadenfreude* of Milton's Satan). Subsequent if not consequent to *Characteristicks*, what Shaftesbury deemed "barbarous and malicious joy" does not flourish in the English novel, the horse-play of Smollett and Burney notwithstanding; it blooms in the novels of Sade, of course, with English echoes in Maturin's late Gothic,[23] but by then the age of Shaftesbury has ended.

In sum, Shaftesbury – and the long list of those he influenced (e.g., Hutcheson, Thomson, Akenside, Hume) – sought to bring joy down from heaven – and at least partially out of the bedroom – to dwell in clubs and assemblies, at tea-tables and coffee-houses, as well as in hills and valleys, in hamlets and on turnpike roads, wherever benevolence and charity might be exercised. They sought to reorient joy away from death and towards ethical life, the life of human flourishing. The degree to which they accomplished this is, alas, the degree to which undergraduates find eighteenth-century literature insufferable.

Fortunately, a truly great literary artist transcends moral programs or univocal aims of any sort. Which brings us to Henry Fielding, a man influenced by but by no means wholly in accord with the Shaftesburian philosophy. I would like to focus on one particularly rich scene from Fielding's *Joseph Andrews* (1742), concerning Joseph's reunion with his beloved Fanny (Book 2, chapter 12), in which the novel concept of ethical joy (joy in doing good, or beholding good accrue to another being) intersects with the erotic *joi* that underlies the Heliodoran narrative form in which Fielding cast his novel.[24] Parson Adams and Fanny have recently arrived at an alehouse in which, unbeknown to them (as to the reader), Fanny's beloved Joseph Andrews occupies another room. They (along with the novel's readers) hear (or read) a song sung "off-stage" by an unidentified singer. The song, a pastoral lyric concerning Strephon's desire for his Chloe, turns upon the familiar troubadour paradox linking the "joy" of desiring with the "woe" of frustrated desire, such as we see, for example, at the end of Sidney's *Astrophil and Stella* (1591): "in my woes for thee thou art my joy, / And in my joys for thee my only annoy." Strephon at first conjures his absent Chloe's image:

> But felt not Narcissus more Joy,
> With his Eyes he beheld his lov'd Charms?
> Yet what he beheld, the fond Boy
> More eagerly wish'd in his Arms.
> How can it thy dear Image be,
> Which fills thus my Bosom with Woe?
> Can aught bear Resemblance to thee,
> Which Grief and not Joy can bestow?

Finally, Chloe appears in the flesh, and Strephon's forlorn plaint segues into a comedic scene of accomplished bliss, complete with "expiring" and "blushing." As the song ends, the narrative advances:

Adams had been ruminating all this Time on a Passage in Aeschylus, without attending in the least to the Voice, tho' one of the most melodious that was ever heard; when casting his Eyes on Fanny, he cried out, 'Bless us, you look extremely pale.' 'Pale! Mr. Adams,' says she, 'O Jesus!' and fell backwards in her Chair. Adams jumped up, flung his Aeschylus into the Fire, and fell a roaring to the People of the House for Help. He soon summoned every one into the Room, and the Songster among the rest: But, O Reader, when this Nightingale, who was no other than Joseph Andrews himself, saw his beloved Fanny in the Situation we have described her, cans't thou conceive the Agitations of his Mind? If thou cans't not, wave that Meditation to behold his Happiness, when clasping her in his Arms, he found Life and Blood returning into her Cheeks; when he saw her open her beloved Eyes, and heard her with the softest Accent whisper, 'Are you Joseph Andrews?' 'Art thou my Fanny?' he answered eagerly, and pulling her to his Heart, he imprinted numberless kisses on her Lips, without considering who were present.

Fielding's narrator explicitly asks the reader to visualize this scene – to become the impartial spectator upon which Scottish moralists constructed a moral philosophy. (As Hutcheson claimed, "joy and love" must be felt "upon observing the actions of agents in some way attached to each other, by prior ties of nature or good offices."[25]) The reader is explicitly asked to feel, at a remove and so less intensely, what Joseph felt; implicitly, the narrator requests that our sympathy, engaged on his behalf, register moral approval of his joy and ardor – his sympathetic joy in Fanny's safety, and his Strephon-like joy in her presence. In case the narrator's cues to our moral approval are insufficient or unavailing, the next paragraph opens by censuring the spectator who has failed to have the appropriate moral response:

> If Prudes are offended at the Lusciousness of this Picture, they make take their Eyes off from it, and survey Parson Adams dancing about the Room in a Rapture of Joy. Some Philosophers [i.e., Shaftesbury and Hutcheson] may perhaps doubt, whether he was not the happiest of the three; for the Goodness of his Heart enjoyed the Blessings which were exulting in the Breasts of both the other two, together with his own.

Adams's is the joy of beholding (rather than effecting) a morally agreeable scene. He feels what the reader of the preceding paragraph ought to have been feeling – but his feeling, presumably unlike the reader's, is attended with wild bodily perturbations. If the ideal reader here, having felt an intellectual joy (or, as Shaftesbury dubs proper aesthetic response, "a reasonable Extasy and Transport" {2:104}), smiles here at the imagined spectacle of the large parson "dancing about the room" (he's prone to such displays), can we account for that laughter without Hobbes' theory of "sudden glory" and a sense of mental pleasure's superiority to physical gyration? But lest the reader feel too comfortable with his intellectual distance, the narrator at first seems to grant the greater intensity of joy to the erotically interested Joseph, whose "happiness was not only greater than the Parson's, but of longer duration: for as soon as the first tumults of Adams's Rapture were over, he cast his Eyes towards the Fire, where Aeschylus lay expiring." Fielding is finally uninterested in deciding between the relative subjective intensities of erotic and ethical joy. Hanging up philosophy, he turns the contest into a joke that moves the narrative along: Adams's joy is less than Joseph's because it doesn't last as long, but that this is so has less to do with the nature of his joy than with his subsequent and grievous recognition that he has inadvertently thrown into a fireplace the copy of Aeschylus he has been compulsively reading for the prior eleven chapters of Book 2 of *Joseph Andrews*.

Character in Fielding's novel is largely determined by characteristic patterns of moral psychology. For Adams, grief continually alternates with wildly physical joy in a pattern of sympathetic moral response that keeps him from attaining the severe Christian Stoicism he consciously professes, but that does not fundamentally detract from the good-natured (if hapless) happiness he embodies. Joseph's moral life, by contrast, hinges on the joys and sorrows of *eros*: his chief passions consist of desire for Fanny, joy in Fanny's presence, compassionate fear for Fanny's safety in her absence, and the regulated desire for revenge on those who separate him from Fanny.[26]

That Fanny and Joseph are repeatedly separated in the novel, however, is due to the uncommonly dangerous and violent England that Fielding imagines. Joseph is mugged and left for dead by highwaymen; there are five attempted rapes on Fanny, a high number even relative to romance and picaresque conventions. Adams and Joseph, for all their good nature, are hardly effective heroes in Fielding's world of sodden country squires who control a corrupt judicature; avaricious publicans; grossly self-interested clergymen (Barnabas, Trulliber); and women of high and low rank whose *eros* results (unlike Joseph's) in a more or less unregulated thirst for revenge (Lady Booby, Betty).

Fielding's moral psychology finds a place, as Shaftesbury's does not, for original malice. As a counterpoint to the ethics of good nature that we find in *Joseph Andrews*, we find as well Mr. Wilson's unchallenged identification of "a Malignity in the Nature of Man, which . . . delights in making another uneasy or dissatisfied with himself," a malignity especially apparent in "the lower Class of the Gentry, and the higher of the mercantile World" (217–18). The novel's readers have earlier seen this malignity instantiated in the interpolated "History of Leonora, or the Unfortunate Jilt" (Book 2, chapters 4 and 6), in which Leonora breaks her engagement to the virtuous barrister Horatio after she has attracted the public attention of the dapper "Bellarmine . . . just arrived from Paris," and thus experienced the greatest joy she has ever known, a specifically *unethical* joy: "Leonora saw herself admired by the fine Stranger, and envied by every Woman present . . . . She had before known what it was to torment a single Woman; but to be hated and secretly cursed by a whole Assembly, was a Joy reserved for this blessed Moment" (109). While Leonora's class status is not specified – she is known simply as the daughter of an avaricious "Gentleman of Fortune" – both the apparent liquidity of the father's assets (no estate is mentioned) and the family's readiness to marry Leonora to a barrister "of a good Family" but relatively slender means suggest that she comes, as Mr. Wilson puts it, from "the higher mercantile World." Had Leonora preserved herself in the malicious joys of *amour-propre*, she might have done just fine by the normative standards of her class; her downfall comes with her relatively selfless erotic devotion to Bellarmine and her subsequent abandonment. Thus it is a modicum of good nature that damns Leonora to a "disconsolate Life" (129).

Is, then, virtue as likely to lead to unhappiness as to happiness in the moral universe that Fielding proposes? The narrator of *Tom Jones* (1749) says as much in his "one Objection" to the doctrine that "Virtue is the certain Road to Happiness, and Vice to Misery in this World" – "namely, That it is not true" (Book 15, chapter 1).[27] Yet *Tom Jones*, like *Joseph Andrews* before it, ends happily. That Adams, Joseph, and Fanny find happiness at the novel's end has less to do with the content of their characters, however, than with the benevolence of the *upper* gentry in the person of

Mr. Booby, *via* the plot manipulations that serve either as a comic analogue of, or a secular substitute for, providential design.[28] As the fourth and final Book of *Joseph Andrews* opens, Lady Booby has hired the pettifogger Scout to have Joseph and Fanny evicted from their home parish, and with the complicity of Justice Frolick they would have ended up in Bridewell, charged with stealing a hazel-twig. The virtuous squire Mr. B., husband to Joseph's supposed sister, Pamela, rescues them from their legal fate, buys Joseph a new suit, and reconciles him to Lady Booby. After Joseph's true, gentle lineage has been established, through the revelations offered by a poor peddler – it turns out that Joseph is really the son of Mr. Wilson, and that Fanny is Pamela's sister – Mr. B. again intercedes by giving Fanny a small fortune, Parson Adams a lucrative benefice, and even the poor peddler a profitable post as an Excise-man. Fielding, in trusting to the good offices of "the great" at his novel's end, negotiates with the class assumptions of the third Earl of Shaftesbury and his "senatorial Whig" optimism: virtue equals happiness, if at all, for and through the disinterested gentleman of considerable resources.

The Politics of (Un)happiness:
William Godwin, Mary Hays, Jane Austen

The patriarchal, magical happiness found at the end of *Joseph Andrews* (as well as of *Tom Jones*) becomes an object of blithe parody in Austen's happy ending to *Northanger Abbey*, one of her novels of the 1790s: "Henry and Catherine were married, the bells rang and every body smiled," and despite the shadow of General Tilney's parental cruelty, "To begin perfect happiness at the respective ages of twenty-six and eighteen, is to do pretty well." Austen began her life of writing at a time when the pursuit of "happiness" had become an intensely politicized affair, with Jacobin novelists (especially Mary Hays) promoting it in tandem with denouncing societal "prejudices," including the patriarchal family, and anti-Jacobin novelists (especially Hannah More and Jane West) maligning it in tandem with supporting traditional familial and societal duties. As Claudia Johnson cogently argues, Austen developed "strategies of subversion and indirection" to criticize patriarchal (though not class) institutions without assuming the polemical stridency of the Jacobins; Johnson notes as well that Austen took the pursuit of personal happiness seriously (though not quite Jacobini-cally) in *Sense and Sensibility* and *Pride and Prejudice*.[29] I would add that Austen managed to write, especially in *Pride and Prejudice*, a novel of relatively unironic happiness by turning a blind eye toward that which poisoned the possibility of happiness for the Jacobin novelists – the doctrine that early circumstances and class prejudice strictly determine, and typically corrupt, individual character.

The Jacobins' fictional emphasis on social fatalism – in effect, on unhappiness and violent death – supplies the flip side of their progressive theoretical program, a thoroughly secular politics of happiness. The Jacobin program, centrally elaborated in Godwin's *Political Justice* (1793), allows for the theoretical, utopian possibility of a perfectly just society, in which "prejudices" – including the belief in rank, entail, primogeniture, and marriage itself – would be eradicated; "luxury" and gross material inequalities would be eliminated; and individuals, unfettered by all but the most minimal government, would conscientiously strive for the public good or "the greatest sum of pleasure or happiness." (In ancient Epicurean fashion, Godwin and his followers equated "happiness" or the *summum bonum* with "pleasure," but pleasure of a tranquil, rational variety.) Godwin maintains, moreover, that "there is no true joy but in the spectacle and contemplation of happiness," and so the greatest joy will attend the greatest collective happiness.[30]

Mary Hays translated Godwin's end-of-history scenario into a passionate defense of a woman's potential power to hasten the *eschaton* through selecting her own sexual partner, in defiance of a constraining code of feminine modesty and outside the legal fiction of marriage. Thus her semi-autobiographical heroine, Emma Courtney, offers herself to the man she desires, Augustus Harley, with a Godwinian appeal to the greatest good: "What is it that we desire – *pleasure – happiness*? I allow, pleasure is the supreme good: but it must be analyzed – it must have a stable foundation – to this analysis I now call you! This is the critical moment, upon which hangs a long chain of events – This moment may decide your future destiny and mine – it may, even, affect that of unborn myriads!" That their relationship might add to a wider felicity in both space and time is due to the ripple effect or outward radiation of rational pleasure and happiness: "I feel in myself the capacities for increasing the happiness, and the improvement, of a few individuals – and this circle, spreading wider and wider, would operate towards the grand end of life – *general utility*"; "From the center of private affections, it will at length embrace – like spreading circles on the peaceful bosom of the smooth and expanded lake – the whole sensitive and rational creation."[31]

Yet Augustus turns a deaf ear to Emma's appeal, choosing to continue in an unhappy marriage out of a questionable sense of "rigid honour" (178), with ultimately dire consequences for all involved. Why does Augustus prove ineducable? The problem, to quote a chapter title from Godwin's *Political Justice*, is that "the characters of men originate in their external circumstances" (I.iv), and while Godwin philosophically maintained "there is scarcely such a thing in character and principles, as an irremediable error" (1:36), in narrative practice he and other Jacobin novelists presented the prejudices acquired early in life as ineradicable, sicknesses unto death. The tragedy of *Caleb Williams* (1794) develops from Mr. Falkland's erroneous but tenacious opinion, acquired through education and ultimately from feudal property arrangements, that his personal honor is of greater value than the lives of other people, including that of his loyal servant, Caleb. A lurid example of the indomitableness of prejudice comes in *Emma Courtney*, when Mr. Montague – Emma's eventual husband, for whom she feels a rational affection – wracked by "senseless jealousies" of Augustus, "stung by false pride" and the thirst for revenge, takes a servant girl as a mistress, kills the illegitimate child he has by her, and then commits suicide (190).

Emma's clipped comment on his long suicide note – "These are the consequences of confused systems of morals" – skirts the suggestion that both his pernicious morality of honor and the homicidal/suicidal acts it led to were the inevitable consequences of his upbringing. The novel raises a further, equally troubling question: whether or not Montague's suicide was in any sense a voluntary rather than conditionally determined act, may it not have been a reasonable one? To quote from his suicide note – given his "obscure consciousness of the prejudices upon which my character has been formed" and *"the inveterate force of habit"* (190), might suicide be the only escape from a habitually bad character? The question rings in Jacobin fiction through to the prospective suicide of Frankenstein's creature that closes Mary Shelley's 1818 novel: given the determining force of circumstances (as of the preordaining Calvinist God that Godwin grew up believing in), what choice does the reprobate have but, sooner or later, to self-destruct?

The creature neatly inverts the eudaimonistic formula that virtue is necessary or sufficient for happiness in addressing Victor, his creator or God: "I was benevolent and good; misery made me a fiend. Make me happy, and I shall again be virtuous."[32] Although the creature's plea to his creator falls on deaf ears, Shelley – like her father, like Mary Hays – presumably hoped that it would communicate directly to her readers, to inspire social and legal changes that might alleviate the burdens of oppressed members of society (women, the poor, slaves) and so make them, in the aggregate, more happy and virtuous. Demonstrating the inescapable effects of socio-economic and ideological circumstances on character, especially in early life, might lead to the gradual transformation of those circumstances and even, perhaps, the utopia that Godwin dared to imagine.

Jane Austen's relation to both the pessimism and possible utopianism of the Jacobin novelists may best be seen in *Sense and Sensibility*, a work that, as Michael Prince comments, stages an unresolved dialogue between "Marianne's secular utopianism" and Elinor's "more cautious art of deliberation."[33] Marianne's is not a utopia of renovated circumstances, however, but a "utopia of her own feelings,"[34] built on an imagination conversant with nature and the verse of genteel rural occupation (Thomson, Cowper), resistant to stifling social conventions, and insulated from the machinations of others (chiefly Willoughby). Marianne quixotically rises above a social world – money-grubbing, social-climbing, and sexually exploitative – that is every bit as bad as that of *Caleb Williams* or Wollstonecraft's *The Wrongs of Woman* (1798), and her nonconformity has been duly praised by recent critics, Johnson and Prince among them.

Yet it should be noted that even Marianne, for all her (pre-)romanticism, never doubts that the accident of wealth is a necessary condition for happiness. On this point, "sense" and "sensibility" do not differ at all. In a conversation with Edward Ferrars on what constitutes happiness, Marianne asks, "What have wealth or grandeur to do with happiness?"

> "Grandeur has but little," said Elinor, "but wealth has much to do with it."
> "Elinor, for shame!" said Marianne; "money can only give happiness where there is nothing else to give it. Beyond a competence, it can afford no real satisfaction, as far as mere self is concerned."

"Perhaps," said Elinor, smiling, "we may come to the same point. *Your* competence and *my* wealth are very much alike, I dare say..." (I. 17, p. 91)[35]

In the course of Austen's novel, Marianne never loses, or has to question, her assumption about the necessity of a competence – she happily enough marries Colonel Brandon, a comfortably landed gentleman, at the novel's end – but she does, however, come to shed some of her other, less useful opinions or "prejudices," particularly her earlier notions that marriage must be founded on a youthful *eros*; that a 35-year-old (Brandon's age) is too old to be loved; and that there should be no second romantic attachments in a life (Brandon had been in love once before). These are small steps for mankind, but large ones for Marianne – and perhaps for the novel of ideas, bound in necessitarian chains through most of the 1790s. One of Austen's main lessons as a moralist – label it progressive or conservative, as you will – is the anti-Jacobin one that individuals can, at least in part, transcend the circumstances that shaped them. Marianne does so in a way that Hays's Emma could not: Emma could only half-regret the indelible impression that the reading of seventeenth-century French romances and later Rousseau's *Julie* made upon her early character, "productive of a long chain of consequences [i.e., her main narrative of *joi* with Augustus], that will continue to operate till the day of my death" (26).[36]

What allows for the concluding happiness of Austen's happiest novel, *Pride and Prejudice*, is both a female character's transcendence of her prejudiced perceptions, or habit of judging with insufficient deliberation (a habit from which even Elinor Dashwood was not exempt), and a male character's palliation of his early-acquired aristocratic pride (a key part of the confused system of morals that led to much death and degradation in Godwin, Wollstonecraft, and Hays). Character can change in Austen, decisively though not radically – Austen's moral therapy is ameliorative, not curative. Of course, her survey of things as they are reveals a majority of subordinate characters who do not change and who are nonetheless accepted – but not respected – in the comedic capaciousness of her novel. The moral shortcomings of the unchanging are revealed through their circumstantial and circumscribed understandings of what constitutes happiness: for Collins it is his own reflected glory from Lady Catherine; for Lydia it is the glory of commanding the attention of many handsome officers (a phantasmal whole for which Wickham will serve as synecdoche); for Mr. Bennet it is the superior laughter of Democritus observing the follies of life. Capable of rising above without relinquishing sympathy for the other inhabitants of Longbourn, Elizabeth Bennet may be the last character in canonical English literature to both consciously aim at and to achieve an Aristotelian ideal of, as she puts it, "rational happiness," a happiness more than incidentally but not quite essentially accompanied by "worldly prosperity."[37]

See also: chapter 7, WHY FANNY CAN'T READ; chapter 9, THE EROTICS OF THE NOVEL; chapter 18, CONVERSABLE FICTIONS.

Notes

1. Methodologically, this article – a portion of a larger literary history of joy – extends the "keyword" approach to cultural-historical understanding inaugurated by Nietzsche's *Genealogy of Morals* (an 1887 philological examination of the shift from "good/bad" to "good/evil") and variously continued by twentieth-century critics and historians such as William Empson, Raymond Williams, and, most recently, J. G. A. Pocock.

2. *Sense and Sensibility*, in *The Novels of Jane Austen*, ed. R. W. Chapman, 3rd ed. (Oxford: Oxford University Press, 1933), 1:158; Elizabeth Inchbald, *A Simple Story*, ed. J. M. S. Tompkins (Oxford: Oxford University Press, 1988), 269.

3. Quoted in Deal Hudson, *Happiness and the Limits of Satisfaction* (Lanham, MD: Rowman and Littlefield, 1996), 49.

4. On Hobbes, Locke, and the "pursuit of happiness" as it develops into the eighteenth century, see my *The Passion for Happiness: Samuel Johnson and David Hume* (Ithaca, NY: Cornell University Press, 2000), 65–70. I have argued elsewhere that Samuel Johnson pioneered a phenomenological understanding of "happiness" that differed signally from the service the term did as *eudaimonia*: see my "Samuel Johnson," in *British Writers: Retrospective Supplement I*, ed. Jay Parini (New York: Scribner's, 2002), 148–49.

5. *The Letters of David Hume*, ed. J. Y. T. Greig (Oxford: Clarendon Press, 1932), 2:366–67.

6. Daniel Defoe, *Roxana*, ed. John Mullan (Oxford: Oxford University Press, 1996), 257.

7. Henry Fielding, *Joseph Andrews*, ed. Martin C. Battestin (Middletown, CT: Wesleyan University Press, 1967), 309–10.

8. Edgar Allen Poe, *The Narrative of Arthur Gordon Pym*, in *Poe: Selected Tales* (New York: Library of America, 1991), 319–50.

9. Daniel Defoe, *Robinson Crusoe*, ed. J. Donald Crowley (London: Oxford University Press, 1972), 89.

10. John Locke, *An Essay Concerning Human Understanding*, ed. Peter H. Nidditch, Book 2 (Oxford: Clarendon Press, 1979), 231.

11. Michel Zink, *Medieval French Literature: An Introduction*, trans. Jeff Rider (Binghamton, NY: Pegasus, 1995), 35–36. See also Moshe Lazar, "Fin'Amor," in *A Handbook of the Troubadours*, ed. F. R. P. Akehurst and Judith M. Davis (Berkeley and Los Angeles: University of California Press, 1995), 61–100, esp. the section "Fin'Amor and Joy," 76–83.

12. C. S. Lewis, *Surprised by Joy* (New York: Harcourt Brace, 1955), 17–18. Lewis continues, "I call it Joy, which is here a technical term and must be sharply distinguished from Happiness and from Pleasure."

13. Horace Walpole, *The Castle of Otranto*, ed. W. S. Lewis (Oxford: Oxford University Press, 1964), 41–43.

14. Denis de Rougemont, *Love in the Western World*, trans. Montgomery Belgion (New York: Pantheon, 1956), 52.

15. Johann Wolfgang von Goethe, *The Sorrows of Young Werther and Novella*, trans. Elizabeth Mayer, Louise Bogan, and W. H. Auden (New York: Random House, 1971), 7, 138.

16. John Bunyan, *The Pilgrim's Progress*, ed. N. H. Keeble (Oxford: Oxford University Press, 1984), 132.

17. Stanley Fish, "*Lycidas*: A Poem Finally Anonymous," *Glyph* 8 (1981): 15.

18. George A. Starr, *Defoe and Spiritual Autobiography* (Princeton, NJ: Princeton University Press, 1965); J. Paul Hunter, *The Reluctant Pilgrim* (Baltimore, MD: Johns Hopkins University Press, 1966).

19. Geoffrey Sill, *The Cure of the Passions and the Origins of the English Novel* (Cambridge: Cambridge University Press, 2001), 92, 100–101; see, generally, 86–106.

20. My reading here of *Robinson Crusoe* is greatly indebted to John Richetti, who has examined the novel's end and means of reconciling liberty with necessity or circumstance (*Defoe's Narratives: Situations and Structures* {Oxford: Clarendon Press, 1975}, 21–62) and Crusoe's growth in the course of the

novel into a practical tactician (*The English Novel in History, 1700–1780* {London: Routledge, 1999}, 67–72).

21. R. S. Crane, "Suggestions towards a Genealogy of the 'Man of Feeling'," *ELH* 1 (1934): 205–30.

22. John M. Robertson, whose 1900 edition of the *Characteristicks* remained the standard edition through the twentieth century, presented Spinoza as a crucial influence on Shaftesbury; Philip Ayres's recent edition (2 vols., Oxford: Clarendon Press, 1999), which supersedes Robertson's, is more skeptical of the influence, but nonetheless cites Robertson's extensive Spinozan annotation to Shaftesbury's *Inquiry Concerning Virtue* in his own notes on the text, 1:303–304. My subsequent references are to Ayres's edition. Shaftesbury's deep and extensive influence on eighteenth-century British literature was first argued by C. A. Moore, "Shaftesbury and the Ethical Poets in England, 1700–1760," *PMLA* 31 (1916): 264–325.

23. See the episode of *Melmoth the Wanderer* (chapter 9) in which "the Parricide" recounts his delight in torturing and murdering an apostate monk and his novice wife.

24. See James Lynch, *Henry Fielding and the Heliodoran Novel* (Teaneck, NJ: Farleigh Dickinson University Press, 1986); more generally, on the Hellenistic roots of the eighteenth-century novel, see Margaret Doody, *The True Story of the Novel* (New Brunswick, NJ: Rutgers University Press, 1996). On the formal prototypes of Fielding's novel, see also Homer Goldberg, *The Art of Joseph Andrews* (Chicago: University of Chicago Press, 1969), 27–72.

25. Francis Hutcheson, *On the Nature and Conduct of the Passions*, ed. Andrew Ward (Manchester: Clinamen Press, 1999), section 3, 48–49.

26. See especially Joseph's dialogue with Parson Barnabas, Book 1, chapter 13, and his emotions during and immediately after Fanny's abduction by a vicious country squire, Book 3, chapters 11–12.

27. Henry Fielding, *Tom Jones*, 783.

28. Those who take Fielding to be the last author to subscribe to "God's plot" include Aubrey Williams, Martin Battestin, and Leo

Damrosch; they are opposed by secularizing readers – John Bender, John Richetti, Ronald Paulson – who see the author himself as responsible for the order that emerges at the end of his novels. For Bender in particular, the order maintained by the novelist is analogous to the surveillance and legal control of the emerging modern state. The controversy is neatly laid out by Charles Knight, "*Joseph Andrews* and the Failure of Authority," *Eighteenth-Century Fiction* 4 (1992): 109–29.

29. See Claudia L. Johnson, *Jane Austen: Women, Politics, and the Novel* (Chicago: University of Chicago Press, 1988), 19 (Johnson quotation), 64 (on *Sense and Sensibility* as a therapeutic novel), and 73–93 (chapter on "*Pride and Prejudice* and the Pursuit of Happiness").

30. William Godwin, *Enquiry Concerning Political Justice and its Influence on Morals and Happiness*, ed. F. E. L. Priestley, 3 vols. (Toronto: University of Toronto Press, 1946), 1:xxv ("Summary of Principles"), 1:447 (4.11). Godwin's utopian vision of a future "system of equality" is worked out in Book VIII, "Of Property" (2:420–554).

31. *Memoirs of Emma Courtney*, ed. Eleanor Ty (Oxford: Oxford University Press, 1996), 116, 118, and 124.

32. Mary Shelley, *Frankenstein* (1818 text), 2:23.

33. Michael Prince, *Philosophical Dialogue in the British Enlightenment: Theology, Aesthetics, and the Novel* (Cambridge: Cambridge University Press, 1996), 241, 246.

34. Ibid., 240.

35. Marianne recalls in her formulation of happiness lines by Pope, a poet she values only less than Thomson, Cowper, or Scott: "Reason's whole pleasure, all the joys of Sense, / Lie in three words, Health, Peace, and Competence," *An Essay on Man* 4:79–80 in *Poems of Alexander Pope*, ed. John Butt (New Haven, CT: Yale University Press, 1951–69), 3.1.

36. Cf. the title character of Wollstonecraft's *Mary* (1788), unable wholly to transcend the crippling, excessive sensibility fostered in part by her youthful reading of Thomson, Young, and Milton. See Gary Kelly's useful

Introduction to *Mary and The Wrongs of Woman* (Oxford: Oxford University Press, 1976), xi–xiv.

37. *Pride and Prejudice*, in *The Novels of Jane Austen*, 2:307 (III. 7). Alasdair MacIntyre provocatively argues, "When Jane Austen speaks of 'happiness,' she does so as an Aristotelian"; indeed, she is "the last great representative of the classical tradition of the virtues." *After Virtue: A Study in Moral Theory*, 2nd ed. (Notre Dame, IN: University of Notre Dame Press, 1984), 240–43.

FURTHER READING

Annas, Julia. *The Morality of Happiness*. New York: Oxford University Press, 1993.

Hudson, Deal. *Happiness and the Limits of Satisfaction*. Lanham, MD: Rowman and Littlefield, 1996.

James, Susan. *Passion and Action: The Emotions in Seventeenth-Century Philosophy*. Oxford: Clarendon Press, 1997.

Lazar, Moshe. "*Fin'Amor.*" In *A Handbook of the Troubadours*, ed. F. R. P. Akehurst and Judith M. Davis. Berkeley and Los Angeles: University of California Press, 1995. 61–100.

Mauzi, Robert. *L'Idée du bonheur dans la littérature et la pensée françaises au XVIIIe siècle*. Paris: Armand Colin, 1960.

Potkay, Adam. *The Passion for Happiness: Samuel Johnson and David Hume*. Ithaca, NY: Cornell University Press, 2000.

Part Three
The Novel's Modern Legacy

15

The Eighteenth-Century Novel and Print Culture: A Proposed Modesty

Christopher Flint

She is very well bred, & expresses herself with much modesty, upon all subjects – which in an *Authoress*, a woman of *known* understanding, is extremely pleasing.

The authorial modesty Frances Burney attributes to Frances Brooke may not be as valued today as it was in the eighteenth century. We have come to consider the "Modest Muse" a significantly limiting concept, often employed to restrict an author's access to or productivity within the print marketplace. Burney's description of the modest "*Authoress*" with whom she shares authorial initials deftly captures the subtle displacements and inhibitions that propriety enforces upon intellectual labor (or, as she puts it, "*known* understanding"). Yet if eighteenth-century authors were encumbered by expectations of modesty, no such burden exists for the twenty-first-century critic. Indeed, recent studies of eighteenth-century fiction and print culture suggest that modern critics might profit from a more modest account of the novel. The print medium has, of course, the advantage of a more concrete and accessible body of lasting evidence than many other communications networks. But since the revival of interest in the history of the book in the last decade, this advantage has often encouraged scholars of eighteenth-century prose fiction to grant the novel a crucial and representative role in the communications revolution of the period.

Any explanation of the relationship between print and narrative fiction should begin, however, by admitting that the novel represents a rather modest part of the history of publishing in the long eighteenth century. As the work of Jan Fergus and Paula McDowell has recently suggested, privileging the novel often hampers the study of eighteenth-century print culture. McDowell observes that "Whereas today, students of eighteenth-century literature are most likely to study novels, one publishing historian estimates that the proportion of all fiction (new titles and reprints) to total book and pamphlet production for the years 1720–9 was only 1.1 percent, rising to 4 percent by 1770."[1] The novel, in other words, was vying for the attention of consumers among a variety of other equally compelling modes of communication in the print sphere. Future work may in fact study the novel's attempts not only to operate within but also to distance itself from a communications network. If so, this work should consider how fiction creates a particular mimetic domain that both reports and distorts those competing modes of imagining a self, community, nation, or world.

The difficulty facing a modest proposal for the composite field of "the novel" and "print culture" is that neither category is particularly manageable, and both are therefore susceptible to reductive explanations and wide-scale claims. At the same time, both fields require interdisciplinary scope. More than ten years ago Roger Chartier urged those concerned with the history of the book to consider the reciprocal relations among three basic categories: the creation of the text (how authors shape the book's written content); the nature of the reader (what skills, access, and modes of reading are brought to the text); and the material state of the book (such as its scribal or printed forms, or means of distribution).[2] These are effectively the terms that recent work on the eighteenth-century British novel has invoked to discuss the function of prose fiction in an emerging print culture. At the risk of seeming to discourse, like Frances Brooke, "upon all subjects," I will examine this scholarship by tracing lines of development, areas of controversy, and implications for the future. Chartier's principal categories – the author, the reader, and the book – may be usefully described as structural, social, and technological determinants. However distinct these may be, they are fundamentally interrelated. I will thus organize the essay into three parts, each one devoted to one of these determinants, but necessarily related to the others as a comprehensive set of practices.

"Author"

I put "author" in quotation marks (much as Burney highlights *"Authoress"* in her remarks about Brooke) because the concept of authorship is routinely in a state of suspension. Over time various theoretical approaches have progressively redefined the instrumental role of the writer in print culture. In the 1960s, Michel Foucault and Roland Barthes famously announced the "disappearance" or "death" of the author. By this, they meant that it was preferable to conceive of the published writer as fulfilling an "author function," the concept by which a given culture draws historically bound assumptions about writing, authority, and originality.[3] This reconfiguration developed, in part, because structuralism, formalism, and new criticism had shifted attention from biographical analysis of the authored text to examinations of the "objective" features of the work itself. In the 1970s, Jacques Derrida claimed that the author's role could only be understood effectively as a discursive attribute deciphered through the process of reading. More recently, as critics increasingly consider authorship a collaborative social, legal, and marketplace enterprise, the equation between the author and "original genius" has consequently been disputed.[4]

Lately, however, the individual author has reappeared, though in chastened form, as a figure whose identity is to be measured in relation to modernity. This has been especially true of recent work that recovers and claims the (often female) novelist as one of the first real emanations of a modern authorial sensibility. The novelist, that is, becomes an avatar of a new but complex articulation of intellectual property, commodification, and modern sensibility.[5] Like the Romantic poets, with whom they share credit for fashioning modern authorship, eighteenth-century novelists supposedly embodied the ideal of the author as a self-sufficient original genius who disdains the market forces that constrain literary production. Studies of this Romantic mode have been effective in both explaining and critiquing the cult of the author that arose in the late eighteenth century. Nonetheless, they tend to produce a limited construction of the author function by seeking too definitive a time frame and too narrow a set of historical causes in order to pinpoint the emergence of the "modern author."

Central to the arguments about the rise of modern Romantic authorship is the assumption that a particular definition of "author," rooted in the emergence of a professional class and a commodity culture, ultimately trumps all other definitions. That a widespread print culture would manifest different modes of authorship seems likely, but to claim from print's impact that one particular kind of author was incarnated for the first time ignores the variety of forms that authorship assumed in the eighteenth century. As various critics have shown, amateur, patronized, polemical, educational, collaborative, oral, coterie, and manuscript forms of authorship persisted into the nineteenth century.[6] It might, therefore, be as useful to consider "author," "writer," or "novelist" as general rubrics that take different historical shapes at different points in literary and critical history and in relation to various cultural determinants.

A print-based analysis may help calibrate, if not resolve, the multiple meanings of such concepts as writer, author, and novelist. Since the 1980s, work on eighteenth-century writing has concentrated especially on economic, legal, and philosophical assessments of the "author" in order to explain the Romantic model that prizes originality, autonomy, and genius. This work has customarily focused on canonical literature (such as that by Pope or Johnson). It has often privileged unique historical events, in particular, legal decisions such as the Copyright Act in 1709, Tonson v. Collins in 1760, or Donaldson v. Beckett in 1774. It has, further, mined theories of authorship published in the eighteenth century, as well as theories of intellectual property and the novel (by, for instance, Catharine Macauley, James Ralph, Clara Reeve, or Edward Young) in order to flesh out historical ideas about the "modern" writer. Summarizing this process, Mark Rose notes that the legal, critical, social, and marketplace conceptions of authorship that arose after the 1740s made a literary work seem the "objectification of a writer's self."[7] Given, however, that the most striking feature of new novels published between 1770 and 1799 is that "the overwhelming majority of them were published without attribution of authorship,"[8] we may be hasty in assuming that either high culture or the legal domain offered much actual self-determining power to most novelists. The scribbling Grub Street novelist, in particular, who hardly matched this "modern" ideal, was frequently situated against writers such as Fielding, Sterne, Burney, or Austen. Yet, as Richard Sher has shown, despite the conceptual impact of the legal and professional dimensions of literary agency, the bulk of professional writers (and therefore very many novelists) still operated within a literary marketplace that protected and rewarded publishers more than authors.[9] Booksellers, in practical terms, did not lose their monopoly powers until after 1800. Furthermore, copyright controversies in the eighteenth century rarely, if ever, involved prose fiction. In fact, novels in the period, especially those produced in "Grub Street," both established competing conceptions of authorship and helped define the Romantic model. Expanding the research on "modern" writing, then, recent scholarship has widened the definitional range of eighteenth-century authorship.

Similarly, the definition of the "novel" has proved as complex a critical issue as authorship. The two categories are, in fact, crucially related, since the novelist's status as an author depended on the status of novels themselves. Current scholarship indicates a general consensus that the mid-century marks the beginning of a "novel culture" in Britain. There are, of course, dissenters from this opinion, such as John Paul Hunter, Cheryl Turner, William Warner, and Ian Watt. But the predominant view seems to be that the 1740s to 1750s were the watershed years. Two main factors have shaped this claim: a fully established commodity economy, and a new market in professional commentators on the novel (particularly in periodical review form). According to Miranda Burgess, "The notion of a distinct and autonomous 'species' of prose fiction was of mid-eighteenth-century provenance,"[10] suggesting that twentieth-century criticism now tends to accept the period's own late self-determination in this regard.

But, as the eighteenth century amply demonstrates, the volatility and variability of the print marketplace was matched by the variety of novels (or, more properly, prose fiction) that appeared. If, to identify a point of origin, we need to drop or add Behn and Defoe (who alternate in being called early novelists and proto-novelists), how do we avoid a self-fulfilling model of history? Richardson and Fielding never referred to themselves as novelists, yet they, along with late Haywood, routinely fulfill both eighteenth- and twentieth-century definitions of the term. Though access to print may have altered the forms of eighteenth-century fiction in significant ways, is print a necessary condition of the novel? Can a novel be a novel without ever appearing in print? Were the manuscripts that Burney and Austen read aloud, or gave to their families to read, novels before or after they were published? Couldn't one simply identify various types of eighteenth-century authorship or different forms of the novel in the period?

Individual authorial cases only complicate matters. If Defoe is a novelist, he is an odd one insofar as he published long works of prose fiction only late in life (and for just five years). These were narratives that he refused to call fiction and to which he never assigned his own authorship. His poetry, polemical works, and non-fiction far outweigh his fictional output. Like many other "novelists" in the period, such as Behn, Fielding, or Inchbald, he published a variety of literary and non-literary works and pursued a number of different professions. Similar issues arise with other authors. Does Haywood become a novelist only in the middle of the century, when she stops publishing short narratives and begins composing long multi-volume affairs like *The History of Miss Betsy Thoughtless* (1751) and *The History of Jemmy and Jenny Jessamy* (1752)? Do print market demands at that point dictate her professional identity? Richardson continued to work avidly as a master printer, even when he was both writing and publishing those monuments of eighteenth-century print, *Pamela* (1740), *Clarissa* (1748), and *Sir Charles Grandison* (1753–4). He then raided these texts to create *A Collection of the Moral and Instructive Sentiments, Maxims, Cautions, and Reflexions of Pamela, Clarissa, and Sir Charles Grandison* (1755), which was effectively a conduct manual, suggesting that such bits of fiction were something other than fiction. Do these activities make Richardson more or less a novelist? Does the *Pamela* media event (during which such items as fans, teacups, and paintings that depicted scenes from the novel were marketed) confer the status of novelist on Richardson because it suggests that writing has finally become so commodified as to be recognizably modern?[11] Then what of the fact that there was a Crusoe media event too (produced through prints, broadsides, redactions for children, pictures, etc.); is it so radically different as to exclude Defoe from the same process Richardson undergoes?

The difficulties in defining what novelists do are continuous and are connected to extensive bibliographical variables. In the recent and indispensable two-volume bibliography, *The English Novel 1770–1829*, James Raven notes that simply identifying novels produced at the time is a constantly evolving task. He nonetheless argues that novels are an identifiable new form in the eighteenth century because they share certain repeated (though diverse) features. Surprisingly, however, the only ones he cites as consistent are "credibility" and "the ability to communicate knowledge and wisdom."[12] Yet Raven's list contains the translation of Rudolf Erich Raspe's *Baron Munchausen's Narrative of his Marvellous Travels* (1786), hardly a credible fiction, maybe not wise, certainly not English. If we include this translation, shouldn't Dunton's 1691 *A New Voyage Around the World* also qualify? As Edward Mangin opines as late as 1808, "The word novel is a generical term; of which romances, histories, memoirs, letters, tales, lives, and adventures, are the species."[13]

The pervasive critical need to narrow the definitions of "author" and "novel" is also reflected in much of the recent attention given to the relation between gender and print culture. From scholars who note the prevalence of women writers in circulating libraries to those who argue for their ascendancy in the marketplace at the close of the century, there has been extensive examination of the rapid increase in women's access to print from the mid-century on. Motivated by a genuine need to counteract male bias in the history of the eighteenth-century novel, such work has resurrected a large group of neglected but highly accomplished writers. Nonetheless, some of this work has potentially skewed the view of the literary landscape by assuming that novels and women novelists were, because of their dramatic rise in numbers, the pre-eminent factor in shaping literate culture in the period. Typical is Ann Mellor's assertion in her provocative *Mothers of the Nation* that "women could, and perhaps for the first time did, dominate the material production of literature."[14] This kind of claim may, however, obscure a more diverse en-gendering of the novel by both women and men.

The re-examination of the relationship between gender and print culture has tended to produce sociological conclusions, often supported by the selective use of statistical data or restrictive definitions of the novel, which merit some qualification. What may apply, for example, to circulating libraries – that they indicate a revolution in what popular literature was read and by whom – may not apply to book consumption generally. For one, religious discourse continued to be, by far, the most pervasive form of printed text. Moreover, there was a wide variety of means to acquire printed matter (including fiction). Book clubs, ranging from those that stocked mostly religious and political material to those that cultivated some interest in prose fiction, preceded the advent of circulating and subscription libraries. In these, male authors and patrons prevailed. Parish libraries, unlikely to carry novels and fashionable periodicals, served readers of both sexes, though were probably relatively unused. There were, furthermore, always a variety of places, from bookstalls and stationers to booksellers' shops, to purchase printed volumes directly, and these texts were frequently, in turn, circulated among family members and acquaintances. It is difficult to conclude from such sources, especially as the majority of transactions have gone unrecorded, that novelists in general, and women novelists especially, had a particularly distinctive purchase on the eighteenth-century reading public. Constituting only four percent of printed matter near the end of the period, the novel can hardly claim to dominate or transform the culture. Similarly, while compilations of women authors, such as that by Cheryl Turner, reveal the impressive contributions of women novelists, and their proportional advance in numbers over the period, they do not prove either dominance or the purported "feminization" of literate culture. According to one recent calculation, "Male writers (292) hugely outnumbered female writers (189). . . . yet the number of individual novels written by men was . . . slightly less than that by women (407 titles compared to 419)."[15] In the early part of the eighteenth century the cultural imaginary was shaped as much by fictional adventure, pirate, and criminal narratives (predominantly written by men) as the now noteworthy novels of amorous intrigue written by Behn, Manley, and Haywood. Later novels ranged across an enormously broad range of types, from oriental narratives to stories supposedly told by inanimate objects, which were embraced equally by women and men.

An exclusive emphasis on gender can, in fact, divert attention from a range of other compelling issues regarding novels and authorship, some of which intersect with gender in interesting ways. Studies of how authors continued to operate within a manuscript tradition or negotiated the conversion from manuscript to print (including, but not limited to, how they related to booksellers or printers), are still needed; these might further illuminate the process of writing as it was understood in the period. Likewise, there is a call for a deeper understanding of the relation between orality and novels (as Margaret Ezell, Nicholas Hudson, and Patricia Michaelson note). More can also be done on novelists and class. While it is true that eighteenth-century novelists were predominantly of the "middling sort," some were aristocrats, and, as several titles suggest, some in the lower classes published novels as well. Reviewers of the period simultaneously discouraged lower-class fiction and recognized its potential wealth of subject matter, as we see hinted in critiques of *The Fortunate Blue-Coat Boy* (1770), of which the *Monthly Review* lamented "What will become of the Reviewers, if this numerous band of charity-boys should follow their comrade's example, and run their callow heads against the press. Mercy on us! what a deluge of histories, memoirs, lives and adventures, shall we have!"[16]

A more integrated approach to authorship would open the field of study by drawing wider rather than narrower boundaries around novel writing. The prose fiction that authors produced in the eighteenth century often projected models of writing and publication that were antithetical to the Romantic conception of authorship and, in some ways, closer to a current understanding of "authorship," as a highly mediated media concept. As the next two sections suggest, the full extent of authorial identity should also be linked to how readers consumed the work of authors (and in doing so, helped define the latter) and how the print industry marketed works of fiction, reminding us that the writer depended on the literary marketplace as much as her or his own "originality."

Reader(s)

The history of eighteenth-century reading, like that of authorship, reveals the complex relationship between production and consumption in the eighteenth-century literary marketplace. As John Brewer notes: "Books, print and readers were everywhere. Not everyone was a reader, but even those who could not read lived to an unprecedented degree in a culture of print, for the impact of the publishing revolution extended beyond the literate."[17] To say that the "revolution" extended to novel reading may be an exaggeration; literacy rates, always difficult to measure with certitude, suggest that the fluency required for the individual silent reading usually associated with novels was not significantly greater by 1790 than it had been in 1720 (in fact, there may have been a decrease in literacy between 1760 and 1780).[18] But "the public" so often addressed in the prefaces and narrative content of novels at this time was one for whom prose fiction was competing on a number of levels.

How do we characterize the reader(s) of eighteenth-century fiction? The parenthetical (s) is meant to indicate the distinction one ought to draw between the conceptual figure of "the reader" and specific historical readers, only a small portion of whom left traces of their reading practices. When Samuel Johnson used the term "common reader" to describe public consumers of print who demanded "engagement and entertainment" he established, as Robert DeMaria notes, a modern designation for the reader which both displaced and reconciled the cloistered scholar and the closeted reader of romances.[19] But the reader that Johnson and many current scholars extol was not an entirely free agent. Readers were also, of course, hectored, bullied, cajoled, and persuaded by authors and booksellers alike. Just as the cultural function of the author may be considered a feedback loop of production and consumption, so too may the reader be best understood as both authorizing and conforming to given texts.

If the author has been, in a sense, demoted in recent years, the reader has been generally promoted, and has, as a result, become radically multifarious. Some critics focus on the representation of readers in fiction (Ellen Gardiner, for instance); some on data about readers of fiction (Raven). Others have begun to examine the role of non-readers' exposure to fiction, fueled in part by the controversies over rates of literacy. Indeed, the full extent of eighteenth-century reading habits needs better accounting. Most research has assumed that silent reading is the primary model of fictional consumption. Lately, however, the work of Barbara Benedict, Ezell, Michaelson, and others, has intimated that, despite long-standing historical claims that print isolates readers in a sphere of private and silent reading, the medium constantly reinforced the social mediations at work in published texts. New questions now range from whether silent reading is really so solitary to how readers regarded an authorial "voice." Eighteenth-century literary criticism frequently commended the reader's ability to amplify a writer's expressions with what Lord Kames called "a ready command of the tones suited to those expressions," or what Priestley regarded as the ordinary reader's capacity to "give the language the assistance we can from pronunciation."[20] Naomi Tadmor argues, moreover, that reading in the eighteenth century often coalesced with other social transactions involving various civic networks. From purchasing, lending, and borrowing books to reading in company or to groups engaged in household or workplace labor, the consumption of texts was often anything but solitary, idle, or frivolous.[21] Raven similarly notes the sociability that public and private libraries fostered. The larger libraries, he argues, "provided space or books for the individual, silent reader, and yet supported, in different ways, the social celebration of books and the communal reading performance." Almost all libraries nourished, he adds, "selection, browsing and the part-reading of a variety of books, but also encouraged concentrated reading, either silently or, as in the case of many domestic libraries, aloud to company."[22]

In reconstructing eighteenth-century readership of the novel, we should therefore acknowledge its communal aspects. Active, if often unrecorded, discussions of fiction, for example, undoubtedly shaped its literary impact. Patricia Crain notes that American readers of British novels, which booksellers imported to the colonies increasingly in the eighteenth century, were admonished, often by novelists themselves, that the seductions of fiction could be counteracted by talking about the novels. In the opinion of a character in William Hill Brown's 1789 novel *The Power of Sympathy* (often called the first American novel): "Conversation only can remedy this dangerous evil, strengthen the judgment, and make reading really useful."[23] This comment echoes the well-documented responses in Britain and America to the perceived moral corruption of prose fiction, especially among women, children, and the lower classes. In America, the essay "Observations on Novel-Reading" argued that "the legislature of the UNITED STATES, would not act beneath their dignity, if they should, among other restraints on the *licentiousness* of the press, lay a very heavy duty on all novels whatsoever for the future – as well those imported, as those printed within their jurisdiction."[24] In Britain, similar concerns were expressed about how the novel, as James Beattie observes in *Dissertations Moral and Critical* (1783), "breeds dislike to history, and all the substantial parts of knowledge; withdraws the attention from nature and truth; and fills the mind with extravagant thoughts, and too often with criminal propensities" (574). While the extent and intensity of these adverse reactions may not, in fact, have been commensurate with the relatively small output of fiction, they do reflect the concern that novel reading produced and the variety of strategies, from proscription to monitoring, that were offered to constrain what many regarded as readers' unregulated habits.

Greater attention to the diversity of "reading" in the eighteenth century may, in fact, alter various assumptions about literary consumption. One of the most famous instances of the *Pamela* media event is the reported jubilation and ringing of church bells when the town of Preston heard, from a public reading of Richardson's novel, that Pamela had finally married her would-be seducer, Mr. B. This story has most often been discussed as a sign of the consumer mania that Richardson's novel stoked, but it also reveals the enormously unfixed nature of reading in the period. If, as Ezell has documented, vibrant forms of social authorship persisted in the eighteenth century,[25] an extensive social readership also probably existed. For instance, there appears to have been considerable reading aloud (though how often novels were orated requires further scouring of memoirs). This attention to orality raises certain fundamental questions. Does a text routinely read aloud carry a different sociological charge than a text read silently and only once? Lord Stanley reported in 1789 that a party to whom he was reading aloud *The Castle of Otranto* (1765), on a foggy, atmospheric, boat trip through the Faroe Islands, was "sorry to leave off the story before we knew to whom the great enchanted helmet belonged."[26] Frances Burney records that her aspiring family routinely read aloud literature (including novels), and she continues to remark on this practice in relation to her domestic life with her husband and son.[27] The mercer and draper, Thomas Turner, and his wife Peggy daily read to one another, including extensive, though intermittent progress through *Clarissa*. As Tadmor observes, the reading was shared between the Turners during arduous workdays in the house and the shop adjoining.[28] Part of a disciplined religious life, it eventually included family, friends, and servants (activities that, in fact, parallel the reading of books in Samuel Richardson's household). Do such acts as these challenge the long-standing assumption that intensive reading (the deep rereading of a select number of texts) gradually replaced extensive reading (the rapid reading of a broad selection) over the course of the eighteenth century? Is it entirely useful, in fact, to separate intensive and extensive reading? Johnson, while admittedly an extraordinary reader, was, according to DeMaria, constantly shifting between different modes of reading that he himself termed "study" or "hard reading," "perusal," "mere reading," and "curious reading." Among the texts he read, those Johnson describes as "captivating" were fictional, but he may have read them in any number of ways.[29]

The recorded experiences of individual eighteenth-century readers reveal not only a wide range of reading modes but also a diverse process of selection. While novel reading seems to have increased in the period, it still accounted for a small portion of overall reading. John Brewer has noted that an avid reader such as Anna Larpent was not consumed by novels. Of the more than 440 titles she read between 1773 and 1783, sixty-eight (or fifteen percent) consisted of English and French novels. While a sizeable number, it is only equal to what she read in history, biography, and political economy, and does not approximate, in terms of repetition, the amount of time she spent studying the Bible, sermons, and pious tracts.[30] Likewise, Stephen Colclough tabulates that the 15-year-old Sheffield apprentice, Joseph Hunter, read in the space of one year (1798) roughly comparable amounts of fiction, travel, divinity, history, and reference works, but much more largely in periodicals and newspapers, in addition to "consumption of sermons at the chapel."[31] More dramatically, perhaps, not one of the many books Walter Shandy enumerates in *Tristram Shandy* (1759–67) is a work of fiction. Novel reading must therefore be understood as a highly contingent form of consumption. Extracts from published material in such records as diaries, logs, memoirs, and autobiographies indicate, for instance, that readers were constantly making strategic decisions about what and how they read. Even where readers obtained and consumed texts probably affected the kind of reading to which they subjected a work. The purported "rage" for reading novels from circulating libraries, for instance, must be understood in relation to how such volumes were presented to the public. Often hastily produced and loaned for only short periods of time, many such texts may have been regarded as largely dispensable reading. A variety of sources, from moral tracts to fire insurance advertisements, complained of hair powder and candle wax in borrowed books, signs of the slovenly and combustible habits associated with bedroom or boudoir reading.[32] That is, we may be attributing to the avid consumption of light reading profound cultural implications that simply reverse the equally overstated denunciations of fictional material by eighteenth-century moral commentators.

In other ways, too, fiction's consumers proved volatile. Reading was, for instance, intimately connected to writing, as the famous examples of Lady Bradsheigh's and Lady Echlin's separate rewritings of the ending to *Clarissa* demonstrate. In such cases as these, reading becomes a resistant act of writing that shows how such readers could be both reactive and proactive figures. At the same time, given that Richardson was inviting written responses to his drafts of the novel, the circuit also worked in the other direction. Clearly, as Richardson was writing his fiction, he was also watching readers read the text, and writing in light of those responses. He was, in fact, still revising his novels in reaction to reader response up until his death. Similarly, the robust market in spurious sequels to Defoe, Richardson, and Sterne's fiction, which, in turn, incited sequels by those writers, signals the interplay of reception and conception that characterizes the novel's economics.

A full understanding of eighteenth-century "novel culture" would need, therefore, to carefully parse these various acts, spaces, and habits of reading. The nature of the evidence already indicates that a monolithic assessment is probably untenable. Admittedly, the access we have to reading practices is very limited and often inconclusive, but the range of reading tactics we can glean from the historical record will broaden our understanding of the variable responses of readers within a probable range of practices. Sterne's (or Fielding's) characteristic addresses to the reader (at once personal and yet comprehending a wide range of possible readers) are, one could argue, the flip side of Austen's frequent last-chapter personalizations of the author–reader relationship. Such textual moments alert us to how eighteenth-century novelists self-consciously cultivated a wide readership and struggled with the seeming paradox of making intimate a relationship that was, in fact, the product of an increasingly anonymous exchange between writer and reader.

Recognizing this complex range of reading is crucial to understanding the novel's cultural function because it both confirms and complicates a major strain in print culture and novel studies, one based on the seminal work of Jürgen Habermas. Nowhere, perhaps, has the instrumental function of the reader been more visible than in discussions of the public sphere. Most scholars of print culture have confronted Habermas' argument that "the commercialization of cultural production,"[33] particularly through the dissemination of printed matter, fostered a uniform public sphere in eighteenth-century Britain (and Europe generally). The popularity of the novel, the increased influence of the press, and advances in the circulation of printed literature in such discourse networks as the coffee house, the library, the music hall, and the theater, fueled public opinion, which became effectively a media event. This activity, in turn, helped create modern nationalism by the end of the century. According to Benedict Anderson (another seminal figure in print history), "print-capitalism" enables the "imagined political communities" necessary to create a unified national identity.[34] As he argues, "fellow-readers" were made aware "via print and paper" that there were "hundreds of thousands, even millions, of people in their particular language-field, and at the same time that only those hundreds of thousands, or millions, so belonged" (47). The unifying and rationalizing effects that Habermas and Anderson describe were, of course, regarded as complementary; their enlightenment force derived from the conviction that an individual's active cultivation of reason would necessarily benefit the social welfare of the state. The effect of rationalizing and consensus-building modes of communication was to create a national unity in which readers could help generate public awareness and reasoned debate. This, largely, is the story that has structured many of the latest studies of eighteenth-century readership and the reception of the novel.

While many authors have been credited with shaping eighteenth-century national consciousness, public opinion is, in fact, most often allied with readers. Part of the successful marketing of eighteenth-century prose fiction resulted, in part, from the mobilization of different mechanisms for distributing published work to readers. As several scholars have shown, these significantly increased means of circulating printed material constituted forms of "cultural technology" that enabled productive social exchange.[35] For Habermas, the novel, especially in epistolary form, played a significant role in fostering personal critical reasoning among readers that helped them participate in the governance of their society.

The close study of print culture, both in its larger, more theoretical orientation and in its often more modest empirical mode, will help dispel or refine certain assumptions about British readership and the role of the public sphere in shaping a nation's governance. A number of scholars have lately complicated the deployment of the terms "public sphere" and "nationalism" in relation to the eighteenth-century novel. Many, for instance, have added the concept of the "counter public sphere" to offset the hegemonic force of Habermas' conceptualization of the public sphere.[36] The insistence on a single public sphere (rather than multiple spheres of public opinion), and a dependence on the distinction between it and a counter public sphere, only partly explains the complexity of the literary marketplace. The similar claim that "Literature" or the "Novel" constituted a counter public sphere also needs some adjustment. A more adequate approach might construe literature as the range of products created by a loose body of actors (authors, publishers, printers, readers, distributors, commentators, etc.) who are themselves at various points active, to various degrees, in various public spheres that intersect, often temporarily, and that function sometimes in agreement, sometimes in contention, and sometimes simply coincidentally.

To account more accurately for the variety of public opinion in eighteenth-century Britain, several scholars have lately begun to apply Pierre Bourdieu's principles of "cultural production" to eighteenth-century prose fiction. Bourdieu's elaborate analysis of the cultural field, in which different public activities (from the literary and artistic to the economic and political) occupy different fields of production, offers a flexible model that can accommodate public dissension.[37] The popularity of a work did not, in all instances, confirm that it was perceived as a culturally central document, and a thoroughgoing analysis of its mode of cultural production might yield a sophisticated explanation of how marketing, reception, and judgment are interrelated. In terms of the novel, relations among authors and the other producers of the printed text also modify how readers might have consumed the fiction they read. Bookseller relations, both in terms of how writers regarded printers and publishers and how the publishing profession managed an author's status, represent one key element in the cultural production of novels. Some of this history can be retrieved by examining the fate of authorship as described within novels or by a novelist's written record, but it would also be helpful to know how other producers, distributors and handlers – from printers and booksellers to reviewers and readers – processed works of fiction.

Reviewing, anthologizing, and canonizing have become, perhaps because they are among the most visible and best-preserved forms of literary reception, the means by which cultural production has most often been studied. Sterne's incorporation not only of such readers as "Dear Sir," "Dear Madam," or "Your Worships," but also of "You Messrs. the monthly Reviewers" who "cut and slash my jerkin," testifies to the writer's market awareness in eighteenth-century literary spheres. But Sterne is only the most overt example of how an author internalizes a whole apparatus of reading, and anticipates a text's dynamic literary reception. As readers come to publish remarks about writers, authors begin to write about their own reading of how readers wrote about them. Professionalized reading becomes a model (or perhaps anti-model) for how to read that is reinternalized in the author's text.

Private reading, then, is only one part of overall reception in the period. It is one of Burgess' insights, for example, that the canonization of earlier novels may have been a response by booksellers to the 1774 Donaldson decision, which limited their propriety rights to copyrighted material.[38] While booksellers continued to compete for new copyrights, they found new editions of older works to be increasingly profitable. The canonization of novels may thus be seen as a consequence, in part, of the development of a literary "marketplace" that the Donaldson decision legitimated. Similarly, reviews often functioned as a means to predetermine reader reception. Various scholars have thus taken Frank Donoghue's lead on eighteenth-century literary reviewing and applied it to the novel.[39] Using such sources as the *Monthly Review, Critical Review, Gentleman's Magazine*, and *London Review*, they have provided insights into the process by which novelists were as much products as producers. Especially noteworthy in recent assessments of this process has been the impact of Barbauld's "Essay on the Origin and Progress of the British Novel," the preface to her edition of *The British Novelists* (1810). But Clara Reeve's *The Progress of Romance* (1785), Vicesimus Knox's "On Novel Reading" (1778), Francis Coventry's "An Essay on the New Species of Writing" (1751), and John Dunlop's *The History of Fiction* (1814), among others, have also received renewed attention for their accounts of the novel as a genre.[40] Many other writers of fiction could be further mined as professional readers – Wollstonecraft's reviews of novels in the *Analytical Review*, for instance, or Smollett's in the *Critical Review*. In addition, the synergy between anthologies and fiction has been treated effectively by Benedict and, in a more concentrated fashion, by Leah Price, who postulates that "a history of the conventions through which novels have been reproduced and reduced could contribute more generally to a genealogy of late-twentieth-century academic criticism."[41] These are areas, then, in which even more critical work can be done (the *Novelist's Magazine* alone is worth a monograph study). Less often studied in detail, though frequently noted, is the mass of fiction that appeared throughout the period in such outlets as periodicals, chapbooks, and other so-called ephemera that surely shaped what value readers accorded novels and novelists. By neglecting these other forms of fiction we may be attenuating a field of cultural production that is more extensive and diverse than conventional definitions of the novel allow.

Ultimately, the wide-ranging reactions to fiction in eighteenth-century Britain indicate the plural nature of print's effects. In their several ways, they attest to the dialectical energy of print as a medium. Prose fiction often endorsed the Enlightenment rationality that seemed implicit in printing technology and yet continuously revealed how communication exceeded the boundaries of rational, reproducible, standardized, and commodified discourse. It is precisely this dynamic that shapes one of the most vexed issues in the history of print: whether increased circulation of, or technological advances in, printed matter transforms how people read, think, and interact socially, or whether such advances are themselves the result of changes in modes of cognition and social behavior. Seeing print culture as either simply effecting, or, conversely, the effect of a revolution in consciousness tends, I would argue, to remove print as an element from the very culture it ostensibly produces. As I propose in the final section, the material texts that readers of fiction consumed in the eighteenth century were hardly stable artifacts that simply mediated the work of the author and the play of the reader.

Book

I have underlined *book* because, of the three areas in print culture that this essay examines, the study of novels as material objects may require less rather than more modesty. Until recently, criticism has barely addressed the brazen display of text or the awareness of the physical life of the book that frequently punctuate fiction from the long eighteenth century. Scholars are just beginning to examine the "printedness" of these texts in close detail, focusing mostly on Sterne or Richardson.[42] But such interest has long been implicit in the study of eighteenth-century fiction. Both Watt and Lennard Davis have asserted that the novel owed its particular existence to print technologies, and Justice has recently called it "the first overwhelmingly commodified type of writing."[43] While these may be overstatements, they reflect a pervasive link between novels and the materiality of books. As Tom Keymer notes, eighteenth-century fiction shows "the readiness of novelists to explore the impact of print technology and publishing format on literary meaning and the reading experience."[44]

To a large extent, this correlation between eighteenth-century novels and print reflects transformations in the production and circulation of texts. In this period, Britain experienced a dramatic consolidation of print technology and dissemination that included the passage of modern copyright law; taxation of printed material; advances in domestic papermaking; the emergence of wholesale marketing, copy-owning congers, and trade sales; the establishment of the modern library system; the appearance of large-scale printing firms; dramatically increased production by provincial presses; the institution of serialized publication and advertising lists in books and periodicals; and the accelerated growth of newspapers, journals, and magazines. These and other innovations unquestionably produced new conceptions of literary expression. Moreover, they seem to support Elizabeth Eisenstein's claim that modern structures of thought derived from the "advent of print" because "the flow of information had been reoriented to make possible an unprecedented cumulative cognitive advance."[45] Certainly by the eighteenth century the link between enlightenment and print was fully established.

Prose fiction in the long eighteenth century provides particularly strong evidence for the assumption that newness, modernity, and print were common bedfellows, even when that principle was derogated. Among canonical writers, for example, Swift's use of asterisks and glosses in *A Tale of a Tub* (1704) or Richardson's manipulation of typographical effects such as fragmented text printed diagonally and upside down, cursive print that imitates a character's handwriting, and creative italics, florets, bullets, and marginal pointing fingers in *Clarissa* reveal their authors' distinct responses to the possibilities of the print medium. Similarly, the varied length of dashes in Sarah Fielding's *David Simple* (1753) or parodic footnotes in Edgeworth's *Castle Rackrent* (1800) show that eighteenth-century novelists of all sorts exploited the expressive function of print. Even more obscure fictions, such as Amory's *The Life of John Buncle, Esq.* (1756), Kidgell's *The Card* (1755), the anonymous *Life and Memoirs of Mr. Ephraim Tristram Bates* (1756), Lady Morgan's *The Wild Irish Girl* (1806), and a host of narratives produced by Sterne's imitators, depend on typographical devices that underline the tension between writing and its public modes of production. Other writers such as Fielding, Haywood, and McKenzie use more conventional effects, such as comic and self-reflexive chapter headings, overly elaborate tables of contents, and parodic prefatory materials, but they also intimate a writer's awareness that authorship derives as much from the material processes of print culture as from his or her own labor.

Such textual display indicates the correspondence implicitly drawn in the period between writing and print production, as it emphasizes both printing-house conventions and the author's relation to the publishing industry. It underscores as well the collaborative aspects of printed texts. Since typographical layout is usually conducted by printers and compositors, authorial interventions reveal the customarily shared creation of published work. While typographical play allows writers to control a text beyond its manuscript phase, it can also reinscribe their dependence. It implies that "modern authors" frequently considered writing in terms of its modes of publication, anticipating the effects of particular techniques from their knowledge of the print trade.

Not all textual self-consciousness in eighteenth-century fiction, however, is presented in the physical layout of the page. The narratives themselves often provide elaborate reflections upon the material effects of print. In one episode from *Tristram Shandy*, whose very appearance in print was considered indecent, Tristram describes the interplay between typographical and narrative content that typifies eighteenth-century literature. In the scene (volume 5, chapters 27–28), a hot chestnut drops into a "hiatus" in the "breeches" of one of the novel's minor characters, Phutatorius. Seeking relief for the pain, he is advised by Eugenius to "send to the next printer, and trust your cure to such a simple thing as a soft sheet of paper just come off the press." As Sterne elaborates the conceit, Yorick and Gastripheres join Eugenius in discussing the variables at work in the application of printed paper to Phutatorius' genital wound. They argue whether the dampness of the paper or the "oil and lamp-black with which the paper is so strongly impregnated, does the business," and whether it is better to spread the latter "thick upon a rag, and clap it on directly" or "so infinitely thin and with such mathematical equality (fresh paragraphs and large capitals excepted) as no art or management of the spatula can come up to." They consider whether the "type" used should be large or small, and whether the text's content contributes to the remedy (Yorick urges them not to employ a text that contains "bawdry," such as Phutatorius' own treatise, which "is at this instant in the press"). The puns here, mixing references to the printing shop and its tools, to masculine virility and size, to textual, sartorial and somatic hiatuses, and to the instruments and consequences of illicit sex, reinforce Sterne's complex integration of social, sexual, and print subjects. Perhaps the most recondite allusion occurs when Yorick complains that spreading the lamp-black too thickly "would make a very devil of it," as it calls to mind both the notorious black page eulogizing Yorick himself in Sterne's own book, and the boys known as "printer's devils" who removed finished sheets from the tympan and thus come to be covered in black. These references, especially those governing the printing house, reveal the degree to which Sterne indulged his fascination with the publishing process. For Sterne, any writer, like Phutatorius, is trapped in an economy in which his own writing returns upon him in unexpected ways. Such moments as this mark the intersection of the writer's discourse with the specific material practices that governed both the aesthetic and economic productions of texts. It also suggests that writing does not necessarily precede but is often coterminous with the printing process.[46]

On a broader level, then, the study of the book (the novel included) needs to account for the role of the printing house in the production of literature. When Swift secretly had the unattributed manuscript of *Gulliver's Travels* (1726) deposited at the bookseller's, he left instructions for it to be published in whatever manner Motte saw fit. Later, Swift somewhat disingenuously complained about the license taken with his manuscript and sought to ensure corrected versions in subsequent editions. Nonetheless, Gulliver's narrative still bears witness to those initial textual decisions, whether made by the bookseller, editor, compositor or pressman. As the elaborate history of editions and editorial decisions that texts undergo certainly attests, a book is invariably a highly mediated version of a given text. Books also retain, of course, the history of contributions made in the print room. Tracing the circumstances that obtain between authors and the various figures of the printing trade can thus serve effectively to flesh out the dense social nature of the published work.

Like the "republic of authors," however, the print industry was also beholden to readers. Many of its material decisions were based on maximizing contact between texts and suitable audiences. As Warner has shown, this objective involved an elaborate mobilization of resources. Applying the term "media culture" to the early modern period, he notes that print media fused "continuity of form (each printed text is the same)" and "portability." These aims reflected new forms of distribution encouraged by a regularized postal system, new turnpikes, and commercial lending libraries. Such socioeconomic changes promoted commodified literary forms such as the novel whose content followed "proven formulas" intended to "win new purchases" and increase "the speed of cultural exchange."[47] However, although hasty or commercially instituted, these formats also intensified the immediacy and personal tone of eighteenth-century fiction. The small octavo and duodecimo formats favored by booksellers for the production of novels not only manifested a particular market attitude toward such literature, they also fostered, as Brewer shows, a companionate attitude toward books. Such volumes could be slipped into a pocket, carried easily to favorite reading locations, and retrieved quickly for immediate reference. As numerous painted, sculpted, engraved, and printed images reveal, more and more people felt personally attached to their books. Furthermore, throughout much of the period, consumers recognized a greater proportion of books by the publisher's rather than the author's name. For instance, the explosion of Gothic narratives fostered by William Lane's Minerva Press aligned their status with the publishing house and the venues at which such works were sold (like Lane's own circulating library) more than with the author. Indeed, the blue covers of these books became, in effect, a trademark means by which the publisher brought books and consumers together and assured readers of the expected content they would be purchasing.

Thus, one of the sobering insights into eighteenth-century culture is that the textual history of most novels in the period dramatizes the author's decreased engagement. Scholars now generally agree, for example, that changes in copyright were not principally about recognizing authorial rights.[48] Similarly, McKenzie notes that the rise of trade publishing led, in practical terms, to "the *dis*sociation of author, printer and bookseller from one another, and all of them from their market, turning books into mere commodities."[49] Perhaps most threatening to authors was the possibility that they were merely products of market forces. John Feather argues that the demand for new books increased the need for writers, and notes that "literary" authors were affected by the evolution and growth of the book trade, with many of them now acknowledging pecuniary motives for writing.[50] Despite the demand, the writing of popular fiction was still mostly characterized by obscure toil, paltry remuneration, and abuse by the bookselling establishment.[51] At the same time, as Brewer notes, it needs to be acknowledged that booksellers were not exclusively motivated by profit; they often regarded their work as contributing to the "republic of letters" in a supportive, ideological, and moral fashion. Many of them, moreover, fared as badly as the authors they supposedly exploited.[52] More work on the relationship, whether intense or slight, between authors, readers, and what we might loosely call "producers" and "distributors" of texts (keeping in mind that writers and printers, for example, may frequently cross over those boundaries), should increase our understanding of the novel's social and economic reach.

Such trade concerns also necessarily complicate our notions of where "composing" occurs. Focusing on the book, in fact, seems a particularly effective way to reveal the interrelatedness of writers, publishers, and readers. On the one hand, it can undermine conventional ways of reading by exposing the material and technological conditions for the production of discourse, challenging received notions about literary exchange. At the same time, however, material study of the book also demonstrates the varied means by which a body of agents that included writers, publishers, distributors, and readers were able to produce, disseminate, consume, and evaluate novels. The behavior of such agents was not simply determined by technology; it also manifested the inventive and unpredictable nature of encounters between people and books.

The physicality of the novel relates, then, not only to the individual textual condition of a work, but also to the manner in which novels were moved and used as physical objects in the cultural landscape. The eighteenth-century British novel, of course, intersects with a series of events that modified its status as an object. It became a culturally sanctioned and institutionalized force that participated widely in a synchronic public sphere fostered by developments in print technology. As a cultural technology that enabled individuals to reconcile personal and civic experience through rhetorical incorporation of the public, it also retained notable traces of disjunction. One major concern in scholarship on novels and the material form of the book thus relates to how, as physical objects, they came to be placed and used in the public sphere. The circulation of the objects in this respect becomes a measure of the dispersion rather than the consolidation of people and things. The history of the novel's materiality, then, also has to confront its more unexpected uses. And, indeed, the novels in the period reveal an obsession with unreaderly uses of text, from curling one's hair or wadding a gun to serving as toilet paper, lining a trunk, or wrapping cheese and fish.

A broad synthetic approach to book production in the eighteenth century will thus enable scholars to deepen our understanding of the material circumstances of literary production in the British eighteenth century. There is still room, that is, for a fuller exploration of the relation between novels and various print contexts. The appearance of fiction in other material forms than the bound book (such as periodicals and broadsides) is still in the initial stages of investigation. Much more can also be said about the interrelation of printed words and printed illustrations or about novels and the reprint market.[53] And the persistent lament of women writers that the "female pen" is not granted equal access to the printed page, despite the notable increase of women novelists, may be better understood in relation to constraints at the level of material production. Despite some instances of typographical play in novels by women, particularly after the publication of *Tristram Shandy*, there are still very few examples compared to those by male writers. That many female novelists were barred from easy access to the printing house or direct negotiation with booksellers (often having to act through male intermediaries) may correlate with their decision to thematize the manipulation of the printed page rather than practice it directly. Explaining this strategy undoubtedly requires a firmer grasp of how novelists such as Frances Burney, Elizabeth Inchbald, Maria Edgeworth, and Jane Austen sublimated their authority over print while preserving the formal integrity of their texts.

Finally, the range of locales within which texts can be situated – from metropole and province to nations, colonies, and empires – complicates assessments of the physical movement of works in the eighteenth-century public sphere. While much has been done to explore connections between Irish, Scottish, Welsh, and English production of prose fiction, other geographies offer fresh possibilities. The eighteenth-century trans-Atlantic trade in publications meant that novels were a part, however modest, of cultural encounters in Asia, the Americas, and the European continent. As Srinivas Aravamudan has recently argued in *Tropicopolitans*, literary critics have to incorporate "*geocultural* histories of production, reception, and institutionalization."[54] Such an approach, joined to the study of the novel's material life, may very well yield revisionary estimates of how the commodification of fiction shaped such categories as class, race, nationality, and ethnicity.

We should attend more, in other words, to the complex ways in which literatures and marketplaces intersect, tracking the various individual agents who were engaged in the conflicting and conflicted activities of eighteenth-century print media. This involves assessing the intricate and highly personal decision-making that authors, booksellers, and printers made to get their products into print, that distributors considered in ensuring wide circulation of their goods, and that readers enacted when purchasing those products. The history of the book is necessarily a diffuse subject that calls into question such categories as authorship, publishing, reading, and material culture; it is, therefore, both a useful interdisciplinary category and a loose and baggy monster that often consumes the very field of study it is meant to constitute. Moreover, since we live in a period whose technological developments seem to portend the end of the book, the study itself may constitute a belated and desperate act. We should remind ourselves, nevertheless, that more books are currently produced per capita in the West than at any other time in history. The digital era, at least for the time being, has increased (some may say exacerbated) books as a cultural medium. Yet in its origins print technology seemed to threaten a book culture centered on scribal and illuminated modes of production. A modest goal, then, might simply be to acquire the sort of "*known* understanding" of the book that Frances Burney long ago admired in Frances Brooke, one that would now comprehend how human agents and such material as paper, feather quills, ink, leather, wood, and metal intersect to produce a diverse print culture.

See also: chapter 1, Crusoe's *Farther Adventures*; chapter 2, Fiction/Translation/ Transnation; chapter 6, Representing Resistance; chapter 7, Why Fanny Can't Read; chapter 16, An Emerging New Canon.

Notes

1. Paula McDowell, "Women and the Business of Print," in *Women and Literature in Britain, 1700–1800*, ed. Vivien Jones (Cambridge: Cambridge University Press, 2000), 136.

2. Roger Chartier, *The Order of Books: Readers, Authors, and Libraries in Europe Between the* *Fourteenth and Eighteenth Centuries*, trans. Lydia G. Cochrane (Stanford, CA: Stanford University Press, 1994), 18.

3. See Chartier, *The Order of Books*, 25–32.

4. Here, the work of such scholars as Chartier, *The Order of Books*, Mark Rose, *Authors and*

Owners: The Invention of Copyright (Cambridge, MA: Harvard University Press, 1993), and Martha Woodmansee, *The Author, Art, and the Market: Rereading the History of Aesthetics* (New York: Columbia University Press, 1994) has been crucial to our understanding of the author's history.

5. See, for example, Miranda Burgess, *British Fiction and the Production of Social Order, 1740–1830* (Cambridge: Cambridge University Press, 2000), Catherine Gallagher, *Nobody's Story: The Vanishing Acts of Women Writers in the Marketplace, 1670–1820* (Berkeley and Los Angeles: University of California Press, 1994), and Ann K. Mellor, *Mothers of the Nation: Women's Political Writing in England, 1780–1830* (Bloomington: Indiana University Press, 2000).

6. See Barbara Benedict, *Making the Modern Reader: Cultural Mediation in Early Modern Literary Anthologies* (Princeton, NJ: Princeton University Press, 1996), Margaret J. M. Ezell, *Social Authorship and the Advent of Print* (Baltimore, MD: Johns Hopkins University Press, 1999), and Nicholas Hudson, *Writing and European Thought, 1600–1830* (Cambridge: Cambridge University Press, 1994).

7. Rose, *Authors and Owners*, 121.

8. James Raven, *The English Novel, 1770–1829: A Bibliographical Survey of Prose Fiction Published in the British Isles* (Oxford: Oxford University Press, 2000), 1: 41.

9. Richard Sher, "Corporatism and Consensus in the Late Eighteenth-Century Book Trade: The Edinburgh Booksellers' Society in Comparative Perspective," *Book History* 1 (1998): 79–82.

10. Burgess, *British Fiction*, 14.

11. The phrase "*Pamela* media event" comes from William Beatty Warner, *Licensing Entertainment: The Elevation of Novel Reading in Britain, 1684–1750* (Berkeley and Los Angeles: University of California Press, 1998), 176–230. He uses it for the extraordinary textual response to Richardson's novel by avid supporters, imitators, critics, censurers, and parodists, but the popularity of *Pamela* was also manifested in other media (painting, music, textiles, ceramics, etc.). See Thomas Keymer and Peter Sabor, *The Pamela Controversy: Criticisms and Adaptations of Samuel Richardson's Pamela, 1740–1750* (London: Pickering & Chatto, 2001).

12. Raven, *The English Novel*, 1: 9.

13. Quoted in Raven, *The English Novel*, 1: 16.

14. Mellor, *Mothers of the Nation*, 88.

15. Raven, *The English Novel*, 1: 41 and 48.

16. Quoted in Raven, *The English Novel*, 1: 127.

17. John Brewer, *The Pleasures of the Imagination: English Culture in the Eighteenth Century* (New York: Farrar, Straus & Giroux, 1997), 187.

18. Brewer, *The Pleasures of the Imagination*, 168.

19. Robert DeMaria, Jr., *Samuel Johnson and the Life of Reading* (Baltimore, MD: Johns Hopkins University Press, 1997), 16.

20. Hudson, *Writing and European Thought*, 112.

21. Naomi Tadmor, "'In the Even My Wife Read to Me': Women, Reading, and Household Life in the Eighteenth Century," in *The Practice and Representation of Reading in England*, ed. James Raven, Helen Small, and Naomi Tadmor (Cambridge: Cambridge University Press, 1996), 167.

22. James Raven, "From Promotion to Proscription: Arrangements for Reading and Eighteenth-Century Libraries," in *The Practice and Representation of Reading in England*, ed. James Raven, Helen Small, and Naomi Tadmor (Cambridge: Cambridge University Press, 1996), 176.

23. Patricia Crain, "Print and Everyday Life in the Eighteenth Century," in *Perspectives on American Book History: Artifacts and Commentary*, ed. Scott Casper, Joanne Chaison, and Jeffery Groves (Boston: University of Massachusetts Press, 2002), 74.

24. Quoted in Crain, "Print and Everyday Life," in *Perspectives on American Book History*, ed. Casper, Chaison, and Groves, 67.

25. Ezell, *Social Authorship*, 141.

26. Maria Josepha Stanley, *The Early Married Life of Maria Josepha, Lady Stanley*, ed. Jane H. Adeane (London: Longmans, Green, 1899), 65.

27. Patricia Michaelson, *Speaking Volumes: Women, Reading, and Speech in the Age of Austen* (Stanford, CA: Stanford University Press, 2002), 137–79.

28. Tadmor, "In the Even," in *The Practice and Representation of Reading*, ed. Raven, Small, and Tadmor, 166.

29. DeMaria, *Samuel Johnson*, 4, 181.

30. Brewer, *The Pleasures of the Imagination*, 194.

31. Stephen M. Colclough, "Procuring Books and Consuming Texts: The Reading Experience of a Sheffield Apprentice, 1798," *Book History* 3 (2000): 30.

32. Raven, "From Promotion to Proscription," 180.

33. Jürgen Habermas, *The Structural Transformation of the Public Sphere: An Inquiry into a Category of Bourgeois Society*, trans. Thomas Burger (Cambridge, MA: MIT Press, 1989), 38.

34. Benedict Anderson, *Imagined Communities: Reflections on the Origin and Spread of Nationalism* (London: Verso, 1983), 40.

35. See, for example, George Justice, *The Manufacturers of Literature: Writing and the Literary Marketplace in Eighteenth-Century England* (Newark: University of Delaware Press, 2002), and Clifford Siskin, *The Work of Writing: Literature and Social Change in Britain, 1700–1830* (Baltimore, MD: Johns Hopkins University Press, 1998).

36. For some of the recent work on literature, the public sphere, and nationalism in eighteenth-century Britain see Rachel Carnell, "Clarissa's Treasonable Correspondence: Gender, Epistolary Politics, and the Public Sphere," in *Passion and Virtue: Essays on the Novels of Samuel Richardson*, ed. David Blewett (Toronto: University of Toronto Press, 2001), Justice, *The Manufacturers of Literature*, Angela Keane, *Women Writers and the English Nation in the 1790's: Romantic Belongings* (Cambridge: Cambridge University Press, 2000), Paul Keen, *The Crisis of Literature in the 1790's: Print Culture and the Public Sphere* (Cambridge: Cambridge University Press, 1999), and Janet Sorensen, *The Grammar of Empire in Eighteenth-Century British Writing* (Cambridge: Cambridge University Press, 2000). Several of these additionally critique Habermas, but see also Mike Hill and Warren Montag, *Masses, Classes, and the Public Sphere* (London: Verso, 2000).

37. See Pierre Bourdieu, *The Field of Cultural Production: Essays on Art and Literature* (New York: Columbia University Press, 1993). Bourdieu's theory must be modified somewhat to accommodate the eighteenth century. In the nineteenth century each field might be limited to "a separate social universe having its own laws of functioning independent of those of politics and the economy" but it would probably be less structured in the prior century.

38. Burgess, *British Fiction*, 158–59.

39. See, for example, Joseph Bartolomeo, *A New Species of Criticism: Eighteenth-Century Discourse on the Novel* (Newark: University of Delaware Press, 1994), and Ellen Gardiner, *Regulating Readers: Gender and Literary Criticism in the Eighteenth-Century Novel* (Newark: University of Delaware Press, 1999).

40. See, for example, Burgess, *British Fiction*, 1–24, and Warner, *Licensing Entertainment*, 1–44.

41. Leah Price, *The Anthology and the Rise of the Novel: From Richardson to George Eliot* (Cambridge: Cambridge University Press, 2000), 11.

42. See Janine Barchas, *Graphic Design, Print Culture, and the Eighteenth-Century Novel* (Cambridge: Cambridge University Press, 2003), Stephanie Fysh, *The Work(s) of Samuel Richardson* (Newark: University of Delaware Press, 1997), and Thomas Keymer, *Sterne, the Moderns, and the Novel* (Oxford: Oxford University Press, 2002), for example.

43. Justice, *The Manufacturers of Literature*, 153.

44. Keymer, *Sterne*, 67.

45. Elizabeth Eisenstein, *The Printing Press as Agent of Change: Communications and Cultural Transformations in Early-Modern Europe* (Cambridge: Cambridge University Press, 1979), 2: 628.

46. For recent work on Sterne's meta-textuality see Christopher Fanning, "On Sterne's Page: Spatial Layout, Spatial Form, and Social Spaces in *Tristram Shandy*," *Eighteenth-Century Fiction* 10 (1998): 429–50, and Keymer, *Sterne*.

47. Warner, *Licensing Entertainment*, 125–26.

48. See Brewer, *The Pleasures of the Imagination*, 133, Chartier, *The Order of Books*, 32, and Siskin, *The Work of Writing*, 109–12.

49. D. F. McKenzie, *Bibliography and the Sociology of Texts* (Cambridge: Cambridge University Press, 1999), 29.

50. John Feather, *A History of British Publishing* (London: Routledge, 1988), 102.

51. See Raven, *The English Novel*, 1: 50–56.

52. Brewer, *The Pleasures of the Imagination*, 155–56.

53. See the relevant essays in the special double issue of *Eighteenth-Century Fiction* entitled "Fiction and Print Culture," vol. 14, nos. 3–4 (2002).

54. Srinivas Aravamudan, *Tropicopolitans: Colonialism and Agency, 1688–1804* (Durham, NC: Duke University Press, 1999), 10.

FURTHER READING

Donoghue, Frank. *The Fame Machine: Book Reviewing and Eighteenth-Century Literary Careers.* Stanford, CA: Stanford University Press, 1996.

Eisenstein, Elizabeth. *The Printing Press as Agent of Change: Communications and Cultural Transformations in Early-Modern Europe.* 2 vols. Cambridge: Cambridge University Press, 1979.

Ezell, Margaret J. M. *Social Authorship and the Advent of Print.* Baltimore, MD: Johns Hopkins University Press, 1999.

Hudson, Nicholas. *Writing and European Thought, 1600–1830.* Cambridge and New York: Cambridge University Press, 1994.

Keymer, Thomas. *Sterne, the Moderns, and the Novel.* Oxford and New York: Oxford University Press, 2002.

McDowell, Paula. *The Women of Grub Street: Press, Politics, and Gender in the London Literary Marketplace, 1678–1730.* Oxford: Clarendon Press, 1998.

16

An Emerging New Canon of the British Eighteenth-Century Novel: Feminist Criticism, the Means of Cultural Production, and the Question of Value

John Richetti

I first read Ian Watt's *The Rise of the Novel: Studies in Defoe, Richardson, and Fielding* (1957) when I was a graduate student at Columbia in the fall of 1960, and in a course on the British eighteenth-century novel Watt was required reading, along with A. D. McKillop's *The Early Masters of English Fiction* (1956). Watt's book was an eye-opener for me, the book that had the most influence on my thinking about narrative when I was a young student, although I gathered more information from McKillop's more complete survey, which included discussions of Smollett and Sterne as well as the other "masters," Defoe, Richardson, and Fielding. Over the forty-odd years since then, the influence of Watt's book has been central and enduring. It is hard to think of a book of comparable continuing influence in its field. *The Rise of the Novel* reinforced the canon of eighteenth-century British fiction and defined the standards by which novels from the British eighteenth century were to be judged. It also helped to make the study of the early novel academically respectable.

In the last twenty years or so, Watt has come under sustained and sometimes savage attack and even repudiation, especially by feminist-influenced critics of the early eighteenth-century novel. Their case is powerful and often persuasive, including as it does a critique of the narrowness of the canon of male novelists that Watt's book helped to solidify, but that he did not, of course, invent or promulgate. Much the same canon, along with extended discussions of other novelists both male and female who were not granted canonical status, had long been on view in such surveys as Ernest A. Baker's 1924–1936 ten-volume *The History of the English Novel*. Baker was a lecturer at University College, London, and his knowledge of narrative in the broadest sense was vast, his book beginning with the Greek Romances and other narratives from antiquity and not reaching the eighteenth-century novel until volume 3, when

he featured a chapter called "The Followers of Mrs. Behn." For all his tremendous
learning, Baker had a simplistic view of the development of the novel as the
emergence of a mature and masculine realism from various kinds of degraded
romances from the seventeenth century, and he developed in volume 3 of his history
a narrative in which Defoe literally invented the modern novel by achieving through
"the irresistible cogency of the circumstantial method" a realism that presented "life
in its fullness . . . the entire mundane scene."[1] Eliza Haywood, like Behn and Manley
before her, received exhaustive but dismissive treatment from Baker, who summed up
all their deficiencies in his evocation of Haywood's works: "she localized her scenes in
a perfunctory way, described her heroines and her heroes in minute detail, and made
them express their feelings in vigorous language; but she does not succeed any better
than they, if as much, in making any of her creations live."[2] Unlike Watt, who
historicized "circumstantial realism" by deriving it from newly emerged socio-
historical conditions in England in the early eighteenth century as well as from a
new philosophical and psychological understanding of the nature and status of the
individual, Baker simply invoked Defoe's literary genius as the origin of this newly
accurate and complete mode of understanding and narration. For all of its dogmatic
simplicity and simple assertiveness, Baker's view of Defoe's superiority to his female
competitors can be defended, or at least better understood, if we remember that all
these writers worked in the expanding commercial literary market and that their
distinct sorts of literary manufacturing were crucially influenced by their differing
kinds of access to the means of literary and cultural production. That is to say, Defoe
as a relatively privileged and educated man (albeit at a Dissenting academy), a
professional merchant with wide experience in the commercial world, and later a
writer and spy for the most powerful politicians of the time was licensed (or licensed
himself) to stage in his fictions a wider ideological drama than his female predecessors
and contemporaries could aspire to. Amatory and sentimental fiction such as they
produced is to a large extent formulaic, aimed at a targeted market, deliberately
partial in its features and effects. Defoe's fiction is also targeted, designed for that
same literary marketplace to appeal to an audience hungry for narratives about
extraordinary individuals who also happen to resemble ordinary people; but his novels
are in addition informed by his self-confident possession of the intellectual means of
production and form thereby a small part of what might be called his larger and lifelong cultural project to represent in his voluminous works the moral, political, and
economic outlines of British society.

　　Some more autobiography is appropriate here. In a doctoral seminar at Columbia in
eighteenth-century English literature, I was assigned to report on a new bibliography
of English prose fiction for the years 1700–1739, the latter date chosen by the
compiler because Richardson had published his ground-breaking *Pamela* in 1740.
W. H. McBurney's *A Checklist of English Prose Fiction: 1700–1739* (1960) sketched out
an interesting history of prose narrative that included only a few familiar names,
Defoe the most prominent. So I subsequently embarked on a dissertation project to
read all of the original English-language titles in McBurney's list and to write a study

of what I came to call "popular fiction before Richardson," which after a bout of paralyzing self-doubt earned me a Ph.D. The dissertation appeared in print in 1969. The material I read in the British Museum for several years in the mid-1960s was hardly unknown, but it had been neglected or even ignored in Anglo-American scholarship during the forties and fifties. Much of what I read was interesting but for me virtually "unreadable." That is to say, these narratives were for the most part crude and ephemeral in various ways: collections of sensational criminal and pirate narratives, last dying words of criminals about to be executed, tedious travel accounts that made you appreciate *Gulliver's Travels* (1726) all the more, as well as narratives influenced by the success of *Robinson Crusoe* (1719), didactic novellas by pious women writers, and the predictable scandal chronicles and overheated amatory novellas, these by women writers, notably Delarivier Manley and Eliza Haywood. In the book that emerged, my thesis was in part that this mass of popular narrative stimulated Defoe to produce his fictions from 1719 to 1724, and ultimately provoked the larger, more substantial, more properly in our sense novelistic literary production that begins in the 1740s with Richardson and Fielding.

When it appeared in 1969, my book earned some wounding scorn in the academic journals but also had some good reviews. Yet even reviewers who liked the book wondered why I had wasted my time with such trashy sub-literature, just as I myself in my epilogue ("The Relevance of the Unreadable") had wondered. Although the term did not exist in those days, if it had I could have answered my critics by saying that what I was doing was literary history driven by "cultural studies" that sought to place literature in its larger historical and cultural contexts and to analyze its social and ideological functions. That sounds like a commonplace now but in the academic climate of the late sixties it was distinctly odd. Retaining as I read in those days a sense of literary value and hierarchy that I had naturally absorbed from my teachers and my reading, I looked as well for density and variety of theme, for control of language, for engagement with complex and serious ideas and issues, and even under the spell of the reigning New Criticism I looked for formal tensions, for the irony and ambiguity that in those days were seen as the marks of literature at its most profound and valuable. I found almost none of those things, and so I made the best of the situation by my version of literary sociology that granted to this material a demotic vigor and socially expressive energy of its own, but also a role in the literary history of the novel whereby it served as a fertilizing muck or productive irritant for the great works of the 1740s.

But something happened in literary studies during the next twenty-five to thirty years, chiefly the feminist re-evaluation and recuperation of women writers and its effects on the evaluation of the traditional male literary canon. As Janet Todd puts it in a recent essay on Aphra Behn, feminist criticism "arose when the aesthetic criticism of high culture was giving way to a social criticism of society, politics, and power [that] brought forgotten women writers like Behn into focus,"[3] and what this revolution in critical thinking meant for the academic study of the British eighteenth-century novel is at the heart of this essay. Only about half of my book dealt with women writers, but during this exciting period of re-evaluation I seem to have played a role as every feminist-oriented critic's whipping boy because of my traditionalist insistence in my book that most of the fiction by women in the early eighteenth century was what I called "entertainment machines," at its best calculated by authors and booksellers to cater to an audience of limited sophistication, offering amatory melodrama and as such the precursor of modern mass-market romance and hence aptly described by my epithet "popular." To be sure, what I freely confess was my elitist contempt for such stuff as it exists nowadays leaked back into my presentation of its eighteenth-century origins. I was more confident or perhaps more arrogant than now, and if the truth were told would rather have been writing about Pope, Swift, Johnson, or Hume, and my evocations of the works of these women writers, especially Manley and Haywood, were less than reverent.

What feminist scholarship and New Historicism, to speak generally, have added to what I wrote more than thirty years ago is a deep understanding that I lacked of the sociocultural significance surrounding the figure of the eighteenth-century woman writer and, since Nancy Armstrong's 1987 book (*Desire and Domestic Fiction: A Political History of the Novel*), of the status of the female self as the essential imaginative basis of the novelistic individual.[4] In a very effective and convincing move, feminist critics have read women's novels as participants in a cultural protest against their underprivileged status as literary producers, so that the narrow amatory subject matter, for example, of Haywood's novellas is by its very restrictiveness an implicit critique and potential subversion of patriarchal oppression, and more specifically a protest against women's denial of access by that oppression to the means of literary production. In a way, the clumsier the fiction the more intense its cultural resonance, the cruder the narrative the more revealing it is of cracks and fissures in the reigning ideology. In some very interesting instances, in much of Aphra Behn's fiction, and in the works of Delarivier Manley and Jane Barker, amatory fiction is convincingly read as a political allegory, with rape and seduction, for example, understood in subversive Jacobite terms as parallel to the violation of Stuart sovereignty in the 1688 Revolution.[5] Or, more generally, relationships between the sexes as obsessively represented in amatory fiction are seen as a rendition of the overseeing political and social order. Always, the strategy of such criticism is to invoke the broadest cultural and socio-political contexts for women's fiction so that the thinness of its representation and the relative poverty of language and form in the women novelists I held up to scorn signify by their very sketchiness and formulaic crudity a fullness denied to women writers and for that matter to female characters in fiction. Toni O'Shaughnessy Bowers puts the case for this approach very cogently and powerfully when she says that in the work of popular women novelists of the late seventeenth and early eighteenth centuries "public issues of authority and accountability" are examined "as issues of gendered power relations, making problematic the assumptions that political relations and intimate relations are essentially different."[6] And Bowers shifts the question of value by bracketing it, asking us rather why we valorize certain works and not others, and suggesting that in "respectful engagement with works we have been trained to resist or dismiss" we might increase our range of literary pleasure.[7]

So the new canon of the British eighteenth-century novel has shifted somewhat, not only with women novelists now sharing the stage with male writers but novels by these men re-evaluated in terms of their representation of female experience. Thus, Defoe's *Roxana* (1724) and *Moll Flanders* (1722) now overshadow *Robinson Crusoe*, and what used to be thought of as Fielding's problematic failure, *Amelia* (1751), takes precedence as a focus for critical discussion over *Joseph Andrews* (1742) and *Tom Jones* (1749). And of course the "feminine" Richardson's ascendancy over the "masculine" Fielding (quite the reverse when I started graduate school forty years ago) is part of this feminizing of the novelistic canon, and it seems fair to say that *Clarissa* (1747–8) now holds pride of place in the canon as the greatest fictional work of the century. Burney's novels later in the century now loom larger than before as the true predecessors of Austen's novels of manners, and once neglected writers such as Sarah Fielding and Frances Sheridan receive the serious attention they deserve.[8] For some feminist critics, this realignment is simply a repetition of the triumphalist narrative of male literary production, with women novelists as the century progresses occupying pride of place as well as dominance in sheer productivity. Thus, for example, Jane Spencer's *The Rise of the Woman Novelist* (1986) deliberately echoes and challenges Watt's title. But feminist critics like Janet Todd and Ros Ballaster go so far as to deny that there is any such thing as a rise, either male or female, of the novel or a progressive improvement in narrative technique in the eighteenth century. More often and more provocatively, the new canon as such critics articulate it rejects older notions of literary value, evaluating fictions instead for their cultural density and resonance, what they reveal about their initial readers and their world rather than for anything intrinsic to them as textual/aesthetic objects. As Ballaster puts it with some force, "The rise in prestige of the novel form through the century does not necessarily betoken increasing sophistication in narrative technique, nor should we allow our analysis of eighteenth-century fiction to be overly determined by the realist aesthetics that came to dominate in the century that followed."[9]

Now to some extent the novel as it emerges in Europe from (say) Cervantes on is always more than an order of words that constitutes an aesthetic object, and the realist aesthetics Ballaster postpones until the nineteenth century may be said to operate in a weaker sense from the end of the seventeenth century. Novels, even early novels from the late seventeenth and early eighteenth century, operate as such by a process we might call pseudo-referentiality whereby the text invites readers to enter a simulacrum of a world that inevitably invites comparison with something defined as actuality, an actuality the text invokes as its guiding force or model. Or in the case of romance, actuality is defined as the realm that the text deliberately avoids or negates but in so doing refers us to. As the founding example of *Don Quixote* (1605) makes clear, novelistic narrative is always as it were pugnacious, in oppositional dialogue in Bakhtin's sense, with other forms and modes of self-expression it declares merely literary and to that extent artificial discourse. The novel thus always highlights as other genres do not its problematic and always urgent relationship to a non-textual world even as it tends to promote its own textual self-sufficiency (which modern critics tend to overemphasize). So I think it can be said that in general we value all novels for their immersion in these relationships, for what they communicate about a world beyond the textual world they occupy. And to come back to my own work on popular fiction, we may say that the narratives I was dealing with and perhaps all eighteenth-century novels ask to be read as cultural as well as aesthetic phenomena, as interventions in an ethical and social world. But for most current eighteenth-century novel criticism such a double valence eliminates value in the traditional sense whereby some novels are better constructed or crafted than others, whereby some novels gesture more effectively in the direction of what the cultural realm values as actuality; all narrative in this new dispensation exists at the same level of socio-cultural meaning and ideological functioning, and high or elite cultural products are purely and simply exercising domination or hegemony. In my small way many years ago, I contributed to this flattening out of value, a shift in literary-historical discourse from aesthetic/intellectual weight to cultural/historical depth and resonance.

The current dominant critical understanding of fiction in early eighteenth-century England is that all narratives are simply part of the jostling for market share in the new world of expanding print media, so that nowadays literary history of the early novel shuns value judgments and offers neutral cultural analysis in which the canonical few merge with all other available titles. But it has always seemed to me that the primacy of the canonical writers is not a patriarchal or deliberate elitist plot to exclude women and popular writers, and indeed Defoe as novelist was nothing if not a popular writer.[10] There is in the work of these writers not so much a superiority in those features of narrative that have come to define the art or literary novel after, say, James and Conrad (although Fielding's and Richardson's novels possess many of the features enshrined by later novelists of narrative sophistication – complexity of character, linguistic control and stylistic variety, and thematic coherence), but rather there is in this main line of eighteenth-century fiction what I want to call a superior socio-cultural fullness and density, an engagement both explicit and implicit, with the ideas and issues of their historical moment. And that superiority can be largely explained in terms of superior or more extensive male access to the means of literary and intellectual production. In the rest of this essay, I would like to explore briefly this redefined or resituated value by looking at two novels, the wildly popular *Love in Excess* (1719), the first novel by Eliza Haywood, and Defoe's last work of fiction, *The Fortunate Mistress* (1724), known now simply as *Roxana*. I want to compare them in terms of their engagement with ideas and issues insofar as such notions cooperate with the evocation of fictional characters in their distinctive expressivity that defines them as narratives and to assign this redefined value to them accordingly.[11]

Love in Excess

Haywood's novel is in three parts, set in France and Italy, clearly influenced by French romances and modeled on English predecessors like Aphra Behn's *Love Letters Between a Nobleman and his Sister* (1684–7). An intricate ballet of would-be lovers striving to come together, an elaborate series of frustrated amorous pas de deux, Haywood's bestseller is artfully constructed and written in an arch and elevated style that fits the exotic aristocratic *mise en scène* her many readers clearly found compellingly romantic. Haywood begins with a historical note: the hero, Count D'Elmont, and his brother, the Chevalier Brillians, have served gallantly in "the late War between the French and the confederate armies."[12] But she quickly moves away from history and plunges into the love affairs promised in the title. D'Elmont finds himself accosted by Alovisa, one of many women we are told who are attracted to his matchless charms: "The beauty of his person, the gaity of his air, and the unequalled charms of his conversation, made him the admiration of both sexes; and whilst those of his own strove which should gain the largest share of his friendship; the other, vented fruitless wishes, and in secret, cursed that custom which forbids women to make a declaration of their thoughts" (39–40). D'Elmont has been smitten by the young Amena, daughter of a gentleman with only a small estate, but his attraction we are told is not deep or serious. He asks her to dance and schemes to seduce her: "not that he was in love with her, or at that time believed he could be touched with a passion which he esteemed a trifle in it self, and below the dignity of a man of sense" (45). During a brief dalliance with Amena, a soft-core encounter in the Tuileries, one of many near consummations in the novel, the lovers are interrupted by a false fire alarm raised by one of the jealous Alovisa's servants, and that determined and already obsessed lady betrays the lovers to Amena's father, who packs her off to a convent. After D'Elmont learns that his brother is in love with Ansellina, Alovisa's sister, he decides to follow "ambition" and marry Alovisa. The narrator explains his calculations in these terms:

> The Count had never yet seen a beauty formidable enough to give him an hour's uneasiness (purely for the sake of love) and would often say, Cupid's quiver never held an arrow of force to reach his heart; those little delicacies, those trembling aking transports, which every sight of the beloved object occasions, and so visibly distinguishes a real passion from a counterfeit, he looked on as the chimera's [*sic*] of an idle brain, formed to inspire notions of an imaginary bliss, and make fools lose themselves in seeking . . . Ambition was certainly the reigning passion in his soul, and Alovisa's quality and vast possessions, promising a full gratification of that, he ne'er so much as wished to know, a farther happiness in marriage. (82–3)

Very soon after this hasty marriage, in Part II of the novel, D'Elmont the skeptic to love is predictably converted to its awful power, smitten by "the matchless Melliora," daughter of his friend, M. Frankville, who on his deathbed makes the Count his daughter's guardian. The rest of the book is an account of the many twists and turns, chances and mischances, that impede the ultimate happiness of these lovers, since Melliora's attraction to D'Elmont is equal in immediacy and intensity to his for her.

All of this characterization and plotting is deeply conventional and highly predictable, and as such doubtless gratifying to the book's original audience precisely for its skillful rendition of amatory formulas. Haywood's narrator has, essentially, two forms of authorial commentary throughout: (1) she admits that the emotional intensities surrounding passion – painful rage and disappointment as well as sweetly intense longing and ecstatic fulfillment – are inexpressible, impossible to render in adequate language; and (2) she distinguishes pretty regularly between authentic love and lower forms of sexual and emotional attraction. Here are representative and somewhat abridged samples of both sorts of commentary:

> There is nothing more certain, than that love, tho' it fills the mind with a thousand charming ideas, which those untouched by that passion, are not capable of conceiving, yet it entirely takes away the power of utterance, and the deeper impression it had [*sic*] made on the soul, the less we are able to express it, when willing to indulge and give a loose to thought; what language can furnish us with words sufficient?...But, if so impossible to be describ'd, if of so vast, so wonderful a nature, as nothing but it's [*sic*] self can comprehend; how much more impossible must it be entirely to conceal it! What strength of boasted reason? What force of resolution?....Honour, and virtue may distance bodies, but there is no power in either of those names, to stop the spring, that with a rapid whirl transports us from our selves, and darts our souls into the bosom of the darling object. (133–4)
>
> How strangely do they deceive themselves, who fancy that they are lovers, yet on every little turn of Fortune, or change of circumstance, are agitated with any vehemence, by cares of a far different nature? *Love* is too jealous, too arbitrary a monarch to suffer any other passion to equalize himself in that heart where he has fixed his throne....*Love*, is what we can neither resist, expel nor even alleviate, if we should never so vigorously attempt it...*Liking* is a flashy flame, which is to be kept alive only by ease and delight. *Love* needs not this fewel to maintain its fire, it survives in absence, and disappointments, it endures, unchilled, the wintry blasts of cold indifference and neglect, and continues its blaze, even in a storm of hatred and ingratitude, and reason, pride, or a just sensibility of conscious worth, in vain oppose it. (182–3)

Notable in these commentaries is their consonance, stylistic and ideological, with the discourse the characters are given. The narrator might as well be a participant in the affairs she describes; she speaks the same language in the same register. Haywood's narrator counts herself as a true believer in love's mysteries, and there is in *Love in Excess* none of the ironic double-voicing to be found in Aphra Behn's *Love Letters* (and for that matter in some of Haywood's later work in the 1740s) whereby readers are encouraged by the narrator's stance to acquire a measure of distance from the characters and situations on display. Instead, Haywood's narrator works to create sympathy and identification between readers and characters, to encourage readers to share as much as possible in these thrilling and passionate encounters, and to hug themselves for their special understanding of passion in its irresistible extremities. The second kind of authorial commentary – the definition and defense of love as pure obsession – is therefore more interesting, a sort of intellectualized response to a potentially wayward or skeptical reader. Haywood's narrator's position at moments like this is implicitly a defense of romance at its purest and most improbable, a rejection of the normal or probable ("mere liking" rather than *LOVE* in capital letters and italics) and an invocation of an irresistible fate ("what we can neither resist, expel, nor even alleviate") that summons up a transcendent emotional universe that cancels personal agency and that is in fact in tension with the secular and pragmatic world of aristocratic libertinism and licensed privilege that is the setting for *Love in Excess* and similar amatory fiction. And indeed D'Elmont begins as a mere seducer and trifling libertine, and there are several other characters in the book who conform to a more realistic profile of desire.

Haywood, it seems to me, brings to this sensationally successful debut as a fiction writer two main resources: (1) her literary experience and knowledge, her fluent grasp of the romance tradition in England of Behn and Manley and similar work in late seventeenth- and early eighteenth-century French writing; and (2) her situation as a woman and as a beginning professional writer, necessarily deprived of full access to the range of educational and intellectual experiences with all the cultural validation and privilege that involves granted to elite male writers. In other words, Haywood's access to the means of literary production of my title was to say the least severely restricted, limiting her or at least predisposing her (for good economic reasons) to a form of narrative that turns its back on ideas and contemporary issues. Haywood's first novel is deliberately restrictive and, to use modern terms, ahistorical and essentialist in its understanding of personality and character, which is grounded in elegant rehearsal and determined repetition of the romance/amatory pattern rather than on significant revision or examination of its assumptions. The form is circular rather than linear. This is not to say that *Love in Excess* (and other amatory fiction and its producers like Haywood) is not full of significance for the history of the novel. Even amatory fiction is part in its way of the Enlightenment project of extending knowledge, and in spite of its overt reactionary and traditionalist commentary on the power of love, *Love in Excess* potentially offers thoughtful readers implicitly critical insights into a leisure class for which erotic and emotional self-expression and exploitation are a defining (and enervating) privilege. In fact, this novel is not one of Haywood's more extravagant and sensational narratives; it is relatively restrained and most of the time moderate as well as elegant, avoiding the normal melodrama of rapacious male seducers and their innocent female victims (and featuring in fact several sexually aggressive and manipulative women). In her avoidance of that simple-minded romantic binary we can glimpse an effort to offer some readers opportunity to draw out such an implicit critique and intellectual understanding of what is otherwise a glamorous cast of beautiful film-star-like characters in an exotic locale. To that extent, we may say that *Love in Excess* occasionally complements excited identification and participation with analysis and a form of knowledge.

Roxana and Compound Interest

Consider next to Haywood's novel Defoe's *Roxana*, published five years later in 1724. The book can be considered Defoe's exploitation of the related genres that Haywood worked in of romance and scandal chronicle, and indeed his title, *The Fortunate Mistress*, echoes and negates the title of one of Haywood's novels published the previous year, *Idalia: or, The Unfortunate Mistress* (1723). *Roxana* represents a reversal and repudiation, indeed a transformation of amatory fiction (dominated in the 1720s by Eliza Haywood) by virtue of its participant narrator whose life is much more than merely scandalous and romantic. Like *Love in Excess*, *Roxana* is concerned with the problem of agency, and here it is specifically female agency in response to paralyzing female dilemmas that is the main theme. But Defoe is able, I submit, by virtue of his relatively unrestricted access to the means of literary production, to render that problem from a number of angles that reveal his full participation as a privileged man and as a political journalist in the cultural and intellectual world of the early eighteenth century. He gives himself the interesting luxury of ventriloquizing a female voice, and indeed, in his voluminous journalism he cultivates a freedom to speak in any number of voices on many subjects. In both specific and general terms, in its representational variety of scene and incident, in its psycho-sexual and moral ambitions, moreover, his novel is a counter-statement to the repetitive thinness enforced by the formulas of the amatory tradition. I want to discuss Defoe's novel in terms of what is never specifically present in *Love in Excess*, except in the most general of terms – money, and money as it impinges particularly on Roxana and her fate and resonates with the economic actualities of the early 1720s in England.

Much attention has been paid in recent years to the intersection of writing and this emerging economic world. The historian J. G. A. Pocock's suggestion that individuals caught up in the new credit-based economic order produced by the early eighteenth-century "financial revolution" were "feminized" by the anxiety created by the market's volatility and uncertainty has proved one of the most fruitful and influential insights for late twentieth-century discussions of the period.[13] Feminist critics, especially, have lately picked up this notion and used it as a key to understanding the dynamics of production in the emerging literary marketplace whose development seems clearly related to the financial transformation of England. In her strongly revisionist book, *Authorship, Commerce, and Gender in Early Eighteenth-Century England: A Culture of Paper Credit* (1998), Catherine Ingrassia finds these new literary and economic realms, writing for the marketplace and credit-based finance, nothing less than homologous activities, interpenetrating and mutually re-enforcing cultural phenomena. For Ingrassia, to give her most striking and original example, Eliza Haywood's erotic novellas feed the sexual fantasies of her readers and thereby mimic the fanciful constructions of speculative credit. Both stock jobbers and the erotic popular novelist, she says very provocatively, "attracted clients seeking participation in an imaginatively constructed 'future,' desiring 'future' returns on the initial investment, either in the form of stock dividends or an enjoyable reading experience." [14] And, further and also provocatively, Ingrassia finds in the structure of amatory fiction, especially in Haywood's case, a metaphor for financial activity in the new credit economy: "The 'love' relationship within Haywood's fiction, the perpetual imagining of an end which must never come, mirrors the implicit understanding on which speculative investment depends: the continued deferral of complete repayment until a date which will, of course, never arrive." [15]

In the same New Historicist spirit, Sandra Sherman brilliantly argued in her 1996 *Finance and Fictionality in the Early Eighteenth Century* that there is an even deeper homology between what she calls the "discourse of credit" and the radically ambiguous truth claims of Defoe's narratives, especially *Moll Flanders* and *Roxana*. Sherman's difficult point is that the essential instability of credit discourse (whereby financial instruments promise what are in fact uncertain returns and creditors and debtors are locked in relationships founded on fragile predictions and unpredictable trends within the instability and volatility of the market) leaks into or infects Defoe's narratives as he "reproduces the very conditions – epistemological confusion – that the market abhors and that compromise his agency." [16] Meaning, as Sherman remarks, in Defoe's fictions lies "in the deferral of meaning," the essential strategy of the credit-based marketplace. I would amend her conclusion here by saying that in the market meaning is temporary or perhaps radically and misleadingly provisional, and that in Defoe's fictions meanings, for his narrators at least, are determined by practical necessity or tactical expediency and to that extent they resemble players in the market.

Both Ingrassia and Sherman argue, then, as if a homology existed between early eighteenth-century narrative fiction and the new credit-based economy. Taking their cue from Pocock, both of them posit a deeply unstable economic order that somehow permeates consciousness and feeling far beyond the stock exchange and the trade in financial instruments. And fiction is more than a simple response or mere representation of the conditions in that market. In its Haywoodian extravagance as well as in its Defoevian ambiguities, fiction is an expression of the ideological conditions produced by the economic order and must – although like other New Historicists, they don't address this issue adequately – also contribute to that order, heightening or intensifying all the anxiety and hysteria that accompany it. Although I admire both of these studies, I want to dissent from their New Historicist faith and to offer in a brief reading of *Roxana* a counter-statement or at least a modification of the Pocockian paradigm of pervasive anxiety caused by the new economic order. My argument is that Defoe in this novel is attempting to shift the ground or the source of anxiety away from economics and indeed treating a certain kind of market as embodied in the steady accumulations of compound interest as a refuge from anxiety and instability, an instability that is of course vividly if metaphorically rendered in the heroine's spectacular career as a courtesan as well as in her lacerating final remorse and madness. In other words, as far as I'm concerned, Defoe in this novel at least is working to neutralize to some extent the determining anxieties that New Historicism treats as inescapable and for those implicated in them imponderable. And of course in making this argument I am claiming the superiority of Defoe's novel over Haywood's precisely by virtue of its deep and also its specific engagement with the economic ideas and issues of the day.

In a sense, my rendition of the role of compound interest in *Roxana* rehearses an old critical debate about the book's meaning – whether Defoe's heroine is a negative moral exemplar of the wages of sin as remorseful madness or an instance of his ability to imagine the triumphantly amoral transformation of a deserted wife into a fabulously wealthy and powerful courtesan who is simply a successful sex worker and business person. That Defoe intended the first seems clear enough, but that his didactic/moral purpose is complicated and contradicted by the self-dramatizations or even the self-creations of his heroine as she gets on wonderfully is also indisputable. It is also another area in which he differs from Haywood, whose narrative is tightly controlled for its various amatory pleasures. Defoe's narrative, we may want to say, is overdetermined in its cultural meanings and resonances, in just the same way (although to my mind more clearly and intensely) that critics like Bowers say amatory fiction is. The issue for me is just how in *Roxana* those two effects balance one another, and it seems to me as I ponder the recent alignment of literature and the new economic order that the steady accumulations of compound interest to which Roxana repeatedly and excitedly draws our attention as she prospers provide precisely the stable opposite of that feminized anxiety in the new credit economy that Pocock speaks of. And in a larger sense, compound interest also supplies two things for this particular narrative: (1) it can be said to serve as a metaphor for the workings of personality, not just in *Roxana* but to some extent in all of Defoe's fictions where that purposeful growth or progressive development we associate with the history of an individual is never quite accurate as a description of the biographical trajectories of his protagonists, whose lives may be said to resemble in their movements the accumulative and transformative energy of compound interest; and (2) compound interest as it is represented by Roxana is a literal rendition of a certain kind of conservatively triumphant financial activity, the reliable economic base on which Roxana's social and moral identity is founded, which accompanies and insures her various feats of survival and prosperity and which also, paradoxically, is yet another source of guilt and remorse for her. On both the metaphorical and literal level, compound interest as evoked in *Roxana* is decidedly enthralling, almost magical: the steady, relentless multiplication of money, principal supplemented by interest plowed back into it, growing, accumulating like an Alpine avalanche, matches in its energy the heroine's transforming personality but contrasts with her quirky and secret singularity and talent for improvisation in its steady and massive impersonality, its unvarying and dependable public and external workings. The market depicted in *Roxana* is steady and invariable, like nothing else in the story, like nothing else in the world dominated by duplicity and disguising evoked by the narrative and mastered by the heroine.

Compound interest in *Roxana* is the risk-free alternative to the dangerous speculative financial instruments and schemes that Defoe railed against twenty years before the novel was published in tracts like *The Villainy of Stock-Jobbers Detect'd* and just a few years before *Roxana* in *The Anatomy of Exchange Alley* (1719). As he remarks in the latter, "Stock-jobbing is play; a box and dice may be less dangerous, the nature of them are alike, a hazard; and if they venture at either for what is not their own, the knavery is the same." Set as it is with some ambiguity during the Restoration, *Roxana* in that sense predates the speculative frenzy of the early decades of the eighteenth century, and the heroine never considers venturing her money that way. But of course the novel actually appears at the height of the South Sea Bubble and, as various commentators have suggested, may be said to have a double time scheme that refers to early eighteenth-century concerns even as it uses a Restoration setting. Roxana's cautious and conservative investments are surely Defoe's comment on the speculative excesses of those years. From the beginning of her affair with a certain Prince in Paris, Roxana can't help but be aware of the instability and fragility of her earning power as a mistress. When she and the Prince return from their Italian journey, she takes stock of her growing wealth:

> In all this Affluence of my good Fortune, I did not forget that I had been Rich and Poor once already, alternately; and that I ought to know, that the Circumstances I was now in, were not to be expected to last always; that I had one Child, and expected another; and if I bred often, it wou'd something impair me in the Great Article that supported my Interest, I mean, what he call'd Beauty; that as that declin'd, I might expect the Fire wou'd abate, and the Warmth with which I was now so caress'd, wou'd cool, and in time, like the other Mistresses of Great Men, I might be dropt again; and that, therefore, it was my Business to take Care that I shou'd fall as softly as I cou'd.... My greatest Difficulty now, was, how to secure my Wealth, and to keep what I had got.[17]

To the courtesan's nervous awareness of her limited earning life, Roxana adds an anxious eagerness to find a means of preserving her wealth, fearing that she might be tricked or swindled, as she tells us a bit later when the Prince, on the death of his wife, repents of their connection: thinking of her wealth, she says, "almost distracted me, for want of knowing how to dispose of it, and for fear of losing it all again by some Cheat or Trick, not knowing any-body that I commit the Trust of it to" (110). Here is nothing less, I suppose, than a specific and clear instance of the anxiety Pocock speaks of, although Roxana is afraid of trickery on the financial level such as she is in her way capable of on the sexual plane. The dangers derive as much from the picaresque pattern the novel is tracing as from any of the conditions peculiar or specific to the new economic order. She consults a Dutch merchant in Paris about the disposition of her wealth, and he becomes the Prince's successor as her lover. Taking her Dutch merchant's advice as she prepares to leave France for England, she converts her "Treasure" in French cash and jewels into bills mainly drawn upon Amsterdam bankers. And as she finally leaves Paris, in one of those precise accountings Defoe makes Roxana so fond of giving us and that modern readers tend to skip impatiently, she summarizes her meticulous financial arrangements: "I deliver'd into his Hands seven Thousand eight Hundred Pistoles in Bills and Money; a Copy of an Assignment on the Town-House of *Paris*, for 4000 Pistoles, at 3 *per Cent*. Interest, attested; and a Procuration for receiving the Interest half-yearly; but the Original I kept myself" (120).

This is the first of several much more detailed and more triumphant financial renderings, but of course they become steadily more elaborate and even fantastic as her assets swell and she becomes truly wealthy and in fact financially secure and independent in her steadily accumulating riches. Once back in England, those assets safely moved through Holland and her bills accepted and paid in London, she receives financial advice from Sir Robert Clayton, a grand but somewhat shady actual contemporary financier. Investing her £14,000 in money in five percent mortgages (rather higher than prevailing rates, apparently, but of course less than one might earn in speculative investments), he counsels a frugality that will enable her to plow the interest back into the principal: "he frequently took Occasion to hint, how soon I might raise my Fortune to a prodigious Height, if I wou'd but order my Family-Oeconomy so far within my Revenue, as to lay-up every Year something, to add to the Capital" (167). He goes so far as to draw up "a Table, as he call'd it, of the Encrease, for me to judge by; and by which, he said, if the Gentlemen of England wou'd but act so, every Family of them wou'd encrease their Fortunes to a great Degree, just as Merchants do by Trade" (167). So in just seven years and about fifteen pages of text her fortune swells to £35,000, "and as I found Ways to live without wasting either Principal or Interest, I laid up 2000 *l.* every Year, at least, out of the meer Interest, adding it to the Principal; and thus I went on" (182). This capital grows even larger, of course, as time goes by, so that at the end of her last cohabitation of several years in London with a nobleman, she has the tremendous fortune of £50,000, "nay, I had the Income of fifty Thousand Pounds; for I had 2500 *l.* a Year coming in, upon very good Land-Security, besides 3 or 4000 *l.* in Money, which I kept by me for ordinary Occasions, and besides Jewels and Plate, and Goods, which were worth near 5000 *l.* more" (202). By modern measure of her wealth, Roxana is a multi-millionaire, worth in contemporary purchasing power upwards of five million pounds; the ledger she offers readers is a wonder of steady accumulation, and it is made even more of a wonder by her mode of living. From the dangerous and ultimately destructive proceeds of selling her body and soul, Roxana finds that the financial order can work its benign magic on her safe and secure investments and render a transformation, as the narrative implies, as significant as the various metamorphoses by which she earns her living. Indeed, her last sexual liaison in London is a high/low point of this interpenetration of the sexual and the financial:

> I may venture to say, that no Woman ever liv'd a Life like me, of six and twenty Years of Wickedness, without the least Signals of Remorse; without any Signs of Repentance; or without so much as a Wish to put an End to it; I had so long habituated myself to a Life of Vice, that really it appear'd to be no Vice to me; I went on smooth and pleasant; I wallow'd in Wealth, and it flow'd in upon me at such a Rate, having taken the frugal Measures that the good Knight directed; so that I had at the End of the eight Years, two Thousand eight Hundred Pounds coming Yearly in, of which I did not spend one Penny, being maintain'd

by my Allowance from my Lord –, and more than maintain'd, by above 200 *l. per Annum*;
for tho' he did not contract for 500 *l.* a Year, as I made dumb Signs to have it be, yet he gave
me Money so often, and that in such large Parcels, that I had seldom so little as seven to
eight Hundred Pounds a Year of him, one Year with another. (188)

It is difficult not to notice the admiration in such passages, as they render an
efficiency, intelligence, and smooth management that readers are at least temporarily
invited to marvel at. Investments of a safe sort provide a tranquillity and stability that
overwhelm any moral qualms and bury remorse or repentance.

Those investments are also diversified, as she makes clear to the Dutch merchant
near the end of the novel, when she finally accepts his marriage proposal and they each
in turn expose their assets in a remarkable prenuptial accounting. Roxana concludes
this opening of their accounts with an interesting proposal whereby they shall live
exclusively from the £2000 a year her principal brings in, so that his capital can
increase, risk-free, by accumulating and compounding its own yearly interest. Her
motive, she explains, is to avoid thereby "mingling my cursed ill-gotten Wealth with
his honest Estate" (260), thus safeguarding her faithful husband from "the Justice of
Heaven, which I had reason to expect would sometime or other still fall upon me or
my Effects, for the dreadful Life I had liv'd" (260).

The scene has a fairytale quality and structure in which their financial revelations
are an unveiling of the transformative magic that money, in a proleptically Marxian
sense, can perform, even as they are in another sense merely a pedantically precise
accounting of their assets. The merchant responds to a test or challenge arranged by
Roxana, a test whereby she can astonish him with her wealth as well as reward him for
his long constancy to her. So she asks him, can he truly transform her into a Lady and
then a Princess? Can he "maintain an expensive *Englishwoman* in all her Pride, and
Vanity?" Does he know whether she has sufficient fortune herself to merit this
elevation? "I am afraid," she concludes, "you keep her in a Figure a great-deal above
her Estate, *at least*, above all that you have seen of it yet? Are you sure you ha'n't got a
Bite? And that you have not made a Beggar a *Lady*?" (255). Roxana is enjoying the
prospect of one of her transformations, one not so distinct from the pseudo-Turkish
dance that made her the King's mistress or the demonstrations to the Prince of her
perfect and unpainted complexion. So these prosaic accountings, these ledgers and
balance sheets, are the ultimate and resolving revelations in her story, outdoing the
merely physical and temporary postures and attitudes of the courtesan, projecting awe
at the workings of money and, of course, at Roxana's acquisition through her investments of the stability and order possessed by those workings. These articulated assets
embody order and regularity, an army of unalterable law that stands in stark contrast
to a narrative otherwise dominated by randomness and dangerous unpredictability,
where luck or mischance seems to rule, and where success and survival are a matter for
Roxana and Amy, her faithful servant and companion, of improvisational balancing
and continuous self-invention and absolute alertness. And we may say that in this
scene Roxana's revelations are the more effective, her most truthful and truly intimate

moment; she reveals her secret stability, her hidden connection to those safe mortgages, and her commitment to that steady and sure accumulation of capital provided by the magic of compound interest.

To be sure, from this moment on Roxana also enters her melodramatic closing sequence, as a lacerating remorse leads to despair, and that guilt over her life as a courtesan is compounded by her fear that she will be exposed by her determined daughter, Susan, as the Lady Roxana. All this can properly be understood as related to the anxieties and epistemological confusions endemic to a market economy that Ingrassia and Sherman make so much of, although in practical terms it also seems like a clumsy moralistic coda to what otherwise would be, like compound interest itself, a story with no foreseeable end. Roxana has been what the market wanted of her, and she has out-performed her rivals in serving the sexual needs (and of course in embodying the fantasies) of her clients. But as much as she exemplifies successful risk-taking and illusionistic promises in her sexual/financial adventures, and to that extent represents a validation of a certain kind of daring speculation that is certainly analogous to financial speculation of a sort that had raged in the early 1720s, Defoe sees to it that she is not overwhelmed by any recognizable financial failure or by direct and anxious participation in a speculative market. Compound interest, with its pattern of steady and sure accumulation, is a better metaphor for the workings of personality and the pattern of history that produce the heroine's concluding guilt. All along, without realizing it, Roxana has been accumulating the materials of remorse, adding and compounding those acts of survival and then of prosperity and triumph that are on another level waiting to reveal themselves as a sum almost beyond measure of guilt. Such guilt is perhaps the negative, the obverse of Roxana's financial triumphs, but its steady accumulation and multiplication seem to follow the pattern of compound interest.

I have had much more to say about *Roxana* than *Love in Excess*, and in the process have been proving my point that Defoe's book far exceeds Haywood's in its cultural density, in the far-reaching historical and ideological resonances that it sets in motion, in the specific and contemporary issues and ideas that it engages and debates both explicitly and implicitly. There's more to say about *Roxana*; it is not a piece of formula fiction and it looks forward to the psychological novel rather than backward to the romance tradition as Haywood's novel does. It is in fact original as well as disturbing, offering a new view of human psychology in a remarkable and pathological individual rather than a classic and reassuring affirmation of emotional inevitability and characteriological predictability as *Love in Excess* does. Perhaps this did not need proving or discussion at quite this length, but one might argue that Haywood's romance is valuable exactly for the contrast it provides with Defoe's work and the substantial originality that it alerts us to in *Roxana*, and finally for the case it allows me to make about the nature of value when considering eighteenth-century fiction.

See also: chapter 11, New Contexts for Early Novels; chapter 15, The Eighteenth-Century Novel and Print Culture; chapter 22, The Novel Body Politic.

Notes

1. Ernest A. Baker, *The History of the English Novel: The Later Romances and the Establishment of Realism* (1929; repr. New York: Barnes & Noble, 1961) 3:225.

2. Baker, *The Later Romances*, 3:117.

3. Janet Todd, "Fatal Fluency: Behn's Fiction and the Restoration Letter," Special issue on "Reconsidering the Rise of the Novel," in *Eighteenth-Century Fiction* 12 (2000): 419.

4. But Michael McKeon in his new introduction to the fifteenth-anniversary edition of his 1987 *The Origins of the English Novel 1600–1740* (Baltimore, MD, and London: Johns Hopkins University Press, 2002) finds such feminist assertions ahistorical and in fact erroneous. He thinks that during the first half of the eighteenth century "gender difference has not yet been sufficiently separated out from status difference to receive direct attention" (xxv).

5. After King Charles II died in 1685, his Catholic brother, James II, had in the view of many English Protestants attempted to undermine the established English Protestant Church by appointing Catholic office-holders, and in what came to be called "the Glorious Revolution" James was forced in 1688 to flee the country, to be replaced by his daughter Mary and her husband, the Dutch William of Orange. They reigned as William III and Mary II.

6. Toni Bowers, "Sex, Lies, and Invisibility," in *The Columbia History of the British Novel*, ed. John Richetti (New York: Columbia University Press, 1994), 70.

7. Ibid.

8. And the University of Kentucky Press has an ongoing series of editions called "Eighteenth-Century Novels by Women," with Isobel Grundy as the general editor.

9. Ros Ballaster, *Seductive Forms: Women's Amatory Fiction from 1684–1740* (Oxford: Clarendon Press, 1992), 23.

10. I've never been entirely happy with this state of affairs, so several years ago, I attempted to stand up for literary value, but a value necessarily redefined in terms of how the novel, early and late, seems to work. See "Ideas and Voices: The New Novel in Eighteenth-Century England," *Eighteenth-Century Fiction* 12 (2000): 327–44. There I attempt to contrast Defoe's overt engagement with particular moral and religious ideas in *Robinson Crusoe*, especially in those sequences when the hero ponders his relationship to the cannibals and in the process invokes a thoughtful reader interested as he is in larger moral, social, and historical issues, and the quite different emphasis of the amatory novella such as Haywood produced in the 1720s, where the narrative emphasis falls on the expressive communication of emotions to a reader conceived of implicitly as eager purely for heightened vicarious experiences.

11. It should be noted that Haywood's later work in the 1740s and early 1750s, beginning with *Anti-Pamela; or, Feigned Innocence Detected* (1741) and culminating in *The History of Miss Betsy Thoughtless* (1751) and *The History of Jemmy and Jenny Jessamy* (1752), engages quite vigorously and self-consciously in a very different manner with what I am calling ideas.

12. Eliza Haywood, *Love in Excess; Or, The Fatal Enquiry*, ed. David Oakleaf (Peterborough, Ontario: Broadview Press, 1994), 39. All further references in the text are to this edition.

13. J. G. A. Pocock, *Virtue, Commerce, and History: Essays on Political Thought and History, Chiefly in the Eighteenth Century*, (Cambridge: Cambridge University Press: 1985), 114.

14. Catherine Ingrassia, *Authorship, Commerce, and Gender in Early Eighteenth-Century England: A Culture of Paper Credit* (Cambridge: Cambridge University Press, 1998), 38–39.

15. Ibid., 88.

16. Sandra Sherman, *Finance and Fictionality in the Early Eighteenth Century* (Cambridge: Cambridge University Press, 1996), 89.

17. Daniel Defoe, *Roxana: The Fortunate Mistress*, ed. John Mullan (Oxford: Oxford University Press, 1996), 105–106. All other references in the text are to this edition.

Further Reading

Backscheider, Paula. "Defoe's Lady Credit," *Huntington Library Quarterly* 44 (1981): 89–100.

Dickson, P. G. M. *The Financial Revolution in England: A Study in the Development of Public Credit, 1688–1756*. New York: St. Martin's Press, 1967.

Dijkstra, Bram. *Defoe and Economics: the Fortunes of Roxana in the History of Interpretation*. Basingstoke: Macmillan, 1987.

Kahn, Madeline. *Narrative Transvestism: Rhetoric and Gender in the Eighteenth-Century English Novel*. Ithaca, NY: Cornell University Press, 1991.

Novak, Maximillian E. *Economics and Fiction of Daniel Defoe*. Berkeley and Los Angeles: University of California Press, 1962.

Richetti, John. *The English Novel in History, 1700–1780*. London: Routledge, 1999.

17

Queer Gothic

George E. Haggerty

Gothic Fiction

Gothic fiction emerged rather suddenly as a popular form of British fiction in the later years of the eighteenth century, starting with Horace Walpole's *The Castle of Otranto* (1764) and extending at least as far as Charles Robert Maturin's *Melmoth the Wanderer* (1820) and James Hogg's *The Private Memoirs and Confessions of a Justified Sinner* (1824). In order to explain the sudden popularity of this bizarrely outrageous yet conventional form, which reached its apex in the 1790s, literary historians have cited aesthetic history, political unrest, literary experimentation, and personal obsession. No single account has been able to establish a reason for the popularity of Gothic writing, nor have critical interpretations felt at all restricted by historical circumstances or aesthetic presuppositions. Gothic fiction has given rise to a wide range of provocative readings, and it has sustained even ahistorical accounts of personality and psyche that would have been unfathomable to those writing these sensational texts.

Recent studies of Gothic fiction, such as those by Emma Clery and Robert Miles, and by Edward Jacobs, have usefully extended the scope of Gothic writing in the eighteenth century.[1] By looking at materials earlier in the eighteenth century and reconsidering a range of writing that has often been ignored, these critics have suggested that the term "Gothic" itself shifts in meaning and cultural significance throughout the period I am considering. In an earlier book, I argued that the opposite of historical specificity, rather vague and often indirect historical associations, served expressive purposes that no amount of historical investigation can explain.[2] The peculiar and often uncanny power of eighteenth-century Gothic fiction still resists attempts to explain it, and as useful as this recent historicizing of Gothic has been, it does not radically change the way "Gothic" functions as a literary device in the period I am discussing. As I shall begin to demonstrate in this essay, a wide range of writers, dispersed historically and culturally, use "Gothic" to evoke a queer world that attempts to transgress the binaries of sexual decorum.

What does it mean to call Gothic fiction "queer"? It is no mere coincidence that the cult of Gothic fiction reached its apex at the very moment when gender and sexuality were beginning to be codified for modern culture. In fact, Gothic fiction offered a testing ground for many unauthorized genders and sexualities, including sodomy, tribadism, romantic friendship (male and female), incest, pedophilia, sadism, masochism, necrophilia, cannibalism, masculinized females, feminized males, miscegenation, and so on. In this sense, it offers an historical model of queer theory and politics: transgressive, sexually coded, and resistant to dominant ideology. While I examine Gothic fiction in order to relate it to the history of sexuality, as articulated by Michel Foucault and others, I also consider recent works of queer theory and cultural studies in order to explore the ways in which this fiction itself is codified. Joseph Bristow offers a useful summary of the emergence of the concept of sexuality in the later nineteenth century.[3] From that perspective these Gothic works predate sexuality's codification. But by predating, they also prepare the ground, as I hope these pages will show, for later developments in sexological studies.

Transgressive social-sexual relations are the most basic common denominator of Gothic, and from the moment in the early pages of Walpole's *The Castle of Otranto* when Walpole's anti-hero Manfred presses his suit on the fiancée of his deceased son (and she flees into the "long labyrinth of darkness" in the "subterraneous" regions of the castle), a Gothic trope is fixed: terror is almost always sexual terror, and fear, and flight, and incarceration, and escape are almost always colored by the exoticism of transgressive sexual aggression.[4] Like other expressions of transgressive desire throughout the eighteenth century, Gothic fiction is not about homo or hetero desire as much as it is about the fact of desire itself. And throughout these works, this desire is expressed as the exercise of (or resistance to) power. But that power is itself charged with a sexual force – a sexual-ity – that determines the action and gives it shape. By the same token, powerlessness has a similar valence and performs a similar function. This creates an odd sexual mood in most Gothic works, closer to what we might crudely label sadomasochism (a binary I will go on to challenge) than to any other model of sexual interaction. That nearly a century of fiction (or more than two centuries depending on how broad the definition of "Gothic" is) would function in this way is in itself queer, and queer too is the manner in which normative sexual relations are articulated and codified; for no matter how tidy, no marriage at the close of a Gothic novel can entirely dispel the thrilling dys- (or different) functionality at the heart of Gothic.

In this essay I approach the question of "queer Gothic" from a number of different directions. In addition to problematizing the representations of same-sex desire in Gothic, a trope that has been variously explained by critics, including myself,[5] I attempt to show the ways in which all normative – heteronormative, if you will – configurations of human interaction are insistently challenged and in some cases significantly undermined. I cannot make too broad a claim because these fictions never significantly challenge the "dominant fiction" of the age.[6] At the same time, however, they occur in a period which had yet to construct the elaborate superstructure of sexuality that

Plate 13.   Horace Walpole's much-celebrated Gothic residence, which inspired *The Castle of Otranto*.

emerged in the age of sexology at the end of the nineteenth and the beginning of the twentieth centuries. Gothic fiction offered the one semi-respectable area of literary endeavor in which modes of sexual and social transgression were discursively addressed on a regular basis; and it therefore makes sense to consider the ways in which Gothic fiction itself helped to shape thinking about sexual matters – theories of sexuality, as it were – and to create the darker shadows of the dominant fiction, that is, the darkness that enables culture to function as a fiction in the first place.

Gothic fiction relies on a set of narrative conventions that barely change from Walpole to Maturin and beyond.[7] Slavoj Žižek explains why such conventions might have the uncanny power that they do. For him, "the Real is the rock upon which every attempt at symbolization stumbles, the hard core which remains the same in all possible worlds."[8] This would begin to explain the common obsessions of Gothic, its seemingly inexhaustible ability to return again and again to common tropes and similar situations. At the same time, however, this promising stability "is thoroughly precarious; it is something that persists only as failed, missed, in a shadow, and dissolves itself as soon as we try to grasp it in its positive nature."[9] So many critical attempts to pin down the Gothic are unsuccessful because of its uncanny structure.[10] For Žižek the function of "the Real" is clear: "All its effectivity lies in the distortions it produces in the symbolic universe of the subject: the traumatic event is ultimately just a fantasy-construct filling out a certain void in a symbolic structure and, as such, the retroactive effect of this structure."[11] This shadow-presence of the real and these distortions of the symbolic are the staple of Gothic fiction. These are primal scenes, if you will, not the secretive private memory of an individual, but the primal reality of the culture at large. It behooves us to look more closely at the queerness of this material so as to recognize its function in the structure of the dominant fiction itself.

I borrow the notion of a "dominant fiction" from Kaja Silverman, for whom this concept explains how cultural prerogatives are given the ascendancy that the "ideological state apparatus" presupposes. In her attempt to analyze the function of marginalized masculinities, Silverman reexamines the Althusserian concept of "interpellation" to include the notion that the "state apparatus" itself is only a "dominant fiction," rather than anything "real." Conveniently for the critic of fiction, she shows the ways in which culture structures itself like a fiction. Like a Gothic fiction? Uncannily, yes. The dominant fiction has a ghostly presence: Silverman argues further that "it is only by defining what passes for 'reality' at the level of the psyche that ideology can be said to command the subject's belief."[12] Gothic fiction attempts to rewrite "psychic" reality for the purposes of extending its own erotic power. In doing so, it shifts the range and complexity of cultural control.[13] Silverman argues that the dominant fiction is more real than any details of concrete reality. The ideological charge is always already at work for Silverman; no writer completely escapes the force of the dominant fiction within which she or he constructs imaginative fictions. In this sense, of course, Gothic fiction can be read as reinscribing the status quo: Gothic resolutions repeatedly insist on order restored and (often) on the reassertion of heteronormative prerogative. At the same time, a non-teleological reading of Gothic – a queer reading – can begin to show the ways in which Gothic works beyond the limits of its structural "meaning" to change the structure of meaning itself. Gothic fiction is about reaching into some undefinable world beyond fictional reality, and that "beyond" can never be pulled back into narrative control. That is why Gothic fiction remains as queer as it is, and it also suggests why and how Gothic remains to challenge the status quo and at the same time to expand its purview.

The Gothic novel, emerging as it does at the moment when the battle lines of cultural reorganization are being formed in the later eighteenth century, shimmers with subversive potential. If the emergence of "the novel" itself celebrates the codification of middle-class values, as several critics have argued, the Gothic novel records the terror implicit in the increasingly dictatorial reign of those values.[14] Gothic fiction, as I have argued in *Gothic Fiction/Gothic Form*, seems particularly, if not aggressively, open to interpretation from social, political, and sexual points of view. The Gothic novel achieves this interpretive license precisely because it reflects in perhaps predictable, but nonetheless often powerful ways, the anxiety generated by the force of culture itself. In its very excess, Gothic fiction thereby challenges the cultural system that both commodifies desire and renders it lurid and pathological.[15]

Matthew G. Lewis

In *The Monk: A Romance* (1796), for instance, Matthew G. Lewis attempts to outrage taste and scandalize propriety in as many sexually explicit ways as he can. The central plot – that of the seemingly virtuous monk Ambrosio, who is seduced by the scheming Matilda, herself disguised as the young novice Rosario – is fraught with uncontrollable sexual desire and motivated by "perverse" sexual transgression throughout. The ambiguous sexuality of Rosario/Matilda provides a backdrop of homoeroticism against which the larger dramas of the plot are played out. When Matilda reveals herself in turn to be an agent of Satan, the catalyst of "perversity," gender recedes as the determining factor in desire. Ambrosio's "lusts" would in any case be difficult to categorize.

After Ambrosio's desire for Matilda cools, he turns his lascivious attentions to the young Antonia, daughter of the proud Elvira, his confidante. Having employed occult arts by means of which to enter Antonia's bedchamber and render her defenseless against his lust, Ambrosio is interrupted by Elvira, who challenges and accuses him. He responds by murdering Elvira in one of the most brutal scenes of Gothic fiction:

> Turning round suddenly, with one hand He grasped Elvira's throat so as to prevent her continuing her clamour, and with the other, dashing her violently to the ground, He dragged her towards the Bed. . . . The Monk, snatching the pillow from beneath her daughter's head, covering with it Elvira's face, and pressing his knee upon her stomach with all his strength, endeavoured to put an end to her existence. He succeeded but too well. . . . The Monk continued to kneel upon her breast, witnessed without mercy the convulsive trembling of her limbs beneath him, and sustained with inhuman firmness the spectacle of her agonies, when soul and body were on the point of separating.

At last he completes his task and gazes on her "a Corpse, cold, senseless, and disgusting."[16]

More than a hundred pages pass before the reader is informed that this woman with whom Ambrosio is struggling on the bed of his proposed sexual violation is in fact his own mother. The excessive emotion of what turns out to be the only "bed scene" in the novel, a scene between a sexually confused young man and his mother, seems in retrospect the emotional center of the work.

Antonia, who is therefore Ambrosio's sister, is not spared the incestuous obsession of the unfortunate friar. Toward the close of the novel, he discovers her in the underground vault of the Convent of St. Claire:

> Naturally addicted to the gratification of the senses, in the full vigour of manhood, and heat of blood, He had suffered his temperament to acquire such ascendancy, that his lust was become madness . . . . He longed for the possession of her [Antonia's] person; and even the gloom of the vault, the surrounding silence, and the resistance which He expected from her, seemed to give a fresh edge to his fierce and unbridled desires. (380)

After Ambrosio accomplishes Antonia's "dishonour" in the "violence of his lustful delirium," he curses her fatal charms and blames her for his fall from grace. He determines further that she must never leave the dungeon. When she tries to escape, he kills her by plunging his dagger twice into her bosom – suggesting at once the murderous impulse harbored within his incestuous desire. For Stephen Bruhn, "the 'Gothic body' is that which is put on excessive display, and whose violence, vulnerable immediacy gives . . . Gothic fiction [its] beautiful barbarity, [its] troublesome power."[17] The "troublesome power" in *The Monk* remains connected to the family in this way because Lewis reserves his bodily excess for such scenes of family intimacy.

These scenes are usually dismissed as merely sensational. It seems to me that however sensationalistic they seem, they are also as political as anything in late eighteenth-century fiction. It is the nature of patriarchy to make incest, for instance, its most basic prohibition; for unless the terms of familial desire are carefully controlled, according to the logic of patriarchy, the fabric of society will break down. Studies by anthropologists such as Claude Lévi-Strauss, and others, have demonstrated that the distribution of power depends on the control of intrafamilial relations by means of an "exchange" of women, and that the incest taboo serves as much a political as a sexual function.[18]

In another context, I have argued that incest is a cultural taboo rather than a "natural" one.[19] That does not make it less deeply encoded as a personal taboo, and when Ambrosio "rapes" and murders his mother Elvira for getting in the way of his desire for Antonia, and in turn rapes and murders his sister Antonia because she comes to represent the hideousness of his own desires, he transcendently violates the most basic law of patriarchal culture. After Ambrosio is informed of his incestuous crimes, during the closing pages of the novel, he is filled with the horror of self-disgust. But I would argue that this horror comes so late that the effect of the incest is at least potentially subversive and that by abusing the relations between himself and his mother and sister he is doing more than giving his villainous character an appallingly misogynist twist. The act of incest is political because it defies the attempt of society to control desire. Cultural critics have suggested that the regulation of marriage ties is a restriction that serves the purposes of the patriarchy; Ambrosio at the very least defies such a restriction in his experiments with "perversion." In raping and murdering the women in his life, moreover, Ambrosio underlines the other, the forbidden desire that Rosario at first represented. At one point in the midst of his nefarious decline, the narrator tells us that in a moment of reflection "he regretted Rosario, the fond, the gentle, and submissive" (232). If Ambrosio must be forced to fulfill the role of the male in patriarchal culture, he does so violently, with none of the subterfuge at work in the society around him. He turns the romantic fiction inside out in order to show that sexuality is always about power and that power, perhaps more importantly, is always about sexuality.

Foucault would argue that this attempt at subversion is not only doomed to failure but is in fact an aspect of the extension of cultural control that he calls "the deployment of sexuality." Foucault claims that sexuality itself becomes a mode of social knowledge and control. "In a society such as ours," he says, "where the family is the most active site of sexuality, and where it is doubtless the exigencies of the latter which maintain and prolong its existence, incest . . . occupies a central place; it is constantly being solicited and refused; it is an object of obsession and attraction, a dreadful secret and an indispensable pivot." But Lewis exposes this "affective intensification of the family space" and ridicules the terms of the Oedipal "fantasy" almost as directly as Foucault does. Lewis seems to understand implicitly what it means to be trapped in a regime that makes sexuality the central, the signal transgression. By turning the Oedipal "fantasy" into vivid and horrifying (fictional) reality, Lewis exposes the very process of cultural control that Foucault came later to describe. What Foucault calls the pathologization of pleasure has its fictional equivalent in a novel like *The Monk*, in which sexuality becomes a form of public madness that defies the culture that would attempt to control, contain, or even know it.[20]

Ann Radcliffe

Ann Radcliffe's evocation of female anxiety in works such as *The Mysteries of Udolpho* (1794) also pushes at the limits of the normative.[21] When Emily St. Aubert first sees the Castle of Udolpho, where she will live with her aunt and her aunt's husband, the nefarious Montoni, it has an almost physical presence for her: "Emily gazed with melancholy awe upon the castle, which she understood to be Montoni's; for, though it was now lighted up by the setting sun, the gothic greatness of its features, and its mouldering walls of dark grey stone, rendered it a gloomy and sublime object. . . . Silent, lonely, and sublime, it seemed to stand the sovereign of the scene, and to frown defiance on all, who dared to invade its solitary reign."[22]

Emily's first view of the castle connects it to its owner, and there is every reason to think that the castle itself, "gloomy and sublime," is a constant reminder of the evil

Plate 14.   Sutton Castle, probably the ruin of a castle in Kent rather than one of the fashionable ruins built for scenic value.

Montoni. Such textbook descriptions of landscape are associated with eighteenth-century concepts of the picturesque or the sublime, inspired by the philosophy of Edmund Burke, whose *Philosophical Enquiry into the Origin of Our Ideas of the Sublime and the Beautiful* (1757) popularized the notion of pleasurable terror and outlined an entire range of techniques for engaging the emotions associated with the Gothic. As Frank Bunting says, "No topic of aesthetic inquiry in the eighteenth century generated greater interest than the sublime."[23] Radcliffean "sublime" always involves a fascination with what is fearful. As Vijay Mishra notes, "the experience of the sublime pushes the imagination to a crisis point, to a point of exhaustion and chaos."[24] This compulsive pursuit of an exhausting and chaotic encounter with the other could be equated with desire, but it is not necessarily a desire for the "owner" of the castle. For Robert Miles, "Radcliffe's picturesque appears to turn on absence – the melancholy viewer is filled with a poignant yearning for something that forever eludes her." Miles goes on to argue that the picturesque "is actually a moment of plenitude, one associated with maternal nurturing. This is because the picturesque moment is for the heroine an instance of artistic self-fulfillment."[25] This is how the picturesque should work, but a scene like this one short-circuits self-fulfillment with the dread associated with the view itself. The more precise rendering of the view makes the terror it invokes more powerful.

Later, when Emily has suffered enough mental abuse from her stepfather to realize that she is in real danger, she finds the dreary castle itself more terrifying and more attractive than anyone who inhabits it: in seeking her aunt in a distant tower, for instance, she "proceeded through a passage, adjoining the vaults, the walls of which were drooping with unwholesome dews, and the vapours, that crept along the ground, made the torch burn so dimly, that Emily expected every moment to see it extinguished." She then looks through "a pair of iron gates" to see "by uncertain flashes of light, the vaults beyond, and near her, heaps of earth, that seemed to surround an open grave" (345). These descriptions are more specific than Walpole's "long labyrinth of darkness," and the details all help to draw a picture that makes understandable the critical desire to connect passages of the castle and passages of memory. Emily seems drawn into these dim, vaporous, and unwholesome spaces; she sees them uncertainly, and she fears for her own safety, even as she insists on penetrating further into the gloom and secrecy of this dark interior. The spectral presence of the castle itself has an alarming "uncanniness," as if Emily, trapped in the passages of repressed memory, recognized in these threatening spaces something about herself that she had always known.[26] David Punter claims that "the Gothic and the sublime best encounter each other on the terrain of memory and forgetting," and that is what Radcliffe accomplishes.[27] Memory itself asks the heroine to confront her deepest fears and darkest desires.

What critics like Clare Kahane have argued so persuasively is that when the "secret" of the castle turns out to be the history of the sexually transgressive Madame Laurentini, this threatening maternal figure becomes, in a way, the "meaning" of the work. "As a victimizer victimized by her own desire," Kahane says, "Laurentini is presented as Emily's potential precursor, a mad mother-sister-double who mirrors Emily's own potential for transgression and madness."[28] "Female Gothic," in other words, confronts the heroine with her own desires and thrills her with the possibility of transgression. In Radcliffe's novels, of course, the transgression remains only a threat, a threat which is contained in the forced conclusions upon which she insists. Emily as heroine cannot transgress, and no one for a moment imagines that she will.

As heroine, however, she can — indeed she must — suffer. Some critics have gone so far as to suggest that the attraction a heroine like Emily comes inexplicably to feel for the inward reaches of the castle is in fact the sign of a repressed masochistic desire for the shadowy Gothic villain hero himself. Cynthia Griffin Wolff calls this figure the demon lover: "Despite the fact that the man is darkly attractive, the woman generally shuns him, shrinking as from some invisible contamination. Too often to be insignificant, this aversion is justified when he eventually proves to be a long-lost relation: an uncle, a step-father, sometimes the biological father himself — lusting after the innocent daughter's chastity."[29] In Wolff's analysis, the demon lover, who "dominat[es] the fiction as its undeniable emotional focus," is secretly attractive to the heroine and becomes the source of a power which releases her from the confines of a sentimental world.

In imagining the possibility of female-female desire in Gothic fiction, however, I would like to return with the maternal obsession that Kahane describes and reinvest it with the erotic potential that is more than merely hinted here. Far more than the Gothic villain, the maternal figure in "female Gothic" holds out the possibility of love, of self-realization, and of escape from the confines of patriarchal culture.

For instance, in Radcliffe's *The Italian; or, The Confessional of the Black Penitents* (1797), which is in some ways a response to *The Monk*, desire is figured differently, but the terms of its challenge to heteronormativity are remarkably similar. Doubly transgressive female-female desire resides at the heart of this novel and gives it structure. As Susan Greenfield has argued, "the Gothic can . . . emphasize the power and potential eroticism of mother-daughter relations."[30] Greenfield claims that the mother can be the object of openly erotic desire only so long as the familial relation is repressed. At the same time, I would argue that *The Italian* and other "female Gothic" works are structured so as to heighten the erotics of maternal relations as vividly and aggressively as Sarah Scott does in *Millenium Hall* (1762).[31] For Ellena di Rosalba, the heroine of *The Italian*, is lost until she finds her mother in the corridors of the convent of the *Santa della Piéta*.[32] Susan Wolstenholme discusses the "*gendered* relationship between audience and spectacle" in Radcliffe's fiction. She also says that "For Radcliffe, writing *The Italian* as a corrective to Lewis's *The Monk*, a text not just less squeamish about rape and incest but actually relishing its own sordid details, decorum veils predatory sex."[33] But it also transforms the predatory into the nurturing, conventual love that instills an uncanny power.

Ellena's melancholic incorporation of the lost mother – her desire for the mother – is played out against her oddly muted love affair with the predictably ineffectual Vivaldi. She wants him, to be sure, but she does not know how to articulate this desire. It is her mother Olivia who teaches her what desire means. Judith Butler says that

> if the assumption of femininity and the assumption of masculinity proceed through the accomplishment of an always tenuous heterosexuality, we might understand this accomplishment as mandating the abandonment of homosexual attachments or, perhaps more trenchantly, *preempting* the possibility of homosexual attachment, a foreclosure of possibility which produces a domain of homosexuality understood as unlivable passion and ungrievable loss.[34]

Ellena and her mother sigh together over the broken body of masculinity because in their love they recognize the loss that a heteronormative narrative represents. But in the end they incorporate that loss into the very heterosexuality that the novel putatively celebrates. What makes this different is the love that they have rediscovered for one another, melancholy and muted as it is. Diane Long Hoeveler argues that "what is at stake in the female gothic novel is psychic and linguistic reconfiguration of parental figures."[35] Gothic fiction offers a range of possibilities as to what forms this "reconfiguration" takes and by what means it is inscribed on the psyches of the heroes and heroines of Gothic fiction.

Charles Robert Maturin

Melancholy is vivid in the characters in Charles Robert Maturin's *Melmoth the Wanderer* (1820) as well. These characters manage not to succumb to the nefarious skill of the infernal Melmoth, the "perverse" emissary who appears in each of the several interpolated tales of the novel to tempt them with "escape" from present difficulties. They do not need to sell their souls to the devil, however, when their bodies have already condemned them to a hell on earth.[36]

In the most famous of the interpolated tales, for instance, "The Tale of the Spaniard," Alonzo de Monçada tells the story of his own incarceration at the hands of the Inquisition. The political abuses of the Inquisition are hideous and disturbing, as are the intrusions of infernal temptation; but Maturin makes the body itself the site of transgression. The body itself, in other words, traps the subject within an ideology that literally dis-members the body for its own purposes. Stephen Bruhm says that "in the experience of terror, the mind imagines a certain physical experience which it reproduces on the body as the experience of pain."[37] That "experience of pain" is dramatized here in gruesome terms. In a sense, Maturin reverses this process to remind us of the relation between psychological and physical suffering, between the mind and the body. When Monçada and a guide are pushing their way through an underground passage, which is so constricted as almost to cause suffocation, Monçada says that he "could not help recollecting and *applying*" a story about a group of travelers exploring the vaults of the Egyptian pyramids. "One of them, who was advancing, as I was, on his hands and knees, stuck in the passage, and, whether from terror, or from the natural consequences of his situation, swelled so that it was impossible for him to retreat, advance, or allow a passage for his companions." When the others realize that this companion threatens their own survival, their guide "proposed, in the selfishness to which the feeling of vital danger reduces all, to cut off the limbs of the wretched being who obstructed their passage." At this suggestion, the companion manages somehow to squeeze himself out of the way. "He was suffocated, however, in the effort, and left behind a corse."[38] What is interesting here is not just the vivid portrayal of the physical effects of fear. Rather, notice that the community of travelers is beset by fear because one individual has "blocked" their passage. They have no trouble planning to free their own way by dismembering the person before them. It could be said that this act, this brutal and self-centered substitute for castration, helps to dramatize the ways in which bourgeois culture handles the individual. Castration, figural or literal, is all there is for those who stand in the way of what the culture values most, in this case its own survival. Punter argues that "Gothic enacts an introjection of the destruction of the body, and thus it introjects death; in so doing it attains sublimity because it is necessary for there to be a circling, hovering, transcendent self which can enact the survival and supersession of physical difficulties, the 'last man,' the wanderer, the ancient mariner."[39] If introjection is a kind of internalization of parental power, here the parental power is writ large, a superego that is represented in this novel as the Catholic church and its offices of the Inquisition.

When, later in his tale, Monçada hears the story of illicit love in the confines of a monastery, the result is strikingly similar. In this case, his companion tells him the story of a novice and his growing sentimental attachment to a young monk. The narrator, a "parricide," gives the following account:

> One evening as the young monk and his darling novice were in the garden, the former plucked a peach, which he immediately offered to his favourite; the latter accepted it with a movement I thought rather awkward – it seemed like what I imagined would be the reverence of a female. The young monk divided the peach with a knife; in doing so, the knife grazed the finger of the novice, and the monk, in agitation inexpressible, tore his habit to bind up the wound. I saw it all – my mind was made up on the business – I went to the Superior that very night. The result may be conceived. They were watched.

After setting a trap for the two, after he is certain that they have arranged to spend the night together, the parricide brings the Superior and other monks to witness the depravity: "we burst into the cell. The wretched husband and wife were locked in each others arms. You may imagine the scene that followed" (205–7).

The convent's Superior, "who had no more idea of the intercourse between the sexes, than between two beings of different species," is so horrified at this spectacle of "two human beings of different sexes, who dared to love one another" (207), that his own sexual proclivities may be called into question. If they are; if, that is, he represents the male-male desire implicit in monastic life, he also helps to explain how what is transgressive in one context becomes the very agent of cultural control in another. The kind of surveillance that comes "naturally" in a convent religious life builds surveillance into its communal system – here has had the salubrious effect of ferreting out male-female desire and extirpating it from the society in question. This transaction succeeds by employing those who would otherwise find themselves in violation of the law they are so desperate to serve.

What does happen is that these lovers are lured, in the hope of "escape," into the underground passages of the convent and there trapped by the parricide in a chamber that is nailed shut and from which they can never escape. Soon they turn on one another, and before the narration ceases, the husband sinks his teeth into the wasted flesh of his mate. This cannibalistic conclusion to a tale of sexual transgression is not unique to Maturin, but it is handled here as a deft reminder of the relativity of desire. Love becomes literally an appetite, and desire becomes indistinguishable from murderous aggression. By walling these young lovers up in the subterranean passage and listening to their moans, the parricide acts out the cultural mechanism that the Gothic harbors at its core.

Queer Gothic

These few examples can begin to suggest how thoroughly invested in same-sex and transgressive incestuous desire the Gothic seems always already to be. "The excess and ambivalence associated with Gothic figures were seen as distinct signs of transgression," Bunting says. "Aesthetically excessive, Gothic productions were considered unnatural in the undermining of physical laws with marvelous beings and fantastic events."[40] It was thought unnatural, too, in the ways personal desires were organized and in the expression of excessive lusts and lurid passions. For Cindy Hendershot, "The Gothic fragments stable identity and stable social order." And "Gothic bodies disrupt stable notions of what it means to be human."[41] I would add that it disrupts stable notions of *how* to be human. In Gothic novels, love between sisters, between mothers and daughters, fathers and sons, again and again challenges the status quo with the very taboo around which the patriarchal system is organized. Other forms of extreme and excessive desire, violent sexuality, victimization, and erotic submission are at work in many of these novels. I call these works queer because there is no way that they merely contribute to the sexual status quo, and it seems to me that in some cases they militate strenuously against it.

Of course, in the larger picture, Gothic fiction did nothing to stop the imposition of sexological thinking at the end of the nineteenth century. But I would like us to reimagine the relation between sexology and the Gothic and to challenge the discussion of sexual violence that has resulted from the rigidities of twentieth-century sexological thinking, especially insofar as it has categorized and dismissed the importance of Gothic fiction. Instead of relying on these rather crude twentieth-century rubrics for classifying sexual activity, I prefer to read these novels as an articulation of principles of pleasure that resist the sexological binaries that Sade and Sacher-Masoch have been made to represent. English Gothic fiction in general, I would argue, and *The Castle of Otranto*, *The Mysteries of Udolpho*, *The Italian*, *The Monk*, *Melmoth the Wanderer*, and an entire range of other novels in particular, offer different ways to speculate about sexuality. If Sade and Masoch have been canonized in attempts to establish a heteronormative system of the sexual imaginary, and if their erotic fantasies have been marshaled to regulate sexological thinking, then the system of sadomasochism should be exposed as a binary as false as any that our culture cherishes.

What a simple, universalized theory of the "connection between cruelty and the sexual instinct" neglects are not only its sources and its specific dynamics, but also its connection to the family and its deep involvement in various forms of same-sex fantasy that Gothic fiction begins to bring more clearly into focus. I think Gothic novels articulate more complex "sexualities," and I would even go as far as to claim, not entirely facetiously, that theories of sexuality that depend on the Gothic – we might call them Walpole-Lewisism, or Lewis-Maturinism, or Radcliffe-Lewisism – would be more varied, more sexually complex, less heteronormative, and more polymorphously perverse than any we have been asked to consider so far in this century of sexological hegemony.

In other words, I think that sexuality needs to be re-historicized in a way that will undo some of the obfuscation that twentieth-century understandings of sexuality have imposed. In an important recent essay, David Halperin demonstrates, by using examples from premodern and early modern culture, situations in which both sexual morphology and sexual subjectivity are richly articulated in literary and quasi-literary texts. He revises our notion of how we can talk about the relation between behaviors and individuals, and he does so by building on Foucault's insights. By using a classical and an early modern example, he argues that "first, sexual acts could be interpreted as representative of an individual's sexual morphology. Second, sexual acts could be interpreted as representative expressions of an individual's secret subjectivity." Halperin is not claiming that either of these understandings is equivalent to the modern notion of sexual identity or, less, homosexuality. Instead, he states that: "We need to find ways of asking how different historical cultures fashioned different sorts of links between sexual acts, on the one hand, and sexual tastes, styles, dispositions, characters, gender presentations, and forms of subjectivity, on the other."[42] This is the challenge facing those of us who hope to "queer" literature of the past: it is not an attempt to read ourselves into the past, but rather it is an attempt to understand how a different culture understood the kinds of extreme expressions of sexual style in the Gothic that no twentieth-century interpretive binary can ever hope to explain.

To build on these observations would be valuable to Queer Studies, to be sure; but it is also a significant addition to our understanding of the history of sexuality. For until we can fathom the extreme sexual behaviors and fantasies of the past, we will not be able to understand the peculiar sexual limitations of the present. In that sense, this approach can contribute to our own liberatory thinking and take us past the essentialist-constructionist controversy into a queer connection that puts us in closer touch with the ways in which sexual practices were organized in the past. Queer Gothic can do that in a way that will make it impossible to forget.

See also: chapter 9, THE EROTICS OF THE NOVEL; chapter 11, NEW CONTEXTS FOR EARLY NOVELS; chapter 21, WHATEVER HAPPENED TO THE GORDON RIOTS?; chapter 22, THE NOVEL BODY POLITIC.

NOTES

1. See E. J. Clery and Robert Miles, *Gothic Documents: A Sourcebook, 1700–1820* (Manchester: Manchester University Press, 2000); and Edward H. Jacobs, *Accidental Migrations: An Archaeology of Gothic Discourse* (Lewisburg, PA: Bucknell University Press, 2000); see also, Kelly Hurley, *The Gothic Body: Sexuality, Materialism,* *and Degeneration in the Fin de Siècle* (Cambridge: Cambridge University Press, 1996).

2. See my *Gothic Fiction/Gothic Form* (University Park: Pennsylvania State University Press, 1989), 14–35.

3. Joseph Bristow, *Sexuality* (London: Routledge, 1997), 1–11.

4. Horace Walpole, *The Castle of Otranto*, ed. W. S. Lewis (1764; Oxford: Oxford University Press, 1982), 27.

5. See, for instance, Eve Kosofsky Sedgwick, *Between Men: English Literature and Male Homosocial Desire* (New York: Columbia University Press, 1985); Judith Halberstam, *Skin Shows: Gothic Fiction and the Technology of Monsters* (Durham, NC: Duke University Press, 1995); see also, "Literature and Sexuality in the Later Eighteenth Century: Walpole, Beckford, and Lewis," *Studies in the Novel* 18 (1986): 341–51.

6. For the concept of "dominant fiction," see Kaja Silverman, *Male Subjectivity at the Margins* (New York: Routledge, 1992); I will return to this idea below.

7. I discuss Gothic conventions in *Gothic Fiction/Gothic Form*, 1–14.

8. Slavoj Žižek, *The Sublime Object of Ideology* (New York: Verso, 1989), 69.

9. David Punter explains the Gothic in similar terms. He says that "Gothic . . . provides an image language for bodies and their terrors, inhabits a point of undecidability in the area of the growth of self-awareness" (*Gothic Pathologies* {New York: St. Martins, 1998}, 14).

10. Tzvetan Todorov made a similar argument about "the fantastic" in his book with that title. For Todorov, however, everything depended on whether or not the supernatural was explained. See *The Fantastic: A Structural Approach to a Literary Form*, trans. Richard Howard (Cleveland, OH: Case Western Reserve University Press, 1973).

11. Slavoj Žižek, *The Sublime Object of Ideology*, 169.

12. Silverman, *Male Subjectivity at the Margins*, 17, 21; see also Žižek, *The Sublime Object of Ideology*, 34.

13. Linda Bater-Berenbaum sees this as a question of repression: "Gothic literature continued to portray all states of mind that intensify normal thought or perception. Dream states, drug states, and states of intoxication have always been prevalent in the Gothic novel because repressed thoughts can surface in them; under their influence inhibitions are minimized, and thus the scope of consciousness widened. Gothic novelists are particularly fond of hypnotic trances, telepathic communications, visionary experiences, and extrasensory perceptions, for these reveal the secret recesses of the mind or powers of increased mental transmission and reception" (*The Gothic Imagination: Expansion in Gothic Literature and Art* {East Brunswick, NJ: Associated University Presses, 1982}, 25). As I argue in the pages that follow, Gothic fiction also dramatizes the surfacing of repressed thoughts and repressed behaviors.

14. The best account of this process remains that presented in Claudia L. Johnson, *Equivocal Beings: Politics, Gender, and Sentimentality in the 1790s* (Chicago: Chicago University Press, 1995); see also, Felicity A. Nussbaum, *Torrid Zones: Maternity, Sexuality, and Empire in Eighteenth-Century English Narratives* (Baltimore, MD: Johns Hopkins University Press, 1995).

15. See my *Gothic Fiction/Gothic Form*, 1–14.

16. Matthew G. Lewis, *The Monk: A Romance*, ed. Howard Anderson (1796; Oxford: Oxford University Press, 1973), 304; further references in the text are to this edition.

17. Stephen Bruhn, *Gothic Bodies: The Politics of Pain in Romantic Fiction* (Philadelphia: University of Pennsylvania Press, 1994), xvii.

18. Claude Lévi-Strauss, *The Elementary Structures of Kinship*, trans. James Harle Bell and Richard von Sturmer, ed. Rodney Needham (1949; Boston: Beacon Press, 1969), 44–45; see also, Emile Durkheim, *Incest: The Nature and Origin of the Taboo*, together with "The Origins and the Development of the Incest Taboo," by Albert Ellis, trans. Edward Sagarin (1898; New York: Lyle Stuart, 1963), 84–86. For a feminist response to these arguments, see Gayle Rubin, "The Traffic in Women: Notes Toward a Political Economy of Sex," in *Toward an Anthropology of Women*, ed. Rayna Reiter (New York: Monthly Review Press, 1975), 157–210.

19. George E. Haggerty, *Unnatural Affections: Women and Fiction in the Later Eighteenth Century* (Bloomington: Indiana University Press, 1998), 27; see further, 26–32.

20. Michel Foucault, *The History of Sexuality*, volume 1, *An Introduction*, trans. Robert Hurley (New York: Vintage-Random House, 1980), 109, 105; see also, Bristow, *Sexuality*, 168–74.

21. For Robert Miles, she is "the great enchantress"; see Robert Miles, *Ann Radcliffe: The Great Enchantress* (Manchester: Manchester University Press, 1995).

22. Ann Radcliffe, *The Mysteries of Udolpho*, ed. Bonamy Dobrée (1794; Oxford: Oxford University Press, 1966), 226–27; further references in the text are to this edition.

23. Frank Bunting, *Gothic*. The New Critical Idiom Series (London: Routledge, 1996), 38–39.

24. Vijay Mishra, *The Gothic Sublime* (Albany: State University of New York Press, 1994), 33.

25. Miles, *Ann Radcliffe*, 123.

26. For a comparison of this novel to Radcliffe's other efforts, see Miles, *Ann Radcliffe*, 129–48.

27. Punter, *Gothic Pathologies*, 10.

28. Claire Kahane, "The Gothic Mirror," in *The Mother Tongue: Essays in Feminist Psychoanalytic Interpretation*, ed. Shirley Nelson Garner, Claire Kahane, and Madelon Springnether (Ithaca, NY: Cornell University Press, 1985), 339.

29. Cynthia Griffin Wolff, "The Radcliffean Gothic Model: A Form for Female Sexuality," *Modern Language Studies* 9 (1979): 98–113, at 102–103.

30. Susan C. Greenfield, "Veiled Desire: Mother-Daughter Love and Sexual Imagery in Ann Radcliffe's *The Italian*," *The Eighteenth Century: Theory and Interpretation* 33 (1992): 73–89, at 74; see also, Johnson, *Equivocal Beings*, 162–63 and 134–35.

31. See Haggerty, *Unnatural Affections*, 88–102.

32. Ann Radcliffe, *The Italian, or The Confessional of the Black Penitents*, ed. Frederick Garber (1797; Oxford: Oxford University Press, 1968), 369–78.

33. Susan Wolstenholme, *Gothic (Re)Visions: Writing Woman as Readers* (Albany: State University of New York Press, 1993), 25, 30.

34. Judith Butler, *The Psychic Life of Power: Theories in Subjection* (Stanford, CA: Stanford University Press, 1997), 135.

35. Diane Long Hoeveler, *Gothic Feminism: The Professionalization of Gender from Charlotte Smith to the Brontës* (University Park: Pennsylvania State University Press, 1998), 23.

36. Bayer-Berenbaum discusses this novel at length, see pp. 75–106; see also Eve Kosofsky Sedgwick, *The Coherence of Gothic Convention* (New York: Methuen, 1986), 15–18; and Bunting, *Gothic*, 91–112.

37. See Stephen Bruhm, *Gothic Bodies* (Philadelphia: Pennsylvania University Press, 1994), 33.

38. Charles Robert Maturin, *Melmoth the Wanderer*, ed. Douglas Grant (1820; Oxford: Oxford University Press, 1968), 192; further references in the text are to this edition.

39. Punter, *Gothic Pathologies*, 17.

40. Bunting, *Gothic*, 6.

41. Cindy Hendershot, *The Animal Within: Masculinity and the Gothic* (Ann Arbor: University of Michigan Press, 1998), 1, 9.

42. David M. Halperin, "Forgetting Foucault: Acts, Identities, and the History of Sexuality," *Representations* 63 (Summer 1998): 108–109.

FURTHER READING

Bunting, Fred. *Gothic*. The New Critical Idiom Series. London: Routledge, 1996.

Clery, E. J. and Robert Miles. *Gothic Documents: A Sourcebook, 1700–1820*. Manchester: Manchester University Press, 2000.

Haggerty, George E. *Gothic Fiction/Gothic Form*. University Park: Pennsylvania State University Press, 1989.

Miles, Robert. *Ann Radcliffe: The Great Enchantress*. Manchester: Manchester University Press, 1995.

Punter, David. *Gothic Pathologies*. New York: St. Martins, 1998.

Wolstenholme, Susan. *Gothic (Re)Visions: Writing Woman as Readers*. Albany: State University of New York Press, 1993.

18

Conversable Fictions

Kathryn Sutherland

Emerging in 1755 from the Herculean labor of producing a *Dictionary of the English Language*, Samuel Johnson engaged proleptically with his critics in a "Preface" whose subject is the impossibility of the task he has just completed. Where the project is conceived on a grand scale, failure, he argues, lies less with the performer than in the size of the undertaking:

> A large work is difficult because it is large, even though all its parts might singly be performed with facility; where there are many things to be done, each must be allowed its share of time and labour in the proportion only which it bears to the whole; nor can it be expected that the stones which form the dome of a temple should be squared and polished like the diamond of a ring.[1]

The defense is characteristically ironic, a show of intellectual muscle behind an apparent disavowal of competence – "I have only failed in an attempt which no human powers have hitherto completed," he boasts (328). But the project was in any case fundamentally flawed – not only by size but by subject: it is a dictionary of the English language. By its very nature, the proposal to bring order single-handedly to the chaos of language anticipates failure on a grand scale: because language, a tool of communication, is incomprehensible except through exchange; its parts become intelligible only in articulation. Unlike heroic endeavor, language is sociable; and because language is not a preparation for social engagement or understanding but is itself engagement and understanding, "words," Johnson infers, "must be sought where they are used" (319). The declared omission from the dictionary of "many terms of art and manufacture" because "I could not visit caverns to learn the miner's language, nor take a voyage to perfect my skill in the dialect of navigation" (323) is further evidence of the methodological vulnerability of the solipsistic dictionary maker. "[I]t had been a hopeless labour," he ruefully concludes, "to glean up words by courting living information" (323). Throughout the "Preface" Johnson keeps in view the heroic singularity of his achievement and the incompatibility of his method and subject: as "living information," language defies every single human effort of explication or regulation and is vivified only in exchange.

As an attempt to explain how things are on a grand scale, inducible from particulars and by a mixture of experience, analogy, and reasoning, Johnson's dictionary project is exemplary. Its simultaneous investment in and undermining of methodological mastery assumes significance in the context of a wide late eighteenth-century enquiry into the power and problems of an economy and culture founded in increasingly divided labor and mutually unintelligible experiences and the paradoxical authority of large-scale narratives both to speak for and to reassociate such phenomena. In pointing to failures of control, omissions, or limits of information in his dictionary making, Johnson, who does "not form, but register the language" (322), reminds the reader that language is "mutable" and subject to "local convenience" (323). He raises, by implication, the distinction (problematic for a printed dictionary) between language as speech and its writeable trace. Where records are written, the opportunity to fix meaning, however tendentiously, is at least possible; in spoken discourse the suspicion of opacity, of unquantifiable individuality, of something hidden is harder to erase. Perhaps this is because sounds cannot be conserved or because they emanate from inside the body – or because, as Jonathan Rée recently put it, "Hearing does not presume as much as vision."[2] The *Dictionary* may store language as words and phrases, but for "living information" we must look elsewhere. In what follows I am concerned with two related topics – the dependency of large-scale narratives of authority on images of visual mastery and the attempts by several women writers at the close of the eighteenth century to promote "local convenience" or understanding by converting insight or seeing into speech, hearing, and "living information." The association of ocular concentration with holistic mastery and of hearing with partial, even passive, understanding provided, then as now, a crudely gendered spectrum for constructing social identity and mapping the production of knowledge. It was by exploiting the opportunities within this division that prose fiction, and indirectly the novel, developed from the late eighteenth century.

We have, since the late twentieth century, become refamiliarized with a form of intellectual engagement which seeks to privilege feminized cultural positions by emphasizing the importance of anecdote, conversation, and local narratives as tools of knowledge. The shift is from "the observing eye" and vision as the route to scientific knowledge to a polyphony of voices. Among anthropologists this way of arguing has gone along with a shift from charting and mapping societies to a concern with what James Clifford described as a search for "partial truths," a less monolithic paradigm for encountering alternative societies than that offered by the observer standing outside, looking in. In the 1980s Clifford called for an anthropology in which "cultures are no longer prefigured visually" but heard as "an interplay of voices, of positioned utterances."[3] And to some extent the admission of a concept of "partial truths" anticipates the objection that in the attention to voices there will always be an asymmetry, whereby some voices will be louder, more privileged than others (obviously, the voice of the anthropologist or ethnographer). Comparable is Richard Rorty's contemporaneous distinction between the two sorts of philosopher – those who address themselves to epistemology, whom he terms "systemic" philosophers; and those who deny the efficacy of constructing epistemologies, whom he terms "edifying" philosophers. Unlike their "systemic" counterparts, for whom visualism connotes structures "erected upon foundations," "edifying" philosophers are "intentionally peripheral" and engaged "in conversation." As Rorty put it, "to see keeping a conversation going as a sufficient aim of philosophy, to see wisdom as consisting in the ability to sustain a conversation, is to see human beings as generators of new descriptions rather than beings one hopes to be able to describe accurately."[4] What he had in mind was philosophy as a kind of transhistorical and transdisciplinary conversation, between poetry, science, history, and other forms of knowledge.

The situation of the intelligent woman making sense of the world by listening to it rather than visualizing it is similarly linked in eighteenth-century thought to the wider uses of conversation. But if the diffident language of auditory perception in which late twentieth-century Western society recognized itself and its relations to others appears to replicate the marked language of cultural feminization of the earlier period, it did so only as an aspect of their shared historical modernity – as a symptom of their self-conscious commercialism. It would be as mistaken to assimilate the relativism of the academic philosopher and anthropologist with that of the earlier female commentator as it would be to suggest that the evident feminized connotations of Literature as a discipline (as distinct from Science or Politics) inevitably favor female authority and opportunity. Just as the ethnographer's voice is never exactly leveled with the voices he hears, similarly, an endorsement of the values implied by a feminized perspective is not precisely equivalent to finding oneself to be female. In this respect, the admittedly dual method of Clifford Geertz's polyphonous ethnography – "to attain what generality it can by orchestrating contrasts rather than isolating regularities or abstracting types" – is both shrewd and honest.[5]

From the end of the eighteenth century, women writers, like Maria Edgeworth, Hannah More, and Jane Marcet, experimentally extended the remit of prose fiction to tackle challenging intellectual and moral subjects, in the process demonstrating a particular relation between women, learning, and speech. Edgeworth's children, for example, are sociable little capitalists, busy laborers turning the world cheerfully into cash, consumer desirables, and meaning. By contrast, the grand specular narrative posits development as a turning inward, a monologic state of self-communion, which in Adam Smith's *Wealth of Nations* (1776) is an act of unalienated self-possession. Carefully structured commentaries on the grand visual narrative of eighteenth-century scientism, the small-scale narratives of Edgeworth, More, and Marcet represent growth as a dialogic process, the development, correction, and adjustment of a literate self within community. They also provide a bridge to the intersubjective delineation of experience which constitutes the reality of the nineteenth-century novel.

Seeing and Knowing: Adam Smith's Grand Narrative

In Book 5 of *An Inquiry into the Nature and Causes of the Wealth of Nations*, in the course of outlining the deleterious effects on the human intellect, the "mental mutilation,"[6] as he terms it, of the division of labor, Adam Smith distinguishes "those few" individuals who, set apart from the normal activity of over-specialized production, are free to observe and to "contemplate" the variety which such multiplied narrowness of occupation brings into existence. He writes:

> In a civilized state . . . though there is little variety in the occupations of the greater part of individuals, there is an almost infinite variety in those of the whole society. These varied occupations present an almost infinite variety of objects to the contemplation of those few, who, being attached to no particular occupation themselves, have leisure and inclination to examine the occupations of other people. The contemplation of so great a variety of objects necessarily exercises their minds in endless comparisons and combinations, and renders their understandings, in an extraordinary degree, both acute and comprehensive. Unless those few, however, happen to be placed in some very particular situations, their great abilities, though honourable to themselves, may contribute very little to the good government or happiness of their society. Notwithstanding the great abilities of those few, all the nobler parts of the human character may be, in a great measure, obliterated and extinguished in the great body of the people. (2:783–84)

Situated in the final section of Smith's treatise, the passage contributes to a seemingly contradictory attempt to outline the regulatory function of government in a free society and thereby to guarantee the conditions for that "natural liberty" which has been its concern throughout. Part of the final overview of a vast, unencumbered, national and international economy, the passage nevertheless appears to hark back to the humble example of pin-making, which in Book 1 chapter 1 illustrated the division of labor on which the whole modern social edifice rests. There Smith noted how in the "small manufactory" for the making of pins each different branch of production is "placed at once under the view of the spectator,"[7] who makes an intelligible whole from its separate specialized operations. According to Diderot, who had described the process for the *Encyclopédie* (1755), the pin involved eighteen distinct processes and was therefore capable of engrossing as many workers.[8] Pin-making, the early democratizing (because trivial) description of the division of labor, and disburdened contemplation, the late heroic prescription for the understanding (and possible salvation) of a society founded upon such division, are united through the comprehensive and uniquely comprehending gaze of the observer. He is an observer who is identified in Smith's opening chapter with the narrator – "I have seen a small manufactory of this kind," "I have seen several boys . . . make, each of them, upwards of two thousand three hundred nails in a day"; while in the late panoramic vision of Book 5 he has become the precipitate of narrative process itself, the personification of its combinatory and comparative practices. For according to the explanatory model that the *Wealth of Nations* constructs, a knowing subject who discerns the totality of its workings is a sheer impossibility. Where social cohesion is guaranteed (as mutual interdependence) and threatened (as the lost integrity of its individual members) by the specialization that the division of labor brings into being, there can be no internal position from which to account for the holistic gaze of the contemplative few; and since society is a totality of partial interests, there can be no external position from which to view it either.[9]

As Vivienne Brown has argued, *Wealth of Nations* is "a largely single-voiced … text"; and drawing on Bakhtin's work on the genre of the novel, she considers the old "Adam Smith problem" (the vexed relation of his economic to his moral theory) in terms of a distribution of voices.[10] According to Brown's Bakhtinian thesis, the metaphor of the "impartial spectator" in Smith's early *Theory of Moral Sentiments* (1759) facilitates the development of a moralized argument in terms of an "interplay of voices," a sympathetic alterity which is not reducible to a single-voiced authorial position, since the interested self and the "impartial spectator" are the oppositional aspects of every human being. *Wealth of Nations*, on the contrary, offers no such distribution of control; instead, the observing subject is detached from his enquiry, a convergence of authorial identity ("I have seen," "I believe," "I understand") and apparently impersonal intellectual design. In this sense, *Wealth of Nations* conforms to Bakhtin's definition of a "monologic" (as opposed to a "dialogic") work by containing "only *one cognitive subject*, all else being merely *objects* of its cognition."[11] *Wealth of Nations* is a self-confounding text — an account of a universal system of exchange which excludes the presence of the other of exchange. What is more, as observer, the "author-monologist" is an unsullied witness to what his narrative orders, inhabiting an impartiality that clears him of the desire for personal gain in a world where such desire is the only motor for action.

What we might call Smith's view from nowhere is a familiar organizational strategy of the grand Enlightenment narrative, where the lordly observer functions as counterpart of or substitute for what is necessarily missing within the configuration of text and society as a total assemblage of partial interests. Observation in these terms is distinctly voluntary and subject to intellectual control. Not consequent upon an outward but an inward act, it might more accurately be described as the act of looking at what is present in order to find what is absent, or as an imaginary perception of unity. In particular, *Wealth of Nations* postulates unity as psychic compensation, an alternative, aesthetic (as opposed to commercial) dimension whose imagined integrity attempts to recoup a preceding, pre-social state (a world of undivided labor before exchange). This aesthetic unity is necessarily at odds with the implied unity of the social text, which comes into being as a structured explanatory system without the aid of an observer. Determined, on the contrary, by the logic of exchange and insatiable desire, social unity is irreconcilable with the aesthetic vision which attempts to explain it and so to satisfy desire.

Adam Smith's description of the transcendent subject, exercising his mind at leisure "in endless comparisons and combinations," is inserted at a significant moment – between talk of women and books – into his argument for the benefits of a state-subsidized system of mass education aimed at combating the mentally impoverishing effects of the division of labor upon the mass of society. His vision of the unencumbered observer, the male economist, comes only paragraphs after his vindication of women's education on the grounds that it trains them to be practical (as opposed to speculative) economists and only pages before his plea for investment in "publick diversions" – poetry, painting, and drama – as an antidote to the social and psychic fragmentation consequent upon the division of labor and specialist production. He writes:

> There are no publick institutions for the education of women, and there is accordingly nothing useless, absurd, or fantastical in the common course of their education. They are taught what their parents or guardians judge it necessary or useful for them to learn; and they are taught nothing else. Every part of their education tends evidently to some useful purpose. (2: 781)

Positioning is all-important; for what this paean to women's education effects in the discursive field of Smith's argument is the feminization and marginalization of the traditional managerial functions of the household as national economic paradigm in anticipation of its disencumbered masculine alternative.

The modern term "economics" did not exist in Smith's time to describe the collectivity of writings on money, trade, and manufacture which documents the wealth of nations. Throughout the eighteenth century, the unattributed term "oeconomy" (from the Greek *oikonomia*) retained as its primary significance "the management of the house" or "domestic regulation." The attributed form "political oeconomy" is cited in the *OED* from James Steuart's *Inquiry into the Principles of Political Oeconomy* of 1767, where he notes: "Oeconomy in general is the art of providing for all the wants of a family, with prudence and frugality... What oeconomy is in a family, political oeconomy is in a state."[12] Behind Steuart lies a system of thinking about the state's role in the management of national provision which runs back through Hume and Cantillon in the eighteenth century, to Petty, Child, and North in the seventeenth, and ultimately to Aristotle. It is this connection between the domestic and the political which Smith is by agreement considered to have loosened.[13] Women are paid in the process a backhanded compliment. As household economist, the female is conditioned by her limited, practical perspective; there is nothing redundant (but also nothing surplus to immediate requirements, nothing that resonates synergistically in the wider sphere) in the effort expended on her education and the return it brings.

One consequence of Smith's method was to be the stricter professionalization of the discourse of the economist; refining the social model he purports to describe, he renders the disciplinary model more exclusive at a theoretic and analytical level. Ignoring women's waged labor as it contributed to the nascent commercial economy both vindicated that economy's ideological extension (the division of public from private interests) and was a necessary stage toward the establishment of the serious (manly) study of economics itself as a discipline of first principles distinct from mere social description.[14] As Rousseau, another grand thinker, has it: "The search for abstract and speculative truths, for principles and axioms in science, for all that tends to wide generalization, is beyond a woman's grasp."[15] Where the female economist is confined to a life of usefulness by the contracted limits of her training, the untrained (because unconfined) male observer commands an apparently limitless prospect, set above the world of subdivided production and beyond the Hegelian "nether world" of the family. The comparison is rich in contradictions which serve to enforce the gendered oppositions of the underlying economic model: against the busy and useful female is set the detached spectator; against every woman's informal labor is set the assimilative and formalizing energy of "those few." Ironically, it is his capacity for "leisure" ("being attached to no particular occupation") which authorizes the Smithian observer, while leisure is the very quality that excludes women from the economy.

Between male and female leisure there is a world of difference. Male leisure assumes the capacity for reflection, for a detachment which has mastered the disorders of experience, controlling while not appearing to possess the subject of inquiry. (In Smith's case the Duke of Buccleuch's patronage provided the practical means for commenting on while standing apart from the world of production.) Female leisure, on the contrary, though associated in Enlightenment discourse (Hume's essays, for example) with a civilizing and moralized ease, at the same time denotes a too-easy consumption of the object of enquiry. In the male, leisure invites inspection – looking around, taking stock of what can be seen, even self-command; in the female, it is potentially an unsettling appetite whose acts of appropriation pose a severe challenge to the detached claims of visual knowing. What Smith finally proposes is an absorbed and gendered accommodation of a set of convergent and potentially disruptive interests – the socially contingent, the feminine, and literacy. Society in its unregenerate form, women, and books stand in opposition to the aestheticizing strategies of the male observer, potential discreditors of his monologizing containment.

Listening and Speaking

In the ideal or grand narrative, an emphasis on observation – the ability to visualize a system, a society – becomes synonymous with understanding. In Western thinking generally, where knowing is grounded in metaphors of seeing, there is an inevitable link between the ideological bias toward vision as the highest sense and the comprehensive, undisputed authority of the monologist. The essayist De Quincey provides a curiously instructive illustration of the power of the visual analogy. Recording in *Confessions of an English Opium Eater* (1821) his excited reading two years earlier of David Ricardo's *Principles of Political Economy and Taxation* (1817), he casts the economist as the visually alert Romantic hero, who gazed like Wordsworth into the unformed abyss, and saw and communicated "the Imagination of the whole." "Mr Ricardo had deduced, *a priori*, from the understanding itself," he enthuses, "laws which first gave a ray of light into the unwieldy chaos of materials, and had constructed what had been but a collection of tentative discussions into a science of regular proportions, now first standing on an eternal basis." Ricardo possesses, he declares, an "inevitable eye."[16] Three years later, in a series of three articles "Dialogues of Three Templars on Political Economy," appearing from March to May in the *London Magazine*, De Quincey defends Ricardo against the charge of confusion of thought and expression in the unlikeliest of terms. Ricardo, he insists, is not confused but, like Kant and Leibniz, falls into the category of "elliptical obscurity," by which is meant "the frequent ellipsis or suppression of some of the links in a long chain of thought." De Quincey explains how "these are often involuntarily suppressed by profound thinkers, from the disgust which they naturally feel at overlaying a subject with superfluous explanations." The elliptically obscure, "so far from seeing too dimly... see too clearly, and fancy that others see as clearly as themselves."[17] Finally, in a late piece, "Ricardo and Adam Smith," for *Blackwood's Magazine* in September 1842, he demands a special reading audience for Ricardo on the grounds of his elliptical obscurity: "it was the *clerus* not the *populus* whom Ricardo addressed: he did not call attention from the laity who seek to learn, but from the professional body who seek to teach. To others, to uninitiated students, he needs a commentary."[18] For De Quincey, what takes Ricardo beyond Smith as an economic thinker is his imposition of system upon a concept of value, not fortuitously in the process rendering its interpretation as value theory intimidatingly obscure. On the contrary, Ricardo actually demonstrates his superior knowledge or insight through a failure of perspicuity. At a time when all social knowledge was increasingly defined by its usefulness – that is, as economic knowledge – Ricardo's obscurity is especially value-laden, marking a significant moment in the professionalization of economic discourse and of knowledge generally.

About the same time as Ricardo perfected his elliptical obscurity, various women writers were busying themselves forging links between the social, the feminine, and literacy, and describing the convergence as an attention to the interplay of voices and partial perspectives. They were rushing, it might be argued, to fill the space allocated to them as mere commentators in the Enlightenment model of knowledge. The wide association in modern times of ocular concentration with masculinity and aural experience with femininity extends certain philosophical assumptions about what seeing and hearing entail: vision being active, detached, and objectivizing, while hearing is passive and selfless.[19] Then again, sound, unlike sight, is sociable and combinatory, and language as sound (of which writing, though visualized, is merely a representation) is not experienced fresh by each user but must be appropriated and adapted from the mouths of others. In this important sense, speaking is (socially) repetitive before it is (personally) expressive. In Stephen Handel's interesting formulation, "Listening is centripetal; it pulls you into the world. Looking is centrifugal; it separates you from the world."[20]

Throughout the eighteenth century a major project for the dissemination and regulation of polite culture, as the endorsement of a widening middle-class commercial society, centered in the uses of conversation. The large number of manuals of conversation in circulation throughout the period suggests a concern to prescribe as well as to cultivate conversation; and while the fashion can plausibly be associated with the ascendancy of the domestic or femininized sphere, the period also saw the counter institution of an exclusively masculine world of discourse – in the coffee-houses and the gentlemen's clubs. Dr. Johnson's definition of conversation as "talk beyond that which is necessary to the purposes of actual business" nicely gestures to a sociability constrained within precise limits, as does the equation of "*Gentleman*" with "Man of Conversation" in *Tatler*, number 21.[21] As Peter Burke has argued, a reiterated correlation in manuals of the time between spending and saving words and money encourages us "to speculate about a possible relation between the rise of silence (or more precisely, controlled speech) and the rise of capitalism."[22] The connection is supported by an entry in the *New General English Dictionary* (1735) of Thomas Dyche and William Pardon, where the meanings of "commerce" extend beyond our modern restricted sense of the commercial to include other forms of social and sexual congress. "Commerce" is here defined as "Trade, Dealing, Traffick, Conversation by Word or Letter, Correspondence of any Kind," suggesting the semantic range within which both "commerce" and "conversation" stand.[23]

The implications, linguistic, social, and gendered, of this convergence of associations are explored in David Hume's writings. In *Essays Moral, Political, and Literary* (1742) Hume outlined how industry, knowledge, and humanity, the three "indissoluble" constituents of advanced commercial society, are all purchased by labor somewhere in the system. "Every thing in the world is purchased by labour," he declares in "Of Commerce," before setting out to show how the most refined products of leisure are simply the deferred products of industry at more inferior levels of production, which is how, in a famous example in "Of Refinement in the Arts," poetry comes to be supported by shipbuilding. In "Of Essay-Writing," a piece withdrawn from later editions of the *Essays*, it is women's capacity for "conversation," their disposition to facilitate social as well as linguistic exchanges, which makes them, in Hume's phrase, "Sovereigns" of the "*conversible*" [*sic*] world.[24] Conversation is also what fits women to be the effective agents of humanity, since, like humanity, conversation represents the refinement of both sexual commerce and economic productivity. Women, Hume argues, are peculiarly equipped to display and engender humanity through their powers of conversation. The implied hierarchy in his social description (industry, knowledge, humanity) may place woman in the highest position but, with the tangible rewards of industry and knowledge outside her range and conversation her only coin, the privilege is precarious.

As a model for discovering knowledge – about the world and one's own place in it – conversation stems from experience: we all hold conversations. Conversation further implies an indispensable social foundation of knowledge: that, if it is true that we must learn and judge for ourselves, it is also inescapably true that we are never self-sufficient to learn and judge; knowledge is part of the process of association. Presenting her *Accidence; or First Rudiments of English Grammar. Designed for the Use of Young Ladies* (1775), the first grammar of modern English explicitly written by a woman for a female audience, Ellin Devis offered this definition: "The true *Use* of Conversation is the perceiving, perhaps adopting, the Ideas of others; the End proposed is, the displaying our own."[25] In the conversational model knowledge assimilates us to one another rather than distinguishing or setting us apart. It implies responsiveness. Hence, the inappropriateness of the term "table talk" to describe the printed record of the oral flow of such great men as Selden, Johnson, or Coleridge. As Henry Nelson Coleridge wryly put it in his preface to Coleridge's *Table Talk* (1835), "I never attempted to give dialogue – indeed, there was seldom much dialogue to give."[26] The conversational model also has a critical use in that it can draw attention to the problems of learning to know. Who decides the limits of a conversation? its subject matter? when it has ended?

Jane Austen is credited with being a pioneer in establishing conversation as the mode of social authority and knowledge in fiction. Through conversation, her heroines reach self and social understanding, and her village communities reach consensus and assert control. Embarking on a career as a writer at the end of the eighteenth century, Austen bears witness to a culture of polite conversation and to the pressures of linguistic and social diffusion which, in the century's closing years, were threatening earlier cohesive ideals. Where in the *Spectator* and Hume's essays conversation and easy-mannered politeness had been figured as the nurturing medium of social virtue, by the 1780s and 1790s manuals for female conduct, like language studies themselves, were colored by a defensive prescriptiveness. Hester Lynch Piozzi's *British Synonymy; or, an Attempt at Regulating the Choice of Words in Familiar Conversation* (1794) is a work concerned to patrol the boundaries between proper and vulgar usage rather than to nourish living exchange. Against such conservative moralism and linguistic demarcation stand radical treatises, like Horne Tooke's *Diversions of Purley* (1786), a determinedly unbifurcated study of the social workings of language in the material world, and polemical attacks on mere female "accomplishments," like Wollstonecraft's *Vindication of the Rights of Woman* (1792). If prescriptiveness and radical challenge haunt the margins of Austen's critical-comic social text, she embraces neither. Instead, she discovers a space which is neither quiescent nor openly interrogative. This space is best imagined as filled with sound – an intricate pattern of *sotto voce* conversations which her characters have with themselves, which the ideal (and misunderstanding) reader has with the reread text, and which, as a consequence of her comically antithetical syntax, the text has with itself and with generic expectations for the novel. Imagining her novels as conversations is to recover their language as performance, as pitch, tone, and voice, as personally invested and opaque – above all, as studies in Johnson's "living information" subject to "local convenience," which includes the convenience of exercising deception and of being misunderstood.

It has recently been suggested that gossip, a conventionally trivialized form of feminine conversation, more accurately identifies both the social register of Austen's fictional community and the novelistic technique of free indirect discourse which she perfected. In free indirect discourse, as in gossip, authority is unlocatable – nowhere and everywhere – its presence multiple and its source ultimately secret. A compulsion to gossip characterizes the intra-group relations of Austen's small societies and a narrative style which works by "disseminating [authority] among the characters" so that it is neither precisely internalized nor merely external.[27] Such small talk may be the sharpest antithesis we have in the period to the objective and omniscient gaze assumed by the synthesizing philosopher – Smith, Wordsworth, or Rousseau. By contrast, gossip's utterances are imitatively replicated and diffused to the point where voices and characters are reinvested in a comically disturbing vocal equivalent of enantiomorphy, unsettling and dramatizing a set of relationships rather than disclosing a permanent truth.

Local Convenience and Living Information

For De Quincey, conversation, even when constrained within the framework of Socratic dialogue, is inappropriate for handling economic truths, because systems of economic thought (like the Romantic imagination itself) cannot be taken part by part but only as wholes. His own *Dialogues of Three Templars on Political Economy* (1824), written as an attempt to simplify Ricardo, contains the internal defense that dialogue constructed by an author for the purpose of demonstrating truths is inevitably monologic, "since I cannot be supposed to have put triumphant arguments into any speaker's mouth unless they had previously convinced my own understanding."[28] By contrast, in a private letter of 1751 to Gilbert Elliot of Minto introducing his *Dialogues Concerning Natural Religion*, Hume acknowledged the problem dialogue presents to the author wishing to do justice to mutual difference and unpredictability in argument, and he speculated as to how the tyranny of monologism might be overcome:

> I have often thought, that the best way of composing a Dialogue, wou'd be for two Persons that are of different Opinions about any Question of Importance, to write alternately the different Parts of the Discourse, & reply to each other. By this Means, that vulgar Error woud [*sic*] be avoided, of putting nothing but Nonsense into the Mouth of the Adversary: And at the same time, a Variety of Character & Genius being upheld, woud make the whole look more natural & unaffected.[29]

Those women writers who champion a tradition of readable economics in the early nineteenth century – Maria Edgeworth, Jane Marcet, and Harriet Martineau – and who communicate it to the most divergent levels of society, do so in terms of a dialogic model which repositions the monologic scientism of its expert definition within a narrative of multiple agency, simulating with some success the shared intellectual activity of different speakers and the impact of new ideas on existing experience.

These female commentators take on the role of elucidating economic meaning through conversation, as though meaning inheres in addressee as well as in addressor. The addressee is a developing reader, often female and always socialized, who is presented dialogically so as to distinguish the stages of female or social development. Theirs are not good conversations in that they do not assume a spontaneous, organic responsiveness or equitable roles for the participants. On the contrary, these are conversations in the way that a well-scripted tutorial might be described as a conversation – constrained talk at the service of a particular purpose, in which the participants play unequal parts. Nevertheless, they are composed from differing voices, differently inflected, and they involve an exchange of perspectives which can destabilize surprisingly any predetermined end. Such conversations transform general propositions into local narrative – that is, into arguments which become true by connecting with what happens in the world and, in particular, with the intellectual capacity and previous experience of the addressee. One consequence is the narrowing and accommodation of the referential dimensions of the expert narrative, of Smith or Ricardo, to the understanding of the developing reader; and, in deciding what is to signify, an affirmation of its necessarily interested and partial status. The text, expert or not, signifies only insofar as its reader is able to make sense of it, which is to say that these dialogues are not so much about economics as about representing economics.[30]

In Edgeworth's innovative economic tales for children, no one is too young to learn the interdependence of subjectivity and society; in the case of her little heroine Rosamond, the reader is introduced to a child who grows in social and personal understanding over a series of narratives. In Marcet's *Conversations on Political Economy*, issued in 1817, the same year as Ricardo's elliptical *Principles*, a fictional instructress, Mrs. B., invites her pupil Caroline to understand the science of political economy on the grounds that, without it, "you might almost as well condemn yourself to perpetual silence." Ignoring the traditional division by which masculine locution demands a voiceless female listener, both teacher and pupil proceed towards a revisionary or, more appropriately, a relocutory adjustment of "the writings of the great masters . . . of Dr. Adam Smith, of Mr. Malthus, M. Say, and M. Sismondi" which allows for their creative misinterpretation and for what Marcet describes as the "collateral" illustration of the thought processes "of an intelligent young person," of the female sex.[31] In direct endorsement of the social text of Smith's great system, Caroline is encouraged to see that economic structures underlie the knowledge she already has – that she was an economist without knowing it. "How very much you have already extended my conception of the meaning of wealth!" she exclaims at the end of her second lesson.

> "And yet I can perceive that all these ideas were floating confusedly in my mind before. . . . All this is perfectly clear: no one can be really ignorant of it; it requires only reflection; and yet at first I was quite at a loss to explain the nature of wealth."[32]

Caroline is expected to exercise her imagination, marshal the knowledge she already possesses in other disciplines (Goldsmith's *Deserted Village* {1770} is singled out for its "ignorance of the principles of political economy") – in short, to further her own learning. "Do not leave everything to me," chides Mrs. B. "Endeavour... to unravel the entangled thread, and discover for yourself."[33] Behind Marcet's influential series of "Conversation" books – *On Chemistry* (1806), *On Natural Philosophy* (1819), *On Vegetable Physiology* (1829) – lies the educational philosophy of members of the Birmingham Lunar Society (Richard Lovell Edgeworth, Thomas Day, Erasmus Darwin, and Joseph Priestley) in claiming science for a wider public. *Conversations on Political Economy* (1816) was her most famous, frequently reprinted, and much admired. "Every girl who has read Mrs. Marcet's little dialogues on political economy," wrote the historian Macaulay in 1825, "could teach Montagu or Walpole many lessons in finance." Marcet was on friendly terms with popularizers like Maria Edgeworth and later with Harriet Martineau; she also knew socially the "experts" Malthus and Ricardo.[34]

Martineau's objection to *Wealth of Nations* is on the very grounds of its large-scale obscurity. As she observes, with heavy condescension, "It is natural that the first eminent book on this new science should be very long, in some parts exceedingly difficult, and, however wonderful and beautiful as a whole, not so clear and precise in its arrangement as it might be." In proposing "Illustrations of Political Economy" for "the people," she argues for the contingent as opposed to the revelatory nature of economic truth, whereby narrative, the telling of stories, is both origin and explanation: "We cannot see why the truth and its application should not go together."[35] For Martineau, narrative, economics, and community share a single birth. This is something like the rebasing D. N. McCloskey recently outlined for modern economic discourse, when she argued:

> Perhaps there is something to treating economics as stories. The advantage would be self-consciousness, though self-consciousness is disparaged by certain economists anxious to manipulate the rules of conversation. Economists would do better to know what they are talking about. Looking on economics as poetry or fiction – or for that matter, as history – gives the economist a place to look in from outside. It is a better place than is provided by the usual philosophies of science; it is a great deal better than the homespun sociologies and philosophies that economists commonly use.
>
> There is another advantage, to the larger culture. Economics should come back into the conversation of mankind. It is an extraordinarily clever way of speaking, which can do much good. The way to bring it back is to persuade economists that they are not so very different from poets and novelists.[36]

Seemingly modest, the methodological alternative proposed by both Martineau and McCloskey in fact entails a more thorough engagement in the effort to bring system (theory) and social processes (animating context) together. Through the fictional density of their imagining, Martineau's moral tales provide a series of localizing footnotes to enrich the dry theory of economics. As the chapter entitled

"Hand-Work and Head-Work" explains, "the practice of the people" needs to be "wiser than the principles of the policy by which they have hitherto been governed."[37] Implicit in her illustrative method is the superiority of illustration over principle – for illustration embodies real practice or knowledge in action. As a reaction against theory, illustration offers the simultaneous endorsement of learning through experience and through fiction.

Marcet and Martineau depend heavily on *Wealth of Nations*, not only for the framework and arguments but also for the examples in terms of which their expositions develop. Beyond this, however, the dialogic models by which they proceed have the effect of reinterpolating into the narrative economy at least the female contribution to labor and value. Perversely, too, both Marcet and Martineau deliberately misinterpret political economy, *contra* Smith, as household economy on a national scale. Marcet even manipulates a male authority into providing her with this explanation when Mrs. B. informs her pupil:

> "I once heard a lady ask a philosopher to tell her in a few words what is meant by political economy. Madam, replied he, you understand perfectly what is meant by *household economy*; you need only extend your idea of a family to that of a whole people – of a nation, and you will have some comprehension of the nature of political economy."[38]

In the context of Smith's masterly redefinition and the restricted feminization of the domestic sphere from the late eighteenth century, this misreading is significant. Informalizing women's labor as extrinsic to the formal structures of his argument, Smith powerfully mystified the relationship between a market economy and the total economy of human existence, at the same time confusing the dynamics of its telling with the dynamics of a material world of production. Marcet will have none of this.

In Edgeworth's three-volume collection *The Parent's Assistant* of 1796, the reader is first introduced to the child Rosamond. At this time, Rosamond is 9 or 10 years old. Usually taken to be a semi-autobiographical figure, Rosamond reappears in *Continuations of Early Lessons* of 1814 and 1815 and in the two-volume series of tales *Rosamond, a Sequel to Early Lessons* of 1821, during the course of which she grows "from ten to thirteen."[39] Rosamond is by any literary standards an engaging child, lively, candid, impetuous, generous, talkative, and self-important – "one of the first real heroines of children's literature."[40] Constantly subject to correction and improvement from her rule-bound parents, she survives their shaping and advice with humor and spirit, accommodating their potentially constricting lessons to her own livelier pace and sense of the joyful possibilities of existence. Learning through direct personal experience, adjusting her behavior in response to particular situations, and discovering how to make a case for herself, Rosamond exemplifies the best of the educational theories of the Edgeworths, father and daughter. Her "ever fluctuating mind" is offered to young readers as "an image of their own." We meet Rosamond for the first time in the tale "The Purple Jar" and for the second in "The Birthday Present."

Both are economic tales, and in both there is the assumption that moral worth, self-restraint, and generosity are direct extensions of an economic behavior which it is never too early to learn; all Edgeworth's children are happy consumers.

In "The Birthday Present" Rosamond spends the half-guinea gift of her godmother in making and extravagantly decorating a work-basket for her cousin Bell's birthday. Rosamond knows Bell is a spoilt child and unworthy of the gift, but she is determined to make a parade of her generosity and at the same time to shame her ultra-rational parents into celebrating their own children's birthdays, something they believe to be unnecessary. Laura, Rosamond's more conformist sister, has also been given a half-guinea by her godmother. Rosamond first accuses her of hoarding her gift, miser-like; but Laura is soon discovered in an act of selfless and useful generosity: she has given the money to a poor little lace-maker who has been badly used by Bell and her peevish, corrupting maid. The story works to its conclusion, in which Rosamond learns to distinguish true from false generosity and moral and economic worth from mere show. "The Birthday Present" is an uncompromisingly social text, giving precedence to women and children and the lower ranks. It is about wise and negligent mothers, about generous and pampered children, about false servants and industrious little workers, who together form a dialogic, interactive community. In terms of narrative and personal development, the children take charge. There is a male authority figure, but in the determining context of the social text his customary role of observer is effectively diminished and rendered impotent. "Rosamond . . . especially at the moment when her present was pushed away with such disdain, had been making reflections upon the nature of true generosity . . . her father . . . stood by, a silent spectator of the catastrophe."[41]

In the fictional lessons of Edgeworth, Marcet, and Martineau, an apparent diffusion of authorial control fashions the social text of narrative – the domain of the female, the child, and the popular – as dominant in contrast to the monologic non-figurative linking of intention and meaning in the philosophical realm of the masculine aesthetic text. This reordering or disordering of priorities redistributes authority in distinct ways: self-consciously peripheral, the female commentator generates meaning through the ability to keep a conversation going. Hers is a knowledge of contingent illustration, which in deciding what is to signify, reaffirms its partial status. These are "conversable" fictions – which, according to Johnson's dictionary definition, implies that they are "fit for company" and "communicative." In an important revisionist essay on Edgeworth's children's fiction, Mitzi Myers set out to show that "women's juvenile writing is sophisticated, revelatory, and culturally significant." She continued:

> It is at once the most neglected genre in the reconceptualization of early nineteenth-century literary history and possibly one of the most relevant to our contemporary rethinking of how literacy and literature shape subjectivity.[42]

The statement is not without irony – we are habituated to the idea that the poetry of Edgeworth's male contemporaries explains our psychic growth in the Rousseau-derived terms of natural, asocial development. What these women writers challenge us to consider are the possibilities for growth through social interaction, or the adventures of "the literate child-in-community."[43]

Finally, this subdivision of prose fiction by women who write *about* others' writings, and *of* and *for* untransformed social arrangements, throws a bridge to the narrative method of the nineteenth-century novel. Persuading Caroline of the importance of taking its study seriously, Marcet noted that the "science of political economy is intimately connected with the daily occurrences of life"[44] – much like the novel, whose values were steadily imbricated through the new century with the economic. Both discourses attempt to offer descriptions of and solutions for the problems of society as it really is. Smith, Marcet senses, is, after all his theorizing, in fact writing history. Maria Edgeworth's little heroes and heroines are members of an industrializing society, intensely interested in practical science and taken on regular visits to workshops. Edgeworth shares with Hannah More, another important conduit into the nineteenth-century novel, a commitment to situated knowledge – knowledge, that is, which is tested in local service. More's tract *The History of Mr. Fantom, the New-Fashioned Philosopher* (issued in August 1797), in her Cheap Repository series, mocks the radical thinkers Thomas Paine and William Godwin with their universal schemes for human advancement, and sets against them the effectiveness of women's narrower, practical aims. Mr. Fantom is "the new-fashioned philosopher," who has "a plan in [his] head for relieving the miseries of the whole world." But "in his zeal to make the whole world free and happy, [he] was too prudent to include his wife." In a section expanded to highlight middle-class women's influential activities for the tract's republication among *Stories for the Middle Ranks of Society* (1818), Mrs. Fantom and her daughter execute several charitable plans to relieve suffering in the local community. Their female heroics, though minutely practical, are dramatically effective. Mrs. Fantom attends to the trivialities of life with an adventurous spirit, while her husband looks on from a philosophic distance. At one point, she rushes out into the night, her pockets "stuffed... with old baby linen," to lend help at the scene of a village fire. Baby linen, it turns out, is just what is needed! Her husband, the philosopher, absents himself. The narrator observes acidly,

> the present distress was neither grand enough nor far enough from home to satisfy the wide-stretched benevolence of the philosopher, who sat down within sight of the flames to work at a new pamphlet, which now swallowed up his whole soul, on universal benevolence.[45]

In this analysis, the very particularity of women's socially assigned roles generates the precise and effective social understanding which eludes the unwieldy universalizing tendency. The village situations from which the Repository series evolved presuppose, like many novels by women in the period, active and mixed interdependent communities in which women find authority.

It is not too extravagant to suggest that More inaugurated the nineteenth-century tradition of gritty female social fiction as displayed in the work of Elizabeth Stone

(*William Langshawe, The Cotton Lord* {1842}, *The Young Milliner* {1843}), Charlotte Tonna (*Helen Fleetwood* {1841}), and Geraldine Jewsbury (*Marian Withers* {1850}). More's barely disguised authorial surrogate Mrs. Jones, a philanthropic widow zealous in the twinned causes of household management and literacy, is the older relation of the socially conscious heroines of later novelists – Charlotte Brontë's Shirley Keeldar and Caroline Helstone, Elizabeth Gaskell's Margaret Hale, and George Eliot's Dorothea Brooke. Like them she discovers her own worth and identity in her relations with children, semi-literate laborers, and victimized women. Like them she inhabits the familiar space of the small group. The type endures, politically muted, in Virginia Woolf's Mrs. Ramsay and Mrs. Dalloway. Their sympathetic identification is with the kind of limited social practices that novels enact, and it exists in direct opposition to what their creators dismiss as the extravagant, self-regarding, and ultimately peripheral heroics of large-scale progressive thinkers.

Like Edgeworth, More possessed an acute ear for talk and the ability to capture something of the variety of real speech. Unlike Dr. Johnson, she did "visit caverns to learn the miner's language" as part of her missionary work in the Mendip communities, and she consciously exploited the sub-literary format and devices of the chapbook. In her Cheap Repository Tracts the sociolectal pressures of particular occupations contribute vital variations to a concept of what English is. There is not a single, monolithic English; and different speech registers allow for fertile misunderstandings which can work effectively to undermine the implementation of what would otherwise be crudely applied moral lessons. Differentiated through speech, More's fictional characters can take on independent agency seemingly at odds with their narrator's didactic function. In *The History of Hester Wilmot* (May 1797) the do-gooder Mrs. Jones chastises Rebecca Wilmot, Hester's mother, for keeping her children from Sunday School. "I see no good in learning, but to make folks proud, and lazy, and dirty," protests Rebecca.

> "Pray," said Mrs Jones mildly, "do you think that young people will disobey their parents the more for being taught to fear God?" "I don't think any thing about it," said Rebecca; "I sha'n't let her come, and there's the long and short of the matter. Hester has other fish to fry."

The exchange continues robustly until Mrs. Jones finally departs, then:

> The moment she went out of the house, Rebecca called out loud enough for her to hear, and ordered Hester to get the stone and a bit of sand, to scrub out the print of that dirty woman's shoes.[46]

This is a moment of triumph – for Rebecca Wilmot over her officious intruder – but also for narrative. Like Edgeworth's Mrs. Pomfret, whose distrust of "Villaintropic folks" is implacable,[47] Rebecca Wilmot represents an irresistible counter-energy to the moral tow of the story and to the bustling, socialized female narrators of the pedagogic tale. Scrubbing out the print of that dirty woman's shoes is on a par with obliterating the "editorial comment" of the omniscient author – a daring strategy which reminds the reader not only of the constructed nature of omniscience but of language's limitless authority to narrate other worlds and other views. Such unadapted fictional figures offer a glimpse of a democratized and heterodox agency which will become increasingly significant in the narrative modalities of the novel in the hands of Gaskell, Dickens, and Eliot as they dedicate the form to exploring multiple, contending, and intersubjective realities. The implied dispersal of authority which distinguishes the nineteenth-century novel finds its origin in the conversational communities of female commentators rising to the challenge of explicating expert narrative to a wider audience.

See also: chapter 8, MEMORY AND MOBILITY; chapter 13, WOMEN, OLD AGE, AND THE EIGHTEENTH-CENTURY NOVEL; chapter 15, THE EIGHTEENTH-CENTURY NOVEL AND PRINT CULTURE; chapter 21, WHATEVER HAPPENED TO THE GORDON RIOTS?

NOTES

1. *Samuel Johnson: A Critical Edition of the Major Works*, ed. Donald Greene (Oxford: Oxford University Press, 1984), 324.

2. Jonathan Rée, *I See a Voice: A Philosophical History of Language, Deafness, and the Senses* (London: HarperCollins, 1999), 46.

3. In *Writing Culture: The Poetics and Politics of Ethnography*, ed. James Clifford and George E. Marcus (Berkeley and Los Angeles: University of California Press, 1986), 12.

4. Richard Rorty, *Philosophy and the Mirror of Nature* (Oxford: Blackwell, 1980), 377–78.

5. Clifford Geertz, *Local Knowledge* (London: Fontana Press, 1993), 13.

6. Adam Smith, *An Inquiry into the Nature and Causes of the Wealth of Nations*, ed. R. H. Campbell and A. S. Skinner. 2 vols. (Oxford: Clarendon Press, 1976), 2:787.

7. *The Wealth of Nations*, 1:14–15.

8. Cited in *The Wealth of Nations*, 1:15 n3.

9. Cf. John Barrell, *The Birth of Pandora and the Division of Knowledge* (Basingstoke: Macmillan, 1992), 89–118.

10. Vivienne Brown, *Adam Smith's Discourse: Canonicity, Commerce, and Conscience* (London: Routledge, 1994), 43.

11. Mikhail Bakhtin, *Problems of Dostoevsky's Poetics*, ed. and trans. Caryl Emerson (Man-

chester: Manchester University Press, 1984), quoted in Brown, *Adam Smith's Discourse*, 43 n33.

12. James Steuart, *An Inquiry into the Principles of Political Oeconomy: Being an Essay on the Science of Domestic Policy in Free Nations*. 2 vols. (London, 1767), 1:1–2.

13. See Keith Tribe, *Land, Labour, and Economic Discourse* (London: Routledge and Kegan Paul, 1978), 80–109.

14. See my "Adam Smith's Master Narrative: Women and *The Wealth of Nations*," in *Adam Smith's Wealth of Nations: New Interdisciplinary Essays*, ed. Stephen Copley and Kathryn Sutherland (Manchester: Manchester University Press, 1995), 97–121.

15. Jean-Jacques Rousseau, *Emile ou de l'éducation*, trans. Barbara Foxley, introduction by P. D. Jimack (London: Dent, 1974), 349.

16. *Confessions of an English Opium Eater*, ed. Alethea Hayter (Harmondsworth, UK: Penguin, 1971), 100–1.

17. *Collected Writings of Thomas De Quincey*, ed. David Masson. 14 vols. (London: A. and C. Black, 1897), 9:49.

18. *Collected Writings of Thomas De Quincey*, 9: 117.

19. Rée, *I See a Voice*, 52–53.

20. Stephen Handel, *Listening: An Introduction to the Perception of Auditory Events* (1989), quoted in Bruce R. Smith, *The Acoustic World of Early Modern England: Attending to the O-Factor* (Chicago: University of Chicago Press, 1999), 10.

21. Johnson is quoted in H. L. Piozzi, *Anecdotes of the Late Samuel Johnson, LL.D.*, ed. Arthur Sherbo (London: Oxford University Press, 1974), 74; *The Tatler*, ed. Donald F. Bond. 3 vols. (Oxford: Clarendon Press, 1987), 1: 165.

22. Peter Burke, *The Art of Conversation* (Oxford: Polity Press, 1993), 140.

23. [Thomas Dyche and William Pardon], *A New General English Dictionary; Peculiarly Calculated for the Use and Improvement of Such as are Unacquainted with the Learned Languages* (London, 1735).

24. David Hume, *Essays Moral, Political, and Literary*, ed. Eugene F. Miller (Indianapolis: Liberty Fund, 1985), 261, 270–71, and 536.

25. [Ellin Devis], *The Accidence; or First Rudiments of English Grammar. Designed for the Use of Young Ladies* (London, 1775), 87; and see Carol Percy, "The Art of Grammar in the Age of Sensibility: *The Accidence ... for ... Young Ladies* (1775)," in *Insights into Late Modern English*, ed. Marina Dossena and Charles Jones (Berne: Peter Lang, 2003), 45–82.

26. *Specimens of the Table Talk of the Late Samuel Taylor Coleridge*, ed. H. N. Coleridge. 2 vols. (London: John Murray, 1835), 1:xxv. On the genre, see F. P. Wilson, "Table Talk," *Huntington Library Quarterly* 4 (1940–1): 27–46.

27. Casey Finch and Peter Bowen, "'The Tittle-Tattle of Highbury': Gossip and the Free Indirect Style in *Emma*," *Representations* 31 (1990): 3; cf. Bharat Tandon, *Jane Austen and the Morality of Conversation* (London: Anthem Press, 2003).

28. *Collected Writings of De Quincey*, 9:44.

29. David Hume, *Dialogues Concerning Natural Religion and The Natural History of Religion*, ed. J. C. A. Gaskin (Oxford: Oxford University Press, 1993), 25.

30. See Greg Myers, "Science for Women and Children: The Dialogue of Popular Science in the Nineteenth Century," in *Nature Transfigured: Science and Literature, 1700–1900*, ed. John Christie and Sally Shuttleworth (Manchester: Manchester University Press, 1989), 171–200; and cf. Patricia Howell Michaelson, *Speaking Volumes: Women, Reading, and Speech in the Age of Austen* (Stanford, CA: Stanford University Press, 2002).

31. [Jane Marcet], *Conversations on Political Economy; in which the Elements of that Science are Familiarly Explained* (London: Longman, Hurst, Rees, Orme, and Brown, 1816), 8 and vii–ix.

32. Ibid., 27–28.

33. Ibid., 29–30.

34. T. B. Macaulay, in *Essays on Milton* (1825), quoted in the *DNB* entry on Marcet. See *Maria Edgeworth: Letters from England, 1813–1844*, ed. Christina Colvin (Oxford: Clarendon Press, 1971); also, Harriet Martineau, "Mrs Marcet," in *Biographical Sketches* (London: Macmillan, 1869), 386–92; and Willie Henderson, "Jane Marcet's *Conversations on Political Economy*: A New Interpretation," *History of Education* 23 (1994): 423–37.

35. Harriet Martineau, *Illustrations of Political Economy*, 3rd ed. (London: Charles Fox, 1832), x–xii.

36. D. N. McCloskey, "Storytelling in Economics," in *Narrative in Culture: The Uses of Storytelling in the Sciences, Philosophy, and Literature*, ed. Christopher Nash (London: Routledge, 1990), 20–21.

37. *Illustrations of Political Economy*, 49.

38. *Conversations on Political Economy*, 17–18.

39. Edgeworth's children's tales have an elaborate bibliographic history, with the contents of volumes printed under the same title but in different editions showing some variety. The first Rosamond stories reappear as part of *Rosamond* (1801). See the bibliography printed in Marilyn Butler, *Maria Edgeworth: A Literary Biography* (Oxford: Clarendon Press, 1972), 504–6.

40. Ibid., 160.

41. Maria Edgeworth, *The Parent's Assistant; or, Stories for Children*. 6 vols. (London: J. Johnson, 1800), 2:41.

42. Mitzi Myers, "De-Romanticizing the Subject: Maria Edgeworth's 'The Bracelets,' Mythologies of Origin, and the Daughter's Coming to Writing," in *Romantic Women*

Writers: Voices and Countervoices, ed. Paula R. Feldman and Theresa M. Kelley (Hanover, NH: University Press of New England, 1995), 109.
43. Ibid., 91.
44. *Conversations on Political Economy*, 9–10.
45. Hannah More, *The Works of Hannah More.* 18 vols. (London, 1818), 4:33–8.
46. More, *The History of Hester Wilmot* (London, 1797), 6–7.
47. Edgeworth, "The False Key," in *The Parent's Assistant*, 1:134.

Further Reading

Barrell, John. *The Birth of Pandora and the Division of Knowledge*. Basingstoke: Macmillan, 1992.

Brown, Vivienne. *Adam Smith's Discourse: Canonicity, Commerce, and Conscience*. London: Routledge, 1994.

Michaelson, Patricia Howell. *Speaking Volumes: Women, Reading, and Speech in the Age of Austen*. Stanford, CA: Stanford University Press, 2002.

Smith, Bruce R. *The Acoustic World of Early Modern England: Attending to the O-Factor*. Chicago: University of Chicago Press, 1999.

Tandon, Bharat. *Jane Austen and the Morality of Conversation*. London: Anthem Press, 2003.

19

Racial Legacies: The Speaking Countenance and the Character Sketch in the Novel

Roxann Wheeler

Henry Fielding employs a typical tool of novelists when he stops the narrative to describe the protagonist's body, lingering on his countenance:

> Mr. *Joseph Andrews* was now in the one and twentieth Year of his Age. He was of the highest Degree of middle Stature. His Limbs were put together with great Elegance and no less Strength. His Legs and Thighs were formed in the exactest Proportion. His Shoulders were broad and brawny, but yet his Arms hung so easily, that he had all the Symptoms of Strength without the least clumsiness. His Hair was of a nut-brown Colour, and was displayed in wanton Ringlets down his Back. His Forehead was high, his Eyes dark, and as full of Sweetness as of Fire. His Nose a little inclined to the Roman. His Teeth white and even. His Lips full, red, and soft. His Beard was only rough on his Chin and upper Lip; but his Cheeks, in which his Blood glowed, were overspread with a thick Down. His Countenance had a Tenderness joined with a Sensibility inexpressible.[1]

Although Fielding's description of Joseph Andrews seems like a decidedly comic send-up of the character sketch, in fact, it differs little from hundreds of serious sketches in other novels from Aphra Behn's 1688 portrait of Oroonoko to Matthew Lewis's snapshot of Antonia in *The Monk* (1796). Conventionally, the character sketch interrupts the narrative for a more or less detailed physical description that makes a subtle transition into an interpretation of the character. The underlying principle of the character sketch is the universality of human nature in its individual manifestation. While much critical attention has been devoted to the moral make-up of characters, relatively little attention has been devoted to the habitual description of a character's appearance. In overlooking the consistent reappearance of the same body and facial features among most protagonists, we have failed to understand that the eighteenth-century novel functions as a technology of racialization. The novel helped make the European face and body desirable and widely disseminated them before they were called on for more specific political and economic work in the decades following the Napoleonic wars.

Fielding's physical portrait, full of cues for readers' interpretation of Joseph, is indebted to two intertwined ways of reading bodies: physiognomy, or the art of translating facial features into character judgment, and racial classification in natural history. A mode of interpretation dating from Aristotle, physiognomy searched the curves and lines of an individual's forehead, the shape of the nose and lips, and the position of the eyes to divine character. Similarly, when it came to arranging the world's people into four, five, or six distinct groups, natural historians, who purported to describe and classify visible nature, noted the general stature, skin color, hair and eye color, and the typical shape of the head and nose. While physiognomy was more of an eighteenth-century guilty pleasure, natural history was a well-respected source of knowledge, epitomizing Enlightenment ideals. Nonetheless, as we shall see, there was a great deal of common ground between them and an overlap with the novel's character sketch.

Usually the character sketch in novels faithfully duplicates the gaze of natural history on the surface of bodies, English or otherwise. Other times, it functions to pique readers' attention precisely because the character's appearance defies its proper natural history category in appearance and behavior, most famously in the cases of Oroonoko and Friday. Novelists employ this standard description of the body's exterior features to establish a relationship between readers and characters. Usually, the novel encodes the proper emotional and aesthetic response to these features. Even as the novelistic sketch treats more fully the character's family, education, and social manners as the century closes, the description of physical appearance remains very general. Indeed, Carl Linné's 1758 description of Europeans in the tenth edition of *Systema Naturae* (a much shorter first edition was published in 1735) reads as a more general version of Joseph Andrews – and most other protagonists in eighteenth-century novels. In regard to complexion, humor, and stature, Europeans are typically "Fair, sanguine, brawny." They have "*Hair* yellow, brown, flowing; *eyes* blue; *gentle*, acute, inventive. *Covered* with close vestments. *Governed* by laws."[2]

Few eighteenth-century scholars have connected the facial interpretation of physiognomy to the global racial sketches of natural history.[3] Thus, the novel has been neglected as a site where this habit of thinking about European character is naturalized. Freely mixing common sense from physiognomy and natural history, the novel unobtrusively forges interest in racial character. In this way, the novel establishes a textual climate conducive to the integration of racial taxonomy and physiognomy, thereby preceding the direction of science, which did not fully integrate them until the mid-nineteenth century.

The discourses of the novel, natural history, and physiognomy converge in their attention to the body's surface. For example, the Royal Society's 1666 instructions to travelers wishing to compose a natural history of a country's inhabitants included some characteristics shared with physiognomy, asking writers to observe "their

Stature, Shape, Colour, Features, Strength, Agility, Beauty (or the want of it), Complexions, Hair, Dyet, Inclinations, and Customs that seem not due to Education. As to their Women (besides the other things) may be observed their Fruitfulness or Barrenness; their hard or easy Labour."[4] Most of these details pertain to the body's surface and require aesthetic judgment.[5] The novel combines racial taxonomy's attention to the stature and color of the body with physiognomy's conclusions that the face reveals the character within. While the eighteenth-century novel often evinces a healthy skepticism about the uncritical conflation of appearance and character, it also proves adept at translating the description of a protagonist's appearance into an overdetermined yet pleasurable, felt quality, not just an abstract visual ideal. Within the novel, narrators or other characters who describe the protagonists typically respond with social approbation or sexual desire. This narrative convention suggests the likelihood of also soliciting readers' cathexis to the uniform physical attributes of British characters, a dynamic that elicits a culturally deep attachment to certain facial features and, eventually, to the qualities of mind that go along with them.

The discourses of the novel, natural history, and physiognomy also converge in their interest in the mind's relationship to physical characteristics. By the end of the century, the novelistic character sketch regularly includes the quality of mind implied in the protagonist's countenance or, sometimes, contradicted by it. Incorporating the lessons of physiognomy, the novel helps establish a cultural investment in the quality of mind connected to ideal European characters and bodies, anticipating natural history's inward turn in mid-nineteenth-century ethnology, which treats "'the whole mental and physical history of the various Types of Mankind.... Ethnology demands to know what was the primitive organic structure of each race? – what such race's moral and psychological character?... and what position in the social scale Providence has assigned to each type of man.'"[6]

In different ways, natural history, physiognomy, and the novel all wrestle with the interpretation of appearance, especially the eloquence of the face. According to art historian Marcia Pointon, the intense focus on the head and face is not a transhistorical phenomenon; it arises in Western art during the sixteenth century in the wake of Renaissance humanism and the discovery of the Caribbean and Americas.[7] It will come as no surprise, then, that in their modern formation, the novel, physiognomy, and racial classification employ the same descriptive technique to animate racial pleasure and desire. As the examples from *Joseph Andrews* (1742) and *Systema Naturae* make clear, descriptions of stature, complexion, hair color, facial features, disposition, situation, manners, and education specify distinct populations in natural history as well as distinct characters in the novel and physiognomy. Following Ian Watt's lead, some literary critics even distinguish the novel from romance by these very details.[8]

Thus, the emergence of modern forms of natural history, physiognomy, and the novel share much more than periodization.[9] Their respective roots lie in Greek philosophy; by the late seventeenth century, they were emerging in their Enlightenment forms through the asymmetric pressures of aesthetics, empiricism, and commerce. Naturalists, physiognomists, and novelists freely plundered the same source material (travel narratives, histories, conduct books, medical treatises, classical philosophy) and each other for evidence on the one hand and for plot lines and characterization on the other hand. They all render identical aesthetic judgments while maintaining somewhat different positions on the stubborn homology between character and appearance that had been the domain of romance. Exalted birth, virtue, and beauty always form a single package in physiognomy and often, but not always, in the novel and natural history. Race is a multiply constituted historical formation, but one of its most enduring strands functions as "a practice of visibility" in which "we read certain marks of the body as privileged sites of racial meaning."[10] The novel was singularly effective in attaching European racial features to the pleasures of narrative.

The Character Sketch in the Novel

In Eliza Haywood's *The British Recluse* (1722), Cleomira uses the techniques favored by natural historians to recall the overwhelming effect of Lysander's clothing, skin, hair, and face:

> He was dressed in a Strait Jocky-Coat of green velvet, richly embroidered at the Seams with Silver; the Buttons were *Brillians*, neatly set in the Fashion of Roses; his Hair, which is black as Jet, was tied with a green Ribbon, but not so straightly but that a thousand little Ringlets strayed over his lovely Cheeks and wantoned in the Air; a crimson feather in his Hat set off, to vast Advantage, the dazzling Whiteness of his Skin! In fine, he was all over Charms.[11]

Cleomira underscores Lysander's sexual impact on her when she reveals to Belinda that it was "fruitless . . . to represent what 'twas I felt!" when she regarded him (170). John Richetti correctly treats this description of "surface particularities" as integral to the "determining circumstances of sexual attraction," although it is the clothes that are particular, not the facial features.[12] The seamless movement between Lysander's sartorial splendor and his irresistible beauty explains Cleomira's desire for him.

The convention of using physical description to account for immediate sexual attraction changes little by the century's end. Ann Radcliffe's *The Italian* (1797) opens with a series of character sketches, and none is more eagerly awaited than the protagonist's. Readers initially share Vivaldi's frustration, since he can see only the general form of the veiled young woman's graceful figure. Thankfully, our curiosity is soon alleviated by a breeze that fleetingly reveals "a countenance more touchingly beautiful than he had dared to image." Vivaldi's emotional response to Ellena's appearance models an ideal reader's pleasure in those same attributes: "Her features were of the Grecian outline, and, though they expressed the tranquility of an elegant mind, her dark blue eyes sparkled with intelligence."[13] Other than perfectly embodying Linné's European racial profile, Ellena's character sketch segues seamlessly from her loveliness to the quality of her mind. The set piece of the character sketch focuses somewhat less intensively on fashion, particularly after the 1780s, when it lingers more on the face and mind. Dress and accessories continue to feature prominently as elements of other characters' approbation and desire, but they are not as central to the sketch itself as in the earlier part of the century.

In the novel, the androgynous physical characteristics of protagonists and the objects of their desire appear surprisingly uniform throughout the century. The sheer repetitiveness of these attributes partakes of the powerful legacy of character types, variously attributed to the neoclassical aesthetic preference for generality and to the influence of print and monetary cultures of the early century.[14] Indeed, Catherine Gallagher and Deidre Lynch both offer astute arguments about the impersonality of *English* characters in the eighteenth-century novel. Gallagher observes that "Typicality is the productive and economical aspect of fiction." Underscoring a connection between natural history and the novel, Gallagher elaborates: "A fictional character, because it refers to nobody in particular, refers to everybody of a certain 'species.' One could say, then, that novelistic depiction, far from being representationally excessive is peculiarly economical."[15] Suggestively, Lynch situates character even more specifically "at the interface of what is particular and what is general" (46). Although neither Gallagher nor Lynch is interested in the actual description of characters in novels, the characterlessness that they analyze also arises from a generalized, though peculiarly European, physical appearance. Linné's method of taxonomy, Samuel Johnson's principles of proper writing, and Joshua Reynolds's sense of taste in painting concur that "perfect form is produced by leaving out particularities, and retaining only general ideas."[16] As Lynch remarks about the human face and its representation, early eighteenth-century Britons were keenly attuned to "the eloquence of the material surface," often defining character as the face, its features, or personal appearance generally (38, 30). The shared terrain of impersonality in the novelistic character sketch and in the scientific racial profile arises from an aesthetically pleasing aristocratic ideal, an ideal that is presented, however, under the guise of empirical observation.

Idealization and Empiricism

As is well known, empirical practice comprises the close observation of daily life, the accumulation of details, and their systematic recording and subsequent arrangement. The inductive method, especially associated with Francis Bacon and Isaac Newton, has long been treated as a primary force that debunked the fanciful in natural history and rid the novel of its romance elements. It is worth recalling that in *The Rise of the Novel* (1957), Ian Watt explicates empiricism's impact on novelistic character in the authorial use of contemporary names and in the practice of situating characters in recognizable streets, theaters, turnpikes, countryside, and ports. Interestingly, physical description does not figure as an empirical tactic in Watt's formal delineation of character.[17] Even though description of bodies and faces seems as if it should spring naturally from empirical practice, the physical character sketch in the novel actually emerges from implicit comparison to the classical body, an aristocratic ideal.[18]

The novel attaches the beautiful physical features of Linné's Europeans to protagonists whose fortunes matter to readers. Moreover, these features, which are supposed to secure the reader's interest, are relayed by narrators and other characters in the idiom of empirical observation, not as the ideal that they were. Recording the satisfaction of a male character in the contemplation of the lead female's appearance, as in *The Monk* or *The Italian*; noting the lead male character's admiration of the protagonist's stature and face, as with Orlando Falkland in Frances Sheridan's *Memoirs of Miss Sidney Bidulph* (1761) or with Roderick Random; documenting the protagonist's pleasure in her own lovely reflection in a mirror or contrasting a character's pristine appearance to weather-beaten country laborers, as in Sophia Lee's *The Recess* (1782), are reality effects that give the *appearance* of employing empirical observation. The novel, then, is well suited to revealing how the ideal face and body acquire cultural cachet and associations with pleasure.

The minimalist sketch in the novel, particularly the description of hair texture, hair color, and nose shape, signifies truth to nature despite its continued idealization of aristocratic-cum-European racial features. This aesthetic preference for the classical, aristocratic body was slowly becoming explicitly racialized as it morphed into the European profile in natural history description and taxonomy. The tension between the empirical method and the idealization of a composite aristocratic body is nowhere more evident than in the racial profiles developed in natural history.

The Racial Sketch in Natural History

As much as rarities captured both scientific and popular imagination, the Royal Society tried to divorce science from novelty as a way to professionalize its pursuits and distinguish itself from dilettantism, eventually by establishing nature's rules rather than its exceptions. Both natural history and the novel retain interest in the new and rare, but their lasting reputations are forged in delimiting the norm, especially in the latter part of the century.[19]

Heralded as a tool of refinement, natural history's main function was to "facilitate the distinction of objects, or to ascertain their relations in the scale of being." Natural history "is the chief source from which human knowledge is derived"; in the inductive spirit of his age, Georges Louis Leclerc, Comte de Buffon, declares that "All our knowledge is ultimately derived from comparison."[20] Comparisons were particularly difficult to make among humans because of their overwhelming similarity. In *An History of the Earth, and Animated Nature* (1774), Oliver Goldsmith claims that "Of all animals, the differences between mankind are the smallest." It is only by comparing the inhabitants of opposite climates and distant countries that "any strong marked varieties in the human species" can be discerned.[21] To fulfill its mission of intellectual and cultural refinement through comparison, natural history tended to record differences, not similarities.[22] Apt comparison was a higher order of knowledge implying judgment, even taste; a person exercising judgment was able to separate one idea from another to avoid being misled by false similarity. The significant claim of common humanity that graced most Enlightenment inquiries frequently did not translate into the details of comparison. This characteristic intellectual disjunction is a troubling legacy of Enlightenment practice.

The influential natural histories of Linné, Buffon, and Johann Friedrich Blumenbach and their popularizers/translators first codified racial ideology in the realm of science. Eighteenth-century natural historians focused on stature and the general shape of facial features as the key to comparison of the world's populations, believing that the heat of the climate accounted for variations of form, height, skin color, and hair texture.

Racial profiles share method and content with the character sketch of the novel. In a bold move, Linné's *Systema Naturae* situates humans with primates and other quadrupeds. This stark arrangement emphasized humans' physical resemblance to animals. Dividing humans into four color groups of alabaster, ruby, sooty, and black in the first edition of his *Systema* in 1735, Linné includes other characteristic physical features and cultural habits, such as the predominant humor, in the revised tenth edition of 1758.[23] The revamped sketches occur under a new category, *Mammalia*, which includes primates, with fore-teeth incisors; *Homo*, however, walks erect and has a naked body, except in a few places covered by hair. *Homo sapiens* is diurnal, varying by education and situation. *Systema Naturae*'s global taxonomy makes sweeping generalizations about bodies and societies, turning description into aesthetic and moral judgments.[24] Linné's expanded 1758 taxonomy and Buffon's original 1749 description of human variety also include the details of nose shape, hair and eye color that composed the lexicon of physiognomists.

Buffon criticized Linné's taxonomy for being too artificial, too systematic: it failed to capture the fluidity of nature. When he treats humans in his *Natural History* (1749), Buffon adopts an expansive, descriptive approach that is supposed to exemplify empirical practice more carefully than Linné's method did. Buffon's claim that only individuals exist in nature seems completely at odds with Linné's taxonomy of *Homo sapiens* and apparently more congenial to the novel. Starting in the north and working his way south, Buffon treats populations according to distinct regions, noting natural differences that arose from climate and the sexual mixture of neighboring or conquering nations (3:74). Following ancient natural history and Montesquieu's *The Spirit of the Laws* (1748), Buffon regards fertile soil, good food, commerce, and proximity to the cooling winds of coastal areas as making all the difference between tawny, ugly people in extremely hot, cold, or mountainous regions and fair, handsome people in temperate climates and gentler landscapes.

This principle means that northern and southern populations fare much worse than geographically middling nations. Accordingly, Laplanders are "uncouth" figures, small in stature, savage in manners, with broad, large faces, flat noses, thick lips, with skin of "a tawny or swarthy hue." Buffon's perception of their physical oddity leads him to suggest that "This race is so different from all others, that it seems to constitute a distinct species" (3:58). Among Africans, who are the southern cognates of Lapps, Buffon found the most variety of any group. While Negroes on the west coast are "sedentary, love cleanliness, and are easily reconciled to servitude" (3:154), the Hottentots of Southern Africa are "a wandering, independent people, frightfully nasty, and extremely jealous of their liberty" (3:155). People in neighboring Natal Territory differ from Hottentots in important ways that Linné's single categorization of Africans masks. According to Buffon, "They are better made and less ugly. They are likewise naturally blacker: their visage is oval, their nose well proportioned, and their teeth are white; their aspect is agreeable, and their hair is naturally crisped" (3:159). Notably, it is to the aesthetic tools of physiognomy – nose shape and agreeable face – that Buffon turns for help in conveying the quality of this population's difference from their neighbors.

Not content with the misguided uniformity of Linné when it comes to Europeans either, Buffon avers that the Greeks, Neapolitans, Sicilians, Corsicans, and Spaniards are more swarthy than the French or British (3:126). This rather general observation about variation in European hues is further refined by comparing the rural laboring classes of Europe to remote savages. Metropolitan and other developed areas produce the most beautiful people: "All those people who live miserably, are ugly and ill made. Even in France, the country people are not so beautiful as those who live in towns" (3:205). Significantly, Buffon does not translate the aesthetic distinction into a moral one. Despite Buffon's declared intention to pursue the fine differences that Linné omits, the end result is often similar because the standard comparison is to the European metropolitan gentleman.

Remarkable for the increased attention to the aesthetic attributes of racial profiles, Blumenbach's series of natural historical treatises confirm the significance of climate's effects on skin color, especially the changeability of complexion, yet they also lay the groundwork for the inward turn of natural history. After the 1790s, natural historians sought to coordinate external features with the deep structure (anatomy) that seemed to give rise to them.[25] Retaining the perspective of basic human similarity affirmed by Linné and Buffon, Blumenbach's increasing fascination with skulls tentatively points to the physiognomical conviction of mid-nineteenth-century race science that the skull shape and the various features of the head relate directly to the mind. By the 1795 third edition of "On the Natural Variety of Mankind" (1775), Blumenbach had absorbed the language of comparative anatomists as well as their tools that measured skulls and racial beauty, but he had not replicated their conclusions about moral or mental attributes. This partial shift in the focal point of natural history registers in the new evidence that Blumenbach offers about the more stable racial features, such as national skull shape, national hair type, and causes of the racial face. The racial face is not a peculiar expression that indexes temperament (that would be physiognomy); rather, the racial face is embodied more generally in the proportion of the countenance's parts, "all of which we see to be peculiar and characteristic to the different varieties of mankind."[26] Blumenbach's interchangeable use of "national" and "racial" as adjectives to denote differences among populations captures a more general transition in thinking from old-style humoral national characters (evident in Linné's reference to the four kinds of humans being phlegmatic, sanguine, etc.) to new-style racial thinking based on anatomical shape and measurement. According to Michael Hagner, Blumenbach adopted the methods of physiognomy without espousing the equation between body shape and character.[27]

Blumenbach espouses the Enlightenment aesthetics popularized by Johann Joachim Winckelmann in selecting a skull from Mt. Caucasus in Georgia as the most beautiful one in his collection because of its spherical perfection. In noting the deviation of all other skulls from this shape, which parallels the degeneration from white skin color, he declares that the bone-deep beauty of whiteness was the primitive, or original, color of humans, naming the entire racial group Caucasian (269). In returning to the novel, we can see its shared fetishization of whiteness with natural history in its depiction of protagonists' faces for our viewing pleasure.

English Complexion and the Character Sketch

Not surprisingly, most Europeans favored themselves as the standard from which all others varied. Indeed, assessments of beauty, because they exercised taste, are a ubiquitous feature of contemporary conversations. A polite man verified his urbanity through aesthetic pronouncements: one result of these habitual references to the beautiful was to reify and naturalize the Enlightenment neoclassical ideal. An important nexus of natural history and the novel, contemplation of complexion gave rise to untold encomiums on beauty. Buffon was typical in believing that the temperate climate "produces the most handsome and beautiful men. It is from this climate that the ideas of the genuine colour of mankind, and of the various degrees of beauty, ought to be derived" (3:205). Some thirty years later an imitator of Buffon, William Frederic Martyn, transforms this general precept and relative standard into a universal perspective: "It is easy to perceive that, of all colours by which mankind is diversified, white is not only the most beautiful to the eye, but also the most advantageous. The fair complexion, if it may be so termed, seems like a transparent covering to the soul."[28] In this typical late-century proposition, climate recedes as the explanatory mechanism as moral and even utilitarian functions predominate. Climate had long been considered a traditional cause of beauty, but civil society was increasingly regarded as crucial to modifying individual facial expressions. Samuel Stanhope Smith, the Scottish-educated first president of Princeton, links attractive appearance to man-made intervention similarly to Buffon, but he offers even more particularities: "all the features of the human countenance are *modified*, and its entire *expression* radically formed, by the state of society."[29] One of the many examples that Smith offers as proof is a 15-year-old Indian at the College of New Jersey who is gradually acquiring "the agreeable *expression* of civil life. The expression of the eye, and the softening of the features to civilized emotions and ideas, seems to have removed more than half the difference between him and us" (61). Smith's observation sutures natural history and physiognomy.

While natural historians understood complexion as easily changeable because of the effects of sun, wind, and altitude, novelists tended to grant this understanding primarily to non-European populations. In fact, Britons' skin color usually functions as an indelible index of belonging. In this way, the novel helps forge and, through repetition, affirm a racial appearance for Britons as surely as taxonomy. White complexion shines through as a defining feature in satirical and serious character sketches alike, at home and abroad. Charlotte Smith's *The Old Manor House* (1793) is typical in reducing the salient difference between Americans and the English to a certain quality of whiteness. In volume 3, Orlando is alternately kidnapped and rescued by the Iroquois. They cut off all of his hair except a long lock on the crown of his head; with his mohawk, "he was distinguished from an Iroquois by nothing but his English complexion."[30] This observation tends both to minimize difference (it's only the complexion that differentiates us) and to connect national identity to complexion in the last instance.

Domestic novels also delight in fair skin color, particularly in its ability to reveal rank and merit. Because whiteness hovers uneasily between these two different ideologies – the one aristocratic and the other bourgeois – it is all the more significant. In *Joseph Andrews*, Fielding describes both Joseph and Fanny primarily through their stature and facial features, which are remarkably the same. With the sketch of Fanny, however, Fielding dwells more on the quality of her skin color and complexion, which are supposed to bespeak her worthiness despite her humble origins. Her shapely arms are "a little redden'd by her Labour, yet if her Sleeve slipt above her Elbow, or her Handkerchief discovered any part of her Neck, a Whiteness appeared which the finest *Italian* Paint would be unable to reach" (152). Fielding explicitly cites the aesthetic tradition of Renaissance painters to conjure up the dazzling whiteness that she shares with Lysander in *The British Recluse*, the Mazzini sisters in Radcliffe's *A Sicilian Romance* (1790), and Antonia in *The Monk*, to name just a few. Then, Fielding draws our attention to Fanny's beautiful face: "Her Complexion was fair, a little injured by the Sun, but overspread with such a Bloom, that the finest Ladies would have exchanged all their White for it" (153). Notably, Fielding distinguishes between the whiteness of her skin color and the sun-kissed complexion of her face and arms, which betray, not unbecomingly, her exposure to the weather while performing outdoor labor. Calling readerly attention to her changeable complexion and to her permanent skin color registers the *frisson* of change in process in which whiteness is becoming a pleasurable racial attribute.

Fielding's character sketch combines the generalities of natural history with the particularities of physiognomy. Fanny's curling chestnut-brown hair is accompanied by a host of physiognomical features that delineate her desirable character: "Her Forehead was high, her Eye-brows arched, and rather full than otherwise. Her Eyes black and sparkling; her Nose, just inclining to the *Roman*;....add to these, a

Countenance in which tho' she was extremely bashful, a Sensibility appeared almost incredible" (152–53). Fanny's physical beauty is inseparable from her character. Her arched eyebrow is an index to her gentle nature, and her high forehead and Roman nose reveal not just her classical beauty but more specifically her loyalty; in a man these features also reveal bravery.

Even in the few novels in which physical beauty is not granted to a protagonist, white skin color still surfaces as the real index of rank and paternal identity. In the unpromising introduction of Humphry Clinker, his clothes are so ragged that his posteriors show, and his physical appearance "was equally queer and pathetic. He seemed to be about twenty years of age, of a middling size, with bandy legs, stooping shoulders, high forehead, sandy locks, pinking eyes, flat nose, and long chin – but his complexion was of a sickly yellow; his looks denoted famine."[31] Despite this unprepossessing first appearance, we are immediately assured that his unseemly nakedness reveals some key information, "that he had a skin as fair as alabaster" (78). While his sallow complexion, linked to health, deceives a viewer, his naturally white skin, linked to his gentleman father, does not. The momentary spotlight on a character's skin color, complexion, shape of nose, and slope of forehead, spans natural history and physiognomy, defining the novel's power to establish an environment conducive to the powerful confluence of these two modes of interpreting beauty and character.

As we have seen with white skin color, natural and civil historians typically explained European physical superiority (moral or political as well) as arising from climate, commerce, or other national improvement; physiognomists explained this same superiority in individuals based on the shape of their various facial features. Together, these ways of seeing offer a comprehensive system for sketching individual, national, and even racial character.

The Facial Character Sketch in Physiognomy

Until recently, there has been little inclination among literary or cultural historians of the eighteenth century to view physiognomy in connection with natural history, presumably because of the debased place of physiognomy in Enlightenment thinking (both Buffon and Blumenbach explicitly divorced their methods from it).[32] Physiognomy, "the talent of discovering the interior of Man by his exterior – of perceiving by certain natural signs, what does not immediately strike the senses," gave whiteness a face.[33] In the domain of physiognomy, the various features of an individual's countenance reflect his or her passions and provide a reliable index to character and express that person's passions, or even soul.[34] Physiognomical principles flout a powerful strain of Enlightenment thinking, helping to unite beauty even more intimately with intellectual acuity and moral virtue. At once referencing the cultural reach of physiognomy and his own doubts, William Hogarth observes in *The Analysis of Beauty* (1753) that the "common received opinion [is] that the face is the index of the mind."[35]

In Sarah Scott's *Agreeable Ugliness* (1754), the protagonist calls on the general principles of Linnean taxonomy and on physiognomical precepts to sketch her character. Such details as dark eyes signify her intelligence, and the nose shape peculiarly reveals her character. Both features denote the quality of her attractiveness, despite the claim that she is ugly. The commonsense of physiognomy makes her face speak to her character:

> My Sister was fair, I was very brown. She was a Picture of my Mother with every Beauty heightened, I an ugly Resemblance of my Father. She had the Superiority in Beauty, I had the Advantage over her in Shape. Her Eyes were of a dark blue, large, and finely formed, but without Fire or Expression, in short they were fine Eyes without Meaning; mine were black, a little too much sunk, tolerably large of very uncommon Vivacity, and seemed to indicate more Sense than perhaps I really had.... My Sister's nose was well-shaped, but rather long; mine was the best feature in my Face ... my Sister's skin was as white as possible, it was neither so smooth or as soft as mine.[36]

The implicit judgment of her sister's vapid beauty and her own vital character relies on the techniques of physiognomy, especially detectable in the seamless transition from her shapely nose and dark eyes to the quality of her mind.

Novels affirm both the ubiquitous tendency to read character from the face and its dangers. A typical example of the perils of relying on physiognomy occurs in *The Man of Feeling* (1771). Initially, Harley is struck by "a fresh-looking elderly gentleman," of whom he later observes: "he never saw a face promise more honesty than that of the old man he had met with."[37] Readers know that this venerable-looking man is actually a card shark and con man who dupes the protagonist. Harley's gullibility repeatedly meets with warnings from other characters and unpleasant lessons about the mistake of reading character from facial features. These two examples from the novels of Mackenzie and Scott somewhat differently capture the use of physiognomy to elucidate contemporary British character. Indeed, protagonists usually benefited from an uncritical application of physiognomical methods and conclusions, but minor characters raised doubts about its universal efficacy.

Physiognomists and novelists share considerable interest in the individual face at rest as well as in the changes that features of a countenance undergo in the course of passion. Johann Casper Lavater, the man most responsible for a resurgence of interest in physiognomy, if not its eventual inclusion in racial science, modernized the principles of physiognomy in the 1770s, and, through hundreds of examples, suggested how to use the shape and placement of facial features to interpret faces. As Lavater puts it, "the moral life of man, particularly, reveals itself in the lines, marks, and transitions of the countenance."[38] Drawing on the insight that "Each trait contains the whole character of man" (Holcroft 2:31), Lavater instructs students to describe an individual's whole form and each particular feature, beginning, as natural historians do, with stature and proportion of limbs. Then, they should proceed to the particularity of forehead, nose, mouth, and chin, especially noting the color, position, size and depth of eyes (2:22). Essentially, this procedure is also the formula for the physical character sketch that novelists use.

Physiognomy did not claim to operate by scientific comparison, yet it relied on study and comparison all the same. The hundreds of plates of European heads and the minute directions about what angles of the forehead, nose, eyebrow, and lips mean affirmed Lavater's claim that "Precision in observation is the very soul of physiognomy" (1:119). The head and face were the most consequential forms to analyze because they housed the brain: "The head of man is, of all parts of the body, the most noble and the most essential; it is the principal seat of the mind, the centre of our intellectual faculties" (Hunter 3:268). Accordingly, the forehead and nose are the shapes most likely to reveal character. The curvature of the forehead, for example, reveals "the propensity, degree of power, thought, and sensibility" (Holcroft 3:163). The gentle Roman noses attributed to Oroonoko, Joseph, and Fanny signify illustrious character and strong leadership.[39] Dark eyes, found to grace most heroic and virtuous countenances in the novel, indicate strength and a certain quality of desirable manliness in men or women (3:171). Even arched or level eyebrows attest to the quality of feminine kindness or masculine understanding, respectively.

Challenging the Lockean common sense of the day, Lavater believes in the formative role of inheritance on the moral and physical person. Indeed, his conviction that the body's shape and the form of its features speak for the entire person leads him to renounce a central Enlightenment tenet: "I know of no error more gross or palpable than the following, which has been mentioned by such great men. 'Every thing in man depends on education . . . and nothing on organization, and the original formation of the body; for these latter are alike in all'" (1:194). Lavater posits that features and forms are inherited as are "moral propensities" (1:197), yet he follows contemporary convention in also believing that time, education, or opportunity could change everything – but not immediately (it could take several generations to eradicate or register a family's change in rank). Even though critics accused him of subscribing to determinism, Lavater did not believe that men were born either vicious or virtuous (1:215) or that there was innate servility (3:25). If physiognomy reveals each person's essence, that essence is not exactly innate.

Despite the implication that physiognomy treats the stripped-down individual, most physiognomical judgments are, of course, deeply culturally conditioned. Predisposition toward high rank and toward Europeans is palpable in Lavater's implicit equation of stature and rank: "there is a proportion, a beauty, of person which announces more virtue, magnanimity and heroism, than another form which is vulgar and more imperfect" (Hunter 1:275). In true Enlightenment fashion, Lavater attempts to make a science out of the way certain facial features elicit revulsion, attraction, or fear; it took patience, training, and hundreds of comparisons to employ his method with integrity. A careful physiognomist studies the face in rest and in motion (technically called pathonomy). Certain times were more propitious than others for interpreting the countenance's true character because these were less affected by humor, the overlay of manners, or the desire to deceive. Not surprisingly, these events, like a sudden meeting or farewell, or a moment of compassion, are also key scenes in novels and plays. Many conclusions based on physiognomy tap into what natural history purported to eschew: the irrational or the prejudicial.

Conventionally, the eighteenth century marks the official decline of faith in physiognomy and the rise of a more scientific view of external appearance. There is considerable merit to this characterization in regard to scientific circles. Natural historians tried to distance themselves from physiognomy, seeing it as unscientific and too particular for the larger generalizations natural history needed to make. For example, Buffon unequivocally declares against it: "there is no analogy between features and the nature of the soul" (2:451). Indeed, Buffon forcefully dismisses the centuries-old conviction that physiognomy reveals anything about a person's natural disposition or faculty of thinking (2:452): "The form of the nose, of the mouth, and of the other features, has no more connection with the natural disposition of any person, than the stature, or size of limbs, with the faculty of thinking" (2:451). Yet he concedes that the motions, posture, and face do convey vital information about the passions and the soul of individuals, just not about the nature of human groups (2:451).

Lavater usually takes the high road in regard to physiognomy's treatment in natural history, choosing to reprint without comment dozens of pages from Buffon's natural history that illustrate his own theory. Once, however, he indulges in testy criticism of natural historians, accusing them of practicing physiognomy even as they claim to eschew it: "Why is Mr. *de Buffon* disposed to allow to the *English* nation more penetration than to the inhabitants of *Lapland*? And why will he decide the question by a simple glance of the eye?" (Hunter 2:22). Criticizing the reductionism of natural history in regard to the human form, Lavater asks: "what is the exterior of Man? – Not merely his naked figure.... Rank, condition, habit, estate, dress, all concur to the codification of Man, every one is a several veil spread over him" (1:25). Lavater, and those scientists who adopted his insights, judge natural history as being inadequate to describing what really mattered about humans.

Despite its official exile from natural history, physiognomy remained integral to a quotidian lexicon among the general population of Britons. As Emma Spary rightly suggests, physiognomy itself may have declined in favor in the nascent sciences, but other genres continued to rely on its methods: "Travel accounts, medical writings, discussions of gender differences and bodies, and books on etiquette all evidenced similar concerns."[40] Most important, however, was the flourishing life of physiognomical principles in aesthetics. There, the Greek ideal had considerable influence on the production of statuary and portraiture and on the cultivation of gentlemanly taste.

This cultural ubiquity of physiognomical applications is the only way to account for the immediate popularity of Lavater's *Essays on Physiognomy* (1774), which in England alone went into twenty editions by the early nineteenth century, from cheap pocket editions to the elaborate folio size with hundreds of plates.[41] Other than embracing familiar aesthetic preferences, another explanation for its immediate appeal lay in the fact that Lavater introduced to this centuries-old impressionistic system a method of measurement to determine how far the nose protruded from the face. His method resembled that of Pieter Camper, a Dutch physiologist who, at about the same time, was developing a technique for determining national beauty and ugliness based on the skull shape and facial angle (a measurement of the angle of imaginary lines projected from the forehead, nose, and chin).[42] In the service of helping artists to distinguish more accurately among various people from around the world, Camper's angle purported to measure beauty based on how closely the facial angle approximated the nearly perpendicular faces of Greek statues: "In both systems, the more acute the profile angle, the more brutal the creature" (Meijer 121).

Decades before Camper and Lavater, Buffon had consulted the perfection embodied in Greek culture. While claiming that statues are merely composite ideals, representing proportions unavailable to individual men, and that we must trust the impression made on our senses by observing real people (empiricism), Buffon persists in using the Greek model to measure perfection in the proportion of body parts to the size of the face (2:460–64). Given this deep enchantment with classical statuary, it is not surprising, then, that skulls and facial angle measurements became, with some tweaking, the new wave of natural history in the nineteenth century, replacing external, environmental theories with more "accurate," bone-deep assessments of racial variety.

Indeed, Lavater the physiognomist describing national types sounds exactly like Blumenbach, the most respected natural historian of the same era, because they are both beginning to view the human form from the skull outward. Round skulls were particularly prized: "in Europeans the vault of the hind-head is more arched, and rounded in form of a globe, than in the Negro, and the African in general." Similarly, "The forehead of the Calmuck [nomadic Tartar] is flat and low, that of the Ethiopian higher and more sharpened." The Calmuck's flat forehead and sunken eyes are translated in the combined languages of natural history and physiognomy: the flatter the forehead, the more it resembles a monkey's and generally reveals signs of "cowardice and rapacity" (Hunter 1:161, 162). Of an Indian skull, description shades into judgment: "The crown of the head is more pointed, the hind-head more shortened.... A scull [*sic*] thus conformed announces a person whose appetites are gross and sensual, and incapable of being affected by mental pleasure and delicacy of feeling" (1:162). To many natural historians of the late century, skulls and skeletons reveal national and gender traits in a way that skin color could not.[43]

The Confluence of Natural History and Physiognomy in the Novel

In examining the novel more carefully in light of the claim that the character sketch sutures natural history and physiognomy in its physical portraits, thereby laying the groundwork for nineteenth-century race science, it is time to glance at the techniques that the genres share. Other than the formulaic physical description of English and

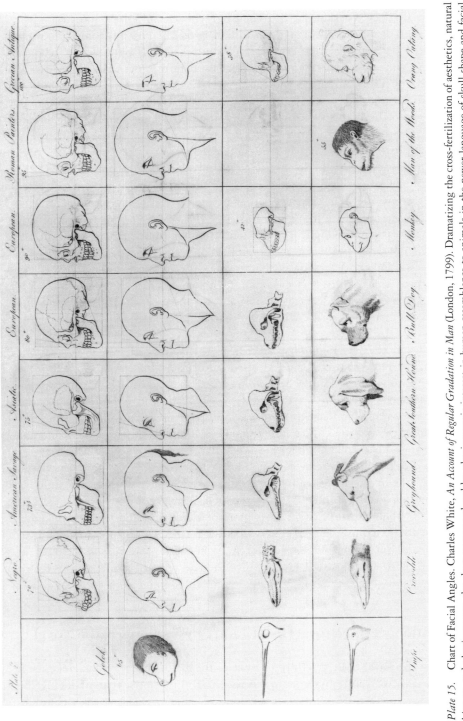

Plate 15. Chart of Facial Angles. Charles White, *An Account of Regular Gradation in Man* (London, 1799). Dramatizing the cross-fertilization of aesthetics, natural history, and physiognomy, the chart portrays the older physiognomic interest in human resemblance to animals in the newer language of skull shape and facial angle. The upper right half of the chart is overdetermined by the association of beauty and humanity, detectable in the doubling of the European figure.

foreign characters, novelists had recourse to the comparative, empirical approach of natural history in bringing together a range of contemporary types. Comparison of the human and animal worlds, particularly to make a satirical point, is a major technique that connects the novel to natural history (and visual satire), most memorably in the monkey twin of the fop Lovel. The well-dressed monkey's cameo appearance in a final scene of Burney's *Evelina* (1778) conjures up Lovel's debased character, which is a paltry imitation of French fashion and manners that has literally made him unmanly, if not inhuman.

Most comparisons operated at the level of distinct types within the same rank. Linné's general method in categorizing *Homo sapiens* was to juxtapose clear-cut opposites; this comparative method gives rise to much of the novel's satire and moral didacticism. In *Tom Jones* (1749), Fielding argues for a beautifully packaged, sympathetic, and generous masculinity in the juxtaposition of opposite types, such as Tom and Blifil. Following Buffon's preference for a method that captures minute differences between similar types, other novelists commonly use comparison with an eye to fine distinction as a strategy for delineating character. Often the characters in question are physically similar or of comparable rank; the key lies in another, crucial detail that distinguishes between a heroine's suitors: the rake Sir Clement Willoughby from the gentle Lord Orville in *Evelina*, the apparently unsteady Clarence Hervey from the gambling Creole Mr. Vincent in Edgeworth's *Belinda* (1801), or the calculated charm of Mr. Elliot from the solid Captain Wentworth in Austen's *Persuasion* (1818). The crucial detail, usually of education or habit, complicates the plot for the characters in the novel, but it is usually presented immediately to readers in the character sketch.

The techniques and pitfalls of physiognomy also appear regularly in the novel. An eloquent face always secures the interest of readers. The most favored countenances were the ones most easily interpreted by others, the ones most ripe for the application of physiognomical principles. Elizabeth Inchbald's *A Simple Story* (1791) follows this formula in the presentation of the Catholic priest turned titled landowner:

> But that the reader may be interested in what Dorriforth says and does, it is necessary to give some description of his person and manners. His figure was tall and elegant, but his face, except a pair of dark bright eyes, a set of white teeth, and a graceful fall in his clerical curls of dark brown hair, had not one feature to excite admiration – he possessed notwithstanding such a gleam of sensibility diffused over each, that many people mistook his face for handsome, and all were more or less attracted by it – in a word, the charm that is here meant to be described is a countenance – on his countenance you beheld the feelings of his heart – saw all its inmost workings. . . . On this countenance his thoughts were pictured, and as his mind was enriched with every virtue that could make it valuable, so was his honest face adorned with every emblem of those virtues – and they not only gave a lustre to his aspect, but added a harmonious sound to all he uttered.[44]

Dorriforth's face is a luminous reflection of his virtuous heart; its expressiveness is as praiseworthy as the goodness it reveals. Moral beauty could create the impression of physical beauty and signify in the countenance that is fair enough to provide, as the natural historian Martyn put it, "a transparent covering to the soul." If it was English politics, European aesthetics, and the romance paradigm that had popularized the equation of high rank, personal beauty, and virtue, then the novel only selectively debunked this powerful cluster of attributes.

Faith in physiognomy, unlike natural history, became interlaced with anxiety about the potential failure of surfaces to reveal truth. Characters who mistake appearance for reality are not treated uniformly in novels. On the one hand, some characters that mistake reality for the surface presentation are routinely viewed negatively as naïve and unthinking. John Moore's *Zeluco* (1786) offers a typical Enlightenment plot of a Neapolitan child improperly educated and spoiled by his mother. Moore invokes the potential danger of relying on physiognomy when courtship and marriage are at stake:

> although some people who pretended to skill in physiognomy asserted, that they could detect the indications of ill-nature[;] . . . in the general opinion, . . . he [Zeluco] was a very handsome man. Rosalia was one of those young ladies who, when they greatly approve of a man's face and figure, are inclined to believe that every other good quality is added thereunto.[45]

On the other hand, a few characters who mistake appearance for reality are often so good themselves that their mistake is a testament to their virtue as much as to their inexperience. This is the case with Parson Adams in *Joseph Andrews*, Goldsmith's Primrose in *The Vicar of Wakefield* (1766), Clarissa, David Simple, and the staple of sentimental literature in general.[46] While Lavater anticipated this objection about physiognomy (he devotes a long chapter to dissimulation), he supports the insight that some real parts of the individual are not changeable: bone structure, eye color, nose shape, and the like, speak for the true character despite efforts to hide or enhance (Holcroft 1:153–55 and chapter 19 generally).

As the earlier example from Radcliffe's character sketch of Ellena in *The Italian* indicates, the most remarkable change in the way that physiognomy figures in novels is detectable especially after 1780, when character sketches more regularly connect the countenance directly to intelligence. This strand of the novel feeds directly into nineteenth-century comparative anatomy and psychology. Two character sketches that feature a palpable change from earlier novels in their descriptions of female characters are Mary Raymond in *The Victim of Prejudice* (1799) and Cecilia (1782). Of Cecilia, Burney writes: "her form was elegant, her heart was liberal; her countenance announced the intelligence of her mind, her complexion varied with every emotion of her soul." Burney associates the mind with the unchanging countenance, distinguishing it from the more mercurial complexion. Similarly, Mary Raymond's self-portrait reflects a countenance that advertises her intelligence in the more specific vocabularies of natural history and physiognomy: she describes herself as "Tall, blooming, animated, my features were regular, my complexion a rich glowing brunette, my eyes vivacious and sparkling; dark chestnut hair shaded my face, and floated over my shoulders in luxuriant profusion; my figure was light and airy, my step firm, my aspect intelligent, and my mind inquisitive."[47] In her incisive analysis of literary character, Deidre Lynch rightly observes that throughout the eighteenth century there are "recalibrations of the relationship between the discourses of character and of physiognomy." One of the important changes that Lynch traces to Romanticism's influence, which follows from physiognomy but bears on racial ideology, is that the face begins to express a unique personality rather than simply registering the passions (272). As these character sketches of protagonists intimate, in the novel, the face also records racial character.

Conclusion

The persistent popular enchantment with physiognomy and a professional faith in natural history help account for the racial work of the character sketch in novels. One of the British novel's most under-recognized but far-reaching achievements is racializing Britons as surely as natural history did. In its overall effect, the novel tends to advertise and ossify a desirable set of androgynous European physical features, which are, however, attached to moral variety. If natural histories touted a consistent and therefore increasingly normative set of physical characteristics, the novel seemed to call a single moral cognate into question with every seducer, harsh father, mercenary lover, or flighty heiress. Overall, the novel's plots and characters tend to illustrate a variety of ranks and behaviors that were the very definition of a liberal, commercial society. The novel did not confirm a British essence as much as advertise the wonderful variety of Britons, even though its protagonists were encased in the standard form, complete with white complexions, curling hair, dark eyes, and slightly Grecian or Roman profiles. Indeed, if there is a British essence, it is variety – just not physical variety.[48]

By the mid-nineteenth century, race science explicitly unites natural history and physiognomy to make claims such as the following a cultural commonplace: "superior physical beauty was the expression of higher mental development" and ugliness was routinely a characteristic of inferior races (Hartley 110–11). As we have seen, traces of these convictions can be found throughout the early modern and Enlightenment periods, particularly in natural history. It is the complementary, positive process of the novel's character sketch – a stable record of beauty, whiteness, and, latterly, intelligence – a process that was largely free of direct comparison in the stark terms of race science that unobtrusively made pleasurable European racial features. As important as it is to seek out the myriad ways that difference operates insidiously, the racial history of Europeans is powerful in its own right with equally profound ways of shaping culture, identity, and desire. The specific contribution of the novel reminds us that the reproduction of society occurs not only through the mechanisms of anxiety and difference but also through mechanisms of pleasure and similarity.[49]

See also: chapter 1, CRUSOE'S *FARTHER ADVENTURES*; chapter 4, AGE OF PEREGRINATION; chapter 10, THE ORIGINAL AMERICAN NOVEL; chapter 16, AN EMERGING NEW CANON.

Notes

I am grateful for the intellectual and editorial suggestions of David Brewer, Virginia Cope, Aman Garcha, and Dian Kriz.

1. Henry Fielding, *Joseph Andrews*, ed. Martin Battestin (1742; Middletown, CT: Wesleyan University Press, 1967), 38.

2. Charles Linné, *A General System of Nature*, trans. William Turton (London: Lackington, Allen, 1802), 9.

3. The major study of physiognomy and the novel is Graeme Tytler, *Physiognomy in the European Novel: Faces and Fortunes* (Princeton, NJ: Princeton University Press, 1982). Reflecting more recent interest in race, two studies unite the efforts of physiognomists and natural historians. In *Race and Aesthetics in the Anthropology of Petrus Camper (1722–1789)* (Amsterdam: Rodopi, 1999), chapter 6, Miriam Claude Meijer provides a superbly detailed, revisionist history of eighteenth-century connections and disconnections between physiognomy and natural history. David Bindman, *Ape to Apollo: Aesthetics and the Idea of Race in the Eighteenth Century* (Ithaca, NY: Cornell University Press, 2002) also studies the connection between physiognomy and race at this time.

4. *Philosophical Transactions {of the Royal Society}* 1 no.11 (1667): 188.

5. In the wake of Watt, literary historians have made much of the effect of the plain style on the language and design of the novel. In *The Origins of the English Novel 1600–1740* (Baltimore, MD: Johns Hopkins University Press, 1987), Michael McKeon devotes an entire section to natural history as a narrative model for the novel based on their joint indebtedness to observation and description (101–6). In a more recent critique of the confluence of the novel and natural history, Amanpal Garcha argues that empiricism gave rise, not so much to the narrative form of the novel, but to moments of non-narrativity, which are most remarkably embodied in the economical character sketch. See Amanpal Garcha, "From Sketch to Novel: Nonnarrative Styles in Victorian Fiction" (Ph.D. diss., Columbia University, New York, 2002), introduction.

6. The quotation from Josiah Nott and George Gliddon's *Types of Mankind* (1854) appears in Robert Young, *Colonial Desire: Hybridity in Theory, Culture and Race* (New York: Routledge, 1995), 66.

7. Marcia Pointon, *Hanging the Head: Portraiture and Social Formation in Eighteenth-Century England* (New Haven, CT: Yale University Press, 1993), 7.

8. Ian Watt, *The Rise of the Novel: Studies in Defoe, Richardson and Fielding* (1957; Berkeley and Los Angeles: University of California Press, 1965), chapter 1, esp. 17–18.

9. McKeon, *The Origins of the English Novel*, chapter 2. See also Robert James Merrett, "Natural History and the Eighteenth-Century English Novel," *Eighteenth-Century Studies* 25 (1991–2): 145–70.

10. Kalpana Seshadri-Crooks, *Desiring Whiteness: A Lacanian Analysis of Race* (New York: Routledge, 2000), 2.

11. Eliza Haywood, *The British Recluse*, in *Popular Fiction by Women 1660–1730*, ed. Paula R. Backscheider and John J. Richetti (New York: Oxford University Press, 1996), 169–70.

12. Richetti's essay cites this very passage: "Ideas and Voices: The New Novel in Eighteenth-Century England," *Eighteenth-Century Fiction* 12 (2000): 327–44, at 338–39.

13. Ann Radcliffe, *The Italian*, ed. Frederick Garber (1797; London: Oxford University Press, 1968), 6.

14. Catherine Gallagher, *Nobody's Story: The Vanishing Acts of Women Writers in the Marketplace 1670–1820* (Berkeley and Los Angeles: University of California Press, 1994) espouses the neoclassical reasoning and Deidre Lynch, *The Economy of Character: Novels, Market Culture, and the Business of Inner Meaning* (Chicago: University of Chicago Press, 1998) investigates the impact of print and the circulation of coins.

15. Gallagher, *Nobody's Story*, 286 and 283. Lynch dates the emergence of "fleshier" characters in the late century, when "Character expanded in an inward direction, and also an outward" (137).

16. Joshua Reynolds, *Discourses on Art*, ed. Robert Wark (1797; San Marino, CA: Huntington Library, 1959), 57.

17. Watt, *Rise of the Novel*, 16, 19. Omitting physical markers entirely, he defines character as "the stable elements in the individual's mental and moral constitution," 272.

18. On the classical body, see John Barrell, " 'The Dangerous Goddess': Masculinity, Prestige, and the Aesthetic in Early Eighteenth-Century Britain," *Cultural Critique* 12 (1989): 101–31; Bindman, *Ape to Apollo*, chapter 2; and Peter Stallybrass and Allon White, *The Politics and Poetics of Transgression* (Ithaca, NY: Cornell University Press, 1986), 105–8.

19. See Gallagher, *Nobody's Story*, 284–85, who cites Maria Edgeworth on the novel's normative function. For the standard in natural history, see Anne Bermingham, *Learning to Draw: Studies in the Cultural History of a Polite and Useful Art* (New Haven, CT: Yale University Press, 2000), 64.

20. Comte de Buffon, *Natural History, General and Particular*, trans. William Smellie, 3rd ed. 9 vols. (1749; London, 1791), 1:xiii, ix, 2:355.

21. Oliver Goldsmith, *An History of the Earth, and Animated Nature*. 8 vols. (London, 1774), 2:212.

22. Michel Foucault, *The Order of Things: An Archaeology of the Human Sciences*, trans. Robert Hurley (1966, New York: Vintage Books, 1994), 142–44, 159.

23. Londa Schiebinger, *Nature's Body: Gender in the Making of Modern Science* (Boston: Beacon Press, 1993), 42 offers a lucid commentary on Linné's additions to the later editions.

24. Europeans have an overall fair appearance; brawny limbs; curling, light-colored hair; blue eyes; gentle and acute in their manner. Africans are "Black, phlegmatic, relaxed," their "*Hair* black, frizzled; *skin* silky; *nose* flat; *lips* tumid; *crafty*, indolent, negligent. *Anoints* himself with grease. *Governed* by caprice." Asiatics are "Sooty, melancholy, rigid." They have "*Hair* black; *eyes* dark; severe, haughty, covetous." They are "*Covered* with loose garments" and "*Governed* by opinions." Americans are "Copper-coloured, choleric, erect. *Hair* black, straight, thick;

nostrils wide, *face* harsh, *beard* scanty; *obstinate*, content, free. Paints himself with fine red lines. *Regulated* by customs" (9).

25. Foucault, *The Order of Things*, 137–38.

26. Johann Friedrich Blumenbach, "On the Natural Variety of Mankind," in *The Anthropological Treatises of Johann Friedrich Blumenbach*, trans. and ed. Thomas Bendyshe (London: Longwood Press, 1865), 229.

27. Michael Hagner, "Enlightened Monsters," in *The Sciences in Enlightened Europe*, ed. William Clark et al. (Chicago: University of Chicago Press, 1999), 175–217, at 201.

28. *A New Dictionary of Natural History*. 2 vols. (London, 1785), entry on "man."

29. Samuel Stanhope Smith, *An Essay on the Causes of the Variety of Complexion and Figure in the Human Species*, ed. Winthrop Jordan (Cambridge, MA: Belknap Press of Harvard University Press, 1965), 50.

30. Charlotte Smith, *The Old Manor House*. 4 vols. (London, 1793), 3:326.

31. Tobias Smollett, *Humphry Clinker*, ed. O M Brack, Jr. (1771; Athens: University of Georgia Press, 1990), 78.

32. For their declared distance from physiognomy, see Buffon, *Natural History*, 2: 451–52 and Blumenbach, *Contributions to Natural History* (1790; 2nd ed. 1806), 297. Alan T. McKenzie, in an introduction to Charles LeBrun, *A Method to Learn to Design the Passions* (1734; Los Angeles: William Andrews Clark Memorial Library, 1980) offers the conventional wisdom: "Physiognomy, perhaps because of its fixity and apparent determinism, earned the distrust of the Augustans and dwindled into a tool of the satirists" (ix).

33. Johann Caspar Lavater, *Essays on Physiognomy*, trans. Thomas Holcroft. 3 vols. (London, 1789), 1:20.

34. Lucy Hartley, *Physiognomy and the Meaning of Expression in Nineteenth-Century Culture* (Cambridge: Cambridge University Press, 2001), 16.

35. William Hogarth, *The Analysis of Beauty* (London, 1753), 203.

36. Sarah Scott, *Agreeable Ugliness: or, The Triumph of the Graces* (London, 1754), 19–20. I follow verbatim the quotation as it appears in Robert W. Jones, "Obedient Faces: The

Virtue of Deformity in Sarah Scott's Fiction," in *"Defects": Engendering the Modern Body*, ed. Helen Deutsch and Felicity Nussbaum (Ann Arbor: University of Michigan Press, 2000), 280–302, at 285–86.

37. Henry Mackenzie, *The Man of Feeling* [1771], ed. Brian Vickers (New York: Oxford University Press, 2001), 43, 52.

38. Johann Caspar Lavater, *Essays on Physiognomy*, trans. Henry Hunter. 3 vols. (London, 1789), 1:15. Graeme Tytler, "Letters of Recommendation and False Vizors: Physiognomy in the Novels of Henry Fielding," *Eighteenth-Century Fiction* 2 (1990): 93–112 attributes the resurgence of physiognomy to the influence of empiricism and "fresh developments in aesthetics" (97).

39. Martha Cowling, *The Artist as Anthropologist* (Cambridge: Cambridge University Press, 1989), 80.

40. Emma Spary, "Political, Natural and Bodily Economies," in *Cultures of Natural History*, ed. N. Jardine et al. (Cambridge: Cambridge University Press, 1996), 178–96, at 191.

41. Cowling, *Artist as Anthropologist*, 19. England published the largest number of editions in Europe.

42. Hagner, "Enlightened Monsters," 200–6 for the way that Camper and Samuel Thomas Soemmerring, a close friend of Blumenbach's, adapted some physiognomical principles into early comparative anatomy.

43. Schiebinger, *Nature's Body*, 156–57.

44. Elizabeth Inchbald, *A Simple Story*, ed. J. M. S. Tompkins (1791; Oxford: Oxford University Press, 1988), 8–9.

45. John Moore, *Zeluco: Various Views of Human Nature Taken from Life and Manners, Foreign and Domestic*, in *The Works of John Moore, M.D.*, ed. Robert Anderson. 7 vols. (1786; Edinburgh: Stirling & Slade, 1820), 5:80.

46. This is the central claim about sentimental heroes in Barbara Benedict, "Reading Faces: Physiognomy and Epistemology in Late Eighteenth-Century Sentimental Novels," *Studies in Philology* 92 (1995): 311–28.

47. Frances Burney, *Cecilia* (1782; New York: Oxford University Press, 1999), 6. Mary Hays, *The Victim of Prejudice*, ed. Eleanor Ty (1799; Peterborough, Ontario: Broadview Press, 1998), 5. Countenances had, of course, been betraying important information throughout the century, just not directly reflecting the character's intellectual faculty. In Eliza Haywood's *The History of Miss Betsy Thoughtless* (London, 1751), Betsy's delight in her newly augmented fortune registers in her body, especially the eyes: "The innate pleasure of her mind, on this occasion, diffused itself through all her form, and gave a double lustre to her eyes and air," 2:236. See Harriet Guest, "A Double Lustre: Femininity and Sociable Commerce, 1730–1760," *Eighteenth-Century Studies* 23 (1990): 479–501, at 494 and 481.

48. Richard Dyer, *White* (New York: Routledge, 1997), 12: "white people in white culture are given the illusion of their own infinite variety."

49. Dyer, *White*, 14 follows this methodology.

FURTHER READING

Brownley, Martine Watson. "Johnson's *Lives of the English Poets* and Earlier Traditions of the Character Sketch in England." In *Johnson and His Age*, ed. James Engell. *Harvard English Studies* 12 (1984): 29–53.

Ketcham, Michael. "The Arts of Gesture: The *Spectator* and Its Relationship to Physiognomy, Painting, and the Theater." *Modern Language Quarterly* 42 (1981): 137–52.

Porter, Roy. "Making Faces: Physiognomy and Fashion in Eighteenth-Century England." *Etudes Anglaises* 38 (1985): 385–96.

Stafford, Barbara Maria. *Body Criticism: Imaging the Unseen in Enlightenment Art and Medicine.* Cambridge, MA: MIT Press, 1991.

Stepan, Nancy. *The Idea of Race in Science: Great Britain, 1800–1960*. London: Macmillan Press, 1982.

20

Home Economics: Representations of Poverty in Eighteenth-Century Fiction

Ruth Perry

Landlords did not annul leases and raise rents two or three times over in the space of a year; nor did they drive land sales up to record levels. It took a parliamentary enclosure to do all this.

> J. M. Neeson, "An Eighteenth-Century Peasantry" (1993)

Nothing can be more shocking to just feelings, than the contrast presented to the eye in a rich high-dressed, and well-inhabited country; where useless acres of what are styled *pleasure grounds*, are an insult to the wretched hut of the hard-working peasant, who for want of land cannot support his family; where against the wall of a park, or the gate of a sumptuous palace, stands the houseless and shivering pauper. . . .

> Edward Mangin, *George the Third* (1807)

Sentimentality can exist . . . only in societies in which money and power are unequally distributed, only where persons of potential moral "worth" suffer "unjustly," that is without regard to their (potential) intrinsic merit.

> Robert Markley, "Sentimentality as Performance:
> Shaftesbury, Sterne, and the Theatrics of Virtue" (1987)

The eighteenth-century novel has been criticized for being concerned only with the lives of the wealthy or at least the middle class – a genre with very little to say about the problems of the laboring class and the poor. Most heroes and heroines of low or indeterminate class origin – such as Tobias Smollett's Humphry Clinker, Henry Fielding's Tom Jones, Frances Burney's Evelina, or Clara Reeve's Edmund – are discovered to have been well-born after all and can claim a healthy inheritance in the end. Jemima, in Mary Wollstonecraft's *The Wrongs of Woman: or, Maria* (1798), may be the unique example of a poor character with a developed subject position in eighteenth-century fiction. A strong and intelligent survivor, her heart hardened by her experiences, Jemima describes the brutal lives of the urban poor.

But poverty is represented in eighteenth-century fiction, this essay argues, with a very direct relation to actual historical conditions at the time. When the novels of the day are consulted, shelter is the basic need most persistently jeopardized by economic hardship. In other words, the troubles of the poor are often summarily represented in the difficulty of paying rent and the threat of being turned out into the world with nowhere to go. Whether in the city or the country, whether cottagers or impoverished persons of the "better sort," whether living alone or caring for young children or old parents, the sufferers in these novels, the worthy poor who give the benevolent heroes and heroines an opportunity of displaying their generosity and sensibility, are more often than not victims of a money economy in which they cannot earn enough to pay for shelter.

From the pages of fiction come the cries of characters evicted from their lodgings, their paltry furnishings auctioned off to pay their debt to the landlord, their children starved – a word that meant both cold and hungry – starved for insufficient food or shelter. Felicia, in Mary Collyer's *Felicia to Charlotte* (1744), visits an "honest but indigent family," a family ruined by the variable market and an unforgiving landlord. Their farm is gloomily silent as she approaches it and inside, "despair and sorrow were painted in the strongest colours" on every face. The farmer explains that he is obliged to "sell the plentiful crop that covered his lands to a vast disadvantage to satisfy his landlord's demands." Despite his know-how and hard work, he was about "to be turn'd out of all his possessions, and perhaps, to glean the fields he himself had sown; and all this for want of a small sum which his landlord had now a particular occasion for" (1:149–50). As the reader knows from the first moment of this dismal account, the benevolent Felicia pays the "small sum" that the landlord requires, obtaining for herself "a delight more exquisite than I have ever experienced" (1:150).

Possessions Seized for Rent

The coin that circulates through many different hands in Charles Johnstone's *Chrysal; or the Adventures of a Guinea* (1760) witnesses the charitable rescue of another distressed family unable to pay their rent. A gentleman on a half-pay pension from the army describes how he was ruined by the expenses incurred by an illness that carried off his three eldest sons and left him unconscious for over a month. When his wife was forced to pawn some of their better "effects" for food, an extremity that "never escapes the watchful eyes of people who keep lodging-houses," the landlady "seized upon the rest, and then turned us out ...." Their benefactor enjoys "the sublimest pleasure the human heart is capable of, in considering how he had relieved, and should further relieve, the sufferings of objects so worthy of relief."[1]

The History of Betty Barnes (1753) opens with the pregnant mother of the heroine-to-be forced from her cottage by parish officers when they learn that her husband has been bound for a sailor, saying "that as she had not been there a year, she had no right to become chargeable." Having nowhere else to go, she walks thirty miles to the village where her husband was born, commences labor prematurely, and is forced to give birth in a barn.[2] An exaggerated example of homelessness and displacement – having her child in a manger – the unhappy woman dies a few pages later, leaving her infant daughter unprotected in the world. In *Lydia; or, Filial Piety* (1755) by John Shebbeare, the landlady's little boy, having heard Lydia's old mother say that she is starving, asks if he can give them his breakfast. This determines his mother to insist upon her rent "before Affairs went worse" (2:267). When they are unable to pay, the landlady becomes angry at Lydia for not being willing to prostitute herself to make the rent. "A fine Virtue indeed, that will not let People pay their Debts!" she says (2: 269). She is particularly eager to get them off her premises before Lydia's old mother dies from hunger, for then she will have the expense of burying her. To add to the pathos, her little son pleads with his mother not to force Lydia and her mother out of the house. The very pattern of heartlessness, this landlady is willing to ruin virtue and expose age for thirty pieces of silver: thirty shillings for three months' lodgings.

Mrs. Bilson, in Sarah Fielding's *The History of the Countess of Dellwyn* (1759), returning from trying to console her husband in debtors' prison, finds her "house in the Possession of Bailiffs; for her Landlord, hearing of the total Ruin of the Family, thought proper to secure himself from Loss, by distraining" (2:169). In Tobias Smollett's *Sir Launcelot Greaves* (1760), a farmer's widow who tries to keep her farm going after her husband dies, runs into arrears with her landlord, who "seized for his rent," after which she is arrested.[3] In Henry Brooke's *The Fool of Quality* (1765–70), an industrious tenant farmer is ruined by a cruel and greedy knight who "borrows" the farmer's rent money a few days before rent day without returning it. The Lincoln attorney who has recently replaced the old agent, Mr. Kindly, seizes the farm and all their goods, "even the beds whereon my wife and children lay, with all their wearing apparel, save what they had on their backs" (293). Needless to say, the benevolent heroes of this novel restore the farm and belongings to the farmer and take suitable revenge on his persecutor.

In the same novel, a family by the name of Clement, cut off by relatives without a cent, are hounded for their rent. At nine in the morning on the day the quarter's rent is due, the landlady enters, followed by constables and appraisers who seize everything in sight, including clothes, for rent, costs, and damages.

> Thus we were turned out, almost naked, to the mercy of the elements. O, how deeply degraded below the birds of the air, the beasts of the forest, or even the worms of the sod, who rightfully claim sustenance from the earth whereof they were bred, and have some hole apart whereto they may creep for shelter! The world, indeed, lay all before us . . . . All hopeless, weak and faint, we took our way, we knew not whither; without home whereto we might travel, or point whereto we might steer. (118)

Like a sad parody of Adam and Eve expelled from the garden, the little family walks on aimlessly until they can go no further. With less right to the space of existence than the lowest worm, their having to pay for shelter – the problem of alienated housing – is depicted as unnatural. Homelessness in a money economy, where property is privately owned and fiercely guarded, is an extreme condition, a deprivation without even the improvised solutions of animals.

The point of multiplying examples of rent distress and eviction is to establish the terms of this literary formula as well as its frequency in late eighteenth-century fiction. The scene appears in the novels of both men and women writers. Robert Bage included several sentimental episodes of eviction in his novels as well. In *Mount Henneth* (1782), one character describes a crowd of people around a small farmhouse where an auction is taking place, and at one of the windows "stood a woman with a young child in her arms, looking mournfully at a new-made grave" (170).[4] He learns that the woman's husband has just died, leaving debts behind. She tells her interlocutor that she has neither "father nor mother, nor brother nor sister... to shelter my little ones," that they are selling up her goods, including the two cows that gave her children milk, and even the bed her late husband died in, which had been a great comfort to her. The benevolent onlookers stop the sale, replace the bed, and offer the bereaved woman employment as a dairymaid in their new utopian community. Bage's later novel, *Man As He Is* (1792), recounts the charitable deeds of the extraordinary Cornelia Colerain, which include paying the rent for a widow with small children and repossessing the milking cow that had been seized by the bailiff. A painting by Miss Colerain depicts another of her charities. It shows "a man suspending his rural labour, and mute with astonishment and fear. Two men had just entered his cottage, sent by the steward of the manor, to take an equivalent for rent. His wife was brought to bed of twins the evening before. They did not take her bed from under her – no – they did not; whatever else they could find they did take" (2:76). That this scene of misery is presented as a painting turns it into an emblem, puts a frame around it within the novel and fixes it, making of it an exemplary story. We have seen its elements before: the woman weakened by childbirth, the family's possessions seized, the emphasis on a bed, the inexorable demand for rent exaggerated by the mediation of a hired executor who does not know the tenants – the steward in this case – and the helplessness of the victims. Miss Colerain's act of charity is converted into a work of art, her impulse first enacted in deed and then memorialized in paint, an act of recording calling attention to itself.

The rent victim in Mary Robinson's *Walsingham; or, The Pupil of Nature* (1797) is not a laborer but an author, hard at work on a tragedy "of no inferior order" when his landlord comes in to demand his rent and to seize his belongings. "Yet give me another week," expostulates the poor man of letters. "Consider my infants; if you drive them into the street they must perish!" "The Lord will protect *them*," replies his heartless persecutor, with a line like a stage villain, "But *I* must be *paid!*" (2:317). As if on cue the landlord's wife enters, crying "Turn the vagabonds out: the bailiff is below; seize their goods...." The bailiff then rushes in, adding his uproar to the scene, only to be upstaged by the sudden appearance of the hero.

Mary Wollstonecraft's *Mary* (1788) includes a rent crisis near the beginning of the novel. The heroine, who has "learned the luxury of doing good" by relieving the necessities of poor fishermen's families, finds her best friend Ann in an hysteric fit because the landlord has sent his agent to Ann's mother for the overdue rent and threatens to seize their goods and turn them out if they do not pay. Wollstonecraft's later novel, *The Wrongs of Woman: or, Maria*, is filled with women who have no place to go, literally as well as metaphorically. Jemima tells of being repeatedly reduced to the wretchedness of no habitation. Boarded with a mercenary wet nurse in a damp cellar as an infant, thrown out of the house as a young woman by her mistress after being raped by her master, she bids her audience to imagine what it was like: "Behold me then in the street, utterly destitute! Whither could I creep for shelter?"[5]

The story of the heroine, Maria, while not driven by poverty, is also about homelessness. Relentlessly hounded from her lodgings by a hated husband, she is drugged and incarcerated by him in that mockery of a safe place, a madhouse. Maria also tells the story of Peggy, whose husband was pressed for a sailor and died abroad. Peggy took in washing to support herself and her children until a recruiting party made off with a large washing hung out to dry. She was forced to pay for it all with the money she had laid by for rent, and the landlord's agent then seized her poor possessions, including her clothes and even her bed. Maria gives her a mattress and a blanket from her own bed, pleads with the landlord to wait for the rent, and collects money from her friends for poor Peggy.

Space and Status

Even when it was not a matter of destitution, impoverishment was always marked by a cramping of space. More than food and clothes, the dimensions of one's habitation – one's living space – were coming to signify one's class and social position. Sidney Bidulph, in Frances Sheridan's novel of 1761, reports to her friend about the conditions of her reduced circumstances:

> "I am now fixed in a very humble habitation. Shall I own it to you, my Cecilia? I was shocked at the change. A room two pair of stairs high, with a closet, and a small indifferent parlour, compose the whole of my apartment."[6]

Although she keeps a servant, can pay for her bread, and has all her clothes from better days, her reduced circumstances are brought home to her, so to speak, by her close quarters. She is shocked by the size and number of her rooms, shocked by how little space she has to call her own.

In *The Vicar of Wakefield* (1766), as the eponymous hero descends the economic ladder, his growing misfortune is registered by a series of smaller and smaller habitations. When a merchant with whom he has invested his fortune absconds, the vicar is forced to move from his large, elegant house, to a one-story cottage "covered with thatch, which gave it an air of great snugness," on one of those idealized but, in fact, almost nonexistent twenty-acre farms which he hopes will support his family.[7] One room serves as both kitchen and parlor – "which" he says philosophically "only made it the warmer." There are three bedrooms in addition; the walls are whitewashed and his daughters' pictures adorn them. Though it is small for his family of six children, the cottage feels cheerfully adequate to the reader.[8] "Better a dinner of herbs where love is, then a stalled ox and hatred therewith."

But the kindly vicar is doomed to sink even further. Later in the novel, when returning home with Olivia, just as he knocks on the door, his "heart dilated with unutterable happiness," the cottage bursts into flames, and the whole family is forced to take shelter in a wretched little outbuilding with "mouldering walls, and humid floor," and to sleep on straw (131). Finally, when the villain has his steward "drive for the rent," and the vicar is arrested and thrown in jail, our hero lodges his wife and daughters cheaply nearby while his sons sleep in a bed in his cell. No longer with a dwelling of his own, this is the nadir of his fortunes before he recovers spectacularly, as befits the hero of an eighteenth-century novel. Goldsmith charts his hero's prosperity in terms of the size and number of rooms he and his family inhabit: his economic and social standing is calibrated in terms of space. Fittingly, we owe this book to Goldsmith's rent debt: when he was arrested by his landlady in 1762 for failure to pay his rent, his friend Samuel Johnson asked if he had any manuscripts to sell, whereupon Goldsmith dug out this novel, which Johnson sold to John Newbery for £60.

As the price of land and the cost of housing rose in the second half of the century (a subject to which I will return), the size and style of one's dwelling place became an increasingly sensitive index of difference in rank. Wealthy citizens, imitating aristocratic privilege, began to think it necessary to their consequence to own an imposing country house with extensive grounds. General Tilney showing off the rooms, the gardens, and the prospects of Northanger Abbey, or Mr. Bingley renting Netherfield in anticipation of purchasing a family estate, are two examples of the phenomenon from the novels of Jane Austen. It came to be the style to display one's wealth by reserving enormous spaces – both indoor and outdoor spaces – for pleasure and show rather than for productive activity.

In Sarah Scott's *The History of Sir George Ellison* (1766), the cousin of the eponymous hero remonstrates with him because the disposition of rooms of his house does not live up to the dignity of his fortune. "Where is the figure in which you ought to appear?" asks Sir William, accusing George Ellison of trying to do away with all social distinction. He should have created a noble suite of rooms on the first two floors of his house, Sir William tells him, because nothing "bears more the air of grandeur than being led through three or four fine rooms, handsomely furnished, before we are brought into that where the master of the house waits to receive us" (2:79). But George Ellison has thrown away that advantage by allowing less conspicuous uses for his magnificent rooms: one is a school-room; another is his housekeeper's; a third has a bed in it for the curate "whenever a rainy evening overtakes him" at his house, and the tutor is given a room that "would not disgrace a palace; tutors are not generally treated with so much ceremony," adds Sir William disapprovingly.

As more and more property was appropriated to exclusive private use, the social meaning attached to the allocation of space became clearer. Parliamentary Acts of enclosure in this period privatized almost a fifth of England's land, and in terms of total agricultural land more than a fourth, monopolizing for single ownership land that previously had been used in common and extinguishing the legal obligations of the property-owner to his neighborhood.[9] The concept of land as privatized property that could exclude all others' use – land that could be bought and sold like any other commodity along with all the living creatures on it – land that could be stripped, dredged, drained, filled, or flooded – came to be more widely accepted, reinforced by stricter laws and penalties that were enforced by stewards and game-keepers on private estates or by bailiffs and justices of the peace in towns. A new appreciation for the visual beauty of nature as well as a scientific interest in the investigation of natural phenomena further complicated the motives for land acquisi-tion and added another dimension to the social meaning of space.

On large estates new parks were created – hundreds of acres set aside for leisure, exercise, or ostentation, acres that in another time would have been farmed or lying fallow. "There was a rough equivalence between income – and even more between social standing – and the size of the park" on these estates, according to John Habakkuk.[10] Even when they did not have acreage to spare, property-owners began to name their places "something-or-other park" for the sake of the connotation. In addition to the well-documented increase in the size of the estates of the great owners,[11] a higher proportion of gentry held land at the end of the eighteenth century than at the beginning, and a lower proportion of small landowning farmers. Artists commissioned to paint family portraits posed their subjects in front of their stately homes and impressive grounds to document and celebrate their property and their lineage – and to establish the connection visually. As Beth Fowkes Tobin has pointed out, these painters tended to obscure the inequities of property ownership as the politics of land ownership became more problematic due to enclosure and the rising price of land.[12]

Goldsmith described this new ethos of land acquisition with broad strokes in "The Deserted Village" (1770).

> The man of wealth and pride,
> Takes up a space that many poor supplied;
> Space for his lake, his park's extended bounds,
> Space for his horses, equipages, and hounds;
> The robe that wraps his limbs in silken sloth,
> Has robbed the neighbouring fields of half their growth;
> His seat, where solitary sports are seen,
> Indignant spurns the cottage from the green....

Silkworms denude the countryside – the fields are robbed for a robe – cottages are removed from the green for the sake of a single huntsman's game, and the space of many poor families is cleared to make way for an artificial lake, stables, and a pleasure park. The rich man's interests take up the space of the poetic lines as they dominate the environs of sweet Auburn. Space is the issue – who will control the space.

It became fashionable to create living paintings on one's property in order to demonstrate one's mastery of it, rearranging woods and streams and meadows to look like painted landscapes in accordance with formal rules of pictorial composition. "All gardening is landscape-painting," said Alexander Pope.[13] In such "improvements," landowners were advised by a new set of professional men, the inventors of landscape architecture, men such as William Kent, Lancelot "Capability" Brown, and Humphry Repton, who taught landowners to lay out their houses and grounds to provide unimpeded vistas for the eye and to enhance the sense of physical as well as social distance from neighboring human habitation. Cottages and even whole villages were torn down if they interfered with the view, and sometimes relocated to a less visible location.[14] The agricultural enterprises, the working farms, were kept out of sight, for as Repton dictated: "the beauty of the pleasure-ground, and the profit of a farm, are incompatible."[15] Thus, new rules of exterior decoration reflected at the level of aesthetics the dissevering of class interests and contact based on shared uses of the land at the same time as they reinforced the ideology of absolute and exclusive ownership.

In Jane Austen's *Mansfield Park* (1814), Henry Crawford urges Edmund Bertram to reorient his house and redesign his grounds in Thornton Lacey to give it the look of "the residence of a man of education, taste, modern manners, good connections" and make it seem the house of "the great landowner of the parish" (chapter 24). Edmund dismisses Henry's suggestions, demonstrating his own fine moral nature in contrast to Crawford's shallow and fashionable if clever instincts. Austen casts her lot with the lower gentry here, with the contented second sons rather than the social climbers, making admirable Edmund's resistance to aristocrat-aping "improvements." It was Austen's genius to be able to use such contemporary issues to deepen her characterizations.[16]

I have been arguing that the amount of space at one's command was increasingly a measure of social standing. Yet the minimum space required for the comfort of the body is an oblong the size of a grave or a mattress. The repeated detail of beds and mattresses in these stories of people down on their luck and turned out of shelter, even their beds distrained for the rent, emphasizes in another way the fetishizing of space in this era of grand buildings and ornamental gardens. The detail of the bed or mattress sold out from under these poor victims seems to argue not merely that beds were a valuable item of furniture, or that beds are synecdoches for the home, but that the new economic dispensation did not leave a symbolic amount of space for the basic needs of the poor. Although estates were getting larger and larger, with pleasure gardens and artificial lakes added to working fields and pastures, less and less provision was made to support the bodies of the laboring poor. If in life, cottages were torn down to provide unimpeded vistas for the eye or to clear the way politically for enclosure of common lands, in fiction, the beds and mattresses of the poor were taken away emblematically, leaving them nowhere to lie down.

The significance of rent is that it requires a person to pay for his or her right to exist in the world. One is not simply born to a place: it must be paid for. To own one's habitation is to live in existential security, whereas to pay repeatedly for the place in which one lives is to be reminded continuously of vulnerability to displacement. Moreover, these fictional scenes of rent distress and eviction emphasize the inexorable nature of rent, its inflexibility, the remorselessness of a cash demand with a time limit. Whether or not rent was a problem for the English laborer in the eighteenth century – and I will come back to that historical question – these fictional confrontations about rent express very graphically the impersonal nature of the new system, the heartlessness of capitalism, above and beyond the cultural reassessment of the value of space.

Sentimentality and Class

And what of the repeated emphasis in these scenes on the "refined pleasures" of benevolence, the exquisite sensations of fellow feeling that so often accompany the acts of charity that relieve those distressed for rent in these novels? In episode after episode, the "luxury of doing good" (Henry Mackenzie's *Man of the World* and Wollstonecraft's *Mary*), the "exquisite delight of doing good" (Collyer's *Felicia to Charlotte*), the "great feasts of [the] soul" (Scott's *Sir George Ellison*), the "sweet gift of doing good to other people" (Brooke's *Fool of Quality*), "the sublimest pleasure the human heart is capable of" (Johnstone's *Chrysal*) – those exalted feelings that accompany benevolence – are embellished in the same breath as the descriptions of the privations of the poor. Why are these "sublime pleasures" an essential part of the formula of scenes of rent distress?

To begin with, the sentimental relish for "the luxury of doing good" keeps the focus of the reader on the subjectivity of the giver, the psychological state of the generous hero or heroine. It is his or her inner life that is supposed to interest the reader, not that of the recently relieved poor. *Their* hyperbolic gratitude is taken for granted; gratitude is assumed to be a less interesting emotion than the exquisite feelings of the giver, compounded of pity, generosity, vicarious suffering and relief, moral superiority, and religious piety. The reader, positioned to identify with the generous hero rather than the distressed victim, experiences this psychological mixture at a second remove. The humane pleasure which the heroic protagonist has purchased with the coin of relief and which the author has described is thus repeated in the reading audience. That these scenes are centered on rent and the basic need for shelter intensifies the exchange, giving the generous protagonist – and hence the reader – more for his money so to speak, primal experience to be had for the reading.

These sentimental scenes imagine the amelioration of one of the most painful immediate effects of capitalism at this time – the displacement of large numbers of people from the villages and counties they thought of as home. For the impersonal relations of the market, these fictions substitute heartfelt benevolence and Christian charity. Both giver and receiver voluntarily re-enroll in a kind of temporary feudalism; the kindness of the generous protagonist compensates for the unraveling of the reciprocal obligations of feudal paternalism, which might have directed the lord of the manor, with his personal knowledge of the families on his land, to forgive their rent payments in their seasons of hardship.

Such scenes of sentimental benevolence in fiction were, according to Robert Markley, one of the means by which middle-class characters and readers imitated the acts and attitudes of paternalistic aristocrats in relation to their laboring poor. In blurring distinctions among the middle and professional classes, the gentry, and the aristocracy, the sentimental generosity celebrated in these scenes of rent distress emphasizes the difference between haves and have-nots, and reinforces the inequality that privilege requires. These acts of disinterested kindness never seek to revise, subvert, or realign existing hierarchies. Rather they prove and perpetuate the very social and economic disparity that they presumably deplore. That is why these scenes have no narrative life – they never go anywhere – but are offered up as static "repetitive tableaux" (in Markley's phrase); they never lead to investigations of the systems that victimize the poor, but look backwards, nostalgically, to a time when the poor were the responsibility of their aristocratic masters.[17] Intense feeling for individual suffering is substituted for anger at systemic injustice.

Nor is it irrelevant that the sufferers in these stories are women alone or with children or whole families – never single men. Whether or not this was a transparent reflection of the economic realities of the day – and it is true that women's wages were on average about half of men's wages, and that two-thirds of the men in debtors' prison had wives[18] – the benevolence formula called for the rehabilitation of whole families. Whole families or at least women capable of reproducing their class – indeed, women often in the very act of reproducing their class – were the sentimental objects of philanthropy in these novels. Families or women with children were the social units capable of reproducing the social relations that underlay the satisfaction of the charitable moment and made it possible to repeat – perhaps in another generation – the possibilities for need, for generosity, and for gratitude.

Such sentimental benevolence as I have been describing was a late eighteenth-century phenomenon, and did not extend very far into the nineteenth century. Lady Louisa Stuart – the granddaughter of Lady Mary Wortley Montagu – writing to Sir Walter Scott, commented on how outdated sentimental fiction had become by 1827. She described an evening in which the company had urged her to read aloud Mackenzie's *Man of Feeling* (1771), their interest revived by Walter Scott's preface to it in Ballantyne's novel library. "The effect," she said, "altogether failed. Nobody cried, and at some of the passages, the touches that I used to think so exquisite – oh dear! they laughed. Yet I remember so well its first publication," she continues, "my mother and sisters crying over it, dwelling upon it with rapture! And when I read it, as I was a girl of fourteen not yet versed in sentiment, I had a secret dread I should not cry enough to gain the credit of proper sensibility. This circumstance has led me to reflect on the alterations of taste produced by time."[19] These politically naïve stories, with their helpless victims and their rescuing heroes and heroines, lost credibility in the period of angrier, violent, more polarized class confrontations of the Luddite and Captain Swing movements. Sentimental fiction featuring scenes of deserving need and responsive benevolence thus occupies a liminal position in the evolution of English class consciousness. The easy harmonizing of class conflict – which is a mark of sentimental fiction – and the belief that the moral authority of good people could counteract the worst effects of an unforgiving cash economy, disappeared along with the hero whose life's work was to rectify injustice.

An Historical Look at Rent

And what was the historical reality that stood behind these formulaic scenes of eviction and restitution? What can historians tell us about the rent distress depicted in this common scenario and the actual levels of rent in the period in relation to wages? Did laboring people in this period have difficulty paying their rent? What is the relation between life and literature, in short, with regard to this matter of rent?

The truth is that historians have not taken rent seriously until very recently. It is a curious fact of historiography that it was not until the early 1980s that rent was even included in price indexes for this period, as though it were a negligible expense. As early as 1974, M. W. Flinn called attention to the need to include rent in assessments of the cost of living for the eighteenth century,[20] but it was not until Peter Lindert and Jeffrey Williamson published their research on English eighteenth-century standards of living in 1983 that rent was for the first time included along with the costs of food and consumer goods for the period.[21] This oversight is less remarkable than it would at first appear when one considers how minor an expense rent had in fact been until late in the seventeeth century.

In the early Middle Ages, tenants held their land "at the will of the lord and according to the custom of the manor" in return for agricultural labor and produce. As tenants' land was passed on from generation to generation, and copied into the manorial records, copyhold tenancies were granted for a lifetime or a period of several lifetimes. In time, the labor requirements were commuted to minimal cash payments. Tenants were expected to pay large initial fees when they came into a holding, or when the lease was renewed, but as late as the seventeeth century, annual rent payments were very small, and had little or no relation to the value of the land being farmed. Copyhold leases often included customary rights such as a widow's free bench or the right to use the resources of adjoining common lands for fuel, grazing, and building and repairing cottages, fences, and outbuildings. Landowners could and did raise the entry fees for obtaining leases, but once a family had a lease, their annual payments for the use of land remained low. What was negotiated in obtaining a lease was the length of time that the land would be held, how tenancies were inherited or sold, and what forms of service or payment, fixed or negotiable, the tenant owed the landowner. In Maria Edgeworth's *Castle Rackrent* (1800), the loyal Thady Quirk remembers back to a time when the lady of the manor demanded her duty fowls, turkeys, and geese, weed ashes, duty labor, heriots, and sealing money whenever a new lease was drawn up.[22] But whatever the variation, the structure of the transaction was the same well into the seventeeth century: a large threshold payment for coming into the lease of a farm, long leases – whether one or several lifetimes – and annual payments that were largely symbolic and in no way tied to the potential profits from the land.[23]

Even at that, tenants could not always afford even these nominal rents, but lived on the credit of their landlords. The shortage of cash in the economy, and declining profits from agricultural goods in the later seventeenth century, meant that some tenants went for years paying little or no rent at all.[24] Landlords had to wait for their arrears or reduce rents – which they were loath to do because that lowered the face value of their estates – or evict tenants who defaulted. But good tenants were in short supply in the late seventeenth century, farmers who kept their buildings in repair and did not plough the heart out of the land. Even through the reign of Queen Anne there were more farms available in many regions of England than there were good tenants to work them, so landlords put up with considerable negotiation about rents and taxes, arrears, repairs and tillage, in order to keep their land occupied.[25]

The eighteenth century saw an end to these unbusinesslike practices. As agricultural prices began to rise and land became more valuable, landlords began to convert lifetime copyhold leases to shorter leases for a term of years or even to tenancies at will, and to charge higher annual rents. Shorter leases permitted more frequent reviews of rent levels and gave the landlord more control over farming practices that protected his land, such as rotating crops, planting clover and ryegrass, or fertilizing. It also allowed renegotiating the respective liability of tenant or landlord for a variety of taxes and for making repairs.

Changes in the use and meaning of the word "rackrent" chart this evolution. In the late sixteenth century "rackrent" meant raising the rent above a fair or normal level, on the analogy of putting a person on the rack, straining his joints to torture him. It mean stretching, forcing, or putting on extreme, oppressive pressure and causing pain. By the later eighteenth century, although these violent connotations lingered, the word simply meant a rent "that represented the full annual value of the holding,"[26] rents in line with the value of the produce raised on that parcel of land. To rent at rack meant to charge a price that the corn or wool or meat raised on that land would bring. To rent at half rack meant to charge half a year's value.

As the value of land came to be judged on the basis of the profits to be made from it, rather than on the basis of the people it had to support, rent did go up, everywhere. The rise in population and the demand for food, in addition to the cultural capital associated with owning land, created a steady rise in the value of land. Rent – whether of agricultural land or urban housing – rose throughout the eighteenth century. All this was theorized by Ricardo, who lived a generation after Adam Smith and could see the significance of rent in the economic balance among landlords, farmers, and workers. Whereas Adam Smith believed that the costs of production (including wages), the price of agricultural products (food), the farmers' profits, and the land-lord's rent were all interdependent and that the market would maintain a natural balance among these constitutive parts, Ricardo believed that whoever owned the land, which was a limited resource, would come in for an ever-increasing share of the national income. Since rent levels were tied to the price of food, he reasoned, and since the rising population drove up demand and hence the price of food, the landlord would benefit from rising prices. The landlord's interest was thus opposed to that of every other class, according to Ricardo. As the population grew, and with it the demand for food, the amount of land on which it could be grown was fixed and so prices would rise – and the proportion of national wealth accruing to landlords would steadily accumulate.[27]

By the end of the century, the power of the landlord over his holdings was more unilateral than it had ever been, replacing the complex forms of proprietorship by peasants in earlier times. Landlords consolidated their holdings, terminating or buying out leases of smallholders and renting to a few large farmers who could afford to capitalize their operations, use modern agricultural techniques for higher yields, and pay higher rent. Larger farmers were believed to be more reliable in their rent payments and less of a nuisance for rent collection. By the end of the century great estate owners and landholding gentry owned more of England and small landowners and yeomen freeholders owned far less.[28]

Studies of individual estate records throughout England show a substantial rise in the rents in the eighteenth century. The estate accounts of Sir Mark Stuart Pleydell in Berkshire show substantial increases between 1738 and 1753.[29] The rents of the Duke of Kingston rose 48% from 1750 to 1790 and the rents of Lord Monson rose 44.5% in the same period. The rents on property owned by Guy's Hospital in London rose 30% between 1762 and 1793. The annual value of the Northcote estate in Devonshire increased eightfold in the second half of the eighteenth century.[30] In Essex, the lack of suitable housing doubled cottage rents from the 1770s into the nineteenth century.[31] A 1997 study of agricultural rent throughout England shows that nominal rents rose twelvefold between 1690 and 1870 and that real rents rose sixfold in that period. Rents rose from "a little over two shillings per acre in the 1690s to a little under eight shillings by the 1770s."[32] Arthur Young estimated that rents more than doubled between 1780 and 1805.[33]

John Clare's account of his rent in Northamptonshire from the late eighteenth century into the early nineteenth century tells the story of rising rents and contracting space as eloquently as any:

> I keep on in the same house that we always occupied and have never felt a desire to have a better – tho it has grown into a great inconvenience since my father first occupied it 35 years ago. It was as roomy and comfortable as any of our neighbours and we had it for 40 shillings rent [a year] while an old apple tree in the garden generally made the rent. The garden was large for a poor man and my father managed to dig it night and morning before and after the hours of labour and lost no time. He then did well – but

the young farmer that succeeded our old Landlord raised the rent and the next year made
four tenements of the house, leaving us a corner of one room on a floor for 3 Guineas a year
[63 shillings] and a little slip of the garden which was divided into 4 parts. But as my
father had been an old tenant, he gave him the choice of his share, and he retained our old
apple tree. Though the ground was good for nothing, yet the tree still befriended us and
made shift to make up the greater part of our rent till every misfortune as it were came
upon him to crush him at once. For as soon as he was disabled from work the old tree
failed to bear fruit and left us unable to get up the rent and when Drury found me out
[discovered him as a poet] we owed for 2 years and was going to leave it the next year. My
father was going to a parish house and I was at Casterton in service where I intended to
remain. And when I met with my unexpected prosperity I never felt a more satisfied
happiness than being able to keep on [in] the old house and to put up with all its
inconveniences. And when I was married, the next door occupier happened to leave his
tenement so I took it and remained on. I have often been urged and advised to leave it and
get a more roomy and better looking house by visitors who gave me no better encouragement than their words and whom I did not expect would be of any service to me in case
their advice happened to lead me into greater inconveniences in the end. So I took no
notice of them and lived on in the same house and in the same way as I had always done
following my old occupations and keeping my old neighbours as friends without being
troubled or disappointed with climbing ambitions . . . .[34]

Clare's account animates the bare historical facts about rising rent and subdivided
space. His affection for his old house, his father's diligent gardening, the apple tree
that befriended them – these details illuminate the changing relation of the subsist-
ence classes to the land. The diminishing largesse of Nature, first the bounty of the
garden together with the apple tree, and then just the tree, and finally nothing at all,
parallels the constriction of space within doors under the management of the new
young landlord. Being confined to a quarter of a house and not being able to afford
even that much but being forced to leave, with no recourse but to send his father to
the poorhouse, when unexpected prosperity enables him to stay and rent another
quarter – this is the stuff of sentimental fiction, complete with a benevolent hero,
Drury, the bookseller who "discovered" Clare and brought his poems to the attention
of the man who published Keats and Shelley. But behind these details that Clare
weaves with homespun elegance is an economic narrative: more money in circulation,
higher costs together with a lower standard of living, the influx of unexpected wealth
from the urban culture, class mobility, new acquaintances interested in his fame and
influence and not in his welfare.

Clare was writing at the hinge of a changing way of life. The next generation would
not remember how much space there had been for a person, both indoors and outside,
nor how hospitable the natural world could feel. By the next generation, three guineas
for two rooms would seem like a bargain, and no one would expect assistance from the
land itself.

I have been arguing that formulaic scenes of rent distress in eighteenth-century
fiction were recording an historically real problem in England at the time, even if

their fairytale solutions were imagined. Why, then, has it taken historians so long to investigate this issue? Although the cost of food and clothing in eighteenth-century England has been assessed and scrutinized since the nineteenth century, it was not – as I have said – until 1983 that the first study was published that included rent in a cost-of-living calculation. There still is no systematic study of housing in eighteenth-century England; the first book on agricultural rent came out only in 1997.

Our modern word for what I have been calling rent distress is, of course, homelessness. It is a new name for an old problem. Public attention to homelessness in the United States in the post World War II period can be dated to the early 1980s. The de-institutionalization of the mentally ill began in the late 1970s and the cutbacks in public programs with the election of Reagan in 1980 increased homelessness. But the depression of 1982 put more people on the street than ever before and social commentators began to notice the problem of homelessness. The Lindert–Williamson article came out the next year, the first article to take rent into account in assessing eighteenth-century standards of living. We study what our world sensitizes us to. The clues to the eighteenth-century phenomenon have been there all along: the novels, the memoirs, the rent rolls. But only when the circumstances of our world make it relevant do we register the meanings of another era. The history of rent is finally being studied by historians – in part because housing and homelessness have become such a problem in our own day. One can read in the plots and tropes of the eighteenth-century novel the literary responses of that era to the way market forces were radically changing the way people lived – including the economics of the home.

See also: chapter 8, MEMORY AND MOBILITY; chapter 21, WHATEVER HAPPENED TO THE GORDON RIOTS?; chapter 22, THE NOVEL BODY POLITIC.

NOTES

1. Charles Johnstone, *Chrysal or the Adventures of a Guinea*, ed. and intro. E. A. Baker (1760; London: Routledge, 1906), 469.

2. Anonymous, *The History of Betty Barnes* (London, 1753), I: 2. Joyce Grossman attributes this novel to Mary Collyer in her "Social Protest and the Mid-Century Novel: Mary Collyer's *The History of Betty Barnes*," *Eighteenth-Century Women* 1 (2000): 165–84. M. Sturge Gretton, in *Three Centuries in North Oxford* (Oxford: Oxford University Press, 1902), 130–31, reports a coroner's inquest of 1773 investigating the case of a woman and her child of 18 months found starved to death on the road near Shipton under Wychwood, Oxfordshire. It was concluded that "they had been turned out of one parish by the overseers so that the expenses of burial might fall on another." Cited in M. K. Ashby, *The Changing English Village* (Kineton, UK: Roundwood Press, 1974), 235.

3. Tobias Smollett, *The Adventures of Sir Launcelot Greaves* (London: 1760–2), chapter 11.

4. Page numbers cited are from the edition in vol. 9 of Sir Walter Scott's Ballantyne library, published in London and Edinburgh in 1824.

5. *The Works of Mary Wollstonecraft*, ed. Janet Todd and Marilyn Butler. 7 vols. (London: Pickering and Chatto; New York: New York University Press, 1989), 1:111.

6. Frances Sheridan, *Memoirs of Miss Sidney Bidulph*, ed. Patricia Köster and Jean Coates Cleary (Oxford: Oxford University Press, 1995), 341.

7. See chapter 7, "Farming Fiction," from my *Novel Relations: The Transformation of Kinship in England 1748–1818*, (Cambridge: Cambridge University Press, 2004), which argues that to be gentlemen farmer on their idealized smallholding was a favorite wish-fulfillment fantasy of this culture while such small farms were, in fact, disappearing.

8. The page numbers cited for this text are from the Oxford World Classics paperback, ed. and with intro. and notes by Arthur Friedman (Oxford: Oxford University Press, 1974), 23–24.

9. See J. M. Neeson, "An Eighteenth-Century Peasantry," in *Protest and Survival: Essays for E. P. Thompson*, ed. John Rule and Robert Malcolmson (London: Merlin Press, 1993), 58.

10. John Habakkuk, *Marriage, Debt, and the Estates System: English Landownership 1650–1950* (Oxford: Clarendon Press, 1994), 61.

11. Mark Overton, *Agricultural Revolution in England: The Transformation of the Agrarian Economy 1500–1850* (Cambridge: Cambridge University Press, 1996), 168.

12. Beth Fowkes Tobin, "The Moral and Political Economy of Property in Estate Portraiture," unpublished paper presented at ASECS in Seattle, WA (March 25–9, 1992), 12. As Tobin lists them, these visual strategies include harmonizing the interests of laborers and masters, and naturalizing the owner's relation to his land.

13. Joseph Spence, *Anecdotes*, ed. James M. Osborn (Oxford: Clarendon Press, 1966), 1: 252; quoted in Carole Fabricant, "Binding and Dressing Nature's Loose Tresses: The Ideology of Augustan Landscape Design," *Studies in Eighteenth-Century Culture*, 8 (1979): 112.

14. John Habakkuk makes this point: "In the hands of Capability Brown and Repton the landscaping of parks became a major art form.... Nor is it a coincidence that the style of gardening associated with Capability Brown was designed to establish vistas and create an illusion of distance." Habakkuk, *Marriage, Debt, and the Estates System*, 60–61. General Tilney, in Jane Austen's *Northanger Abbey*, showing off his power and wealth to a nearly oblivious Catherine Morland, promises that he will leave a cottage visible from the drawing-room windows at Woodston because she thinks it "a sweet little cottage." General Tilney peremptorily says to his son, "Henry, remember that Robinson is spoken to about it. The cottage remains." Vol. 2, chapter 11.

15. From *Observations on the Theory and Practice of Landscape Gardening*, quoted in Howard Newby, *Country Life: A Social History of Rural England* (London: Weidenfeld and Nicolson, 1987), 19.

16. For an extended investigation of Austen's attitudes towards land management and "improvements," see Alistair M. Duckworth's *The Improvement of the Estate: A Study of Jane Austen's Novels* (1971; Baltimore, MD: Johns Hopkins University Press, 1994).

17. Robert Markley, "Sentimentality as Performance: Shaftesbury, Sterne, and the Theatrics of Virtue," in *The New Eighteenth Century*, ed. Felicity Nussbaum and Laura Brown (New York: Methuen, 1987), 210–30.

18. Paul H. Haagen, "Eighteenth-Century English Society and the Debt Law," in *Social Control and the State: Historical and Comparative Essays* (Oxford: Basil Blackwell, 1985), 222–46, esp. 224.

19. *Lady Louisa Stuart: Selections from her Manuscripts*, ed. James Home (New York: Harper & Brothers, 1899), 234–35.

20. M. W. Flinn, "Trends in Real Wages, 1750–1850," *Economic History Review*, 2nd ser., 27 (1974): 395–411.

21. Peter H. Lindert and Jeffrey G. Williamson, "English Workers' Living Standards During the Industrial Revolution: A New Look," *Economic History Review*, 2nd ser., 36 (1983): 1–25. The cost-of-living index presented by these authors included rent for the first time. In their words, "While the classic indices all omitted this important part of the cost-of-living, ours includes a rent series based on a few dozen cottages in Trentham, Staffordshire (just outside Stoke-on-Trent). While the data base is narrow, it does apply to a housing stock of almost unchanging quality" (9). Earlier studies that did not include rent were R. S. Tucker, "Real Wages

of Artisans in London, 1729–1935," *Journal of the American Statistical Association* 31 (1936): 73–84; E. W. Gilboy, "The Cost of Living and Real Wages in Eighteenth-Century England," *Review of Economic Statistics* 18 (1936): 134–43, reprinted in A. J. Taylor, ed., *The Standard of Living in Britain in the Industrial Revolution* (London: Methuen, 1975), 1–20; E. H. Phelps Brown and S. V. Hopkins, "Seven Centuries of the Price of Consumables Compared with Builders' Wage Rates," reprinted in E. M. Carus-Wilson, ed., *Essays in Economic History*, vol. 2 (London: E. Arnold, 1962), 179–96 and *A Perspective of Wages and Prices* (London: Methuen, 1981). For a recent contribution on this subject, see Charles H. Feinstein, "Pessimism Perpetuated: Real Wages and The Standard of Living in Britain during and after the Industrial Revolution," *Journal of Economic History* 58 (1998): 625–58. Feinstein argues that the cost of living in the late eighteenth century was even higher than that calculated by Lindert and Williamson and that real wages were even more depressed.

22. Edgeworth's note in the glossary explains weed ashes: "By ancient usage in Ireland, all the weeds on a farm belonged to the farmer's wife, or to the wife of the squire who holds the ground in his own hands. The great demand for alkaline salts in bleaching rendered these ashes no inconsiderable perquisite." Maria Edgeworth, *Castle Rackrent and Ennui*, ed. Marilyn Butler (Harmondsworth, UK: Penguin, 1992), 131. When a tenant died, his or her executors or heirs were expected to hand over the best animal on the farm to the landlord, a customary duty called a heriot.

23. Mark Overton, *Agricultural Revolution in England: The Transformation of the Agrarian Economy 1500–1850* (Cambridge: Cambridge University Press, 1996), 30–35.

24. The study of agricultural rent in England prepared by Turner, Beckett, and Afton includes a graph of the rent arrears as a proportion of agreed rents, from 1690 to 1910. It shows the periods of hardship during which tenants could not pay their rents.

M. E. Turner, J. V. Beckett, and B. Afton, *Agricultural Rent in England* (Cambridge: Cambridge Unversity Press, 1997), 180.

25. Craig Muldrew, *The Economy of Obligation: The Culture of Credit and Social Relations in Early Modern England* (Basingstoke: Macmillan, 1998), 107; D. R. Hainsworth, *Stewards, Lords and People: The Estate Steward and his World in Later Stuart England* (Cambridge: Cambridge University Press, 1992), 52–72. The account in 1700 and 1701 of the Shropshire parish of Myddle by Richard Gough corroborates in this local history the accounts given by Muldrew and Hainsworth of widespread, often uncollectable, rent debt. See *The History of Myddle*, ed. David Hey (Harmondsworth, UK: Penguin, 1981), 59, 92, 131, 179, 228.

26. Mark Overton, *Agricultural Revolution in England*, 151.

27. Whereas Adam Smith had believed that rents, wages, and profits would be shared equally by landlords, laborers, and farmers, Ricardo theorized rent as the surplus after laborers' wages and farmers' capital outlay and profit margin were deducted: all supererogatory profit – such as came, for example, from the greater productivity of better agricultural techniques or extremely fertile land – was the landlord's due. *The Works and Correspondence of David Ricardo*, ed. Piero Sraffa (Cambridge: Cambridge University Press, 1962), I, "On the Principles of Political Economy and Taxation," xxxv–xxxvi, 67, 327–37; Adam Smith, *An Inquiry into the Nature and Causes of the Wealth of Nations*, ed. James E. Thorold Rogers. 2 vols. (Oxford: Clarendon Press, 1880), 1:151–53.

28. Mark Overton, *Agricultural Revolution in England*, 168.

29. Janie Cottis, "A Country Gentleman and his Estates, ca. 1720–68: Sir Mark Stuart Pleydell, Bart., of Coleshill, Berkshire," in *Town and Countryside: The English Landowner in the National Economy, 1660–1860*, ed. C. W. Chalklin and J. R. Wordie (London: Unwin Hyman, 1989), 37.

30. P. J. Keeley, "A Devon Family and their Estates: the Northcotes of Upton Pyne,

1660–1851," in *Town and Countryside*, ed. C. W. Chalklin and J. R. Wordie, 177.

31. T. L. Richardson, "Agricultural Labourers' Wages and the Cost of Living in Essex, 1790–1840: A Contribution to the Standard of Living Debate," in *Land, Labour, and Agriculture, 1700–1920: Essays for Gordon Mingay*, ed. B. A. Holderness and Michael Turner (London: Hambledon Press, 1991), 69–90, esp. 74–75.

32. M. E. Turner, J. V. Beckett, and B. Afton, *Agricultural Rent in England*, 228. See also the review of this book by Gregory Clark in the *Journal of Economic History* 58 (1998): 206.

33. Arthur Young, "An Enquiry into the Progressive Value of Money in England," *Annals of Agriculture* 46, no. 270 (London, 1812): 104, quoted in B. E. S. Trueman, "The Purchase and Management of Guy's Hospital Estate," in *Town and Countryside*, ed. C. W. Chalkin and J. R. Wordie, 73.

34. John Clare, *John Clare By Himself*, ed. Eric Robinson and David Powell (Ashington, UK: Carcanet Press, 1996), 116–17. Thanks to Anne Janowitz who gave me her copy of this book! I have silently corrected the spelling and some of the punctuation in the passage quoted.

FURTHER READING

Frank, Judith. *Common Ground: Eighteenth-Century Satiric Fiction and the Poor*. Stanford, CA: Stanford University Press, 1997.

Hammond, Barbara, and J. L. Hammond. *The Village Labourer 1760–1832*. London: Longmans, Green, 1911.

Hill, Bridget. *Women, Work, and Sexual Politics in Eighteenth-Century England*. New York: Basil Blackwell, 1989.

Linebaugh, Peter. *The London Hanged: Crime and Civil Society in the Eighteenth Century*. Cambridge: Cambridge University Press, 1992.

Neeson, J. M. *Commoners: Common Right, Enclosure and Social Change in England, 1700–1820*. Cambridge: Cambridge University Press, 1993.

Snell, K. D. M. *Annals of the Labouring Poor: Social Change and Agrarian England 1660–1900*. Cambridge: Cambridge University Press, 1985.

21

Whatever Happened to the Gordon Riots?

Carol Houlihan Flynn

Arguably the most traumatizing event that Londoners had experienced since the Great Fire of 1666, the 1780 Gordon Riots shut London down for almost a week. Deliberate and successful attacks on places of authority demonstrated to the nation the power of the people in the street determined to tear down institutional structures supporting, among other things, the unpopular and unsuccessful war in America. The Gordon Riots became, briefly, London's prophetic preview of the storming of the Bastille, a storm contained, but one that shook the confidence of a nation. The financial and psychological costs of the riots are still incalculable and were, more importantly, quickly repressed, almost disappearing from cultural consciousness. Just this unspoken and unrepresentable nature of the riots interests me. What does the critical absence of the Gordon Riots mean to our understanding of the eighteenth-century novel's ability to absorb, to recognize, even to transform civic violence?[1]

Certainly Charles Dickens saw opportunity in the riots, a fictional space that he argued had not been filled for sixty years. In his preface to *Barnaby Rudge* (1841), Dickens writes that "No account of the Gordon Riots having been to my knowledge introduced into any work of Fiction, and the subject presenting very extraordinary and remarkable features, I was led to project this Tale."[2] He overlooks George Walker's *The Vagabond: A Novel* (1799),[3] Maria Edgeworth's *Harrington* (1817),[4] and Thomas Gaspey's *The Mystery; or Forty Years Ago. A Novel* (1820)[5] in this sweeping statement, but essentially his point is valid. His is certainly the first novel to make the Gordon Riots its centerpiece.

Why did it take sixty-one years for the meaning of the Gordon Riots to become the focus of a major novel? We know, thinking of the Holocaust, the Japanese Internment, the Partition of India that created Pakistan, the Chinese Revolution, and the Vietnam War, that novels representing traumatic materials can take decades to emerge. There is no doubt that the Gordon Riots traumatized the nation, creating a state of repression reinforced by the government and by the self-censorship endured by a people alarmed by their own capacity for destruction. Much of the fictional and critical suppression can be directly connected to the French Revolution and its terrifying and stimulating implications, but even before the Revolution, the riots themselves produced an internalized terror connected to a notion of an Englishness under siege. To tell the story of the Gordon Riots in the eighteenth-century novel, one needed either to be satirically driven, like Walker, to burlesque and reduce the riots' significance, or radically brave enough to represent the riots' social meaning. Radically brave becomes almost oxymoronic in the 1790s and the early part of the nineteenth century.

Dickens's claim to originality in turning the riots into fiction begs the question: who was there at the time able to make them present in a "work of Fiction"? William Blake becomes the most attractive literary witness, present at the destruction of Newgate, literally in the front row, and he is said to have created *Albion Rose* to commemorate that moment of liberation. Blake may be the only eighteenth-century poet who seemed seriously inspired by the riots, expressing his fascination with fire, passion, and destruction in cryptic and mythological works that turn London into a Marriage of Heaven and Hell, a site of Innocence and Experience. William Cowper wrote a minor poem lamenting the loss of Judge Mansfield's library, Samuel Johnson, Ignatius Sancho, Hester Thrale, several Burneys, Edward Gibbon, and Horace Walpole less formally discussed the event in memoirs and letters, Edmund Burke and Thomas Paine more formally in *Reflections on the French Revolution* (1790) and *The Rights of Man* (1791–2). But there was no poet like John Dryden writing *Absalom and Achitophel* (1681) to head off the Monmouth Rebellion, no novelist like Henry Fielding incorporating the confusing and threatening days of the Jacobite Rebellion of 1745 into the very plot of *Tom Jones* (1749). In a letter to Johnson, James Boswell asked why he had not written more fully on his own experience "during the barbarous anarchy. A description of it by DR. JOHNSON would be a great painting; you might write another *London*."[6] But Johnson never did, and the riots disappeared from the cultural consciousness. They soared, they burned, they scorched, and vanished. While dazed Londoners strolled through the "ruins" of the city, expressing their panic and dismay, after the first frantic weeks most witnesses stopped talking, at least in print.

In the 1790s, Jacobin writers like Mary Wollstonecraft, William Godwin, Robert Bage, and Thomas Holcroft avoid the riots in their fiction. Their literary productions might make some of the same attacks on unequal distributions of power that drove some of the rioters out into the streets, but their novels resist rather than act. The Jacobins imagine spaces where they are put under surveillance in oppressive circumstances, not spaces in which they can fight back. Talking back, Godwin's Caleb Williams and Wollstonecraft's Maria discover, leads to frustrating and self-destructive encounters with people in power. Only Godwin, in *St Leon* (1799),[7] represents a riot, hardly a revolutionary event, but a frightening demonstration of the atavistic power of the mob, the sort of beasts that attacked Joseph Priestley's laboratory in Birmingham.

Perhaps, in 1841, Dickens could finally incorporate the riots in his fiction because they represented his own conservative fears about the power of the people taking to the streets. By deploying the Gordon Riots in his novel, he was able to assume a potent imperial detachment to defuse the radical implications of Gordon and his "Malcontents." Over the years, the riots became a background that he could incite and manage, always in juxtaposition to his vision of "old England," home of the beloved Maypole and the Golden Key. The riots could be represented when they ceased to matter.

To better understand the ways that the Gordon Riots resisted representation in the eighteenth century, we first need to question interpretations of Lord George Gordon's "mad" character and descriptions of the riots themselves. Gordon's slippery position makes him almost ideally unreadable. Mad, he becomes the unspeakable icon of resistance whose cause can be dismissed as nonsensical. Thus the riots will continue to be seen as unknowable and unspeakable. Secondly, Blake's position, both physical and metaphorical, in the debate over the meaning of the riots, is crucial to examine. Was he an unwilling bystander or an animated rioter freeing the prisoners at Newgate? Was he a political radical or a rabid dissenter crying "No Popery"? His presence in the heart of the riots points to the ambiguous meanings we can make of the event. Finally, we will look at novelistic treatments of the riots before *Barnaby Rudge* – Walker's *Vagabond*, Edgeworth's *Harrington*, and Gaspey's *Mystery*, as well as Godwin's representation of the Birmingham Riots of 1791 in *St Leon*, to consider how difficult it was for novelists to record "mob" violence, particularly when they were sensitive to the political issues that erupted in the streets. But before we try to know Lord George Gordon, we need briefly to look at what took place in London between 2 and 8 June 1780.

A Short Version of the Gordon Riots

Lord George Gordon, President of the Protestant Association, Member of Parliament, met 60,000 persons in St. George's Field, Southwark on June 2, 1780, to present a petition so heavy with names – 44,000 of them – that it could barely be carried to the Houses of Parliament. The petition called for the repeal of the Catholic Relief Bill of 1778 that eliminated some of the restrictions against education and property rights that Catholics in England and Wales had endured since the reign of William III. The bill also made it possible for Catholics to be recruited to fight for the British against the American colonies. Gordon, speaking "No Popery," also argued that the bill was designed to trick Catholics into waging war against a noble people. After hours of speeches, the crowd of 60,000 left in four divisions, one of them come down from Scotland, to march towards Westminster, jamming all the roads along their way. They waited outside while Gordon presented the petition to the House of Commons. When the petition did not go forward, after hours of hostile actions taken by Gordon's supporters against Members of Parliament trying to enter the House, the House of Commons adjourned and the crowd was sent home. Some began, instead, almost a week of rioting that essentially closed down London.

Plate 16.   An engraving of the army encampment in St. James Park during the Gordon Riots.

At first the objects of attack were primarily Catholic: the private chapel of the Sardinian ambassador, the Bavarian embassy's chapel, Roman mass houses and the houses of known Catholics. Then the rioters turned towards places of power, pulling down houses of the mighty: George Saville, who had introduced the Catholic Relief Bill, Justice Hyde, and Lord Mansfield, as well as the police office of Sir John Fielding. They also attacked and destroyed many important jails—Newgate, Clerkenwell, the Fleet, the King's Bench, and the Borough Clink. After making an unsuccessful attack on the Bank of England, the rioters, most sensationally, burnt down Langdale's Distillery in Holborn. As a consequence, 800 to 1,000 people (almost all of them rioters) died, 450 were arrested, 160 were brought to trial, and 25 (most of them young boys) were hanged. Gordon was tried for treason, but acquitted. The financial cost of the riots is estimated to have been in the hundreds of thousands of pounds.

Knowing Lord George Gordon

If you are going to write a novel about the Gordon Riots, you need to have a character in the novel called Lord George Gordon. Gordon, known as "Lord George Gordon" as he was the younger son of the third Duke of Gordon, is the perfect dramatic figure, and Dickens is the first novelist to deliver him as a lank-haired, fiery-eyed loony who speaks mysteriously and tenderly of his plans to wreak havoc. In creating such a cracked protagonist, Dickens carries on the tradition of the mad, bad Gordon, one that can be found from the start in Thomas Holcroft's "Narrative." It is remarkable to see Holcroft, later known as a radical Jacobin novelist and member of the Society for Constitutional Information (1792), writing in 1780, under the name of William Vincent, *A Plain and Succinct Narrative of the Gordon Riots*, a conservative description of the events that he deemed deeply threatening to the nation. The mob he describes is "desperate" and "infernal," made up of "insatiable and innumerable fiends," driven by "their own inordinate appetites."[8]

The "succinct narrative" gives us two different pictures of Gordon. Holcroft first describes Gordon, "head of the Malcontents in Scotland," those who rioted over the Relief Bill in 1779, as a man of "eccentric and desultory character" who is often a subject of ridicule in the Houses of Parliament. He "has the manners and air of a modern Puritan; his figure is tall and meagre, his hair strait and his dress plain." The bad hair will in later descriptions of Gordon become not only straight, but also red (signifying his Scottish identity) and lank (in other words, not powdered). Gordon puzzles Holcroft by not acting the way a lord should, looking and acting in fact like a Commonwealth man. He addresses the public in a private and accessible manner, sounding like William Prynne, the earless William Prynne, rather than the "noble Commoner he should be."[9] Holcroft's first description is contradicted by two pages of "Anecdotes" at the end of the narrative, probably added on to fill out the pamphlet, most likely written by the Whig journalist, James Perry. The "Anecdotes" praise Gordon for his independence and integrity and for resisting bribes that Lord North offered him to give up his seat in Parliament. "He possesses a great fund of wit and humour, and his temper is withal so sweetened with the quality of good nature, that he has never been known to sacrifice it at the shrine of satire." More significantly, "should [he] fall a sacrifice to his zeal on the present occasion, no man ever received a greater share of public respect, than his Lordship will no doubt meet with."[10] Uneasiness about "his zeal" characterizes both narratives in spite of their radical difference in tone. Zeal, in both a religious and political context, is one of the reasons, I think, that Gordon is not usually regarded as a serious revolutionary and is seldom allotted revolutionary space. Or perhaps it is more accurate to say that when he does take up revolutionary space, he appears ridiculous and awkward in it.[11]

Gordon's culturally constructed awkwardness – the hair, the zeal, the sincerity – is not appreciated by his biographers. J. Paul de Castro, after laboring to understand the riots and the "lunatic apostle"[12] who inspired them, ends with stern scorn for his subject. On the question of "mental derangement" he "cannot suppress the feeling that had he been well cuffed when indulging his unbridled insolence ... much of his vanity would have disappeared." Castro finally decides that Gordon's early death can only be regarded as "a national blessing."[13] Christopher Hibbert finds Gordon erratic and impressionable from the start, enlisting eighteenth-century sources to support his derisive contempt for the man, beginning *King Mob* with Walpole's judgment that "they were, and are, all mad," and following with his own opinion that "the exasperated judgment was not entirely groundless."[14] Such contemporary sources disparaging Gordon's "mental derangement" are not difficult to find. Ignatius Sancho writes "a very imperfect sketch of the maddest people – that the maddest times were ever plagued with," driven by "the insanity of Ld G. G. and the worse than Negro barbarity of the populace."[15] Even Thomas Paine, while he defends the rioters for acting against the essential "want of happiness," finds "the person called Lord G—G—'a madman.'"[16]

It may seem too easy to attack in the first decade of the twenty-first century Castro writing in the 1920s and Hibbert in the 1950s, but their anecdotes and biases recycled from hostile eighteenth-century sources color most treatments of Gordon even now, crucially affecting the way that Gordon is still interpreted as the mad leader of the riots. The reasons that Hibbert finds Gordon mad are complicated by his contempt for social attitudes that could be seen to be revolutionary fifty years later. As the *Succinct Narrative* recognized, Gordon's temper was full of sweetness. What might seem so mad, or should I say maddening, about the earnest Gordon to his contemporaries and to his early twentieth-century historians is his inability to deploy satire in an age that depended upon at least some sort of satirical bottom. Earnestly holding his salon in his prison cell at Newgate with Jews and radicals, and preserving his foreskin to prove his conversion to Judaism, Gordon addresses cultural problems in a literal way that makes him too transparent to be ignored.[17]

Hibbert reports wryly that from his first day as a midshipman in the navy, horrified by a shipment of biscuits crawling with weevils, Gordon complained to the captain and aligned himself with his men, "as a sort of seaman's lawyer, odd, talkative, erratic, and somehow lovable." Hibbert does not make this zany love for the underdog sea-dog sound like a good thing. Found to be "a damned nuisance" by the Admiralty Board, Gordon, "the emotional and meddlesome young officer" fails to be promoted. "In the West Indies his impressionable, emotional nature was appalled by the "bloody treatment of the Negroes." His admiration for Americans, "kind and simple . . . honest and free, already aware of their great destiny" was "wholehearted and uncritical," while "his entry into politics was marked by that ebullient, erratic enthusiasm which had characterized his life in the Navy."[18]

In spite of Hibbert's irritation with Gordon's egalitarian ways, his "King Mob" emerges as a public figure who begins to sound a lot like Lord Edward Fitzgerald, revolutionary icon of the United Irish and its failed Revolution of 1798.[19] Both men, younger noble sons from colonized kingdoms, were raised by generous, impulsive, aristocratic women who encouraged their sons to learn their native heritage, and to embrace Irish and Scottish ways. Yet Gordon, learning Gaelic, playing the pipes, wearing tartan trews while attending to the problems of a downtrodden and angry people, is characterized as zany, excessive, and ridiculous, while Fitzgerald, learning Gaelic, dancing reels, and wandering through the countryside to drink poteen and sympathize with the locals, remains to this day one of the great romantic Irish revolutionary figures. Perhaps Fitzgerald, marginalized by his location in Ireland, did not threaten England in the way that Gordon could and did. For Scotland is not across the water from England, but north, over Hadrian's broken-down wall.

When Gordon crossed the border, head of the 12,000 "Malcontent" Scots come down to meet him in St. George's Field, he represented a political as well as a religious threat to the Union itself. He, and more importantly his followers, the sailors and apprentices, the dissenters, the soldiers on half-pay, the Afro-Britons, many ex-slaves pressed into naval service – proto-revolutionaries – would continue to forge alliances through the eighties and nineties. The rioters knew how to build things and how to tear them down, they were the managers and workers of plantations and building sites in London, and they would make the middling and upper classes in London realize their power to create and destroy.[20] Perhaps that is why Fitzgerald, mutilated hero, incapable of bringing off the great rising of 1798,[21] that famous failed Irish revolutionary moment, could be safely canonized, while Gordon, acquitted of high treason, but still waging war against the institutions of the empire until his death, would become a cracked, slightly comic figure scorned for his mad and unreliable ways. His compromised, almost illegible reputation teaches us the dangers of dissent, the real cost of speaking against empire.

Reading the Riots

Iain McCalman, John Nicholson, and Peter Linebaugh, following George Rudé, politicize the Gordon Riots as events signifying more than religious zealotry and drunken, frenzied mob action. McCalman explores Gordon's ties to Scottish nationalism, and through that to "a wider revolutionary ferment" that would involve "libertarian Dissenters, radicals, and pro-American revolutionaries."[22] When McCalman imagines Gordon, zealous Protestant, anti-Catholic, converted to Judaism as a Jacobin Revolutionary, he comes closest to solving the problem that Gordon's zealotry inevitably causes. Zeal seems more plausible when it works for political rights than when it drives religious persecution. Colin Haydon complicates this analysis when he brings anti-Catholicism back into the riots. To avoid Gordon's religious zealotry, he argues, is to turn the riots into a politically liberating event, when actually they were conservative in nature, "true blue," preserving the Protestant status quo and enshrining an "English" moral economy that depended upon anti-Catholic restrictions. For Haydon, the British Anglicans and Dissenters, sailors and merchants, constructed their idea of nation around an ideological center that was deeply anti-Catholic.[23] Thus radical Dissenters like Blake could insist upon both religious liberty *and* "No Popery." The rioters could have had conflicting motives as they dismantled prisons to free "true blue" rioters or to bring down the state or both, working always with deliberate precision to reach their goals.

Rudé was the first historian to insist upon the rioters' workmanlike precision. Revising the notion of the drunken, lurching, fiendish rhythms of a crowd out of control, a fireball cleansing the streets of London, collapsing finally upon itself, Rudé makes the case for a "[deep] social purpose" behind the riots, "a groping desire to settle accounts with the rich, if only for a day," and for the "calculated and careful behavior of the rioters."[24] Contemporary witnesses sometimes noticed this behavior, but their observations were frequently overwhelmed by qualifications, and often forgotten. One thing was certain to the eighteenth-century observer. The rioters made deliberate attacks on places of power. Three particular targets demonstrate the control that the "mob" attempted to deploy against spaces of commerce and empire: Justice Hyde's house, Newgate, and Langdale's Distillery. The power that they exerted often seemed to be misread and misunderstood. In fact, the misreading itself could have made early fictional representation of the riots impossible.

Hyde's Poor House

Most accounts of the firing of Hyde's house simply report that it was pulled down and destroyed, "in less than an hour."[25] After reading the Riot Act earlier in the day, Hyde was receiving his deserts. Susan Burney sends her sister Frances in Bath a fulsome account that incorporates the conflicted interpretations of what was happening down the street. From her window, she watches rioters throw furniture out into the street and make six fires "at distances sufficiently great to admit of one or 2 People passing between them...the wretches...seemed like so many *Infernals*."

> One thing was remarkable, & convinced me that this mob was secretly directed by some body above themselves – they brot. an *Engine* with [*sic*] them, & while they pull'd Hyde's House to pieces & threw every thing they found in it into the flames, they order'd the Engine to [*sic*] play on the neighbouring Houses, to prevent their catching fire – a precaution wch. it seems has been taken in every place that these lawless Rioters have thot. fit to attack.

Neighbors entreat the crowd "not to keep up so strong a fire before their Houses," for "fear they would soon catch & that the whole street wd. be in a blaze nothwithstanding the Engine."

> Upon this the Ringleaders gave the word, & away they all ran past our windows to the bottom of Leicester Fields, with lighted firebrands in their hands, like so many furies – Each carried something from the fires in our street that nothing might escape – they made in Leciester Fields one Great Bonefire of them – the Women like the Furies were more active & busy in the business than the Men – & they continued pulling down Pannels, Doors, & c till between two & 3 in the Morning to keep up the Bonefire & totally destroy the Poor House."[26]

Burney's report certainly contradicts Holcroft's. It didn't take less than an hour to bring down Hyde's house; it took about seven, and it also took the passive cooperation of the militia. Burney describes the mob "shouting & clapping the soldiers as they pass'd on their back & one of these even joined in the huzza." Her account also contradicts herself, and in that way is a classic treatment of the riots. Infernal Furies always bring along their own fire engine and take burning movables out of the street to save the neighboring houses. Just this disjuncture between diabolic frenzy and cool calculation complicates the early descriptions of the mob in action.

Burney sees their infernal smoky visages, but she also supplies us with an interesting view of a certain charity that the "lawless Rioters" always demonstrate, as well as a class-driven judgment that such calculated courtesy could only come from "somebody above themselves." As the Archbishop of York judged, "no mob acted without a number of well-dressed men to direct them." One man "dug out of the ruins of a house . . . had ruffles, with a large diamond at his shirt breast."[27] Horace Walpole disagreed. In his copy of *The Trial of Lord George Gordon* (1781), when he comes to the claim that the magnitude of the attacks "leave[s] no doubt that greater designs then at first appeared were opening to the public," he wrote in the margins that "yet not the smallest proof of any such design has been discovered."[28]

Theft was rare in the riots, even though Dickens puts golden treasures under the looters' beds, plunder that never seemed to materialize in the real riots.[29] Destruction and demolition of property was the end in view. Sancho reports that when the Sardinian ambassador "offered 500 guineas to the rabble to save a picture of our Saviour from the flames, and 1000 guineas not to destroy an exceedingly fine organ: the gentry told him, they would burn him if they could get at him and destroyed the picture and organ directly."[30] A new iconoclasm was being born, one that needed to be refuted by reports of plundering, drunken infernals.

Gin Lane

In the burning of Langdale's Distillery, the rioters prove themselves in anecdotal and journalistic reports to be drunken beasts that deserved their blazing deaths. Thomas Langdale, a Catholic, owned a large distillery in Holborn, where he had stockpiled gin to avoid impending duties. He had been offering bribes of drink and money all through the Riots to keep his distillery intact, knowing that if it were fired, it would go off like a bomb, and he even went so far after the fire to claim £2000 in bribes as part of his damages. Imagine a distillery full of people being bribed by drink not to burn it. The distillery was fired, possibly a fire engine was pumping gin onto the fire, and streams of poisonous unrectified gin spilled into the streets. The scene is then described several ways. Holcroft reports that the liquor running down the middle of the street "was taken up by pailfuls, and held to the mouths of the besotted multitude; many of whom killed themselves with drinking non-rectified spirits, and were burnt or buried in the ruins. Eight or nine of these miserable wretches have been found and dragged out."[31] Henry Angelo reports that the morning after the fire, he saw several dead bodies near the distillery, "the greater part . . . had made themselves drunk in the premises." This report is overwhelmed by the authority of Horace Walpole, whose description informs Dickens's account and can still be found in Peter Ackroyd's recent history of London where he writes, "Some hundreds are actually dead about the street with the spirits they plundered at the distiller's; the low women knelt and sucked them as they ran from the staved casks."[32] The victims of the Langdale fire become complicit in their own deaths, victims of their beastly appetite. Walpole's image of low women, sucking the burning breast of the street, recycles Hogarth's indictment in *Gin Lane* of at least one low woman, child tumbling from her unnatural breast. Hundreds did not die, maybe eight or nine, but Walpole's image sticks because the "public" wanted it to stick. It is as if the twenty-one people drowned in the Great Boston Molasses Flood of 1919 were blamed for having a sweet tooth.

Ignatius Sancho, who so often seems to protect himself from the implications of his cultural critique in ironic asides, makes a singular and startling observation about the Langdale disaster. "The greatest losses have fallen upon [Langdale] and Lord M[ans-field]; the former, alas! has lost his whole fortune; — the latter, the greatest and best collection of manuscript writings, with one of the finest libraries in the kingdom. — Shall we call it a judgement? — or what shall we call it? The thunder of their vengeance has fallen upon gin and law — the two most inflammatory things in the Christian world."[33] Sancho stands outside the culture that he both emulates and distrusts in making the connection between the oppression and volatility of the man-made law and the equally volatile oppression of spirits.

Sancho's contemporaries seemed less able to make such a leap. The implications of the riots paralyzed even those who would later become more revolutionary in their thinking. Holcroft, reporting the attack on the Bank, the burning of the prisons, the attack on Blackfriars Bridge, imagines that "had half the mischief the Mob had threatened been effected, nothing less than national bankruptcy and destruction could have ensued."[34] No doubt it seemed far better that the terrifying implications of the destructive power of the crowd disappear. Burke, traumatized by the attack upon his own house and upon his person, preserved the terror in his hysterical meditation upon the violation of the Queen's body, but others equally political fled from the riots. It was easier to imagine Gordon to be a maniac jailed for attacking Marie Antoinette and ridiculed for his romance with Judaism and for his attempt to keep convicts from being sent to Botany Bay.[35]

Blake Delivers Newgate

Blake stood at Newgate, in the front row of the mob, perhaps one of the few contemporary observers who understood what he was seeing: men and women, the sort that Susan Burney called "Infernals," acting in a civilized and disciplined manner. Contemporary reporters agree upon the discipline of a demolition team that Holcroft finds

> in this instance, as well as every other, amazing .... They broke open the doors of the different entrances, as easily as if they had all their lives been acquainted with the intricacies of the place, to let the confined escape .... Thus was the strongest and most

durable prison in England, that had been newly erected, and was not yet finished, and in the building of which the nation had expended immense sums demolished.

Newgate had been rebuilt between 1770 and 1778. The rioters dismantled a state-of-the-art prison two years old[36] with the precision emphasized in the "Exact Representation of the Burning, Plundering, and Destruction of Newgate." Linebaugh notes that the "Representation" demonstrates

> several interesting incidents in the behaviour of the mob: a blacksmith removing a thief's shackles; drinking from pots and bottles; the distribution of leaflets; the approach of the fire-engines; the insignia of cockade and flag; the victory trophies of chains and keys; the street fights against the constabulary where the arms are clubs, wheel spokes, pikes, axes and cutlasses. It is a scene, neither orderly nor horrific, in which a hundred countenances are watching and gestures both brutal and tender are performed.[37]

Blake at Newgate invites us to confront the divided, oppositional interpretations of the Gordon Riots. The facts seem simple and few, preserved by Alexander Gilchrist, an early Blake biographer:

> Blake long remembered an involuntary participation of his own . . . the artist happened to be walking . . . through Long Acre, past the quiet house of Blake's old Master, engraver Basire . . . and down Holborn, bound for Newgate. Suddenly, he encountered the advancing wave of triumphant Blackguardism, and was forced (for from such a great surging mob there is no disentanglement) to go along in the very front rank, and witness the storm and burning of the fortress-like prison, and release of its three hundred inmates. This was a peculiar experience for a spiritual poet, not without peril, had a drunken soldier chanced to have identified him during the after weeks of indiscriminate vengeance.[38]

This "involuntary" action of Blake can be read several ways, representing just what is at stake in understanding why he can be found so close to incendiary action. G. E. Bentley seems to attack the pro-revolutionary critics like David Erdman and Linebaugh when he cites Gilchrist as a "reliable, vastly influential, and irreplaceable" source.[39] The "spiritual poet" didn't mean to be at Newgate; he was forced to stand there in the front row by the blackguards in the mob.

Erdman, Linebaugh, and Stanley Gardner read Blake's presence at Newgate as a sign of his commitment to the people of London. Erdman, finding Gilchrist "patently incorrect" on much of Blake's politics, sees the delivery of Newgate as the inspiration for Blake's *Albion Rose*, designed or at least imagined in 1780. Erdman cites the inscription "WB INV 1780" engraved on *Albion Rose* "sometime in 1796 or later" as proof of this direct connection between the riots and Blake's own artistic production of "Albion r[ising] from where he labour'd at the Mill with Slaves," dancing "the dance of Eternal death." Linebaugh builds upon this analysis, comparing the delivery of Newgate "with the central action of Milton's Samson pulling down the house of oppression," alluding to "slavery, Africa, escape, death, destruction, revolution and freedom."[40] Gardner finds the aspirations and frustrations of the mob shaping Blake's revolutionary thinking. Besides, he argues, Blake, the quintessential Londoner, could have freed himself from the mob and darted down countless streets and paths out of harm's way.[41] He wanted instead to stay put in front of the incendiary mob bringing down Newgate.

I like the idea of Blake delivering Newgate to forge a new and shining Jerusalem, but Haydon's insistence on bringing anti-Catholicism back into the Riots complicates Blake's presence at the prison's demolition. Blake the Dissenter could have stood up front shouting "No Popery"; Blake the radical could have been dismantling the prison to free the poor little vagabonds driven into crime. The Gilchrist anecdote endorsed by Bentley seems designed to save Blake from his revolutionary self. Gilchrist, terrified of "Blackguardism," turns Blake into a tranquil and spiritual artist who, like his old engraving master, James Basire, belongs in "quiet houses," unmolested, protected from "drunken" soldiers who might identify him as part of the mob. Gardner argues that "the spiritual poet" would "applaud the troops who refused to fire . . . . It all must have spoken Blake's mind . . . "[42] [or] part of his mind, the part that constructed some of the most revolutionary arguments against the authority of the state ever written in the eighteenth and nineteenth centuries. But Blake also backed away from his more literal representations of poverty and civic indifference, those early portraits of chimney sweeps, little vagabonds, and dropped children. Constructing an Albion filled with mythological figures often hard to read, he made it difficult for the authorities in the nineties to pick him up for sedition, however incendiary his vision. His cryptic and compelling productions signal a retreat.

Rewriting the Riots

The Gordon Riots were forgotten on behalf of a greater national effort to imagine an impregnable Britain, not a place where its state-of-the-art Bastille, two years old, has been gutted, but a nation with no room for Gordon's commitment to revolutionary change. In the forgetting, the riots seem to decay, turning into sensational material necessarily emptied of meaning. There's a reason for this. The disciplinary nature of the novel makes it difficult for the novelist to break out of its restraints. Imagining the rioter, the novelist is forced either to identify with the mayhem and internalize its disorder, or self-protectively to contain the rioters and their leader. How does the novelist deal with the "character" Gordon? If he is appreciated for his sincerity (or rather patronized for it in an age of satire), he is also feared for his zeal. Riots impelled by that sincere zeal threaten public order, and even more, produce when unchecked, a narration that can get out of control. To enter into the Gordon Riots is to take a side. The choice is clear – attack them with an anti-Jacobin vigor or run with the vulgar.

This could be the reason that the Jacobins stay clear of the dilemma altogether. Under surveillance, they displace mob violence to save their own skins.

Mobs swirl in and out of novels by Fielding, Samuel Richardson, Burney, Monk Lewis, Tobias Smollett, and Maria Edgeworth, but for the most part, eighteenth-century novels do not present sustained treatment of the *mobile vulgus* free to roar through the streets. The literary mobs themselves seem to be ad hoc, lasting a page or two, 5,000 bodies congregating around Amelia and Billy Booth, or the handful surrounding Cecilia going mad in the street.[43] The Gordon Riots went on for days, involving strategies of deployment, meeting places, synchronized activity, providing almost too much material to contain.

Four novels written between 1799 and 1820 represent, in varying degrees, the difficulty that rioting mobs bring to the novel form. Two narratives written in 1799 bizarrely connect and controvert such materials. In *St Leon* Godwin translates the Birmingham Riots of 1791 to sixteenth-century Pisa, Italy. His riot takes up six pages of narrative. In eighteen pages, Walker burlesques Godwin's "political justice" in *The Vagabond*, imprisoning Godwin (Stupeo) in Newgate, where he is anachronistically freed by the Gordon rioters. Edgeworth's *Harrington* (1817) represents the Gordon Riots obliquely in fifteen pages that are more concerned with anti-Semitism than the political anger and anti-Catholicism that fueled the Gordon Riots. Gaspey's *The Mystery; or, Forty Years Ago* (1820) treats the Gordon Riots extensively in 105 pages in the first volume of a novel that goes on for another 800 pages careening through Africa, an exhaustive tour of empire at its most racist, most athletic, most vile. In all four novels, the Gordon Riots recede in significance as they deploy and contain political unrest.

The Vagabond and *St Leon*: The Failure of Idealism

Walker exults in the failures of Godwinian "political justice." Every time the words are mentioned in his anti-Jacobin novel, the safe drops out of the fifth-floor window to flatten the speaker. Walker's editor, W. M. Vanderhoeven, suggests that *The Vagabond* is an "anti-novel," sacrificing plot, character, and chronology in an "inter-textual tissue of political innuendo, malicious gossip and quotations from a wide range of (mainly) reformist writers."[44] (It is also wickedly funny.) Walker uses the Gordon Riots as well as the Birmingham Riots to pillory what he sees as dangerous practitioners of theoretical and material revolution. His Candide-like anti-hero, Frederick Fenton, disciple of Stupeo, believing in the "germ of justice, generosity, and magnanimity"[45] of the mob, leads the attack upon Newgate, where he discovers and frees his mentor imprisoned for his Godwinian attitudes toward private property. Walker kills Stupeo off in the Gordon Riots, only to resurrect him three years later to witness the attack on the house of Dr. Alogos (Priestley). Alogos, Stupeo, and Fenton emigrate to America, where, after they are fleeced by Gilbert Imlay's land scams, Stupeo is tied to the stake and set on fire by Indians. "Such was the termination of that enlightened great man, who...endeavoured to kindle the world...but expired himself in the midst of a blaze."[46] The Gordon Riots don't depress Walker, but rather stimulate his gleeful destruction of their meaning, providing local color and an urban stage for the mutual cruelty of rioters, "sons of nature," and philosophers.

In *St Leon*, Godwin, writing in the same year, uses the mob to act out his own disappointment. For Godwin, the riots signify the end of revolutionary idealism, leaving behind only smoke and ashes. Gary Kelly finds that *St Leon* suffers from "conflicting excesses" of plot and character, arguing that the novel's forced fusion of the philosophical and Gothic novel approaches a nihilistic distrust of reform. The protagonist is "in part a portrait of the apostate Burke, the renegade reformer, who dazzled by the pomp of chivalry, abandoned the cause of humanity for an empty show." Like Falkland, St. Leon strives for a chivalric mastery that ultimately turns him into a self-absorbed monster who gains the philosopher's stone at the expense of his family's being destroyed by his alchemic gifts. St. Leon, also modeled upon Joseph Priestley, is assaulted by the vulgar mob offended by intellectual and physical gifts that he tries to bestow upon an ungrateful populace.[47] "Villain, renegado, accursed of God!" I heard from every side. . . . Exterminate him! . . . It was the roaring of tigers, and the shrieks of cannibals. Sticks, stones, and every kind of missile weapon . . . fell in showers around me."

Alarmed, St. Leon seeks advice from a nobleman in Pisa who dismisses the mob as "a mere material machine . . . as light and variable as a feather." On his way home, however, he sees the mob embodied. Standing on "higher ground," he watches the mob "armed with clubs, and others with torches." "Clattering their arms, and pouring out vehement execrations," they vow to return to level his house the next day.[48]

Retelling the Birmingham Riots, and uncannily foreshadowing the mob's action represented in his daughter's novel, *Frankenstein* (1818), Godwin describes the final scene of destruction from a distance. He and the nobleman "saw flames ascend. We recognized the shouts of infernal joy with which they witnessed the catastrophe." His friend suddenly turns misanthropic, sounding like a character in Mary Shelley's novel of scientific hubris, lamenting that "No sooner did a man devote himself to the pursuit of discovery which, if ascertained, would prove the highest benefits to his species, than his whole species became armed against him." The next day, St. Leon learns that the mob had seized upon his "so simple-hearted, so noble" Hector, his "Negro servant," and "inflicted on him every species of mockery and of torture; they killed him joint by joint, and limb by limb. – The pen drops from my lifeless hand." St. Leon, writing his testament many years later, "lifeless," yet ironically immortal and perpetually on the move, remembers looking back, "the heart wounded spectator of the ruin," onto "the last cloud of mingling smoke and flame ascend[ing] from the ashes of my villa. The blaze sunk, its materials were nearly consumed, and it yielded an uncertain and fitful light."[49] As the "last man," he witnesses the fitful dying light of the Jacobin illuminati. The plans of Priestley, of Godwin, like the plans of Dr. Frankenstein, another infamous benefactor of mankind, are doomed to fail.

Godwin's treatment of the mob says much about his own pessimism, but also about the way that depictions of mob violence can turn conservative and containing. "You are Italians," St. Leon shouts out to the crowd before they start throwing their sticks and stones. "Show yourself worthy of the honour with which your name is heard in every corner of the habitable world!"[50] Instead they show their teeth and claws, cannibals and tigers every one. He blames the mob for its excesses, expressing an inverted idealism that demands such a monstrous, Swiftian picture of mankind. Looking down onto the "last cloud of mingling smoke," Godwin watches his own dreams turning into ashes, creating a mob that he will not join. Read against Walker's unforgiving satire, Godwin sounds unfortunately like a repentant Stupeo, but then, the "enlightened" Stupeo would never, in Walker's literary prison, be able to repent.

Harrington: Reformation of Riotous Space

In *Harrington* (1817), Maria Edgeworth uses the Gordon Riots to address anti-Semitic stereotypes that an American Jewish woman, Rachel Mordecai, found in her work. To answer her critic's accusation of representing Jews as "by nature mean, avaricious, and unprincipled,"[51] Edgeworth set out to trace the development of a positive hatred of Jews inculcated in a young boy six years old. Her opening scene powerfully presents the traumatic materials of prejudice. Watching "an old man . . . holding a great bag slung over one shoulder, walk[ing] slowly on, straight forwards, repeating in a low abrupt, mysterious tone, the cry of '*Old-clothes*,'" young Harrington resists going to bed until his maid threatens to "call Simon the Jew there . . . and he shall come up and carry you away in his great bag." The nurse proceeds to terrorize the boy with even more lurid stories of Jews who " . . . steal poor children . . . crucifying . . . them at their secret feasts and midnight abominations," and make pies "of the flesh of little children." The boy sees "faces around me grinning, glaring, receding, advancing, all turning at last into . . . the same face of the Jew . . . and that bag in which I fancied were mangled limbs of children."[52]

This powerful prose terrifies the reader even as the text attempts to probe didactically the foundations of prejudice. Significantly, it is more disturbing than Edgeworth's representation of the Gordon Riots. When she writes about the riots, she collapses them into the controversy surrounding the Jew Bill of 1753. Introducing Harrington's father, a hardened anti-Semitic MP still fighting against the naturalization of Jews in England ten years after the Jew Bill had failed, Edgeworth locates public displays of anti-Semitism in the domestic sphere. Young Harrington delights his father at a dinner by toasting "No Naturalization Bill – No Jews," and going on to the drawing room to visit the ladies, he explains that the Jews cannot be naturalized because they are "naturally unnatural." "Kisses and cakes in abundance" reward his bigotry.[53]

By 1780, Harrington has learned to overcome his anti-Semitism and to seek out Jewish thinkers at college. We find him in love with Berenice, the daughter of

Montenero, a wealthy Spanish Jewish art collector. The Gordon Riots become a space of heroic possibility in which Harrington can prove his love for the girl, as he protects her and her father. Why? Because somehow the riots, not even called the Gordon Riots, only described as anti-papist, also seem to be directed against the Jews. Lord George and his 44,000 signatures, and his 60,000 protestors gathered at St. George's Field, don't even enter into the picture. Instead, "from the smallest beginnings, the mischief grew and spread; half-a-dozen people gathered in one street, and began the cry of 'No popery! – no papists! – no French.'"[54]

The events of the riots are sketchily represented: the destruction of Mansfield's house, Newgate, the Fleet, the King's Bench, and popish chapels blaze across the page in two sentences. Edgeworth uses the riots for her own purposes, indirectly connecting Gordon's conversion to Judaism to the anti-Semitic riots without a name.[55] Rioters shout out "No wooden shoes, No Jews," as they storm the streets looking for Catholics and Jews to assault. Harrington saves the family, but the real hero of the piece turns out to be an Irish orange-woman. As Edgeworth explains, orange-women had special relationships with London Jews, since it was "a customary mode of charity with the Jews, to purchase and distribute large quantities of oranges among the retail sellers." The orange-woman offers herself as the protector of "her Jewels, the Jews." Smoking her pipe and speaking her broad brogue, she fools the mob to run off for the militia, who disperse the rioters and save the day.[56] Eventually, Harrington gets the girl, who turns out to be Christian, not Jewish at all, and the riots, described in a frantic fifteen pages, become sensational material to provide a plot turn. Edgeworth transforms the Gordon Riots into a piece of theater that exploits picturesque Irishness while she attempts to placate the irritated Jewish American, Rachel Mordecai, with her attack on Jewish stereotypes. Mordecai, by the way, was not that pleased that Berenice, daughter of the Spanish Jew, was a Christian after all.[57] The nameless riots, emptied of meaning, become blank space, ready to be written on.

The Mystery; or Forty Years Ago. A Novel

It is 1820, and the "mystery" is incest, or at least fear of incest that blocks the romance between Charles Harley, a poor but well-educated officer in the Navy, and Amelia, daughter of Sir George Henderson, wealthy, benevolent, who thinks but cannot say that Charles is his son. It seems he seduced his wife's cousin, and when she became pregnant, convinced her to marry his clueless friend Harley and travel to India to start a new life. The lady, however, lied, and after miscarrying the putative son of Henderson on the journey to India, made Sir George believe for decades that Charles, actually the son of Harley, conceived on the journey, was his. That way he would send Charles to good schools in England and give him great expectations, denying him only his daughter Amelia, for obvious reasons. It all gets settled in the end, late in volume 3, when Sir George receives a posthumous letter from the dead mother of

Charles. It is 1820, and incest is fashionable, and even more pleasing when it is mistaken.

The title, *The Mystery; or Forty Years Ago*, suggests that Thomas Gaspey joined the two events – the Gordon Riots, and the sensational domestic and national materials of "the mystery" with ambivalence. He gives the unspeakable riots voice, but only as background for the romance of Charles and Amelia and perhaps more significantly for the romance of empire. Charles, known hereafter as Harley, born in India, declaims from the start his love of England, where slavery and tyranny have been banished. He attacks the "measureless arrogance" of the wealthy Europeans in India, "who cannot pass even from one apartment to another, without causing some half dozen of his fellow-creatures to move with him, to fan him, to shade him." "I know not," Harley claims, "whether I would not prefer mingling with the menials who swell his train, to acting the part of the bloated idol himself." Knowing "not," Harley can retain both his indignation and his disgust, but still remain open to capitalistic options that he will later enjoy in his adventures in Africa. What he does know is that he is not "a leveller." "The absurd and chimerical scheme of making all equal, never entered my mind."[58]

To enter the romance of the riots, Sir George and Harley travel to London, only to be stopped by throngs along Holborn. One hundred five pages follow, approximately 10 percent of the novel, representing the riots in vivid, dramatic detail. Thousands of persons march by, their hats decorated with blue ribbons.[59] The post-boy tells them that the thousands seen are "but a *small* part of ten divisions . . . with Lord George Gordon at their head," marching to demand repeal of the Relief Act, peace with America, and an end to the national debt. Such an absurd notion "produce[s] an involuntary burst of laughter from Sir George and Mr. Harley."[60]

In London, Harley and Sir George learn about the violence in Parliament: how the "disheveled hair, torn clothes, and bespattered face" of an assaulted Member of Parliament give evidence "of the violence of the mob."[61] And then they are out in the thick of it, Amelia joining them in the coach to witness the riots. "'Who are those rough dirty-looking men, that are running backwards and forwards?' enquired Amelia."[62] Newgate becomes the dark heart of the riots, a place of horror "no language can adequately describe." The rioters' "countenances . . . presented all the appalling characteristics that ferocity, senseless fanaticism and the love of depredation could supply to complete the deformity of the human visage."[63]

Ned Dennis, the hangman, making a raucous and disorderly appearance, confesses, "I likes a little rioting as well as another." He and Mr. Snowball, "a man of colour . . . depraved as any of his white brethren" quarrel when Snowball suggests that the hangman cannot make his usual profit from the hangings if the jailed are free: "You won't have the clothes, and you won't bleed them before they go off."[64] The entire exchange with Dennis makes it hard not to believe that in spite of his claim to be the first novelist to introduce the Gordon Riots in a work of fiction, Dickens had certainly consulted *The Mystery* when he was writing *Barnaby Rudge*. His rowdy and acquisitive Dennis relishes "the smalls" he gets from "friend[s] that's left off sich incumbrances for ever: this coat too . . . and as to my hat . . . Lord! I've seen this hat go up Holborn on the box of a hackney-coach – ah, many and many a day!"[65] Such a macabre portrait suggests Dickens's indebtedness to Gaspey's irreverent characterization of the hangman. We know that Dickens thought of him while writing *Barnaby Rudge*; he made a reference to "Gaspey – Chief Executioners chapter" – in his diary in 1839.[66] Unlike Gaspey, however, who stuck to "the facts," and spared Dennis's life, Dickens hanged him, getting full mileage out of his wheedling, venal, carnal character and then punishing him for his sins.

As bad as the rioters can be, the authorities are worse. Beaten by the mob, Harley is taken for a rioter, and hauled off to the magistrate where he escapes hanging only through the intervention of Sir George. Protesting the arbitrary power of the magistrate, Harley learns that "appearances was against you." "Certainly," Harley replies, "I looked like one in distress, and, of course could have no claim on your humanity or your justice."[67]

Denied the hand of Amelia, who might after all be his sister, Harley plunges into the dark realms of empire. The plot shift seems important. Gaspey represents the riots both ways, as an assault on the dignified life of gentlemen and ladies, and as an event that exposes the rotten underpinnings of the authorities that the riots threaten. After questioning British justice, Gaspey writes 800 more pages of adventures exalting the white man teaching Africans how to bake bread while warning against hearts of darkness ready to burst. Gaspey writes like Defoe crossed with Godwin foreshadowing Dickens; he pumps up, blows up, and finally shakily recuperates the dreams of empire. He exposes more injustices than Dickens can, but he does it awkwardly, in haste, even if he is delivering 1,000 pages to his reader to digest.

Lieutenant Harley joins his ship and heads for the infamous Goree, a slave-trading extension of the British empire where he meets genteel-seeming Governor Wall, "one of the meanest, most rapacious and basest villains, on earth." Major Houghton educates Harley in the ways of the world ruled by Wall. He "flogged a man to death, while on his way from England," flogged a slave to death in Goree, and gives his soldiers brandy "in lieu of their pay." When they become drunk, he flogs them with "thieves' cat."[68] Adventures abound. Harley is captured by the French, escapes, swims to shore, wanders around the jungle being Robinson Crusoe, and is rescued by utopian Africans, the Pholies, living in Sambarra who, like Spenceans in England, believe in sharing the wealth. They give him land to build his own western-style house, and help him to erect it. He teaches them how to make clay pots. Boiling water does occasionally scald an unwary Pholie, but the benefits of the new luxuries certainly outweigh the inconveniences.[69]

When his house mysteriously burns down (not every African adores his whiteness), Harley takes off, packing up some "gold" that he "found" in the Spencean Pholie village, and travels through the continent. His female servant follows him into other adventures until she's conveniently taken off by a tiger and shot dead by her rescuers, saving him the "embarrassment" of dealing with her African subject position, and her color, once they reach civilization.[70] He's enslaved twice, amasses wealth and

admiration from Africans adoring his white supremacy and from an English inheritance waiting for him back home, and finally makes his way back to the coast where he
meets Houghton, who's been suspended by Wall. Hankering to get to Timbuctoo
(the real Daniel Houghton will die in the effort),[71] Houghton continues to regale
Harley with stories of Wall's illegal and tyrannical conduct, all the worse because it is
"offered not by a savage...but by a country-man, and still more, by a pretended
friend."[72] Readers in 1820 would remember Joseph Wall, infamously hanged at
Newgate in 1802. At Goree, in 1782, he ordered, without a trial, that five soldiers,
ringleaders of a troop of sixty demanding back pay, be flogged 800 lashes by black
slaves. After hiding from the law for twenty years, he returned, expecting to be
acquitted, and was executed instead before a cheering crowd of 60,000. Beginning
with the Gordon Riots, so unruly and demoralizing to the English elite, Gaspey ends
his novel gesturing towards a "savage" crime committed by a genteel-seeming
governor married to the daughter of a Scottish peer.[73] Harley returns home, conveniently wealthy, where he finally wins the hand of Amelia, conveniently not his sister,
his success framed by "horrors."

Gaspey's narrative falters, pressured by state authority, sexual authority, and the
inevitable power of whiteness. His conventional, almost lifeless figures move through
preposterous adventures. But what he does with and to the Gordon Riots reveals why
Dickens could eventually use them for his own purposes. The unspeakable riots
allowed both Gaspey and Dickens a way to gauge the threats attacking a shaky
cultural foundation, one that might even deserve to be erased. They both depict the
"deformed" countenances of members of the mob determined to destroy authority
brick by brick. And both seem to face the price that empire exacts, and the reward
that it bestows upon a Harley sold into and out of slavery, upon a Joe Willet who loses
an arm fighting for king and Protestant country. In gesturing toward Wall's brutal
reign, one that will end in sadistic floggings, Gaspey unsettles the conventional happy
ending, making it difficult for the reader not to ponder the cost of empire. Dickens
was more shameless than Gaspey in using the riots to discipline his readers. Enforcing
the law, he pushes us into the cozy corners of the Golden Key, home of his locksmith
hero, a sign of the signification of the science of incarceration that Linebaugh
recognizes as one of the legacies of the Gordon Riots.[74] This doughty locksmith
stands ready to deliver us to Newgate if we resist.[75] And if we are good, we can settle
into the high camp of cozy, under the sign of the Maypole, celebrating an England
that could only exist in a fiction paid for by arms lost in the Salwanners.

Continuing the Riots

The absence of the Gordon Riots in the eighteenth-century novel takes on an uncanny
power at this particular time. When the governments of the United States and Great
Britain have committed themselves to fight terrorism in unpopular wars, it is
essential to imagine how to resist, in presence, in writing, out loud. There is no

doubt that the repressive measures that the British government took against writers deemed seditious helped to silence dissent in the 1790s. These acts of repression resulted in evasive and edgy literary productions that avoid or displace active, vulgar responses to civic violence while they make the Gordon Riots' resistance to the war in American mysterious and unreadable. The riots themselves literally seem to disappear. To avoid the historical trap of submission, dissenters in this present culture might need to become vulgar, reproducing the disciplined activities of the *mobile vulgus*, at least in print. Or we can wait forty or sixty-one years to reconstruct versions of what we let happen. Perhaps I make it sound too simple, a vulgar proposition, but the absence of the Gordon Riots in eighteenth-century literature underscores the need to speak the unspoken.

See also: chapter 17, QUEER GOTHIC; chapter 20, HOME ECONOMICS; chapter 22, THE NOVEL BODY POLITIC; chapter 23, LITERARY CULTURE AS IMMEDIATE REALITY.

NOTES

1. Sources for the Gordon Riots come from Thomas Holcroft's *A Plain and Succinct Narrative of the Gordon Riots: London, 1780*, ed. G. Smith (Atlanta, GA: The Library, Emory University, 1944); J. Paul de Castro, *The Gordon Riots* (London: Oxford University Press, 1926); Christopher Hibbert, *King Mob: The Story of Lord George Gordon and the London Riots of 1780* (Cleveland, OH: World Publishing, 1958); George Rudé, "The Gordon Riots: A Study of the Rioters and their Victims," in *Paris and London in the 18th Century: Studies in Popular Protest* (London: Fontana/Collins, 1974); John Nicholson, *The Great Liberty Riot of 1780* (London: Panther, 1985); Peter Linebaugh, *The London Hanged: Crime and Civil Society in the Eighteenth Century* (London: Allen Lane, The Penguin Press, 1991); Ian Gilmour, "The Gordon Riots," in *Riots, Risings and Revolution: Governance and Violence in Eighteenth-Century England* (London: Hutchinson, 1992), 342–71; Colin Haydon, "The Gordon Riots," in *Anti-Catholicism in Eighteenth-Century England, c. 1714–80* (Manchester: Manchester University Press, 1993), 204–45; Iain McCalman, "Controlling the Riots: *Barnaby Rudge* and Romantic Revolution," in *Radicalism and Revolution in Britain, 1775–1848*, ed. Michael T. Davis (London and New York:

Macmillan Press and St. Martin's Press, 2000), 207–28.
2. Charles Dickens, *Barnaby Rudge: A Tale of the Riots of 'Eighty'* (London: Folio Society, 1987), xviii.
3. George Walker, *The Vagabond: A Novel*, ed. W. M. Verhoeven (Peterborough, Ontario: Broadview Press, 2004).
4. Maria Edgeworth, *Harrington*, ed. Marilyn Butler and Susan Manly, in *Novels and Selected Works of Maria Edgeworth*, vol. 3 (London: Pickering & Chatto, 1999).
5. Thomas Gaspey, *The Mystery; or, Forty Years Ago. A Novel.* 3 vols. (London: Longman, 1820).
6. James Boswell, *Life of Johnson*, ed. R. W. Chapman (Oxford: Oxford University Press, 1998), 1062.
7. William Godwin, *St Leon: A Tale of the Sixteenth Century*, ed. Pamela Clemit in *Completed Novels and Memoirs of William Godwin*, Vol. 4 (London: Pickering & Chatto, 1992).
8. Holcroft, *A Plain and Succinct Narrative of the Gordon Riots*, ed. Smith, 26, 27, 29.
9. Ibid., 18.
10. Ibid., 40–41.
11. Nicholson and McCalman are most sympathetic to Lord George Gordon's revolutionary sensibility; other historians supportive of

the rioters tend to dismiss Gordon as eccentric and mad.

12. Castro is citing Horace Walpole, who writes, "It is to be hoped that this man is so mad that it will soon come to perfection," *The Gordon Riots*, 19.

13. Ibid., 248.

14. Hibbert, *King Mob*, 15.

15. Ignatius Sancho, *Letters of the Late Ignatius Sancho, An African*, ed. Vincent Carretta (New York: Penguin, 1998), 217.

16. Thomas Paine, *The Rights of Man*, introduced by Eric Foner (New York: Penguin, 1985), "Part Two," p. 166, "Part One," p. 50.

17. "In Birmingham, he was circumcised and 'preserved with great care,' so Wraxall said, 'the sanguinary proofs of his having undergone the amputation,'" Hibbert, *King Mob*, 225.

18. Ibid., 19–21.

19. See Stella K. Tillyard, *Citizen Lord: Life of Edward Fitzgerald, Irish Revolutionary* (New York: Farrar Strauss and Giroux, 1998).

20. Peter Linebaugh and Marcus Rediker discuss the political and cultural alliances forged by sailors, slaves, and commoners in *The Many-Headed Hydra* (Boston: Beacon Press, 2000).

21. Tillyard, *Citizen Lord*, 240–79.

22. McCalman, "Controlling the Riots," in *Radicalism and Revolution*, ed. Davis, 213–14.

23. Haydon, "The Gordon Riots," in *Anti-Catholicism in Eighteenth-Century England*, 224, 235, 242–43.

24. Rudé, "The Gordon Riots," in *Paris and London*, 289.

25. Holcroft, *A Plain and Succinct Narrative of the Gordon Riots*, ed. Smith, 25.

26. Susan Burney, *The Susan Burney Letters Project*, "Letter Extract 2: The Gordon Riots, St. Martin's Lane," London, 8 June 1780, *http://www.nottingham.ac.uk/hrc/projects/burney/letters/gordon.phtml*, 2–3.

27. Castro, *The Gordon Riots*, 217.

28. *The Trial of George Gordon, Esquire commonly called Lord George Gordon for High Treason at the Bar of the Court of King's Bench, on Monday, February 5ᵗʰ, 1781* (London, 1781). Taken in shorthand by Joseph Gurney. Walpole's copy is in the Houghton Library, Harvard University.

29. Rudé, "The Gordon Riots," in *Paris and London*, 281–82; Dickens, *Barnaby Rudge*, 382.

30. Sancho, *Letters*, ed. Carretta, 219.

31. Holcroft, *A Plain and Succinct Narrative of the Gordon Riots*, 29.

32. Hibbert, *King Mob*, 158. Peter Ackroyd, *London: A Biography* (London: Bantam Doubleday Dell, 2003), 302.

33. Sancho, *Letters*, ed. Carretta, 222.

34. Holcroft, *A Plain and Succinct Narrative of the Gordon Riots*, ed. Smith, 28.

35. Nicholson argues that Gordon's attempt to prevent prisoners from being shipped to Botany Bay is a significant and revolutionary attack upon the "institutionalized cruelty of English society," *The Great Liberty Riot*, 84–87.

36. Holcroft, *A Plain and Succinct Narrative of the Gordon Riots*, ed. Smith, 25.

37. Linebaugh, *The London Hanged*, 342.

38. Alexander Gilchrist, *Life of William Blake*, 36–37, cited in Stanley Gardner, *The Tyger and The Lamb and The Terrible Desart* (London: Cygnus Arts, 1998), 23.

39. G. E. Bentley, Jr., *The Stranger from Paradise: A Biography of William Blake* (New Haven, CT: Yale University Press, 2001). Bentley finds Gilchrist's *Life of William Blake, 'Pictor Ignotus"* to be "reliable, vastly influential, and irreplaceable," 448.

40. David V. Erdman, *Blake: Prophet Against Empire* (Princeton, NJ: Princeton University Press, 1954), 6–10; Linebaugh, *The London Hanged*, 368–70. E. P. Thompson's *Witness Against the Beast: William Blake and the Moral Law* (New York: Norton Press, 1993) connects Blake to militant theories of millennialism.

41. Gardner, *The Tyger and The Lamb*, 21, 24.

42. Ibid., 25.

43. Henry Fielding, *Amelia*, ed. Martin C. Battestin (Middletown, CT: Wesleyan University Press, 1983), 519–21; Frances Burney, *Cecilia, or Memoirs of an Heiress*, ed. Peter Sabor and Margaret Anne Doody (Oxford: Oxford University Press, 1988), 896–98.

44. Walker, *The Vagabond*, 38, 12–13.

45. Ibid., 106.

46. Ibid., 241.

47. Gary Kelly, *The English Jacobin Novel, 1780–1805* (Oxford: Clarendon Press, 1976), 232, 216, 214.

48. Godwin, *St Leon*, ed. Clemit, 233–35.

49. Ibid., 236–38.

50. Ibid., 233.

51. Susan Manly, "Introductory Note" in *Novels and Selected Works of Maria Edgeworth*, 3: xxvii–xxviii.

52. Edgeworth, *Harrington*, 168–69.

53. Ibid., 178–79.

54. Ibid., 285.

55. Neville Hoad, "Maria Edgeworth's *Harrington*: The Price of Sympathetic Representation," in *British Romanticism and the Jews*, ed. Sheila A. Spector (New York: Palgrave Macmillan, 2002) sees Edgeworth conflating the Catholic Relief Bill and the 1753 Bill for Jewish Naturalization, 124. "There is no record of damage to Jewish property. In 1780, the violence took place far from the Jewish quarters." The only reference I have found to Jewish connections to the Gordon Riots is in Holcroft, *A Plain and Succinct Narrative of the Gordon Riots*, ed. Smith: "the very Jews, in Houndsditch and Duke's Place, were so terrified that they followed the general example, and, unintentionally, gave an air of ridicule to what they understood in a very serious light by writing on their shutters, 'This house is a true Protestant,'" 30.

56. Edgeworth, *Harrington*, 285–86.

57. Manly, *Novels and Selected Works of Maria Edgeworth*, 3:xxiii.

58. Gaspey, *The Mystery*, 1:38–40.

59. Ibid., 1:69.

60. Ibid., 1:74–75.

61. Ibid., 1:107.

62. Ibid., 1:122.

63. Ibid., 1:128–29.

64. Ibid., 1:131–33.

65. Dickens, *Barnaby Rudge*, 288.

66. Thomas Jackson Rice, *Barnaby Rudge: An Annotated Bibliography* (New York and London: Garland Press, 1987), 67, conjectures that Dickens was familiar with *The Mystery* and with Gaspey.

67. Gaspey, *The Mystery*, 1:147–52.

68. Ibid., 2:6, 12, 16.

69. Ibid., 2:206–7.

70. Ibid., 2:256–57.

71. Daniel Houghton was an African explorer who served at Goree and received funding to visit Timbuctoo, but never got there. *Dictionary of National Biography*, Leslie Stephen and Sidney Lee, ed. (Oxford: Oxford University Press, 1900), 9:1314.

72. Gaspey, *The Mystery*, 3:155–62, 168.

73. Linda Colley discusses Wall in *Captives* (New York: Pantheon Books, 2002), 328–32. Wall receives a fulsome biography in the *Dictionary of National Biography*, 20:551–52.

74. Linebaugh, *The London Hanged*, 365–66. "Joseph Bramah . . . not long after the Riots published a book describing a revolutionary change in locksmithery, *A Dissertation on the Construction of Locks*," (London, 1785).

75. Repelled by the "Tink tink tink" of chapter 41, Dickens's paean to the sunny power of the "honest" locksmith, Nicholson finds *Barnaby Rudge* "a hymn to prisons," 197–200.

FURTHER READING

Colley, Linda. *Captives*. New York: Pantheon Books, 2002.

Erdman, David. *Blake: Prophet Against Empire*. Princeton, NJ: Princeton University Press, 1954.

Gardner, Stanley. *The Tyger and The Lamb and the Terrible Desart*. London: Cygnus Arts, 1998.

Haydon, Colin. "The Gordon Riots." In *Anti-Catholicism in Eighteenth-Century England, 1714–80*. Manchester: Manchester University Press, 1993. 204–45.

McCalman, Iain. "Controlling the Riots: *Barnaby Rudge* and Romantic Revolution." In *Radicalism and Revolution in Britain, 1775–1848*, ed. Michael T. Davis. London and New York: Macmillan Press and St. Martin's Press, 2000. 207–28.

Nicholson, John. *The Great Liberty Riot of 1780*. London: Panther Press, 1985.

22

The Novel Body Politic

Susan S. Lanser

I can usually count on my students to be surprised when they read *Frankenstein*. Schooled in popular images, they don't expect the "monster" to be a fleshed-out character, let alone a sympathetic being who began his conscious life "glowing with love and humanity." So when the creature heretofore represented only as a "vile insect," a "demon," an "abhorred monster" begins to speak, and speaks for six full chapters, their experience of the novel is transformed. The creature himself knows full well that his fate rests on his voice: his first demand, all the more insistent against Victor's repeated refusals, is to be heard. It is a demand presented, moreover, as a civil right: "by human laws," he says, even guilty subjects must be allowed "to speak in their own defense."[1]

In giving the creature an "eloquent and persuasive voice" and in locating in his ability to speak for himself his only chance to be recognized as human, *Frankenstein* (1818) articulates the terms of participation not only in a human community but, I will suggest, in a body politic. Mary Shelley's novel gives the part of a speaking subject to a singular, non-human being who nonetheless makes claims to human rights. He establishes his claim by exposing the gap between external perception and internal worth; rejected on sight as "hideously deformed and loathsome," he relies on words to demonstrate the "natural inclination" for "Fellowship" and the commitment to "the common good" that Locke posits as "the very Soul of a Politick Body."[2] Hence the pivotal place of De Lacey's blindness in the creature's chances to be heard; hence the creature's need to speak through the educated discourse of enlightened Man; and hence too his tragic impulse to silence those who do not hear but only see and spurn. When this nameless being is identified as "Frankenstein" in popular culture through a symbiosis of creature and creator, and when Victor ends up applying to himself the terms of monstrosity, we see even more vividly the novel's uncertainty about which bodies shall be entitled to the "rights of man."

I begin with *Frankenstein* because it lays bare the dynamics through which, I will suggest, the eighteenth-century English novel stages the project of forming a politics.

Whether we take the creature to stand in for women, for the people (dystopically, the "mob"), for the physically "imperfect," for enslaved or colonized Others, for the "human condition," or simply for his literal and idiosyncratic self, the workings of Shelley's plot unfold from the creature's denied claims to the subjectivity that eighteenth-century revolutions came to accord some men. An eighteenth-century novel in structure and setting, *Frankenstein* leads back to struggles about participation in the body politic that are enacted and contained through the forms of fiction and the strategies for reading it. With recourse to the conception of politics articulated by the philosopher Jacques Rancière, I want to ask how the eighteenth-century English novel redistributes speaking bodies in social space and how we might account for discrepancies between fictional and historical constructions of "Politick Bodies." As a telling limit case, I also want to revisit the important question Lynn Hunt raises when she asks why women, so central to the eighteenth-century novel, were so resoundingly denied the "rights of man."

The Voice of Politics

Since the shift in literary studies from various formalisms to various historicisms in the 1980s, the conviction that the novel is "political" has become a scholarly commonplace. Building upon the work of such pioneering theorists as Erich Auerbach, Mikhail Bakhtin, Lucien Goldmann, Georg Lukács, Ian Watt, and Raymond Williams, a voluminous scholarship has analyzed the "rise" of the novel in relation to the emergence of European social, economic, and political modernity. Yet claims that the novel is political continue to encompass a broad range of notions both of politics and of the ways in which novels might inscribe those politics. Scholars whose work is anchored in "politics" do not necessarily define the term: the word does not appear, for example, in the index of Nancy Armstrong's *Desire and Domestic Fiction: A Political History of the Novel*, and in Fredric Jameson's *The Political Unconscious: Narrative as a Socially Symbolic Act* "politics" is delineated only through the vast claim that "everything is 'in the last analysis' political."[3]

By the same token, the conceptions of politics that underwrite studies of fiction range from a strict focus on affairs of government to the entire spectrum of power relations that structure human intercourse. Theories about the ways in which politics might be inscribed in a novel are likewise diverse: some scholars focus on manifest content, others on the shared ideological underpinnings of public and private life, still others on the ways in which textual and political structures might be homologous. Clearly the majority of eighteenth-century novels would fare quite differently within these varied conceptions of novel politics: at the one extreme, for example, *Pride and Prejudice* (1813) might be considered apolitical or anti-political in its failure to engage the urgent public issues of its day; at the other extreme, Austen's novel could be seen as nothing *but* politics, and the distinction between novels that are political and those that are not, to quote Fredric Jameson, would simply be a "symptom ... of the reification and privatization of contemporary life."[4]

I hope here to mediate these polarities through a specific understanding of politics that I believe characterizes the eighteenth-century novel in particular. I want to suggest that through its (re)distribution of speaking bodies, the novel engages the pressing eighteenth-century question of who shall participate in civil society, in what ways, and with what rights, of who shall have public power and whose interests shall be recognized and served. It is, of course, during the period coextensive with the "rise" of the English novel that the meaning of a body politic undergoes a dramatic shift: from a sovereign head, who confers rights according to particular stations, to a legislative body representing citizens by whose consent that body governs and whose rights, newly deemed "natural," it is designed to protect. It is worth noting that eighteenth-century novelists from Delarivier Manley and Daniel Defoe to William Godwin and Mary Wollstonecraft were as engaged with questions of governance as with questions of narrative: John Richetti's comment that except for Samuel Richardson, "the major male novelists of the mid-century were polemical and political writers first and novelists only as the literary marketplace led them to it" could be extended to many of the female and male novelists of the later eighteenth century as well.[5] It is thus striking but not anomalous that the philosopher who seems to have coined the phrase "rights of man" published his wildly popular novel *Julie, or The New Héloïse* (1761) and his politically radical *Social Contract* (1762) barely a year apart.[6]

That the concept of representation links discourse and politics has been recognized at least since Thomas Hobbes's *Leviathan* (1651). But the two modes of representation are aligned in a particularly fruitful way by the philosopher Jacques Rancière in *Disagreement: Politics and Philosophy {La Mésentente: politique et philosophie}*. For Rancière, politics happens when the existing "order of domination is interrupted by the institution of a part of those who have [had] no part." That is, some part of humanity that has been relegated to lower ("animal") status disrupts the dominant order by making a claim to rights that is "totally foreign" to the status quo. Politics can thus be understood as "whatever shifts a body" from its assigned place as a non-part(y) into the part(y) of universal humanity.[7]

In Rancière's view, voice enables politics: it is the articulation of subjectivity in language that allows bodies to shift. Political subjects emerge "through a series of actions of a body and a capacity for enunciation not previously identifiable within a given field of experience, whose identification is thus part of the reconfiguration of the field of experience." Democracy, then, may be understood as "the way of life – in which the voice ... usurps the privileges of the logos."[8] In Slavoj Žižek's rephrasing of Rancière, politics happen when a particular constituency "not only demand[s] that their voice be heard against those in power" and becomes "recognized as included in the public sphere, on an equal footing with the ruling oligarchy," but also "present[s] themselves as the representatives, the stand-ins, for the Whole of Society, for the true Universality." Hence the "elementary gesture of politicization" is the paradoxical move through which the single case claims to stand for the universal, "destabilizing the 'natural' functioning order" of the social body through the "identification of the non-part with the Whole."[9] The argument that "women's rights are human rights" makes just this move to locate woman as the universal human subject whose claims are not "special interests" but basic requisites.

The current movement for "gay rights" provides a particularly vivid illustration of Rancière's understanding of politics. From a nonexistent part(y) of people whose sexualities had been deemed subhuman (shameful, sinful, sick), there has emerged a set of voices claiming the status of universal subjects in a way that has unsettled the social body. Across the relatively short span of two or three decades, "gay" has become a political distinction reconfiguring the social and legal spheres. In its wake, the US Supreme Court has struck down sodomy laws, at least three countries and the State of Massachusetts have legalized same-sex marriage, South Africa has written gay rights into its Constitution, and myriad social practices in diverse democracies have provided new institutional recognition to a part of society that had no part, indeed whose abjection made them vulnerable to arrest, firing, blackmail, commitment to mental institutions, and other abrogations of their human rights. The emergence of "gay rights," then, entails precisely the redistribution of speaking bodies that Rancière counts as the instantiation of a politics. Insofar as these rights remain contested, a gay politics continues; when this (or any) part of humanity becomes fully integrated into the social body, it ceases to be the site of a politics in Rancière's sense.

In the eighteenth century, multiple constituencies not before included, from un(en)titled prosperous white men to enslaved Africans, began to claim their part, in a widespread movement that culminated in the radical project of the French Revolution to create a common body without any sovereign head. Since it was the absence of representation that precipitated political action, most of these struggles began not in formal institutions of government but in the "courts of public opinion" enabled by a burgeoning print culture in what Jürgen Habermas has famously called the "bourgeois public sphere." But while Habermas imagines politics as a "rational debate between multiple interests," Rancière sees it as a "struggle for one's voice to be heard and recognized."[10] This makes the "political animal" first of all "a literary animal" bent on undoing "the relationships between the order of words and the order of bodies that determine the place of each." The "multiple fracture lines" thus produced forge a gap between "the inegalitarian distribution of social bodies" and "the equal capacity of speaking beings in general." For Rancière, this production of a gap works best through the "case" or "demonstration" that creates "the world where argument can be received and have an impact," where the "structure of relationship between the common and the not common can be worked out."[11] Hence, for example, the crucial role in gay movements of multiple instances of "coming out" – by media celebrities, elected officials, relatives, colleagues, and fictional characters – in "case histories" that emphasize the speakers' ordinariness and hence their universality as human beings.

What's Novel about Politics

Politics in Rancière's sense relies on two qualities paramount to the novel: its basis in the individual story and the centrality it accords to the represented voice. Rancière speculates that a narrative rendering of political claims "operates more clearly when the names of subjects are distinct from any social group identifiable as such."[12] This distinctiveness is certainly true of *Frankenstein*'s nameless creature, who can stand allegorically for any number of social entities seeking a political part. The creature begins his conscious life as a model citizen in the sense imagined by liberal philosophers such as John Locke and Jean-Jacques Rousseau. Schooled by observing and imitating humanity and reading its cherished books, he has strengthened a natural dispensation for kindness toward those near him and empathy for those afar. His mastery of language coincides with his exposure to history, so that he weeps over the "hapless fate" of the colonized, regrets the social sins of poverty, admires "peaceable lawgivers," and feels "the greatest ardour for virtue" and "abhorrence for vice."[13] His efforts at communion with humans are rooted in actions for the common good: he becomes an "invisible hand" replenishing the De Laceys' store of wood and sympathizes with their joys and sorrows. Although he recognizes his physical otherness, he "persuaded" himself that when his neighbors, who seem to be paragons of sensibility, "become acquainted with my admiration of their virtues, they would compassionate me, and overlook my personal deformity," extending "friendship" rather than "turn [me] from their door."[14] In other words, the creature expects as his due a place in the human community, a manifestly political claim in the eighteenth century to "life, liberty, and the pursuit of happiness" on which constitutions were founded and the "rights of man" were based.

Yet at what becomes a turning point in his story, the creature finds himself driven out of this community. When he throws himself on the mercy of the blind De Lacey but is torn from him and beaten by Felix, the being who is trying to claim a part where he has had no part experiences the failure of an attempted politics. The pattern of benevolent participation and violent rejection is repeated when the creature saves a young girl from drowning and is shot by her father, and the dynamic turns vengeful when he seeks to "educate" young William to accept him but is reviled as a "hideous monster" and "ugly wretch."[15] Refused a part in human society, the creature finally places his hopes in a separate sphere, asking Victor to fashion him a likeness with whom he can live apart from humanity "in the interchange of those sympathies necessary for my being." In the creature's only usage of the word, he demands a mate "as a *right* which [Victor] must not refuse to concede." Victor agrees that he "had no right to withhold from him the small portion of happiness which was yet in my power to bestow."[16] Yet he does withhold this "happiness" in fear that ceding *any* power to the creature and his "kind" will mean losing *all* of it – and to a "race" that "might make the very existence of the species of man a condition precarious and full of terror."[17] Whatever one takes Shelley's creature to represent, *Frankenstein* enacts the rejection of a politics, a refusal to make a part among speaking bodies for the creature who has no part.

Recognizing the potential of the novel to enact political contest through individual cases gives new force to Mikhail Bakhtin's argument that the "fundamental condition, that which makes a novel a novel," is "the *speaking person and his* [sic] *discourse*," a discourse that always entails "a particular way of viewing the world" and that "strives for social significance."[18] The flexibility of its voices gives the novel a special capacity to redistribute social bodies through its deployment of their speech, constituting or *pre*-constituting a politics in Rancière's sense. Certainly the early English novel builds itself around this pre-eminence of the speaking voice, which is produced through a new range of formal strategies from memoirs, eyewitness accounts, and exchanges of letters to quoted speech, extended dialogues, and "third-person" narrators with distinctive personalities. These mechanisms converge with new notions of whose speech is worth hearing, notions put forth, not coincidentally, by a socially wide range of authors, many of whom previously had no part in literature; a majority of English novelists would not have been entitled, for example, to elect, let alone to stand as, Members of Parliament: some were Dissenters, some lacked property, many were female. The dominant characters in many novels – women, orphans, bastards, middling sorts – also lack those rights that signify the fully human; as Paula Backscheider notes, the predominant "narrative point of view" in the eighteenth-century novel "was that of the Other," and even novels that "strengthened the status quo" tended "to give the central or sustained major voice to the non-dominant position," implicitly asking those with power to recognize the "importance of other subjectivities."[19] When speaking voices lay some kind of claim or present some kind of case that exposes and rejects the distance between a particular body's categorical position and the place of universal humanity, then the novel is engaging in the gesture of politics, of undoing the "order of bodies" through the "order of words."

It is in this sense that I want to claim the eighteenth-century English novel as "political." Without denying other ways in which one might speak of politics in the novel or the novel as politics, I argue here that a defining project of the early English novel in particular is to alter the order of speaking bodies, creating parts for those who have had no part and thereby enacting the scheme of politics. A quick survey of some canonical eighteenth-century novels points to just this movement at the heart of each. Moll Flanders begins as the orphaned daughter of a mother transported to a plantation for petty theft; from criminal and convict she turns wealthy "gentlewoman" with a plantation of her own. Robinson Crusoe, a mere youngest son of the "middle sort," moves from merchant sailor to king of his island to wealthy colonial. Pamela, of course, moves from being Mr. B.'s servant to becoming his wife, and Tom Jones starts out as a lovable bastard thought to be of low birth and ends up – his probable illegitimacy notwithstanding – as Squire Allworthy's heir, while Blifil moves from presumptive heir to exile in an exchange of bodies based on Tom's superior virtues or at least on his less reprehensible vices. Fanny Hill, daughter of poor but pious parents, unwittingly enters a life of prostitution, learns to profit from it, and is rewarded in the end with a married life in the "bosom of virtue," an estate in the country, legitimation for her children, and "every blessing in the power of love, health, and fortune to bestow."[20] The ladies of *Millenium Hall* (1762) move from dependents to proprietors, from pawns in the schemes of others to architects and legislators of their separate world. Evelina moves from unacknowledged orphan of "obscure birth" to cherished daughter of a nobleman and wife of a peer. Fanny Price enters Mansfield Park as a poor relation and ends up running it. And Olaudah Equiano's *Interesting Narrative* (1789), to take a non-fictional if arguably fictionalized example, moves its author-protagonist from slave to entrepreneur, from African to Englishman, from capital to capitalist.[21] Whether the character's movement is cynical or earnest – the move of a Fanny Hill or a Fanny Price – in each instance it is movement that reaps social rewards.[22]

The gesture of each of these narratives is to rearrange its speaking bodies, and particularly the body of its protagonist, to make a place for one(s) who had no place, so that a previously unrewarded subject gains a share in the rights or benefits of the novel's entitled group. While the circumstances vary widely, in most cases the subjects of movement have not simply claimed but earned their new status – whether by dint of virtue, industry, or crass cleverness – in ways that at least implicitly call into question the previous distribution of social parts. This pattern supports a change in social value from birth to worth and from entitlement to enterprise: those rewarded with movement are either admirably virtuous or admirably enterprising and the fact that virtue and enterprise are the criteria for their legitimation suggests the terms on which this particular society is willing to make a place for those who had no place.

Through these deployments of speaking bodies the novel enables, as no other genre has done before it, the mechanisms for ordinary readers to identify with ordinary characters of a sort usually deemed unfit to be serious literary, let alone political, subjects. This does not mean that all of these novels dramatize a full-blown shift in the social order or explicitly recognize the claims of a designated group; it is worth recalling Backscheider's astute observation that minoritized voices also get deployed in eighteenth-century novels that affirm the status quo. But even a discourse that presents the mobile body as an exception suggests the fragility or permeability of the system as a whole. If Evelina's membership in the ruling class affirms its right to continue ruling, if *Tom Jones* (1749) reasserts the validity of primogeniture and gentry blood, the more progressive movements of *Moll Flanders* (1722), *Pamela* (1741), *Millenium Hall*, and *The Interesting Narrative* insert a new part and arguably a new politics.

Clearly the movements of fictive bodies do not in themselves alter history, and John Bender wisely reminds us that we will never know for sure how much social change the novel caused because we have no similar but novel-free society as a basis for comparison.[23] It seems likely, however, that the cumulative effect of these novelistic movements was to alter and expand the culture's sense of who deserved a part, who could stand in for the universal subject, and thus who could generate a politics in Rancière's sense. Lynn Hunt has argued that by fostering the reader's identification with ordinary individuals seeking their autonomy, the novel laid "the psychological foundation of democracy and human rights."[24] That the two countries in which the novel first emerged were also the two countries in which the "rights of man" were most widely debated provides supporting circumstantial evidence. So does the fairly close relationship in class terms between the redistribution of speaking bodies in the novel and the political regimes of the late eighteenth century.

In this regard, it is important to acknowledge the limits to the social rearrangements that both the novel and the revolutions of the eighteenth century engineer. The proliferation of individualized and different-seeming persons may mask both the fairly limited social mobility that these novels actually engineer and the fact that the novel's range of social movement decreases as the century goes on, with *fewer* rather than *more* upstarts like Pamela and Moll being rewarded. The near absence of laboring-class speaking voices (especially of male characters) from eighteenth-century fiction reminds us that the novel served the interests of two constituencies in particular: a rising entrepreneurial middle sort aspiring to gentry status, and a gentry aspiring to make virtue, education, and manners more important than titled rank. The novel's failure to give a part to the lowest classes both precedes and strikingly parallels the political reconfigurations of the late eighteenth and early nineteenth centuries. When the Estates-General convened in France in 1789, even the Third Estate was peopled by bourgeoisie and lesser nobility: despite the street actions of the "sans-culottes," the new constitution did not make the poor full citizens.[25] The 1832 Reform Act that dramatically increased English suffrage still enfranchised at best one man in five, and voting rights in the new United States were initially restricted on the basis of taxable property. For both good and ill, then, the patterns of privilege that emerge in the eighteenth-century novel get repeated in the political shifts enacted by reformist England, republican America, and revolutionary France. The novel doubtless did not cause these patterns of privilege, but surely it helped to legitimate them to its literate readers, who also stood to gain the most from this newly expansive but also limited formation of the body politic. When Marthe Robert describes the novel as at once "revolutionary" and "middle-class," then, she is also pointing, however unwittingly, to the limits of revolutionary achievement in both fiction and history.[26] As the story of what Georg Lukács and Lucien Goldmann have called the "problematic individual," the novel as it emerges by the end of the eighteenth century has delimited its notion of both individuals and their problems along class lines.

But the parallel between fiction and history falters in the case of women: among the most prominent speaking subjects in the novel, women are the most glaringly absent from the body politic as it is reconfigured at the end of the eighteenth century. Despite a flurry of discourse on women's rights in the 1790s, the English Parliament never seriously considered women in its project of political reform. In France, except for a few unheeded voices such as those of Jean-Antoine-Nicolas Condorcet and Olympe de Gouges, even the revolutionaries who, as Hunt notes, "took such public and vociferous stands in favor of Protestants, Jews, free blacks, non-property owners, and even slaves ... did nothing for or actively opposed granting rights to women."[27] Nor were women's rights taken up by the Constitutional Convention that formed the new United States. Hunt thus recognizes a "paradox" that complicates her argument that the novel served as a catalyst for social change: "if women could be shown [in the novel] to be so noble, so intensely human, so longing for freedom, then how could they be deprived of their rights?"[28]

In one sense, the paradoxical difference between novel and society that Hunt describes is actually neither difference nor paradox. If we locate politics as Rancière does in the movements of speaking bodies, then the dissonance between the novel and eighteenth-century political revolutions in fact dissolves. For the novel confers on women little more entitlement to *rights* than did the governing bodies of France, England, and the United States. Among the novels I named earlier, only Sarah Scott's *Millenium Hall* addresses the status of women *as* women, fulfilling the claims for independence of (some upper-class) women and according them rulership over a more-than-domestic domain. The movements of characters like Pamela and Fanny Hill, Evelina and Fanny Price, are status movements; while these characters sometimes challenge gender biases, women's political or legal independence is not their goal. Moreover, *Millenium Hall* is not a conventionally plotted novel about a single "problematic individual" but a utopia in which the women's struggle for autonomy and authority lies safely in the retrospectively narrated past. And while the women of Millenium Hall have moved from dependents to philanthropic entrepreneurs who live a life of their choosing, they also operate within a space apart – rather as *Frankenstein*'s creature wished for himself, and on not wholly dissimilar grounds. Tellingly, in Scott's sequel to the novel, *Sir George Ellison* (1763), it is a man who tries out the women's economic program in the outside world.

But to the extent that the pervasive presence of women as speaking bodies in the novel failed to set in motion the case for women's rights, Hunt's "paradox" does offer a telling limit case to her argument, and mine, that the novel inaugurates a politics. Nancy Armstrong has claimed that through the eighteenth-century novel the "modern individual" became "first and foremost a woman."[29] If so, what does it mean for a person or group to stand as the quintessential "modern individual" while lacking civil representation and legal autonomy? Conversely, if the novel could not redistribute female bodies to create a part(y) *for* women, rather than simply consolidating middle-class hegemony *through* women, then how fairly can we really speak of a novel body politic? If the eighteenth-century novel does redistribute women's bodies, then why the dramatic gender gap between the novel body politic and the body politic of history? I will suggest that in this sense, what Hunt posits as a paradox between the novel and history stems from a contradiction within the novel itself, and one that requires us to scrutinize the ways in which the eighteenth-century novel can defer or deflect the very politics that it inaugurates.

Clarissa's Politick Body

I believe that the eighteenth-century English novel does attempt a politics of women's rights, but in ways that complicate and compromise the rather sanguine picture of the genre that I have advanced thus far. I want to begin exploring these complications by reading Samuel Richardson's *Clarissa* (1748) as an investigation of women's rights. While *Moll Flanders, Pamela, Fanny Hill* (1749), *Evelina* (1778), and *Mansfield Park* (1808) focus on a woman's rise in rank, riches, or respectability, what generates the action of *Clarissa* is a question purely of sex, or rather sex within a privileged-class framework: whether a virtuous, intelligent, gentry-class paragon of a woman may be entitled to the status of universal human, and on that basis be allowed to claim the rights of (a) man. Although she is the youngest child and female, Clarissa is accorded specific, traditionally male legal and financial rights when her grandfather's will makes her "independent of them all."[30] The will inaugurates a politics by giving Clarissa a part where there was no part, moving her from a legal and economic nonentity into the position of civil subject that only the men of her family have occupied. That Clarissa did not choose this new subjectivity matters little in view of her desire to keep it; that she cedes back to her father some rights of management does not alter her status as proprietor nor – more importantly – compromise her sense of herself as independent in person. She readily claims the right to stand against what she comes rather insolently to identify as "my father's authority, as it is called" and to recognize that authority as hostile to women's interests: "my Father . . . has not (any more than my Brother) a kind opinion of our Sex."[31] Richardson explicitly presents Clarissa as an exemplary case: as her friend Anna Howe tells her, "every eye . . . is upon you with the expectation of an example."[32]

Clarissa plays out this conflict set in motion by a woman's claim to rights within a social order – the Harlowe family – that is bent upon denying them. It is Clarissa's declaration of independence, at least as much as her economic privilege, that propels the Harlowes forcibly to attempt the one political arrangement – marriage – that can turn her from sovereign subject to *feme covert*, from participant in the family's social contract to sexual subordinate. The ensuing family politics – what Mrs. Harlowe calls a *"caballing"* – thus seeks to deprive Clarissa not simply of rights to property but of rights to self, and Clarissa's deployment of the terms of freedom and entitlement – her insistence upon "liberty of speech" and the right "to tell my own story," her belief in the "justice" of her cause, her claim for women of *"manly* virtue[s]" – all suggest a subject who is insisting on full humanity. The struggle between Clarissa and her family is a struggle for power as well as rights, a struggle between "enjoy[ing] that independence to which [her grandfather's] will has entitled me" and her subjugation to a father who "will be obeyed" or "you are no child of mine!"[33] Clarissa's refusal to marry Solmes is clearly not only the rejection of one odious suitor but an insistence on autonomous subjectivity rather than subjection as wife. Significantly, she seems able to make her claims because of the legal privilege she already enjoys: she wishes the "right and power" to "be made sole, as I may call it, and independent, for such the will as to that estate and the powers it gave (unaccountably, as they all said), made me."[34] Anna Howe's repeated critiques of male rule and female subordination only under-score this position and make of it a wider political argument than Clarissa herself puts forth.

Plate 17. Meeting of the Patriotic Women's Club at the time of the French Revolution. The women read reports of the National Convention sessions aloud and took up collections to help the needy families of patriots.

But the scenario that I have been describing is the starting point and not the ending of *Clarissa*. The novel unfolds, of course, not as the triumphant vindication of Clarissa's rights, but as the strategic struggle to deny them. *Clarissa* enacts this abrogation by reducing its heroine from singular subject to sexual subordinate, from a *person* insisting on her right to choose to a *body* who cannot prevent herself from being raped. In the end, of course, Clarissa amasses an "army of texts" to exonerate herself, to destroy Lovelace, and to take back the headship of her family. But this reclamation, such as it is, comes at the cost of her life. The visible turning point lies in the double meaning of her vow to return to "my father's house," which confirms that what Lovelace still reads as a temporal – hence political – struggle will be only a spiritual return.

Yet the force of civil law does allow Clarissa's will – in both senses – to exert its authority from beyond the grave. She is able to decree the disposition of her body, which now is not to be touched "but by those of my own sex" nor to be "unnecessarily exposed" to view; she is able to publicize Lovelace's deception by circulating his letters; and she is able to dispose of her lands and monies through direct bequests and through a fund, administered by women, to assist the "honest, industrious, labouring poor."[35] The family members who have denied her rights lose power even over their own happiness: her parents hardly outlive her, her siblings remain miserable in a "justice" that even her brother acknowledges is his due as repayment for his "vile and cruel treatment." Without denying the intricacies of Richardson's *magnum opus* or the ways in which Clarissa herself complicates a simple view of her, it does not seem exaggerated to say that in terms of the novel's body politics, Clarissa dies for women's rights: sacrificing herself in a dramatic display of the consequences of sexual subjugation, she resurrects her subjectivity and her social power through words.

But unlike the cheerful upward-bound novels I described earlier, *Clarissa* maps the movement of its speaking bodies by setting the claims she advances in conflict with the imperatives of plot: Clarissa does not survive to take her part. Moreover, her claims remain more or less private ones enacted within the family circle: she refuses, for example, to prosecute Lovelace in a court of law. And it is uncertain whether the empathy she receives from those who have loved her would move her readers inside or outside the novel to support a more general claim for women's civil rights. Each of these three factors complicates *Clarissa*'s potential to render a gendered politics. And with few exceptions, other eighteenth-century English novels that make a case for women's rights take a similarly tragic trajectory, enacting a denial, deferment, displacement, or derailment of those claims. In the wake of the French Revolution, for example, several English novels – Mary Hays's *The Victim of Prejudice* (1799), Eliza Fenwick's *Secresy* (1795), Amelia Opie's *Adeline Mowbray* (1805) and, most dramatically, Mary Wollstonecraft's posthumously published *The Wrongs of Woman; or, Maria* (1798) which I will discuss below – feature heroines whose rejection of subordination does them in.

I want to suggest, moreover, that the three factors limiting *Clarissa*'s ability to instantiate women's rights pervade eighteenth-century fiction in ways that render the novel a fragile mechanism for moving women from claims of rights to their realization beyond or even within the text. That is, the attempt to create a part(y) for women in the eighteenth-century novel is contingent and arguably compromised in at least three ways: through disjunctions between the claims of speaking voices and the workings of plot; through a circumscription of movement to the domestic or private realm; and through a separation of personal empathy from political entitlement – or, to use terms advanced by Barbara Johnson, of lyric from legal personhood.

The Reluctance of Plot

The first complication I want to examine is the tension common to many eighteenth-century novels between the claims of bodies and their movements in time and space. The denial of women's part reminds us that politics as Rancière conceives it is a two-phased affair. It entails not simply the articulation of new claims on behalf of previously unheard speaking bodies, but the movement of those bodies toward the achievement of the claims. In the novel, claims and movements sometimes operate along different axes, forging a dissonance between what is uttered and what is achieved. The eighteenth-century English novel is far more likely to deploy voices of narrators and characters that speak for women's rights than to move bodies into places where they can achieve them. Indeed, one feature of the novel is precisely its capacity to set forth a wide range of ideas, wishes, and polemics with which its plot does not have to come to terms. Discourse in the novel is highly elastic and potentially detachable from plot; this is why it was possible for Samuel Richardson to select out bits from his three huge novels and publish them as *A Collection of the Moral and Instructive Sentiments, Maxims, Cautions, and Reflections, Contained in the Histories of Pamela, Clarissa, and Sir Charles Grandison.*

Through this discursive flexibility, the very form of the novel may encourage a gap or tension between the utterances of voices and the movement of characters. Whether this gap stems from the novel's mandate for probability – in Clara Reeve's 1785 description, to "deceive us into a persuasion…that all is real"[36] – or from deeper resistances to women's participation in the social contract, the result is that the eighteenth-century novel is more willing to voice women's wrongs than to secure their rights. *Clarissa* is rich in pronouncements, most of them in the voice of Anna Howe, about the inequities of patriarchy and the wrongdoings of men, yet Anna too capitulates to marriage despite repeated insistence that she never will. Defoe's *Roxana* (1724) articulates quite vividly this gulf between the case for rights and the conventions of submission in a telling dialogue between Roxana and her Dutch suitor when Roxana observes that

the very Nature of the Marriage-Contract was … nothing but giving up Liberty, Estate, Authority, and every-thing, to the Man, and the Woman was indeed, a meer Woman ever after, that is to say, a Slave … that while a Woman was single, she was a Masculine in her politick Capacity; that she had then the full Command of what she had, and the full Direction of what she did; that she was a Man in her separated Capacity, to all Intents and Purposes that a Man cou'd be so to himself; that she was controul'd by none, because accountable to none, and was in Subjection to none; … [and] that whoever the Woman was, that had an Estate, and would give it up to be the Slave of *a Great Man*, that Woman was a Fool, and must be fit for nothing but a Beggar; that it was my Opinion, a Woman was as fit to govern and and enjoy her own Estate, without a Man, as a Man was, without a Woman; … and if she gave away that Power, she merited to be as miserable as it was possible that any Creature cou'd be.

To this passionate discourse, the Dutch merchant can only evoke the conventional social plot: unable to "answer the Force" of her argument, he reminds her that "the other Way was the ordinary Method that the World was guided by" and that he expected Roxana would "be content with that which all the World was contented with."[37] Roxana does eventually marry the merchant, but if her tortuous fate maps onto neither the conventional plot nor the one she imagines, one could also argue that the woes that come back to "haunt" her begin when she leaves her "fool" of a first husband and her five children for a "single" life.

In this tension between speaking bodies and their fortunes we can see what Lucien Goldmann calls "the internal contradiction between individualism as a universal value produced by bourgeois society and the important and painful limitations that this society itself brought to the possibilities of the development of the individual."[38] Setting aside the not insignificant fact that *Frankenstein*'s plot devolves around the fate of a world without women, it is worth remembering that here too it is the creature's discourse that carries forward the claim of entitlement that the plot denies. One might also recall Radclyffe Hall's 1928 *The Well of Loneliness* as a novel that instantiates a claim of humanity on behalf of homosexuals but denies its protagonist Stephen the same-sex relationship that Hall herself lived out with Una Troubridge, when the novel marries off Stephen's "feminine" partner Mary to a man. In each of these cases, plot blocks the redistribution in social space of the new part(y) advanced by discourse.

The utterances of speaking voices, then, may well be the formal location for the novel's most progressive impulse, the place where the foundation for a politics resides, the site of what Raymond Williams identifies as the "emergent" ideology that heralds change, with plot most commonly enacting a "dominant" or even "residual" ideology.[39] The very separability of discourse, its capacity to be extracted and anthologized (in Leah Price's sense[40]), preserves the claim to rights and at the same time detaches that claim from the necessity of its narrative fulfillment. This flexibility of discourse, I suggest, also leads critics to seize upon speech rather than plot to establish a novel's feminist possibilities. Thus we may cite Lady Catherine de Bourgh's criticism of entailment, Charlotte Lucas's jaded view of marriage, or Elizabeth Bennet's rebukes to Darcy while the plot of *Pride and Prejudice* rolls merrily toward its marital ends.

The distinction between voice and plot gives formal contours to Marthe Robert's observation that the novel is simultaneously democratic and conservative, that its "uncontested freedom" is nonetheless parasitic on "the material world whose reality it purports to 'reproduce.'"[41] The novel's freedom, I suggest, is far more a property of its speaking persons than of the plots in which they operate. If Fredric Jameson is right to claim that some kind of "political unconscious" structures all novels, then the irreconcilable tensions between voice and plot in eighteenth-century fiction seem to me to be revealing a contest over whether politics, in Rancière's sense of the word, should exist at all.

The Rights of Privacy

The contest is further complicated, I submit, by the propensity of eighteenth-century novels to redistribute women's speaking bodies within a purely private space, not so much fulfilling *or* denying a speaker's claims to rights as transforming them into movement of a different kind. The vast majority of eighteenth-century novels play out the question of a female body politic within the arena of "private" or "domestic" life — and in ways even more circumscribed than *Clarissa*, which raises legal and economic issues that many novels about women do not address. The question that then arises is whether these representations of private life may be taken as a *stand-in* for the public realm, and thus an impetus toward a politics, or as a *substitute* for that realm and thus a displacement or deflection of women's public agency. This is a key question, for example, around which critical responses to Nancy Armstrong's *Desire and Domestic Fiction* have revolved: does the domestic authority granted to women in fiction reclaim women's power or replace it? Do the politics of the private map the opportunities for women's civil rights or confirm women's curtailment to a separate space? Put in the terms articulated by Carole Pateman, does the enactment of a sexual contract – arguably the project of myriad novels built around a marriage plot – locate women outside the realm of the social contract or serve as its proving ground?[42] Feminist scholarship has long been divided on this point: Mary Poovey's *The Proper Lady and the Woman Writer*, for example, sees the domestic plot as a diminution of women's rights, while Eve Bannet's *The Domestic Revolution* argues that domestic representations enact forms of government by virtue of the analogy between state and family that was in place well before the eighteenth century.

Clearly there is no single answer to this question. Rather, the distinction is one between what I would call metaphoric and metonymic reading practices.[43] Metaphoric readings like Bannet's view the domestic social body as homologous to the body politic, so that whatever rights and powers are accorded women in the domestic sphere stand in for, and arguably encourage, public rights and powers. Metonymic readings, on the other hand, see the domestic sphere in contiguous relation with the public body and read the space of the family as a displacement of women's power even when the woman is "in charge" of the household and the husband's power appreciably diminished; these can only be diminutions of civil rights. This might well be Lennard Davis's position when he argues that "what plot does is refocus [the possibility of massive social change] into less threatening visions of personal and familial reform."[44] John Richetti, on the other hand, implies a metaphoric practice of reading when he says that the novel is centrally concerned with the "domestic and political" question of "who rules and who serves and who benefits from the arrangement."[45]

The power of a novel to advance an effective politics on behalf of women, then, would seem to rest heavily on this difference of view about the relationship of domestic to public life. Within a metaphoric reading, *Clarissa* is testing out the possibility for (gentry) women to be full participants in the social contract, and the novel becomes a concerted attempt to prevent this autonomy by other "parts" with contrary investments. This reading of *Clarissa* entails a transfer of meaning between domains; it is supported by Clarissa's own insistence that "the world is but one great family,"[46] which arguably lets the Harlowe family stand in for society at large, and is further reinforced by the text's deployment of societal concepts like "justice," "liberty," "independence," "rights," and "power." But the case can also be made that Clarissa's essentially private drama unfolds because of her confinement within the family, and that one tragedy of the novel is that Clarissa herself never challenges nor seeks redress outside from this separate and contained world. Moreover, the metaphoric argument is more difficult to make with respect to a novel such as *Evelina*, in which whatever claims exist for women's rights come not from Evelina herself but from equivocal characters such as Mrs. Selden, and in which the "young lady's entrance into the world," as the novel is subtitled, does not seem to define "the world" in terms that encompass civil rights.

Nowhere is the contest between metaphoric and metonymic reading enacted more frequently, I suspect, than in disagreements over whether Jane Austen's shifting bodies produce or fail to produce a politics. Claudia Johnson, who has made the most persuasive case for a "political" Austen, necessarily does so upon the claim that "the private is political."[47] But she also recognizes the conservative limits to which Austen's novels may lead. Does Knightley's move into Hartfield when he marries Emma signify a yielding of patriarchal power? Is there a shift in the body politic when Anne Elliot moves from being a "nobody" to a distinct somebody, not only winning back Wentworth but winning a man who says to her, "For you alone I think and plan"? Does Mrs. Croft's taking the reins from the Admiral – certainly a challenge to Sir Charles Grandison, who sees such a gesture as odiously masculine – signify a usurpation of the highest levels of military competence?[48] Or do all of these subtle redistributions of bodies provide a safe and separate realm for female action that will never challenge the important "rights of man"?

One approach to this dilemma lies not in choosing between these two ways of reading but in recognizing them as able to be mediated over time. Thus the small gesture in a metonymic realm may be at once a circumscribed expression of power and a harbinger of larger shifts to come. That is, by enacting a "family drama" in which one or more women who previously had no part begin to claim parts as women, the novel both proposes and defers a politics. Perhaps both the immediate failure and the long-term success of women's rights devolve in part from this dual status of the domestic plot – in and out of fiction – at once to mirror and to contain. Indeed, this enactment of rights at the private level may be a particular necessity for realizing the movement of women's bodies precisely because a sexual contract underwrites the social contract and must be subverted if the social contract is to include women as a full part.

The Limits of Empathy

Both the tension between voice and plot and the domestic circumscription of most eighteenth-century novels about women help to explain the gender gap Hunt recognizes between the novel and the social body politic. But we may also need to rethink Armstrong's claim that the modern individual was a woman, and Hunt's hypothesis that empathy became the basis for rights, by considering discontinuities between the modern individual as a psychological and as a political subject and thus also between empathy and entitlement. For when texts create a disparity between claims and movements, especially when the characters themselves do not recognize the gap between the two, then the very representation of interiority that produces our identification with the character encourages us to accept the contours of the character's own desires. Empathy and rights may even operate in opposition, so that identification with a character's struggles can find its fulfillment not in action but in grief – as in the weeping for Clarissa enacted at the novel's end by characters who were never disposed to grant Clarissa rights. A story like Maria Edgeworth's "The Grateful Negro" (1804) is a vivid case in point. It shows deep concern for mistreated slaves, setting up the loyal and trustworthy Caesar as the heroic slave who claims a part of humanity and with whom readers can empathize. Yet the text explicitly denies the wisdom of abolition and uses Caesar himself as a vehicle of identification with that denial when he chooses fidelity to his master over support of the slaves' revolt. Here the very rendering of the character as "three-dimensional" through the representation of his conflict between freedom and loyalty fosters an identification of the reader with the character's desires.

We might better be able to understand this contradiction between empathy and rights through a distinction Barbara Johnson has made between "lyric" and "legal" persons. Johnson suggests that there are "two different ways" in modern society "of stating what a person is." What she calls the "lyric person" is one recognized as having human feelings, wishes, complexity: the lyric person is "emotive, subjective, [and] individual." The "legal person," on the other hand, is politically entitled: "rational, rights-bearing, [and] institutional."[49] When Shylock makes his famous speech, "Hath not a Jew eyes? . . . If you prick us, do we not bleed?" he claims for Jews the status of lyric person. *The Merchant of Venice* has no interest whatsoever in giving Jews legal rights: on the contrary, in the climactic court scene, Shylock is deprived even of his right to be a Jew. The psychologically complex characters constructed by novels are almost always representations of lyric persons, but they may or may not be legal ones, and plots like that of "The Grateful Negro" take the very gap between lyric and legal persons as their subject. One could say that *Tom Jones* makes a legal person out of a lyric one – an heir out of a lovable bastard, while *Clarissa*, conversely, takes away Clarissa's chance for legal personhood and turns her into a figure of increasing emotional complexity and lyric suffering (although her own last testament does exert legal force beyond the grave). Characters who feel and who stimulate feeling in readers, in short, are not necessarily seen as entitled to legal rights.

In this case, the very dynamic of the novel that gives speaking voices their efficacy may also be encouraging a separation between the psychological and the political. The rendering of the "grateful Negro's" inner struggles between his loyalty to his master and longing for liberation fosters the reader's identification with the character's desires, and when the plot confers psychological but not legal humanity, our empathic identification with Caesar encourages us to accept *his* acceptance of his continued enslavement. This gap between empathy and rights answers Lynn Hunt's question, which I transmute here: if slaves could be found to be so noble, so human, so deserving of freedom, then how could they be deprived of their rights? In "The Grateful Negro," it is the good slave himself who "chooses" to be deprived of his rights. A poem like Anna Barbauld's "To the Poor" (1825) enacts a similar move by empathically addressing those

> Whose bursting heart distains unjust controll,
> Who feel'st oppression's iron in thy soul,
> Who drag'st the load of faint and feeble years,
> Whose bread is anguish and whose water tears –.

And yet Barbauld's point in this poem is emphatically *not* to argue for civil rights, for she then enjoins the poor to "Bear, bear thy wrongs" and "Bend thy meek neck beneath the foot of power!" because the "Lord above" will be kinder to them than the "Lords below." In moving the poor not to better conditions but to heavenly rewards, Barbauld also moves the reader away from the claims of politics.[50] Novels can easily lead us from claims of humanity to similarly plotted outcomes that defuse the political potential of those claims, all the more if that outcome is made to coincide with the character's own desires. If a female character is willing for her "separate Rights" to be "lost in mutual love," as Anna Barbauld exhorts in another poem,[51] then it may be only the most resisting reader who objects.

It is thus worth reconsidering the radical claims to which Lennard Davis points in his *Resisting Novels*, a work rather more neglected by scholars of the eighteenth-century novel than it might have been had it not been published in that banner year that brought us McKeon's *Origins of the English Novel*, Armstrong's *Desire and Domestic Fiction*, and Bender's *Imagining the Penitentiary*. Davis sees novels as elaborate cultural defense mechanisms that avoid rather than advance a politics: "novel reading as a social behavior helps prevent change." Through a "collective obsession for following the lives of fictional folk," says Davis, readers not only avoid political challenges, but are "lowered further into that dehumanizing pit from which they are trying to escape."[52] Certainly, "The Grateful Negro" enacts such a refocusing by shifting the problem from collective revolt to personal loyalty. If, as Hunt suggests, women are indeed the most prominent site for identificatory empathy in eighteenth-century fiction, characters through which readers of both sexes can yearn for the "impossible – and therefore tragic – but nonetheless believable, quest for autonomy,"[53] then readers may be invested in limiting the autonomy a character can realize. One real-world effect of the novel, in other words, may be to redirect the novel's readers towards empathy as a substitute for politics. This may be one reason why the novel, often in politically radical but tragic form (for example, in Godwin's *Caleb Williams*, 1794, or Hays's *The Victim of Prejudice*, 1799) flourished in non-revolutionary England during the 1790s but not in revolutionary France.

From Wrongs to Rights

But if the project of a politics is indeed the project of modernity, as I have suggested, then these various strategies of containment – plot, circumscription in the domestic, the deflection of rights into empathy that splits legal from lyric persons – are necessarily unstable practices, as a look back at *Frankenstein* makes clear. It may be worth noting that, in some sense, the longings the creature puts before Frankenstein are rather "feminine" desires: desires for affection, for sympathetic congress, for love returned. But Shelley's novel rejects this possibility of a metonymic refuge when Victor refuses to fashion a mate to dwell with the creature in a separate place. In so doing, the novel also demonstrates the dangerous consequences of separating plot from discourse by refusing a politics, for it is the failure to heed the creature's voice that generates the tragic events of *Frankenstein*. One must remember that the creature's "humanity" exists from the outset, and his turn toward murderous rage is the *effect* and not the *cause* of his deprivations; in his own words: "I am malicious *because* I am miserable"; "Let [man] live with me in the interchange of kindness, and instead of injury I would bestow every benefit upon him with tears of gratitude at his acceptance"; "if I cannot inspire love I will cause fear."[54] In a similar way Shylock has warned Antonio and his compatriots, "If you wrong us, shall we not revenge? . . . The villainy you teach me I will execute," although the early modern *Merchant of Venice* keeps Shylock from a revenge that the post-revolutionary *Frankenstein* exacts.

This language of threat in *Frankenstein* is surprisingly close in import and hardly more fierce in spirit than Abigail Adams's famous warning to her husband in 1776, as she questions John Adams's "passion for Liberty" when he refuses to curb the tyranny of husbands against wives. Adams suggests that if the *voices* of women – their claims to a politics – are not heeded, the *plot* of the new republic will change: "If particular care and attention is not paid to the Laidies we are determined to foment a Rebelion, and will not hold ourselves bound by any Laws in which we have no voice, or Representation." This warning, no less radical for having taken more than a century to begin to be realized, establishes a potential plot that Adams hopes the "Founding Fathers" will avoid. That John Adams, writing back on 14 April, "cannot but laugh" at Abigail Adams's "extraordinary Code of Laws" also reflects his fear precisely *of* a politics: "We have been told that our Struggle has loosened the bonds of Government every where; that Children and Apprentices were disobedient – that schools and colleges were grown turbulent; that Indians slighted their Guardians and Negroes grew insolent to their Masters. But your letter was the first Intimation that another Tribe more numerous and powerfull than all the rest were grown discontented."[55]

Does this not sound like Victor Frankenstein's fears of the creature, who might produce a tribe of offspring more numerous and powerful than the human race? That John Adams's fear is fear of women's power *over* men is also manifest: "We have only the Name of Masters, and rather than give up this, which would compleatly subject us to the Despotism of the Peticoat, I hope General Washington, and all our brave Heroes would fight." And when Abigail Adams retorts that "Arbitrary power is[,] like most other things which are very hard, very liable to be broken – and, notwithstanding all your wise Laws and Maxims we have it in our power not only to free ourselves but to subdue our Masters, and without Violence throw both your natural and legal authority at our feet,"[56] she is insisting that a change in the body politic is inevitable. The redistribution of speaking bodies is the plot of modernity, a plot that may emerge from the denial as much as from the granting of rights. Even a conservative narrative like "The Grateful Negro" carries a bit of warning, for although the slave revolt is quelled, the cruel master "was never afterwards able . . . to shake off his constant fear of a fresh insurrection among his slaves" and ends up returning to England to live "in obscurity and indigence."[57] Narratives that affirm the status quo, then, are also likely to leave a residue: a surplus or gap or contradiction between speaking voices and moving bodies that continues to trouble the social order so that it must be taken up again, both in and beyond novels, until it gets worked out. Perhaps both the short-term failure and the long-term success of a cause such as women's rights devolved in part from this duality of the novel both to advance and to contain a politics. This makes the novel a genre not simply about particular movements but about the very problem of movement.

Michael McKeon has suggested that by the end of the eighteenth century the novel has so well separated the rising individual from larger social conditions that "the autonomy of the self consists in its capacity to enter into largely negative relation" with a society it must learn to resist.[58] For female characters, however, the "autonomy of the self" could not even be realized without an active engagement with social conditions. Ideally, such a fictional project would align discourse and plot, public and domestic space, lyric and legal personhood, in a heroic gesture toward the necessity of a feminist part(y). Mary Wollstonecraft's *The Wrongs of Woman; or, Maria* takes on just this mandate to vindicate the rights not only of its characters but of women as a caste, and it does so through several formal practices that distinguish it from the novels I have thus far discussed. *The Wrongs of Woman* gives voice to characters from different social classes who together expose the consequences of women's exclusion from the political order, uncompromisingly insisting that it is the lot of all women from which these characters are suffering. This means that individual solutions are rendered unworkable, all the more as the novel refuses a distinction between domestic and public issues by making a husband's powers a matter for legal reform. Thus Maria must take her divorce case to a court of law in which she pleads for an equality within the social contract that rests on women's becoming universal subjects. And so closely does the novel connect Maria's and Jemima's desires with their civil status that to empathize with them all but requires one to support their political and legal rights.

But *The Wrongs of Woman* achieves this alignment of psychological and political subjectivity, of discourse and story, of domestic and public "spheres" at severe textual cost: the novel is unable to choose among the diverse – comic and tragic – possibilities for resolution that Wollstonecraft sketched out before her death. This short-circuiting of an outcome makes *The Wrongs of Woman* an "interrogative text" in Catherine Belsey's sense – one that opens options by "splitting the subject" and indeed splitting the plot.[59] More than any other eighteenth-century novel, I think, *The Wrongs of Woman* enacts the "speaking out" that founds a politics by insisting that those wrongs can be righted only *through* a politics. When the eponymous Maria takes her case to court – where it necessarily founders – *The Wrongs of Woman* also makes clear the impossibility of resolving within a work of fiction problems that fiction did not create. Wollstonecraft's uncharacteristic difficulty in completing the novel, her attempt at so many different alternatives to resolve the plot, propels the resolution to a place outside the novel, affirming Lukács's reminder that "the conflict between what is and what should be... cannot be abolished in the [life sphere of the novel] wherein these events take place."[60]

If *Frankenstein* shows the dangers of a politics unheeded, *The Wrongs of Woman*, literally its mother-text, illustrates both the potential and the limitations of novel politics. By allowing the movements of speaking bodies only insofar as they can operate with the "life sphere" of fiction, Wollstonecraft's unfinished novel exposes the fragility of the genre's ability to advance the politics that the eighteenth-century novel also seems bent on trying out. In those cases where the genre is successful in its project, we can indeed speak of a genuinely novel body politic. Where it fails, it often fails grandly, rather as Abigail Adams's proposal fails, in ways that not only offer lessons for the future but that inaugurate its possibilities.

See also: chapter 17, Queer Gothic; chapter 20, Home Economics; chapter 21, Whatever happened to the Gordon Riots?; chapter 23, Literary Culture as Immediate Reality.

Notes

1. Mary Wollstonecraft Shelley, *Frankenstein or The Modern Prometheus: The 1818 Text* (London: William Pickering, 1993), 81 and *passim*.
2. Shelley, *Frankenstein*, 99; John Locke, *The Second Treatise of Government* [ca.1681], §135, in *Two Treatises of Government*, ed. Peter Laslett (Cambridge: Cambridge University Press, 1960), 357.
3. Fredric Jameson, *The Political Unconscious: Narrative as a Socially Symbolic Act* (Ithaca, NY: Cornell University Press, 1981), 20.
4. Ibid., 20.
5. John Richetti, *The English Novel in History 1700–1780* (London: Routledge, 1999), 14.
6. On the history of the words "rights" and "rights of man," see Lynn Hunt, "The Paradoxical Origins of Human Rights," in *Human Rights and Revolutions*, ed. Jeffrey N. Wasserstrom, Lynn Hunt, and Marilyn B. Young (Lanham, MD: Rowman and Littlefield, 2000), 3–17. As Rousseau's *Emile* (1762) makes explicit, Rousseau's notion of the "rights of man" is decidedly gendered.
7. Jacques Rancière, *Disagreement: Politics and Philosophy* [*La Mésentente: politique et philosophie*], trans. Julie Rose (Minneapolis: University of Minnesota Press, 1999), 11, 17, 30.
8. Ibid., 22, 35.
9. Slavoj Žižek, *The Ticklish Subject: The Absent Centre of Political Ontology* (London: Verso, 1999), 188. As Žižek recognizes, this claim to represent the whole does carry the danger of a new hierarchy in which those previously without rights claim in their turn to be the only legitimate subjects.
10. Ibid. Habermas outlines his concept of the "bourgeois public sphere" in *The Structural Transformation of the Public Sphere*, trans. Thomas Burger (Cambridge, MA: MIT Press, 1991).
11. Rancière, *Disagreement*, 37, 42, 58.
12. Ibid., 59.
13. Shelley, *Frankenstein*, 99, 108.
14. Ibid., 107, 109.
15. Ibid., 121.
16. Ibid., 122–24.
17. Ibid., 143–44.
18. Mikhail Bakhtin, "Discourse in the Novel," in *The Dialogic Imagination*, trans. Caryl Emerson and Michael Holquist (Austin: University of Texas Press, 1981), 332–33, emphasis Bakhtin's.

19. Paula Backscheider, *Revising Women: Eighteenth-Century "Women's Fiction" and Social Engagement* (Baltimore, MD: Johns Hopkins University Press, 2000), 9–10.

20. John Cleland, *Memoirs of a Woman of Pleasure* (1749; London: Penguin, 1985), 39, 223.

21. Equiano's narrative is autobiographical, but Vincent Carretta has argued that it manifests some fictional qualities; see "Olaudah Equiano or Gustavus Vassa? New Light on an Eighteenth-Century Question of Identity," *Slavery and Abolition* 20 (1999): 96–105.

22. The claim of worthy mobility is complicated, of course, if we see Pamela as a crass opportunist, as Fielding did, or view Moll as an unrepentant fiend, as some critics have argued. Yet in substituting calculation for virtue, such characters arguably show another path of movement toward social rewards.

23. John Bender, *Imagining the Penitentiary: Fiction and the Architecture of Mind in Eighteenth-Century England* (Chicago: University of Chicago Press, 1987), 5.

24. Hunt, "The Paradoxical Origins of Human Rights," 13–14.

25. The most radical of the Revolutionary French constitutions would have achieved universal male suffrage and many characteristics of what we might now call a welfare state. It was adopted, however, just weeks before "Thermidor" (in July 1794), the downfall of the Jacobin regime of Robespierre.

26. Marthe Robert, *Origins of the Novel* [*Roman des origines et origines du roman*], trans. Sacha Rabinovitch (Bloomington: Indiana University Press, 1980), 4.

27. Hunt, "The Eighteenth-Century Self," chapter from an unpublished book, 25. I am grateful to Lynn Hunt for allowing me to cite this chapter, which develops more fully the arguments advanced in her 1999 Clifford Lecture for the American Society for Eighteenth-Century Studies and in her essay "The Paradoxical Origins of Human Rights."

28. Ibid., 23–24.

29. Nancy Armstrong, *Desire and Domestic Fiction: A Political History of the Novel* (Oxford: Oxford University Press, 1987), 4.

30. Samuel Richardson, *Clarissa, or, The History of a Young Lady*, 3rd ed. (London, 1751; rpt. New York: AMS Press, 1990), 1:41.

31. Ibid., 1:49.

32. Ibid., 1:4.

33. Ibid., 1:30, 49–50.

34. Ibid., 1:75.

35. Ibid., 8:97, 110–11.

36. Clara Reeve, *The Progress of Romance* (London, 1785), 2:111.

37. Daniel Defoe, *Roxana, or, The Fortunate Mistress* (1724; Oxford: Oxford University Press, 1964), 148–49.

38. Lucien Goldmann, *Towards a Sociology of the Novel* [*Pour une sociologie du roman*], trans. Alan Sheridan (London: Tavistock, 1975), 12.

39. See Raymond Williams, *Marxism and Literature* (Oxford: Oxford University Press, 1977), 121–27.

40. See Leah Price, *The Anthology and the Rise of the Novel* (Oxford: Oxford University Press, 2000).

41. Marthe Robert, *Origins of the Novel*, 4–5.

42. See Carole Pateman, *The Sexual Contract* (Stanford, CA: Stanford University Press, 1988).

43. I refer here to the famous distinction of Roman Jakobson between substitutionary or metaphoric language and the language of metonymy or contiguity. "Two Aspects of Language and Two Type of Aphasic Disturbances," *Selected Writings II: Word and Language* (The Hague: Mouton, 1971), 239–59.

44. Lennard Davis, *Resisting Novels: Ideology and Fiction* (New York: Methuen, 1987), 218–19.

45. Richetti, *The English Novel in History*, 4.

46. Richardson, *Clarissa*, 1:4.

47. Claudia L. Johnson, *Jane Austen: Women, Politics, and the Novel* (Chicago: University of Chicago Press, 1988), xx.

48. I am grateful to Leslie Jansen for pointing out this antecedent to Austen's famous "taking the reins" scene. See *Sir Charles Grandison*. Vol. 6, letter LV.

49. Barbara Johnson, "Anthropomorphism in Lyric and Law," *Yale Journal of Law and the Humanities* 10 (1998): 550.

50. Anna Barbauld, "The Poor," in *The Poems of Anna Letitia Barbauld*, ed. William

McCarthy and Elizabeth Kraft (Athens: University of Georgia Press, 1994), 129.

51. Barbauld, "The Rights of Women," in *Poems*, 121–22.

52. Davis, *Resisting Novels*, 17, 22.

53. Hunt, "The Eighteenth-Century Self," 21.

54. Shelley, *Frankenstein*, 123, emphasis mine.

55. *The Book of Abigail and John: Selected Letters of the Adams Family 1762–1784*, ed. L. H. Butterfield et al. (Cambridge, MA: Harvard University Press, 1975), 122–23, 127 (letters of 31 March and 14 April 1776).

56. Ibid., 123, 127 (letters of 14 April and 7 May 1776).

57. Maria Edgeworth, "The Grateful Negro" in *The Works of Maria Edgeworth* (London, Pickering and Chatto, 2003), Vol. 12.

58. Michael McKeon, *The Origins of the English Novel 1600–1740* (Baltimore: Johns Hopkins University Press, 1987), 419.

59. See Catherine Belsey, *Practical Criticism* (London: Methuen, 1987), chapter 4.

60. Georg Lukács, *Theory of the Novel*, (Cambridge: MIT Press, 1973), 122.

FURTHER READING

Backscheider, Paula. "The Novel's Gendered Space." In *Revising Women: Eighteenth-Century "Women's Fiction" and Social Engagement*, ed. Paula Backscheider. Baltimore, MD: Johns Hopkins University Press, 2000. 6–15.

Bannet, Eve. *The Domestic Revolution: Enlightenment Feminisms and the Novel*. Baltimore, MD: Johns Hopkins University Press, 2000.

Hunt, Lynn. "The Paradoxical Origins of Human Rights." In *Human Rights and Revolutions*, ed. Jeffrey N. Wasserstrom, Lynn Hunt, and Marilyn B. Young. Lanham, MD, and Oxford: Rowman and Littlefield, 2000. 3–17.

Jameson, Fredric. *The Political Unconscious: Narrative as a Socially Symbolic Act*. Ithaca, NY: Cornell University Press, 1981.

Johnson Barbara, "Anthropomorphism in Lyric and Law" *Yale Journal of Law and the Humanities* 10 (1998): 549–74.

Lanser, Susan S. *Fictions of Authority: Women Writers and Narrative Voice*. Ithaca, NY: Cornell University Press, 1992.

Rancière, Jacques. *Disagreement: Politics and Philosophy* [*La Mésentente: politique et philosophie*], trans. Julie Rose. Minneapolis: University of Minnesota Press, 1999.

23

Literary Culture as Immediate Reality

Paula R. Backscheider

In recent years, a great deal of attention has been given to the influence of the literary marketplace, manuscript culture, print culture, and media culture somewhat to the neglect of the non-commercial side of writers' consciousnesses. At every moment, not only what their contemporaries were writing and to what ends they were experimenting but also what had been written in the past to what purpose and with what reception lived in eighteenth-century writers' consciousnesses as did a recognition of the cultural capital and exchange value of each genre. Defoe wrote poetry and novels; Behn, Haywood, Smollett, and Goldsmith poetry, novels, and plays; Fielding and Burney plays and novels, and Johnson poetry, a play, and an Oriental tale. Various stories – often economic – have been offered to explain authors abandoning one genre for another. For some of these writers, additional, more or less familiar theories circulate to explain the abandonment of the more prestigious and lucrative theater for the novel – Johnson's and Smollett's lack of theatrical talent, Burney's patriarchal discouragement, Walpole's buy-out of Fielding-the-dramatist. Admittedly there are compensatory stories, such as Behn's recognition of prose fiction's potential power as political propaganda and Fielding's consummate talent as novelist. John Dryden knew exactly what he was doing in *Absalom and Achitophel* (1681) when he eschewed drama to turn a biblical paraphrase into formal verse satire: claiming and demonstrating what Antonio Gramsci has identified as the superior moral and intellectual position that maintains power. To choose to write fiction was more than an economic and talent decision, and to incorporate other genres – either as full examples or shadowy traces – a habitual practice and often a deliberate and telling hegemonic move made within a literary milieu that was deeply familiar and nuanced to them, one as powerful and constitutive as the market.

Novelists were a subculture within the literary community, sharing a distinctive "web of significance"[1] colored at every point by awareness of other writers and genres. They practiced within a culture of strong acceptance of a hierarchy of genres, as is obvious from the considerable anxieties they demonstrated with their various attempts to identify the novel with more prestigious forms. Genre, therefore, was a major part of the schema that was a fundamental constitutive element in their composing and compositions. These writers worked at tables on which genres were laid out like an artist's paints and brushes – or like a surgeon's scalpels and forceps.

The eighteenth century is somewhat anomalous in literary history, and some of the major contrasts to other periods are the number of writers who wrote in multiple genres, the number who actively scrutinized literary culture, their rising sense of the relationship between a nation's global reputation and its literature, and, of course, their awareness of creating an *English* novel. Perhaps no text illustrates the relationships eighteenth-century writers had to genres as fully as Henry Fielding's *Tom Jones* (1750). Fielding self-consciously aligns his text with some genres, parodies some, embeds some, calls attention to others, and yet claims to be creating a new genre. Perhaps most interesting are those that are constitutive, such as epic, which is overtly invoked, and classical and Renaissance satire, which, as in Smollett's novels, are silently employed. Fielding came to *Tom Jones* after proving himself the most creative dramatist of the eighteenth century and after the success of *Joseph Andrews* (1742), a text more satiric than novelistic. The excess and ebullience of *Tom Jones* speaks of authoritative command and confidence, and it is obvious but atypical evidence of a constitutive literary milieu.

For many writers in every time, as it is for Fielding, the literary milieu is one of the dominant aspects of their world. For a subset of these writers (and I would not include Fielding in this group), literature is dominant in shaping a schema, the term psychologists use for the complex, unconscious knowledge structures that organize past reactions and experiences. To a significant degree, they form schema by which they interpret the world, recognizing, ordering, and articulating experience through past and present literature. For example, their reading and seeing plays shaped schema of how people relate and what were likely outcomes of events and actions. When Eliza Haywood's Betsy Thoughtless suddenly realizes that her actions are like Betty Modish's in Colley Cibber's *The Careless Husband* (1704), the link arises from this schema. More than allusion, intertextuality, or even cultural myth or archetype, such moments are constitutive ways of ordering, interpreting, and communicating experience and meaning; they allow the mind to construct analogies and models and to solve problems. At every point, then, literary culture must be factored in, its relative weight gauged for each individual writer at the time of each production, and the possibility that it was fundamentally constitutive considered. Simply, a constitutive element "makes a thing what it is." It has "the power to institute, establish, and enact" (*American Heritage Dictionary*, *Webster's New World Dictionary*).

Hypothesizing literary consciousness as an unusually dominant schema may provide a way of approaching two tantalizing questions for novel critics influenced by Mikhail Bakhtin. The first as formulated by Michael Holquist, a major translator, editor, and Bakhtinian theorist, is, "How can reality appear to be immediate if it comes to us in *forms?*"[2] The second regards Bakhtin's "unremitting emphasis" on dialogic elements that are external to the text:[3] How exactly are they activated? I want to consider these questions with several highly artificial literary works while hypothesizing literature as providing an unusually influential schema for their authors. Above all, I am exploring the ways that texts that call attention to their artificiality and even aestheticism can be apprehended as in the zone of maximal contact with immediate reality. The novelistic zone is described repeatedly by Bakhtin: "a zone of contact with the present in all its openendedness"; "a zone of maximally close contact between the represented object and contemporary reality in all its inconclusiveness – and consequently a similarly close contact between the object and the future."[4] Openended, predictive, immediate – these have become the defining words for powerful novels. How does an especially artificial, self-conscious form initiate the feeling of *immediate* reality? How can such a text become the bridge that relates text and context, thereby releasing the full dialogic potential of a text? How can such texts make concepts that do not originate in lived experience find application in experience?

My case-study texts are Nathaniel Lee's *The Princess of Cleve*, a play based on the English translation of *La Princesse de Clèves* (1678) by Marie-Madeleine Pioche de la Vergne, comtesse de Lafayette [produced in 1682];[5] Eliza Haywood's *The History of Miss Betsy Thoughtless* (1751) and Oliver Goldsmith's *The Vicar of Wakefield* (sold 1762; published 1766), two important mid-century novels with markedly different tones and intertextualities; and, finally, *Julia, A Novel, Interspersed with some Poetical Pieces* (1790) by Helen Maria Williams, which was inspired in part by Johann Wolfgang von Goethe's *Die Leiden des Jungen Werther* (1774). Literary culture is a constitutive, deep structure in all of these texts, and these writers make genres "heroes," "master categories" within a text, but, I argue, they exploit the fact that genre is both within and external to the text, therefore composing multiple interpenetrations between text and lived experience.

The cross-genre pairing of the first case represents the reality of drama's importance at the end of the seventeenth century, the cross-Channel pairings of the first and last capture the importance of literature from France in the early period and from Germany for the later, and the cross-gender pairings add another constitutive consideration. Through these texts, I join other contributors in this book in reminding readers of the reality of the European literary community and consciousness, of the deceptiveness of constructed trajectories of the "triumph" of the novel over other genres, and of the temptation to overestimate the number of novels published in the century and readers' alleged preference for them over other reading material. Incidentally, the texts call to mind the steady pressure that poetry and drama exerted on the novel, the ubiquity of mixed forms, and the century's assumption of permeable genre boundaries.

These authors share three characteristics important for my inquiry: they employ and integrate numerous genres to which they call attention; their texts were recognized in their own time as eccentric and innovative; and all of them had strong authorial identities, strong enough to be external dialogic elements. Before I take up individual cases, I will describe them briefly in these terms.

La Princesse de Clèves is often described as the "first modern" novel, and it was recognized shortly after publication as a new genre, "the *galant* history."[6] The reaction to it was extraordinary in both France and England and its influence on English fiction is well known. Lee, writing in this same culture and replicating the mixed nature of his source, called his play "this farce, comedy, tragedy, or mere play" in the dedication. Tara and Philip Collington summarize: "Just as La Fayette's novel represents a groundbreaking generic hybrid, composed of history, fiction, memoir and romance, Lee's play seems an incongruous mixture of distinct dramatic forms."[7] Critics have demonstrated that Lafayette's novel is richly indebted to the drama of her time, thereby passing along to Lee another level of genre speech acts. The history of Lee's and Lafayette's texts became intermingled and cast a long arc, for Lee's play, like many plays, was more successful as reading material than in production. It was first published in 1689, the year after the prose English translation of the novel was reprinted. The best descriptions of the relationship among these texts may be April Alliston's conception of correspondence and flow, "a sharing of conventions – formal, narrative, thematic, and iconic."[8]

The range of literary allusions is exceptional in both *Betsy Thoughtless* and *The Vicar of Wakefield*; commentary on Goldsmith's novel has recognized this fact since its publication, and much recent criticism of *Betsy* is devoted to explicating the work that various embedded genres perform. Haywood's novel is composed out of romance, domestic fiction, *Bildungsroman*, conduct book, and drama, and employs major episodes from *La Princesse de Clèves*. Goldsmith's includes, among others, romance, fable, sermon, ballad, allegory, elegy, song, periodical essay, and idyll. In addition to poetry, *Julia* includes elements of the conduct book, picturesque nature description, and allusions to plays, all of which are thematically and ideologically constitutive rather than merely metaphoric. Goethe's novel has been said to mark the beginning of modern German prose. Both letters about travel and lyrical descriptions of scenery with the viewers' emotional responses were literary rages, and the appeal of epistolary fiction was rising all over Europe. Werther writes an ode, and, in addition to *Ossian*, other trendy cult texts play a part, as do the newly published letters between the poet Friedrich Klopstock and his wife Meta.

All of these English writers were well-known literary presences. Lee had already had ten plays produced, two in collaboration with Dryden and four that had been great hits. His *Lucius Junius Brutus* (1680) and *The Massacre of Paris* (1689) had been banned, and his and Dryden's *The Duke of Guise* (1682) postponed for four months. Known for his spectacular effects, lyrical language, and hard, public drinking, Lee had an ambivalent relationship to the court in an especially turbulent time. By 1751, Haywood had written in most of the important and influential genres of the period and created or advanced several. She was acutely aware of the functions literature performs in society and the claims made for genres. For instance, *The Adventures of Eovaai* (1736) is a stunning "advice to a *princess*" within a romance and also a vitriolic contribution to anti-Walpole propaganda. She had written dramatic, political, and periodical literature in addition to her many novels, had been proprietor of her own bookseller's shop in Covent Garden, and had been arrested for seditious libel.[9] As Maureen Harkin says, Goldsmith's "life and career [were] anchored in the theatres and clubs, salons and reviews that constituted the literary sphere in mid-century London."[10] With Edmund Burke and Joshua Reynolds, he was a founding member of Samuel Johnson's Club; Haywood was part of the Hill and Fielding circles. Both were vigorous participants and analysts of literary and print culture, as proved by publications such as Haywood's *Invisible Spy* (1755) and Goldsmith's *An Enquiry into the Present State of Polite Learning in Europe* (1759).

Williams was also a star in the literary sky, already being hailed as a poetic genius.[11] At age 21, she had published *Edwin and Eltruda* (1782), a metrical tale about the Wars of the Roses, and then made all the papers with *An Ode on the Peace* (1783), a post-American war reflection on the benefits of peace, and with *Peru* (1784), a condemnation of Pizarro's conquest of the Indians. The 1786 collection of her poems listed over 1,500 subscribers, and William Wordsworth's first published poem is an appreciation, "On seeing Miss Helen Maria Williams weep at a tale of distress" (*European Magazine*, March 1787). During the time she wrote the novel, Williams was part of a glittering literary and political circle, hosted salon-style gatherings at her home in Bloomsbury, and was something of an epitomizing spectacle. Samuel Johnson, Frances Burney, Charlotte Smith, Anna Barbauld, and Whig Members of Parliament were her friends. She took for granted an audience who shared similar interests, and the full title of *Julia* suggests its generic self-consciousness.

Lee's and Williams's texts are composed in some of the most rigid forms of their time, and those by Haywood, Goldsmith, and Williams repeatedly draw attention to literary forms and conventions, thereby highlighting the inseparability of mode of representation and substantive, mimetic content. All of these texts argue that the novel's zone of maximal contact goes beyond reference to socio-historical specifics. Rather they tap into the overwhelming power of what a people *feels* to be reality. Schiller described *Werther* as "compressing" the temper of the time, and Raymond Williams describes "thought as felt and feeling as thought" in some texts. Primarily through investigating dialogic elements external to the text, my essay pushes toward an understanding of this effect.

The Princess of Cleve

Nathaniel Lee's *The Princess of Cleve* is an angry diagnosis of the drama and court of his time and prophetic commentary on immediate society and on prose fiction. For his circle and his audience, the French romances and continental novels were well known, and, in fact, so were the historical events and individuals described in Lafayette's novel.[12] They read them, discussed and corresponded about them, and other plays had dramatized episodes from them, as John Banks had Scudéry's *Artamenès, ou Le Grand*

Cyrus (1649–53) in his *Cyrus the Great* (1695). The publication of the English translation, *The Princess of Cleve. The most famous Romance. Written in French by the greatest Wits of France. Rendred into English by a Person of Quality, at the Request of some Friends*, in 1679 made the wildly popular, much discussed and debated *La Princesse de Clèves* even more widely available and discussed.

The novel was about a crisis moment, the Princess's recognition of her love for a man not her husband, both men important courtiers. At that time, comedy, "hard" and city, and heroic tragedy were obsessed with crisis moments and political and sex intrigues. Lee repeatedly juxtaposes episodes from the novel and set pieces from these three dramatic forms. He has been identified as the "outstanding creative figure" of his time because of his command of the full resources of the theatre,[13] and perhaps no other dramatist could have produced a play that simultaneously deployed and critiqued the deep structures and defining strategies of the major genres in current circulation.

As Lee brings his audience into the play with its familiar plot, it gradually becomes more novelistic, thereby making the play and the novel so inseparable as to offer cynical reinterpretations of Lafayette's text and to generate prescient commentary on "novel." His major tactic is to reproduce scenes from the novel with quotations of Lafayette's most significant lines while depending upon a repertory of discourses and strategies from a variety of kinds of plays in complicated and brilliant ways, as key scenes and the ending to the play show. For example, Act II.iii stars the Princess, bringing the audience back to the text of the novel with his rendering of the moment in which the Princess begs the Prince to take her away from the court. In this scene, however, Lee has imposed his own interpretations of the Princess and Nemours onto Lafayette's text and converts dramatic irony and juxtaposed speeches and scenes, all frequent theatrical strategies, into something approaching novelistic voyeurism. Thereby he produces a shocking moment of revelation about the tragedies *and* comedies of his time and generates quite different meanings for the plot and characters in *La Princesse de Clèves*. His play opens *in medias res* on the morning after the Princess's marriage, and thereby focuses on the central motivational factor in the novel: that the Princess did not know what love was when she married the Prince. Against the backdrop of the other characters' lust and gratification, Lee has the Prince recognize he loves her but that she cannot love him. Symbolically, Lee has Cleve call his wife by her maiden name, "Chartres," throughout the play. In the play, the Princess is already in love with Nemours. Act I concludes with her situation rendered into a creative variant on the dilemma of the heroine of a she-tragedy. She says:

> Methinks I see fate set two bowls before me –
> Poison and health, husband and Nemours . . .
> . . . .
> But when Nemours my fancy does recall,
> The bane's so sweet that I could drink it all.
> (I.iii.195–200)

Lee changes the meaning of the Princess's attraction to Nemours and, in fact, gives it greater thematic significance. In a speech that makes her sexual desire unmistakable, the Princess tells her maid that she has dreamed of Nemours, who brought her "Dissolving pains, and swimming, shuddering joys." The Nemours she loves is different, too. Lee understood that many, perhaps most, of his audience would have a strong impression of Nemours's character, so he takes drastic measures to alter it. The play opens with Nemours and Bellamore requesting that a eunuch sing an exceptionally explicit song about a wet dream and with allusions to Nemours's insatiable bisexual appetites. This beginning belongs with the obscene verse exchanged and published by rakes like John Wilmot, Earl of Rochester, not to the novel, heroic tragedy, or even to "hard" Restoration comedy. Like this fifth constitutive genre, his circle's poetry, the first two acts of the play include many references to sexual arousal, to pressing needs for release, and to satisfaction gained as often through fantasized gratification as through sexual acts. Lee thus turns the Princess into one more bedazzled woman and transforms Nemours from the glittering aristocrat into what he calls him in the dedication, "a ruffian reeking from Whetstone's Park," a whore's alley. Nemours speaks lines that none of the characters in Lafayette's novel would and often with an anti-Catholic twist to please Lee's audience. In insisting all men are the same, he says, "Did I not see Father Patrick, declaiming against flesh in Lent . . . yet protest to the ladies, that fat arm of his, which was a chopping one, was the least member about him?" (II.iii.38–42). Thus, the princess in the play is not awakened to what love is by acquaintance with an admirable man but is at the beginning of a long line of English heroines including Eliza Haywood's Belinda in *The British Recluse* and Richardson's Clarissa who prefer the dangerous, seducing rake to a steady, mundane man (Haywood names Belinda's suitor "Worthly"). In the key eavesdropping scene, Nemours exults in the play: "She loves, she loves, and I'm the happy man." He gloats over her "daring virtue" and his triumph over such a "chaste mind." In the novel, he is "desperately in love," and as jealous as her husband for "he could not imagine she had so violent a passion for him, as to need recourse to so extraordinary a Remedy" (162–3). In the play, his triumph is not about love but power, and his words point to Lovelace's aggressive desire in *Clarissa* (1748). Lee quickly juxtaposes another scene in which Marguerite, Nemours's true witty match, enters disguised, and he woos her by telling her he is "primed and charged" and "can fit [her] every way."

In the novel, the Prince is the heir to his father's achievements in battle, diplomacy, and state administration, and in Lee's play his language is that of high tragedy. His dialogue contrasts to Nemours's protean language and to that of the characters in the subplot, whose discourse is from low comedy, or what had already morphed from city and sex comedies into the novelistic language of ephemeral English prose fiction with titles such as *The Death and Burial of Mistress Money* (1678). Remarkably, Lee includes summaries of what would become ubiquitous novel plots and, therefore, his play contributes to the recognition of how early this emergent genre mobilized writers' anti-novel discourse. Marguerite accuses Nemours: "And thou villainy, treachery, perjury, all those monstrous, diabolical arts that seduce young virgins from their innocent homes, to set 'em on the highway to hell and damnation" (4.1.199–202). From Haywood through Goldsmith, such plots dominate courtship novels, and Lee's ability to conflate the meanings of "highway" as the physical road taken and the metaphysical path to eternity anticipates the discourse of novels that exploit what Umberto Eco defined as ambiguous words, as in Robinson Crusoe's "improvements" and Clarissa's "law."

Another example of Lee's anticipation of English novel plots is when Nemours says at the beginning of Act IV: "How it fires my fancy to steal into a garden, to rustle through the trees, to stumble up a narrow pair of backstairs, to whisper through the hole of the door, to kiss it open, and fall into thy arms with a flood of joy." Behn's Philander does exactly this in Part I of *Love Letters between a Nobleman and his Sister* (1684). The obscene double meaning, so obvious in Lee's lines, is always lurking in the novel of amorous intrigue and is unleashed by the reader as much as by the writer, as Richardson's *Pamela* (1741) would notoriously demonstrate. Lee is drawing upon what would become the content of English novels by Eliza Haywood, a detailed mapping of a woman's emotional life. The Princess and Marguerite are contrasting case studies, and their characters and fates are marked almost as much by these fictions as by the dramatic genres to which they belong. Just as Aphra Behn will move inside the Sylvia of Part I of *Love Letters* to reveal an amoral, lustful adventurer in Part III, Lee moves inside Marguerite's witty and suffering conventional lines to reveal her lust and suggest that Nemours reads her aright. Lee absorbs these fictions and is one of the first dramatists to exploit the fascination with the moods behind prescribed social actions and the motive behind actions. Putting the two *Cleves* together reveals how differently explorations of character, motive, and contextual mores were depicted and for what different ends they were done in the two genres.

Robert Hume argues rightly that Lee is exposing the "hollowness" of the value systems of both heroic/*précieuse* tragedy and Carolean sex comedy,[14] but Lee also exposes and critiques what he saw in the novel's characters and those who admired the book. In doing so, he identifies and sometimes uses major novel strategies. Nemours's ability to change discourses and levels within discourses implies his – and the novel form's – dangerous heteroglossia, the quality that allows accusations of a lack of a fixed, readable value system and, therefore, characters without firm identities and a text without a moral. The master of the hostile takeover, such novelistic rakes prefer not to rape or to enter into the mutually beneficial contract of companionate marriage. At times, Nemours's language, like Lovelace's, is so exaggerated as to approach parody of the discourse, potentially laying bare the false contract of equality that the language of the *précieux* performs.

Lee sometimes anticipates novelistic readers. He rejects dramatic irony and makes his audience voyeurs like Nemours, seeing but not confessing to seeing that, rather than a vision of a perfect love, lust drives the Princess. Eavesdropping and voyeurism do not produce the same effects as dramatic irony, and Lee both exploits theatrical dramatic irony and, as novelists will come to do frequently, implicates the audience by engaging them in the questions being discussed about the novel. As *Le mercure galant* illustrates, readers were accustomed to regarding many French fictions as written to encourage discussion and judgment: "Which character suffered more?" "Was the Princess wrong to take the desperate gamble of telling her husband?" Lee raises questions that novelists will assume to be central to the form, including "What are Nemours' motives and is there any change at all in his character?" Lee exploits this reader position to reveal how voyeurs see what they want to imagine experiencing. Like Jane Austen's deliberate eavesdroppers, Nemours wants to obtain information that flatters him and helps him determine a course of action. The audience learns nothing that they do not already know, and so their focus is on the puzzle of Nemours's character, not on watching the implications of something they know will come about. They are engaged as novelistic readers, either seeking to understand Nemours as spies do[15] or identifying with him as voyeurs do. They view him in different places with characters with whom he is unselfconscious and arrogantly honest about himself. He makes the audience witnesses to knowledge they would prefer not to have confirmed more often than he grants them the empowering anticipation that dramatic irony creates.

In his dedication, Lee had compared Nemours to the statue of the naked gladiator in Hyde Park, which "they may walk by and take no notice," and his play to a series of plays in which libertines were taken as mere diversions. By creating a Nemours behind the Nemours of Lafayette's novel and relating him to the type characters of sex comedies even as he shows his effect on the elevated couple of a heroic tragedy, he arrests those who would "walk by" the destruction such a man wreaks. Thoroughly disaffected with the court by this time,[16] Lee has discovered a safe way to point out the kind of survivors it breeds and to compare its sexual licentiousness to Whetstone's Park. Again and again, Lee attacks people seeing what they want to see, and by merging the reading community with the theatrical one produces new results. The objects of anti-novel discourse in the first decades of the eighteenth century were continental romances and novellas and the texts by Behn, Manley, and Haywood like them. As Lee's examples of plots show, they were saturated in sex, especially extramarital sex. In his exposé of Lafayette's novel, he attacks Lafayette's discourse, her elegant language that masks the "reek" of her characters with a desirable, "polite," "cultured" façade. He sees clearly that the language and the trappings — Edenic gardens, glittering balls, and beautiful people — make the fictions more dangerous. He anticipates, then, the attack on novels as fantasy machines fostering destructive behavior and unrealistic hopes. Replacing the fantasy of learning what the heights of love were through the symbolism of sexual ecstasy would be fantasies of rising in social status by attaining gentility through the symbolism of elegant language. Simultaneous with the recognition of the death of the Cleves' "fanatic" language, Lee saw the chimera of Nemours's ventriloquism and its implications. Defoe, like Lee, saw the danger of a protean character who could master discourses and languages, who rose from the novel of amorous intrigue but could perform king's mistress and Quaker matron. In the shifting discourse of characters like Nemours, Poltrot, and Roxana were the seeds of what would be attacked as hypocritical, hegemonic middle-class morality – the polite, elevated, even moralistic, masking the crass and carnal.

In the conclusion, Lee brilliantly set in motion discourses in dialogic relationship to each other. Poltrot from the low plot continues to mirror the upper characters by pledging faithfulness to Celia "in serge, grogram or crepe," the discourse of parody of the City's commercial values familiar from city comedies and English novellas. Nemours describes women and Marguerite in prose, promises yet another Restoration comedy wit combat ("Now thou shalt see a battle worth the gazing.... but I'll swing into friendship because I love her"). He dismisses the Princess in the language of high tragedy's intermingling of its love and war imagery ("With flying colors, and with beat of drum,/Like the fanatic..."). The Princess's incredible actions belong to a genre whose time, Lee sees, is passing not only because of the sordid modern world but because of the "new" genre that others, including Jonathan Swift, would see as a dangerous, corrupting force. Idealism such as the Cleves' is simply irrelevant – "fanatic," as Nemours calls the Princess. What Hume calls a "bleakly sardonic treatment" of it is common in the later novel, sometimes washed lightly in nostalgic longing and sometimes a source of tragic endings but more often discussed as "knight errantry," as Defoe styles it in *Roxana* (1724).

Mid-Century Anger

The History of Miss Betsy Thoughtless (1751) and *The Vicar of Wakefield* (1766) give two shockingly contrasting pictures of domestic life and, formally, they are highly idiosyncratic. Amazingly, early reviews of them begin the same way:

Of *Betsy*: "We are almost at a loss what to say of a performance, in the perusal of which we have had some entertainment ...."
Of *The Vicar of Wakefield*: "this very singular novel...." and "Through the whole course of our travels in the wild regions of romance, we never met with any thing more difficult to characterize, than the Vicar of Wakefield; a performance which contains beauties ...."[17]

Goldsmith's novel is known for its "simple" style, and Haywood's fits Michael Holquist's conception of "roiling mass of languages."[18] William Thackeray called Goldsmith "the most beloved of English writers"; he and others described him as having "a pure kind heart," and Marshall Brown observes that "Goldsmith has counted to many as the most agreeable writer of his age."[19] No one would ever say such things about Haywood, and critics are chipping away at this description of Goldsmith.

Exceptionally aware of genre formulas, audience-pleasing conventions, and the cultural capital of various forms, and with strong authorial identities, Haywood and Goldsmith create two of the first English novels in which the dialogized relationships among author, narrator, protagonist, and characters are highly visible. Each is orchestrated to bring to the fore genuine public sphere issues, thus actualizing what Bakhtin identified as "the basic distinguishing feature of the stylistics of the novel" (263). These novels further projects born with the proliferation of novel writing. Like Defoe and Penelope Aubin, Goldsmith saw resistance to traditional morality and the transmitters of this morality, "religious treatises . . . moldy on the booksellers' shelves in the back shops." He imagined, as Aubin observed, that the novel could become a new way of teaching morality.[20] Early reviews and comments on *The Vicar of Wakefield* praised it in just these terms, claiming it the bearer of Christian piety and core virtues. As Haywood had always done, she saw the novel as a space for social critique, for exposing the harsh implications for individuals in accepted practices and oft-repeated pieties. Both understood power and its disseminated pressures and cruelties, and the ways that institutions public (prisons) and private (marriages) are disciplining and regulatory, and, if the public is attentive, destructively normative.

The author is strikingly and unusually present in *Betsy*. Haywood counted on knowledge of her long career as an expert on relations between the sexes and her identity as the great "arbitress of passion," *the* best-known writer of modern love stories.[21] Some of her character names, embedded subsidiary stories, and, at times, the narrative voice call attention to the Haywood who, for a while, had published five novellas a year. As early as chapter 3, she begins, "We often see, that the less encouragement is given to the lover's suit, with the more warmth and eagerness he prosecutes it; and many people are apt to ascribe this hopeless perseverance to an odd perverseness in the very nature of love; but, for my part, I rather take it to proceed from an ambition of surmounting difficulties . . ." (39). Miss Forward's boarding school story has the lover's linguistic excess and the sad, generalized morals familiar to Haywood readers. Mr. Wildly proclaims, "My angel, . . . how heavenly good you are." Miss Forward propounds: "But, oh! Let no young woman depend on the first profession of her lover" (108). By producing a near parody of her own style, showing her command of it with such verbal fun as "angel" and "heavenly good" and a 1720s tale, she establishes an authoritative author-function even as she lets her readers know that she is the author whose work they have long enjoyed.[22] One of the most remarkable feats in the eighteenth-century novel is Haywood's calling attention to her expertise by setting in motion a dazzling variety of examples of the language of courtship in the first quarter of *Betsy*. In chapter 1, Haywood dismisses Richardson's *Clarissa* as "the story of Piramus and Thisbe," from which Master Sparkish, Miss Forward's first teen-age suitor, has learned and then puts into play as subject and content the ideology-inflected languages of love alive in her culture, literary and "real." Despairing over Trueworth and harassed by her brothers, she falls victim to Munden's cynically controlled, just-right discourse; notably he is often silent or his discourse unrepresented, thereby allowing all of the characters to write their impressions or hopes onto him.

Haywood's narrator often sounds, as Christopher Flint and Shea Stuart say, like a conduct book,[23] but Haywood also creates a repertory of tones including arch and pseudo-omniscient ones. The narrator often disapproves of Betsy, harping on her vanity, frivolity, enjoyment of power, and even capacity for malice. In a typical sentence, the narrator contends, "there are not many who are possessed of [vanity] in that immoderate degree Miss Betsy was" (94). The narrator's voice oscillates among being close to Haywood's, departing from it, and opposing it, thereby creating a dialogic contest. As Andrea Austin observes, Haywood heaps up "in insistent detail" episodes that contradict the narrator's view of Trueworth, and of Betsy.[24] The author function, the narrator's mostly calm omniscient voice, and Betsy's initiation into the situation of women join the points of view of Lady Mellasin, Lady Trusty, and the exemplary Mabel to capture the fact that marriage as an institution was in crisis and the culture actively rethinking what it and the gendered roles of husbands and wives should be. These voices are as culturally and ideologically inflected as those of the suitors, and exhibit a wide range of approaches to women's situation and to marriage. The interpenetrations of the public into the private and the *Realpolitik* consistently represented in Haywood's presentation of the situations and relations between the sexes throughout her career are formidably contrasted to comfortable patriarchal and domestic clichés through this dialogism.

Betsy is, like my other examples, a transitional text with pre-emergent structures of feeling and literary paradigms. It is also a key text in the shift away from courtship to critiques of marriage, a movement begun on the stage. The Mundens' marriage is a "modern marriage," and its ugly plot and even its details are familiar from a series of plays that includes Fielding's *The Modern Husband* (1732). The crassest part of these marriages is the coercion of the wife to have sex to advance her husband, a situation initiated on the stage, built into Betsy's encounter with L——, found in novels throughout the century and featured in Mary Wollstonecraft's *Maria* (1798). Haywood was singularly well prepared to write a transitional novel that absorbs literary culture at the deep structural level. Her familiarity with French fiction is a major constitutive element in her work; as late as *Betsy* is in her career, that fact is still true; the conduct book, of which she had written eight,[25] and, of course, domestic fiction like Mary Collyer's *Felicia to Charlotte* (1744) and Richardson's *Pamela* along with the drama, the genre she described as her true love, make this novel what it is. Haywood's experience with drama is longer and deeper than many critics recall. In addition to acting and writing plays, she co-rented the Haymarket Theatre for performances and had recently expanded and published the two-volume *Companion to the Theatre* (1747). In fact *Betsy* may have something of the same relationship to a play that Lee's *Princess* has to a novel. In *The Dramatic Historiographer* (1735), Haywood describes Cibber's Lady Betty Modish as having "Honour and Sense; but Vanity and Affectation sometimes obscures the Brightness of her other Qualifications. She prides herself more in a Croud of Admirers, than in the Character of a prudent Woman."[26] This is obviously a description of Betsy, and the novel spins out experiences, emotions, and implications for such a character. *Betsy*, thus, may be an elaboration, the psyche behind the play's character, used, as Lee's Nemours is, to critique a society.

Haywood creates a schema like her own through which Betsy apprehends and articulates experiences. A representative section begins with Sir Ralph comparing himself to Marplot in Susannah Centlivre's *The Busie Body* (1709) and ends with an event suggested by William Wycherley's *The Country Wife* (1675): Munden "seized [her beloved pet squirrel] by the neck, and, throwing it with his whole force against the carved work of the marble chimney, its tender frame was dashed to pieces" (507). Violence in this and other mid-century novels tends to break out unexpectedly and ferociously. The movement from *The Busie Body*, a happy humours comedy of marriage performed more than 250 times between 1709 and 1750, to *The Country Wife*, a cynical "hard" comedy, mirrors the progress of the Munden marriage. Allusions to plays provide access to Betsy's thoughts and feelings. Her fears and the narrator's ominous warnings compete with the commonplace story of Betsy's engagement. Once she realizes the marriage will happen, she quotes Monimia, who was warned to beware men for they are all false, from the tragedy *The Orphan* (1680) by Thomas Otway: "I have bound up for myself a weight of cares; / And how the burthen will be borne none knows" (488). Immediately after this reflection, she and Munden have their first argument, precipitated by Betsy quoting Leonora in Dryden's *The Spanish Fryar* (1680), a play about legitimate power: "bonds without a date they say are void" (491). Haywood recreates her schema through which Betsy apprehends and articulates experiences. Every quarrel between Betsy and Munden begins with a performance of social forms, as in Betsy's genteel efforts to be a forbearing wife and Munden's middle-class reasonableness, and ends with passionate outbursts of individualism. That the squirrel is violently killed before the wife's eyes in a domestic novel but an impotent threat in a "hard" Restoration comedy raises the stakes. In this scene and the threat to Betsy's pin money, Haywood produces socially symbolic moments. She pulls window curtains aside to expose the tyranny, disappointment, and routine desperation in modern marriage.

Haywood reworks a key scene from *La Princesse de Clèves* in *Betsy*, and it is an exemplary illustration of her ability to activate external dialogic elements. As Haywood so often does, she hails a "taste culture," a group that responds in more or less uniform ways to a given set of cultural stimuli or "fantasy triggers." She gives her readers pleasure by sharing what they enjoy and evoking a scene they are gratified to recognize.[27] She then unsettles them by explicating, rewriting, or deconstructing it. In the highly charged encounter in a garden, Trueworth discovers Betsy contemplating the miniature of him that she has secretly purchased. Like the Princess, whom Nemours has found reflecting on his portrayal in a picture of the siege of Metz, Betsy is carelessly and, therefore, revealingly dressed. Their bodies and their hearts are exposed. *Paradise Lost* (1667) made gardens the site for guileful seductions initiating women into the end of Edenic youth, but *La Princesse* established the paradigmatic scene of *adult* decision. In novel after novel, a sadder, wiser heroine confronts and decides about her future. Her freedom, happiness, and identity are at stake. In Lafayette's and Haywood's texts, both heroines are widows, a state to which society granted more wisdom and independence than to any other condition of women's lives. They can choose the next chapter in the plot that is their lives, and these choices are socially symbolic.

Haywood's version of Lafayette's scene, like Lee's, strips away the polish that obscures harsh realities. Trueworth no less than Munden has suddenly exposed his violent, peremptory temper, and in this episode he shows himself to be worse than Nemours, for he "threw his arms about her waist, not regarding the efforts she made to hinder him, and clasp'd her to his breast with a vehemence, which in all his days of courtship to her he never durst attempt" (609). David Macey points out that Trueworth has "a newfound sense of authority" over her and takes "a liberty which . . . is decidedly uninvited and, under the circumstances, altogether improper."[28] Betsy repulses him and speaks the Princess's line, "Farewell for ever" (610), but, like the Princess, she has learned what love is: "the accident [of his finding her with his portrait], which had betrayed the secret of her heart to him, had also discovered it to herself" and "she was conscious that while she resisted the glowing pressure of his lips, she had felt a guilty pleasure in the touch" (610, 612). In both, sexual desire, lust, plays an unusually prominent part in a fiction that styles itself as polite and somewhat elevated. In both cases, the women's sexuality is strangely repressed or sublimated, "domesticated" as James Turner would say, even in spite of the number of Betsy's suitors and the rape attempts.

Working back from this scene, Trueworth looks uncomfortably like Nemours. Selected for Betsy by her impulsive, violent brothers, Trueworth is certainly rakish, as his affair with and brutish casting aside of Flora demonstrate, and the disrespect he shows Betsy is characteristic of his self-assurance. He never doubts that Betsy has an illegitimate child and he is, as Andrea Austin argues, "false, to Betsy, to Harriot, and to Flora."[29] Betsy, left free to marry as the Princess is by the death of her spouse, recognizing herself "a sacrifice" to her family's and friends' "persuasions," states firmly that the choice of her second husband is going to be hers and "the chief inducement" will be "an infinity of love" (630). Like Harriet in George Etherege's *The Man of Mode* (1676), she tests Trueworth, requiring what he calls *his* year of "probation," "the painful penance" that *she* "enjoined." Unlike Nemours, who had powerful people attempt to bring the Princess out of retirement and then broke her injunction and went to her sanctuary, Trueworth has with obvious resentment observed the social forms that he had taught her were so important and returns to claim "recompense" for his "submission" (626).

Opinion about the meaning of Betsy's marriage to Trueworth is beginning to be as disputed as the Princess's final retirement. Rather than interpreting the Princess's refusal to marry Nemours as an expression of autonomy and escape from the misery of a marriage to a man incapable of faithfulness, negative readings of the conclusion of *La Princesse* now seem to prevail. At this moment in the early history of the prototypical adult-choice garden scene, Haywood does not follow hers with, for instance, extended episodes of equalizing discourse that make the ending of Austen's *Pride and Prejudice* so light and bright, or with any of the devices later writers use to foreground the heroine's discernment and independence and the couple's meeting of minds. Instead, the reader has the example of Munden (and other novel heroes, including Richardson's B.) quickly assuming tyrannical, arbitrary, angry patriarchal power.

To some extent, the year of probation correlates to the scene in which the gaze is reversed and the Princess watches Nemours lying vulnerably in a garden. However, Trueworth's two acts of taking possession, physically in the garden and then completely one day after the year of mourning ends, seem more a part of Haywood's consistent portrayal of the unequal power between the sexes than a joyous reunion.[30] Leslie Richardson has argued that the seduction-rape plots of eighteenth-century fiction are actually "self-ownership" plots,[31] and although Betsy has the wit and "militant virtue" of later heroines, they still bring about her undoing. Rather than making a statement about the possibility of women's autonomy and freedom, Haywood deliberately creates ambiguity and vexed possibilities. She provides a standard happy ending, but a coquette so reformed and chastened casts a shadow from which it is hard to step free. Macey, for instance, speculates that Haywood is calling "attention to the sacrifices that a new code of female conduct demanded from women who, like Betsy, aspired to lead independent lives";[32] certainly the episodes and characters of thoroughly depressing marriage novels such as Frances Sheridan's *The Memoirs of Miss Sidney Bidulph* (1767) are in *The History of Miss Betsy Thoughtless*.

What Haywood has done is compose one of the best examples of a text dialogized, and therefore still alive with contending structures of feeling and interpretations, one almost equally animated by external contexts (including its standard romance ending) and internal elements. Indeed, Bakhtin asserted that an author's dialogic relationship to other languages is a "fundamental constitutive element" of novels, and he considered genres to be languages (46–7). Genres, the only speech acts both within a text and external to it, allow Haywood to provide readerly pleasures even as she, like Lee, critiques social institutions and the genres that allow an audience to pass the statue of a naked gladiator without noticing *naked*, *gladiator*, or the national values that a monument inscribes. The squirrel with its suddenly snapped neck and dashed frame is a good symbol of the power and violence that maintain the sex-gender system – a power masked by theatrical comedy and by society's unwillingness to admit it.

The world of *The Vicar* is as chaotic as that of *Betsy*, and both texts are filled with wild jolts in tone and sudden shifts in genre. Arching an eyebrow at *Clarissa* as Haywood had, Goldsmith gives us a now conventional part-persuasion, part-kidnapping plot – Lee's "villainy, treachery, perjury, all those monstrous, diabolical arts that seduce young virgins from their innocent homes, to set 'em on the highway to hell and damnation." *Betsy*'s chaos is depicted, of course, while *The Vicar*'s is the nature of the narrative itself. Filled with frauds, the book may be a fraud. As part of an over-the-top seduction of Olivia, two prostitutes disguised as aristocrats discuss coterie manuscript circulation, still a prestige form of publication. Olivia, who has dressed as an Amazon for the family painting, runs away with Thornhill, the serial seducer, because she feels desire and ambition. Mixed motives are thematic in the novel, and a defrauder like Jenkinson can turn into a deliverer. The master of an impressive mansion can be the butler.

Amidst this chaotic, uninterpretable world filled with frauds, in many interpretations the Vicar is supposed to stand like a beacon: a plain, good man. Goldsmith puts him in a narrative, however, that seems to be aligned with the reflexive, meta-novel projects of *Tristram Shandy* (1760–7) and *Tom Jones*.[33] The number of hardships visited on him and his endless fountain of statements of endurance are broken up by little domestic set pieces in which, for instance, the family dances, plays games, or sings. Primrose often behaves like a fool but carries out a prison reform. Goldsmith deconstructs and turns novelistic plots against themselves even as he uses them as critiques for things as they are. The bizarre conclusion begins with George Primrose, believed to be fighting in the West Indies, appearing before the Vicar and his former love, Arabella Wilmot, as a member of an itinerant acting company. This and other coincidences are justified with this amazing analogy provided by the Vicar:

> Nor can I go on, without a reflection on those accidental meetings, which, though they happen every day, seldom excite our surprize but upon some extraordinary occasion. To what a fortuitous concurrence do we not owe every pleasure and convenience of our lives. How many seeming accidents must unite before we can be cloathed or fed. The peasant must be disposed to labour, or the shower must fall, the wind fill the merchant's sail, or numbers must want the usual supply.[34]

This quotation epitomizes the problem of interpreting the text and its varied responses. The ridiculous and the pragmatic, the idiosyncratic and the philosophical are glued together. The peasant "must be disposed to labour" – by inclination or necessity? Does the Vicar mean the former and Goldsmith point to the latter? "Numbers must want the usual supply" – why is this clause made deliberately strange? Do people want in the economic sense? "Numbers" – is that a reference to the luxury-hungry mob that Goldsmith and others saw coming to characterize the nation? This mixture of references to class, Providence, commercialism, and consumerism is, of course, underpinning motivations and explanations throughout the novel, and part of the fraud of the novel is Goldsmith's refusal to take up the novelist's usual responsibility for sorting them out and encouraging judgments about them.

Shortly afterwards, the Vicar is in prison. The disorganized scene in which he gives a sermon while the prisoners play various tricks on him yields to the next step in the chaotic, improbable ending in which his son George lands in jail with him and Sir

William Thornhill, a.k.a. Burchell and therefore another fraud, arrives in fine *deus ex machina* style.[35] He has even studied physic as "amusement," writes a prescription, and heals the Vicar's burned arm. Is Goldsmith pointing humorously to his own flirtation with medicine and his greater, instantaneous power as an author? On stage this conclusion would be more ridiculous than in a sensibility novel, and this may be Goldsmith's point. Such an exaggeration of the good rewarded and the bad punished becomes parody but allows an illusionist faith in the goodness of humankind that has often been folded into an interpretation of the text and Goldsmith's good nature. Using Gay's cynical provision of an audience-satisfying ending to *The Beggar's Opera* (1728), Goldsmith amuses the audience, but two images of power hint at more ominous implications. Olivia is married to Thornhill, and, as in some of Haywood's novels, given power over him because she controls the money. Once coerced, she is now able to coerce, and this union without reconciliation punishes the guilty. Sir William has been described as moody and eccentric throughout the novel, and a brief glimpse of his predator fangs comes when he discovers the Primrose family has gone through his pocket-book. He says, "I could hang you all for this" (80). This same assumption of absolute power is evident in the ending when he peremptorily orders the release of George, who is accused of a duel challenge and attempted murder and is vulnerable because of his class.[36] His proposal that Sophia marry Jenkinson with a £500 gift from him to get them started is both cruel and, as the Vicar observes, "hideous." It is a stretch to suppose that the reader is to see his naked power united with the Vicar's virtue.

Primrose offers archaic although nostalgic values while Sir William represents a disquieting picture of the best possibility of the modern world, the union of wealth and power that seems to drop down on plots and characters, sometimes providing a "magic solution" and sometimes causing severe disruption and suffering. We have, then, a different kind of dialogism, one in which residual structures of feeling provide an absorbing, escapist, admonitory fable while emergent structures of feeling and contemporary anxieties about what the world is really like roil and impact every aspect of life. Shortly after hearing Johann Gottfried von Herder read *The Vicar* to them, as something of a lark Goethe and a friend sought a country clergyman "with an intelligent wife and a pair of amiable daughters" near Strasburg. Goethe goes in disguise like Sir William and says he found himself "actually in the Wakefield family." There are two daughters, and when a son comes home, Goethe writes: "I could scarcely help exclaiming, 'Moses, are you here, too!'"[37] Goethe is seeking, and for a while thinks he has found, an isolated, domestic circle surviving from the past, something rather like the dying community in *The Deserted Village* (1770). This idealization of the *Volk* and their "pure human sentiments" is a piece with the time's avid collection (and forging) of folk art and antiquities.

Goethe provides a striking example of readers' desire to enter and believe in the Vicar's mental world. He was also one of the first to identify it with Romanticism, but I would argue that the most significant and largely unnoticed strain of Romanticism in *The Vicar* is the recognition that Sensibility requires victims. Later, in *Essay on the Theatre; Or, A Comparison between Sentimental and Laughing Comedy* (1773), Goldsmith attacked empty sentimentality, and *The Vicar* contrasts to plays in which spectators are taught to "applaud" "faults and follies" and see "folly, instead of being ridiculed, . . . commended" (3: 212) because of its attention to the forces selecting and making victims, the moral and social implications, and its prophetic elements. His moral seriousness and strong social critique distinguish much later work, including that of the abolitionist poets. Julie Ellison counsels:

> Sensibility is not simply a taste for pathos but a varied, contested, and ambivalent discourse of emotional action.
>
> Sensibility, moreover, is almost by definition the culture of a colonial, mercantile empire. . . . The literature of sensibility is inconceivable without victims and its victims are typically foreign, low, or otherwise alien and estranged.[38]

These are the forces in *The Vicar of Wakefield*.

Behind the sentimental Primrose family with their patriarch who never saw a "righteous man forsaken, or his seed begging their bread" (4: 26), roil the forces of empire – wealth, power, capitalism, commodification, and foreign exile. George, after all, is sold into colonial service by the scheming Thornhill; not only does Thornhill get rid of a rival but he also puts the Vicar in debt to him, thereby, of course, gaining the power to coerce and imprison him. Throughout his career, Goldsmith sees Britain's colonies as the sad destination of British victims. The depopulation that Goldsmith defends in the dedication of *The Deserted Village* to Joshua Reynolds is, as he admits, not something people in England see about them. But it was something the Irish and Scots saw frequently, and offices such as Crisp's had existed since at least the mid-1600s.

The Vicar's forbearance and his sermons about the hopes of the next world actually emphasize the arbitrariness and hypocrisy in this world. "It is among the citizens of a refined community that penal laws, which are in the hands of the rich, are laid upon the poor," the Vicar observes, a prose version of a line from *The Traveller; or, A Prospect of Society* (1764): "Laws grind the poor, and rich men rule the law" (line 386). "Refined community," the phrase slides by like the statue of the naked gladiator. The repeated juxtapositions of the allegedly refined, those attempting to imitate refinement, and those unaware or incapable of meeting this standard are consistent with his career-long attacks on the gentility movement's tangible effects on the social fabric. Just how radical Goldsmith's attention to the kinds of victims portrayed in the novel was is captured by Frances Burney: "He advances many very bold and singular opinions – for example, he avers that murder is the sole crime for which death ought to be the punishment, he goes even farther. . . ."[39]

Like Haywood, Goldsmith had an unusual, distinguishing identity as an author and a figure in the print culture when he published his novel, one which puts him in a similarly oscillating relationship to his narrator. Goldsmith had become a reviewer for Ralph Griffiths's influential *Monthly Review* at age 27, written the ambitious *Present State of Polite Learning in Europe* (1759) and the popular *Citizen of the World* papers, and, as reviews of *The Vicar* mention, published *The Traveller*. His authorial identity, while colored by a reputation for some sentimentality, was primarily that of a *wandering* literary and social arbiter. Much that he wrote, including *The Traveller*, demonstrated a firm confidence in his judgments, but they also presented him as an exile or at least an outsider casting a somewhat melancholy eye over whatever he experienced. *The Traveller*, then his "signature piece," begins: "Where'er I roam . . ." (line 7).

Because Goldsmith's social critique had been so consistent and the personae so distinctively wrought, readers would feel Goldsmith's presence. Sometimes reinforcing, sometimes ironizing, sometimes ridiculing the Vicar as Haywood had her narrator, Goldsmith manages in a novel often read as a self-contained pastoral idyll to produce a text with strong dialogic elements from outside the novel. In fact, we cannot believe in the Vicar. Even if Primrose is the narrator, he is in "a Tale," and repeatedly the iron control of an author acting as master of genres and omniscient determiner of events, one so omniscient as to be free of every convention, every literary form, and every probability, asserts itself. The comparison between the structured, deliberate text and, for instance, Primrose's incoherent, pretentious discussions with Jenkinson and the butler are but two obvious examples of the rupture.

The Vicar's sermon advice to wait for the next world is famously that of oppressors and those without hope of genuine reform. Sir William makes some people do the right thing and tempers injustice with wealth and raw power, as Harkin says, demonstrating the "gulf between efforts to persuade and actual power."[40] Because what happens is so individual and so far outside the state's legal institutions, Sir William's actions cannot be called justice. As Goldsmith weans the reader from Primrose as Swift had readers from Gulliver in Book 4, he exposes Primrose's ignorance and even dishonesty (as when Primrose thinks he understands Seneca's *De Providentia*). By the end of the text, Goldsmith brings this dialogism of author function, Primrose, and the narrative itself with Sir William as the dominating presence to the fore and creates a zone of contact with the incomplete evolution of a particular present. John Bender has pointed out that England lived under what he calls a "tactical" government, one characterized by concealed motives, covert maneuvering, and illusion-producing rhetoric. As he says, "The motif of disguise itself becomes a figure for the idea that efficacious governance strives to work invisibly as a mode of control rather than through personal action."[41] Sir William has tried to hide and even deny his power, and Thornhill to keep his machinations and power hidden, but Sir William is finally provoked into wielding a naked sword.

The complicated dialogism of the novel mirrors the complicated world in which Goldsmith and his contemporaries lived, one in which various stories/explanations/narratives, all bathed in recognizable *national* ideologies, were being deployed to maintain a hegemony even as event after event contradicted accounts of the moral nature of the English people and their government. Goldsmith's work points to the union of sentimentality and politics in the later abolitionists' attacks on England's hypocritical claims to being a land of liberty. He makes present, in both senses of the word, (1) an immediate reality that is mythologized and already believed to be "forever England," (2) one that is unpleasantly real for many people, and (3) one that sketches the situation created by the politics and economic policies of the time.

In a scant twelve years, the rising anger of the British people about the abuses of power and wealth and the growing skepticism about the law as remedy for injustice proposed by Goldsmith's novel broke out in events we have largely forgotten: the storming of Newgate during the Gordon Riots, the pro-Wilkes demonstrations leading to the Massacre of St. George, and the depiction of John Howard, the prison reformer, on the stage by quietly radical writers such as Elizabeth Inchbald. Goldsmith's chaotic novel mirrors the chaotic, uncertain world, and the Vicar's many lectures the turmoil of caesurism. Goldsmith's generation clutched England's insular, pastoral image and resisted thinking of itself as a commercial, imperialistic nation. Betsy Thoughtless has no home; she is constantly out of harmony with wherever she finds shelter; Primrose creates a home anywhere, even prison. Yet Betsy rents and lives alone and seems autonomous in her country retreat while the Vicar's apparent domestic sanctuaries always prove to be false, either because of natural disasters or human invasion. All kinds of disruptive people seem able to just walk into Primrose's home, yet his claims and little tableaux of the family circle overwhelm the memory of his vulnerability. Therein lies the appeal of *The Vicar* – as in the most satisfying popular culture, Goldsmith exercises fears and fantasies and then contains them, deftly substituting an ending that reassures and reinscribes comforting plot conclusions and mythic stories to live by. This was a strategy that would become more common; rather than breaking out as it does in Smollett's novels, rage would be clothed in "realistic" episodes about which readers were forced to draw conclusions and in sentimental tales depicting the horrible treatment of fellow humans that carried implied condemnation of Britain's moral economy.

Helen Maria Williams and the Poetic Novel

Helen Maria Williams's *Julia, A Novel, Interspersed with some Poetical Pieces* (1790) is steeped in the literary culture of the time when the public was under the spell of fashion novels, arty descriptions of nature, sensibility, romanticism, and poetry. It was the kind of novel that "everyone" had to read, was read aloud, discussed in society gatherings, and mentioned in plays. Its sensibility, graceful style, picturesque descriptions, global reach, and easy integration of the arts assured its respect and popularity. Fashion novels, of which *Evelina* (1778) is the most famous, arose in the 1760s and were fashionable objects as well as recorders of fashion.[42] They were written in a polished, elegant style and depicted fashionable behavior, usually in both city and country, and editorialized in various ways on them. Numerous charming, affected, and gauche characters moved through a series of pastimes; money and sensibility figured large, and the admirable young couple overcame obstacles.

Julia begins like a fashion novel; at age 19, contrasting young ladies are reunited in London. An opening scene is at a ball where a coterie of envious women mock their rivals and display their own ineptitude on the marriage market. Charles Seymour "makes a hasty calculation of the difference between a hundred thousand pounds at Bengal, and ten thousand in the Bank of England," overcomes his fear that the East Indian fortune will go down in a ship, and courts "it."[43] We learn that "eating has become a science" that men are supposed to discuss with discriminating knowledge of ingredients, that card assemblies are frequent, and that, like the repertoire of a street musician, "fashionable conversation is not very extensive" (1: 38–9). The editorializing in a fashion novel is often like this, judgments rendered through brief satiric portraits or witty similes with roots in the observations of Restoration drama's most perspicacious worldlings. Her contemporaries recognized and praised her technique. For example, the reviewer in *The Monthly Review* calls the mercenary Charles Seymour a picture "of our modern men of the world."[44] These novels often engaged serious domestic and political issues but were easy to read for the surface plot. Embedded in *Julia*, for instance, are critiques of marriage and electioneering as parts of a speculative economy,[45] and, as there was in some of her early poetry, strong anti-war sentiments.

The plot has some resemblance to that of *La Princesse de Clèves*, surely a fashion novel in its own right. The heroine meets Frederick Seymour and immediately feels what fashion novels describe as the virtuous woman's sensation of love for him. He is, however, engaged to Charlotte Clifford. He falls passionately in love with Julia but marries Charlotte as his honor dictates. Julia is even more persecuted by her lover than the Princess, because family relationships continually throw her in his presence and, unlike the Princess and Betsy Thoughtless, she has no alternate place to live. Like the French romances, *Julia* engages her readers in the characters' dilemmas. For instance, when Mr. F—proposes marriage to Julia, readers are asked if they do not think she should have accepted to "put a final end to her present perplexities, and perhaps banish for ever" Frederick's passion for her (1: 187). Most of the novel describes Frederick's uncontrollable attraction to Julia, Julia's attempts to avoid him, and their shared struggle to behave honorably and to protect Charlotte, who is also a likeable, intelligent character. When Charlotte finally learns of her husband's feelings, she also acts with complete propriety, which means never revealing that she knows. Like the Prince of Clèves, she learns a painful lesson and "no longer mistook attention for tenderness, and kindness for love" (2: 155).

The depth and integration of the literary culture in this fashion novel is unusual and suggests Williams's literary schema. By page 36, Julia has written two poems and attended a performance of John Home's *Douglas* (1756) starring Sarah Siddons, a play

Plate 18 This frontispiece to *Solitude Considered with Respect to Its Influence upon the Mind and the Heart* (1796), by Johann Georg Zimmermann, surrounds the woman with fashionable art objects, including the sheet music before her. Her furniture and dress hint at the book's European past, as the English edition was translated from J. B. Mercier's French translation of the original German.

to which Williams refers twice more in the novel. The most admirable characters in
Julia enjoy reading parties, share newly written poems with each other, and delight in
arty outdoor scenes, all aspects of the novel that reviewers appreciated and that show
Williams's grasp of her society. In 1790 poetry represented what French romance, heroic
tragedy, and hard comedy had in 1680. Even lower middle-class people sent each other
occasional poems, and readings and recitations of poetry and writing *ex tempore* were
popular evening entertainments. Williams is unusually skilled in using verse to develop
characters and in illustrating the social pleasures of poetry. Frederick writes sonnets and is
selected to read two poems from Scotland. The "Song" by a man and "Ballad" by a woman
conform to gendered notions of poetic forms and parallel the separation of Frederick and
Julia. Small touches show her developing consistent characters; Mr. F—, Julia's suitor,
loses his brother in war and produces letters that mention the divisions caused within
families and between lovers when they fight on opposite sides in the American war. It is
he who reads the prescient poem, "The Bastille, A Vision."

How carefully Williams structured her novel is clear from the poetry. Two sonnets
by Julia, an early one on hope and the despairing one to peace, which Charlotte is
discovered crying over, are paralleled in movement from optimism to pessimism by
"The Linnet," a poem in which the bird is rescued from a cat and flies joyously away,
and "Elegy. On finding a young Thrush in the street," which begins, "Mistaken Bird"
and concludes with the bird's falling into a grate (2: 27). The elegy can be read to have
allegorical applications within the novel, both for the characters, especially Frederick,
as they succumb to depression, and for the political conduct of nations. From writing
poetry, Williams had learned to use balance and metaphorical repetition as constitutive structural devices.

As in Goldsmith's and Haywood's novels, protagonist, narrator, and author function are strongly dialogic elements. Julia is introduced through poetry.[46] She "discovered at a very early age a particular sensibility to poetry," and the narrator gives us
a gently mocking portrait of the epitome of an aspiring poet. Her first poem,
composed at age 8, "displayed, with great diligence, her whole stock of classical
knowledge; and obliged all the heathen gods and goddesses, whose names she had
been taught, to pass in succession, like the shades of Banquo's line" (1: 13) In contrast,
her "An Address to Poetry" displays discriminating taste in melodic, dignified ottava
rima. Williams prefaces the poem with a paragraph that skillfully defends poetry
writing, which Julia's exemplary father had encouraged because "a propensity for any
elegant art was a source of happiness" (1: 13). She represents her culture, for, like her,
even minor characters express their thoughts through literature and are drawn to
literary moments of pathos and sensibility. For example, understanding Captain F—
depends upon his comparison of himself to Home's noble Douglas: "I do regret, like
Douglas, 'to be cut off glory's course' – 'which,' added he . . . 'never mortal was so fond
to run!' " (1: 244). Williams replicates her schema in her characters, as they articulate
experience and aspiration through literature.

The narrator, who has a distinct voice descended from Henry Fielding and Laurence
Sterne, interprets by means of literary experiences and a variety of genres. This

voice contrasts in tone to those assigned to Julia and other characters. Although the authors and texts mentioned by the narrator and the characters are often the same, the narrator usually refers to moments of dry wit or clear-sighted analysis of human nature, as in a reference to Richard Sheridan's *The School for Scandal* (1777) when she cold-heartedly appraises the Clifford family portraits: "at a sale of pictures, [they] would perhaps have sold no better than aunt Deborah and her flock of sheep" (1: 78). Williams does not hesitate to give this voice a presence and artistic agency. At one point, the narrator says, "I think I see . . . ," "I see the old man . . ." (1: 62) in giving us a Primrose-family moment in her sketch of Julia's grandfather, a venerable old man whose piety, relationship with his tenants, and pride in having "served his king and country" are stark contrasts to the complicated maneuverings and hidden motives of the London characters. Like so many fashion-novel writers, Williams is conscious of an England that has passed. Grandfather Clifford, like the Trustys in *Betsy*, represents behaviors and structures of feeling associated with English values of the first decades of the century.

Admirable as Julia is, she is less intelligent, witty, and perspicacious than the narrator. Watching the suffering characters from above with a kind of detachment, albeit sympathetic, the narrator counters the voices of excessive sensibility and melodrama. The relationship between the narrator's style and that of the characters' releases new layers of socio-linguistic heteroglossia. That the narrator can think by means of literary imports, show characters doing the same, and explain characters' states of minds through literary allusions reveals Williams's ability to set all of these domains in dialogic relationship to each other. These literary speech genres from the past, the contemporary art scene, and the fashion novel in which she was writing reveal what Williams is identifying as the dominant "spirit" in each and also the contrast between narrator and heroine.

The greater the conflict between the narrator's and character's languages, the more clearly ideology stands out and, as in Goldsmith's and Haywood's texts, the more it contributes to the didactic purposes of the book. Holding up the mercenary, the sociable, and even the sensibility characters to scrutiny, the narrator generates a separate, moral worldview that leaves intact the difficulties in which the characters find themselves. In this construction, Williams was following the inspiration for her novel, Goethe's *Die Leiden des Jungen Werther*, the sensational and sensationally popular novel with the same plot situation. Williams was taking up a challenge in *Werther*:

> We hardly dare to express in words the emotions with which Charlotte's soul was filled during the whole of the time, both in relation to her husband and to her unfortunate friend. But, knowing her character, we may form some idea of her frame of mind; *a perceptive feminine reader may be able to fathom her soul and feel with her.* (Emphasis mine)[47]

In Lee's cross-genre, cross-gender play, he had featured Nemours, the character of his sex, and Williams does the same. Goethe's triangle was Charlotte (Lotte), her admirable but rather dull husband Albert, and Werther; Williams's has two women and concentrates on the "persecuted" Julia rather than Frederick, her Werther character. Goethe's call to someone who can "fathom her soul" and feel what she does has echoes in a rich history of passionate, destructive love, including the lines in Pope's *Eloisa to Abelard* (1717): "Such if there be, who loves so long, so well; / Let him our sad, our tender story tell; / The well-sung woes will sooth my pensive ghost; / He best can paint 'em, who shall feel 'em most" (lines 363–66). Goethe sounds this note in the editor's introduction, in which he bifurcates his readers, as Fielding and Sterne most notably had. Some ("ihr," the plural of the first paragraph) will feel "Bewunderung," wonder, amazement, admiration; a few ("du," the singular used for personal friends), "who are labouring under the same distress," are invited to accept the book as a friend.

Goethe's "editor," like Williams's narrator, finds the situation unfortunate, highly unusual, and one to be carefully scrutinized, both for its private implications and its public resonances. In the revision, Goethe increases the distance between the editor's voice and Werther and, most significantly, raises doubts about Werther's perceptions of people and events as the editor imposes order more firmly on Werther's last two and a half weeks. In version two, Goethe tightens and smoothes but also emphasizes the transitions from discourse to discourse.[48] By choosing not to use the epistolary form of *Werther*, Williams has far more control of interpretation and can less intrusively replicate the mixed condemnation, affirmation, and sympathy toward Frederick that the editor shows toward Werther.

Most readers would have recognized Frederick as a Werther character and noted Williams's revisions. Goethe reproduced the common novelistic situation of a woman pulled between a dangerous libertine and a steady, middle-level working man. Not only is Werther a libertine in his thinking and assumption of privileges in matters of love, but there are hints, such as the references to his relationship with Lenore in the opening letter, that suggest he has practiced this philosophy as Richardson's Lovelace had. At one point Lotte says to Werther, "Oh! why were you born with this impetuosity, this persistent passion for everything that you once touch!" (432). This is an exact description of Frederick's obsessive attachment to Julia.

Like many novelists, including Richardson, in the second edition Goethe attempted to make these mundane, reliable, kind men more attractive. Williams gives her Charlotte some of the characteristics of Goethe's, such as her love of dancing, but, rather than a persecuted wife, she gives us the situation of the English courtship novel – a virtuous single woman besieged by a man who believes he has the right to act on his desires. Goethe paints a man with a defective, sick relationship to the world around him, but Williams portrays a man who tries to be a good, honorable husband and, had he not been pre-engaged and then obsessed with Julia and his feelings, might have been a good, happy husband. Both novels are filled with artistic, moving nature scenes, and the characters are inseparable from literary allusions. Some of the most beautiful passages in *Werther* are the early descriptions of nature, a source for him as for Julia of almost boundless religious happiness.[49] Again and again, Williams revises *Werther*. In their first meeting, Werther and Lotte share the experience of a thunderstorm through recollections of Klopstock's popular description of a storm in *Die Frühlingsfeier* (*Spring Celebration*, 1759) while Julia meets Frederick when he nearly rides down a cottager's toddler.

The climactic scene in *Werther* is his reading his translation of "The Songs of Selma" and "Ossian's Last Hymn" from *The Poems of Ossian* to Lotte. Even those reading *Julia* as a Wertheriad would have experienced a sudden *frisson* at the point where Frederick and Julia encounter the engraving of Lotte at Werther's tomb. As they rather awkwardly flip through modish engravings Julia's uncle has brought her, this one causes a crisis. In Goethe's scene, Lotte's love for Werther surfaces powerfully, she orders him away, and his suicide rapidly follows. The scene is deeply intertextual. Lotte and Albert have played out several of the scenes and moods in the sad marriage of the Prince and Princess of Clèves. In their last scene, Lotte speaks the Princess's line to Werther: "You shall never see me again!" (118). Williams deliberately brings *Werther*'s climax to mind with Frederick's description of "the vain efforts of prudence" to subdue passion like his and Julia's agonized line: "I see no end of my conflicts but in death" (2: 203–4). Here Williams explicates the danger of *Werther* as she makes clear the power of literature to be "reality" and model a human condition, in this case one for which Lotte's and Goethe's "Be a man" seems a sad, even impossible solution.[50] By replacing Werther's botched suicide, with his thrashing body and leaking brains, with Julia's "beautiful" mourning at Frederick's deathbed as he dies from fever, she appears to understand how aesthetics can influence ethical judgments and asks her readers to reject self-murder.

At that moment, Williams actualizes the potential of the image of a language to be an "exhibition of its 'spirit,' its ideological structure."[51] Friedrich Schiller described *Werther* as "compressing" "everything that nourished the reflective character...: impassioned, unhappy love, sensibility towards nature, religious feeling, a penchant for philosophical contemplation, and finally, to leave nothing out, the sombre, formless, melancholy Ossianic world."[52] The "Ossianic world" had given way to "Werther fever," a threatening move from a fascination with a lost world to a "modern" sense of isolation, hopelessness, and a romanticizing of suicide. Werther's mind has been constituted through a literary sequence as compelling as the contextual movement from *Ossian* to *Werther*. As he starts his new life, he reads Homer, whose stories have "no beginning and no end, a rounded universe blossoms into all-embracing life,"[53] then Ossian, and finally Gotthold Lessing's *Emilia Galotti* (1772), a love tragedy found beside the body of Karl Jerusalem.

Jerusalem, an acquaintance whose suicide helped inspire *Werther*,[54] and Goethe were well aware of a tradition of linking suicide to specific texts. In many accounts, Charles Blount and Thomas Creech had killed themselves after reading John Donne's *Biathanatos* in 1684 and 1700 respectively. Allegedly Joseph Addison's *Cato* (1713) encouraged a wave of suicides, and Richard Steele felt compelled to criticize the "cult of Cato"; daggers and swords gained favor as suicide instruments.[55] The press made much of the suicide of a Miss Glover, a young lady who left a copy of

Werther under her pillow, and the novel has the reputation of being the model for "artist-suicide in the Romantic age."[56] *Werther* was especially pernicious within this tradition because the character's reasons were both philosophical and romantic, two of the three categories recognized.[57] Opinions about suicide were surprisingly mixed and freely discussed in England; for sixpence in 1786 the public could attend debates on topics such as "Is suicide an act of courage?"[58] A persistent fear that "the English malady" inclined them to suicide played a part in the fascination with it.[59] At different times, the public seemed persuaded that suicide was on the rise, and casual mentions of strikingly large numbers, such as Goldsmith's in *The Vicar*, were common ("we daily see thousands who by suicide shew us they have nothing left to hope," 160). Engravings – and silhouettes, porcelain, fans, tins, and other objects decorated with scenes from *Werther* – sold well for decades, and psychologists today still use the term "Werther effect" for imitative rather than individually motivated suicide.

Writing in the "age of Werther," when Julia desperately turns away from the image, it is impossible to tell if she is condemning suicide or frightened by the possibility that Frederick or even she herself is imagining it. *Werther* and the "poetic" literary culture of her time provide the deep structure of her novel as she activates the images of languages and sets them in socio-historical motion. They allow her to put the spirit of Ossian, whom she knew by then to be a fraud, beside "Werther fever," in some ways a shorthand for the excessive sensibility that had swept her own nation. She didactically condemns the excessive, self-indulgent sensibility that would become the wild, uncontrolled passion of the French Revolution's Reign of Terror. Frederick, who spent so much time on the continent and met Charlotte there, is a threatening, coercive European sensibility. The plays of Kotzebue, *Werther*, and the uncontrolled passions of the French Revolution were un-English. One reviewer complained that Julia's "principles are so fixed that nothing can tempt her to act wrong, and as she appears like a rock, against which the waves vainly beat, no anxiety will be felt for her safety,"[60] but her English rationalism and virtue are the "common sense" that her country needed in a time when German and French sentiments sometimes seemed to be sweeping English people away. As the *Werther* scene makes clear, it is not her virtue but her survival that is at stake. Frederick's fever is symbolic of his burning, obsessed brain, and his conversation is so threatening because seductive, literally infectious.

Williams rewrites the story of a time's indulgence in melancholy, "enthusiasm," and sensibility that turns a psychological crisis into a corrective story of nationhood. Her representation of a literary discourse different from her narrator's and heroine's is as deliberate and revelatory as Lee's departure from his genre. She, at least as much as he, activates a dialogism that makes external discourses and events part of the novel's structure. The meaning of the text and its engagement with immediate reality, then, is produced by the relation between the text and the context, in this case both heavily dependent on cues drawn from a complex, multinational literary culture. The poem "The Bastille," written from the point of view of a prisoner, is near the end of

Julia and is a poem filled with dread even as it expresses hope for Liberty and Freedom. Williams wrote to Hester Thrale Piozzi that she appreciated "literary conversation, a fine library, charming music and sweet walks," but "I must renounce them a little while for the sublimer delights of the French Revolution."[61] *Letters Written in France*, published the same year as *Julia*, begins with a fervid account of Fête de la Fédération, the first Bastille Day celebration of the ideals of unity and "probably the most elaborate public spectacle in European history." This and seven more eyewitness books would make her "a foreign correspondent, interpreting French history to readers in England" and "an architect of radical sensibility."[62] *Julia* demonstrates that Williams stood on a precipice, already grasping the theatricality and sublimity that British people seized upon to interpret events in France.

Conclusion

How do forms come to be apprehended as reality, as pure concepts of understood experience? Sadly, as Goldsmith noted in his *Essay on the Theatre*, an audience may weep over a play's homeless family in spite of having just given a contemptuous glance at a beggar. Paradoxically, these texts with their extreme literariness, abrasive implausibility, and self-conscious aestheticism have that mysterious power to arouse interest. The seductiveness of Goldsmith's fable-family, the intensity of Werther's inner life, and the absorbing nature of the situations that Lafayette and Williams create detach readers from history *in order to engage them with a time's structures of feeling*. All are "crisis texts," written at times of social and political unrest and, more significantly, when the society that produced them was poised breathlessly on a fulcrum between two worldviews. Such texts, as all of these did, provided paradigms for transitions in progress and for future texts and modes of thought.

In thinking of the immediate reality activated by these texts more than references to contemporary events, kinds of people and current issues and opinions come to the fore. An author for whom literature is a dominant schema activates the power of other genres and the images of literature. Like a river narrowed by rocky cliffs and then released, the force is augmented and concentrated. When Lee is blending theatrical strategies with novel scenes and lines, he is funneling by means of his schema to expose the value systems of both and strongly condemn the uncritical audience. The fact that this schema is a major means of analogizing and problem solving is especially clear with these writers. Goethe, for instance, recognized immediately the parallels between Werther and Berrathon in *Ossian* and easily saw that Werther was so appealing because "All young men saw themselves as Hamlet."[63] Even more effectively than "realistic" fiction, novels animated by such schemata can give the "spirit of the time" form while alluding to actual events or reproducing them in mimetic, archetypal, or symbolic ways. Although members of the audience may not have a strong literary schema, the way the author composes the relationship between text and context brings recognition to the surface, spreads, and intensifies it as a mode of interpreting experience. As Raymond Williams says, the text defines "a social experience which is still in process, often indeed not yet recognized as social but taken to be private, idiosyncratic, and even isolating." The texts analyzed here were greeted this way, and they, as art and literature often do, provide examples of some of "the very first indications that . . . a new structure is forming."[64] Literature for them seems to be an experience with the world, and although literature delivers an experience unlike any other and may not structure readers' thought as it does these authors', the texts often produce a different and profound effect.

Apparently paradoxically, since they refer back so insistently to earlier literature, these texts capture a pre-emergent worldview. All are mixed genre, bringing an exceptionally large number of literary kinds into the text because they are trying to say or do something new, to capture a new reality. Because genre is the only dialogic element both within the text and external to it, it can activate the greatest number of images of languages, each with its own mood and ideological structure. The carefully controlled language and form in *La Princesse*, *The Vicar*, *Werther*, and *Julia* point to the large mass of languages outside of them and highlight their absences, while Lee and Haywood bring them into the text. Both strategies produce heteroglossia and images of conflict. Reality is mediated through the form, but also facilitated and heightened. Again paradoxically, each of these texts has been experienced as highly coherent, unified, and even economical, yet they all make ideological contradictions and unresolved problems in the culture highly visible. The mixture of genres brings speech acts into grating juxtapositions, thereby strongly illuminating ideologies and structures of feeling by means of contact with others. They create a form to give expression to a particular climate, one that is recognized but has not yet been articulated. Reality, like the shifts in socio-literary languages, becomes a disjunction in an illusionist text, and the very papering over of contradictions makes them more visible. As John Bender says of *The Vicar of Wakefield*, "breaks in tone, conflicts in representational method, and tensions among generic expectations" make some texts "peculiarly revealing" of political and social contradictions, and "the very contrivance of formal coherence out of disparate materials allows us to glimpse" what Raymond Williams calls "cultural emergence."[65] The word "modern" insistently recurs: "first modern novel," "modern marriage," "modern men of the world," "modern novel," "modern German prose," "modern sense of isolation." In each case, "modern" registers an awareness of change, a vague sense of the threat of standing on a precipice above a chasm of unknown depth.

In the space between the triangular poles of the mimetic, actual events, and literary conventions, a sense of a reality emerges. Strangely, sometimes the less realistic and mimetic the text, as with *Werther*, the more powerfully it seems to model a structure of feeling. Once set in their immediate context, how much they captured currents in the culture becomes strikingly apparent; for instance, a year before Goethe published *Werther*, Jean-Paul Marat published *Les Aventures du jeune comte Potowski*, a novel "in which suicide is present on nearly every page."[66] Current theorists of popular culture recognize that the "danger" and "subversiveness" of such forms come from the ability to fuse myth texts (archetypes) and specific, culturally immediate materials.

Werther observes, "Ossian has crowded Homer out of my heart. To what a world this glorious poet has introduced me!" "A world," Goethe writes. The worlds of the Princess of Clèves, of Primrose, of Werther became seductive places, and Lee, Haywood, and Williams created alternatives. In the reading and rereading, revising and adapting, some texts, like these six, become markers and catalysts in major shifts in human perception. Both Lee and Williams recognized such a shift and that the texts they adapt had unleashed a dangerous, "poetic" – and, therefore, apparently amoral – power. *La Princesse* and *Werther* challenged "reality" and expectations about human behavior, Lee and Williams bring them back down to earth, thereby demonstrating their recognition of the novel form's power to obscure, mislead, or even hide as well as to reveal. Lee is in dialogue with Lafayette's idealizing audience, and Williams is presenting a didactic performance for the entertainment, enlightenment, and correction of her readers. Williams goes farther than the other writers in taking the step many Romantics would by attempting to move her readers to reject one *Weltanschauung* and enact her ideology.

Literature and literary schema become the bridge that relates text and context and thereby releases the full dialogic potential of the text. A second connective between text and context created by these writers is a dynamic among author, narrator, and protagonist, possible because the writers had strong literary identities to their contemporaries. In every case an overarching intelligence, one greater and broader than the narrator's, hovers. For example, the Vicar of Wakefield's limitations become increasingly evident, as do the predictive nature of Lee's anti-novel discourse, the doubts cast upon the reliability of the narrator's view of Betsy Thoughtless, and the didactic nature of *Julia*. All of these case-texts also challenged interpretations of other texts and expectations about human behavior. They simultaneously reflect and reflect on contemporary culture while invoking past values. Both Haywood and Goldsmith bring these things violently together, and controversies about decisions characters make swirled around *La Princesse de Clèves*, *Werther*, and *Julia*.

The feelings and expectations released from the genres accentuate socially symbolic moments in the texts and capture the spirit of an age. The "reality" of the text feels "immediate" and delivers heightened satisfaction or anxiety because it is both content and form, external and internal. Lee's *The Princess of Cleve*, for example, captures the coming class mobility and mingling as surely as it does disaffection with the court, its mores, and its aristocracy. Haywood's second novel, *The British Recluse*, is an isomorphic story, half written in romance discourse and half in novel language. Lee's play is a pre-emergent example of this awareness, just as Goldsmith's is of didactic romance/moral Romantic. Of the novels discussed here, four were first novels, making them, perhaps, especially sensitive to the external genre voices around them. In Goethe's lyric prose, Williams recognized the spirit of her age and saw its dangers.

Haywood saw the conflict between Lafayette's heroine's longing for autonomy and Richardson's normative image of marriage and drew together a panoply of disciplining forces concentrated on Betsy. The range of external speech acts is great, including such things as Lady Trusty's reminder, "consider how odd a figure a woman makes who lives apart from her husband" (511).

These texts created out of their authors' extraordinary literary schemata give form to a climate searching for expression. Not only is this climate English but it is British, European, and even global. The conjunction of *La Princesse*, *Werther*, and *Julia* brings to the surface the depth and breadth of *European* literary culture and how nations shared but also tried to differentiate themselves from structures of feeling. The novel is about "social existence," and Georg Lukács saw Werther searching for a new form of it. In 1914 he encapsulates one of the obsessive quests of eighteenth-century novel writers: "as the objective world breaks down, so the subject, too, becomes a fragment, only the 'I' continues to exist, but its existence is then lost in the insubstantiality of its self-created world of ruins."[67] This is what many reviewers saw as the danger of *Werther*, that readers would mistake the "self-created world of ruins" for "the whole" of the world revealed to them. Lukács certainly saw the symbolism of Werther's initial reading of Homer, and Goethe once remarked that "Werther praised Homer while he retained his senses, and Ossian when he was going mad."[68] British novelists tended to wash the greatest continental imports in a form of English skepticism and rationalism, as Lee and Williams did. Writers increasingly accepted the responsibility for initiating their readers, as Stuart says of Haywood, "not in the didactic sense of the way the world should be, but in the sense of the way the world is."[69] In doing so, they grappled with social problems, and multiplied titles such as Bage's *Man As He Is* (1792), Godwin's *Things as they Are: or, The Adventures of Caleb Williams* (1794), and Inchbald's *Such Things Are* (1787). The multiplicity of "worlds" and the complexity of interpretating "reality," however, increasingly occupied writers and led to the intense plumbing of obsessive individuals in William Godwin's *Caleb Williams*, the global sweep of Charlotte Smith's *The Young Philosopher* (1798), and the brilliance of Scott's clashing of structures of feeling in *The Heart of Midlothian* (1818).

See also: chapter 2, FICTION/TRANSLATION/TRANSNATION; chapter 5, MILTON AND THE POETICS OF ECSTASY; chapter 6, REPRESENTING RESISTANCE; chapter 20, HOME ECONOMICS.

NOTES

I would like to thank my research assistants, Heather Hicks, Sara Brown, and Lacey Williams for their work on this project.

1. My conception of "culture" depends upon Clifford Geertz, *The Interpretation of Culture* (New York: Basic Books, 1973); see especially 9.

2. Michael Holquist, *Dialogism: Bakhtin and His World* (London: Routledge, 1990), 151.

3. A number of Bakhtinian theorists call attention to the dependence of dialogism on external contexts; "unremitting" is David Shepherd's word, "Bakhtin and the Reader"

in *Bakhtin and Cultural Theory*, ed. Ken Hirschkop and David Shepherd (Manchester: Manchester University Press, 2001), 94.

4. Mikhail Bakhtin, *The Dialogic Imagination*, trans. Caryl Emerson and Michael Holquist, ed. Michael Holquist (Austin: University of Texas Press, 1981), 7, 11, 31 *et passim*.

5. I accept Robert D. Hume's reasoning about the date, "The Satiric Design of Nat. Lee's *The Princess of Cleve*," *Journal of English and Germanic Philology* 75 (1976): 119–20. John Downes in *Roscius Anglicanus* says that Lee wrote the play for Dorset Gardens before the Union of the companies. The play was first published in 1689 and may have been revived in that year.

6. This point is made in "Introduction: *La Princesse de Clèves* and the History of the French Novel" by Faith Beasley and Katharine Ann Jensen, eds., *Approaches to Teaching Lafayette's 'The Princess of Clèves'* (New York: MLA, 1998), 1, and see Elizabeth C. Goldsmith, "Lafayette's First Readers," 31–32, in the same book.

7. Tara Collington and Philip Collington, "Adulteration or Adaptation? Nathaniel Lee's *Princess of Cleve* and Its Source," *Modern Philology* 100 (November 2002): 203.

8. April Alliston, *Virtue's Faults: Correspondences in Eighteenth-Century British and French Women's Fiction* (Stanford, CA: Stanford University Press, 1996), 19–20. See also Margaret Cohen and Carolyn Dever's cultural field of "intersections and interactions," "Introduction," *The Literary Channel*, ed. Cohen and Dever (Princeton, NJ: Princeton University Press, 2002), 2–27.

9. Catherine Ingrassia, *Authorship, Commerce, and Gender in Early Eighteenth-Century England* (Cambridge: Cambridge University Press, 1998), 108–16, and Paula R. Backscheider, "Introduction," *Selected Fiction and Drama of Eliza Haywood* (Oxford: Oxford University Press, 1999), xiii–xxxvi, and "The Shadow of an Author: Eliza Haywood," *Eighteenth-Century Fiction* 11 (1998): 79–102.

10. Maureen Harkin, "Goldsmith on Authorship in *The Vicar of Wakefield*," *Eighteenth-Century Fiction* 14 (2002): 335, and see Frank Donoghue, *The Fame Machine: Book Reviewing and Eighteenth-Century Literary Careers* (Stanford, CA: Stanford University Press, 1996), 86–124. Harkin points out that Goldsmith "took the nature of modern literary culture in general and the position of the writer in particular as a frequent topic for his essays and journalism, and for his two longer critical works," 326.

11. See "Domestic Literature," *The New Annual Register . . . To which is Prefixed, A Short Review of the State of Knowledge, Literature, and Taste*; the *European Magazine* 17 (June 1790) prints three pages of "Sentiments and Similes" that the reviewer compiled as evidence of her "superior style," 435–38. Long reviews appeared in the *Monthly Review* 2 (1790), 334–36; *Analytical Review* 7 (1790), 97–100, and *Walker's Hibernian Magazine* (1790–1), 455–58. Deborah Kennedy writes that Williams's literary reputation was "firmly established" by her *Poems*, *Helen Maria Williams and the Age of Revolution* (Lewisburg, PA: Bucknell University Press, 2002), 30–34.

12. How vexed the terms "romance," "novel," and "novella" were and efforts to distinguish among them are much discussed. I shall use "novel" for prose fictions of the period as a blanket term because of this essay's relationship to Bakhtin's theory of novelization. On the familiarity of events and individuals, see Collington and Collington, "Adulteration or Adaptation?" 225, and for a good account of the historical personages in Lafayette's novels, see Alliston, *Virtue's Faults*, 33–77.

13. Cf. Philip Parsons, "Restoration Tragedy as Total Theatre," in Harold Love, *Restoration Literature: Critical Approaches* (London: Methuen, 1972), 28.

14. Hume, "The Satiric Design of Nat. Lee's *The Princess of Cleve*," 135–38.

15. This reader position becomes that of judge; see Paula R. Backscheider, "The Novel's Gendered Space," in Backscheider, ed., *Revising Women* (Baltimore, MD: Johns Hopkins University Press, 2000), 15–18.

16. J. M. Armistead says that Lee's favorite subject was "the mental pathology of political leadership" and describes the passing of the circle of court playwrights, their codes of conduct, and their dramaturgy, *Nathaniel Lee* (Boston: G. K. Hall, 1970), 161–62; quotation, 175.

17. Quotations are respectively from the *Monthly Review* (October 1751), quoted in Christine Blouch, ed., *The History of Miss Betsy Thoughtless* (Peterborough, Ontario: Broadview Press, 1998), 637; the *Critical Review* 21 (January 1766), 439, and the *Monthly Review* 34 (January 1766), 407. Quotations from *Betsy Thoughtless* are from the Blouch edition.

18. Holquist, *Dialogism: Bakhtin and His World*, 69. Christopher Flint compares the conflicting voices in the Goodman-Mellasin home to "the divisive and heretical babble of Nimrod and his followers," *Family Fictions: Narrative and Domestic Relations in Britain, 1688–1798* (Stanford, CA: Stanford University Press, 1998), 215, 221.

19. William Thackeray, "Sterne and Goldsmith," in *The English Humorists of the Eighteenth Century* in *The Four Georges* (Boston: De Wolfe, Fiske {n.d.}), 281–82; Marshall Brown, *Preromanticism* (Stanford, CA: Stanford University Press, 1991), 113, and see John Lucas, *England and Englishness* (Iowa City: University of Iowa Press, 1990), 55. Brown notes that "not even namby-pamby Philips wrote so simply" as some of the verses in *The Deserted Village*, 128, and on *The Vicar*'s reputation as simple, see 141–42.

20. Penelope Aubin, "Preface to the Reader," *The Strange Adventures of the Count de Vinevil and His Family*, in *Popular Fiction by Women, 1660–1730: An Anthology*, ed. Paula R. Backscheider and John J. Richetti, (Oxford: Clarendon Press, 1996), 114–15; and see Harkin on Goldsmith and the author as moral instructor, "Goldsmith on Authorship," 328–44.

21. The reviewer in October 1751 in the *Monthly Review* implies that he knows who the author is.

22. On the continuities from Haywood's early work, see my "The Story of Eliza Haywood's Novels," in *The Passionate Fictions of Eliza Haywood*, ed. Kirsten Saxton and Rebecca Bocchicchio (Lexington: University of Kentucky Press, 2000), 19–47.

23. Flint, *Family Fictions*, 208 *et passim*; Shea Stuart, "Subversive Didacticism in Eliza Haywood's *Betsy Thoughtless*," *Studies in English Literature* 42 (2002), 559–75.

24. Andrea Austin, "Shooting Blanks," in Saxton and Bocchicchio, eds., *The Passionate Fictions of Eliza Haywood*, 266–67, 276–78. She points out that Haywood uses references to other texts to show that Betsy is less gullible than the narrator suggests, 276.

25. Flint categorizes them and points out their importance to *Betsy Thoughtless*, *Family Fictions*, 208. In the essay in this volume, Srinivas Aravamudan reminds us that 36 percent of all novels read in Britain between 1660 and 1770 were translations of French novels.

26. Eliza Haywood, *The Dramatic Historiographer* in *Selected Works of Eliza Haywood II*, ed., Christine Blouch, Alexander Pettit, and Rebecca Hanson. 3 vols. (London: Pickering and Chatto, 2001), 1: 43.

27. On women's continued familiarity with French romances, see April Alliston's perfectly worded description, *Virtue's Faults*, 12–13, 19–21, 74–76.

28. J. David Macey, "'Where the World May Ne'er Invade'?" *Eighteenth-Century Fiction* 12 (1999): 84–85. For quite different purposes, Macey analyzes these scenes together.

29. Austin, "Shooting Blanks," 277.

30. Compare Macey, "'Where the World May Ne'er Invade'?" 85, 99–100, and Ann Leone, "*La Princesse de Clèves* and the Politics of Versailles Garden Design," *Mosaic* 27 (1994): 25–48.

31. Leslie Richardson, "Who Shall Restore my Lost Credit?" *Studies in Eighteenth-Century Culture* 32 (2003): 19.

32. Macey, "'Where the World May Ne'er Invade'?" 87.

33. Brown's line of argument about narration, which refers to Defoe, Fielding, Sterne and others, could be interpreted to support my opinion, *Preromanticism*, 164–65.

34. Oliver Goldsmith, *The Vicar of Wakefield*, in *Collected Works of Oliver Goldsmith*, ed. Arthur Friedman, 5 vols. (Oxford: Clarendon Press, 1966), 4: 167. All citations to Goldsmith's texts are from this edition.

35. Brown insightfully calls the novel a "carnival text," *Preromanticism*, 175–80.

36. If the duel occurred at the time of the quarrel, the charge was manslaughter. George, however, has sent a challenge, thereby

opening him and all who participated, even seconds, to the charge of murder. Juries seemed to acquit gentlemen who followed the code of honor even if they killed an opponent, but the legal system worked to prevent the practice from spreading to the lower classes, J. C. D. Clark, *English Society, 1688–1832* (Cambridge: Cambridge University Press, 1985), 111–16.

37. Johann Wolfgang von Goethe, *The Autobiography of Johann Wolfgang von Goethe*, trans. John Oxenford. 2 vols. (Chicago: University of Chicago Press, 1974), 2: 35–45.

38. Julie Ellison, "The Politics of Fancy in the Age of Sensibility," in *Re-visioning Romanticism: British Women Writers, 1776–1837*, ed. Carol Shiner Wilson and Joel Haetner (Philadelphia: University of Pennsylvania Press, 1994), 228–29.

39. Quoted in G. S. Rousseau, *Goldsmith: The Critical Heritage* (Boston: Routledge and Kegan Paul, 1974), 53.

40. Harkin, "Goldsmith on Authorship," 344.

41. John Bender, "Prison Reform and the Sentence of Narration in *The Vicar of Wakefield*," in *The New Eighteenth Century*, ed. Felicity Nussbaum and Laura Brown (New York: Methuen, 1987), 169, and see also 182–87.

42. I have defined and discussed this genre at length in "Fashioning Novels, Novelizing Fashions," *Eighteenth-Century Genre and Culture*, ed. Dennis Todd and Cynthia Wall (Newark: University of Delaware Press, 2001), 190–217. See also Kristina Straub's introduction and accompanying selected reading in the Bedford Cultural Edition of *Evelina* (Boston: Bedford, 1997).

43. Helen Maria Williams, *Julia, a Novel*. 2 vols. (New York: Garland, 1974), 1: 48–49. Quotations are from this edition.

44. *Monthly Review* 2 (1790): 335.

45. Ingrassia has described this economy in *Authorship, Commerce, and Gender*, see especially 96–136, and see J. G. A. Pocock, "The Mobility of Property," in *Virtue, Commerce, and History* (New York: Cambridge University Press, 1985).

46. On Julia as a sensibility heroine and poetry as part of that, see Kennedy, *Helen Maria Williams*, 46–51, and Eleanor Ty, *Unsex'd Revolutionaries: Five Women Novelists of the*

1790s (Toronto: University of Toronto Press, 1993), 73–84.

47. I have used both versions of *Werther*, occasionally collating the German editions, and there are differences significant to my argument. The second includes the Bauernbursch episode, another parallel to Werther's case, for instance. The separation between editor and Werther is present in both versions, but significantly revised especially through the differing conclusions beginning with 6 December. Quotations unless otherwise noted are from the translation by Victor Lange of the second version, reproduced in *Goethe* (New York: Holt, Rinehart, and Winston, 1949), 104. I occasionally refer to the translation of the first edition by William Rose in *The Permanent Goethe*, ed. Thomas Mann (New York: Dial Press, 1948). The publication history of *Werther* in Great Britain is complex. Robert Dodsley published the first translation in 1779, but Daniel Malthus had worked from the 1777 French translation of *Les Passions du jeune Werther* by Philippe Charles Aubry and, like the other English translators, had omitted sections. The revised second edition of *Werther* came out in 1787 but was not translated into English until much later. Williams's cosmopolitan circle probably read it, but passages in her novel suggest she had the first in mind; which and how many versions Williams read cannot be determined. Anna Seward's *Louisa, a Poetical Novel* (1784) is sometimes identified with Wertheriads, and she probably discussed *Werther* with her. Williams was not the only writer to give Charlotte voice; see *Eleonora: From the Sorrows of Werther* (London, 1785) and William James, *The Letters of Charlotte during her Connection with Werther* (London, 1786).

48. Compare Rose's translation, 430–46, with Lang, 95–101.

49. Katharina Mommsen and Richard Koc relate *Werther* to German pietism, "Introduction," *Die Leiden des Jungen Werther* (New York: Suhrkamp, 1987), and see xvii.

50. Williams, *Julia*, 2: 105; Rose translation of *Werther*, 432; Goethe also makes this line of Charlotte's part of a prefatory poem added to the second book of the 1775 second edition.

51. Ken Hirschkop, "Introduction" to *Bakhtin and Cultural Theory*, ed. Hirschkop and Shepherd, 22.

52. Friedrich Schiller, *On Native and Reflective Poetry*, quoted in Martin Swales, *Goethe: the Sorrows of Young Werther* (New York: Cambridge University Press, 1987), 96–97.

53. Georg Lukács, *The Theory of the Novel*, trans. Ann Bostock (Cambridge, MA: MIT Press, 1989), 55.

54. On parallels between *Werther* and Jerusalem's and then Goethe's lives, see the brief, clear "Introduction" by Mommsen and Koc, *Die Leiden*, ix. They note that Goethe's allusion to Lessing's play may be interpreted as Werther committing suicide to insure virtue, the motive of the heroine of the play, 149 n. 14.

55. Richard Steele, "The Christian Hero," in *Tracts and Pamphlets by Richard Steele*, ed. Rae Blanchard (New York: Octagon Books, 1967), 11–15, 23. Georges Minois, *History of Suicide: Voluntary Death in Western Culture*, trans. Lydia Cochrane (Baltimore, MD: Johns Hopkins University Press, 1999), 179, 183, 187, 189, and on the large number of English characters who kill themselves, 223–24. The phrase is Minois's, 218.

56. The *Gentleman's Magazine* reported this event and called *Werther* a "pernicious work" (July 1784), 964–65. The city council of Leipzig on petition of the theological faculty made it illegal to sell copies of the book or to wear "the Werther costume"; the ban was in force from 1775 to 1825, Swales, *Goethe*, 97. On artist-suicide, see Tobin Siebers, "The Werther Effect: The Aesthetics of Suicide," *Mosaic* 26 (1993): 16.

57. The third is that of the repentant criminal. The categories are discussed by Germaine Necker de Staël in *De l'influence des passions sur le bonheur des individus et des nations* (Lausanne, 1796), 239–45.

58. Advertised in *The Times* (24 February 1786); noted in Minois, *History of Suicide*, 210.

59. See Minois, *History of Suicide*, 217–19, 223–28.

60. *Analytical Review* 7 (May-August 1790): 99.

61. Quoted in Deborah Kennedy, *Helen Maria Williams*, 14.

62. Neil Fraistat and Susan S. Lanser, "Introduction," *Helen Maria Williams, Letters Written in France, in the Summer 1790* (Peterborough, Ontario: Broadview Literary Text, 2001), 16 and 9 respectively. Biographical information on Williams is from this source, 16–29, and Deborah Kennedy, *Helen Maria Williams*.

63. Quoted in Mommsen and Koc, *Die Leiden*, 137 nn. 7–13 and xi.

64. Raymond Williams, *Marxism and Literature* (Oxford: Oxford University Press, 1977), 132–33.

65. Bender, "Prison Reform," 177–78, and Williams, *Marxism and Literature*, 119–41.

66. Minois, *History of Suicide*, 306.

67. Lukács, *The Theory of the Novel*, 53–54.

68. Quoted in Mommsen and Koc, *Die Leiden*, "Introduction," xiii.

69. Stuart, "Subversive Didacticism," 559.

FURTHER READING

Alliston, April. *Virtue's Faults: Correspondences in Eighteenth-Century British and French Women's Fiction*. Stanford, CA: Stanford University Press, 1996.

Brown, Marshall. *Preromanticism*. Stanford, CA: Stanford University Press, 1991.

Clark, J. C. D. *English Society, 1688–1832*. Cambridge: Cambridge University Press, 1985.

Cohen, Margaret, and Carolyn Dever, eds. *The Literary Channel: The Inter-National Invention of the Novel*. Princeton, NJ: Princeton University Press, 2002.

Lucas, John. *England and Englishness*. Iowa City: University of Iowa Press, 1990.

Index

History of Miss Betsy Thoughtless (Haywood):
  authorial presence in, 514–15; dialogism in,
  515, 518; language of, 514–15; literary
  schema in, 505, 516–18; marriage in, 515,
  517–18; narrator in, 515
Hobbes, Thomas, 330; *Leviathan*, 483
Hoeveler, Diane Long, 392
Hogarth, William: *The Analysis of Beauty*, 429;
  Before, 223, 224
Hogg, James: *The Private Memoirs and Confessions of
  a Justified Sinner*, 383
Holcroft, Thomas, 431, 460, 463, 467, 468
Hollingworth, Brian, 111
Holmesland, Oddvar, 101
Holquist, Michael, 505–6, 513
homelessness, 442–5, 455 *see also* rent
Homer: *Iliad*, 53
homosexuality: and incest taboo, 256
Hottentots, 426
Howard, John, 523
Hudson, Nicholas, 349
Huet, Abbé Pierre Daniel: *Traitté de l'origine des
  romans*, 51, 52–3, 54, 63
Hulme, Peter, 98, 102
Hume, David, 409; *Essays Moral, Political, and
  Literary*, 407; *History of England*, 323
Hume, Robert, 511, 513
Hunt, Lynn, 482, 487–8, 489, 496, 497, 498
Hunter, John Paul, 327, 346, 431; *Before Novels*,
  98–9
Hurd, Richard, 105
Hutcheson, Francis, 332
Hyde, Justice, 466–7

identity: bourgeois, 25–6, 29; British, 25–9,
  142–3, 151, 430–1; English, 33, 35, 40, 42;
  instability of, 65, 68, 400, national, 144,
  244, 251; Scottish, 146–7, 454–65
Ides, Evret Ysbrants: *Three Years Travels from
  Moscow Over-land to China*, 39, 42
"Illuminati": immorality of, 254–5; racialization
  of, 255–56
illustration: and learning, 412
imagined community, 237, 238, 239
imperialism: and identity in travel writing,
  101–4; *see also* colonialism
incest, 9, 236, 248–56, 388; and colonialism,
  236–7, 251; and commerce, 249–51;
  endogamy as, 247, 249; and Gordon Riots,
  475; and Gothic fiction, 388–9, 395, 474–5;

in *Julia and the Illuminated Baron*, 254–5; in
  Moll Flanders, 248–50, 251; in *The Monk*,
  388–9; and national space, 251, 256; and
  novel, 236, 248, 250; as political act, 388–9;
  in *The Power of Sympathy*, 251–2, 253–4;
  taboo, 250–1; unwitting sibling, 248–56
Inchbald, Elizabeth, 13, 282, 347, 523; *A Simple
  Story*, 289, 290, 321, 435–6; *Such Things Are*,
  534
Incorporating Union, 144–5
India, 35, 36, 43, 91, 93
inductive method, 423
Ingelo, Nathaniel, 221
Inglis-Jones, Elisabeth: *The Great Maria*, 316
Ingrassia, Catherine, 1–15, 245, 246, 380;
  Authorship, Commerce, and Gender, 374
innovation: and the novel, 506–8
Ireland: debate over Union with England, 111
irony, 511–12
Islam, 75–7, 80–2, 93

Jacobin writers, 322, 334–5
Jacobite rebellion (1745), 150
Jacobites, 149, 151
Jacobs, Edward, 383
Jakobson, Roman, 495
Jameson, Fredric, 483, 494; *The Political
  Unconscious*, 482
Jefferson, Thomas, 323
Jenyns, Soame, 171
Jesuits, 37, 38, 39, 41, 44
Jewsbury, Geraldine, 415
Johnson, Barbara, 492, 497
Johnson, Charles: *The Sultaness*, 69
Johnson, Claudia, 108–9, 334, 496
Johnson, Samuel, 227, 349–50, 351–2, 399, 407,
  423, 446; *Dictionary of the English Language*,
  13, 399–400; *Journey to the Western Islands of
  Scotland*, 211; *Rasselas*, 77
Johnstone, Charles: *Chrysal*, 442, 449
Joseph Andrews (Fielding): classical language in,
  178, 181; and education debates, 168–9,
  173–4, 175–7, 178–85, erotic in, 227;
  happiness in, 334; joy in, 324, 331–33;
  literacy in, 168–9, 173–85; natural history
  and physiognomy in, 428–9; physical
  description in, 419–20
Journal of the Plague Year (Defoe), 192–8; as fiction
  of population, 192–5; mobility in, 193–4; as
  novel of memory, 196

Oroonoko (Behn), 97, 126, 256, 323; contractual
episteme in, 240–6; happiness in, 323; honor
in, 242–4; hybridity of, 99–101, 239–41;
and novel, 221, 239–40; realism in, 62–3; as
surveillance chronicle, 62–6; and translation
63–4; as travel writing, 97
"Other": in Defoe's fiction, 28, 37, 38, 103, 131;
in novel, 142, 217, 486
Ottaway, Susannah R., 302
Ottoman empire, 78
Ovid: *Sappho to Phaon*, 225
Owenson, Sydney, 111

Paine, Thomas, 414, 460, 464
Painter, William: *The Palace of Pleasure*, 54
Pallavicino, Ferrante: *Coriere Svaligiato*, 216
Pamela (Richardson), 4, 5, 7, 88, 214, 239,
511, 515; "collusive resistance" in, 147–9;
and genre, 82–3, 221, 239; heated debate
and "novel panic" over following
publication, 149, 226–7; influence of
oriental tale on, 82, 83–4; and literacy, 168,
172–3; media event, 351; Pamela's resistance
in, 148–50; and politics, 486; praise of by
Hill, 226, 231; revisions of, 150; subject
positions in, 149; 486; Tory ideology of,
148–50
Pamela Censured, 226–7
Paradise Lost (Milton), 118–25, 129, 516; as an
oral narrative, 117, 118; ecstasy in, 118–25,
129; and fancy, 121–4; generative power of,
119; "Hail wedded Love" passage, 119–20;
influence of, 119, 124; joy in, 325; sexuality
in, 119–20
Parker, William Riley, 117
parks, 447
Parsons, Talcott, 250–1
Pateman, Carole, 495
patriarchy, 278
Patriotic Women's Club, 491
patronym, 255
Peabody, Reverend W.O., 314–15
Percy, George: "Discourse of Virginia," 103
Percy, Thomas: *Hau Kiou Choaan*, 88–91, 90
periodical essay, 60
Perry, Ruth, 11, 441–55
perversity, 387–90
Petty, William, 191, 193
phantasia, 121
philosophers: systemic and edifying, 401

physiognomy, 13, 420–1, 426, 427, 428, 437; in
aesthetics, 432; definition, 429–30; facial
character sketch in, 429–33; and natural
history, 421, 432, 433–7; and novel, 420–2;
practice of, 431–2; and racial taxonomy, 420,
423–4
picturesque, 54, 112, 390
Piozzi, Hester Lynch, 307; *British Synonymy*, 408
pirates 26, 32–3, 35
Plain Dealer (newspaper), 264
Plumptre, Anne, 282; *Antoinette*, 290
Pocock, J.G.A., 87, 246, 374, 377
Pococke, Edward, 82
Poe, Edgar Allan: *The Narrative of Arthur Gordon
Pym*, 324
poetic novel, 523–31
poetry, 506, 526; distinction between romance
and, 52
Pointon, Marcia, 421
politeness, 263–4, 278
political arithmetic, 191–8
politics: claims of bodies in, 483, 493; and
domestic sphere, 494–5; definition, 482; of
happiness, 322, 334–7; and novel, 485–6;
"political bodies," 482–3; voice in, 483; and
women, 489–90
Pollak, Ellen, 247, 248
Poovey, Mary: *The Proper Lady and the Woman
Writer*, 495
Pope, Alexander, 323, 448; *Dunciad*, 266; *Eloisa to
Abelard*, 528
popular fiction, 367, 370
population, 11, 191–211; as aggregate subject,
193; and colonial expansion, 199–201;
emigration seen as cure for redundant, 204;
figuring of gypsies and veterans as
"redundant," 206, 210; growth in rhetoric
surrounding "useless," 203, 204, 206; luxury
seen as threat to growth of, 198–9
pornography, 229–30
Porter, Dennis, 98, 106
Potkay, Adam, 11, 321–37
poverty, 8, 11, 441–55; cramping of space as mark
of, 445–6; history of rent, 451–5;
representation of rent distress and eviction in
fiction, 442–5, 449; and sentimental
benevolence, 449–51
Pratt, Mary Louise, 98
Premo, Terri, 299–300
Price, Leah, 355